The American Home
Garden Book and
Plant Encyclopedia

The American Home Garden Book and Plant Encyclopedia

by the Editors and Staff of

The American Home

Published by M. Evans and Company, Inc.,
New York, and distributed in association with
J. B. Lippincott Company, *Philadelphia and New York*

Contents

The Rewards of Gardening

Gardening, like most things, is largely what you make it. And you can make it anything you will — an art, a science, a hobby, a game. It can be an easy-going avocation or a serious pursuit, an infinite pleasure or a vital concern. It's a creative visual art because it involves design, color, texture, form; and it's an applied science because it takes in such disciplines as agronomy, chemistry, plant physiology, genetics. As a means of relaxation it can be the most pleasurable of pastimes, and as a game it can be as competitive as you like. At its best, whatever you make it, it's one of the most rewarding endeavors in the world.

Gardening of sorts has been going on since the earliest beginnings of civilization, and undoubtedly will continue as long as there's a civilized way of life. Fundamentally it's always pretty much the same, but in every one of its component parts it's always undergoing change. Year in and year out there are new plants, new uses for them, new problems, new solutions, new theories and techniques. And as time proceeds, the changes come faster and faster. In recent years they've occurred so rapidly that even professionals have been hard pressed to keep abreast of their fellow-workers' discoveries.

The amateur, of course, can be as up-to-date or as old-style as he likes. He doesn't actually *need* power tools, the latest chemical fertilizer, or the newest varieties of plants. He may, indeed, choose not to have them. But he *does* need a reliable source of information to turn to when faced with gardening problems. And that is what this guide is intended to be.

Over the years, it has been evident that readers of *The American Home* are more than casually interested in plants and gardens. The magazine has published many hundreds of articles on almost every phase of gardening—

comprehensive, many-page features on major subjects, and short, meaty items on specific techniques — and we have answered thousands upon thousands of questions on even more subjects than we have had space to discuss in our articles. The responses of readers to our articles and the subject-matter of their questions have, to a large degree, determined the shape of this book.

It is not, and it could not be, a *complete* garden guide, for the truth is there's no such thing. But it *is* a comprehensive, basic handbook. We have included in it just about everything American Home's gardening readers have shown an interest in since the magazine was started. We have not prepared it for the benefit of horticultural experts, amateur or professional, who have ample sources of whatever special information their interests require. But it is our hope that America's home gardeners — the countless intelligent people who enjoy working with plants and who want their homes to look more than merely presentable — will find in this reasonably compact volume all the finger-tip facts they really need.

The American Home Garden Book is *not* a collection of articles reprinted from the magazine. All the text has been newly researched and newly written for this project. It is as current and as usable as we can make it. And it has been arranged exclusively for your convenience. The *Contents* will tell you where to look for the broad, general phases of gardening; the *Plant Encyclopedia* will give you in a nutshell the basic facts on some 2,000 plants; and the *Index* will direct you to every specific subject covered by the book. If it serves your needs as we hope it will, our *Garden Book* will have been well worth all the effort that has been expended on it.

The Editors

The American Home Garden Book and Plant Encyclopedia

1

Soil: Garden Loam

If primitive man had fully appreciated the nature of soil, some tribe or race would certainly have worshipped it as a major god. True, early peoples did have their earth gods and goddesses, but never regarded them as vitally important. Nor did they show any realization of the vital role soil plays in the lives of living creatures.

Soil is the most complex and least understood material with which man works. In general, however, the owner of a small property needs only to know the type of soil on his own land, so that he may add whatever is needed for good plant growth. The end product at which he aims, resembles no natural soil found anywhere. Rather, it is a synthetic material, created by his manipulation of the native earth. All the same, he should understand something about the way soil functions.

He should realize first that soil is not just a mechanical mixture of clay, sand, and gravel, which supports plant roots; nor is it a bank into which a certain amount of fertilizer can be poured to stimulate a certain amount of growth, which is then removed to close the account.

Soil is a community of living organisms, ranging from microscopic fungi and bacteria to the roots of great trees that penetrate all its layers and draw upon every corner for sustenance. As the gardener manipulates this community, he must observe certain rules or risk losing a valuable asset.

The fertilizer he applies will feed his plants directly only to a very limited extent. Several other agencies will seize upon applied plant foods and conserve them, so that, later, plants can absorb them indirectly. As fertilizer elements in solution (fertilizers can move only when in solution) gravitate downward between the grains of soil, some of the dissolved minerals they contain are attracted by clay particles that help compose true soil. Other elements are absorbed by organic matter. Even

11

more active will be micro-organisms — tiny bits of living matter that need nourishment just as higher plants do. As they live and die, micro-organisms first conserve, then release, plant foods. Thus the effect of a single application of fertilizer is extended over a period of days or weeks.

ELEMENTS OF A TRUE SOIL

With this crudely sketched picture of a soil in action, the elements essential to its make-up can be seen. Mineral matter such as clay and sand are the framework — providing mechanical support for plant roots and living quarters for soil life. Water is another vital element: plants live strictly on a liquid diet. Because soil contains life, it must also have air to supply oxygen and carbon dioxide — gases vital to living organisms.

Part of the carbon dioxide in soils comes from the digestion of organic matter by micro-organisms. True soil cannot exist unless it contains some organic matter, much of it so well digested that it has formed humus. In this stage, the soil is so finely divided that most of its particles act as colloids. That is, they will float suspended in water.

TYPES OF SOIL

Soil types are defined according to their mechanical make-up or texture. Texture refers only to the size of the soil particles and has nothing to do with the structure or organization of these particles in layers. Some of the particles are so fine that they cannot be seen under an ordinary microscope. Under an electronic microscope they appear as flat flakes or plates. Clay particles vary in diameter from about 2/25,000ths of an inch (.002 millimeter) to sizes too small to measure. Silt may measure as much as .05 mm. Gravel, the largest particles usually considered as part of a soil, may measure up to an inch across.

The way a soil works under a tiller or plow depends a great deal upon its texture. As a rule, the more sand and gravel it contains, the easier it is to handle. Organic matter also tends to separate the adhesive clay and silt particles so they do not form a solid mass.

Clay and silt work in the the opposite way. They are so fine that water does not move freely through them, but acts as a glue to hold the particles together. When mixed with sand, the fine particles wash between the coarser sand grains. This can cause trouble if the ratio of clay to sand is less than one to three.

SOIL AMENDMENTS

Old-time garden books often recommend adding sand to clay soils to make them more workable, but this can be both costly and hazardous. If too little sand is used, clay flowing between the grains acts like cement, making the soil hard and unworkable.

Chemical soil conditioners introduced a few years ago proved impractical for garden use, but they did alert gardeners to the need for modifying natural soils to make them more suitable for plants. These chemicals worked on the theory that a chemical with a negative electric charge will attract one with a positive charge. The products were so efficient that each particle could attract over 200 particles of clay, but their cost was prohibitive. Less efficient products do the job well enough, and improve the soil in other ways. Partially or thoroughly decayed organic matter added to the soil does an excellent job in making clays and silts more porous and easier to work. It is difficult to use too much. If too little is applied, the effect is not the same as when too little sand is used.

Another material that pulls clay particles together in little clumps is lime. While most clays found in the United States are acid, a few are alkaline, and lime should not be used on these.

Perhaps the cheapest way to loosen clay soils, if the raw material can be had for the hauling, is to add steam cinders, the hard-burned ashes formed when coal is burned in high-pressure boilers. These tiny clinkers are practically inert and very porous. They need to be conditioned for use, however, for by-products of combustion contain harmful sulfur compounds, making this material unsafe when fresh. Allow steam cinders to weather for at least 6 months, then screen them through a ¼-inch mesh (hardware cloth with 16 holes to the square inch). Use the fine particles as a soil amendment. The coarse particles can be used for fill.

SOIL AS A HOME FOR BACTERIA AND FUNGI

Two of the most important processes in nature are the carbon and nitrogen cycles. In the first, carbon tied up in decaying plant tissues is released and returns to the air. In the second, nitrogen tied up in plant proteins is similarly released for use by other plants. If it were not for these cycles, all the carbon in the world and perhaps much of the free nitrogen would eventually be locked up in the organic matter of dead plants and animals, leaving the living ones to starve. It is bacteria and fungi that break down the complex organic compounds locked up in plants and reduce them to simple, soluble plant-food elements. Similarly, dying bacteria release growth-stimulating substances, sometimes called plant hormones, which help produce stronger roots. Shade-loving plants in particular seem to need these naturally occurring hormones.

Anything that provides food and moisture for soil bacteria and fungi thus contributes to plant growth. Since these too are plants, with the same food requirements as higher ones, they need fertilizers in order to grow. The addition of plant foods to soil feeds them more directly than it does the higher plants, as we have seen. If they are not supplied with plant foods, particularly nitrogen, they rob the soil of nutrients to such a degree that green vegetation begins to turn yellow.

The addition of undecayed organic matter to soil starts up such a reaction. For example, corn cobs are often used as a mulch. When applied without the addition of extra nitrogen, plants whose roots are under such mulch begin to turn yellow. If some source of quickly available nitrogen is added, the yellow soon disappears.

Plants with green leaves are able to use carbon dioxide from the air in their manufacture of carbohydrates — the energy foods on which all the world runs. But bacteria and fungi have no green leaves. They must draw sustenance from decaying vegetable matter. Corn cobs are high in sugars and starches, but low in nitrogen. By supplying nitrogen, we allow them to work on the job of breaking down organic matter without robbing the soil. Here, then, is a first principle in applying organic matter to soils. If the organic matter is not completely decomposed, nitrogen must be added to avoid starving garden plants.

SOIL NUTRIENTS

The nutrients discussed here are those that comprise "built-in" or native fertility. Added nutrients, in the form of fertilizers, will be discussed later. The most vital single source of built-in fertility is humus. By maintaining the humus content of soil, with compost or by green manuring, no deterioration in native fertility need be experienced. In some cases, however, such as under the sod of a lawn, it is all but impossible to increase humus content by adding these sources of organic matter. Fortunately, grass is able to create its own humus through death and annual renewal of its hair roots.

Organic matter is more than a source of fertilizer. Even if it has been thoroughly rotted down, it still is a valuable soil amendment. It acts as a sponge to blot up fertilizer and hold it until needed by plants. It serves as a home for soil bacteria and fungi. In fact, these uses are more important than its feeding function, which commercial fertilizers and plant foods can perform with greater efficiency.

COMPOSTING

Organic matter is often composted — allowed to go through decay and break down to humus, the finely divided fluff which resists further decay so strongly that a single application of humus may last 50 years or more in soil.

Composting is a simple process. A layer of organic matter 2 or 3 inches thick is sprinkled lightly with a complete fertilizer. Since the fermentation and decay of this material will be somewhat acid, a small amount of ground limestone can be used also, but is not necessary. (It may be added later.)

This layer is then covered with 2 or 3 inches of good garden loam. If the soil is dry, it should then be watered. If the place selected for the compost pile is well drained, first soak it thoroughly. Continue to add layers of organic matter and soil, sprinkling each with fertilizer. Hollow out the center of the pile slightly to hold water, thus helping to keep the composting material moist.

After 4 or 5 weeks, break down the entire pile and fork over the compost so that it is thoroughly mixed. If it is brown and crumbly, it can be screened and the fine particles distributed where needed. All coarse materials should go back in the pile.

Not all organic matter can be reduced to humus. Only that which contains lignin, a component of wood, will serve. Dried blood, for example, a highly valuable organic fertilizer, will not produce humus, nor will most meat and fish wastes. This does not mean they should be excluded. They are valuable as a source of food for the micro-organisms.

Materials for Composting

Since the heat generated in the process of decay kills germination, even weeds that have gone to seed can be used. Contrary to general belief, oils and greases do not harm compost. Weeds are conducive to the formation of humus and, though they break down slowly, they add to the life of the product.

Anything that will rot can be used. Leather scraps, old clothing, hair, wood shavings, waste grains, table scraps, bones, and plants pulled from the garden are all worth using. A covering of 4 inches of soil over the pile will confine odors. When turning the pile, if the odor is strong, add a little superphosphate.

GREEN MANURING

Organic matter can be added to the vegetable garden by sowing cereal rye in late fall and plowing it under in spring. Rye will grow even under snow and produce an amazing amount of green matter at a season when no growth seems to be taking place.

THE VALUE OF pH READINGS

Ascertaining whether soil is acid or alkaline is important in gardening, but analysis is often neglected because it seems so mysterious. Actually, it is as easy as reading a thermometer.

The pH scale by which soils are rated runs from 0.0 to 14.0, with 0.0 as the most acid and 14.0 as the most alkaline. Halfway between, the acid and alkaline forces are balanced, so this point is considered neutral. Readings can be taken in two ways, with an electric pH meter, which measures resistance and shows it as a pH reading, or by means of chemicals that turn various colors with changes in readings. Most seed stores and garden centers stock inexpensive kits which show reactions by means of a color change in a chemical solution.

Such tests are important because most of the food elements plants need are completely available only through a fairly narrow pH range. If a soil has a pH between 6.0 and 6.9, slightly on the acid side, all the chemicals which plants need for growth are in soluble form and can be taken up by roots. This presupposes, of course, that they are actually in the soil. Merely changing pH will not make available an element that is lacking.

If pH goes above 6.9, certain elements begin to lock up in an insoluble form. Iron, copper, and zinc are among these. For example, if oaks, rhododendrons, blueberries, and other plants which have a high iron requirement, are overlimed, the iron cannot be absorbed and their leaves turn yellow. Iron chlorosis makes the plant look sick, and it really is. If the pH is increased still more, phosphorus is locked up too, an equally serious matter. Similar reactions on the low end of the scale take place when readings drop below 5.9.

There are, of course, exceptions to this rule of 6.0-6.9. Certain plants such as azaleas, rhododendrons, blueberries, camellias, gardenias, and others, have adapted themselves to living in soils that are quite acid, say as low as a pH of 5.0.

Adjusting pH

If a soil reading is too low for the crops being grown, ground limestone is the best material to increase it. In clay soils, 7 pounds to 100 square feet should raise pH one full point. In sandy soils, use half that much.

Sulfate of ammonia, which supplies nitrogen in addition to changing pH, is a good material to lower the pH reading. Use 6 pounds to 100 square feet of soil on clay, 3 pounds on sandy soils. Sulfur will also reduce pH: 2 pounds to 100 square feet on clay, 1 pound on sand.

BASIC SOIL REQUIREMENTS

While for many plants the degree of alkalinity or acidity of a soil (the pH) is highly important, for the majority the soil's physical condition — its tilth — is what counts. Most garden plants give the best performance in a crumbly soil that allows air as well as water to reach the roots. Even those that require alkaline or acid conditions must at the same time have soil of good physical properties.

2

Annuals, Biennials, and Perennials

North America supports as wide a variety of native plant species as any great land mass of the world. These range from zero-hardy roses and dwarf shrubs (like low-bush blueberry) to the sub-tropical and semi-arid species of Mexico. They include a tremendously diverse group of Temperate Zone prairie and woodland plants, grasses, bulbs, and other herbaceous plants; vines, shrubs, and trees.

Even more amazing than the wealth of native species is the richness of color, form, and climatic adaption of the exotics — plants from other countries — that have been introduced only to disappear without being accepted by gardeners. Although we are able to grow many more kinds of plants than the British in their cool, humid, maritime climate, the true plantsman must envy the tremendous variety of plants found in English catalogs. Many of these are much more at home with us, yet have never caught on.

Too many gardeners grow half a dozen annuals and perennials, fearing to tread unfamiliar ground, but for those who dare, a rainbow of blossoms is possible. Let us look first at the annuals.

ANNUALS

A WORD TO THE NEW GARDENER

One of the most challenging activities facing those who sponsor gardening as a national hobby is that of helping the beginner gain experience in growing plants. Each year hundreds of thousands of new home-owners move from the city into suburban homes. Their only experience in growing plants has been a sansevieria on the window sill or a pot of chives in the kitchen. Perhaps the only flower they can name is a rose.

All too often, a novice is thrown into gardening by impulse. Shopping in a store that handles garden materials as a grocery sideline, he sees a wrapped rose bush. This is his first plant purchase — a red Hybrid Tea rose, one of the most difficult of all plants for the inexperienced to grow. He will be lucky if it has not languished on the counter for weeks, practically dead. Let us hope he does not fail and give up gardening in disgust!

Obviously, the best way to learn how to grow plants is to grow them. But which are best for beginners? The easiest and least expensive class are annuals that are sown as seeds in early spring, bloom quickly, and finish their life cycle in a single year. Any mistakes made are automatically erased by the frost that kills all annuals in the fall.

An ideal planting would include short rows of 50 to 100 different annuals, to give the beginner broad experience. Unfortunately, few home grounds afford that much space. Instead, the beginner's first purchase might well be a package of one of the mixtures of annuals sold under such names as "Surprise Garden Mixture" or "Rainbow Mixture." These are usually made up by blending 50 to 100 different annuals as a basic formula, to which are added many novelties and rare plants. Because such a mixture contains seeds of plants from the four corners of the globe, the seedlings that come from it can thrive under a wide variety of conditions. Whether the soil is rich or poor, the weather hot or cold, something is sure to grow. And whatever does grow will be thrilling to the novice gardener.

To learn how annuals adjust to different conditions, try this experiment: Divide the seeds into two lots, sowing half the packet as early in spring as the soil can be worked. Then, when the apple trees bloom and the tall late tulips are opening, sow the rest. If the weather is normal, the first sowing will produce a variety of plants quite different from the second. The first will consist largely of true hardy annuals that can survive in cold, wet soil. The second will also include a few hardy annuals, but tender and half-hardy annuals will predominate.

This will be your introduction to annuals, one of the most valuable types of flowers. But this need not end your gardening for the year. When frost has killed the annuals, pull them up, turn the soil over with a spade, and plant spring-flowering bulbs such as tulips and daffodils in the bed. These are very easy to grow, because the flower is already formed inside the bulb. When a gardener has grown annuals and bulbs for a year or two, he should be ready to try other plants — even roses.

ANNUALS FROM SEED: *Start with a flat of topsoil. Cover with ½" of vermiculite or ground sphagnum moss. Level off and tamp firm.*

Press thin slat into surface to make seed rows — ⅛" to ¼" deep and 2" apart. Sow seed ⅛" or so apart.

Gently cover and level off with hand. Very fine seed is best sown on surface and not covered. Water with fine spray. Stand in sunny window. Check surface daily; keep it just moist.

Annuals can be sown in coldframes 2 to 4 weeks earlier than outdoors; in hot-beds, up to 2 months earlier. Sowing in flats or pots makes it easier to use cold-frame later for transplanted or potted seedlings.

Transplant seedlings when about this size. Set about 2" apart in flats of topsoil, making holes with dibble and pressing soil around roots. Keep in window. Use liquid plant food. Set plants out when frost danger is past.

ANNUALS ARE VERSATILE

Although often recommended for the beginner, annuals are also the favorite plant material of many skillful amateurs. Without them, the true gardener's ideal of "continuous bloom" would be impossible. As spectacular as certain perennial flowers can be in their season, even the most elaborate border would have its dull moments without annuals.

Today's small suburban lots, with their severely plain ranch houses, practically dictate plantings in straight lines and narrow bands. About the only decorative material that can be squeezed in will be a ribbon of bedding plants along the combined walk and drive, a few more in a simple bed under the picture window, and perhaps a slightly less formal planting along the property line opposite the drive. Because of the need for intense, concentrated bloom in the limited space available, perennials would be difficult to use unless foliage alone would be acceptable for long periods of time. Since few perennials retain their fresh green color after flowering, annuals provide the best answer to the needs of modern small suburban homes.

CULTURE OF ANNUALS

Annuals are divided into three groups — hardy, half-hardy, and tender. Hardy annuals may be sown in either early spring or late fall. Spring sowing should be done as soon as the soil is workable. Follow exactly the cultural instructions on the seed packets. As a rule, hardy annuals do not grow well if sown after the apple trees have dropped their blossoms or tall late tulips have faded.

Half-hardy annuals are somewhat more resistant. They can be sown while the soil is still cool, but as a rule cannot tolerate more than a light frost after germinating. They should be seeded when the apple trees and tall late tulips are in full bloom.

Tender annuals cannot tolerate cold wet soil and will usually rot if sown before the petals have fallen from the apple blossoms, or when tall late tulips fade.

ANNUALS FOR WINTER SOWING

Certain annuals are quite hardy; if sown in fall just before the ground freezes, they will lie dormant until spring. They will germinate long before most soils can be spaded, grow and produce flowering plants much earlier than spring-sown seed.

A useful trick for covering the deteriorating foliage of spring-flowering bulbs is to sow the seed of hardy annuals soon after the bulbs have been planted. The annuals begin to flower when the tulips fade and continue to bloom well into summer. However, since most annuals hardy enough to be grown in this way do not like summer heat, replacements should be made in early July. For this purpose warm-weather annuals can be grown in peat-fiber or bagasse pots and held in a coldframe until needed. They may then be set out without removing the pot, thus avoiding the risk of transplanting in midsummer.

This method of growing hardy annuals can be used to attain the dream of every true gardener — continuous bloom. Bulbs in early spring, fall-seeded annuals until July, and bedding plants in summer will still leave a period in fall when spectacular bloom can be had with hardy chrysanthemums. The plants for this autumn show need not occupy space in the bed when not in flower. Since they can be transplanted even when in full bloom, they can be grown elsewhere and moved into place after the summer-bedding plants begin to go. If the budget will allow, they can even be purchased from nurserymen who sell them in flower, planted in splint baskets or tar-paper pots.

The following annuals can be planted in the fall, when temperatures will remain below 40°: alyssum, annual poppy, calendula, California poppy, candytuft, celosia, centaurea, cleome, coreopsis, cosmos, euphorbia, *Impatiens balsamina*, kochia, larkspur, nicotiana, petunia (small-flowered varieties), portulaca, *Salvia farinacea*, sweet peas.

ANNUALS BY COLOR

Since annuals are used largely to provide masses of color, it is important to know their hues exactly. Mistakes are often made in assuming that "red" is true red and "pink" really pink.

When red annuals are being selected, a distinction should be made between those of orange-scarlet hues and those that are closer to the purple section of the spectrum — the ruby-crimson. The same distinction should be made in selecting pink annuals. Those that contain considerable salmon or yellow in their color will clash with pinks that are closer to rose or lavender. While the same holds true of yellows, these are less likely to cause trouble, unless they are so deep in tone as to approach orange. In the following list, red annuals are divided into orange-reds and ruby-crimsons, while pinks are listed as rose-pinks and salmon-pinks.

Those not too well versed in the use of color often recommend a mass planting of white flowers as a "harmonizer" between discordant colors. The term is inept since the planting does not actually harmonize the colors, but weakens them by suppressing brilliancy and reducing the intensity of all the colors. This is advisable only if the purpose is to produce a softer effect. The gardener who expected strong, brilliant, and striking contrasts will be disappointed.

A better way to achieve harmony is to omit white entirely and use only colors which blend well. If this cannot be done, a soft creamy yellow is a much better choice than white as a harmonizer. It does not kill the brilliancy of colors as much, and it does have a color value of its own. Two zinnias are of exactly the right color for this purpose — 'Ice Cream' in the giant-cactus class and 'Isabellina' in the older giant-flowered group.

FLOWERING ANNUALS

	Height (in inches)	Color
Abronia umbellata, Sand Verbena	6	Rose-pink
Adonis annua, Pheasant Eye	12-18	Bright red
Ageratum houstonianum, Garden Ageratum	6-16	Blue to lavender
Alonsoa acutifolia, Maskflower	24-36	Scarlet
Alyssum maritimum, Sweet Alyssum	8-12	White
Amaranthus caudatus, Love-lies-bleeding	36	Deep pink to crimson
Ammobium alatum, Winged Everlasting	24-36	White
Anagallis arvensis, Pimpernel	6	Scarlet, white
Antirrhinum majus, Snapdragon	8-36	Orange, yellow, red, white
Arctotis grandis, African Daisy	24	White with blue shadings
Argemone mexicana, Mexican Poppy	24-36	Yellow, orange
Asperula orientalis, Blue Woodruff	9-12	Blue
Borago officinalis, Borage	12-24	Blue
*Brachycome iberidifoli*a, Swan River Daisy	12-18	Blue
Browallia speciosa, Sapphire Flower	18-24	Blue
Calendula officinalis, Pot Marigold	12-24	Yellow, orange
Callistephus chinensis, China Aster	18-30	Blue, lavender, pink, red, white
Celosia, Cockscomb	12-36	Yellow, orange, red
Centaurea cyanus, Bachelor Button	12-24	Blue, pink, white
C. imperialis, Giant Imperial	24-36	Blue, pink, white
Chrysanthemum carinatum, Annual Chrysanthemum	24-36	White, yellow
Clarkia elegans, Clarkia	24-36	Purple, pink, white
Cleome spinosa, Spider Flower	48-60	Magenta, white
Collinsia bicolor, Chinese Houses	18-24	White, blue, violet
Collomia biflora, Chilean Plume	12-24	Orange-red, scarlet
Convolvulus tricolor, Dwarf Morning-glory	9	Blue
Coreopsis drummondi, Golden Wave	12-24	Yellow, orange
C. tinctoria, Calliopsis	24-30	Yellow with red-brown markings
Cosmos bipinnatus, Cosmos	48-72	Crimson to white
C. sulphureus, Yellow Cosmos	36	Orange-yellow
Cuphea ignea, Cigar Flower	12-18	Scarlet
Cynoglossum amabile, Hound's Tongue	18-24	Blue
Delphinium ajacis, Annual Larkspur	18-48	Blue, lavender
Dianthus chinensis, China Pink	12-18	Pink, red, lilac, white
Dimorphotheca hybrida, Cape Marigold	12-18	Orange, yellow, white

	Height (in inches)	Color
Downingia pulchella	3-6	Blue
Emilia flammea, Tasssel Flower	18	Orange to scarlet
Eschscholtzia californica, California Poppy	12-24	Yellow, orange
Felicia bergeriana, Kingfisher Daisy	6-8	Blue
Gaillardia pulchella, Indian Blanket	12-20	Yellow with rose-purple markings
Gilia capitata, Thimble Flower	24	Blue
Godetia amoena, Farewell-to-spring	24	Pink to white, lavender, red
Gypsophila elegans, Annual Baby's Breath	12-15	White
Helianthus annuus, Annual Sunflower	6 to 12 feet	Yellow to orange
Heliotropium arborescens, Heliotrope	24-48	Purple shades
Hunnemania fumariaefolia, Mexican Tulip Poppy	18-24	Yellow
Iberis amara, Rocket Candytuft	12	White
I. umbellata, Globe Candytuft	12-16	Pink, red, purple
Impatiens balsamina, Garden Balsam	18-24	Pink, purple, white
I. holsti, Patience Plant	18-24	Red, pink, white
Ionopsidium acaule, Diamond Flower	4	Violet, white
Lathyrus odoratus, Sweet Pea	12-72	Various
Lavatera trimestris, Annual Tree Mallow	36	Rose-red, white
Layia elegans, Tidy Tips	12-20	Yellow with white tips
Leptosyne stillmani, Golden Wave	18	Yellow
Limonium suworowi, Annual Statice	12-18	Blue to lavender
Linum grandiflorum rubrum, Flowering Flax	12-24	Crimson
Lobelia erinus, Edging Lobelia	4-8	Blue
Lupinus, Lupine	12-36	Yellow, blue, purple, pink
Lychnis coeli-rosa, Rose of Heaven	12-15	Rose-pink
Malcomia maritima, Virginia Stock	8-12	Purple, pink, red, white
Malope trifida, Mallow-wort	24-36	Rose-pink to purple
Mathiola bicornis, Evening-scented Stock	15	Purple
Matricaria inodora, Scentless Camomile	12-24	White
Mimulus fremonti, Monkey Flower	8	Crimson
Mirabilis jalapa, Marvel of Peru	24-36	Pink, red, yellow
Nemesia strumosa, Nemesia	12-24	White, yellow, pink, purple
Nemophila insignis, Baby-blue-eyes	6	Blue
Nicotiana affinis, Flowering Tobacco	20	White
Nierembergia caerulea, Cupflower	9	Violet-blue
Nigella damascena, Love-in-a-mist	18	Blue, white
Nolana triplicifolia, Chilean Bellflower	6-12	Blue with white markings
Oenothera drummondi, Texas Evening Primrose	12-20	Yellow
Oxypetalum caeruleum, Southern Star	12-18	Blue

If you have space in windows, try transplanting seedlings into 2½" pots. When potting, press soil firm with thumbs and forefingers. Stand pots in trays or flats and keep in full sunlight. Later, transplant outside.

Feed annuals with a complete plant food about once a month. Don't overdo or you'll have all leaves, no flowers. In cutting beds, where looks are not important, mulch heavily to save weeding, hoeing, and watering time.

	Height (in inches)	Color
Papaver rhoeas, Corn Poppy	24-36	Red, pink, white
Petunia hybrids, Garden Petunia	8-18	White, red, purple
Phacelia campanularia, California Bluebell	8	Blue
Phlox drummondi, Annual Phlox	10-18	White, pink, purple
Portulaca grandiflora, Moss Rose	4-8	Pink, red, yellow, white
Reseda odorata, Mignonette	12-24	Greenish yellow
Rudbeckia bicolor, Black-eyed Susan	24	Yellow with black centers
Salpiglossis sinuata, Painted Tongue	24-36	Yellow, red, blue
Salvia farinacea, Blue Sage	24-36	Blue
Sanvitalia procumbens, Golden Stars	6	Yellow
Saponaria calabrica, Soapwort	6-9	Pink
Scabiosa atropurpurea, Sweet Scabious	24-36	White, red, pink, purple
Schizopetalon walkeri, Almond Flower	10	White
Silene armeria, Sweet-William Catchfly	12-24	Pink
Silybum marianum, Holy Thistle	24-48	Red-purple
Tagetes, Marigold	10-48	Yellow, orange
Tithonia speciosa, Mexican Sunflower	72	Scarlet, orange
Torenia fournieri, Wishbone Flower	12	Violet, blue, yellow
Trachymene caerulea, Blue Laceflower	24	Blue to purple
Tropaeolum majus, Nasturtium	12-48	Yellow, orange, red
Ursinia pulchra, Orange African Daisy	10-18	Orange
Venidium fastuosum, Jewel Daisy	18	Orange
Verbena erinoides	12	Lilac
V. hortensis, Common Verbena	10	Red, purple, blue
Vinca rosea, Periwinkle	12-24	White, pink
Zinnia elegans, Zinnia	12-36	All colors except blue

BIENNIALS

Biennials occupy a niche which cannot be filled by any other flower. Tall graceful spires of foxglove, clustered bells of *Campanula medium*, pert and saucy English daisies, and fragrant wallflowers are an intimate part of the garden picture.

A true biennial makes a mature plant that does not flower the same year that seed is sown. It blossoms the following summer, sets seed, and dies. Some of the plants we grow as biennials do not follow this pattern exactly because they are actually short-lived perennials. Among them are hollyhocks, sweet Williams, English daisies, and pansies. All of these, if they happen to survive in the garden, will produce a few flowers the second summer. However, they are so unreliable handled in this way that it is better to pull them out and start anew.

While the need for constant replacement may seem unnecessary, it can be advantageous. Most perennials have a short season of bloom. Biennials, on the other hand, can be taken out after this short period and replaced, either with potted annuals or with clumps of chrysanthemums.

Once biennials have been started in a garden, the only problem is one of raising replacements and moving these into position in fall. There is no break in the continuity so long as the current year's seeding is able to produce mature plants. The real trick is to judge when to sow.

Following British recommendations of sowing dates is a mistake often made. Usually, these call for sowing in June. This is fine for England, where June night temperatures may average about 50°, but all wrong for the United States. Note particularly the sowing times given in the list below, designed to adapt the seed to the best temperatures available.

CULTURE OF BIENNIALS

All of the species grown as biennials prefer a rich soil containing liberal amounts of well-decayed organic matter. Soil should have a pH of not lower than 6.5. Although biennials prefer a moist soil, they cannot stand wet feet. Withhold water somewhat towards fall so that they do not go into winter in too soft a condition.

THE BEST OF THE BIENNIALS

Althaea rosea (Hollyhock). Undoubtedly one of the best of our background plants. Self-seeded plants should be ruthlessly destroyed and new seed planted. Otherwise colors deteriorate and doubles become singles. Sow seed as early in spring as soil can be worked. Seeds should be sown in July or August for bloom the following year. The type has red, pink, or white single flowers, but improved forms have a wide range of color shades, as well as double and semi-double forms.

Bellis perennis (English Daisy). British gardeners are looking for a reliable weed-killer to destroy this flower. If it escapes to their lawns, it can be a terrible pest. Less rugged here, it is difficult to start from seed. It likes cool nights and warm days. Sow it in August under lath or burlap shade and keep the beds moist with a fine spray. Hold the plants over in the coldframe until spring, then plant them between tulips, just emerging from the soil. About 6 inches high, English daisies bloom in spring. The dainty flowers are white, pink, or deep rose.

Campanula medium (Canterbury Bells, Cup-and-Saucer Flower). Although cup-and-saucer is sometimes listed as *Campanula calycanthema*, it is a variety of *C. medium*. Both produce lavish violet-blue or pink flowers in early summer, then die. The hardest part of their culture is keeping them alive over winter. They resent the least moisture in the center of the crown. For both *Campanula medium* and digitalis, try to think of winter protection as a tent instead of an overcoat. The idea is to keep out excessive moisture, including snow and rain. Experts use a wide wooden shingle canted across the plant and supported by a stake at one end. Then evergreen boughs are thrown over the shingles to break the wind. This device keeps water out of the center of the crown, the cause of most winter losses. Sow seed in early spring, not in June as usually recommended.

Cheiranthus allioni. See *Erysimum asperum.*

Cheiranthus cheiri (English Wallflower). If the winter is not too severe, this startling flower will grow in the open — notably in the South — and will flower in January and February even when covered with drifting snow. Sow seed as early as possible (January and February in the South; indoors at the same time in the North). Plants once established can be grown from cuttings. In the North, bring them into flower in coldframes for sensational, richly fragrant winter bouquets. Yellow flowers on 1-ft. plants.

Delphinium (hybrids) and *Delphinium chinensis.* Some gardeners will be surprised to see these treated as biennials, but over much of the United States and Canada, they are best handled as such. The new Pacific Giants, for example, as magnificent as they are in California (where they are true perennials) are much better treated either as annuals or biennials from the Rocky Mountains eastward. If left in for a second year's bloom, many of the plants will be dead the following spring.

One requirement of delphinium must be kept in mind: the seed germinates poorly or not at all at temperatures above 60°. It can be sown in a cool greenhouse between Christmas and New Year's Day. This sowing will produce strong plants that will flower in early summer. If these are then cut back (remove only the flower stalk, no leaves) they will send up another shoot in fall. The plant should then be discarded. A spring sowing in a cool frame will produce seedlings that will flower late in fall, after which they can be left in for possible spring blooms. After that they are best discarded.

Dianthus barbatus (Sweet William). While this species will live over winter, the flower heads and florets will be smaller. Start new plants each year. The modern variety 'Wee Willie' is grown as an annual and flowers with the marigolds. Unless flower heads are kept picked, it dies.

If a coldframe is available, cuttings can be made from old plants in August and carried over to be set out in spring. Otherwise, sow seed each April and transplant in August. Usually 1-2 ft. high with red, pink, or white flowers.

Digitalis (Foxglove). What has already been said about wintering Canterbury bells applies equally to foxglove which needs particular care in wintering. Start seed in April in a coldframe and winter them in the frame. Set out the plants in spring. The very deep clay pots known as rose pots are ideal for growing individual plants. Roots and leaves are poisonous.

In some locations, for reasons no one can explain, April seedings may fail to flower: if this happens, try August seeding in the frame. Once plants are established, old roots can be split up after flowering and off-shoots used for producing new plants.

One of the most stately and beautiful flowers to grace the spring garden, digitalis, especially *D. purpurea,* the species most commonly grown (2-4 ft. high) produces charming white, rose, purple, or yellow flowers. Many intermediate shades — especially delicate pinks — are available among the newer hybrids. Cool, moist growing conditions are ideal.

Erysimum asperum. (Siberian Wallflower). Seeded in May, it will flower the following May. Keep the flowers picked; otherwise it will die as soon as seed is set. The plant can also be seeded indoors in February or March, for late fall flowering. At that season, however, it must compete with chrysanthemums.

Lunaria biennis (Peter's Pence or Honesty). Flowers lilac-purple followed by silver seed pods used as everlastings in winter bouquets. An old-fashioned favorite. Self-sows and may be pesky. Fragrant flowers on 1½-2½ ft. flower stems.

Myosotis sylvatica and *M. dissitiflora* (Forget-me-not). Technically, forget-me-nots are classed as annuals or perennials, but most are grown successfully as biennials in the U.S. The most delicate shade of blue is found in the varieties of *M. dissitiflora.* Plants grow about 8-9 in. high and bloom April-June. They often self-sow, so that plants perpetuate themselves just like perennials.

Viola tricolor hortensis (Pansy). Needs cool nights to germinate. Sow seed in mid-August, using a fine spray to cool the soil if the weather stays hot. Protect plants in frames as described under coldframes (Chapter 14).

PERENNIALS

The ability to produce a succession of bloom with perennials might well be taken as the badge of a real gardener. Coming as they do from all over the temperate areas of the world, north and south of the equator, their cultural needs are highly varied. Thus, great skill is required to grow them within a single garden.

Too often, inexperienced gardeners look on perennials as a quick and permanent answer to the problem of borders. "Once planted, forever done" is a beautiful dream, but sooner or later the gardener wakes to the realization that his "permanent" plantings require constant renewal. A perennial border which is not substantially redone at least every five years is definitely on the downgrade.

This should in no sense be taken as an argument against perennials.

Despite the work entailed, they are among the most rewarding of all plants when well grown. No others can produce quite the sensational burst of bloom we enjoy from peonies, Oriental poppies, daylilies, iris, or phlox when these are at their peak. True, each may bloom only a short period in the garden, but if plantings are made so that one major flower follows another, spring, summer, and fall can be a succession of striking displays.

It is in this piling of glory upon glory that British gardeners excel. An English perennial border in June is a garden sensation that must be seen to be believed.

Since the greatest problem in arranging a border is to reconcile different flowering seasons with the need for color harmony, the list that follows indicates color and month of bloom. Further description of the different plants is given in the Plant Encyclopedia.

Because no perennial border can possibly maintain an uninterrupted flow of bloom, supplemental plantings of bulbs or annuals can be made to fill in wherever needed. Too, a regular place should be provided for biennials and bulbs. Particularly with the earliest perennial to bloom, the Christmas rose (*Helleborus niger*), are the first small colorful bulbs of the season welcome. The Christmas rose may bloom when snow is on the ground in winter, and continue into March.

FLOWERING PERENNIALS
(Not including bulbs or vines)

	Height (in feet)	Color	Time of bloom
Acanthus mollis, Bear's Breech	2	Rose-lilac to white	July-Aug.
Achillea species, Yarrow	1-3	Yellow, white	June-Sept.
Aconitum species, Monkshood	4-6	Blue, yellow, white	Aug.-Sept.
Actaea species, Baneberry	1½-2	White	May-June
Adenophora lilifolia, Ladybell	2-3	Blue	July-Aug.
Adonis amurensis, Amur Floss Flower	1½	Yellow	May
A. vernalis, Spring Ox-eye	1½	Yellow	May
Aethionema grandiflorum, Persian Stone Cress	1-1½	Rose-pink	May-June
Ajuga reptans, Carpet Bugle	½-1	Blue-violet	May-June
Alchemilla vulgaris, Lady's Mantle	1½	Greenish yellow	July
Alyssum saxatile, Basket-of-gold	1	Yellow	April-May
Amsonia tabernaemontana, Blue Shadow	2	Blue	May-June
Anchusa azurea, Alkanet	3-4	Blue	June-July
Anemone japonica, Japanese Anemone	2-3	Rose-purple	Sept.-Oct.
A. pulsatilla, Pasque Flower	1	Blue, purple	April
Anthemis tinctoria, Golden Marguerite	2-3	Yellow	July-Aug.

	Height (in feet)	Color	Time of bloom
Aquilegia species and hybrids, Columbine	1-3	Blue, yellow, purple, white	May-Aug.
Arabis albida, Wall Rock Cress	½-1	White	April
Armeria maritima, Common Thrift	1	White, rose-pink	May-June
Aruncus sylvester, Goatsbeard	5-7	White	June-July
Asclepias tuberosa, Butterfly Weed	3	Orange	July-Aug.
Asperula odorata, Sweet Woodruff	¾	White	May-June
Asphodeline lutea, Jacob's Rod	2-3	Yellow	June
Aster species	1-4	Various	Aug.-Sept.
Astilbe species, False Spirea	2-3	White	July
Aubrieta deltoidea, Purple Rock Cress	½	Purple to pink	June
Baptisia australis, False Indigo	4-6	Blue	June
Begonia evansiana, Hardy Begonia	1½	Pink	July-Aug.
Bergenia cordifolia, Siberian Saxifrage	1½	Pink	May
Bocconia cordata, Plume Poppy	6	White	July-Aug.
Boltonia asteroides, Giant Aster	4-8	White	Aug.-Sept.
Brunnera macrophylla, Siberian Forget-me-not	1½	Blue	May
Callirhoe involucrata, Poppy Mallow	1	Purple	June-Aug.
Caltha palustris, Marsh Marigold	1½-2	Yellow	April-June
Campanula species, Bellflower	1-5	Blue, purple, white	June-Aug.
Cassia marilandica, Wild Senna	3-4	Yellow	July-Aug.
Catanache caerulea, Cupid's Dart	1½-2	Blue	July-Aug.
Centaurea macrocephala, Showy Knapweed	3	Yellow	July-Aug.
C. montana, Mountain Bachelor Button	2	Blue	June-July
Centranthus ruber, Red Valerian	2½	Red	June-July
Cerastium tomentosum, Snow-in-summer	½	White	June
Ceratostigma plumbaginoides, Plumbago	1	Blue	Aug.-Sept.
Chelone species, Turtlehead	2-3	White, red	July-Aug.
Chrysanthemum species	1-3	White, yellow, red	July-Sept.
Cimicifuga racemosa, Black Snakeroot	5-8	White	July-Aug.
Clematis fremonti, Prairie Bell	1½	Purple	May-Aug.
C. heracleaefolia, Dwarf Chinese Clematis	2½	Blue	Aug.
C. integrifolia, Dwarf Virgin's Bower	3	Blue, white	June-July
C. recta, Dwarf Chinese Clematis	3	White	June-Aug.
Convallaria majalis, Lily-of-the-valley	¾-1	White	May
Coreopsis grandiflora, Perennial Tickseed	2	Yellow	July-Aug.
Coronilla varia, Crown Vetch	1-2	Pink	June-Oct.
Delphinium species and hybrids, Larkspur	3-6	Blue, white	June-July
Dianthus species, Pink	½-1½	Red, pink, white	June-July
Dicentra eximia, Plumy Bleeding-heart	1½-2	Pink	May-July
D. spectabilis, Bleeding-heart	2-2½	Pink	May-June

	Height (in feet)	Color	Time of bloom
Dictamnus albus, Gas Plant	3-4	Reddish, white	June
Doronicum species, Leopardbane	2	Yellow	May
Echinacea purpurea, Purple Coneflower	2-4	Purple	July-Aug.
Echinops ritro, Globe Thistle	2	Blue	July-Aug.
Epimedium species, Barrenwort	1	Red, white, yellow	May-June
Erigeron speciosus, Showy Fleabane	1½-2½	Rose to purple	June-July
Eryngium species, Sea Holly	1-2	Blue	July-Aug.
Erysimum asperum, Siberian Wallflower	2½	Yellow to orange	May-June
Eupatorium coelestinum, Hardy Ageratum	2-2½	Blue	Aug.-Sept.
Euphorbia corollata, Flowering Spurge	2½	White	July-Aug.
Gaillardia aristata, Blanket Flower	2-3	Yellow-orange	June-Aug.
Galega officinalis, Goats-rue	2-3	Purple-blue	June-Aug.
Gentiana species, Gentian	½-3	Blue, yellow	July-Sept.
Geranium sanguineum, Blood Geranium	1-1½	Red, purple, white	June-July
Geum chiloense, Common Avens	1½-2	Scarlet	June-Aug.
Globularia vulgaris, Globe Daisy	1	Blue	May
Gypsophila paniculata, Baby's Breath	2-3	White	July-Aug.
Helenium autumnale, Sneezeweed	3-6	Yellow	Aug.-Sept.
Helianthemum nummularium, Sun Rose	1	Yellow	July
Heliopsis laevis, False Sunflower	3-5	Yellow to orange	July-Aug.
Helleborus niger, Christmas Rose	1	White to purple	Nov.-Feb.
Hemerocallis species and hybrids, Daylily	1½-4	Orange, yellow, red, blends	June-Sept.
Hesperis matronalis, Dame's Violet	2½	Pink to purple	June-July
Heuchera sanguinea, Coral Bells	1½-2	Red	June-July
Hibiscus moscheutos, Swamp Rose Mallow	3-7	Rose-pink, white	Aug.-Sept.
Hosta species, Plantain Lily	2-3	Blue, lavender, white	July-Aug.
Iberis sempervirens, Perennial Candytuft	1	White	May
Iris species	1-4	Various	May-July
Lamium maculatum, Spotted Dead Nettle	1-1½	Red-purple	May-Aug.
Lavandula spica, Lavender	2-3	Lavender	July-Aug.
Lavatera assurgentiflora, American Tree Mallow	8-10	Pink to purple	July-Aug.
Liatris species, Gayfeather	2-4	Blue-purple	Aug.
Limonium sinuatum, Sea Lavender	1-2	Blue	July-Aug.
Linaria dalmatica, Toadflax	2-4	Yellow	July-Aug.
Linum species, Flax	1-2	Yellow, blue, white	June-July
Liriope muscari, Lily-turf	1-1½	Blue-purple	July-Aug.
Lobelia cardinalis, Cardinal Flower	2-4	Scarlet	Aug.-Sept.
L. siphilitica, Great Blue Lobelia	2-3	Blue-purple	Aug.-Sept.
Lupinus polyphyllus, Perennial Lupine	3-5	Purple, white, yellow	June-Sept.

	Height (in feet)	Color	Time of bloom
Lychnis species, Campion	¾-2½	White, pink, red	June-July
Lysimachia vulgaris, Golden Loosestrife	3-4	Yellow	July
Lythrum salicaria, Purple Loosestrife	3	Purple-red	July-Aug.
Malva moschata, Musk Mallow	2	Pink, white	July-Aug.
Mertensia virginica, Virginia Bluebell	2-3	Blue	April-May
Mimulus luteus, Monkey Flower	3	Yellow	July-Aug.
Monarda didyma, Oswego Tea	3	Scarlet	July-Aug.
Myosotis scorpiodes, Forget-me-not	1½	Blue	June-Aug.
Nepeta species, Catnip	1-3	Blue, purple, white, pink	July-Aug.
Oenothera missouriensis, Missouri Primrose	1	Yellow	July-Aug.
Ostrowskia magnifica, Giant Bellflower	5	Blue	July-Aug.
Paeonia species, Peony	1½-3	White, pink, red	May-June
Papaver species, Poppy	1-3	Red, yellow, white	May-June
Penstemon glaber, Beardtongue	1-2	Blue, purple	July-Aug.
Petalostemon purpureum, Tassel Flower	3	Purple	July-Aug.
Phlox paniculata, Garden Phlox	3-4	Pink, purple, white	July-Aug.
P. subulata, Ground Pink	½	Various	May
Physostegia virginiana, False Dragonhead	3-4	Violet-pink, white	July-Aug.
Platycodon grandiflorum, Balloon Flower	2-3	Blue	June-Aug.
Podophyllum peltatum, Mayflower	1½	White	May
Polemonium species, Jacob's Ladder	1-3	Blue	May-June
Potentilla nepalensis, Nepal Cinquefoil	2	Red	July-Aug.
Primula species, Primrose	½-2½	Yellow, purple, white	April-June
Pulmonaria angustifolia, Cowslip Lungwort	1	Purple, blue	April-May
Ramonda nathaliae, Serbian Queen	½	Lavender-blue	June
Ranunculus acris flore-pleno, Buttercup	2-3	Yellow	May-June
Rudbeckia fulgida, Coneflower	2	Yellow-orange	Aug.-Sept.
Salvia species, Sage	2-3	Blue, purple	June-July
Saponaria officinalis, Bouncing Bet	2	Pink, white	May-Sept.
Saxifraga species, Rockfoil	½-2	Yellow, white, rose-pink	May-July
Scabiosa caucasica, Blue Scabious	2-3	Blue, lavender	July-Aug.
Sedum species, Stone Cress	½-1	Yellow, white	June-July
Shortia galacifolia, Oconee Bells	¾	White	May-June
Silene species, Catchfly	½-1	Pink, purple, red, white	June-Aug.
Solidago species, Goldenrod	4-5	Yellow	Aug.-Sept.
Stachys species, Woundwort	1½	Purple, white	June-July
Stokesia cyanea, Stokes Aster	1½	Purple-blue	Aug.
Tanacetum vulgare, Tansy	3	Yellow	July
Teucrium chamaedrys, Germander	1-2	Red-purple	Aug.-Sept.
Thalictrum species, Meadow Rue	3-4	White, yellow, purple	June

	Height (in feet)	Color	Time of bloom
Thermopsis caroliniana, Yellow False Lupine	4	Yellow	June
Thymus serpyllum, Creeping Thyme	¼	Red-purple	June-July
Tradescantia virginiana, Spiderwort	3	Red, purple, blue, white	May-Sept.
Trillium grandiflorum, Great White Trillium	1½	White	May
Trollius species, Globe Flower	2	Yellow, orange	May-June
Tunica saxifraga, Coatflower	¾	Lilac, pink	June-July
Uvularia grandiflora, Bellwort	1½	Yellow	April-May
Valeriana officinalis, Garden Heliotrope	4-5	Lavender, pink, white	July-Aug.
Veronica species, Speedwell	1-2½	Blue, lilac	May-June
Viola species, Violet	½-1	White, purple, yellow, blue	May-Aug.

3

Daylilies, Lilies, and Phlox

At first glance, lilies, daylilies, and phlox seem to have little in common. True lilies belong to the genus lilium, daylilies to the genus hemerocallis. Both are members of the lily family, but phlox is a broad-leaved plant, miles away from the others botanically.

We group them together here because they spell one thing — reliable summer bloom. When the great wave of spring colors has ebbed, they take the stage, enlivening a border that would otherwise be dull. Their gay colors lack blues and purples, but these can be supplied by blue-flowering perennials such as certain campanulas (particularly *Campanula carpatica*, used as a low edging plant), fall asters, and one or two reliable aconitum species. Blue annuals, too, can be spotted here and there in the border.

HEMEROCALLIS

Most of the improvements in daylilies have been effected since World War II, although enthusiasm for the plant as a subject for intensive breeding was largely initiated much earlier by Dr. A. B. Stout. He was, of course, aided and abetted by others who revolutionized the appearance of this flower. Before his time, the color range included only yellow and orange. This was augmented in 1929 by the introduction of the rose-colored *Hemerocallis fulva rosea* from China. However, it was not until later that the introduction of the new color had much influence on commercial varieties.

One factor, of tremendous importance to results, is the existence of three different types of hemerocallis varieties. One is the so-called dormant type which succeeds in the North, going through a winter rest period as part of its life cycle. Varieties in this group were bred largely by Northerners, using *Hemerocallis flava*, *H. fulva*, and *H. fulva rosea* as their major sources. While these flower well, they bloom for much shorter periods in the South than the next type, and are therefore less popular there.

The second type includes evergreen varieties, largely produced by southern breeders, which keep blooming in "flushes" all summer and fall. Because of their longer flowering season, and flowers that are often more striking than those of the dormant group, evergreen varieties are used almost exclusively in the South.

The third group is "all things to all men." It includes varieties in which the long-flowering habits of the evergreen varieties and the ability to withstand winter have been rather successfully combined.

South of the Kentucky-Tennessee line, hardy evergreen varieties should be selected along with true evergreens. North of that line, dormants, combined with hardy evergreens are preferable. These lists have been adapted from the popularity poll conducted by the American Hemerocallis Society and thus include only widely distributed varieties.

SELECTED LIST OF POPULAR DAYLILIES

DORMANT VARIETIES

'Atlas': Midseason; light yellow, chartreuse shadings.

'Bess Ross': Midseason; brilliant scarlet, green throat.

'Blythe Spirit': Midseason, light yellow.

'Capitol Dome': Midseason; buff yellow.

'Cartwheels': Midseason to late; deep yellow.

'Chetco': Midseason; creamy primrose, melon pink touches, green throat.

'Daafu': Midseason to late; rosy pink, golden throat.

'Evelyn Claar': Midseason; salmon pink, golden throat.

'Fairy Wings': Midseason; pale yellow, pink tint, green throat.

'Flying Saucer': Midseason; light yellow.

'Francis Fay': Early to midseason; melon pink.

'George Cunningham': Midseason; deep melon pink.

'Golden Chimes': Early to midseason; clear chrome yellow.

'Golden Song': Midseason; golden yellow, greenish throat.

'Green Valley': Midseason; light yellow.

'Hearts Afire': Early to midseason; brilliant carmine red.

'Kindly Light': Midseason; rich yellow, spider-petalled.

'Lady Inara': Early to midseason; pink and yellow blend.

'Limonero': Early to midseason; lemon yellow, jade green throat.

'Louise Russell': Midseason to late; delicate pink.

'Lucky Strike': Early to midseason; light dawn pink blend.

'Magic Dawn': Midseason; light melon pink, yellow green throat.

'Marguerite Fuller': Midseason to late; pale yellow-chartreuse.

'Midwest Majesty': Midseason; creamy pale yellow.

'Midwest Star': Midseason; pale yellow.

'Multnomah': Midseason to late; apricot overlaid with pale pink.

'Nashville': Midseason; cream yellow and orange.

'Neyron Rose': Midseason; bright rose, darker veins, cream bands.

'Nina Rebmen': Midseason; amber yellow and pink.

'Painted Lady': Midseason; cinnamon over golden yellow.

'Pink Damask': Midseason; rose pink, yellowy green cup.

'Pink Imperial': Midseason; porcelain pink, wide yellow throat.

'Pink Orchid': Early to midseason; salmon, shell-pink blend.

'Pink Prelude': Midseason; rosy pink with flesh-pink midribs.

'President Rice': Midseason; deep orange-gold.

'Rare China': Midseason; blend of yellow and rose.

'Revolute': Late midseason; light lemon green.

'Ringlets': Midseason; bright gold miniatures.

'Ruth Lehman': Midseason; melon pink touched with paler pinks.

'Shooting Star': Midseason to late; light creamy yellow.

'Splendor': Midseason; rosy crimson.

'Tootie': Midseason to late; clear, soft pink.

'The Doctor': Midseason; bright vermilion scarlet.

EVERGREEN VARIETIES, STRICTLY FOR SOUTHERN PLANTING

'April Breeze': Early to midseason; light greenish lemon.

'Bright Dancer': Early (reblooming); bright red.

'Capri': Midseason (reblooming); pale rosy apricot.

'Captain Russell': Midseason; lavender, light ivory bicolor.

'Cosette': Early (reblooming); warm yellow dusted with rose.

'Delectable': Midseason to late; melon pink.

'Delta Girl': Early; very pale, almost white.

'Dorcas': Early; burnt orange.

Why daylilies bloom so long: Today's flower (A); yesterday's (B); last week's (C); tomorrow's (D); and one for next week (E).

Setting out daylilies: Juncture of tops and roots should be at soil level. Space far apart to allow several years of uncrowded growth.

Hardy daylilies multiply pleasantly fast without becoming invasive. With a little care, they grow larger and have more flowers each year.

To divide an old clump without losing a season of blooms, dig only half of it this year. Separate dug half into single units and reset.

'Drama Girl': Midseason (reblooming); flamingo pink.

'Garnet Robe': Midseason (reblooming); oxblood red, yellow-green throat.

'Gay Lark': Midseason; pink.

'Golden Galleon': Midseason (reblooming); deep apricot.

'High Noon'; Midseason; deep cadmium yellow.

'Jake Russell': Early to late midseason; gold with velvety sheen.

'June Rhapsody': Early midseason; pink.

'Lime Frolic': Midseason; light gold with lime green throat.

'Luxury Lace': Midseason to late; lavender pink.

'Melotone': Midseason; soft yellow with touch of pink.

'Nantahala': Early; orangey-yellow.

'Naranja': Midseason to late; deep, clear orange.

'Nobility': Midseason to late; light yellow.

'Picture': Early to midseason; light rose pink.

'Pink Reflection': Early midseason; pink with small gold throat.

'Playboy': Early midseason; deep, bright orange.

'Prima Donna': Midseason; peach tones, blended pink and yellow.

'Queen of Hearts': Midseason; bright rose red.

'Quincy': Midseason; pale peach beige, banded reddish purple.

'Ruffled Pinafore': apricot yellow with rose glow at ends of petals.

'Side Show': Early (reblooming); buff yellow with green throat.

'Silver Sails': Midseason; very light creamy yellow, almost white.

'Soleil d'Or': Early (reblooming); lemon gold, sepals lavender edged.

'Summer Love': Midseason (reblooming); rich golden yellow.

DORMANT "EVERGREEN" VARIETIES FOR PLANTING NORTH OR SOUTH

'Alan': Midseason to late; cherry red.

'Bailey Walker': Midseason; melon in pink-gold blend.

'Colonel Joe': Early to midseason; light lemon-yellow.

'Colonial Dame': Midseason; light apricot banded with pale rosy tan.

'Cradle Song': Early (reblooming); medium yellow.

'Garden Sprite': Early to midseason; apricot with pink flush.

'Golden Dew Drop': Early (reblooming); orange-yellow.

'Jack Frost': Late midseason; pale lemon-yellow.

'Jade Crest': Midseason; chrome yellow.

'Lime Painted Lady': Midseason; light yellow-chartreuse.

'Marie Wood': Early midseason; true, full pink.

'Marionette': Midseason to late; yellow with mahogany band.

'Miss Jessie': Midseason; orchid mauve, light yellow bicolor.

Salmon Sheen': Midseason (reblooming); salmon pink.

'Show Girl': Early midseason (reblooming); orchid pink with deeper veins.

'Wide Eyes': Early (reblooming); yellow with wine-red "eye."

CULTURE OF DAYLILIES

One of the endearing qualities of the daylily is its ability to survive almost any abuse and still bloom. Clumps resulting from garden escapes have been known to survive and compete aggressively with grass and weeds for half a century or more. This does not mean they should be neglected, but does indicate an inherent vigor which makes the daylily a unique subject. For one thing, you can walk through the fields of a grower, pick out the varieties you want, dig them with a ball of earth and move them for miles. Plant them the next day, water well, and they will grow with practically no sign of having been moved.

If you want to increase your stock of a certain variety, dig it at almost any time of the year and divide it. On the other hand, daylilies can be allowed to go for years without dividing and still flower. They are not fussy about soil, though they thrive especially well in a rich prairie loam.

Specialists have a hard time trying to find diseases among them; their ills are insignificant. Simple spraying with a general insecticide will take care of practically any pest that attacks them. (Such attacks are rare.) Water them if you want to force bloom in summer, but they will survive without it. In short, plant them 3 feet apart in any soil, and if they get 4 hours or more of sun a day they will flower for you.

IMPROVED MODERN DAYLILIES

Those who remember daylilies only as tawny or yellow roadside escapes that flowered in July and quickly faded, can scarcely credit the improvement achieved in the quality of bloom during the past two decades. Perhaps the most striking improvement has been in color. With the introduction of the variety 'Rosalind,' the first pink "break" in the genus, breeders had a much wider color range with which to work. Today, the modern hemerocallis can be had in every color except blue. The range is from the palest primrose yellow through gold, orange, and buff to deep bronze; and from a delicate seashell to deep ruby-red. The newer melon shades are subtle blends of peach, copper, buff, and pink, plus all the pastel colors between. Modern reds are astonishing in their brilliance, and the deep purple shades must be seen to be believed.

At first these colors were solid; today bicolors (even tricolors) are com-

TYPES OF LILY FLOWERS: *Trumpet-shaped blooms (1) include this Golden Clarion, also regal and Easter lilies. Bowl-shaped lilies (2) are typical of gold-band and several new hybrids. Chalice-shaped upright clusters (3) include many Mid-Century varieties. Small recurved blooms (4) include Fiesta Hybrids. Large recurved blooms (5) are found on varieties of* Lilium *speciosum.*

mon. Striped, eyed, and banded flowers further increase the range of color combinations.

A weakness of the daylily, even in today's improved varieties, is its poor value as a cut flower. Individual blooms last only a day, closing at sundown. However, this defect is being remedied; a few varieties are now in commerce that not only stay open a full day but last overnight and are still fresh the next morning.

The earliest daylilies begin to bloom in May with late iris, and continue into June. Other varieties take up the procession during July and August — the big months for this flower. A few still carry on into early September. Repeat bloomers may carry a few flowers later in the fall. Varieties of the dormant-evergreen and evergreen types can be depended on for succession bloom over a much longer period of time.

LILIUM: THE TRUE LILY

True lilies, like their hemerocallis cousins, have been completely changed in character during the past two decades. Formerly delicate and extremely difficult to grow, the lily is now a dependable bulbous flower, filling a definite place in the summer border.

Always considered one of the loveliest of flowers, the lily was a specialist's flower, hard to grow and whimsical in its behavior. British horticulturists in Queen Victoria's time had a standard test of a gardener's worth: "Has he bloomed *Lilium giganteum*?" To have produced the 12-foot stems of this stupendous plant, with its dozen or more nodding white trumpets, was indeed a feat to qualify the lucky gardener for horticultural immortality.

Other lilies in the past were almost as difficult to keep alive. Even the ubiquitous Madonna lily has always been a perverse species, refusing to live under apparently ideal conditions, then surviving for years where conditions were anything but good. Our former Easter lily, *Lilium harrisi*, grown for years in Bermuda, is another example. So is *Lilium auratum*, the gold-banded lily of Japan — a glorious mosaic of white, gold, and crimson, as redolent as a Grasse jasmine distillery and as unpredictable as weather. It might survive for a generation, perfectly happy, in some woodland glade, only to sicken and die almost overnight.

Lilies still suffer from a reputation for fickleness, a fault which cannot be attributed to modern hybrids. The time has come for present-day gardeners to realize that lilies have come of age and are today one of our most valuable flowers for summer bloom. Nor is their season confined to summer; it is possible to find early species and varieties that flower in May and June, and at least two reliable September lilies can be had.

Whenever a modern named variety is available that is as good as, or an improvement on, an old species, always select the new variety. Even

though it may not be greatly superior, the fact that it has been raised
from seed within comparatively recent times means that it has not been
propagated widely, and it is more likely to have been raised under disease-
free conditions. As a result, newer varieties are usually much more free
of the diseases, such as mosaic and botrytis, which tend to make the older
varieties and species short-lived in the garden.

In height, the lily genus ranges from about 20 inches to 8 feet. In color
range, the modern lily shows remarkable advances. Solid colors from pure
white to deep purple — with clear yellow, cinnabar-red, and orange in
between — are available, and the same colors striped, or splashed with red,
purple, or black dots. Perhaps the most striking colors of all are found in
hybrids of *L. auratum* and *L. speciosum* — huge saucers of white or primrose yellow, variously marked with vivid reds and crimsons — as rich
as an Oriental rug.

WHERE TO GROW LILIES

Although definitely not adapted to full shade, most lilies prefer some
shading around their roots. They do well in light, filtered shade such as is
found under a honey-locust tree. The ideal situation is a sunny border
where their roots are shaded by low-growing, shallow-rooted plants. A
mulch over their roots will definitely improve results. This can be left on
from year to year. Since all lilies (except Madonna and Nankeen) prefer
an acid soil, an acid peat makes an excellent mulch. Another good material is oak leafmold. Vermiculite is also good. Perlite, though a good
mulch, is too white and glaring.

Avoid mulches high in sugar and starch, such as ground corn cobs,
fresh straw, and grass clippings. If these are used, they should be composted for a year before they are applied. Old sawdust that has been in a
pile outdoors for several years makes a good mulch if it has turned brown.
Fresh sawdust is definitely bad.

LILY SOIL

The ideal lily soil, according to one specialist, is so loose and friable that
an arm can be thrust into it up to the elbow. This is a bit of hyperbole, but
it does illustrate what we are after — an extremely loose soil, high in well-
rotted organic matter, in which air can move freely but which is so spongy
that it will hold water and remain constantly moist without being soggy.
This ideal would be impossible to attain without the liberal use of organic
matter. Since the only lily in the following list that prefers alkaline soil is
Lilium candidum (and its hybrid *L. testaceum*), the use of acid peatmoss
or oak leafmold is logical. There are some lime-*tolerant* lilies such as *L.
cernuum, L. hansoni, L. longiflorum, L. martagon, L. monadelphum,* and

L. regale, but since these will also grow in acid soil, a pH of not more than 6.0 to 6.5 is best.

FERTILIZERS FOR LILIES

A superstition, and one which may account for some failures with lilies in the past, is that they should not be fertilized. This idea has been refuted by the work of Dr. S. L. Emsweller of the U.S. Department of Agriculture, who has proved definitely that lilies are heavy feeders and should be given fertilizer if they are to do well. However, *organic* fertilizers *do* stimulate fungus diseases. This, perhaps, is the basis of the notion that lilies do poorly when fed. A balanced chemical fertilizer with minor elements included is best. Some gardeners mix about a spoonful of *ureaform nitrogen* (which is *not* urea, *per se*) in the soil when planting a bulb.

VARIETIES

Although the skill of the modern plant breeder is largely responsible for the present upsurge in the popularity of lilies, there are still a number of older species and varieties which flower at a season when no modern hybrid ever blooms.

The enthusiast will probably want to include *Cardiocrinum giganteum,* in spite of its temperamental growth. It must be planted in a soil that is half leafmold, preferably in a glade in open woods facing south but sheltered from the harsh rays of the sun after about two in the afternoon. Bulbs of several sizes should be planted, since the plant flowers only once, then dies, leaving smaller offsets to carry on. For fuller description and other lily species, see the Plant Encyclopedia.

LILIES FOR AMERICAN GARDENS
Short (Under 30 inches)

	WHITE	YELLOW	ORANGE	RED	PINK
MAY		'Golden Chalice' 'Golden Wonder' *L. pumilum* 'Butterball'	*L. pumilum* 'Golden Gleam'	*L. pumilum*	
JUNE	'Achievement' *L. martagon album*	'Croesus' 'Destiny' 'Prosperity' *L. amabile luteum*	'Coronado Hybrids' 'Harmony' 'Joan Evans' 'Sunstar' 'Valencia' 'Paisley Strain'	'Cinnabar' 'Enchantment' 'Fireflame' 'Paprika' 'Tabasco' *L. amabile L. concolor L. concolor* 'Coridion'	*L. japonicum platyfolium* *L. martagon L. rubellum*

	WHITE	YELLOW	ORANGE	RED	LILAC	PINK
JULY	L. longiflorum 'Croft' L. longiflorum 'Estate' L. longiflorum 'Tetraploid' L. formosanum pricei		'Palomino' L. tsingtauense			L. cernuum
AUG.		L. wilsoni flavum	'Victory'	L. papilliferum		

Medium (2½ to 4 feet)

	WHITE	YELLOW	ORANGE	RED	LILAC	PINK
JUNE	L. candidum	L. hansoni 'Buttercup' L. monadelphum				
JULY	'Green Dragon' 'Green Magic' 'Olympic Hybrids' 'Olympic Select' 'Sentinel Strain' 'Emerald Strain' 'Emerald Isle' 'New Era' 'Bright Star' 'Stardust' L. taliense L. polyphyllum	'Citronella' 'Golden Wedding' 'Royal Gold' 'Golden Clarion' 'Golden Spendor' 'Limelight' 'Moonlight Strain' L. regale	'Shuksan' 'Bronzino' 'African Queen' 'Copper King' 'Happy Day'	'Afterglow' 'Sunset' 'Burgundy'	'Pink Perfection'	'Verona' L. kelloggi L. lankongense L. wardi
AUG.	'Empress of China' 'Flying Cloud' 'Imperial Silver' 'Empress of Japan' 'Angel Wings' 'Imperial Gold' L. auratum platyphyllum L. auratum virginale L. browni australe L. formosanum 'Wallace Strain'	'Golden Showers' L. parryi	'Gingersnap' 'Jack-Pot'	'Empress of India' 'Imperial Crimson' 'Jillian Wallace' 'Red Band Hybrids' L. martagon dalmaticum	'Pink Glory'	'Potomac Hybrids'

	WHITE	YELLOW	ORANGE	RED	PINK
SEPT.	L. speciosum 'White Champion'				'Mapleton Strain' L. speciosum 'Red Champion' 'Superstar'

Tall (Over 4 feet)

	WHITE	YELLOW	ORANGE	RED	PINK
JULY	'Black Dragon' 'Black Magic' 'Carrara'	'Helios' 'Luna'			'Inspiration'
AUG.	'Ivorine' 'Silverine' 'Silver Sunburst'	'Sunlight' 'Good Hope' 'Golden Sunburst'	'Coraline' 'Orange Sunburst' 'Thunderbolt'	'Jamboree'	
SEPT.	L. formosanum wilsoni		'T. A. Havemeyer'		

LILY CLASSIFICATION

For years, lily classification has been in a state of confusion because of the many new hybrids introduced during the past two decades. Every effort on the part of botanists to classify these has failed. They based their separations on such features as leaf characteristics, short or long pedicels, dark or light pollen, only to discover that when two species are crossed, results are not uniform. In the same group from the same parents, one seedling will have long pedicels while its sibling may have short. All possible characteristics may emerge from a single cross.

In an effort to bring some order out of chaos, Jan de Graaff of Gresham, Oregon, who has been responsible for many of the new hybrids, has set up a classification based first on origin and then on parentage. Although this classification has not yet been adopted by any official group, it has been approved in principle by the Royal Horticultural Society and has been referred to a special committee of the North American Lily Society for further study.

About the only disturbing feature of this classification (and this may be changed by 1964, the earliest date an official list can be put out), is the use of Asiatic, Oriental, and Chinese as classification divisions. While there are good reasons for this division, the terms may be confusing because they refer to the same areas of the world. The ten proposed divisions are as follows: Asiatic, Martagon, Candidum, American natives, Longiflorum, Chinese trumpet lilies, Aurelian hybrids, Oriental hybrids, a division for varieties and hybrids not included in other divisions, and last, a division to contain all true species.

PERENNIAL PHLOX

Unfortunately, we cannot say about hardy phlox what has already been said about lilies and daylilies. While there has been substantial progress in developing new varieties, practically all of the work has been done abroad, and new varieties are slow in showing up in American commerce. Many of our best varieties are still 20 to 30 years old. This is remarkable in a flower so often neglected or taken for granted in the garden and nursery.

An old superstition holds that phlox "reverts" to the original magenta-pink of the wild species from which it was bred. This arises from the fact that old plants are allowed to go to seed when the standard practice should be to cut away the faded flower heads. The seeds fall to the ground in winter, usually landing in the old stems of an established clump, and germinate. When the seedlings bloom, they are usually of the magenta-pink of the species. Because of their greater vigor, they often crowd out the old clump, giving the impression that they are the original plants, mutated in color.

Actually, examples of phlox mutating or reverting are very, very few. If new colors *do* appear in an old planting, keep them if they are desirable, but root them out if not. One way to avoid confusion is to dig old clumps every 3 years, divide the plants into single-stem divisions, and reset these in freshly worked soil.

Because of their ability to survive in spite of abuse, phlox are seldom given good culture. They thrive best in a rich, moist soil that does not dry out in summer. Don't plant them closer than 10 inches apart: red-spider mites and mildew thrive between plants set too closely.

One condition often observed in phlox is the browning and dropping of lower leaves about the time they come into bloom and later. This condition is blamed on many things (including rust, red-spider mites, and mildew) but is actually physiological — the effect of a shortage of both potash and phosphorus in the soil. True, other pests do move in after the leaves have been weakened, but these are secondary. This condition can be avoided by adding extra superphosphate to the soil when resetting the plants every third year, and by sprinkling wood ashes or muriate of potash on the surface of the soil yearly.

PHLOX VARIETIES

Most of these are *Phlox paniculata* varieties but those marked *P. suffruticosa* are shorter in stature and earlier in bloom.

SHORT: 15 to 20 inches   MEDIUM: 20 to 30 inches   TALL: over 30 inches

WHITE

'Marie Louise' T   Snow-white

'Mia Ruys' S
   Clean white — *P. suffruticosa*

'Miss Lingard' M
   Soft clear white — *P. suffruticosa*

'White Admiral' T   Pure white

'World Peace' T
   Large head, late bloomer

WHITE WITH ROSE OR CRIMSON EYE

'Mt. Everest' T   Delicate rosy eye   'Prime Minister' M   Red eye

LIGHT PINK TO DEEP ROSE

'Columbia' T
   Light pink, lavender shading

'Fairyland' T   Delicate shell-pink

'Fairy's Petticoat' T
   Pinkish lavender, darker eye

'Pinkette' M
   Palest of the rose pinks

LIGHT PINK TO DEEP SALMON

'Daily Sketch' T
   Salmon with red eye

'Gaiety' M   Clear salmon, early

'Lillian' S
   Shiny salmon-pink —
   P. suffruticosa

'Queen of Tonga' T
   Striking salmon with red eye

'Salmon Beauty' M
   Salmon-rose, white eye

'Sir John Falstaff' T
   Rich salmon-pink, large truss

RED AND SCARLET

'Adonis' T   Intense crimson

'Charles Curtis' T
   Bright scarlet-orange

'Cheerfulness' T   Salmon-red

'Jean' M   Blood-red eye, scarlet

'Leo Schlageter' T
   Orange-scarlet, deep glowing
   color

'Shenstone' T
   Rich cherry-red, dark eye

'Thunderbolt' T   Tangerine-red

ORANGE

'Orange' M True orange color

LAVENDER AND VIOLET

'Blue Boy' T Deep violet-blue

'Lilac Time' T
Deepest violet
(not lilac-colored)

'Little Lovely' s
Violet with white eye
P. suffruticosa

'Progress' M
Light violet, purple eye

'Rosy Blue' M
Closest to true lavender

'Toits de Paris' M
Deep violet

'Widar' M White, violet eye

4

Bulbs, Tubers, and Corms

Through ages of adaptation, many plants have developed underground storage members to help them survive during periods of adversity. This period might be a drought, a long cold period followed by a short growing season, or other unfavorable conditions.

Some plants must always be in a hurry. Woodland flowers that grow under deciduous trees must grow rapidly for a few weeks in spring before the forest canopy develops. In that short space of time they must produce their complete stem and leaf structure, bloom, and set seed. After that, they sink into dormancy until the following spring. The food that bulbs store during this short growing period must support the entire growing cycle the following year, even though the soil at that time of year is not high in nutrients.

In some plants the need for developing a bulbous storage organ may have been lost through eons of evolution, yet the plant continues to develop bulbs because no natural condition has made its ability to store food a disadvantage. Most lilies now thrive in rich soil and remain in constant growth, yet continue to produce bulbs which apparently are no longer needed.

WHEN IS A "BULB" A BULB?

The trade custom of calling any lumpy underground structure a bulb may not be good botany but is too well established to ignore. A garden-center operator will offer "100 Gladiolus Bulbs for $5" on the same counter with "Five Giant Dahlia Bulbs for $5," though the first is a corm and the second a tuber. For the record, a true bulb is made up either of fleshy scales (as in the lily) or of tunics (concentric coats, as in the onion and tulip) surrounding a basal plate from which the bud grows and becomes the aboveground plant. A corm is similar to a bulb, but is solid instead of being made up of scales. A tuber is a thickened underground stem with buds on the sides or top. A rhizome is a thickened underground stem with the growing tip at one end or at a joint.

Because some bulbous plants come from the tropics, they will not survive winters in the temperate zone and are grown as summer-flowering species. The bulbs are dug before freezing weather begins and stored indoors. These will be discussed later.

Among the best-known hardy bulbs is the tulip, of which about 100,000,000 are planted in the United States each year. A typical true bulb, it produces a plant in early spring, flowers less than a month after emerging, grows for a short time after flowering, then dies down until the following spring. It is one of the so-called Dutch bulbs, grown for centuries in Holland along with crocus, chionodoxas, hyacinths, narcissus, scillas, and snowdrops.

An "off-beat" bulb is the lycoris or hardy amaryllis, which flowers in late summer. Several species of crocus flower in late fall, having apparently adapted their life cycle to take advantage of the brief period when foliage has been thinned out by approaching winter but the soil has not yet frozen. The colchicum follows a similar pattern, as do several other bulbs.

If given reasonable care, hardy bulbs are among the easiest of all plants to grow. Indeed, if most beginning gardeners were given a few tulips and narcissus for their first project, the satisfaction they would derive from growing them would go a long way toward making them confirmed gardeners. In most bulbs the flower is already laid down, so that unless conditions for growth are highly unfavorable, they are sure to bloom.

CULTURE OF BULBS, TUBERS, AND CORMS

Recalling how bulbs evolved to overcome periods of adversity, we can get a good idea of their needs. Since most bulbs originated in parts of the world where water is often scarce, they dislike excessive moisture. Good drainage is essential to their well-being. If water ever stands in an area, do not plant bulbs there.

A rich soil is a disadvantage. Most bulbs developed where soils were thin — the tulip, for instance, in the mountains of Asia Minor. If they are planted where more food is available than is needed when mature, the bulb will proceed to split into bulblets. Moved to a poorer soil, these little bulbs will increase in size, and in two to four years they will flower. If left in the same rich soil, however, they will grow slightly and divide again. Gardeners often have this difficulty. Their tulips flower well the first and second years, then divide and send up only single leaves.

The ideal soil for most Dutch bulbs is a good sandy loam containing considerable humus (but no fresh organic matter). Such a soil is not over-rich, drains well, yet holds enough moisture for normal growth. In very poor soils, some fertilizer should be used, but not organic material such as sewerage sludge or sheep manure. Adding well-decayed organic matter is good practice. Also a complete chemical fertilizer should be used, one that will supply not more than 1 pound of actual nitrogen to 1,000 square feet.

Bulbs for forcing indoors are discussed in Chapter 11.

Organic Matter and Fungi

The reason for ruling out organic matter which has not gone through decay is that such matter nourishes certain fungus organisms that damage bulbs. A disease called tulip fire is caused by the botrytis fungus, picked up from decaying organic matter as the shoot emerges from the soil. At Beltsville, Maryland, the U.S. Department of Agriculture showed that when organic fertilizers were used on gladiolus plantings, three to four times as much disease developed as when no fertilizer was used.

Many old-time garden books recommend using large quantities of bone-meal for bulbs. This is probably as safe as anything, but it releases prac-tically no fertility which bulbs can use. In most gardens where annuals and perennials are fed during the summer, *no fertilizer* should be the rule for bulbs.

One exception to this rule is the lily. Although a true bulb, it thrives in rich soil. As previously mentioned, Dr. S. L. Emsweller of the Depart-ment of Agriculture has shown in careful experiments that lilies are heavy feeders. Also, he has shown that a complete chemical fertilizer is a better source of nutrition than one based on organic materials.

Planting Depths

Many difficulties with bulbs are traceable to planting at the wrong depth. Directions often say to "plant 3 inches deep" without explaining whether you are to measure from the top of the bulb or the base. In every instance, where planting depths for bulbs are mentioned in these pages, they are to the *top* of the bulb.

Some bulbous plants are able to form a new bulb above the old if planted too deeply, but this is not universal. Others are able to produce contractural roots which will pull the bulb down if it is planted too shal-low. The safest practice is to try to plant at the recommended depth.

Sometimes, the right level is hard to determine. At other times, the ideal must be sacrificed to convenience. The lighter the soil, the deeper a bulb can be planted. However, the minor bulbs are exceptions to this rule. If the soil is suitable for bulbs in the first place, they will do well at the

HOW TO PLANT BULBS: Dig a hole about 8″ deep, mix a handful of plant food with soil at bottom, then cover with enough soil to make the hole the right depth for the type of bulb being planted.

TUBEROSES — *set 6 or more bulbs per hole, 4″ deep, 4-6″ apart.*

DAHLIAS — *plant singly, large types 5-6″ deep, 2½-3′ apart; small types 4-5″ deep, 1½-3′ apart.*

PERUVIAN DAFFODILS — *set in clumps of 3 to 6, 4″ deep, 4-6″ apart.*

Bulbs of Tigridia, the tigerflower or shellflower, should be planted 6 to 12 bulbs in a hole, 4" deep, 4" apart.

IRIS TYPES: *Tall Bearded — Typical division you buy is one rhizome with fan of leaves. (A) Plant in good, well-drained soil and cover with ½ to 1" of soil. (B) Divide crowded clumps, discarding old center rhizomes. (C) Reset in groups pointing growing ends outward to avoid crowding.*

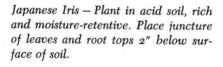

Japanese Iris — Plant in acid soil, rich and moisture-retentive. Place juncture of leaves and root tops 2" below surface of soil.

Siberian Iris — Plants can remain undisturbed for 10 years, so set out to allow clumps 2' in diameter. Root tops should be 1" below surface.

depth indicated, whether the soil is light or heavy. The tendency of narcissus and tulips to split into smaller bulbs is somewhat suppressed by
deep planting. Where tulips are planted for a single year's bloom, they
will probably put on a somewhat better show if planted only 4 inches
deep. Where permanence is desired, plant them 5 inches deep in heavier
soils, 7 inches deep in sandy loam.

Planting Time

Practically all bulbs are available only in fall; hence, they should be
planted then. Some, such as the crown imperial and all of the smaller
minor bulbs, are quite perishable. They should be planted as soon as they
are delivered, if possible.

There are exceptions, however. If tulips are planted too early, they
may make top growth and a sudden freeze might penetrate the soil and
kill the flower bud. This happens most often the first year. Once planted,
the tips are less likely to emerge early. For this reason, planting of tulips
should be delayed until mid-October over most of the East and Middle
West.

To Dig or Not to Dig

Many customs having to do with growing tulips originated during
Victorian times on the big estates in Europe, under climatic conditions entirely different from ours. The tulips grown were of the single early type,
which flower long before the tall late tulips and are less easily injured by
being dug. They were grown by the thousands and dug as soon as the
flowers began to fade. They then were "heeled in" where they could ripen
off, and were immediately replaced by bedding plants such as English
daisies, forget-me-nots, and pansies, which remained in place for only a
short time before they, too, were replaced with geraniums, lantanas, and
other summer-bedding plants.

Such a program has no place in the average American garden, yet we
persist in digging tulips as though we were following a mid-Victorian
schedule. Digging is not necessary if the bulbs are planted fairly deep and
if the soil around them does not reach 85° by August 1. The temperature
can be determined by removing a spadeful of earth at that time and inserting a thermometer.

Soil temperatures can be reduced if petunias, alyssum, or similar shallow-rooted annuals are sown over the bulbs, Where a bed slopes south
or is in sandy soil, the readings are likely to be too high, and the bulbs
should accordingly be dug and stored. Do not do so, however, until every
trace of green has disappeared from the leaves. Not until then has food
manufactured in the foliage been withdrawn into the bulb for storage.

Avoid placing bulbs where air temperatures go *above* 80° or *below*

55°. Too low a temperature causes roots to form at the base and the flower bud to grow prematurely.

In warm parts of the country soil temperatures usually do not fall rapidly enough to start tulips rooting in early winter. They can be grown in these areas only if the bulbs are dug and stored at above 55° until late fall, then placed in cold storage for six weeks at above freezing but below 50°. When planted after this treatment, they will grow normally.

TULIPS

The most conspicuous of all spring-flowering bulbs, tulips, should be given first consideration in spring-garden plans. No other group of plants can offer a more brilliant early display, more concentrated color, or a wider range of tints and shades. A gardener can use tulips as an artist uses pigments to paint striking pictures. From the purity of white found in the variety 'Glacier' to the sooty near-black of 'Queen of the Night,' he has at his command practically every known hue except pure blue.

Most gardeners cheat themselves of several weeks of tulip bloom. Moved by the magic of the name Darwin, they confine their plantings to this late-flowering type, ignoring tulips which could substantially extend the flowering season. Each of the following has its place in continuous bloom from before the frost is completely gone until the first perennials flower in May.

While most of these belong in the rock garden because of their small stature and delicate flowers, several new varieties bred from *Tulipa fosteriana* have caught the public fancy and are being planted widely. The first of these was 'Red Emperor,' with huge 7-inch flowers of fire-engine red on 12-inch stems. This has been followed by 'Holland's Glory,' the 'Big Boss,' 'White Emperor,' and others. New varieties of this breeding are still being increased for future introduction. They are extremely early, flowering with the first narcissus. Though invaluable for spots of brilliant color in their season, they should not be overdone. Their season is quite short and if the weather turns unseasonably warm in April, they may last only a day or two. Fosteriana varieties have made the 'Duc Van Thol' tulips obsolete. However, the *T. fosteriana* hybrids are of no value for forcing. In Europe, the 'Duc Van Thols,' still used for this purpose, are made to flower at Christmas time.

SINGLE EARLY TULIPS

More of these are planted in Sweden and Germany in one season than all the varieties we plant combined. Their virtues include early bloom, clear clean color, and short stature. They are perfect for planting in masses because their short stiff stems are not easily snapped off by wind.

WHITE: 'Diana,' 'Lady Boreel,' 'White Beauty,' 'White Hawk,'
YELLOW: 'Chrysolora,' 'King of the Yellows,' 'Mon Trésor,' 'Rising Sun,' 'Yellow Prince'
YELLOW-SCARLET: 'Keizerskroon'
RED: 'Brilliant Star,' 'Vermilion Brilliant,' 'Couleur Cardinal'
ORANGE: 'General de Wet,' one of the most fragrant, 'Prince of Austria'
PINK: 'Cottage Maid,' 'Diadem,' 'Flamingo,' 'Pink Flamingo'

DOUBLE EARLY TULIPS

Although these may seem heavy and clumsy, in bloom they form such solid mats of color that they are unsurpassed for mass effects.

WHITE: 'Boule de Neige,' 'Schoonoord'
YELLOW: 'Couronne d'Or,' 'Van der Hoef'
RED: 'Imperator Rubrorum,' 'Vuurbaak'
RED-YELLOW: 'Orange Nassau'
ORANGE: 'Maréchal Niel,' 'Toreador'
PINK: 'Murillo,' 'Peach Blossom,' 'Triumphator'

TRIUMPHS AND MENDELS

These form an intermediate group which bridges the season of the single and double early varieties with that of the tall late tulips. Not too readily available at retail, they are widely used for commercial forcing because they flower early, yet are taller than other early tulips. Outstanding varieties are 'Elizabeth Evers' (soft rose and white), 'Kansas' (snow-white), 'Telescopium' (clear violet), and 'Ursa Minor' (butter-yellow).

TALL LATE TULIPS

Distinctions between the Cottage, Darwin, and Breeder classes have all but been erased by new varieties introduced since World War II. At one time Cottage varieties were somewhat shorter and were different in color range because yellow was included. The Breeders were very tall, murky-colored varieties with blocky, oblong flowers. Darwins were intermediate in height, with unusually brilliant colors, but without yellow.

Today all this is changed. One of the biggest of all blocky tulips is a Cottage; there are brilliant yellow Darwins, and even a bright orange Breeder. It is foolish to consider these as separate classes — they should be studied as a whole even though they may be separated in catalogs. When a brilliant orange Breeder like 'Dillenberg' is grown alongside a dusky black Darwin like 'Queen of the Night,' the absurdity of separating them into different groups is obvious. Any good catalog will list a wide range of tall tulip varieties for specific uses.

LILY-FLOWERED AND PARROT TULIPS

Formerly limp, oddly shaped flowers of no particular beauty, these have been so improved that they are now worthy of a place in any garden. Because of their unusual forms they are difficult to blend with other tulips and are best planted together.

Flower arrangers are particularly impressed by the artistic forms and unusual coloration of the newer Parrots, which are sports of Darwins. Outstanding varieties are 'Blue Parrot,' 'Black Parrot,' 'Fantasy' (salmon-pink), 'Gadelan' (soft lavender), 'Sunshine' (bright butter-yellow), and 'Sundew' (bright red).

NARCISSUS, DAFFODILS, AND JONQUILS

In England, the terms have quite different meanings from ours. Botanically, all flowers in this section are species of narcissus, but in the United States they may be called daffodils without bringing down the wrath of purists. However, the use of the term jonquil for the entire class is definitely wrong. This word is applied only to *Narcissus jonquilla*, often catalogued as *Jonquilla simplex*, a very small narcissus with rush-like leaves and a small long-trumpet flower, to its hybrids, and to two similar but little-known species. Because of the many forms of narcissus or daffodils, they are classified in 11 categories:

1) Trumpet: yellow, white, and bicolor with trumpet as long as or longer than perianth.

2) Large-cupped: yellow and bicolor flowers with large cups.

3) Small-cupped: dainty cups distinctly smaller than the surrounding petals.

4) Double: *N. tazetta* with its hybrids, and others.

5) Triandrus: hybrids of *N. triandrus* with several nodding flowers to a stem.

6) Cyclamineus: hybrids of *N. cyclamineus* with single yellow flowers.

7) Jonquilla: hybrids of *N. jonquilla*.

8) Tazetta (Poetaz): *N. tazetta* and hybrids with with double or clustered flowers.

9) Poeticus: *N. poeticus* and hybrids; single flowers.

10) Species: various wild forms.

11) Miscellaneous: all others.

Except for *N. tazetta* and its hybrids, most daffodils are hardy anywhere in the United States. The tazetta hybrids, which include the 'Paperwhites,' are most commonly flowered indoors in winter.

Varieties are being produced at such a rapid rate that any published list would be obsolete almost immediately. Although British and Irish breeders are placing new kinds on the market at $100 and up, the Dutch are turning out new ones at a much more modest price. These are usually marked by strong, sturdy stems, heavy-textured flowers, and by the ability to multiply rapidly. Any good specialist's catalog will list 100 or more narcissus.

Basal rot, mosaic, nematodes, and bulb fly are four pests which occasionally infest daffodils. Except for basal rot, which can sometimes be cured by soaking the bulbs in an organic mercury solution, all are so difficult to cure that the bulbs are best dug up and destroyed. To avoid introducing basal rot with new bulbs, dip them in an organic mercury solution. This can be bought under a number of trade names. (*Note:* Mercury compounds are poisonous.)

BULBOUS IRIS

These are listed here instead of with other iris because they require completely different handling. Also, they are listed with bulbs in catalogs. The three types — superficially much alike — are known as Dutch, Spanish, and English. All are hybrids of *Iris xiphium,* although some authorities put the English iris in a separate group, *I. xiphioides.* These grow up to 18 inches tall, and are valuable in the bulb garden because their color range includes rich blues and purples that are missing in tulips and narcissus.

Unfortunately, while they can withstand freezing, they grow so rapidly when planted that they are likely to be killed by an early freeze. They are best planted just before the soil freezes. After flowering, the foliage should be allowed to die down before the bulbs are dug and stored for the summer. Because the bulbs are fairly inexpensive, some gardeners treat the plants as annuals, planting new bulbs each year. In California and along the eastern seaboard south of Virginia, the bulbous iris are hardy and multiply rapidly.

An interesting miniature is *I. reticulata,* the netted iris. It grows about 3 inches tall and blooms very early. The flowers, a rich deep purple with gold veins, have an intense violet fragrance. This iris makes a delightful pot plant. (See House Plants.)

HYACINTHS

It it were not for their heavenly fragrance and distinctive flower form, only gardeners living south of Washington, D.C., would grow hyacinths. North of that city, it's advisable to mulch them to insure their survival over the winter. Because of their delightful scent, however, they are planted and protected by heavy mulches, where necessary, against too early growth in spring.

For outdoor planting, the bedding grade of hyacinths should be used. If the giant bulbs offered for forcing are planted in the perennial border, their flowers are too large and top-heavy to stand upright and they must be staked.

Hyacinths should be planted 6 inches deep in light, well-drained soil enriched with compost or some other form of humus. A mulch of straw, oak leaves, or evergreen boughs should be applied to keep the soil frozen as late as feasible in the spring.

Double varieties appear attractive in catalogs, but are so formal as to be almost priggish in a flower already stiff and upright in its single form. Among the best of the singles are the following:

WHITE: 'La Grandesse' and 'L'Innocence'

VIOLET: 'King of the Violets'

RED: 'Roi des Belges' and 'La Victoire'

PORCELAIN BLUE: 'King of the Blues' and 'Grand Maître'

PALE PINK: 'General de Wet' and 'Lady Derby'

PURE PINK: 'Queen of the Pinks'

DEEP PINK: 'Gertrude'

MEDIUM BLUE: 'Queen of the Blues'

NATURALIZING BULBS

A lightly wooded slope where the grass does not need to be cut is an ideal place for naturalizing daffodils, and there are few more cheerful sights than the gleaming yellow and white of their massed flowers. If bulbs are tossed and planted where they land, an informal effect is assured.

The red of hyacinths is a harsh carmine, not a pleasing color to many. There are really no good clear yellows, but creamy yellows include 'City of Haarlem' and 'King of the Yellows.' To most gardeners, they are not particularly pleasing.

MINOR BULBS

These are minor only from the viewpoint of interest shown in them by American gardeners. Actually, some of the most striking garden effects, such as the gorgeous sheets of blue *Scilla nutans* in English woods, the gold of crocus in spring, and the lovely white bells of snowdrops as winter fades, can be enjoyed only when these delightful small bulbs are planted. Gardeners who neglect minor bulbs curtail their gardening season by at least a month. The earliest flowers of spring (unless it be late blooms on the Christmas rose or flowering of *Cornus mas*, the cornelian cherry), are the snowdrops, winter aconites, and crocus that flower often before the late drifts have melted.

Chionodoxa (Glory-of-the-snow). Resembling the scillas, but with white centers to the bright blue flowers. There is also a pure white form. About 3 inches tall. They should be lifted every fourth or fifth year and thinned. Plant 3 inches deep.

Crocus (Dutch Crocus). Flowers open close to ground with striped up-turned cups of solid or purple, white and blue, also pure yellow. Grass is not the ideal spot for them; they are lovely planted in clumps in the front of perennial borders. Plant 1 to 2 inches deep.

Eranthis (Winter Aconite). This tiny yellow "buttercup" is usually the first true flower of spring. The bulbs resent being out of the soil and must be planted as soon as possible after they are received. Plant 1 inch deep.

Fritillaria. Two widely planted forms. One is *F. meleagris*, the guinea-hen flower, which has small nodding bells checkered like a guinea-hen's feathers. The other is *F. imperialis*, the crown imperial, one of the most impressive of early spring flowers. Three-foot-tall stems are capped with clusters of yellowish or brick-red flowers suggestive of a coronet. The plant needs a mulch when grown north of the Ohio River. The strong musky odor of the flowers is objectionable to many; plant it to the rear of the perennial border. Plant 3 inches deep.

Galanthus (Snowdrop). The species most commonly sold is *Galanthus nivalis*. It often flowers in January or February south of the Ohio River, and will spread and form large mats of snowy flowers if seed is allowed to ripen. In the South, *Galanthus elwesi* is larger and more showy, but may die out in the North. Plant 1 to 2 inches deep.

Leucojum vernum (Snowflake). Because it flowers about a month later than snowdrops (which it resembles except for being taller), the snowflake is often neglected. It grows about 6 inches tall. Plant 1 to 2 inches deep.

Muscari (Grape Hyacinth). One of the best of the minor bulbs, the grape hyacinth spreads to form great sheets of blue in light woodsy shade. The variety 'Heavenly Blue' is the one most widely planted in the United States. There is a white form also. Plant 3 inches deep.

Ornithogalum unbellatum (Star of Bethlehem, Sleepy Dick). This grows so freely that it can become a pest if it competes with other flowers. Star-like white flowers with an interesting touch of green appear some-what later than other minor bulbs; sometimes called summer snowflake. Plant 2 inches deep.

Scilla (Squill). *Scilla sibirica* is another of the free-flowering blues which form great sheets of color in lightly shaded woods. The English wood hyacinth, *S. nutans*, is difficult to find in America, though it can be made quite at home here. *S. hispanica* (formerly called *S. campanulata*) is a lovely thing and comes in white, pink, and blue. It flowers quite late. The blue form is particularly lovely when planted close to the tree peony 'Reine Elizabeth.' Plant 2 inches deep.

SUMMER-FLOWERING HARDY BULBS

Allium (Flowering Onion). The onion, leak, and garlic are all alliums, and this has worked against their flowering relatives. *A. moly*, the daffodil garlic or lily leek, is an old European favorite. Its 18-inch flower stalks make a brave show with their yellow globes in June. *A. giganteum* lives up to its name by producing stalks 6 feet tall topped with bluish lavender balls of flowers nearly a foot in diameter. A spectacular flower, but the tips of its leaves are likely to be injured by freezing in spring. Other species of allium are available from specialists. See Plant Encyclopedia for listing of species.

Camassia esculenta (Wild Hyacinth). Tall spikes of blue flowers in late June. The plants like rich, moist soil. Plant them 5 inches deep.

Lilies: See Chapter 3.

Lycoris (Hardy Amaryllis). This striking, fragrant pink flower appears suddenly in August on a 3-foot stem, and resembles the tender greenhouse amaryllis. No foliage is produced at this time; it appears in spring, grows for a while, then disappears.

AUTUMN-FLOWERING BULBS

Colchicum. Sometimes called autumn crocus. The flowers appear in fall without any foliage. The following spring, thick lush leaves appear (like those of a vigorous tulip), grow for a while, and die. This bulb is the source of colchicine, a drug used by plant breeders to stimulate mutations. The plant is poisonous if eaten.

Crocus (Autumn Crocus). Three species — *C. sativus* (saffron crocus), *C. speciosus*, and *C. zonatus* — are commonly sold. Several other rare species can be had on special order from Holland. These interesting plants are not common here because they are difficult to ship, often opening their flowers while still packed. Immediate planting is necessary.

Sternbergia (Autumn daffodil). Actually a close relative of the amaryllis, this produces in fall a flower like a yellow crocus. Not large or impressive, but interesting at this season of the year. Plant 6 inches deep.

TENDER BULBS

These vary in hardiness, some surviving as far north as Washington, D.C., without special protection, while others often do not survive on the Gulf Coast, Florida, or in warmer parts of California.

Many of these tender bulbs are grown as summer-flowering plants in the North, dug after the first light frost, and stored in a root cellar. They may present storage problems because, except for gladiolus, they need a temperature of about 55° — the same as required for storing squash and pumpkins.

Others can be handled as tub or pot plants for terrace, patio, or porch decoration, and carried over in a sun-heated pit or cool greenhouse where growth is held stationary until the return of brighter sunshine in late winter.

Achimenes. Grown as pot plants for porch decoration. They are striking in hanging baskets, with brilliant blue saucer-like flowers on trailing stems. The rhizomes are very small and are usually salvaged by drying off the pot, then sifting the soil through a screen with 16 meshes to the inch (¼ -inch hardware cloth.) Plant just below the surface of soil in a greenhouse or sunny window in March.

Acidanthera. Handles like gladiolus, though a longer growing season is needed. When grown in the North, plant about 6 bulbs in a 12-inch bulb pan. One species, *A. bicolor* (white and purple), can be grown outdoors as far north as the Alabama-Tennessee line. Plant 4 inches deep in the ground, 2 inches deep in pots.

Agapanthus (Blue Lily-of-the-Nile). *A. africanus* (catalogued as *A. umbellatus*) is a popular veranda plant from the 19th century. Long straplike leaves are topped by enormous umbels of clear, sky-blue, lily-like flowers. The variety mooreanus is smaller and easier to handle in tubs, with darker blue flowers. A mature bulb of *A. africanus* may need an 18-inch tub. Plant with tip of bulb just below soil surface.

Alstroemeria (Peruvian Lily). If well mulched, this can survive as far north as Columbus, Ohio. Has survived in Washington, D.C., without protection. Can also be dug and stored for the winter, but the tubers are quite brittle and care is needed. Lovely lily-like flowers in bright colors — yellow with garnet splashes, yellow and orange spotted, pink, rose. The hardiest species is *A. aurantiaca.* Plant tubers 2 inches deep.

Amaryllis (Belladonna Lily). Interesting flowers, somewhat more tubular than the greenhouse amaryllis, with a strong vanilla fragrance. Mostly clear rose-pink, but white and blush-pink varieties are known. Hardy in California, along the Gulf Coast, and sometimes as far north as the Tennessee-Alabama line. They flower on 18-inch stems in August without the foliage, which appears in spring, then dies down. Transplant in June and July when dormant. Do not plant deeper than 1 inch.

Amaryllis advena (Oxblood Lily). A neglected semi-hardy bulb. Survives at the U.S.D.A. Plant Introduction Station, Glenn Dale, Maryland. Blood-red drooping trumpet flowers appear in fall in umbels on stems 12 inches tall. A situation in full sun on rich soil suits it. Plant 6 to 8 inches deep, a little less in the South. Mulch yearly with an organic material such as compost or rotted manure.

Anemone coronaria ('St. Brigid' and 'De Caen' Anemones). These unusual anemones produce tubers that can be as hard as bone, yet when soaked and planted will grow, even ofter a storage period of 3 to 4 years. They are not too hardy, yet do not like heat. Grown mostly as winter flowers in California and on the Gulf Coast. In the North, they grow in pots in well-protected coldframes and are set out for early color in the perennial border. Will also flower as summer bulbs in New England and in the Pacific Northwest. Colors are brilliant shades of red, blue, purple, and pink. Plant 4 inches deep.

Babiana (Baboon Flower). Hardy to North Carolina, sometimes surviving farther north with protection. Has foliage like an iris. Red flowers (or purple, blue or yellow) on 12-inch stems resemble freesias. Plant 3 inches deep.

Begonia tuberhybrida (Tuberous Begonia). One of the most striking tender plants for partial shade, producing camellia-like flowers in tones of salmon, pink, white, and yellow. Often grown in *full* shade, where it fails to flower. It needs filtered sunshine (as through elms or honey locusts) all day, but will flower later in fall if it also gets full sun up to 9 a.m. and after 6 p.m.

Light loose soil, constantly moist but never soggy, is best. Start tubers in March in a mixture half sand, half peat. When roots are well developed, pot in 4-inch pots and set outdoors when all danger of frost is over. Carry bulbs over winter in 55° storage in vermiculite or sand.

Brodiaea (Triplet Lily). Lavender and bluish star-like flowers. Sweet, but not striking. Too uncertain to be worth growing north of Washington, D.C. *B. uniflora*, the spring starflower, is a pretty thing at the edge of woodlands. Plant 2 inches deep.

Caladium (Fancy-leaved Caladium). Outstanding foliage plants to provide color in shade where flowers are scarce. Many varieties with mottled and veined leaves in tones of green, pink, red, and white. *C. candidum*, white and green, is overplanted. Not hardy, even in the South, but must be carried over in storage until settled warm weather and then planted in rich moist soil. Will grow in full sun, contrary to common belief. In the North, start tubers in February or March in a half-peat, half-sand mixture. Keep them damp and when roots are well started, place in 4-inch pots for setting outdoors.

Calochortus (Mariposa Lily, Globe Tulip, Star Tulip). Those called mariposa lilies may have flowers 5 to 6 inches across on 24-inch stems, in yellow, lilac, pink, citron, rose, or orange, mostly with a contrasting dark blotch. Star and globe tulips are fragrant and smaller, colored yellow, rose, lilac, or white. They do beautifully in California in sandy acid soil, but are not at all reliable in the East. Plant in fall, 2 to 3 inches deep.

Canna. Modern cannas are a far cry from the old-fashioned bright red flower with coarse green leaves that was standard planting for court houses and cemeteries in the early 20th century. Colors now include pale coral, soft yellows, and many other attractive shades and tints. Because of their reliable blooming habits, they make excellent plants for extending the flowering season of the perennial border. Not hardy north of Georgia,

A well-planned border of annuals: giant zinnias in the back, celosia "Forest Fire" in the middle, and dwarf yellow marigolds for front edging.

Daffodils are excellent for permanent naturalistic plantings. Here they are combined with basket-of-gold and dwarf phlox. Later they will be overplanted with summer annuals.

Lilies, with their fine summer blooms, are among the loveliest and most useful of all garden plants. This is a Mid-Century variety "Destiny".

Tuberous begonias bring color to your shady summer garden. They thrive and bloom in spots where sun-loving annuals and perennials sulk.

but from there south they are often left in the soil. Farther north, store in winter at 45° to 50°. Start up in March and set outdoors in rich, moist loam when danger from frost is over. Tip of rootstock should be just below surface of soil.

Cooperia (Rain Lily). Flowers open after rain. This plant prefers a dry, poor soil, grows 12 inches tall, and produces whitish flowers tinged inside with red. It can be grown farther north than its native Texas, but must be carried over winter in storage with other tender bulbs. Plant 2 inches deep in sandy soil.

Crinum (Crinum Lily). Grown outdoors in the South, where they are known as milk-and-wine lilies, but impractical in a greenhouse or sunroom because of the enormous size of the bulb. *C. longifolium* and *C. moorei* will survive outdoors with protection up to the Tennessee-Alabama line, sometimes even farther north. Should be planted with neck of bulb exposed.

Dahlia. This tender plant from the mountains of Mexico cannot stand frost, yet likes cool growing conditions. Plant where roots are shaded, and use a mulch to keep soil cool. In really hot weather, use a fine spray, whenever possible, to reduce temperature.

Start tubers outdoors in spring when apple trees bloom. Old clumps should be divided into single tubers, each with a piece of the stem on which is a live bud. Plant 6 inches deep in a soil that is not too rich. Place stake at neck end of tuber before filling hole. Tie plant to stake as it grows.

Dig clumps after first light frost kills foliage. Store in dry vermiculite at 40° to 50°.

The Unwin dahlias can be easily grown from seed.

Freesia. Hardy outdoors in Florida and along the Gulf Coast if planted 3 inches deep. They will flower only in winter: they do not like heat. For pot culture, see House Plants.

Galtonia candicans (Summer Hyacinth). Usually catalogued as *Hyacinthus candicans*. The common name describes this flower well. Its fragrant white bells are produced on tall slender stalks. Plant bulbs 6 inches deep in a rich loamy soil that does not dry out, but is not soggy. Flowers will appear in May. After foliage has died down, store for the winter.

Gladiolus. See Chapter 15.

Hymenocallis calathina (Peruvian Daffodil). Catalogued as *Ismene calathina* and also called spider lily, which well describes the flower. Among the most fragrant of all tender bulbs. Plant 4 inches deep in rich soil in full sun. In the North, allow bulbs to remain in the soil until frost kills the foliage, then dig, and store at 50° to 55°. Be careful not to injure the fleshy roots; these should be left intact so the food they contain can be drawn into the bulb. Even in the South, where the Peruvian daffodil will survive in the soil, it flowers much better if dried off and stored for the winter.

Ixia (African Iris). Similar to freesias in form, but taller. Unusual colors, including peacock blue, purple, crimson, yellow, and white. The flowers close on dark days, but bud colors are still interesting. Short-lived if planted outdoors, though they will survive in North Carolina. Can also be grown outdoors in the North if planted in November, heavily mulched. In spring, remove the mulch gradually. Plant 5 inches deep in loose, rich soil.

Kniphofia (Red-hot Poker or Torch Lily). Not a bulbous plant, but its fleshy roots are handled much like bulbs. Among the brightest of all garden plants — brilliant orange and yellow, scarlet and orange, and bright yellow spikes 15 to 30 inches tall make striking accents in the perennial border. Plant with the crown level with the surface. Dig after the first light frost in areas north of Philadelphia and store in a root cellar with a temperature just above freezing. Reset in April. Hardy south of Philadelphia.

Lycoris (Guernsey Lily). May be catalogued as *Nerine sarniensis*. Needs sharp drainage (a layer of broken brick 12 inches below surface is suggested), rich soil, and full sun. Plant bulbs 4 inches deep in August when they are dormant and mulch lightly in winter. Hardy to the Tennessee-Kentucky line and as far north as Washington, D.C., on the East Coast. Flowers usually garnet-red, but other colors are available.

Ornithogalum (Bird's Eye or Darling Chinkerichee). *O. arabicum* is of the easiest culture, but does not survive long. Flowers are star-like with a distinctive black eye, borne in clusters on 18-inch stems. Last well as cut flowers. *O. thyrsoides aureum*, the darling chinkerichee, has remarkable lasting qualities as a cut flower. Stalks are cut in Africa and shipped dry to the United States, where they open in water and last for weeks. Not reliably hardy except in California and on the Gulf Coast.

Polianthes tuberosa (Tuberose). The intense fragrance makes this a perennial favorite. Spikes of star-like flowers in September and October on 3-foot stems are excellent for cutting. While plants will usually survive in the garden if not dug, they will not bloom. Store tubers over winter at 55°. Plant in April in the South, in May in the North. Started in pots in March, plants will flower in August.

The double variety, 'The Pearl,' is the most beautiful but after flowering once, the tubers split into smaller ones which will not bloom again for three or four years. The 'Mexican Everlasting,' a single form, does not have this fault. Plant both single and double tuberoses 4 inches deep in full sun.

Sparaxis (Wandflower). Much like tritonia, but smaller, with flowers that resemble freesias, but in deeper, richer colors. Plants grow 6 to 12 inches tall. Not hardy north of South Carolina. Plant 3 inches deep.

Tigridia (Shellflower). Brilliant flowers of scarlet, orange, and deep yellow, with darker mottling at the base. These last only a day but are borne in succession in July and August on stems 24 inches tall. Plant in late

May 4 inches deep in light sandy loam. Treat like gladiolus, but store for the winter in vermiculite or sand. Do not divide the crowns in fall: wait until ready to plant.

Tritonia (Montbretia). Hardy outdoors only in California or, with protection, along the Gulf Coast and Georgia seaboard. *T. crocata*, the flame freesia, is brilliant scarlet with interesting mottlings. These plants are more difficult to grow than gladiolus and, unless their particular colors are needed, are not worth growing in competition with them. Plant 4 inches deep in light loamy soil with a pH of at least 6.5. They flower in July and August.

Watsonia (Bugle Lily). Related to the gladiolus and by some considered a superior flower. Culture is the same. Unfortunately, bulbs are usually sold in the fall, so must be purchased then and stored over winter. In California they are planted in fall. Dormancy period is short, so it is wise to pot bulbs in late February and carry in a cool greenhouse until planting time.

Zantedeschia (Calla Lily). The calla lily has been thrown by botanists from one genus to another so often that it is a wonder the public ever finds it listed. The rhizomes are handled as tender bulbs and stored over winter, except from North Carolina south. They prefer rich soil and do best if they have some light shade in the heat of day. An ideal plant for pool-side planting in the North in summer.

Best handled in pots and the pots plunged outdoors. When flowering stops, lift the pots and lay them on their sides. In winter, water pots only enough to prevent soil from becoming dust-dry. The rhizomes should not shrivel. Start again in February or March, setting them out when the weather is warm and settled. Storage temperature should be above 50° or the rhizomes will rot. Lift in September before night temperatures turn cool. *Z. aethiopica*, the common variety, has large green leaves and clear white trumpets on flower stalks to 30 inches. Very fragrant. *Z. albomaculata* is similar but smaller and has spotted leaves. *Z. elliottiana* has butter-yellow flowers. *Z. rehmanni*, with white-spotted leaves, is smaller and lower-growing than the others. Flowers vary in color from pale pink through lavender-red to violet-red and rose-red.

Zephyranthes (Fairy Lily). Here are some of the better native American species among bulbs. Sometimes called rain lilies, a name better applied to *Cooperia pedunculata*. Plant zephyranthes bulbs 3 inches deep in acid soil that is preferably constantly moist. In cold climates they can be handled like gladiolus corms and stored over winter. *Z. atamasco* (Atamasco Lily) has single white lily-like flowers on 12-inch stems in April. Hardy as far north as Virginia. *Z. candida*, 8 inches tall, will survive with protection to New Jersey; to Virginia without protection. Crocus-like flowers are produced in August. *Z. grandiflora* is a beautiful pink species, hardy only in the Gulf States.

5

Trees: Major and Minor Landscape Subjects

If you want to be remembered after you are dead, plant a tree. Choose the right species, and it will continue to grow long after you are gone — a living memorial.

While many of us will be planting for our grandchildren, we can plant for our own pleasure, too. Many species make surprising growth in a comparatively short time. We can even achieve beauty overnight if we want to pay the price expert movers ask for transporting and planting a large tree.

Fortunately, modern landscape architects and gardeners have learned to value trees of lower stature than the forest giants which once dominated every landscape plan. Today there is a greater demand for species that do not exceed 30 to 35 feet in height. Even city tree men have come to appreciate the beauty of low-growing trees for street planting — trees they would have scorned a decade or two ago. Where they fit, no one can deny the beauty of the avenues planted to such lovely things as *Magnolia soulangeana* and the flowering crabs.

We cannot overlook the contribution made by the Dutch elm disease to this wider use of flowering trees. While not all of this trend toward variation is fear-inspired, it has made us realize the danger of monoculture — the planting of an entire city to a single species which may be wiped out in an epidemic from abroad. Even today, there are ordinances on statute books of many cities and villages, barring the planting of any trees on

parkways other than *Ulmus americanus*. Fortunately, they are being ignored as obsolete by progressive tree men.

This does not mean that American cities, towns, and villages should
abandon all control over street planting and permit a hodgepodge of trees
to replace dead American elms. The beauty of a street planted to a single
wisely selected species cannot be denied.

There is a practical aspect, too. Spraying for disease and pest control
becomes simplified, and pruning and other care can be given all the trees
at the same time. If other species are used for other streets, the work of
city tree men can be spread over the season, since maintenance schedules
for different kinds will vary. The only danger occurs when an unexpected
disease or insect passes from tree to tree and demolishes an entire street
planting in a year or two.

All that is said of street planting applies equally to trees on private
property.

Home-owners should be as much concerned with the fate of specimens
beyond the sidewalk line as they are with their own trees. If street plantings are entirely of elms, now is the time to consider what would happen
if these became diseased and no effective program for replacement had
been planned. It would be wise to plant trees of a different species between the house and sidewalk, so that if disease should strike, the home-
owner would not be without some tree cover.

TREES AS A PERMANENT FEATURE

A tree comes closer than any other living thing to being permanent. Its
selection and planting, therefore, demand more thought than any other
class of plants. For information on hardiness in choosing trees, see later
in this chapter. All too often, a tree is chosen merely because someone has
a volunteer seedling to contribute or some local nursery is overstocked.
Instead of accepting these offerings at once, try to visit an arboretum or
other public garden and study the kinds that do well and look most attractive in your vicinity. Because a tree is such an important landscape feature,
the owner of a small property where there is room for only one or two,
needs to give special attention to his selection. He has a more difficult
task than the man who can plant with a lavish hand and also afford to
experiment.

HOW TO PLANT A TREE

When you plant, remember that a tree will be in the ground a long, long
time and that the soil at its roots may remain undisturbed for a century or
more. You will then understand the need for doing a good job in preparing both the surface soil and the subsoil.

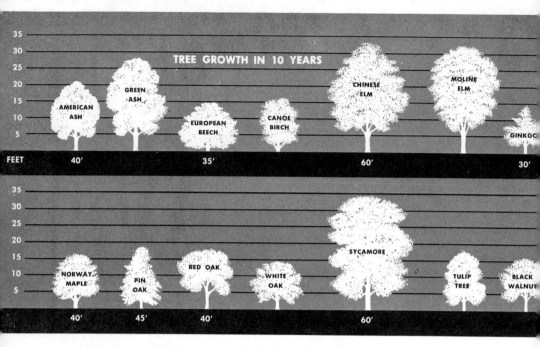

The shape and rate of growth of trees are important things to remember before you plant the saplings in your garden. The chart above shows characteristic

Balled and Burlapped Specimens

Many trees are moved today with a ball of earth, in answer to the demand for instant beauty. Such specimens are heavy and difficult to manipulate into a prepared hole. This means that the job is often done hastily and without much thought of what will happen later. If this hole is filled with rich, loose loam (as is often recommended) the ball may sink deeper and deeper as the soil settles. This is harmful in several ways. Newly formed roots are broken and the tree may gradually sink below the level at which it can make its best growth.

To prevent this, balled and burlapped specimens should be set on a firm flat stone laid in the bottom of the hole, as recommended for shrubs. If no stone can be found, use bricks. Such support should hold the tree in place so that after the soil has been filled in and settled, it will not be more than an inch or two lower than at the nursery.

The fill around the ball should be of the best soil available. The subsoil is better discarded. If the topsoil is not good, it should be replaced. In any event, all the organic matter possible, up to one-third the total bulk of the soil (one-half in the case of magnolias and swamp and pin oaks) should be added before filling in around the ball. Add a pound of superphosphate

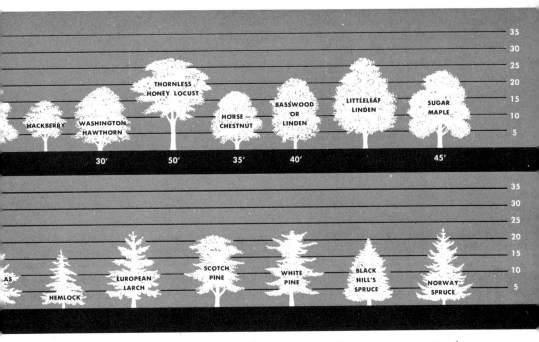

shapes and ten-year growth of trees under average conditions in most parts of the country where they are found.

to every bushel of soil. Since this fertilizer element cannot be worked down from the topsoil, it will be available to the tree's roots only if included during planting.

Bare-root Stock

Where a number of trees must be planted, balled and burlapped stock is too costly for many pocketbooks. Even when only one or two trees are involved, a new home-owner who has mortgaged all visible income to make payments on his property will hesitate to invest in trees whose cost may reach three figures or more. Bare-root stock of young trees can be planted safely and will often be as successful as expensive large specimens, if properly cultured. The shock of transplanting often disturbs a larger tree more than it does a young and vigorous sapling.

Seven Rules for Planting

FIRST: *Don't be stingy with the size of the hole.* Although the roots of the tree being planted have been cut back, new feeder roots can fill a mass of earth twice the diameter of the remaining roots in an amazingly short time. Make the hole at least twice as wide as the roots, and at least half again as deep as seems necessary.

SECOND: *Put the best earth in the bottom of the hole.* This is because most new roots will grow downward.

THIRD: *Enrich the soil that lies two to three feet below the surface while you have a chance.* As indicated under directions for balled and burlapped specimens, soil for filling the hole should be mixed with at least one-third to one-half its bulk with some form of well-decomposed organic matter such as peatmoss, leafmold, or compost. (These forms of organic matter will continue to feed the tree for as long as fifty years.) Add also at least one pound of superphosphate to each bushel of soil, as explained above.

FOURTH: *Cut back injured roots to clean wood.* But avoid cutting roots unnecessarily. There is no worse sin in tree pruning than removing roots to make the tree fit a small hole. Instead, make the hole larger.

FIFTH: *Place the roots in as natural a position as possible.* If the tree has spreading roots, build up a cone of earth in the bottom of the hole. This should be firmed by tramping so that later it will not settle too much. Set the tree on this cone, with the roots spread out as naturally as possible, then fill over them with prepared soil. Tramp firmly on the soil, but not too heavily, after planting.

SIXTH: *Fill the hole with water after tramping.* Let the water soak in, add more earth, and water the ground again. A firmed soil will not settle.

SEVENTH: *Do not allow newly planted trees to weave or sway in the wind.* Established trees gain resilience when their tops are buffeted, but newly planted specimens are not yet firmly enough anchored to take storms without damage. The new tree should be tied either to a stout stake close to its trunk or to three stakes set a few feet distant, so that it will not sway, no matter how hard the wind blows.

CARE AFTER PLANTING

As soon as the tree is planted, even before it is staked, the entire trunk should be wrapped with special tree tape. This consists of two layers of crinkled kraft paper stuck together with asphalt. Pulled tight around the trunk, the tape expands as the tree grows. Wrap the tree from ground level up to where it begins to branch.

This wrapping serves three purposes. It keeps out insects that might attack the bark; conserves moisture that might otherwise evaporate through the bark, slowing up the transport of food and moisture from the roots to the branches; and it prevents mechanical injury, sunscald, and winter damage by animals.

If the tree is planted in an exposed position, the use of one of the protective latex sprays that slow evaporation is recommended. This gives the bark, branches, and even the leaves a thin coating which permits respiration but prevents excessive water loss. Even if the tree is not in an exposed position, such protection is valuable the first winter after planting.

MOVING TREES FROM THE WILD

Although root-pruned, nursery-grown trees should be used whenever possible, a home-owner may want to move a sapling or even an older tree from a woodland. If possible, the specimen selected should be prepared for planting a year ahead of time. Dig a trench 18 inches for saplings, farther for bigger trees. Fill it with rich loose soil into which new roots can grow. When the tree is dug, the new ring of hair roots formed in the trench should be included with the larger roots.

Hollies from the wild present a special case. These can be moved only with a ball of earth, and even then it is difficult. Experts recommend removing the foliage by cutting off every leaf with a pair of scissors. This is a tedious job but usually means the difference between success and failure. The same method has been used with evergreen azaleas and rhododendrons, but is not universally successful.

ON PRUNING TREES

Perhaps more trees are ruined by incorrect pruning than by complete neglect. At the same time, unless their early growth is guided by corrective pruning, structural faults may develop which will cause premature breakdown or permanent harm.

Reasons for Pruning

Why prune trees? The first principle of pruning should be: *know why you are cutting;* if you don't know, lay down the pruning tools at once. Here are some basic reasons for pruning:

1) To balance loss of roots during transplanting or grading. Nowadays this is less important than formerly because we can now reduce water loss by wrapping the trunks of newly planted trees and by spraying the tops with wilt-proofing coatings.

2) To direct growth in newly planted trees so that they will assume the form we have in mind. While it is unwise to force growth in an unnatural pattern, judicious pruning can modify the final form to some extent. Pruning at this stage is easier on both the tree and the owner: a 6-inch limb is harder to cut away than a twig that is starting in the wrong direction.

3) For sanitation and pest control. Beginning rot in an old tree can often be halted, and the useful life of the tree extended, by early attention to small lesions and dead branches.

4) To prevent the formation of narrow crotches. If delayed until the crotch has formed, a misshapen tree will result.

Tree-wells, lined with stones or tiles, supply air to roots. Raising the soil level more than a foot or so may suffocate a tree unless a well is used. Oaks, beeches and most evergreens are particularly sensitive.

5) To remove lower branches of street trees for passage of cars and pedestrians. Also to clear sight lines for a view down the street and to form an attractive picture.

6) To renew vigor of old trees. Removing excessive wood from elms, for example, will divert food and water to the remaining limbs and force stronger growth.

When to Prune Trees

If a cut is made when sap is rising rapidly in spring, much of the food and moisture intended for the branch that was removed will be directed into the dormant buds just below the cut and force them into strong growth. Obviously, if strong growth is *not* wanted, it is better to prune later, when growth has slowed.

Cuts made in spring heal over faster than those made later, and new shoots formed by the sprouting of dormant buds will be more mature and more cold resistant when winter comes. Spraying operations, often done when trees are dormant, may also affect time of pruning. If excess wood is removed in advance, the area to be covered is decreased considerably. For these reasons, most tree pruning should be done in late winter or early spring, just before the sap rises. (For details of pruning operations and minor tree surgery, see Chapter 22.)

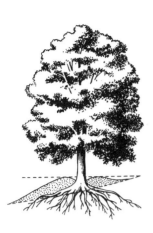

Lowering the soil level around a tree can be disastrous, too. Use a soil-mound (left) or raised bed (right). Brick or masonry walls should be built with drainage holes at the bottom.

SELECTING WOODY PLANTS FOR HARDINESS

Hardiness to factors other than cold is a special problem, mainly involving the selection of plants which have become adapted to a particular environment. The mild, humid climate of the Pacific Northwest has generated many plants which collapse if brought into the dry, rigorous climate of the Middle West. Desert plants, resistant because of such mechanisms as water-storage organs, thick coverings that retard moisture loss, and similar devices are equally subject to injury if planted in humid surroundings.

For this reason, the chances of acclimatizing a desert plant to the more humid East are slim. Centuries of gradual adaptation might do the trick, but this is for philosophers to ponder, not for gardeners to try. Adaptation to cold, however, if possible at all, can sometimes be built up in a couple of years. This offers some hope that a less hardy plant can be moved 100 to 200 miles north of its normal range and gradually inured to the rigors of a less favorable environment. However, there is a distinct line of demarcation between true tropical species and species capable of developing cold resistance. This lies in the ability of a plant to withstand the formation of frost crystals within its cells, without rupturing the cell wall. This ability varies from season to season and is not present during the periods of most active growth — spring and summer.

To resist cold, a plant must go through a state known as dormancy, one of the least-understood phases of plant growth. It takes place in three stages: pre-freezing preparation, actual winter sleep, and awakening. The first step — preparation to resist cold — is a slowing of growth. In areas north of the Ohio River, if you observe woody plants about mid-August, you will notice that terminal growth on branches and twigs has ceased. Although the tree may have been growing rapidly through June and July, as though on signal, in August all this activity ends.

No change in temperature seems responsible. Weather Bureau readings will show many seasons when June and July are cooler than August, while in other years the reverse may be true. One change in conditions that may possibly set off this action is the quality of sunlight. Since June 21, the sun has been sinking lower and lower in the south with each passing day. Its rays must pass through an increasingly thick layer of air, screening out the blue end of the spectrum (which has a stimulating effect on the top growth of plants). Now daylight is strong in red, which affects the growth-regulating chemical system of the plant. Just how all this works is an unsolved problem.

But notice the twigs that have stopped elongating. Instead of growing at the tips, they are now swelling in diameter. This indicates that they are absorbing food that will be needed to grow leaves in spring. Stored as starches and sugars, this food must be sufficient to produce an area of leaf surface so tremendous that a mature tree could never find its equivalent in the cold ground. Most of the plant nutrients in the soil are not available anyway at this time. They are locked up in the bodies of soil organisms that will not be active until much later.

Cold gradually changes stored starch into sugar, so that by spring, this soluble food is ready to move. This is why maple sap is sweet in spring: it is rich in sugars converted from starch by the winter cold.

This stored food serves still another purpose. As it replaces some of the water inside plant cells, it lowers their freezing point. The ability to withstand cold is largely due to this stored food which allows water in plant cells to freeze without rupturing cell walls.

All this would be mere academic discussion were it not for one fact. Hardiness in woody plants can be increased slightly (often enough to enable a plant to grow 100 to 200 miles farther north of its normal range) by feeding it well at the time when twig elongation has stopped, and diameter increase has begun. In the area north of the Ohio River, this would be about August 15, just south of that line about September 1. This is no time to feed slow-acting organic fertilizers. Completely soluble high-nitrogen chemical tree and shrub foods should be used. If they can be dissolved in water and applied in liquid form, so much the better.

A classic example of the ability of woody plants to adapt to a hostile environment are the giant California redwoods that stood near Geneva, N.Y., from 1880 (when they were planted by the famous old nursery firm of Elwanger and Barry) until 1940, when they were killed in the Armistice Day freeze that saw the thermometer register a 60-degree drop in 24 hours. Less dramatic, but perhaps of more importance to the home gardener, are many cases where evergreens such as Hicks yew and American hollies have been kept alive in Iowa and Nebraska by enthusiasts who have fed them liberally in mid-August.

GROWTH-REGULATING CHEMICALS

Once plants have gone into rest, it is equally important that they emerge from it when warm weather returns in the spring. Preparation for winter and the return to life are under the control of an amazing system of growth-regulating chemicals. Those that stimulate growth have been pretty well studied and reported on in scientific literature. Those that prevent growth are only now being studied intensively.

For simplicity's sake, we might call the first group "hormones" and the second "counter hormones." As fall approaches, the counter hormones are built up to such a point that they prevent the hormones from allowing the plant to grow. As long as the counter hormones are active in the plant, it cannot resume growth. The counter hormones are gradually destroyed by cold; by spring, they can no longer hold back the growth-stimulating hormones.

Scientists feel that the difference in hardiness between plants from the southern edge of the temperate zone and those from farther north lies in the amount of counter hormones the plants are able to manufacture.

This suggests that whenever possible, woody plants should be purchased from nurseries located in the same hardiness zone as the garden in which they are to be grown, or only slightly to the north of that zone.

However, this is not an absolute barrier to the use of stock from an area south of you. An amazing fact is how quickly woody plants can "learn" to build up larger stores of counter hormones. This process apparently takes about two years, though in some cases three may be needed. The redwoods previously mentioned were covered during the first three winters with a wooden shed filled with leaves. After the third winter they grew too large and no protection was given.

ADAPTING LESS HARDY SPECIES

This ability to adapt is fortunate for the gardener who wants to try exotic species which are likely to be cold-sensitive. The usual practice in handling such specimens is to give them special protection for at least two winters and then let them go with minimum protection. Their chance of survival is better if additional precautions are taken. For example, a tree from some area in the South where adequate summer rainfall is the rule, might be attempted in Illinois or Indiana, where summer droughts of two to three weeks are common. The exotic specimen would require regular watering even though native trees do not. Much of what is called winter-killing is actually the effect of a summer drought which has so injured the bark of woody plants that it is unable to transport water. This in turn affects the ability of the tree to store food, which must be dissolved in water in order to move. During *dry* periods the bark of such transported trees or shrubs should be washed down daily with a fine spray of water.

Importance of Location

The location of less-than-hardy specimens can be a critical factor in their survival. Avoid a spot where prevailing winds can wipe out moisture either in winter or summer. Try to plant them so that they will be in shade during the winter. This is easy to do. Set them so their tops are in full sun about July 1, but so that the shadow of buildings or evergreen plantings shade them as the sun drops to the south with the coming of winter.

For the first two years at least, mulch the soil around such a specimen heavily to slow up freezing of the soil and thus give the roots a chance to attain maximum growth before cold weather begins.

Air drainage is another factor to consider. Cold air flows downward and this means that a plant in a depression will be subjected to more cold than a plant on top of a slope. Too, the effect of the downhill flow should be studied. If a tender specimen is located in a "tunnel" of dense planting that runs up and down a hill, be prepared for trouble. Perhaps the ideal location for a marginally hardy species is just below the crest of a hill, with trees and shrubs around serving as protection from cold winds.

Protective Sprays

Old-time British gardeners sometimes applied a thin glue wash to specimens of doubtful hardiness. Today similar protection, or better, can be provided by using one of the products based on latex or a plastic which can be sprayed onto the bark of deciduous trees and onto the foliage and bark of evergreens, both broad-leaved and needled. Such coatings slow up moisture loss and help conserve the latent heat of the plant. It is important to remember that these materials should be applied at *above-freezing* temperatures. Spray deciduous shrubs as soon as the foliage has dropped; evergreens a little earlier.

Delayed Winter Injury

Sometimes branches or even whole trees or shrubs leaf out normally in spring and even set flowers, then wilt suddenly and die within a few days. This puzzling and upsetting behavior is often due to winter injury.

As already explained, spring growth depends upon stored starches and sugars. If the bark which feeds a branch is killed by the cold, the branch is still able to leaf out and may even produce flowers, using only the food stores of the previous year. But if the bark has been killed below the branch, there is no way to replace the food for further growth and the branch dies. If all the bark on the trunk of a tree has been killed, the entire top may leaf out normally, then collapse with dramatic suddenness.

When such injury occurs, the best course is to examine the soil. If it is too dry, the answer is obvious. If too wet, holes bored with a post-hole auger under the drip of the branches and filled with dry peatmoss might do some good. If these simple remedies fail, wait three weeks, then if the tree shows no signs of putting out new leaves, it is finished.

Inexperienced tree men, called in after such a collapse, often recommend an expensive course of feeding, spraying, and other treatments, none of which do much good. About the only other condition which might cause such a sudden collapse is a gas leak, something to suspect if a gas line runs nearby. However, by the time the leak is discovered, this tree also has been fatally damaged.

TALL HARDY DECIDUOUS TREES

Properties on which two- and three-story houses have been built require tall trees, but they are not always easy to obtain. In recent years, the demand for trees to replace stricken elms has particularly emphasized the need for, and the lack of, sizable specimens in most areas. You may have to settle for something less than your ideal unless you are prepared to have stock shipped from a distance.

Most of the trees listed below mature at a height of not less than 40 feet and can be grown north of Zone 6. For the exact range, however, see the Plant Encyclopedia. Those which have conspicuous flowers are marked CF.

Acer negundo, Box-elder
A. platanoides, Norway Maple
A. pseudo-platanus,
    Sycamore Maple
A. rubrum, Red Maple
A. saccharinum, Silver Maple
A. saccharum, Sugar Maple
Aesculus hippocastanum (CF),
    Horse Chestnut
Betula lenta, Cherry Birch
B. nigra, River Birch

B. papyrifera, Canoe Birch
Carpinus betulus,
    European Hornbeam
Carya alba, Mockernut
C. lacinosa, Shellbark Hickory
C. ovata, Shagbark Hickory
Catalpa bignonioides (CF),
    Indian Bean
C. speciosa, Western Catalpa
Celtis occidentalis, Hackberry
Cladrastris lutea (CF), Yellow-wood

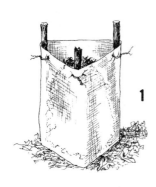

1

2

3

4

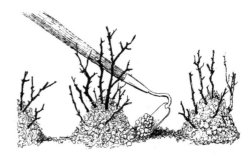

5

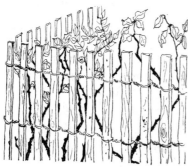

6

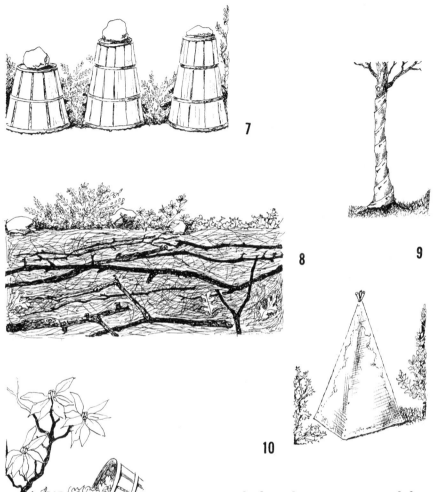

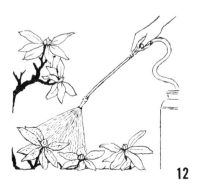

Shrubs and trees grown toward the northern edge of their hardiness zones need protection from sharp winter winds and deep frosts. Here are some of the easiest and most reliable methods: 1) Burlap screen around posts; 2) A roof of burlap; 3) A large burlap screen for several plants; 4) A screen of woven reeds; 5) Mounded earth around roots; 6) A snow fence barrier; 7) Inverted baskets over small plants; 8) Straw or hay anchored with branches; 9) A spiral tree-wrap; 10) A teepee construction; 11) Mulching; 12) Plastic spray to prevent moisture loss.

Diospyros virginiana,
    American Persimmon
Eucommia ulmoides,
    Hardy Rubber Tree
Fagus grandifolia, American Beech
F. sylvatica, European Beech
Fraxinus americana, White Ash
F. excelsior, European Ash
F. pennsylvanica, Red Ash
F. quadrangulata, Blue Ash
Ginkgo biloba, Maidenhair Tree
Gleditsia triancanthos,
    Honey Locust
Gymnocladus dioica (CF),
    Kentucky Coffee Tree
Juglans cinerea, Butternut
J. nigra, Black Walnut
Larix decidua, European Larch
Liquidambar styraciflua,
    Sweet Gum
Liriodendron tulipifera (CF),
    Tulip Tree
Maclura pomifera, Osage Orange
Magnolia acuminata,
    Cucumber Tree
M. fraseri, Fraser Magnolia
Morus alba, White Mulberry
M. rubra, Red Mulberry
Nyssa sylvatica, Tupelo
Phellodendron amurense,
    Amur Cork Tree
Platanus acerifolia, London Plane
P. occidentalis, Buttonwood
Populus acuminata,
    Plains Cottonwood
P. alba, Abele
P. balsamifera, Cottonwood
P. bolleana, Bolleana Poplar
P. candicans, Balm of Gilead

P. nigra italica, Lombardy Poplar
P. tremuloides, Quaking Aspen
Quercus alba, White Oak
Q. bicolor, Swamp White Oak
Q. borealis, Northern Red Oak
Q. coccinea, Scarlet Oak
Q. macrocarpa, Burr Oak
Q. palustris, Pin Oak
Q. prinus, Chestnut Oak
Q. velutina, Black Oak
Robinia pseudoacacia (CF),
    Black Locust
Salix alba, White Willow
S. alba vitellina, Golden Willow
S. pentandra, Laurel Willow
Sassafras variifolium, Sassafras
Sophora japonica (CF),
    Chinese Scholar Tree
Sorbus aucuparia,
    European Mountain Ash
Tilia americana (CF),
    American Linden
T. cordata (CF), Little-leaf Linden
T. euchlora (CF), Crimean Linden
T. heterophylla (CF),
    Southern Linden
T. platyphyllos (CF),
    Big-leaf Linden
T. tomentosa (CF), Silver Linden
T. vulgaris (CF), Lime Tree
Ulmus americana, American Elm
U. fulva, Slippery Elm
U. glabra, Scotch Elm
U. parvifolia, Chinese Elm
U. pumila, Siberian Elm
Zelkova serrata, False Elm

LOW-GROWING HARDY DECIDUOUS TREES

The more nearly dwarf forms of trees have acquired new importance during the past two decades because of the development of the one-story house. Many are interesting for their conspicuous flowers. In the list below these are identified by the letters CF. Included are species that will mature at from 10 to 40 feet, heights suitable for landscaping modern home grounds. Such trees find a place, too, in the landscaping of multi-story houses.

The use of small species as street trees is relatively new in the United States, but in Holland, France, and other European countries, flowering cherries, globe lindens, and others have been used for years. They cast adequate shade and are easier to maintain. With the increase in the ranch-type house, village and city tree men are beginning to question the wisdom of planting streets to forest giants. Flowering crabs, hawthorns, saucer magnolias, and flowering dogwoods have been used recently with stunning effect in a number of street plantings.

Acer campestre, Hedge Maple

A. circinatum, Vine Maple

A. ginnala, Amur Maple

A. japonicum, Full Moon Maple

A. palmatum, Japanese Maple

A. pensylvanicum, Moosewood

A. spicatum, Mountain Maple

A. tataricum, Siberian Maple

Aesculus carnea (CF),
    Red Horse Chestnut

Alnus vulgaris, Black Alder

Amelanchier canadensis (CF),
    Shadblow

Caragana arborescens (CF),
    Siberian Pea Tree

Carpinus caroliniana,
    American Hornbeam

Carya glabra, Pignut

Catalpa ovata,
    Japanese Catalpa

Cercidiphyllum japonicum
    Katsura Tree

Cercis canadensis (CF), Redbud

Chionanthus virginicus (CF),
    Fringe Tree

Cornus alternifolia (CF),
    Pagoda Dogwood

C. controversa (CF),
    Giant Dogwood

C. kousa (CF), Kousa Dogwood

C. mas (CF), Cornelian Cherry

C. nuttalli (CF), Pacific Dogwood

Crataegus cordata (CF),
    Washington Thorn

C. lavallei (CF),
    Lavalle Hawthorn

C. mollis (CF), Downy Hawthorn

C. monogyna (CF),
    English Hawthorn

C. oxyacantha (CF),
    'Paul's Scarlet' Hawthorn

Elaeagnus angustifolia,
    Russian Olive

Euptelea polyandra,
    Autumn Flame Tree

Euonymus atropurpureus, Wahoo

E. europaeus, Spindle Tree

E. latifolius, Bleeding-heart Tree

Fraxinus 'Moraine,' Moraine Ash

F. ornus (CF), Flowering Ash

Halesia carolina (CF),
    Carolina Silverbell

Hippophaë rhamnoides,
    Sea Buckthorn

Hovenia dulcis, Raisin Tree

Koelreuteria paniculata (CF),
    Golden-rain Tree

Maackia amurensis (CF),
    Amur Yellow-wood

Magnolia denudata (CF),
    Yulan Magnolia

M. salicifolia (CF), Anise Magnolia

M. soulangeana (CF),
    Saucer Magnolia

M. watsoni (CF), Watson Magnolia

Ostrya virginiana,
    Hop Hornbeam

Oxydendrum arboreum (CF),
    Sourwood

Populus simoni, Simon Poplar

Prunus americana (CF),
    American Wild Plum

P. persica (CF), Flowering Peach

P. serotina (CF), Black Cherry

P. serrulata (CF),
    Japanese Flowering Cherry

P. subhirtella (CF),
    Rosebud Cherry

Pyrus arnoldiana (CF), Arnold Crab

P. baccata (CF), Siberian Crab

P. coronaria (CF), Garland Crab

P. floribunda (CF), Showy Crab

P. halliana (CF), Hall Crab

P. ioensis var. (CF), Bechtel Crab

P. sargenti (CF), Sargent Crab

P. spectabilis (CF), Chinese Crab

P. theifera (CF), Tea Crab

Rhus glabra (CF), Smooth Sumac

R. typhina (CF), Staghorn Sumac

Salix caprea, Goat Willow

S. discolor (CF), Pussy Willow

S. elegantissima,
    Thurlow Weeping Willow

S. lucida, Shining Willow

S. matsudana contorta
    Corkscrew Willow

S. nigra, Black Willow

Sorbus americana,
    American Mountain Ash

Styrax japonica (CF),
    Japanese Snowbell

S. obassia (CF),
    Fragrant Snowbell Tree

Syringa amurensis (CF), Amur Lilac

S. japonica (CF),
    Japanese Tree Lilac

S. pekinensis (CF), Peking Lilac

Xanthoceras sorbifolium (CF),
    Yellowhorn

Zanthoxylum americanum,
    Prickly Ash

HARDY NEEDLE-LEAVED EVERGREENS

The overplanted city or suburban home, threatened by a tidal wave of ominous green, for a time led landscape architects to avoid needled evergreens. Such plantings usually sheltered a home-owner who wanted his grounds to look neat all year with little attention.

Fortunately, evergreens have been rescued by an appreciation of their true landscape value. Where a permanently fixed, solid feature is needed, nothing else can take their place. A common problem on small properties is the tendency to cut a corner and walk across the lawn. If some solid evergreen is planted in this spot, it will suggest going around it. A similar purpose is served by the solid planting at an entrance door which says to the visitor, "This is where you enter."

These two uses call for shrub-like evergreens rather than trees. However, there are similar situations that call for taller solid plantings, whether these are the striking accent of a fine Colorado blue spruce against a darker background at some focal point in a garden or the distinctive pattern of a Japanese table pine to throw an interesting shadow against an otherwise monotonous wall. In considering evergreens, we find their range of adaptation much narrower than that of deciduous trees. Northern conifers refuse to grow well south of the Ohio River, and southern species are reluctant to adapt themselves to northern cold. Information on the range of the trees in the following list may be found in the Plant Encyclopedia.

The majority of these trees reach a height of not less than 40 feet. Under favorable circumstances, many grow to 100 feet or more.

Abies concolor, White Fir
A. cilicica, Cilician Fir
A. homolepis, Nikko Fir
A. lasiocarpa, Rocky Mountain Fir
A. nordmanniana, Nordmann Fir
A. veitchi, Japanese Purple-cone Fir
Chamaecyparis lawsoni,
    Port Orford Cedar
C. nootkatensis, Alaska Cedar
Juniperus chinensis,
    Chinese Juniper
Picea abies, Norway Spruce
P. bicolor, Alcock Spruce
P. engelmanni, Engelmann Spruce
P. glauca, Skunk Spruce

P. glauca albertiana,
    Black Hills Spruce
P. omorika, Siberian Spruce
P. polita, Tigertail Spruce
P. pungens, Colorado Spruce
Pinus cembra, Swiss Stone Pine
P. densiflora, Japanese Red Pine
P. flexilis, Limber Pine
P. griffithi, Himalayan Pine
P. monticola, Western White Pine
P. mugo, Swiss Mountain Pine
P. nigra, Austrian Pine
P. parviflora, Japanese White Pine
P. ponderosa, Bull Pine
P. resinosa, Norway Pine

P. strobus, White Pine

P. sylvestris, Scotch Pine

P. thunbergi, Japanese Black Pine

Pseudolarix amabilis, Golden Larch

Pseudotsuga taxifolia, Douglas Fir

Sciadopitys verticillata,
　　Japanese Umbrella Pine

Taxus cuspidata, Japanese Yew

Thuja occidentalis,
　　American Arborvitae

T. orientalis, Oriental Arborvitae

Torreya nucifera, Japanese Cedar

Tsuga canadensis,
　　Canadian Hemlock

T. caroliniana, Carolina Hemlock

T. diversifolia, Japanese Hemlock

T. sieboldi, Oriental Hemlock

TENDER TALL TREES

Many of the less hardy species listed below can be grown as far north as Philadelphia in favorable situations but, even there, might suddenly be killed in an unfavorable winter. They are interesting planted on large properties where their occasional loss in a test winter will not be serious. In places where there is room for only one or two trees, planting them would be risky.

Planted north of their normal range these half-hardy species seldom attain full size, because of their curtailed growing season. *Paulownia tomentosa,* a 50-foot tree in South Carolina, is a 20-foot tree in New Jersey.

Southern gardeners are fortunate because many northern species grow well there.

Acacia decurrens (CF),
　　Silver Wattle

Acer macrophyllum, Oregon Maple

Arbutus menziesi (CF), Madrona

Betula maximowicziana,
　　Monarch Birch

Brachychiton acerifolium (CF),
　　Flame Tree

B. populneum (CF), Kurrajong

Carya pecan, Pecan

Castanea sativa, Spanish Chestnut

Casuarina cunninghamiana,
　　Australian Beefwood

C. equisetifolia, Horsetail Tree

Cedrela sinensis (CF), Toona

Celtis australis,
　　California Hackberry

Ceratonia siliqua, St. John's-bread

Cinnamomum camphora,
　　Camphor Tree

C. cassia, Cassia-bark Tree

Cornus nuttali (CF),
　　Pacific Dogwood

Davidia involucrata, Dove Tree

Ficus macrophylla,
　　Moreton Bay Fig

F. retusa, Shady Fig

Firmiana simplex,
　　Chinese Parasol Tree

Gordonia lasianthus (CF),
   Loblolly Bay
Grevillea robusta, Silk Oak
Halesia monticola (CF),
   Mountain Silverbell
Jacaranda acutifolia (CF),
   Jacaranda
J. cuspidifolia (CF), Violet Tree
Juglans californica,
   California Walnut
J. regia, English Walnut
J. rupestris, Texas Walnut
Libocedrus decurrens,
   Incense Cedar
Liquidambar formosana,
   Formosa Sweet Gum
Magnolia grandiflora (CF), Bull Bay
Melia azedarach (CF), Chinaberry
M. azedarach var. (CF),
   Texas Umbrella Tree
Paulownia tomentosa (CF),
   Empress Tree

Phoenix canariensis,
   Canary Island Palm
Populus fremonti,
   California Cottonwood
Quercus agrifolia,
   California Live Oak
Q. ilex, Holly Oak
Q. lobata, California White Oak
Q. nigra, Water Oak
Q. phellos, Willow Oak
Q. rubra, Red Oak
Q. suber, Cork Oak
Q. virginiana, Live Oak
Roystonea regia, Royal Palm
Tilia petiolaris,
   Weeping White Linden
Umbellularia californica,
   California Laurel

TENDER NEEDLE-LEAVED EVERGREENS AND EUCALYPTUS SPECIES

Araucaria araucana, Monkey Puzzle
A. bidwilli, Bunya Bunya
A. excelsa, Norfolk Island Pine
Cedrus atlantica, Atlas Cedar
C. libani, Cedar of Lebanon
Cephalotaxus drupacea,
   Green Plum-yew
C. fortunei, Purple Plum-yew
Chamaecyparis lawsoniana,
   Port Orford Cedar
C. obtusa, Hinoki Cypress
C. pisifera, Sawara Cypress
Cryptomeria japonica,
   Japanese Temple Cedar

Cunninghamia lanceolata,
   China Fir
Cupressus arizonica,
   Arizona Cypress
C. sempervirens, Italian Cypress
Eucalyptus amygdalina,
   Peppermint Gum
E. botryoides, Bastard Mahogany
E. globulus, Blue Gum
E. maculata citriodora,
   Lemon-scented Gum
E. polyanthemos, Australian Beech
E. robusta, Swamp Mahogany
E. rostrata, Red Gum

E. *rudis,* Desert Gum

E. *sideroxylon,* Red Ironbark

E. *tereticornis,* Gray Gum

E. *viminalis,* Manna Gum

Juniperus barbadensis,
    Bermuda Juniper

J. excelsa, Greek Juniper

J. mexicana, Ozark White Cedar

Libocedrus decurrens,
    Incense Cedar

Pinus canariensis,
    Canary Island Pine

P. caribaea, Slash Pine

P. cembroides, Mexican Stone Pine

P. coulteri, Big-cone Pine

P. halepensis, Aleppo Pine

P. pinea, Italian Stone Pine

P. radiata, Monterey Pine

P. taeda, Loblolly Pine

Podocarpus elongatus,
    African Yellow-wood

P. macrophyllus, False Yew

Sequoia gigantea, Redwood

S. sempervirens, Giant Redwood

Taxodium distichum, Bald Cypress

Thuja orientalis, Oriental Arbovitae

Torreya californica,
    California Nutmeg

T. taxifolia, Stinking Cedar

SMALL TREES FOR WARM CLIMATES

The development of air conditioning, which made the one-story house and its flat, exposed roof practical (if not economical) in warmer climates, has in turn increased demand for low-growing trees. Here are some suggestions.

Acacia baileyana (CF),
    Winter Acacia

A. *longifolia* (CF), Sidney Wattle

Albizzia julibrissin (CF), Silk Tree

A. *lebbek* (CF),
    Woman's-tongue Tree

Aralia chinensis (CF),
    Angelica Tree

Arbutus unedo (CF),
    Strawberry Tree

Broussonetia papyrifera,
    Paper Mulberry

Castanea crenata,
    Japanese Chestnut

Cercis chinensis (CF),
    Chinese Redbud

C. *siliquastrum* (CF), Judas Tree

Chamaerops humilis,
    Low Fan Palm

Chionanthus retusus (CF),
    Chinese Fringe Tree .

Cocos australis, Coco Palm

C. *plumosa,* Queen Palm

Cordyline australis,
    Australian Dragon Tree

Cornus florida (CF),
    Flowering Dogwood

Crinodendron dependens,
    White Lily Tree

C. *patagua,* Red Lily Tree

Delonix regia (CF),
    Royal Poinciana

Diospyros kaki,
    Japanese Persimmon

Eriobotrya japonica (CF), Loquat

Ficus carica, Common Fig

F. lyrata, Fiddleleaf Fig

F. retusa, Malayan Rubber Tree

Gordonia alatamaha (CF),
Franklin Tree

Halesia diptera (CF),
Silverbell Tree

Ilex aquifolium, English Holly

I. cassine, Dahoon

I. opaca, American Holly

I. vomitoria, Yaupon

Laburnum alpinum (CF),
Scotch Laburnum

L. anagyroides (CF),
Golden-chain Tree

Lagerstroemia indica (CF),
Crape Myrtle

Laurocerasus officinalis,
Cherry Laurel

Leucadendron argenteum,
Silver Tree

Magnolia fraseri (CF),
Fraser Magnolia

M. tripetala (CF), Umbrella Tree

Metrosideros tomentosa (CF),
Iron Tree

Olea europaea, Olive

Paliurus spina-christi,
Jerusalem Thorn

Parkinsonia aculeata, Ratama

Phoenix reclinata,
Spiny Feather Palm

Poncirus trifoliata (CF),
Hardy Orange

Prunus angustifolia (CF),
Chicksaw Plum

P. armeniaca (CF), Apricot

P. ilicifolia (CF), Holly Plum

Pterostyrax hispida (CF),
Epaulette Tree

Pyrus species (CF), Crabapples

Schinus molle (CF),
California Pepper Tree

Stewartia pseudo-camellia (CF),
False Camellia

Trachycarpus fortunei,
Windmill Palm

Ungnadia speciosa (CF),
Mexican Buckeye

WOODY PLANTS WITH GOOD AUTUMN FOLIAGE COLOR

Few areas of the world enjoy the autumn explosion of color that occurs in the United States. Soil, rainfall, and temperatures must be just right to change the green of the leaves to scarlet, gold, and purple. The trees and shrubs listed below will enliven the autumn landscape when their foliage changes color.

SHRUBS

Berberis thunbergi	Japanese Barberry	Orange-scarlet
Cornus mas	Cornelian Cherry	Red
Euonymus alatus	Winged Burning-bush	Rosy scarlet
Fothergilla major	Witch Alder	Orange & scarlet

Hamamelis mollis	Chinese Witch Hazel	Golden-yellow
Rhus typhina	Staghorn Sumac	Flaming scarlet
Sassafras albidum	Sassafras	Yellow, orange & scarlet
Viburnum	Viburnum	Shades of red & scarlet

TREES

Acer circinatum	Vine Maple	Orange to scarlet
A. ginnala	Amur Maple	Red
A. macrophyllium	Oregon Maple	Brilliant yellow to orange
A. pensylvanicum	Moosewood	Clear yellow
A. platanoides	Norway Maple	Yellow
A. rubrum	Red Maple	Brilliant yellow & scarlet
A. saccharinum	Silver Maple	Yellow
A. saccharum	Sugar Maple	Yellow, orange & scarlet
Amelanchier canadensis	Shadblow	Red
Betula papyrifera	Paper Birch	Gold
B. pendula	European Birch	Gold
Carpinus caroliniana	American Hornbeam	Orange & scarlet
Carya ovata	Shagbark Hickory	Yellow
Cornus florida	Flowering Dogwood	Scarlet
Crataegus cordata	Washington Thorn	Orange-scarlet
C. crus-galli	Cockspur Thorn	Orange-red
Fagus grandifolia	American Beech	Bright yellow to bronze
F. sylvatica	European Beech	Red
Ginkgo biloba	Maidenhair Tree	Clear Yellow
Gymnocladus dioica	Kentucky Coffee Tree	Yellow
Liquidambar styraciflua	Sweet Gum	Purple, yellow, scarlet, orange
Liriodendron tulipifera	Tulip Tree	Yellow
Nyssa sylvatica	Black Gum	Red
Oxydendrum arboreum	Sourwood	Brilliant scarlet
Populus grandidentata	Bigtooth Aspen	Yellow
P. tremuloides	Quaking Aspen	Gold & scarlet
Pyrus calleryana	Chinese Sand Pear	Yellow & scarlet
Quercus alba	White Oak	Crimson to purple
Q. coccinea	Scarlet Oak	Scarlet

| Q. *palustris* | Pin Oak | Scarlet |
| Q. *rubra* | Red Oak | Scarlet to crimson |

VINES

Celastrus scandens	Bittersweet	Yellow
Euonymus radicans coloratus	Bronze Wintercreeper	Maroon-bronze
Parthenocissus quinquefolia	Virginia Creeper	Scarlet
P. tricuspidata	Boston Ivy	Scarlet

THE DUTCH ELM DISEASE SPRAY CONTROVERSY

The loss of a large percentage of American elms, with the impending loss of the remainder unless Dutch elm disease can be controlled, has generated a controversy in which the basic problems have not been satisfactorily clarified. The disease is caused by a fungus which is carried from tree to tree by elm-bark beetles. One means proposed for checking it is to use sprays against the beetles; but sprays of all kinds have of late come under fire.

Bird lovers contend that spraying for the control of Dutch elm disease (a) does not control or protect trees, (b) that it kills birds by the thousands, and (c) that it prevents the operation of natural checks and balances which would control all types of pests.

Tree lovers contend that (a) without spraying, the elms would be killed off in a year or two once the disease invaded a community, (b) that injury to bird life is grossly exaggerated and can be prevented entirely by spraying at the proper time, (c) that natural checks and balances do not operate in the case of an imported disease, and (d) that centuries would be needed to develop a natural control, by which time all the elms would be dead.

Overlooked in the heat of discussion are several other aspects of the problem that are just as important. The first is that if elms are not sprayed, they will succumb to the disease and be destroyed in a short time, leaving the streets denuded. With the elms gone in towns where they have been almost exclusively planted as street trees, the nesting places for birds have gone, too, and the tree-nesting birds have moved elsewhere. To many other kinds of birds, trees are a source of food which may consist of buds, fruits, leaves, or of insect pests that infest them. So no matter what is done, the bird population will be affected.

Another factor overlooked is the effect that spraying wide areas for mosquito and fly control has on the food supply of the bird population.

Spare the trees: Old trees give charm and character to this new terrace of a new house. The builders' bulldozers managed to avoid them; the wooden seat helps scooters and tricycles to do the same.

Such spraying is done during the height of the feeding and nesting season of birds. It is far more destructive to bird life than the limited spraying of elms in very early spring before birds return, and it accounts mainly for the disappearance of insect-eating species such as the wren.

Imbalance of Nature

As a whipping boy, the destruction of natural balance may be a useful idea, but it offers no practical answer to the problem. A disease invading a new area is without natural controls, which can be developed only over a long period of time.

We cannot deny that the "balance of nature" has been upset. This process began when the first forests were destroyed in New England and Virginia during colonial days. It has progressed relentlessly ever since. Consider the millions of acres of forest and brush cut in the last decade for toll roads alone; this has had far more effect on the bird population of the country (through the destruction of available nesting sites) than all the Dutch elm disease spraying to date. The devastating effects of air pollution, the rapid intercommunication between foreign lands (which brings in new pests without natural enemies), plus hundreds of other factors are working to upset the balance of nature every day. About the only way the world can be returned to the interplay of natural forces is by an atomic war which will destroy all mankind.

To return to the elms themselves, no one will deny that, whether we spray or not, the Dutch elm disease will continue to take its toll. To eradicate it completely from North America would call for a complete cover spray on every existing elm in every state and county where the disease is established. This would obviously be so costly that it will never be undertaken — although it would cost less than sending one man to the moon.

To Spray or Not to Spray?

An infected beetle can fly at least 1,000 yards. Even if a tree has been sprayed, that beetle can stab it and pass on the causative fungus before it is killed. With trees on private property largely unsprayed, treating street trees provides no assurance they will survive.

If this is the case, why spray? It is a matter of simple economics. Despite the lack of complete success with spray programs, they do reduce the chance of infection. Thus instead of all elms in a city dying in 2 to 3 years, their loss can be spread over 10 to 20 years. In a town with thousands of trees lining its streets, the removal of 5 to 10 per cent of its elms a year is a vastly different problem from cutting them all down within a year or two.

With the smaller yearly loss, removal can usually be handled by the permanent forestry crews, at no increase in the budget. With a crash program, outside crews must be called in at a cost of as high as $100 a tree for removal. The alternative is to leave the dead elms standing, a stark ugly reminder of a shortsighted program.

Bird-Lovers' Responsibility

This does not mean that those concerned for bird life should stop all resistance to spraying. They have a right to insist that what spraying is done is done properly — long before migrating birds return. They should insist that the safest possible chemicals be used, that all bird baths and pools where birds may drink be covered, that no spray be applied so heavily that it drips to the ground to contaminate the soil and be picked up by earthworms, and that no pools of spray solution accumulate in tree crotches, empty tin cans, or other places. They should be vigilant to see that no mad, thoughtless campaigns, such as the badly managed spraying for the fire ant in the South, be staged.

Tree-Lovers' Concern

By considering fairly all aspects of the elm controversy, we should be able at least to delay the loss of our precious elms. Perhaps in time an effective cure can be found. If not, underplanting existing trees with species not subject to serious diseases should be contemplated by every home-owner. Oftentimes, a tree can be located between the street and the house in such a way that it will not interfere with existing specimens but will replace them if they are destroyed.

6

Shrubs and Hedges

The modern trend away from the use of massed shrubbery may help to simplify maintenance, but it does so at a sacrifice of interest. Today, when an entire property can frequently be seen at a glance, the effect is apt to be monotonous, unless, by some rare chance, the house stands in a dramatic situation — perhaps with a vast backdrop of distant views. Another weakness of sparse planting is that if the owner wants to use his property for outdoor living, he finds himself in a goldfish bowl, with his every move visible to the curious public.

Shrubs are beautiful in themselves and useful as screens and backgrounds. While an old New England house may be picturesque with a single lilac bush as decoration, we must realize that it fits a time and a place which bear little resemblance to life today.

Fine gardens have been created by leaving the choice of woody plants to the landscape architect, but these do not satisfy the true gardener who finds individuality, even personality, in plants. Unless we have a personal feeling for the shrubs we use, much of the joy of gardening is lost.

Landscape architects, unfortunately, are not always interested in the finer differences in the characteristics of shrubs. If a plant of *Euonymus alatus compactus* suits exactly the same space as a fine specimen of *Viburnum tomentosum*, most will select the less expensive euonymus. They are chiefly interested in shrubs as items of mass and line, not as fascinating plants with innumerable subtle differences. Much of this seeming indifference has been forced upon them, for keeping costs down is a constant battle that must be won if services are to be sold. It is ideal when the landscape architect's eye for design can be paired with the home-owner's personal taste.

Before any major selection of shrubs is made, a visit to an outstanding arboretum, public park, or even cemetery will pay dividends. Mount Auburn Cemetery in Boston, founded by the Massachusetts Horticultural Society, surpasses some arboretums in the quality of its plants. Lakeview Cemetery in Cleveland is the goal of garden-club pilgrimages in spring because of its superb collection of woody plants. Visit these places at different times of the year, if you can. In spring, spectacular bloom may hide the fact that, when not in flower, a certain shrub is ungainly or poor in foliage. Again, the ugly duckling of spring may be a lovely swan when tinted by autumn.

PLANTING SHRUBBERY

Unlike the perennial border or vegetable garden, which can be torn up and remade at the end of the season, shrub planting is a more or less permanent affair — sometimes too permanent. Many an overgrown planting lives on in tangled confusion, worth little as outdoor decoration because the owner fails to give it his needed attention.

Because shrubs are so permanent, great care must be given to their placement and planting. It takes courage to set a 3-foot *Viburnum tomentosum* in a space designed for its ultimate spread to 12 feet, but unless this is done, a vast amount of moving and shifting must be undertaken as the planting matures. A prime cause of overgrown plantings around older houses is the owner's negligence when filler shrubs should be removed.

A fact often overlooked in setting out shrubs is that few of their roots will be in topsoil. Even experienced landscapers often make a big show of bringing in several inches of black topsoil, then plant the shrubs with their roots in unadulterated subsoil. A hole for a shrub should be at least a foot deeper and a foot wider than the root it is to hold. Fill it with good soil to encourage the roots for at least the first growing season.

When balled and burlapped specimens are used, the hole should be just as deep. However, to prevent the heavy mass of soil and roots from sinking too far into the soft surrounding earth, the ball should rest on a hard stone or on a pillar built of hard-burned brick. This should elevate the plant so that it stands about an inch below the level at which it grew in the nursery.

Mistakes are often made in filling around the newly set plant. Proper filling does not imply merely throwing loose dirt into the hole. The soil must be settled thoroughly around the roots until they are in complete contact with it. At the same time, the heavy-footed nursery worker has retarded growth on many trees by overdoing this tramping down of the fill. Trees and shrubs with so-called "slip bark," such as cherries and magnolias, are particularly susceptible to injury by tramping. Much of the settling can be done with water, which washes loose earth into any empty spaces without packing it too hard.

PLANTING A SHRUB: *First, dig good-sized hole, mix damp peatmoss with soil at bottom, firm soil so it will not sink. (1). Bare-root shrub — Spread roots (2). Work soil in among roots, pressing firm, until hole is three-fourths full.*

Burlapped shrub — Top of earth ball should be at soil line (1). Cut burlap loose and tuck down firmly (2). Container-grown shrub — Carefully remove container and set ball in hole with top at soil level (3).

Soil and water — Add soil, pressing firm, until hole is three-quarters full (1). Fill balance of hole with water (2). Allow to drain, then fill with soil. Shape surface like a saucer, and mulch to prevent crusting.

The wealth of plants available to American gardeners is vast and wonderful, but the trend toward standardization is driving from the market many marvelous plants for which there is no established demand. The lists which follow include only commercially available species and varieties.

FACING SHRUBS

Much of the woody plant material offered for landscaping is taller than 4 feet and may grow from 12 to 20. If used alone, such tall shrubs either present a solid, abrupt wall if they are covered with foliage down to the ground, or show naked branches until leaves appear. A few species form interesting patterns when they are bare.

But all too often the lower branches of shrubs are ungainly and need to be concealed by the low-growing species landscape architects call facing shrubs. These range in height from almost prostrate to about 3 feet. The following list names hardy evergreen shrubs that can be used for facing, or to form low masses where these are needed.

Andromeda glaucophylla,
    Bog Rosemary
Arctostaphylos uva-ursi, Bearberry
Buxus japonica koreana,
    Korean Box
Daphne cneorum, Garland Flower
Empetrum nigrum, Crowberry
Erica carnea, Winter Heath
Euonymus radicans carrierei,
    Shrub Wintercreeper
Kalmia angustifolia, Sheep Laurel
Ledum groenlandicum,
    Labrador Tea

Leiophyllum buxifolium, Sleek-leaf
Mahonia repens, Creeping Barberry
Pieris floribunda,
    Mountain Fetterbush
Taxus baccata repandens,
    Dwarf English Yew
T. cuspidata nana,
    Dwarf Japanese Yew
Thuja occidentalis globosa,
    Globe Arborvitae

HARDY EVERGREENS 3 TO 8 FEET

This is a most difficult group to classify because hardiness in evergreens, both broad-leaved and needled, is not a matter of temperature alone. Species hardy in snowy Maine may die without apparent reason much farther south. Winter moisture, both in the air and in the soil, plays a much greater role here than in the case of deciduous shrubs.

Placement must always take into account the fact that evergreens give off moisture all winter, even when the soil is frozen. They should not be placed where prevailing winds blow against them across wide, flat areas. Watch out particularly for "tunnels" formed by long lines of trees or other heavy plantings which are open toward the prevailing wind. Cold, dry winter air rushing up such a tunnel can kill an evergreen that might otherwise be hardy a hundred miles or more farther north.

Winter sun is a hazard too. Many broad-leaved evergreens can be grown north of their normal range if they are planted on the north side of a hedge or wall. In June their branches are in full light, but as the sun sinks to the south as the year progresses, they will be in increasing shade until, by the time freezing weather comes, they are completely shaded.

The use of mechanical protection, such as wrapping in burlap or surrounding the entire plant with a cage of leaves, is frowned upon by some garden enthusiasts, but often it saves valuable specimens. One of the pleasures of gardening is being able to grow plants which others in your vicinity do not have. While winter protection may seem like taking unfair advantage of your neighbors, they have the same privilege if they will exercise it.

A question of classification arises when the narrow-needled coniferous evergreens are under consideration. Many of the species and varieties used by landscapers may be planted as 3 to 8-foot specimens and, because they are slow growing, they will remain at that height for a number of years. An example is the Hinoki cypress, which at maturity has horticultural forms which may remain low for 30 to 40 years under northern conditions. When these are used in home landscaping, their ultimate height may not be too important. However, those who are responsible for landscaping public areas, where plantings may be considered more or less permanent, might do well to keep these limitations in mind.

Many of the more rapid-growing species planted while small, are used for home landscaping with disastrous results. All over America twin blue spruces are seen, which were planted 20 or 30 years ago as attractive 5-foot specimens on either side of a front door. Today they threaten to crowd the house off its foundations, and are an obstacle to visitors trying to enter the front door. In the following list, an effort has been made to eliminate all such plants.

Berberis julianae,
    Wintergreen Barberry

Chamaecyparis obtusa varieties,
    Hinoki Cypress

Cytisus scoparius, Scotch Broom

Euonymus patens,
    Evergreen Burning-bush

Ilex crenata convexa,
    Boxwood Holly

I. crenata microphylla,
    Small-leaf Japanese Holly

Juniperus chinensis pfitzeriana,
    Pfitzer Juniper

J. sabina, Savin Juniper

J. squamata meyeri, Meyer Juniper
Kalmia latifolia, Mountain Laurel
Leucothoë catesbaei, Fetterbush
Pinus mugo mughus, Mugho Pine
Taxus baccata repandens,
    Dwarf English Yew

T. canadensis, Canadian Yew
Thuja occidentalis compacta,
    Dwarf Arborvitae
T. occidentalis globosa,
    Globe Arborvitae

DECIDUOUS SHRUBS PROSTRATE TO 3 FEET

Amorpha canescens, Leadplant
A. nana, Dwarf Leadplant
Amygdalus nana,
    Dwarf Russian Almond
Berberis thunbergi minor,
    Dwarf Japanese Barberry
Caryopteris incana, Blue Spirea
Ceanothus americanus,
    New Jersey Tea
Chaenomeles japonica,
    Dwarf Flowering Quince
Cotoneaster adpressa,
    Creeping Rockspray
C. horizontalis, Rose Rockspray
Cytisus albus, Dwarf White Broom
C. nigricans, Spike Broom
C. purgans, Provence Broom
C. purpureus, Purple Broom
Daphne mezereum, Mezereon
Deutzia lemoinei compacta,
    Dwarf Deutzia
Diervilla lonicera, Gravelweed
Hypericum aureum, St. Johnswort
H. bucklei, Carolina St. Johnswort

H. moserianum, Goldflower
Jamesia americana, Shagbark Shrub
Lonicera dioica, Small Honeysuckle
Myrica gale, Sweet Gale
Potentilla fruticosa,
    Shrubby Cinquefoil
Prunus besseyi, Sand Cherry
Rhododendron molle,
    Chinese Azalea
Rhus canadensis, Fragrant Sumac
Ribes alpinum, Alpine Currant
R. grossularia, Gooseberry
Rosa nitida,
    New England Wild Rose
R. spinosissima, Scotch Rose
R. varieties,
    Polyantha & Floribunda Roses
Spiraea bumalda 'Anthony Waterer,'
    Spirea
Symphoricarpos albus, Snowberry
S. mollis, Creeping Snowberry
Xanthorhiza simplicissima,
    Yellow-root

DECIDUOUS SHRUBS 3 TO 8 FEET

Once the group from prostrate to 3 feet is complete, classification becomes more difficult. Many species in the following list will remain in the 3- to 8-foot classification, but occasionally may have a spurt in growth, due to some unusually favorable condition and reach a height of 10 to 15 feet.

Acanthopanax sieboldianus,
    Five-leaved Aralia
Amelanchier stolonifera,
    Dwarf Juneberry
Aronia arbutifolia, Red Chokeberry
A. melanocarpa, Black Chokeberry
Baccharis halimifolia,
    Groundsel Bush
Berberis thunbergi,
    Japanese Barberry
B. vernae, Coral Barberry
Buddleia davidi, Butterfly Bush
Callicarpa americana,
    French Mulberry
C. dichotoma, Beautybush
C. japonica, Japanese Beautybush
Calycanthus floridus, Sweet Shrub
Caragana maximowicziana,
    Russian Pea Shrub
Caryopteris incana, Bluebeard
Chaenomeles lagenaria,
    Japanese Quince
Clethra alnifolia,
    Sweet Pepperbush
Cornus alba, Coral Dogwood
C. amomum, Silky Cornel
C. racemosa, Gray Dogwood
C. stolonifera, Red-osier Dogwood
Coronilla emerus, Scorpion Senna
Corylopsis pauciflora, Winter Hazel
Cotoneaster divaricata,
    Spreading Rockspray
C. hupehensis, Chinese Rockspray
C. lucida, Hedge Rockspray
Deutzia gracilis, Slender Deutzia
D. lemoinei, Lemoine's Deutzia
Diervilla rivularis,
    River Bush Honeysuckle
D. sessilifolia, Wood Honeysuckle

Elaeagnus argentea, Silverberry
E. multiflora, Gumi
Elsholtzia stauntoni, Mint Shrub
Euonymus alatus compactus,
    Winged Burning-bush
E. americanus,
    American Burning-bush
Forsythia, various species,
    Golden Bells
Halimodendron halodendron,
    Salt Tree
Hamamelis vernalis,
    Spring Witch Hazel
Hydrangea arborescens grandiflora,
    Snow-hill Hydrangea
H. quercifolia, Oakleaf Hydrangea
Ilex verticillata, Winterberry
Itea virginica, Sweet Spire
Kerria japonica, Japanese Rose
Kolkwitzia amabilis, Beautybush
Lespedeza thunbergi, Bush Clover
Ligustrum vulgare, Common Privet
Lonicera ledebouri,
    California Honeysuckle
L. morrowi, Morrow Honeysuckle
L. syringantha, Lilac Honeysuckle
Myrica caroliniensis, Bayberry
Nemopanthus mucronata,
    Mountain Holly
Neviusia alabamensis, Snow Wreath
Philadelphus species, Mock Orange
Physocarpus opulifolius, Ninebark
Prunus tomentosa, Nanking Cherry
Pyracantha coccinea, Firethorn
Rhododendron species, Azaleas
Rhodotypos tetrapetala, Jetbead
Ribes odoratum, Golden Currant
Robinia hispida, Rose Acacia
Rosa species & varieties, Roses

Rubus odoratus,
   Flowering Raspberry

Sorbaria aitchisoni,
   Kashmir False Spirea

Spiraea species, Spireas

Weigela species, Weigelas

DECIDUOUS SHRUBS 8 TO 20 FEET

Where to draw the line between trees and shrubs is often a difficult problem. Almost any upright-growing shrub can be trained to a single stem like a tree. Certain trees, if allowed to form several trunks, make useful shrubs with more mass and less line value in the landscape than they would provide if grown with a single trunk. Some of the species listed below are grown both ways, and may even be listed again in the chapter on trees. An excellent example of dual use is *Euonymus europeaus*, which may go by the name spindle tree in one role and be called European burning-bush in another.

Amorpha fruticosa, Bastard Indigo

Benzoin aestivale, Spicebush

Caragana arborescens,
   Siberian Pea Shrub

Colutea arborescens, Bladder Senna

Cornus alternifolia,
   Pagoda Dodwood

C. mas, Cornelian Cherry

Cotoneaster species, Rocksprays

Elaeagnus augustifolia,
   Russian Olive

Enkianthus campanulatus,
   Bellflower Tree

Euonymus bungeanus,
   Winterberry Euonymus

E. europaeus,
   European Burning-bush

Exochorda giraldi,
   Redbud Pearlbush

E. racemosa, Pearlbush

Hibiscus syriacus, Rose of Sharon

Hippophaë rhamnoides,
   Sea Buckthorn

Ligustrum species, Privet

Lonicera species, Honeysuckle

Magnolia stellata, Star Magnolia

Parrotia persica, Iron Tree

Philadelphus varieties,
   Mock Oranges

Photinia villosa, Christmas Berry

Poncirus trifoliata, Hardy Orange

Prunus cerasifera pissardi,
   Pissardi Purple-leaf Plum

P. triloba, Flowering Plum

Pyrus (malus) species and varieties,
   Small Flowering Crabs

Rhus cotinoides,
   American Smoke Tree

R. cotinus, Purple Smoke Tree

Rhododendron species, Azaleas

Sambucus species, Elders

Shepherdia argentea, Buffalo-berry

Syringa varieties, Lilacs

Tamarix parviflora, Saltbush

Viburnum species, Viburnums

Vitex agnus-castus, Chaste Tree

TENDER SHRUBS FOR WARMER CLIMATES

Some species that are hardy in the North do not survive in the South. Among these are species of ribes, ledum, and a few others, but most of those listed for the North can be grown also in the South.

PROSTRATE TO 3 FEET

Ardisia crispa, Coral Ardisia

Buxus microphylla koreana,
    Korean Box

B. sempervirens suffruticosa,
    Dwarf Boxwood

Ceanothus prostratus, Mahala Mat

Cotoneaster dammeri,
    Trailing Rockspray

Daphne genkwa,
    Lilac Garland Flower

Diosma ericoides, Breath-of-heaven

Fothergilla gardeni, Dwarf Alder

Hypericum coris,
    Corsican St. Johnswort

H. olympicum, Greek St. Johnswort

H. patulum,
    Japanese St. Johnswort

H. reptans, Creeping Goldflower

Indigofera decora, Chinese Indigo

Lonicera pileata,
    Privet Honeysuckle

Ononis fruticosa, Rest-harrow

Pernettya mucronata, Prickly Heath

Rhododendron species, Azaleas

Turraea obtusifolia, Ribbon Flower

Ulex europaeus, Furze

3 TO 8 FEET

Aucuba japonica, Golddust Tree

Berberis buxifolia,
    Magellan Barberry

B. darwini, Darwin's Barberry

B. julianae, Wintergreen Barberry

Carpenteria californica,
    California Mock Orange

Cotoneaster species, Rocksprays

Cytisus canariensis,
    Genista (of Florists)

Deutzia scabra, Rough Deutzia

Erica mediterranea, Darnley Heath

E. stricta, Corsican Heath

Escallonia rubra, Escallonia

Fontanesia phillyreoides,
    Syrian Privet

Fremontia californica, Flannel Bush

Fuchsia species, Fuchsias

Gardenia jasminoides, Cape Jasmine

Grevillea thelemanniana,
    Jewel-flower Shrub

Hakea pugioniformis, Dagger-leaf

Hibiscus rosa-sinensis,
    Chinese Hibiscus

Hydrangea macrophylla,
    House Hydrangea

Indigofera gerardiana,
    Himalayan Indigo

Leycesteria formosa,
    Himalayan Honeysuckle

Ligustrum species, Privets

Mahonia beali,
    Leatherleaf Holly-grape
Meratia praecox, Wintersweet
Myrtus communis, Common Myrtle
Nandina domestica,
    Heavenly Bamboo
Perovskia atriplicifolia, Silver Sage

Raphiolepis indica,
    Indian Hawthorn
R. umbellata, Yeddo Hawthorn
Rhodendron species, Azaleas
Ribes sanguineum, Winter Currant
Veronica (Hebe) species,
    Shrub Veronicas

8 TO 20 FEET

Callistemon lanceolatus,
    Lemon Bottlebrush
C. rigidus, Stiff Bottlebrush
Chilopsis linearis, Desert Willow
Clerodendron trichotomum,
    Harlequin Glory-bower
Cotoneaster frigida,
    Himalayan Rockspray
Duranta repens, Skyflower
Elaeagnus species, Oleasters
Erica arborea, Tree Heath
E. scoparia, Besom Heath
Escallonia montevidensis,
    Escallonia
Eugenia paniculata,
    Australian Brush Cherry
Fatsia japonica, Fatsia
Lagerstroemia indica, Crape Myrtle
Laurus nobilis, Laurel
Melaleuca armillaris,
    Drooping Bottlebrush

M. decussata, Lilac Bottlebrush
M. hypericifolia, Dotted Bottlebrush
Michelia fuscata, Banana Shrub
Nerium oleander, Oleander
Photinia villosa,
    Low Christmas Berry
Punica granatum, Pomegranate
Rhododendron species,
    Rhododendrons & Azaleas
Rhus integrifolia, Sourberry
R. laurina, Laurel Sumac
R. ovata, Sugarberry
Spartium junceum, Spanish Broom
Staphylea colchica,
    Caucasian Bladdernut
Tecoma stans, Yellow Elder
Tetrapanax papyriferum,
    Rice-paper Plant
Viburnum odoratissimum,
    Sweet Viburnum

HEDGES

In places where garden information is dispensed, a common complaint is trouble with the hedge. The logical counter is, "What kind of a hedge is it?" Four times out of five the answer will be, "Hedge? Why it's a hedge, of course."

In this exchange, the garden authority knows without further identification that he is dealing with privet. To four people out of five, hedge and privet are synonymous. As a result, few nurserymen ever try to sell anything else. The result is privet — miles and miles of privet — extending monotonously across the face of America. This leads the sophisticated gardener in turn to despise and shun the species. In some landscape circles, the comment, "He specified privet!" is enough to damn a man's professional reputation.

While privet is a fairly satisfactory plant for hedges, gardeners should realize that it does have some distinct disadvantages, not the least of which is that it is common. Even more important, they should appreciate the fact that almost any shrub can be used as a hedge. In the famous hedge collection at the Morton Arboretum near Lisle, Illinois, and in similar collections at the Arnold Arboretum, and the Cornell Plantations near Cornell University, there are more than 150 combinations of hedges, trimmed and untrimmed.

The principal objection to privet is overuse. A second is that the most widely planted species, *Ligustrum ovalifolium* or California privet, simply is not hardy in the areas for which it is most widely sold. This statement may seem like sheer effrontery to the nurseryman in New York State or Michigan who has sold it for years, yet a study of the record will show that it must be listed as tender north of the Ohio River. True, its roots do survive when the tops are winter-killed, but at least a full year is needed before it recovers its mature size, and then it is often cut back the following year by another cold spell.

Add to these disadvantages the susceptibility of privet to a die-back disease which may take out an entire hedge in a year's time, and it certainly has enough counts against it to encourage consideration of other shrubs.

There are many species that can fill every purpose for which privet has been used in the past, and fill them with distinction. Think for a moment of the gorgeous fire kindled by *Euonymus alatus compactus* in autumn when it turns a brilliant cerise-red, unlike any other foliage color in the landscape. Then compare this show with the dull gray-yellow of dying privet.

Even so common a hedge as Persian lilac is neglected in many parts of America. Hardy from Canada into northern Alabama and Georgia (it is the one lilac that does well in the South), it should be one of our better hedge plants, yet it is difficult to find enough stock in nurseries to plant a 100-foot hedge.

WHAT IS A HEDGE?

Perhaps a stumbling block in the way of other plants, is the popular concept of a hedge. In the United States (perhaps less so in Canada where British traditions are strong) a hedge to most people is a row of privet across the front of a suburban lot — a sort of living fence, kept low

An oleander hedge and a groundcover of strawberries and trailing juniper link this well-landscaped home to its natural hillside setting.

so as not to hide the house from the street. Anything taller than four feet is considered "unfriendly" or "unneighborly." Even the modern picture window, revealing every detail of the family's life, has failed to alter this feeling. In some suburbs, developed by speculative builders, it is often possible to see completely through such a window — through its twin at the back of the house and into a second set of windows in the house across the street. Every movement inside is visible to the passing public.

Rebelling at such togetherness, a progressive soul will occasionally "plant out" the peeping world at both front and rear of his property. This is not necessarily a solid barrier of unrelieved monotony, but may be a composition of shrubs or small trees of similar habit, so planted as to obscure all direct sight lines. Or if the property is small and space between the house and walk limited, he may of necessity select a narrow-growing species of proper height to give privacy, and clip it in a formal manner to save space.

Here, then, are three types of hedge — low, fence-like barriers; tall, irregular plantings that obscure and hide; and the tall, formal clipped hedge. To these three we might add the wall-like hedge for limited space, formed by planting vines on a supporting structure, and the almost prostrate low line of demarcation created by growing English ivy or *Euonymus radicans* over a low arch of chicken wire.

For the tall, informal, irregular planting that might be placed across the back lot line to give privacy to an outdoor living area, practically any

For a more formal front entrance, the owners chose a waist-high hedge of Japanese yew. Individual clipped yews set off the doorway.

shrub with fairly dense foliage can be used. This would exclude such loose airy plants as tamarisk or rose acacia, giving preference to those with solid foliage such as *Viburnum lantana* or *Lonicera tatarica*. If use is to be made of outdoor areas in winter, or if the picture window is too open, evergreens should be considered. Such a rear-line planting might be combined with the idea of a private bird sanctuary. (See Chapter 16.)

VINE WALLS

Where space does not permit more than a few inches for a tall dividing wall, and where a brick or stone structure would obstruct the movement of air, a wire or wooden trellis, completely clothed with vines, is a valuable device. This need not occupy more than 6 inches in width, including the vines, where the narrowest possible hedge will take up many times that space.

CLIPPED VS. NATURAL HEDGES

As already indicated, clipped hedges save space. However, they add a note of formality to the landscape which may not always be desirable. If the property is laid out in simple straight lines and is at least semi-formal in treatment, this is not objectionable. If, however, the plan is less formal, the trimmed hedge does not fit in as well. Even on such a property, how-

How to repair a hedge, if neglect has let it grow tall and scrawny: In late winter or early spring, cut it back close to the ground (1). When new growth is a foot or so high, cut back to a quarter of its height (2). Keep cutting new growth, top and sides, until hedge is dense and of proper size.

ever, a touch of formality might not be too much out of place as the house is approached.

At the same time, the owner of a clipped hedge must realize that he is tying himself down to a job that must be done, if not by himself, by hired help, two to five times a year. Here the advantage of using clipped conifers rather than deciduous material is soon apparent: evergreen hedges usually need clipping only twice a year. The first shearing should be done when spring growth is about half-mature, usually in June in the North. At this time, half the new growth formed in the current year is cut away. This forces two buds to sprout farther down the branch, producing a thicker plant. In summer, a second clipping may be needed to cut away any shoots which have made too vigorous a growth following the first shearing.

Evergreens should never be cut back beyond the current year's growth. They do not retain living dormant buds for more than two years; if cut back to the old wood, they cannot grow out again. Two exceptions to this rule are hemlocks and yews, both of which can tolerate more shearing, if necessary.

In contrast to this twice-a-year-shearing, a hedge of California privet may have to be sheared five times if it is to appear neat. A long clipped hedge of practically any height demands mechanical equipment such as electric hedge shears. No longer can yardmen be employed for 50 to 75 cents an hour to do this tedious work.

Perhaps the best compromise between shearing and natural growth is to form the hedge right after planting and in its second year of growth, than allow it to grow untrimmed. In later years, an occasional use of the shears to remove branches that are straying too far out of line will be all that is needed. For such a hedge, however, a slow-growing shrub such as *Euonymus alatus compactus* should be selected.

LOW RIBBON HEDGES

Hedges less than 12 inches high are the most difficult of all to maintain, and should be avoided if possible. However, there are situations (for example, a low border around rose beds) where nothing else will serve. Perhaps the best plant for this purpose is not a shrub at all, though it has shrubby character. It is germander (*Teucrium chamaedrys*). A little less formal in habit, but capable of being restrained if not allowed to spread, is *Pachistima canbyi*, cursed with the ugly name of rat-stripper, yet a lovely small holly-like plant. Both species are hardy north.

Where boxwood survives, there is nothing finer than Korean box (*Buxus microphylla koreana*). This is hardy as far north as the Great Lakes and into Michigan. Its one fault is that in winter its foliage turns an unattractive olive-green color, but new growth in spring is fully as attractive as that of common boxwood. Farther south the dwarf box (*Buxus sempervirens suffruticosa*) makes a lovely low hedge. It is used extensively in the plantings of Colonial Williamsburg.

A number of dwarf Japanese yews are also available, often selections from seedlings by local nurserymen. These do not have wide distribution but can be discovered by inquiry at better nurseries.

The box barberry (*Berberis thunbergi minor*) is another excellent low edging that stays neat. Both green- and red-leaved varieties are available.

LOW HEDGES

DECIDUOUS SHRUBS THAT CAN BE HELD TO 2 FEET

Berberis thunbergi erecta,
    True-hedge Barberry
Chaenomeles japonica alpina,
    Alpine Flowering Quince
Ligustrum vulgare lodense,
    Lodense Privet
Lonicera claveyi,
    Clavey Dwarf Honeysuckle
Ribes alpinum, Alpine Currant

Rosa species, Roses
Rosa varieties,
    Polyantha & Floribunda Roses
Salix purpurea nana,
    Dwarf Purple Willow

EVERGREENS THAT CAN BE HELD TO 2 FEET

Picea glauca conica,
    Dwarf Alberta Spruce
Pinus mugo mughus, Mugho Pine

Taxus varieties, Yews
Thuja occidentalis pumila,
    Dwarf Globe Arborvitae

HEDGES 2 TO 5 FEET

DECIDUOUS SHRUBS

Berberis koreana, Korean Barberry

B. mentorensis, Mentor Barberry

B. thunbergi, Japanese Barberry

Chaenomeles lagenaria,
Flowering Quince

Cotoneaster lucida,
Hedge Rockspray

Euonymus alatus compactus,
Dwarf Burning-bush

Ligustrum species, Privets

Physocarpus monogynus,
Mountain Ninebark

Prinsepia uniflora, Hedge Prinsepia

Rosa varieties,
Floribunda & Grandiflora Roses

EVERGREEN SHRUBS

Berberis julianae,
Wintergreen Barberry

Chamaecyparis obtusa varieties,
Hinoki Cypress

Euonymus patens,
Evergreen Burning-bush

Ilex crenata convexa,
Boxwood Holly

Pinus mugo mughus, Mugho Pine

Taxus canadensis, Canadian Yew

T. cuspidata & varieties,
Japanese Yew

T. media & varieties, Hybrid Yew

Thuja occidentalis varieties,
American Arborvitae

TALL HEDGES (6 to 30 feet)

DECIDUOUS TREES AND SHRUBS

Acer campestre, Hedge Maple

A. ginnala, Amur Maple

Caragana arborescens,
Siberian Pea Tree

Carpinus betulus,
European Hornbeam

Crataegus species, Hawthorns

Euonymus alatus,
Winged Burning-bush

E. europaeus, Spindle Tree

Hibiscus syriacus, Rose of Sharon

Lonicera maacki,
Manchurian Honeysuckle

L. tatarica, Tatarian Honeysuckle

Prunus spinosa, Blackthorn

Rhamnus species, Buckthorns

Syringa species & varieties, Lilacs

Viburnum species, Viburnums

EVERGREENS

Tsuga canadensis,
Canadian Hemlock

T. caroliniana, Carolina Hemlock

HEDGES FOR WARM CLIMATES

2 FEET OR LESS

Buxus sempervirens suffruticosa,
    Dwarf Boxwood
Pernettya mucronata, Prickly Heath

Taxus baccata repandens,
    Dwarf English Yew

2 TO 5 FEET

Abelia grandiflora, Glossy Abelia
Buxus sempervirens,
    Common Boxwood
Diosma ericoides, Breath-of-heaven
Lantana camara, Yellow Sage

Laurocerasus officinalis,
    English Cherry Laurel
Lonicera nitida, Box Honeysuckle
Pittosporum tobira, Tobira

6 TO 30 FEET

Acacia longifolia, Sydney Wattle
Carissa grandiflora, Natal Plum
Casuarina equisetifolia, Beefwood
Chamaecyparis lawsoniana,
    Lawson Cypress
Cupressus sempervirens,
    Italian Cypress
Eugenia paniculata australis,
    Australian Bush Cherry

Ilex vomitoria, Yaupon Holly
Laurocerasus caroliniana,
    Carolina Cherry Laurel
Poncirus trifoliata, Hardy Orange
Viburnum odoratissimum,
    Sweet Viburnum

7

Vines: Third-Dimension Landscape

An important difference between British and American gardening lies in the lavish use of wall plantings abroad. Not only are climbers used extensively in England, but many species that we grow as woody shrubs are displayed or espaliered against stone walls. Even the newest garden is thus given an atmosphere of age and permanence.

By contrast, our unclad garden walls and bare brick houses seem raw and unfinished. Even public buildings that might have been planted originally by some knowledgeable landscape architect are often stripped of their plantings later on in the mistaken theory that vines will "destroy the mortar." As a result of our mistrust of climbers, we seldom find a building or wall in America which has been deliberately landscaped with this third dimension in mind.

America is rich in climbing and clinging plants that can be used on walls — far richer, in fact, than Great Britain. Of these, the vines mentioned below are readily available, and adaptable to many sections of the United States and Canada.

One function of vines, in addition to their artistic value, is temperature control. A well-maintained covering of a close, tight vine such as Boston ivy on the south wall of a brick or stone house can reduce internal temperatures several degrees on a hot day. Where air-conditioning equipment is installed, a covering of vines can reduce its load substantially. This cooling is due both to deflection of the sun's direct rays and to the evaporative cooling by moisture given off by the leaves. A wall covered with vine foliage may give off as much as a barrel of water on a hot day.

Semi-tropical vines, lushly covering a trellis, turned this lanai into a shady retreat from summer in Los Angeles.

Put vines to work: Star Jasmine softens the severe lines of a contemporary redwood screen. And the fragrance is delicious.

Three sets of climbers on a stake fence mean privacy plus charm for this city garden.

WALL SCRAMBLERS

Some vines have no special mechanism for climbing but ascend by scrambling or leaning against their support. Once they reach the top, they sprawl or scramble across. If not given support of some kind, they will keep piling up until they gradually lift themselves above surrounding vegetation. These are the scramblers:

Ampelopsis japonica,
  Porcelain Creeper
Clematis montana,
  Mountain Clematis
C. vitalba, Traveler's Joy

Rosa, species and varieties,
  Climbing Roses
Vitis kaempferi,
  Japanese Ornamental Grape

TWINERS

Some vines climb by winding their stems around a support, others by grasping with their tendrils any nearby twig or branch. Because of their need for this type of support, they are of no value for covering walls. They are best grown on trellises or pergolas to which they can be tied when training. The following are twiners:

Actinidia arguta, Tara Vine
A. polygama, Silver Vine
Akebia quinata, Five-finger Vine
Aristolochia durior,
  Dutchman's Pipe
Celastrus, various species,
  Bittersweets
Clematis, various species,
  Clematis
Humulus japonicus, Hop Vine

Ipomoea pandurata,
  Perennial Moonflower
Lonicera, various species,
  Honeysuckles
Periploca graeca, Grecian Silk Vine
P. sepium, Chinese Silk Vine
Polygonum auberti,
  Silver Lace Vine
Pueraria hirsuta, Kudzu Vine
Wisteria floribunda,
  Japanese Wisteria
W. sinensis, Chinese Wisteria

CLINGING VINES

Far from being weak and unable to hold themselves upright, most clinging vines are aggressive, vigorous, and able to take over any wall on which a tip can find space. Most of them climb by clinging to their supporting wall with holdfasts or suction cups which adhere even after a vine has died. The mistaken idea that they eat away mortar is due to the fact that the weight of a mature, vigorous specimen of English ivy or Virginia creeper is often sufficient to pull off spalling stone or crumbling mortar when these holdfasts refuse to let go. The vines should not be blamed for this; any wall too weak to support such weight is of little value as a shelter or a barrier. Actually, because they ward off snow and rain, vines can prevent water from entering a wall and weakening it.

Of all vines useful for reducing summer temperatures and winter heat losses, the clinging species are the best. They form a dense mat of foliage that acts like an umbrella. These are among the most useful:

Ampelopsis brevipedunculata,
    Porcelain Creeper

Campsis 'Madame Galen,'
    Trumpet Creeper

Hedera helix, English Ivy

H. h. baltica, Baltic Ivy

Hydrangea petiolaris,
    Climbing Hydrangea

Parthenocissus quinquefolia,
    Virginia Creeper

P. tricuspidata, Boston Ivy

HERBACEOUS CLIMBERS

For quick effects, annuals are essential. This does not mean that their use should be restricted to temporary plantings. Often a certain place, such as a kitchen door facing south, needs summer shade, though in winter the sun is welcome. Here an annual vine does its job and is out of the way when not needed. Herbaceous perennials behave similarly. Because they can expend so much of their energy in flowering rather than in forming dormant buds to enable them to survive winter, herbaceous vines usually flower much more lavishly and for a longer period than woody ones. No woody plant can possibly match the show staged by a 'Heavenly Blue' morning-glory at its best. All annual vines climb by twining and need thin supports around which to wrap their stems and tendrils. Some in the list below are biennials or perennials, but may be grown as annuals.

HERBACEOUS VINES

Boussingaultia baselloides,
    Madeira Vine

Calonyction aculeatum, Moonflower

Cardiospermum halicacabum,
    Balloon Vine

Centrosema virginianum,
    Butterfly Pea

Cobaea scandens,
    Cup-and-saucer Vine

Cucurbita, various species,
    Ornamental Gourds

Dioscorea batatas, Cinnamon Vine

Dolichos lablab, Hyacinth Bean

Ecballium elaterium,
    Squirting Cucumber

Ipomoea, various species,
    Morning-glories

Lathyrus latifolius,
    Perennial Sweet Pea

L. odoratus, Sweet Pea

Momordica balsamina,
    Balsam Apple

M. charantia, Balsam Pear
Phaseolus coccineus,
    Scarlet Runner Bean
Quamoclit sloteri,
    Cardinal Climber

Thunbergia alata,
    Black-eyed Susan Vine
Tropaeolum majus, Nasturtium

TENDER CLIMBERS FOR FLORIDA AND CALIFORNIA

Antigonon leptopus, Coral Vine
Aristolochia elegans, Calico Flower
Azara microphylla,
    Chilean Wall Vine
Bignonia capreolata, Cross Vine
Clematis texensis, Scarlet Clematis
Clerodendron thomsoniae,
    Bagflower
Clianthus dampieri, Glory-pea
Doxantha unguis-cati,
    Cat's-claw Vine
Eccremocarpus scaber,
    Glory Flower
Gloriosa rothschildiana, Glory Lily
Hoya carnosa, Wax Plant
Ipomoea leari, Dawnflower

Jasminum officinale, Italian Jasmine
Lapageria rosea,
    Chilean Bellflower Vine
Lonicera sempervirens,
    Coral Honeysuckle
Passiflora, various species,
    Passion Vine
Phaseolus caracalla, Corkscrew Vine
Rosa, various species,
    Climbing Roses
Stephanotis floribunda,
    Madagascar Jasmine
Tecomaria capensis,
    Cape Honeysuckle
Thunbergia grandiflora, Skyflower
Trachelospermum jasminoides,
    Confederate Jasmine

8

Landscaping: the Investment that Grows

An investment of $1,000 in landscaping begins to pay dividends the moment the plants are in the ground, and it continues to do so with each passing year. This is a factor the home-owner should consider, whether he expects to remain where he is for years, or knows that his stay is limited.

A system for evaluating shade trees in all parts of the United States has been worked out by the National Arborist Association and the National Shade Tree Conference. Four classes of trees are listed in seven geographical areas, and five degrees of quality are recognized, from 100 down to 20 per cent. The basic measurement of a Class 1 tree in perfect condition is the size of the trunk 4½ feet above the ground, and the basic value is $6 per square inch. To obtain the measurement, use a king-size gauge or caliper; square the diameter, and multiply the result by 0.7854 to obtain the square inches in the trunk at breast height. If you have a Class 1 tree in perfect condition, use this figure to multiply $6. Thus a tree with a 20-inch diameter will have a trunk measurement of 314.2 square inches in cross section (20 x 20 x 0.7854). At $6 per square inch, this tree would have a value of $1884. If it is a Class 3 tree (a weeping willow, for example) instead of an oak, its value would be 60 per cent of $1884, or $1130.

Lists of trees and full details of how to figure their value can be obtained for a dollar from the National Arborist Association, Wooster, Ohio.

LANDSCAPING FOR PLEASURE

But, values aside, landscaping pays its way in pleasure and in comfort. A satisfaction often overlooked by new home-owners is the cleanliness value of planting. Not until you have tried to survive in a newly completed house surrounded by a sea of mud or dust can the dirt-suppressing qualities — let alone erosion-control ability — of a good lawn be appreciated.

Too often building projects are launched by bulldozing to extinction every trace of living green — mature trees, shrubs, and grass. The greatest loss is the trees, which can be replaced only at considerable cost and even then must grow for several years before their shade is more than a promise. If trees must be planted, their placement should be studied with great care to avoid shading the lawn and garden areas more than is necessary. At the same time, the coolness they provide should creep over the house when the heat of the sun is greatest.

Privacy is often possible only by proper placement of landscape features. This is peculiarly a problem on small suburban lots where living space is extended outdoors. All too often considerable sums are invested in outdoor barbecues and terraces which are abandoned when the owner finds that his family is living in full view of his neighbors. A few well-placed tall shrubs or small trees can often salvage such an investment.

Perhaps the landscaping asset most difficult to assess is beauty. People are not all alike in their appreciation of color, line, and mass, yet a sensitive person is aware of beauty in every well-planned garden. Living with a beautifully planted home can be an experience as emotional as owning a great work of art.

THE ROLE OF THE PROFESSIONAL

Many a home-owner has decided to consult a landscape architect, only to find that the professional man seems completely uninterested in a commission to design a home property. Thinking that he may have consulted the wrong man, he may try other firms, only to find them equally indifferent. This often kills all interest in doing a good landscaping job. Frustrated, he plants a few mediocre shrubs or second-rate evergreens and calls it a job. From then on all he does is mow the grass and rake fallen leaves.

What owners of small homes do not appreciate is that landscape fees are based on a percentage of cost and that, unless a client is prepared to spend between $5,000 and $10,000, most established firms cannot afford to handle such work. Even if the home-owner is willing to make such an investment, he may still be turned down by a busy firm. The reason is simple: residential work usually means nothing but headaches for the firm. Every time a tree or shrub dies or a brown spot develops in the lawn, the landscape architect will be called in instead of the nurseryman who did the job and is responsible.

Some smaller offices will do a domestic plan for a set fee, say about $350, with the understanding that it includes no services whatever and that the purchaser must make his own planting arrangements. But this eliminates two of the most valuable aspects of professional service — supervision and know-how.

This leaves a home-owner with two alternatives: One is to seek the services of a landscape nurseryman — a hybrid between the landscape architect and the nurseryman. While the architect does not deal in stock, the landscape nurseryman either grows all he sells or has an established source of supply. His services can be anything from surprisingly good to wretchedly poor. His weakness is that he usually recommends only material that he grows himself. Often this will not fit the design that is best for one's property. The second alternative is to study the simple principles involved and apply them yourself.

MAKING YOUR OWN PLAN

How to Begin

In a stationery store buy a pad of graph paper, ruled in tiny squares. Try to get the kind that has a larger unit of measurement printed over the smaller squares. Some have 10 by 10 small squares inside a larger unit, while others have 12 by 12. Most people find the 10 by 10 easier to work with because decimals can then be used. On the other hand, the 12 by 12 can show inches and feet.

Using this paper, draw a plan of your property, as large as your paper will allow, to exact scale. Locate accurately the house and garage and any other fixed features such as trees. Then, with rough circles or ovals, indicate where the main features of your planting should be.

What Do You Want?

Now the planning comes down to your own terms. What do you want to do in your backyard, in your garden? Set down everything, no matter how trivial it seems. Do you want an outdoor spot for sun bathing? What about games such as croquet, putting practice, bowls? Have you thought of a children's play yard, swings, gym, and sandbox? What about a place to store cordwood for the fireplace?

How pleasant it would be to have a spot outdoors for reading or sewing. Think twice before you build a barbecue for outdoor dining (many are used only a few times), but if you do, provide electric connections for appliances, and shelter for radio, matches, pillows, and furniture.

A compost pile is not attractive, nor is a vegetable garden always a thing of beauty. They might be concealed behind a hedge along the back

MAKING A LANDSCAPE PLAN: *Materials — Drawing paper or graph paper, several sheets of tracing paper, ruler and pencil. First, on drawing or graph paper, make a scale drawing of your property. Include desirable or necessary features to be retained (good trees, septic tank) or added (fence, screen planting). Next, draw rough circles or ovals to indicate where main areas of the plan should be (1).*

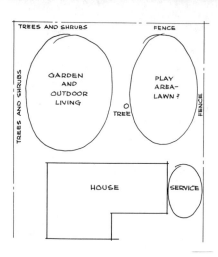

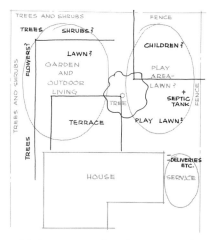

Make a new drawing on tracing paper and begin converting circles and ovals into definite shapes and sizes.

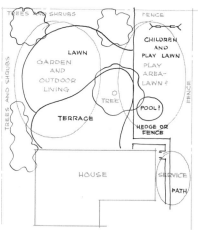

On another tracing-paper drawing start experimenting with more exact shapes, locations for specific items.

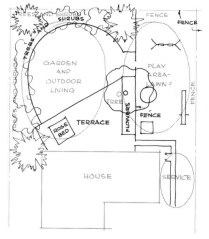

Make more drawings, reworking shapes, adding details, until plan is complete.

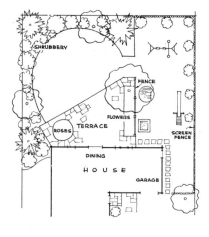

The final plan: it may be your fifth, fifteenth, or fiftieth try.

of the lot. And do not dismiss the idea of a backyard hobby center or workshop if your family is inclined towards craftsmanship. A small building to house a workshop can take the pressure off the basement, or provide work space if a basement is lacking.

True hobby gardeners will want a nursery for cuttings, sick plants, and the propagation of perennials. The low-cost plastic greenhouse brings this luxury item within reach of everyone. Hotbeds and coldframes should be squeezed into even the smallest property. And do not forget the drying yard. Even housewives with fancy dryers want to sun blankets and pillows. The dog run, rabbit hutch, and poultry pens have a place in semirural areas. If saddle horses are kept, prevailing winds from the stable should blow away from the house. Most important, make allowances for driveways with off-street parking for guests.

When the schedule is completed, chances are that it will be too long and formidable to contemplate. Now study functions that can be combined. The drying yard, if used only a few times a year, can be laid out by providing for clotheslines that cross part of the drive. Sun bathing and game areas might also use the same area: you cannot do both at the same time. And some ideas you thought interesting at first may now be dropped as not worth the effort.

Scale Model

The next step is to estimate the amount of space each item will occupy and cut out bits of paper to scale. These can be juggled around the scale plan to see where they fit best. Keep in mind their purposes while deciding where they belong. If a play area for children is in the plan, remember to locate it where it can be seen from a window. Do *not* locate it where the driveway can become part of the playground. Not only would it be unsafe, but it would be too hot for play when the mercury soars.

If possible, the rubbish-burner, compost heap, and vegetable garden should be cut off from the rest of the property by a 5-foot fence or hedge at the back of the garden. On the other hand, if the distance out to the rubbish-burner is too great, it may become inaccessible in bad weather. Coldframes might also go into this rear area, but hotbeds are better near the house. Since most hotbed heating today is done with electric cables, voltage drop may be too great if the run is long.

On tracing paper, now convert your circles and ovals into definite shapes and sizes for the garden features you want. Make another, more refined drawing on tracing paper, always adding more details.

Trying Out the Plan

Once the features have been decided upon, they should be tested practically. Large areas can be outlined by staking the corners and running a string around the outside edge. The ground area for smaller features (the grill or rubbish-burner, for example) can be cut from a large carton to exact dimensions tested on the spot. You can then move them around until you find the best location for each.

When a plan is tested this way, errors in placement are easily seen. For example, as you imagine yourself frying a hamburger on the proposed grill, you can picture the smoke smudging the white paint on a wall of the house that is too close. Or the spot for the garbage pail, viewed from the street, turns out to be most unattractive. Once these inconsistencies are corrected, the final design can be formulated.

Design Within the Lot Lines

The first principle, except for those with a distant view, is to define and concentrate the design within the lot lines. Despite an American prejudice which frowns on tall fences and concealing walls, do not hesitate to use them for privacy. Often they can be arranged so that they do not appear to be shutting out your neighbor.

A stiff, formal hedge may seem unfriendly, but an irregular, informal mixed planting of shrubs, none over 6 feet tall, around the back and two sides of your lot, will appear to be planned as a background for flower borders, not as a barrier. Also, a 6-foot hedge will give privacy as effectively as one that is 10 feet tall.

A hedge will do even more if your property is on a busy street, and particularly if it is a corner lot. It will serve as a sound trap for the squeal of brakes and the racket of busy trucks. Flashing headlights that punch holes in the darkness of night will be diverted, too, by thick shrub plantings. On a corner lot, however, a hedge may become a traffic hazard.

One drawback to a heavy planting along three sides of a property is that it sometimes develops into a heat trap where air hardly stirs and where plant diseases flourish. A way to avoid this is to leave gaps in the shrub border. Not only will gaps permit air to move freely, but they will also allow access to adjoining properties if the neighbors are congenial. In fact, there is nothing wrong with working in cooperation with neighbors on all three sides when planting; this tends to cut down any feeling of opposition.

If space is at a premium, as it is on small lots, remember that a fence will occupy only 4 inches of space, a hedge 4 feet, or even more.

Appropriate Plants

Avoid overplanting at all costs. Too many landscaped homes are cluttered with such great masses of shrubs and trees that no room is left for flowers. In fact, it has been said that the worst competitor the seedsman and plantsman have is the nurseryman who pre-empts all available space without thought for the color and beauty of the flower garden.

So far, little has been said about actual plants except to suggest shrubs for hedges. Species and varieties are discussed and lists given in Chapter 6. However, the matter of appropriateness of material cannot be ignored. Take, for example, the shrubs or evergreens that are used to mark the front door. Remember that visitors look *in* at a property before entering and must be guided properly.

Problem 1, then, is to enable a visitor to locate the front door. Not long ago, this was done by planting a pair of Colorado blue spruces on either side. In many of our older suburbs, these now tower 15 to 20 feet above the house itself and completely hide the entrance. The foundation planting of scraggly shrubs that accompanied them has grown into a jungle.

Older houses set high on stone foundations still need some form of planting to hide the ugliness of the walls. On the whole, plant selections are being made today with a greater discretion.

A foundation planting around a modern spreading house is unthinkable, although many old-time nurserymen still advise it. They are also repeating the old mistake they made with Colorado blue spruces, compounding the error by using red cedars and arborvitae, which grow even faster.

Nevertheless, the front door must be indicated somehow. A good choice is the compact burning-bush, *Euonymus alatus compactus*. This is massive, slow growing, and can be kept trimmed to a height of 5 or 6 feet. If an evergreen is wanted, the Hatfield yew is bulky and fairly upright.

PRINCIPLES OF PLANNING A LANDSCAPE

A garden plan should be sound, should have a good design, be in proper scale and proportion, and have balance and unity. These are the five principles.

Design

This means the all-over scheme, which should be logical. Traffic should flow along proper paths to avoid foot lanes across the grass. It shouldn't be necessary to push a power mower completely around the house to reach some remote corner of the lawn. The kitchen doors should be accessible for deliveries and service calls. Fuel-oil pipe lines should not have openings on the lawn because even the most careful driver sometimes spills a little oil. Access should not be blocked to outside service meters.

A most important element in design which is often overlooked is that of sight lines. When you look out the window, what do you see? What do you not want to see? Since passers-by can see in as clearly as you can see out, experiment both ways.

Landscape with the practical in view: The terrace does triple duty as play yard, outdoor living room, and groundcover. Hardy, permanent planting, like the fringe of low junipers, is tough and blends with the natural setting.

Scale

Landscape architects during the past two decades have had to revise completely their thinking about scale. Accustomed to thinking in terms of houses 35 feet tall, framed by forest trees that towered 80 to 90 feet above the sidewalk, they found the modern ranch house a frustrating subject. The forest giants were completely out of scale. So were the elaborate masses of shrubs in foundation plantings. More and more nurserymen are now called upon to supply hawthorns, flowering crabs, dogwoods, and other small trees rather than oaks, elms, and maples.

A rule to follow in setting the scale for trees to frame a house is that the trees should not be more than two to three times the height from ground to ridge pole. A house 15-feet high needs trees not over 45 feet tall, and 30- to 35-foot trees would be even better. Taller ones seem top-heavy.

Proportion

This is often confused with scale, which has reference to the size of an individual unit. Proportion is the ratio of all objects in a landscape to the whole. A good example of the need to consider the relation of several objects at once is seen in the problem discussed above — that of marking the doorway. The left side of the door towards the drive might be planted

In this peaceful city garden, a stake fence, ensuring privacy, makes a fine background for permanent shrubs and seasonal blooms. The planter of old brick continues the curve of the terrace around a dichondra lawn.

with a shrub which is smaller in scale than the one on the right. The thought is to lead the eye from the left (nearest the drive and entrance walk) to the door. If, however, a still smaller shrub had not been planted to the left of the first, the difference in proportion would have been disturbing.

The same principle applies in designing the rest of the property. A two-story garage to serve a one-story house (not common, but they can be found) would obviously give too much weight to the garage.

If an existing feature is out of proportion and cannot be changed, the landscape architect's remedy is to "plant it out." Suppose that a towering wall on neighboring property is out of proportion to your house. By screening it with trees that form an interesting pattern against it, you can break up its apparent size.

Balance

The shrubs planted alongside the doorway as suggested above also illustrate balance — in this case asymmetrical balance. Elements of different sizes are used, but those on one side "weigh," or balance, the single specimen on the other side. If the smaller shrub to the left had been omitted, the one on the right would have been out of balance, and out of proportion, too, even though correct in scale for the size of the door.

Exterior designs are becoming more and more simple with less ornamentation and fewer architectural details. This tendency is dictated by rising building costs. Formal plantings, which use symmetrical balance, seem monotonous and uninteresting when placed against the plain exteriors of ranch houses. While asymmetrical balance is much harder to accomplish, it is more interesting and should receive preference.

Unity

When scale, proportion, and balance are all just right, unity is practically assured. Most amateur designs fall down in this one feature, largely because home-owners are reluctant to eliminate offending features. As a result, we may see a Victorian gazebo left to destroy the unity and beauty of an otherwise modern garden. Sometimes it takes courage to attain unity, but the result is rewarding.

HOW TO PROCEED AFTER PLANNING

Once the plan is complete and the elements to be included have been brought into a design, the first step is to move in big plant material such as trees and shrubs (the latter balled and burlapped properly). Work on drives and walks can proceed at the same time. These heavy operations should be finished before lawns are laid and flower borders begun. Fortunately, the trees being moved today are smaller, and it is no longer necessary to wait until winter to move mature specimens with a frost ball.

Some specialists are even willing to move trees in full leaf, protecting them with a wilt-proofing spray to keep them from drying out after planting. However, if this is to be done, get a written guarantee and make sure the seller is reliable.

Drives

Although gravel, crushed stone, and similar materials are commonly used for drives, these often bring cries of anguish from housewives when it rains. No matter how many times male members of the family are admonished to wipe their feet, bits of stone and gravel defile carpets. Think twice before you pass up the blessings of blacktop, concrete, or paving brick. They cost more, but are worth it.

Keep in mind too that visitors will arrive in cars. Doubling the width of the drive will provide space for parking and there will be less lawn to cut. Some city ordinances limit the width of the opening at the street curb, in such cases, the drive can be regulation width at the street, but gradually widen toward the house until it is widest at the landing platform in front of the steps. The side of the drive away from the house can be kept straight, but the side toward the house sloped in. Using the drive as an entrance walk is common practice and saves cutting up the front lawn with a ribbon of brick or concrete.

Walks

Wherever space between landscape features narrows so that the weight of foot traffic and power equipment is concentrated, use paving of some kind to form a walk rather than wear out the grass at this point. Generally speaking, however, the fewer the walks, the better. When they are used, they should lead somewhere. If they curve or bend, make the bend seem essential by planting an imposing shrub so that it seems as if the path had to go around it.

Changes in Level

When grading must be done, a chance is afforded to add interest to a property. The least desirable way to grade is with a steep grassed slope that must be mowed. Costliest, yet best, is a stone wall that forms a terrace. However, broken concrete — often available free — looks like limestone when laid in a wall and allowed to accumulate dirt. Plant rock-garden plants in the chinks, and it becomes a work of art.

Old railroad ties are cheap and have interesting color. Laid up crib

Front yard planning is important. Here a simple design is dressed up with unusual plants: cutleaf Japanese maple near doorway, amoena azaleas under window, false cypress and tulips in the foreground.

fashion to a height of several feet they look very attractive. Since most discarded ties have rotten spots in them, these should be cut out and treated with a penta solution or with copper naphthanate. Do *not* use creosote: it kills plants.

A FEW ADDITIONAL HINTS

Don't reveal the entire landscape scheme of a property at once; try to preserve a little mystery. A beautiful rose bush or flowering magnolia behind the garage, to be discovered as you turn a corner, makes a pleasant surprise. Other features can be planned if the property is studied for corners that are not readily visible.

Modern mosquito abatement programs make outdoor living practical for many nights during the summer, but do not solve the problem of rain. When planning outdoor living space, be sure to provide some shelter from sudden showers other than a trellis or pergola.

A fountain in the garden gives an illusion of coolness.

If you live where snow falls, consider snow removal. Some plans allow so little room beside the drive that there is no place to throw shoveled snow. If not damp, soggy, and heavy, snow *can* be thrown on top of a shrub border if this is done carefully. However, this is definitely poor practice.

The entrance planting of this Southern California home is made up of tropical and sub-tropical trees and foliage plants. The groundcover of succulents becomes a brilliant carpet of flowers twice a year.

9

Lawns and Groundcovers: Backdrop of Landscaping

"When you have selected the right carpeting, your home decorating is half done." This comment from a leading interior decorator applies with equal force to every landscaping plan — the exterior decoration of the home. A lawn is the carpeting background against which the shapes and colors of flowers, trees, and shrubs are displayed to best advantage.

In addition to this role, a lawn serves many other purposes which a beginner may not appreciate. It suppresses mud and dust, provides a floor for games, and furnishes space for footpaths and lanes along which garden equipment can be trundled. Unless these practical uses are considered and the proper species or mixture is selected for them, serious problems can arise. Another service of grass is that it suppresses glare and heat reflection. This function should be kept in mind when driveways are laid out. Grass substituted for concrete reduces temperatures from 3 to 6 degrees.

NOT ALL LAWNS ARE ALIKE

Lawns should be planned to suit the needs of the individual family. The luxurious turf of a well-kept putting green should not be the goal of the average home-owner. Such a lawn requires almost constant attention and expense, plus high professional skill. The bentgrasses that usually compose a green are difficult, fickle, and subject to disease. One kind requires mowing three or four times a week, and the best greens are mowed daily. A bentgrass lawn might provide a hobby for a retired man with little else to occupy his mind, but for a busy man with a family it is sheer folly.

Perhaps the simplest lawn is the kind that can be created around a semi-rural home, set in several acres of land. Simply mowing the existing native grasses and supplying fertilizer now and then will result in a lawn good enough for the purpose it serves. A home-owner has a harder problem if he lives where a lawn must take the impact of heavy traffic, due perhaps to a bus stop on his parkway or the fact that half a dozen active children and a dog use it for a playground.

A step above these two types is the lawn for a man who wants his home neat and clean, but has neither the time nor money to maintain a luxury lawn. His problem may be complicated by sunny and shaded areas and by isolated patches of soil of low fertility. Most lawns today fall more or less into this last category. What is wanted is high-quality-at-reasonable-cost turf. Such lawns are maintained at a reasonably high level to avoid "summer brownout," are mowed often enough to look well-groomed, and are planted to disease-resistant grasses.

GRASS SELECTION: KEY TO PROPER USE

No single species can qualify for all the uses to which a lawn is put. Only tough coarse grasses can survive under heavy traffic. Dainty fine-leaved species make a lovely lawn, but one that wears poorly and may be subject to disease.

Yet no one grass has complete immunity to disease. There are striking differences in resistance even among the improved varieties of common Kentucky bluegrass, a basic group for northern lawns.

The season of use is important too. Zoysias are a justifiable luxury around a beach cabin or summer cottage used only during warm weather. The same lawn would be an irritation in the North around a home that is used twelve months of the year, because it browns out in early fall to a dull grayish tan, and remains thus until spring.

MIXTURES: THE KEY TO BETTER LAWNS

Since no grass has all the qualities needed for a lawn, to select a blend of several species is usually the soundest practice. Some might question this, arguing that good qualities would be diluted as well as poor ones. Fortunately this is not true, since many grass weaknesses are due to diseases or insects moving freely from one plant to the next. Such easy passage may be interrupted when individual plants are separated by plants of a different variety or species. If one species is weakened or destroyed, the better adapted grasses quickly take over the empty space.

Another argument in favor of mixtures is that few lawn-makers are able to estimate existing conditions accurately. A man may say that his lawn is in full sun because he happens to see it only at a time of day when sunshine reaches it; actually it may be shaded for most of the day.

Soil types, too, are difficult to judge. Even in the richest soils there may be patches where drainage is poor, or where it is so efficient that the soil is always dry. When properly blended mixtures are sown on such problem areas, they tend to adapt themselves to conditions, the most suitable grasses surviving while the others die out.

SINGLE SPECIES LAWNS

Some grasses should not, however, be sown or planted in mixture. Of these, zoysia, one of the South's luxury grasses, is an excellent example. When planted near its northern limit (roughly the Ohio River), and bluegrass creeps in, it is never at its best. Bluegrasses in this area go dormant in summer and the zoysia cannot fill in rapidly enough to heal the gaps. Then in the fall, zoysia browns out with the first frost, leaving green patches of bluegrass.

A decade or two ago, bentgrasses were blended with bluegrasses in almost every lawn mixture, and quality was measured by the amount of bent included. This was sound practice with the original common Kentucky bluegrass, which was so badly hit by leaf-spot diseases in midsummer that it either died out or faded to a sickly yellow green. With the advent of 'Merion' Kentucky bluegrass, this changed. Its deep, rich green color in midsummer made the paler bentgrasses look diseased and undernourished. Today, bentgrasses are considered weeds in bluegrass lawns.

'Merion' Kentucky bluegrass is perhaps the choicest of all modern cool-season grasses. It can be grown in pure stands, particularly north of a line drawn between Chicago and New York City. South of that area it should only be grown in mixture to overcome the possible effects of two diseases which attack it.

GRASS REGIONS OF THE UNITED STATES AND CANADA

North America can be divided roughly into three grass regions. (See map.) In Region A only cool-season grasses should be grown. Attempts to use even so hardy a warm-season grass as zoysia in this zone have been generally unsatisfactory. Region B is a band where the warm- and cool-season grasses supplement each other, neither dominating the lawn all year. In Region C warm-season grasses predominate, but because cool-season grasses will grow during the winter, the latter are used for winter color.

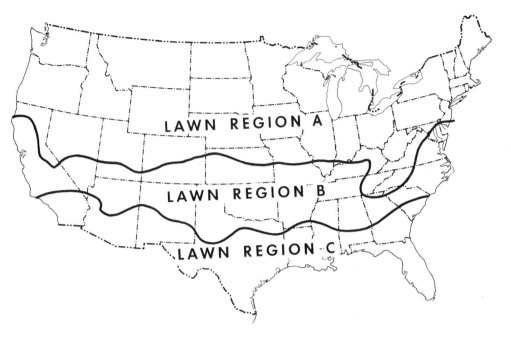

COOL-SEASON GRASSES: REGION A

The dominant grass in Region A is common Kentucky bluegrass and its improved varieties. The latter, largely introduced since World War II, were selected for various qualities and are described below. However, while Region A is shown as extending across the Great Plains, this semi-arid region is too dry to meet the heavy moisture demands of bluegrass. This region, stretching from the Kansas-Missouri line to the Rocky Mountains, still has many unsolved lawn problems, perhaps the most important of which is the need for a well-adapted attractive turf-grass species.

COMMON KENTUCKY BLUEGRASS. Despite its name, Kentucky bluegrass was brought to that state in packing hay by early English settlers. It grows luxuriously in spring and fall, but is subject to "brownout" in summer. Though this condition is called dormancy, it is actually the result of leaf-spot diseases that kill off the tops.

'MERION' KENTUCKY BLUEGRASS. Perhaps the best cool-season grass available. Deep-rooted and highly resistant to leaf spot, it retains its rich, deep color longer than any other. South of a line drawn from Omaha to Pittsburgh, it may be attacked by a root-rot fungus, but this can be controlled chemically. It is also subject to rust because it is in active growth when rust spores are flying. This, however, is serious only on the Great Plains: in other sections it can be controlled by culture.

'ARBORETUM,' 'DELTA,' 'NEWPORT' AND OTHER IMPROVED BLUEGRASSES. Each has been selected for some special quality. 'Delta' is a vigorous, early starter and fills in — it is particularly good to supplement 'Merion.' 'Arboretum' is resistant to the root rot which affects 'Merion' in Region B.

'Newport' has good early spring and late fall color. All, however, are as subject to leaf-spot diseases as common Kentucky bluegrass. Only 'Merion' is resistant to these.

BLUEGRASS MIXTURES. Because of the multiple-resistant factors in a mixture of several improved bluegrasses, such blends usually give more satisfaction than straight grasses. Authorities agree that for Region A, mixtures should contain between 40 and 45 per cent 'Merion,' plus two or three other grasses, to which is added a resistant fine-leaved red fescue such as 'Pennlawn.'

If conditions are reasonably good, such a mixture will probably result in a lawn that is about 80 per cent 'Merion' within three to four years, with poorer soil patches taken over by the 'Pennlawn' fescue. The other bluegrasses will never be totally crowded out and will be ready to fill in if for some reason 'Merion' fails.

FINE-LEAVED FESCUES. On dry sandy soils or those naturally low in fertility, varieties of red fescue will survive where bluegrasses die. They are also the best shade grasses available in the North (except for the special use of 'Highland' noted under bentgrasses). Two types of red fescues are in commerce. Chewings' fescue, a non-creeping form, tends to grow in bunches. It is fine-leaved and a deep, dull blue-green in color. It has been largely replaced by creeping red fescue, except in mixtures with bluegrasses, where its tendency to form bunches is overcome by other grasses. Like many other red fescues, it is highly susceptible to leaf-spot diseases.

Creeping red fescue is like Chewings' except for its creeping habit. Three improved varieties, however — 'Illahee,' 'Penn State,' and 'Pennlawn' — are more disease resistant, have better color, and do not bunch. Of these, 'Pennlawn' is the best, with the highest disease resistance and a color which more nearly matches that of the bluegrasses. Also, it will tolerate closer mowing.

TALL FESCUES. The closest we have to a universal variety is either 'Alta' tall fescue or 'Kentucky 31' tall fescue. Both grow well from Maine to California and from the Gulf of Mexico to Canada. If these were only fine-textured, they would make superb turf grasses. Unfortunately, seeded at the rates usually given, they produce coarse, bunchy clumps which have created a serious problem in lawn maintenance. They are so weedy in appearance that many weed-control authorities receive more requests for methods of controlling them than for crabgrass.

This does not mean that tall fescues are worthless; for some purposes they are indispensable. They are perhaps the only grasses available that will survive under heavy traffic. 'Alta' fescue was used during World War II to "pave" emergency landing fields and more than once absorbed the impact of a bomber landing.

If tall fescues are sown for severe-use lawns, they should be seeded at a high rate and never in mixture. Use from 8 to 10 pounds to 1,000 square feet. At this rate, the plants are too crowded to form clumps and, as a result, produce finer blades. This is definitely not a cheap lawn; when seeded at this rate, the cost may be 3 to 4 dollars per 1,000 square feet for seed alone.

BENTGRASSES. Pure stands of bentgrasses, although considered the finest of northern grasses when perfectly grown, are definitely not for the home lawn. Formerly, seeds were mixed with bluegrasses and, as a result, many old lawns are now contaminated with bent grasses that have run wild. These wild bents are particularly annoying when they invade lawns planted with 'Merion' Kentucky bluegrass, for they form disfiguring light-colored patches.

Bentgrasses are still grown in mixture to some extent in cool, moist regions of the Pacific Northwest and in New England. They are less difficult to grow in such areas but still need some attention to keep them free from disease.

'Velvet' bent is perhaps the world's most luxurious grass when it is healthy. The blades are so fine that it is hard to see individual plants. Like all bents except 'Highland,' it demands great care. It will tolerate close mowing ($\frac{3}{16}$ths to $\frac{3}{8}$ths of an inch) and must be cut three or four times a week. Its fertility needs and water requirements are high. 'Kernwood,' 'Piper,' and 'Raritan' are improved varieties of 'Velvet' bent.

True creeping bents can be grown from seed ('Seaside' and 'Penncross') or started vegetatively by planting sprigs or stolons ('Arlington,' 'Congressional,' 'Cohansy,' 'Old Orchard,' 'Pennlue,' and 'Toronto'). Their requirements are the same as those of velvet bent.

Colonial bent does not creep vigorously, though it does produce short stubby rhizomes which enable it to form a dense turf. Although far from being a carefree turf species, it is less fussy than other bents.

'Highland' bent, although a form of true Colonial bent, and at times a useful grass in shade, requires a warning. An upland variety, it has lower water and fertility needs than other bents and is less subject to disease. When grown in open sunshine, it is an ugly grass, producing a long, straw-like sheath that remains behind when the grass is cut. Even so, it is often used in cheap mixtures to give them a false air of quality. In shade, where it does not develop the typical strawy sheath, it thrives and produces a dense green turf, even when competing for food and water with the hungry roots of trees. It is the grass to try in shade when nothing else will grow. If it fails, use a non-grass groundcover.

POA TRIVIALIS. Although widely recommended for use in shade and a universal ingredient in shade mixtures, it is a grass of limited usefulness. It burns badly in sunlight and is highly susceptible to leaf-spot diseases. Its one value is in rich shaded soil where moisture is plentiful. Although included in most shade mixtures, it is less desirable than either 'Highland' bent or the red fescues. Use only where excess moisture is a problem.

WARM-SEASON GRASSES: REGION C

Although separated from Region A by a fairly wide band of country, Region C and its grasses should be treated before Region B. The problems of this intermediate region will be better understood after a survey of the northern cool-season grasses and southern hot-weather types.

Despite its uniformity in temperature, Region C is far from uniform in its other characteristics. Moisture varies from the heavy rainfall of the Gulf States to arid conditions in the Southwest. Alkaline soils of the Southwest have little in common with the acid red clays and sands found from Georgia through Alabama.

Insect resistance is highly important in the Southeast, though ravages of chinch bugs can now be halted almost at once by a relatively new insecticide called Diazinon.

BERMUDA GRASS. Not many years ago, this was regarded as a worse lawn weed than crabgrass. Even the introduction of 'U-3' Bermuda, first of the fine-leaved varieties, failed to break down prejudice against it. However, with the development of such varieties as 'Tiflawn,' 'Tiffine,' 'Tifway,' 'Tifgreen,' and 'Sunturf,' Bermudas became respectable, and today (along with the fine-leaved zoysias) are the backbone of high-grade turf in the Southeast. There are varieties, too, notably 'Ormond,' 'Sunturf,' 'Texturf 1-F' and 'U-3,' which are among the better grasses for the Southwest. Except for 'U-3' (of which seed is available, but does not come true), all must be planted as sprigs or plugs, or laid in sod.

All Bermudas have high fertility requirements but can thrive on moderate moisture as long as they are not allowed to become really dry. Disease resistance is high. Unfortunately, they do not tolerate shade well. They do best when mown at a height of about 1 inch. Because they turn brown with the first frost, Bermudas are usually overseeded with rye grass for winter color.

BAHIA. Bahia grass is cheap, easy to grow, and one of the few southern grasses which can be seeded. It is fairly tolerant of shade. It seems to do well in Florida, otherwise is inferior to similar grasses used in the South. If used at all, the variety 'Pensacola' should be purchased: most other bahia grasses are grown for hay.

CARPET GRASS. Often confused with St. Augustine, carpet grass does not produce as heavy a sod and is somewhat more yellow-green in color. It has some advantage over St. Augustine in that it will grow on poor, wet, acid soils such as are found in spots along the Gulf of Mexico. Mow weekly to a height of 1½ to 2 inches. If it grows too long between mowings, the seed heads are disfiguring. Carpet grass grows readily from seed sown in spring after the soil has warmed up.

CENTIPEDE GRASS. Except that it will survive with minimum care, this grass has little to recommend it. It is less shade tolerant than St. Augustine, coarser than Bermudas, slow to establish, and wears poorly. While it can be grown from seed sown in spring after the soil is warm, it is by far the most costly grass seed in commerce. It can also be started from sprigs. Do not overfeed; it thrives on low fertility. Do not use lime; it likes acid soils. Iron chelates or ferrous ammonium sulfate will help keep it green.

ST. AUGUSTINE GRASS. Northerners who move south are often shocked when told that this is not a vigorous strain of quackgrass, but a desirable lawn species. They dislike its coarseness — the flat, hard stems and broad, flat leaves. But after they have tried to grow finer grasses, they often accept St. Augustine and even learn to love it.

Actually this grass has much to commend it — rich blue-green color, tolerance of shade and sun, and aggressive, quick growth. Its one big weakness is lack of resistance to brown-patch disease and to attack by chinch bugs, but new fungicides and insecticides are now available for controlling these.

St. Augustine is not usually hardy 150 miles north of the Gulf of Mexico. Despite its rugged looks, it is not as durable under traffic as either Bermuda or zoysia. For athletic fields, it is a poor third to tall fescues. Because of its high iron requirements, St. Augustine grass thrives best when given iron chelates, dried blood, or some other good source of iron. Two improved varieties are 'Bitter Blue' and 'Florentine.'

ZOYSIA. Once established, a zoysia lawn is perhaps the ultimate in high-grade turf in the South. Underfoot it feels like a thick broadloom carpet laid over foam-rubber padding. It will endure traffic probably better than any grass other than tall fescues.

Although root-hardy to twenty below zero, zoysias will brown out with the first frost and not resume growth in spring until the weather turns hot. They are not supposed to be particularly drought resistant, but they green up more rapidly after a drought than any other turf grass.

Fertilizer requirements are high. Because the blades are tough and stiff, a rotary power mower is needed to cut zoysias. A lawn can be established only by plugs or sprigs.

Varieties include 'Meyer' (which has the widest range) and 'Emerald,' which has somewhat better color than 'Meyer,' spreads faster, but is not quite as hardy. Tenuifolia (actually a separate species) has the finest foliage, but is quite tender. Matrella (another species) and 'Flawn' are similar to 'Emerald,' but slower growing.

SUMMING UP

Mixtures are not as popular in the South as in the North except where cool-weather grasses are overseeded in winter. These might be called companion grasses rather than mixtures, since their purpose is not the same as for mixtures for the North.

For fine-leaved turf that can match and even surpass northern lawns, the newer Bermudas and zoysias should have first preference. Because these are both quite trouble-free, they should head the list. The only exception might be where an extremely busy home-owner prefers the less exacting centipede grass.

Zoysia might be discounted slightly because of its slow growth and failure to suppress weeds the first year or so after planting. This would not be a problem if sod were laid. Bermuda covers rapidly. In shade, St. Augustine should be given top rating, with zoysias next in shade tolerance and better in texture.

COMPANION GRASSES IN WINTER

Rye grass, a coarse, ugly species in the North, produces a luxurious show of green in the South if sown in late August (north of Birmingham, Alabama) to October (along the Gulf Coast). Because of its lack of heat resistance, it kills out the following summer, but not always in time to prevent the crowding of better grasses. For this reason, many are turning to overseeding with 'Highland' bent, which is not quite as aggressive and also kills out in southern heat. This bent is superior to bluegrasses for the purpose because it comes more quickly from seed. A few sprigs may survive in summer, but not enough to create a problem.

Red fescues are also used for overseeding, and present no real problems the following season.

GRASSES IN THE INTERMEDIATE BELT: REGION B

It has been said that any grass that will produce a lawn in St. Louis will grow anywhere. Certainly, the intermediate region presents more problems than any similar region in North America. Winter temperatures are so low that the more southern species, such as St. Augustine and centipede, are worthless, and hot, dry summers work against success with bluegrasses, red fescues, and bent. ('Highland' bent has been reasonably successful in shade.) Between these two handicaps, most home-owners in this region seem happy even with crabgrass. Golf clubs with low budgets actually depend on this weed for summer fairways. However, this defeatist attitude overlooks the tremendous advances made since World War II in developing new grasses.

Perhaps the best solution for Region B lawns is the planting of zoysias. At the northern limits, 'Meyer' is perhaps best, but 'Emerald' should be tried elsewhere. Its longer growing period adds about 10 to 14 days to the time it remains green.

Unfortunately, zoysia is such a slow starter in spring that if overseeded with rye grass or other species, it suffers from competition this far north.

For this reason, the use of dyes, winter paints, or colorants has become popular in this region, both on zoysias and Bermudas. These lawn paints are being improved constantly to make them seem more natural. The only objection to their use is cost.

For shaded areas, zoysia does fairly well in Region B, although growth is slowed. 'Highland' bent has been reasonably successful in St. Louis. Others report modest success with "Pennlawn' fescue, 'Merion' or 'Arboretum' bluegrasses, or with mixtures of all these. Even though a poor shade grass in the North, protection from hot sun seems to help Kentucky bluegrass and its varieties in this area.

The best Region B variety of bluegrass seems to be 'Arboretum,' which originated in St. Louis. It is more resistant to the fungus *Helminthosporium sativum*, which causes root rot. In this region, mow all bluegrasses, even 'Merion,' at a height of 2 to 2½ inches.

Because the new fine-leaved Bermudas do well in full sun, they should be considered for this region, particularly south of Missouri and Kentucky. The hardiest variety is 'U-3,' which does well even in St. Louis.

SPECIAL PROBLEMS OF SOUTHWESTERN LAWNS

Perhaps the most difficult grass problem in the Southwest is to acquire and hold humus on dry, sandy soils. With little grass cover to help build native fertility, everything grasses need for growing must be supplied artificially.

Since grass roots do not go deep, a 12-inch layer of good soil is all that need be built up. If cost is not a factor, remove all sand over the area to a depth of a foot. Then lay down a barrier of tar paper or plastic film. Over this, fill in whatever organic matter is available to a depth of about 4 inches. This can be garbage, leaves, sawdust (even pine sawdust), sewerage sludge, peatmoss, pine needles, or straw. Dust this liberally with ammonium sulfate, then replace the sand. Water it thoroughly to settle the mixture and let it stand one month before seeding.

When the lawn is finally made, the plastic or tar-paper barrier will hold back fertilizer and organic matter that otherwise would drain off rapidly. As grass roots are formed, they will gradually build up a mat of organic matter. By the time the barrier rots away, enough true soil will have formed to keep the lawn going.

Instead of fertilizer, use 40 pounds per 1,000 square feet of a mixture made up of equal parts of peatmoss, sewerage sludge, iron sulfate, ammonium sulfate, and dried sheep or cattle manure. Water in thoroughly as soon as applied.

On this prepared soil, try the new fine-leaved Bermudas such as 'Ormond,' 'Sunturf,' 'Texturf,' or 'U-3.' These are for areas with a long frost-free period. If the grass goes dormant for a short time in winter, lawn paints can be used. However, in warmer sections this dormant period is so short that it can be endured.

Zoysias deserve a trial, though they are not widely used as yet. For higher altitudes with cool nights, 'Merion' Kentucky bluegrass blended with 'Newport' Kentucky bluegrass has been successful.

FERTILIZERS FOR LAWN GRASSES, NORTH AND SOUTH

Fertilizer practices have been revolutionized since World War II. Present practices, based on research at State Experiment Stations, now call for about four times as much nitrogen as was formerly recommended, while high rates of phosphorus and potash are no longer considered necessary. The need of some grasses for additional iron (which reduces infection by certain turf diseases) is now being recognized.

A rule of thumb can be laid down for all vigorous grasses that build a heavy sod and are in active growth for a long period of time. For such grasses, the use of 1 pound of actual nitrogen to 1,000 square feet for every month between the last frost in spring and the first frost in fall, should result in good quality growth.

In the Chicago area, this growing season can be reckoned from May 1 to October 1, a period of five months. In practice, bents and bluegrasses in this area require from 4 to 8 pounds of nitrogen to 1,000 square feet each season. In the South, use 6 to 9 pounds for zoysias and Bermudas.

(For information on figuring the nitrogen content of various fertilizers, see Chapter 19.)

Other Food Elements

Since other elements needed by grasses are limited in quantity, these feedings can be done with high-nitrogen fertilizers such as ammonium nitrate, ammonium sulfate, urea, and ureaform if these are more economical. To supply the small amounts of phosphorus, potash, and other elements needed, a single feeding once a year with a good, mixed, lawn fertilizer can be made in addition to these straight nitrogen products. In the North, this might well be applied in early September. (A good way to remember the time is to set aside Labor Day for the job.) Fall feeding has one advantage — it feeds the plant at a time when it is making new root growth and so builds up a stronger sod. Spring feeding stimulates top growth more than it does roots.

In the South, however, spring feeding is preferred, particularly when a grass is growing close to its northern limit. For some reason not yet determined, warm-season grasses are not stimulated into making root growth by fall feeding.

Poor-soil Grasses

The one-pound-per-month rule does not apply to poor-soil grasses such as red fescues in the North or centipede and carpet grasses in the South. These need a general fertilizer in spring at a rate to supply not more than 1 pound of nitrogen to 1,000 square feet. If growth seems poor, 1 pound of nitrogen can be given once or twice more in summer — not oftener.

Feeding Mixed Lawns

When grass-seed mixtures are sown, feeding should be planned to suit the needs of the dominant grasses in the mixture. If bluegrasses make up more than 50 per cent of a blend, feed them at their preferred rate. If fescues or centipede grass dominates a mixture, use less.

ESTABLISHING A NEW LAWN

Except for *Poa trivialis* in the North and carpet grass in the South, the first requirement for a lawn is good drainage. No lawn grasses can stand being waterlogged very long. Soil can be improved and fertilizers applied later, but drainage must be considered when a lawn is made.

In any soil where grass will grow, a slope of ⅛ to ¼ inch per foot allows water from heavy, sudden showers to drain off without causing washing. If the area is low and water stands after rains, underground drainage should be provided. This is usually a job for a professional, but do-it-yourself gardeners can get directions and help from their county agent or county farm advisor. Check the ability of the soil to absorb water by pouring several pailsful in low spots. If it stands for several hours, drainage tile is needed.

Since tiling takes time, it should be done the season before planting, to allow the soil to settle. What is the season for planting? This differs. In the South, all sprigged or plugged lawns should be planted in spring — also seeds of practically all the warm-season grasses.

Ideally, northern lawns should be seeded as soon as night temperatures begin to fall in August, usually about the 15th. Except at the southern edge of Zone A, September 15 should be about as late as grass is seeded. For every day that seeding is delayed after September 20, the prospect of a stand is reduced about 10 per cent. A lawn planted after October 1 is almost certain to fail.

This does not, however, preclude spring planting, if a new lawn must be made and August is months away. Spring-seeded lawns will give the owner more problems, yet he will have made substantial progress by August and his lawn will be farther ahead.

To get seed germination in spring calls for extra care in watering. Set sprinklers so they will cover the entire area, and turn them on for 20 minutes in the morning and again for 20 minutes at night. As soon as daytime temperatures reach 80°, turn them on for an additional 30 minutes at noon. This program will germinate seeds from May sowing in six days.

A mistake often made in preparing soils for lawns is to go too deep. This means that the loosened soil, however it has been worked, must settle to its original level. Usually it settles unevenly. Four inches is deep enough to work the soil. Add a source of organic matter, such as peatmoss or compost, as the soil is being tilled. Apply also 25 to 35 pounds of a good mixed lawn fertilizer to every 1,000 square feet and work it in.

Rake or drag the bed level. A section of extension ladder makes a good drag. Tie one end of a rope to the top rung and the other to the bottom rung. Drag the ladder sideways across the tilled earth and it will cut down high spots and fill low ones.

Seed is best sowed with a spreader; hand-seeding at the low rates needed for some modern grass varieties is hard to manage. As soon as the seed is sown, roll the earth with a medium-weight roller (not more than 50 pounds weight for each foot of the roller's width) to press the seed firmly into the soil.

Then turn on the sprinklers as recommended under spring sowing. If seeding is done in fall, less moisture may be required because of reduced evaporation, but the soil should be constantly moist.

MOWING

Start mowing as soon as the new grass is 3 inches tall — not before. If mowed before the seedlings are well-rooted, the plants may be pulled out. Once mowing has begun, maintain the same height the year around. (Obsolete practices recommend raising the height of cut during the summer, largely to control crabgrass. Modern chemical controls make this practice unnecessary.) The following heights are recommended:

'MERION' KENTUCKY BLUEGRASS: 1 inch. Common and other varieties of Kentucky bluegrass: 1¼ to 1½ inches except on south edge of Region A and through Region B, where a 2- to 2½-inch cut helps keep the soil cool.

FESCUES: 1¼ to 1½ inches in shade, 2 inches in sun.

BENTS: Cut at rate recommended for the variety. If in doubt, consult a local golf-course superintendent.

ZOYSIAS: Can be mowed as short as ¾ of an inch or as long as 2 inches.

BERMUDAS: ¾ to 1 inch.

ST. AUGUSTINE: 1½ to 2 inches.

BAHIA: 1½ to 2 inches.

EIGHT STEPS TO A HEALTHY LAWN

1) *Feed the soil before you work it.*

2) *Work the soil with digging fork (or plow) about 4 inches deep.*

3) *Rake it smooth — but don't pulverize it.*

4) *Feed again for quick, vigorous growth.*

5) *Choose the right seed, and sow evenly with spreader.*

6) *Use back of lawn rake or light roller to set seed.*

7) *Mulch lightly with straw or hay.*

8) *Sprinkle slowly until soil is thoroughly moist.*

CARPET GRASS: 1 to 2 inches.
CENTIPEDE GRASS: 1½ to 2 inches.

Proper mowing is the most important single operation in turning a mass of unrelated seedlings into a true lawn. Most owners do not mow often enough. In the North, cool-season grasses often need mowing twice a week in early spring and late fall when growth is rapid. Few grasses can stand being left uncut for more than a week.
(For turf diseases see Chapter 23; for weed control see Chapter 20.)

GROUNDCOVERS

In dense shade or burning sun, where grasses will not grow well, a carpeting of other plants can provide outstanding beauty. Baltic ivy, running myrtle, or bronze-leaf wintercreeper is far superior to a poor stand of grass in the heavy shade of trees; and on dry sunny banks — where even the toughest grass has a hard time — yarrow, crown vetch, or one of the prostrate junipers look attractive.

Tests have proved that no species of grass known will survive permanently in a given area if total light intensity is less than one-fourth that of full sunlight, and few will dispute the difficulties encountered on steep banks in full sun. Yet for some reason, the use of groundcovers is considered by many as a confession of failure with grass. Gardeners will struggle for years trying to make grass grow in difficult locations rather than turn to other plants.

Groundcovers need not be merely masses of green foliage without relief. A sunny bank ablaze with 'Max Graf' rose is a beautiful sight; so is a shaded woodland carpeted with lily-of-the-valley. *Ajuga reptans*, the carpet bugle, can be had in varieties with bronze, maroon, or green-and-white variegated foliage. It can be kept trim by occasional high mowing. Keeping such covers free of weedy grasses is no longer a problem. The weed-killer Dalapon will destroy even quackgrass without injuring broad-leaved plants.

GROUNDCOVERS FOR SHADY PLACES

Since groundcovers are used most in shady areas, the following list has been made as extensive as possible. It includes some species found only in the nurseries of specialists. Plants that retain their foliage during the winter are marked E, but are not necessarily true evergreens. Those marked F, can be depended upon for some bloom in shade, and the ones marked V are represented by several species. Descriptions of these plants are given in the Plant Encyclopedia. Some groundcovers are so aggressive that they tend to become weeds, but they are among the most valuable

There are suitable ground-covers for almost any diffi-cult spot in sun or shade. They reduce maintenance substantially, add touches of lovely texture. Here are four of the most popular:

Vinca minor, *myrtle;*

Hedera helix, *English ivy;*

Liriope, *lily-turf;*

Convallaria majalis, *lily-of-the-valley.*

because they fill in rapidly and resist hardships. Six such plants are marked R for reliable in the list immediately below.

Aegopodium podagraria (R),
  Goutweed
Ajuga reptans (FR), Carpet Bugle
Arenaria (VF), Sandwort
Asarum canadense, Wild Ginger
Asperula odorata, Sweet Woodruff
Chiogenes hispidula (E),
  Creeping Snowberry
Convallaria majalis (FR),
  Lily-of-the-valley
Coronilla varia (F), Crown Vetch
Dianthus arenarius (F), Sand Pink
Duchesnea indica, Mock Strawberry
Epimedium alpinum (EF),
  Common Epimedium
Euonymus obovatus,
  Running Bittersweet
Galax aphylla (EF), Galax
Gaultheria procumbens (E),
  Wintergreen
Hedera helix (E), English Ivy
Heuchera sanguinea, Coral Bells
Hosta (VFR), Plantain Lily
Hypericum calycinum (F)
  Aaron's Beard
Lamium maculatum (F),
  Spotted Dead Nettle

Linnaea borealis (F), Twinflower
Mahonia repens, Creeping Barberry
Menispermum canadense (E),
  Moonseed
Mitchella repens (E),
  Partridge-berry
Myosotis scorpioides (F),
  Perennial Forget-me-not
Nepeta hederacea (F),
  Creeping Jenny
Ophiopogon japonicus (FE),
  Dwarf Lily-turf
Pachistima canbyi (E), Rat-stripper
Pachysandra procumbens,
  Allegheny Spurge
P. terminalis (ER), Japanese Spurge
Primula (VF), Primrose
Ranunculus repens (F),
  Creeping Buttercup
Sagina subulata (E), Pearlwort
Sedum (VF), Stonecrop
Vinca minor 'Bowles,'
  Bowles' Myrtle
Viola (VF), Violet

SUN-TOLERANT GROUNDCOVERS

Those that are marked F flower to some extent. Those with foliage that lasts well into the winter are marked E, but are not necessarily evergreen. Plants designated V are represented by various species.

Aegopodium podograria, Goutweed
Ajuga reptans (F), Carpet Bugle
Akebia quinata, Five-finger Vine

Arabis alpina (F),
  Alpine Rock Cress
Arctostaphylos uva-ursi (E),
  Bearberry

Artemisia stelleriana (F),
  Beach Wormwood
Ceratostigma plumbaginoides (F),
  Plumbago
Cornus canadensis (E), Bunchberry
Coronilla varia (F), Crown Vetch
Cotoneaster (v), Cotoneaster
Dianthus (VF), Pink
Gypsophila repens,
  Creeping Baby's Breath
Helianthemum nummularium (F),
  Sun Rose
Iberis sempervirens (F),
  Perennial Candytuft
Lonicera japonica (EF),
  Japanese Honeysuckle
Lysimachia nummularia (F),
  Pennywort
Mahonia repens (E),
  Creeping Barberry
Matricaria tchihatchewi (F),
  Turfing Daisy

Mentha (v), Mint
Nepeta hederacea (F),
  Creeping Jenny
N. mussini (F), Dwarf Catnip
Ophiopogon japonicus (F),
  Dwarf Lily-turf
Phlox (VF), Trailing Phlox
Polemonium reptans (F), Bluebell
Polygonum (VF), Fleeceflower
Ranunculus (VF), Buttercup
Rosa 'Max Graf' (F),
  'Max Graf' Rose
R. wichuraina (F), Memorial Rose
Saponaria (VF), Soapwort
Thymus serpyllum (F),
  Creeping Thyme
Veronica (VF), Speedwell
Vinca minor 'Bowles,'
  Bowles' Myrtle
Viola (VF), Violet

GROUNDCOVERS FOR FLORIDA

Ajuga genevensis, Geneva Bugle
Asparagus plumosus,
  Fern Asparagus
Bignonia venusta, Flame Vine
Cuphea hyssopifolia, Bush Cuphea
Dichondra carolinensis, Dichondra
Dolichos hosei, Sarawak Bean
Euonymus radicans, Wintercreeper
Ficus radicans, Trailing Fig
F. pumila, Creeping Fig
Gelsemium sempervirens,
  Carolina Yellow Jessamine
Hedera canariensis, Algerian Ivy
Hemerocallis (VE), Daylily
Juniperus conferta, Sand Juniper

Lantana montevidensis,
  Trailing Lantana
Lippia canescens, Lippia
Liriope muscari, Blue Lily-turf
Lonicera japonica,
  Japanese Honeysuckle
Mesembryanthemum edule,
  Hottentot Fig
Mitchella repens, Partridge-berry
Ophiopogon japonicus,
  Dwarf Lily-turf
Peperomia crassifolia, Peperomia
Pilea microphylla, Artillery Plant
P. nummulariaefolia,
  Creeping Charley

Saxifraga sarmentosa,
   Strawberry-geranium
Selaginella (v), Selaginella
Spironema fragrans, Spironema
Trachelospermum jasminoides,
   Confederate Jasmine

Tribulus terrestris, Puncture Vine
Vinca major, Periwinkle
Wedelia tribolata, Wedelia
Zebrina pendula, Wandering Jew

Various ferns may also be effectively used for groundcovers.

GROUNDCOVERS FOR CALIFORNIA

All of the groundcovers recommended for the North or for Florida can be used in some part of California. Use the Florida list for warmer parts of the state, but be sure moisture and soil conditions are favorable. The Department of Ornamental Horticulture, University of California, Los Angeles, recommends, in addition, the following list. Because of their limited range, not all of these plants are discussed in the Plant Encyclopedia. Consult local nurseries or write to the above address for further information.

Low groundcovers: *Carex texensis, Cyperus gracilis, Dichondra carolinensis.* Also, lippia, mesembryanthemums, and various sedums.

Shrubs: *Plumbago capensis* and species of carissa, cistus, correa, hebe, helianthemum, and veronica.

California natives: *Baccharis pilularis, Ceanothus gloriosus, C. griseus horizontalis,* and native buckwheats (eriogonum).

Woody vines (these make excellent groundcovers): *Hedera canariensis, Lonicera japonica, Philadelphus mexicanus, Sollya heterophylla, Trachelospermum jasminoides, Vinca minor,* and species of bougainvillea, distictis, and pandorea.

Herbaceous perennials: *Ajuga reptans, Erigeron mucronatus, Lotus bertheloti, Oenothera childsi, Ophiopogon japonicus, Polygonum capitatum, Sagina procumbens, Veronica filiformis,* various bergenias and primulas.

Needled evergreens include many prostrate species, but they are expensive.

ANNUALS AS GROUNDCOVERS

For sunny areas almost anywhere in the United States, any quick-growing annual that hugs the ground can be used as a temporary groundcover. Among these are sweet alyssum, ageratum, annual pinks, English daisies, dimorphotheca, forget-me-nots, lobelia, dwarf marigolds, nierembergia, petunias, annual phlox, portulaca, and verbena.

10

The Rose:
World's Favorite Flower

The rose is easily man's favorite flower, pampered and cherished beyond all others. It flourished in the gardens of ancient Greece and Rome, in Persia, and in China. During centuries of cultivation, roses have been modified in so many ways that those grown today bear little resemblance to the wildlings from which they sprang. While they have become increasingly varied and beautiful, hybrids of the present have lost the ability to compete with other plants. To survive and remain attractive year after year they require special attention. Though some, even a few Hybrid Teas, continue to live when neglected, their flowers deteriorate.

This does not mean that the culture of roses is difficult or mysterious. It *does* mean, however, that, if you want roses, certain fundamentals must be observed.

CULTURE OF ROSES

Location

First consideration in selecting a site for a rose garden should be for air circulation and air drainage. Soil is not as important as often represented; it can be modified. But roses do not do well where air cannot move over them freely. All too often, a rose garden is surrounded by a tall evergreen hedge for decorative effect. This condemns the gardener to a constant battle with blackspot and mildew. When there is a choice, pick a spot where the air moves freely, but not one where the plants will have to bear the force of the unbroken west or north wind in summer and winter.

SIX STEPS IN PLANTING A ROSE: *Dig a hole 2' wide, 2' deep. Mound soil at bottom; press firm to prevent sinking.*

Spread roots over soil mound and adjust height so bud-union (knob on stem) is just below surface of soil.

Add soil, working it in around roots and pressing it firm.

Continue adding soil and firming it until hole is three-quarters full.

Fill hole with water. When it has drained, add soil but don't press firm.

Mound soil to protect stems from sun and wind. Level it in about two weeks.

In the Middle West and South, light filtered shade at noon is beneficial. This should be no heavier than that cast by a honey locust or white ash trimmed high. Not all varieties need this protection, but if one corner can be so located, the ones that fade badly in bright sun or in other ways show they don't like the summer heat can be gradually moved into that spot. All roses, however, need five hours or more of direct sunshine a day.

Whatever part of the property is selected, it should have good drainage. Garden roses cannot tolerate wet ground.

Many unnecessary words have been written about special soil preparation for roses. What they need most is a loose friable soil, well filled with humus.

Planting

Any rose worth planting (except a miniature) ought to have a hole dug for it at least 2 feet deep and 2 feet square. In the center of this hole, build up a cone about 12 inches high of the best topsoil taken from the hole. If this soil is not good, either find some that is, or add extra compost and a handful of fertilizer and work this over thoroughly. The idea of the cone is to direct the roots of the plant outward. Set the unwrapped plant on top of this cone with the roots spread out across the soil.

Now fill in, using only good topsoil. When the roots are covered and the hole is about half full, step into it (both feet) and press down the soil so that it is in firm contact with the roots. Now run in water until the hole is full and let it settle. Fill the rest of the hole with soil. Pile extra soil around the plant, and remove it a little at a time when the top shows signs of growth. Leave a slight dish — not too deep — to hold water; but if drainage is not as good as it should be, omit this.

The bud union, or knuckle, determines the depth of planting. Wherever possible, this should be at ground level, to stimulate the production of new "drives" from the dormant buds. Sunshine on the bud union helps do this.

However, in regions with severe winters, ground level is not always safe. Even though earth is brought in to protect the plant against freezing, this is never as well-settled as the soil in the bed and does permit some frost penetration. For this reason, in areas where earthing up for winter protection is needed, the knuckle should be 1 to 2 inches under the soil. Then, if the top is winter-killed, there will still be live dormant buds below the surface but above the union to produce a new top.

Fertilizers

Much nonsense has been written about the "ideal" formula. While obviously a product with a formula of 0-20-20 might be out of balance for most gardens, practically any *complete* mixed plant food will feed roses.

If it has everything in it plants need, roses will take what they want. The rest may be wasted, but the value of this waste will probably be far less than the cost of running a soil analysis.

There *is* some advantage in using the long-lasting forms of fertilizer such as ureaform nitrogen (but it must be mixed with other plant-food elements in order to be complete) since these will not have to be applied as often.

Most fertilizer programs provide too much plant food. More roses are killed by overfeeding than by starvation. There is no formula for feeding a rose. Each garden offers different conditions, and the right amount must be learned by trial and error. Feed a little and watch. When growth seems to be slowing up, see what effect another small dose will produce.

The one admonition in feeding is to discontinue early enough in fall to permit the wood to ripen and go into winter in a firm condition. If it is soft and green, as it will be if fed too late, it can be killed by a sudden cold snap.

Water

Conditions attributed to a lack of fertilizer are often due to a lack of moisture. Plant nutrients cannot be used unless they are dissolved in water. This does not mean you should flood the beds. The soil should be kept moist but not waterlogged.

Insect and Disease Control

Some gardeners never see blackspot or mildew on their roses, or the infestations are so light they can be ignored. This, however, is unusual. In most parts of the United States and Canada regular spraying for disease and insect control is urgently necessary.

Since most people garden only on week ends, a seven-day program is probably best. Ideally, a spray every five days would be slightly better, but seven is nearly as good. Use a mixed insect-and-disease spray. (Dusts are less effective, but can be used if time does not permit the application of a spray; a dust that *is* applied is more effective than a spray that is *not*.)

Most seed stores and garden centers carry broad-spectrum chemicals that will control a wide variety of pests. Some are specially prepared for use on roses and are so marked. Follow the directions carefully: they are put on the package for your protection as well as for the protection of your plants.

ROSE PRUNING

Before you start to prune a rose bush, study it carefully and notice how it grows. No one can lay down rigid rules for this operation, which in the hands of an expert is an art. Experience is important, but by following certain basic principles, the beginner can do a better job than the gardener who cuts just to cut.

There are two instances when drastic pruning may be in order. The first is when a rose is newly planted and the shape of the bush is being determined. Since the ideal plant should be well "clothed" from the ground up, low pruning (which is not otherwise desirable) is usually recommended at this time. Leave only three or four strong canes, cut the others back to the main stem, being careful not to bruise the bark at the base of the cane. The remaining strong canes should then be cut back, leaving two or three good buds at the base of each. Be sure the top bud faces outward on each cane. Any branch that grows from these buds will grow in the direction it is pointing. By "aiming" the buds outward, you prevent a tangle of weak branches in the center.

At the same time, there is no point in wasting that space in the center. Later, you can aim one well-placed bud to fill it. However, in damp cool regions where mildew is a problem, leave the center open so that sunlight can reach the base and help dry the plant quickly in the morning.

The second time when severe pruning is needed is when roses are uncovered in spring (in areas where hilling-up is practiced) and you find that the canes have been killed back. (Winter-killed canes are brown or black instead of a healthy green.) The dead canes must be cut back to live wood. Again, remember to aim all buds properly.

When winter-kill is not evident, how low should you prune? A principle to remember is that for every inch of wood you lose above 10 inches (measuring from the ground up) you will lose 10 per cent of your early bloom. This means that if canes are cut back to 8 inches, perhaps to produce a more shapely plant, you will have 8 blooms where you might have had 10. Try never to cut lower than 10 inches.

This still is not the whole story. How *high* can we cut? Here there is the problem of adjusting all plants to a uniform height if they are growing in beds and must look well together. In this case, the height is determined by the weakest grower in the bed.

If individual bushes are grown, remember that the more foliage the plant has, the more food it can manufacture and the more vigorous it will be. For this reason, try to let the bush grow as tall as is feasible for its location.

Summer Pruning

Every time a flower is cut for the house or a faded bloom is removed, you are pruning, whether you call it that or not. Always leave at least two or three buds on the stem from which a flower is cut. The buds, incidentally, are at the base of the leaf stem. Often there are two or three weak leaves below the point at which the flower is removed. Cut these away because the buds at their base will produce poorer flowers.

If you want long-stemmed perfect flowers, remember that the fewer the leaves left on the stem, the longer the new stem will be. However, it will take longer to bloom. If you want an abundance of flowers, allow more leaves to remain.

Disbudding

To produce top-quality flowers, most Hybrid Teas and all Floribundas should be disbudded. This is a simple operation. When the flower buds begin to swell, you can see that there are several of them in a cluster. As soon as you can do so without damaging the largest bud, pinch out all the others.

Suckers

These are often a problem, more so with plants from some nurseries than from others, but more and more growers are "de-eyeing" their under-stocks when the bushes are harvested in the field. This cuts away the dormant buds on the roots from which suckers arise. However, if a severe winter completely kills the top above the knuckle, buds too small to be removed in the de-eyeing process will often come to life and produce sprouts. Suckers can usually be detected because their foliage is different from that of most desirable varieties. The real test, however, is to see whether they come from below the knuckle or above it. If below, cut them away, taking as much as possible of the ring of buds at the base of the shoot without cutting into the wood of the root.

If there is no growth whatever from the plant above the knuckle, better dig it up and throw it away. But be careful not to confuse suckers with the highly desirable low-break buds that emerge just above the bud union. If the bush is planted with the union below the surface, scrape the soil away before doing any cutting to be sure of the source of the sucker.

Special Pruning

HYBRID PERPETUALS. In spring, remove all canes older than two years. If the plant is strong, leave four to five canes; if weaker, three to four. If any heading back is to be done, wait until after flowering in June bloom, then never leave fewer than five to six buds on the headed-back cane. Do not try to keep these strong-growing roses cut down in order to grow them in the same bed as Hybrid Teas.

CLIMBERS. Ramblers flower only on one-year-old wood. As soon as a cane has flowered, cut it back to three or four buds. These will grow vigorously and flower the following summer. Select the number of canes you want to fill the trellis or fence on which the plant is growing and cut away the rest.

Large-flowered climbers bloom only on old wood; do only as much cutting back as is needed to keep the plant within bounds. Whenever possible, try to train some of the canes horizontally. This directs the sap flow in such a way that flower buds are formed rather than vegetative growth, and the cane blooms more freely.

FLORIBUNDAS. Treat like Hybrid Teas. They do resent hard pruning, however. Try to avoid cutting them back severely.

SHRUB ROSES. Cut out all old weak wood, leaving several canes on strong-growing species, about four on weaker growers. Cut back the side branches on these canes (the twiggy growth) to stubs with two or three buds. On roses that bloom only once, this should be done right after the flowers fade to give them time to form new flower buds for the following year.

PROTECTION FOR ROSES

Mulching

Mulching is preferred to regular cultivation because roses are at best poor root-makers. Stirring the soil with hoes or other tools inevitably destroys some roots. However, a sticky wet mulch, high in organic matter, is an ideal breeding place for the wintering-over stage of blackspot. Whenever possible, use relatively inert materials such as rice hulls (which are largely silica), buckwheat hulls, or vermiculite. Corn cobs are widely used but have the disadvantage of being fairly high in sugar, which fungi can use for food.

If a high-organic mulch is used, it should be removed soon after the fall rains begin and weed growth has slowed. Put it on the compost pile with some extra nitrogen to rot it down. In areas where winter protection is needed, do not replace it until the following spring. In less rigorous climates, a fresh mulch can be applied at once or replaced in spring.

Winter Covering

Where air temperatures drop to 10° F. or lower for 24 hours, winter protection of some sort is needed. At the southern limits of this area, it need not be anything more elaborate than burlap shade or loose pine boughs to ward off winter sun.

However, the farther north you go, the more roses need clean soil piled around the main stem. If zero readings can be expected for more than 24 hours, earth piled at least 10 inches high is recommended. Start as soon as a killing frost has removed the foliage. Sometimes frost will hold off for weeks beyond the normal date. In this event, the danger of a sharp sudden freeze catching soft growth is great. Artificially defoliate the plants and begin hilling up. Be ready to finish the job if a freeze is threatened.

North of the southern shores of the Great Lakes, as in upper New York State and Wisconsin, an additional covering of evergreen boughs or several inches of straw is advised.

Although all sorts of weird devices have been recommended for rose protection, year in and year out none of these will afford the protection that clean soil gives.

Climbers should be on hinged trellises when grown in colder parts of the country, so they can be laid down and covered with loose straw, corn stalks, or similar protection. One precaution: when straw, corn stalks, or pine boughs are used on top of soil, be sure to wait until a sharp freeze has occurred. If this type of protection is applied before field mice have moved into winter quarters, they will set up housekeeping there and live in luxury on fresh green rose shoots. They have even been known to dig down and eat shoots below the surface.

Many of the questions that arise about roses can be answered by visiting one of the great public gardens where they are displayed.

ROSES AS CUT FLOWERS

Cut roses when partly opened, preferably in the afternoon of a sunny day. Don't cut more stem than you need (unless the plant has grown too tall), and make the cut one-quarter inch above a husky five-part leaf.

Immediately after cutting, condition or "harden" the roses for an hour or two before using them in an arrangement, bouquet, or corsage. Here's how:

First wash off any soil or spray residue on the leaves and remove lower leaves that would be below the water line in your vase. Scrape off the thorns below the leaves with a sharp knife.

Make a new, sharply slanting cut at the end of the stem and scrape a little bark off the lower inch or so. This will help the rose absorb water. Now place the roses in room-temperature water deep enough to come up to the lower leaves. Stand container in a cool spot, out of drafts, and in an hour or two the roses will be ready for use.

Roses that have wilted — either because they were not placed in water soon enough or from being in a draft — can usually be revived by this procedure:

Cut off the lower inch or so of the stem, at a slant, and make two scrapes one to two inches long at the base. Place the scraped part in *hot* water — not boiling, but a little too hot to hold your hand in — and leave them in the water till it cools. Then place them in *cold* water up to the base of the flowers. In an hour or so they should be completely revived and strong enough for arranging.

Keep your bouquet or arrangement away from heat and drafts and, of course, add water as necessary to keep the stems well immersed.

Roses considered the best for cutting are listed by color in the accompanying table:

BEST GARDEN ROSES FOR CUTTING

Grouped by Color

	A.R.S. Rating	Date	Number Of Petals	Fragrance	Plant Height
DARK RED					
'Carrousel'	9.0	1950	20	Moderate	Tall
'Chrysler Imperial'*	8.8	1952	40–50	Intense	Med.
'Crimson Glory'	9.1	1935	30	Intense	Tall
'Nocturne'*	8.1	1949	20–28	Intense	Tall
'Mirandy'*	7.7	1945	40–50	Intense	Tall
MEDIUM RED					
'Etoile de Hollande'	8.1	1919	35–40	Intense	Tall
'Grand Duchesse Charlotte'*	8.1	1947	25	Slight	Med.
'Starfire'*	8.1	1958	25–30	Moderate	Tall
'New Yorker'	8.0	1947	35	Moderate	Tall
'El Capitan'	7.9	1959	30	Slight	Tall
LIGHT RED OR DARK PINK					
'Charlotte Armstrong'*	9.0	1940	35	Moderate	Tall
'Montezuma'	8.6	1955	32–40	Slight	Tall
'Rubaiyat'*	8.2	1946	25	Intense	Tall
'Tallyho'*	8.4	1948	35	Intense	Tall
'Red Radiance'	7.9	1916	20–25	Intense	Tall
MEDIUM PINK					
'Queen Elizabeth'*	9.0	1954	37–40	Moderate	Tall
'Duet'*	7.7	1961	25	Slight	Med.
'Pink Favorite'	8.2	1956	21–28	Slight	Tall
'Pink Peace'	7.6	1959	50–65	Intense	Tall
'Show Girl'	7.6	1946	15–20	Moderate	Med.
LIGHT PINK					
'First Love'	8.0	1951	20–30	Slight	Tall
'Pink Princess'	7.7	1939	30–40	Intense	Tall
'Picture'	8.0	1932	30	Slight	Tall
'Radiance'	7.9	1908	23	Intense	Tall
DEEP YELLOW					
'Lowell Thomas'	7.7	1944	35–40	Moderate	Med.
'Gold Glow'	7.8	1959	35–40	Moderate	Med.
MEDIUM YELLOW					
'Eclipse'	8.1	1935	25-30	Moderate	Tall
'Burnaby'	8.1	1954	56	Slight	Tall
'Buccaneer'	7.3	1952	30	Moderate	Tall
'King's Ransom'	—	1962	—	—	Tall
LIGHT YELLOW					
'McGredy's Yellow'	7.5	1933	30	Slight	Med.

	A.R.S. Rating	Date	Number Of Petals	Fragrance	Plant Height
WHITE					
'White Knight'*	7.2	1957	28–35	Slight	Med.
'McGredy's Ivory'	7.2	1930	25–30	Moderate	Med.
'June Bride'	7.5	1957	30	Moderate	Tall
'White Queen'	7.3	1958	30	Moderate	Med.
'Pedralbes'	7.4	1935	30	Slight	Med.
ORANGE AND ORANGE BLEND					
'McGredy's Sunset'	7.5	1936	40	Moderate	Med.
'Mrs. Sam McGredy'	7.9	1929	40	Moderate	Med.
'Mojave'*	7.4	1954	25	Moderate	Med.
'Aztec'	7.7	1957	22–28	Moderate	Med.
'Hawaii'	7.7	1960	—	Intense	Med.
APRICOT BLEND					
'Paramount'	7.8	1950	30	Slight	Med.
YELLOW BLEND					
'Peace'*	9.6	1945	40–45	Slight	Tall
'Garden Party'*	7.7	1959	35	Slight	Med.
'Sutter's Gold'*	8.1	1950	30–35	Intense	Tall
'Lady Elgin'	7.7	1957	35–48	Moderate	Tall
PINK BLEND					
'Tiffany'*	8.8	1954	25–30	Intense	Tall
'President Herbert Hoover'	7.7	1930	25	Moderate	Tall
'Mission Bells'*	7.8	1949	40–45	Moderate	Tall
'Confidence'	8.3	1953	28–39	Moderate	Tall
'Good News'	8.4	1940	50	Intense	Tall
RED BLEND					
'Mme. Henri Guillot'	8.4	1935	25	Slight	Tall
'Saturnia'	8.1	1936	20	Moderate	Med.
MAUVE OR LAVENDER					
'Sterling Silver'	6.9	1957	30	Intense	Med.

* All-America Rose Selections award winners.

A CHOICE OF ROSES

There are some half-dozen types of rose — the Hybrid Tea, Hybrid Perpetual, Floribunda, Polyantha, climbing rose, miniature rose, and, in a class by itself, the Mermaid. But the rose most people want is the Hybrid Tea, the ideal rose — long-stemmed, with perfect, pointed buds that open into high-centered fragrant flowers. These flowers are quite large, exceeded in size only by the older Hybrid Perpetuals. They are borne in clusters of two to five buds, but are disbudded to a single flower when perfect specimens are wanted. Practically all Hybrid Teas are budded on an understock of some other species. This leaves a bud union or "knuckle" where the top of the understock was cut off and the bud formed a new top. Management of this bud union is a vital part of modern rose culture.

HYBRID TEA VARIETIES

Many fine old-time roses are still worth planting if they can be had in good stock, but unfortunately they are usually grown for cheap markets. There are those who contend, and not without reason, that a fine specimen of 'Kaiserin Auguste Victoria' is the equal of any white rose grown today. 'Condesa de Sastago,' with its brilliant flag-of-Spain coloring — red and yellow — and its fragrance, is hard to equal even among the newer bicolors. It takes a good specimen of 'Christian Dior' or 'Crimson Glory' to surpass the aged 'Etoile de Hollande' when the latter is well grown. However, the following list is largely devoted to the better new varieties.

Where a rose is mentioned as an AARS Winner, this means that it was tested in over 20 gardens located throughout the United States and was rated by competent judges for all-over excellence. AARS (All-America Rose Selections) winners are excellent roses for beginners because they do well almost everywhere.

'CARELESS LOVE.' A rather shapeless rose, a sport of 'Red Radiance,' it is well worth growing because of its interesting color variation. Flowers on the same bush may vary from clear carmine splashed and striped with white through pure pink to a mixture of rosy pink and apricot yellow. Fragrant.

'CHARLOTTE ARMSTRONG' (AARS Winner). One of the great roses of all time, a rose-carmine to clear red. Vigorous healthy plants often 50 to 60 inches tall. Fine fragrance. Disbud to single bloom for specimen flowers.

'CHICAGO PEACE.' Far and away the best of the many sports of 'Peace.' Like its parent in every respect, including vigor, size, floriferous habit, and lack of fragrance; it differs only in color. The flowers retain the vivid pink of the parent, but the white has disappeared, leaving a brilliant gold and rose blend unmatched in any modern rose.

'CHRISTIAN DIOR.' Almost too opulent to be named for the designer who has tried to make American women elegantly svelte. Flowers of from 50 to 60 petals are a lush crimson, shading into an iridescent scarlet. A strong, upright bush.

'CONFIDENCE.' Although introduced in 1951, this is a better rose than the newer 'Garden Party' among the blends, with more "lift" in its coloring. Tints of pale flesh, pink, and rose are delicately highlighted with gold. Flowers are fragrant, long, and pointed.

'CRIMSON GLORY.' Perhaps the country's best-loved rose, this flower has as rich a fragrance as can be found in any rose. The color is a rich velvety red. Although 'Christian Dior' has more petals and fuller centers, its color cannot compare with the deep, glowing red of 'Crimson Glory.'

'CHRYSLER IMPERIAL' (AARS Winner). A crimson red with a hint of blue in it. Paint manufacturers tried to match the color but finally gave up in despair. The fragrance is excellent and the plant healthy.

'FORTY-NINER.' In cool weather this slightly fragrant rose excels, but in the heat, 'Condesa de Sastago,' is better. Same red-and-yellow flag-of-Spain coloring.

'GARDEN PARTY' (AARS Winner). This is a rose that creates controversy. Many find its delicate coloring delightful — a soft ivory with palest apple-blossom pink. Others find it much too weak. The bud is beautiful — long and slender like that of 'Charlotte Armstrong.'

'GOLDEN MASTERPIECE.' Until the introduction of 'King's Ransom,' this was considered the finest of all yellows. It is slightly deeper in color and many still prefer it. Fragrant.

'HELEN TRAUBEL' (AARS Winner). One of the country's favorite pink-apricot-rose blends. An outstanding bicolor on a plant as good as the flower. A consistent winner at shows. Fragrant.

'INVITATION.' One of the better coral blends with shadings of orange and salmon. Huge flowers with a fine fragrance. High-centered flowers opening from long, slender buds.

'JOSEPHINE BRUCE.' A truly black rose has been a breeder's goal for years. While not black, this is a deep maroon with black shadings. Lasts beautifully as a cut flower, but needs a light background for proper display.

'KING'S RANSOM.' Just the color you might expect — glittering gold. Huge 6-inch flowers borne on a vigorous, healthy plant. Hard to choose between this and 'Golden Masterpiece,' but for flower size, this wins.

'KORDES PERFECTA.' A spectacular blend. Ivory petals with vivid shocking-pink edges. Those who like 'Garden Party' dislike this as a rule, and vice versa. Very fragrant.

'MEMORIAM.' Perhaps the closest to a perfect pink rose. Like an old-fashioned Hybrid Perpetual but with a long pointed bud and a high center. Flowers 5 inches across with 50 to 60 petals. In some lights the petals have a fluorescent glow which lifts the pink out of the commonplace.

'MIRANDY' (AARS Winner). Its rich fragrance distinguishes this rose. Color is garnet red but it needs heat to develop well.

'MME. HENRI GUILLOT.' This rose is visible across a large garden — bright coral, red, and orange flowers contrast strongly with the deep green foliage. Not new, but no other rose in its class.

'NEW YORKER.' The opposite of 'Mirandy' in that this is at its best in cool, moist weather. One of the brightest of all red roses, and fragrant.

'PEACE.' This might be called the 'American Beauty' of the 20th century. One of the great roses of all time. Huge white to ivory flowers flushed gold at the base and with changeable pink lights. Will grow anywhere and should be in every garden despite its lack of fragrance.

'SUTTER'S GOLD.' Perhaps the most fragrant yellow rose. The buds are beautiful, but the fully opened flowers are shapeless.

'THE DOCTOR.' Not too reliable, but when its huge rose-pink flowers open under favorable conditions from long, beautifully shaped buds, no rose in the world can surpass it. But grow it only if you have other pink roses not quite as miffy.

'TIFFANY' (AARS Winner). Most freely blooming of all pinks. Clear pink flowers with a hint of gold at the base. They have unusual lasting quality as a cut flower and fine fragrance.

'VIRGO.' If it were not for the fact that the long white buds are sometimes tinged with pink, this would be a top-rated variety. If you have room for two white roses, this is the one for #2 place.

'WHITE KNIGHT' (AARS Winner). The only white rose ever to win an All-America award. Flowers are 5 inches across with more than 50 petals. Aristocratic in form and purity of color. Good for cutting. This should be #1 choice as a white rose.

HYBRID PERPETUALS

These are difficult to find commercially, but are well worth searching out. They are much hardier than Hybrid Teas, surviving zero readings without protection. They lost favor about forty to fifty years ago because they bloomed only once, in late June or early July. Since then, the cane-renewal system of pruning has brought them back into favor with informed gardeners, who now expect them to bloom in season with the Hybrid Teas.

The June bloom on well-grown Hybrid Perpetuals must be seen to be believed. A single bush may carry 100 five-inch roses. In form they are globular or flat, sometimes called cabbagy by those who do not like them. Despite this, no rose in existence is more striking or pleasant to the eye than a well-grown Hybrid Perpetual at the height of bloom.

Here is where the now defunct 'American Beauty' rose belonged. Florists gulp and say nothing when customers order roses under this name, but the last roses of this varity grown in commerce were cut in 1938. What buyers are usually given is 'Better Times,' a really superior rose.

That Hybrid Perpetuals will have a revival seems almost certain. Specialists are increasing stocks of varieties and are selling them. North of the Chicago-New York line, they are definitely worth planting. Losses from winter-killing are practically nil, even without hilling.

The color range, while wide, lacks the yellows and scarlets of modern Hybrid Teas, but it is rich in creamy pinks, lavender-rose, deep glowing red, and near-black crimsons. Modern taste shuns the lilac to violet tints found in these delightful flowers, just why is hard to say. The variety 'Reine des Violettes,' introduced in 1860, is one of the most delightful of these. Its petals are a bluish-violet at the tips, deep magenta in the body of the flower, and a rich lilac pink in the center. It is easy to imagine Queen Victoria dining with a bouquet of these roses on the table.

VARIETIES OF HYBRID PERPETUALS

(This list has been checked against lists of specialists, and only those available in commerce today are listed.)

'ARRILAGA.' A "modern" variety, introduced in 1929. Enormous plants, 7 to 8 feet tall with masses of soft pink to vivid pink fragrant flowers much like those of a Hybrid Tea.

'BARONNE PREVOST.' A true rose-pink flower of typical Hybrid Perpetual form, fragant. May seem a bit cabbagy to many, but a lovely flower.

'BARONESS ROTHSCHILD.' Soft rose to creamy pink huge-cupped double flowers with delightful scent. The plant is shorter than most Hybrid Perpetuals. Can be used with the Hybrid Teas, but it is hard to make it bloom after June.

'CLIO.' Huge double globular pink flowers with a flesh-pink center. Very fragrant. Flowers may ball in wet weather because of too many petals. A heavy plant about 5 feet tall.

'FRAU KARL DRUSCHKI.' If this rose had fragrance, it would be the greatest rose in the world. Plants may grow 10 feet tall and bear 100 or more white blooms. However, it is better to prune it hard and make it repeat. For larger flowers, disbud the clusters.

'GEANT DES BATTAILES.' A dwarf-growing variety with very fragrant crimson-red flowers, rather smallish but very double. Repeats regularly.

'GENERAL JACQUEMINOT.' Scarlet-crimson buds open to clear red flowers. This was *the* red rose of Queen Victoria's time, and is still one of the best. May bloom again in fall, but cane pruning doesn't help this one. Let it grow. Very fragrant.

'GEORG ARENDS.' Sometimes listed as a Hybrid Tea because it blooms regularly in summer. Flowers also have the Hybrid Tea form. Color is a true soft rose-pink. Fragrance is light but pleasant.

'HENRY NEVARD.' A giant red flower with intense fragrance that repeats regularly. Six- to 7-foot plant.

'MARCHIONESS OF LONDONDERRY.' Huge cup-shaped, soft pink fragrant blooms. Plant is thornless and about 6 feet tall.

'MRS. JOHN LAING.' The closest of all the Hybrid Perpetuals to a constant bloomer. Fragrant clear pink flowers, cup-shaped, and very double. Fairly short plant that will not look out of place with Hybrid Teas.

'PAUL NEYRON.' So fragrant that its odor was used for years as a standard of comparison. The blooms are enormous, 6 to 7 inches in diameter, but not too well-formed, often splitting across the flower. A museum piece, but worth having.

'REINE DES VIOLETTES.' Modern rose enthusiasts shudder when a rose that "blues" is mentioned, but this variety, with bluish tips on its petals is lovely. The body of the flower is a rich magenta (another *bête noire* of

Planning meant success: The shape of lawn and walk, the naturalistic plantings of groundcover and flowers to take advantage of rock formations, the use of shrubs — each plays its part in this well-designed landscape.

Groundcovers: Here English ivy is used for edging and combined with myrtle (periwinkle) in the center. The yellow-flowered vine on the lamp-post is Carolina jasmine.

The rich, deep color of "Crimson Glory" has made it a favorite hybrid tea rose for over a quarter of a century.

*Sometimes the key to good landscape design is knowing when to stop planting.
This simple garden preserves all the charm of its New England setting.*

color "authorities"), fading into a soft lilac pink in the center. A lovely, fragrant flower on a plant up to 8 feet tall.

'ROGER LAMBELIN.' A floral freak, but lovely. The flowers resemble a carnation more than a rose and are bright crimson-red, streaked and splashed with white.

GRANDIFLORAS, FLORIBUNDAS, AND POLYANTHAS

These form a group of three different types, somewhat related in their habits and breeding. All are recurrent bloomers. The name Grandiflora is a misnomer, implying as it does that the flowers are very large. Actually, they are smaller than either Hybrid Teas or Hybrid Perpetuals, though borne very freely. They resulted from crosses between Floribundas and Hybrid Teas, in which the good qualities of both types were supposed to be blended. A number of excellent Floribundas came out of the crosses, but a few grew much too tall to be included in beds with other roses. The name Grandiflora was applied to these to form a separate class.

Their main use is as a background for shorter roses. If they were not so expensive, they would make splendid flowering hedges. However, they are no more winter-hardy than the Hybrid Teas and offer some problem in covering them where winter protection is necessary.

Floribundas were originally called Hybrid Polyanthas, since they were largely developed by crossing the small Polyantha with Hybrid Teas. They tend to be taller than the former, with larger flowers, but flowering in clusters like the Polyantha parent. They are more winter-hardy than Hybrid Teas, often surviving unharmed without protection along the Chicago-New York line. However, winter protection is a wise precaution.

Of all roses, the Floribundas are probably the most satisfactory for the beginner. Even if left unsprayed and unpruned, they manage to survive and bloom.

The older Polyanthas, now largely relegated to the greenhouse as forcing roses for Easter and Mother's Day, still have a place in the outdoor garden for low hedges and edging. Perhaps the brightest of all roses in color is the Polyantha, 'Gloria Mundi,' a scintillating neon orange color.

GRANDIFLORA VARIETIES

(Some of these may be catalogued as Floribundas, having been introduced before the invention of the Grandiflora class. However, in habit they belong here.)

'BETTY PRIOR.' When used as a Floribunda, this always seemed out of place because of its vigorous shrub-like habit. Its fragrant flowers, however, are single while other Grandiflora varieties are double. Nonetheless, moving 'Betty Prior' to this class would simplify matters.

'EUTIN.' This is another tall-growing, vigorous Floribunda that really belongs here. It bears enormous clusters, often up to 100 individual double blooms, on long, arching stems. An outstanding hedge rose with a slight fragrance.

'GOLDEN GIRL.' A tall-growing 'Eclipse' describes this. Its yellow flowers are as fine as most Hybrid Teas and make excellent cut flowers.

'JOHN S. ARMSTRONG' (AARS Winner). A rich, deep red, with flowers as fine as most Hybrid Teas. A vigorous, healthy bush with many canes, ideal for a hedge.

'MASQUERADE.' Usually listed as a Floribunda, but grows 5 feet tall. Enormous clusters of slightly fragrant flowers opening yellow, turning coral-pink, then rich red.

'PINK PARFAIT' (AARS Winner). Ice-cream sundae colors — rose-pink to coral on a typical Grandiflora bush. Quite fragrant.

'QUEEN ELIZABETH' (AARS Winner). This is one of the great roses of the century, a Floribunda able to hold its own with any Hybrid Tea. The fragrant individual flowers are a beautiful clear true rose-pink and are borne in abundance. Do not plant this with Hybrid Teas: it will make them look puny.

'STARFIRE' (AARS Winner). An unusual color — a currant red that does not fade in direct sunshine. Bronzy foliage enhances it. Fragrant.

FLORIBUNDAS

Originally these were called Hybrid Polyanthas. They were developed by crossing Hybrid Teas with the small-flowered Polyanthas. They combine the qualities of both types with the hardiness of the Polyanthas.

'CIRCUS' (AARS Winner). Urn-shaped, high-centered buds open bright yellow and orange, then burst into brilliant tones of orange, scarlet, pink, cream, and apple pink. Fragrant. Makes an excellent cut flower.

'FASHION' (AARS Winner). A gorgeous coral-pink overlaid with gold. Considered among the top ten Floribundas. Fragrant.

'FIRE KING' (AARS Winner). Covered all season long with brilliant vermilion-red flowers that resemble Hybrid Teas. Musk fragrance.

'FLORADORA' (AARS Winner). One of the most brilliant of all roses, a vermilion-scarlet-orange of burning intensity. Nicely formed individual blooms with a slight fragrance.

'GARNETTE.' For many years the florist trade absorbed all the stock of this variety available. It is without question the longest-lasting of all roses as a cut flower. The color is a deep garnet red. Flowers are borne in clusters of 10 to 20, each a perfect bouquet. Slightly fragrant.

'GOLD CUP' (AARS Winner). The best yellow Floribunda. Individual flowers are 3 inches across and sweetly fragrant.

'GOLDEN SLIPPERS.' A new break in color — an almost fluorescent neon orange-red that changes and blends to gold, pastel orange, and clear apricot.

'GRUSS AN AACHEN.' An old European variety, used as bedding plants. Flowers profusely all summer long. Individual blooms are shapeless, but en masse they form a cloud of creamy white touched with pale salmon. Slightly fragrant.

'IVORY FASHION' (AARS Winner). With all the good qualities of its parent, 'Fashion,' in ivory-colored flowers. The best near-white Floribunda for cutting or garden display. Fragrant.

'JIMINY CRICKET.' Might be called a masculine 'Cecile Brunner': just right for a buttonhole flower in a mannish color. Bright red at first, changing to orange and finally to clear coral pink. Fragrant.

'LAVENDER GIRL.' The buds belie the name at first because of their red tinge. When open, however, they are a clear, fresh lavender that does not fade in sunshine. Individual blooms are quite large, 3½ inches across. Fragrant.

'LITTLE DARLING.' Another perfect corsage or buttonhole flower — brilliant red and yellow, melting to orange and yellow, and finally to soft coral-pink. Spicy fragrance.

'MOULIN ROUGE.' One of the best reds for cutting; rivals 'Garnette' both in color and lasting qualities, but is less formal in shape. Semi-double flowers in great clusters that can be cut to form whole bouquets. Slightly fragrant.

'PINOCCHIO.' Parent of many newer Floribundas and still one of the best. Fat, round buds of coral and gold are borne in clusters. Fragrant.

'RED PINOCCHIO.' Like the preceding except for color, which is a rich, deep carmine.

'ROSENELFE.' Unusually lovely flowers like miniature gardenias in form but a silvery rose-pink. A constant bloomer. Fragrant.

'SPARTAN.' Lives up to its name in vigor and hardiness. Flowers are a vivid orange-scarlet and fragrant, an unusual quality in this color.

POLYANTHA VARIETIES

One of the parents of modern Floribundas, the Polyanthas are still worth planting for their good qualities. They are usually lower-growing; and hardier than Hybrid Teas or Floribundas.

'CAMEO.' Semi-double salmon-pink flowers turning to soft orange-pink. Slightly fragrant.

'CAROL ANN.' Smallest of this class, about 12 inches tall, covered with salmon-orange flowers in clusters.

'CECILE BRUNNER.' The favorite buttonhole rose of generations of estate-owners, yet grown in cottage gardens everywhere. One of the best-beloved roses of all time. Fragrant. Also known as the 'Sweetheart rose.' Flowers are a soft flesh-pink flushed with cream and yellow. A sport, 'Mrs. Finch,' has intensified, deep shades of the same colors. 'Perle d'Or' is even tinier in size in a clear peach-pink without heavy shading.

'CHATILLON.' A magnificent variety where masses of clear, bright pink flowers in great billows are needed. Blooms profusely all summer. Fragrant.

'GLORIA MUNDI.' This rose should be planted near others only after careful consideration of colors. It is one of the most vivid hues imaginable, a strident fluorescent orange-scarlet that can be seen for hundreds of feet. Purple and blue flowers are about the only ones not killed by it.

'THE FAIRY.' Not really a Floribunda, but must be classed somewhere. This is one rose that can be neglected and will still bloom. If not kept in bounds by pruning, will form an enormous shrub 12 to 15 feet across. Might be considered a Grandiflora except that growth is in width rather than height and the flowers are minute, more like Polyanthas. They are clean pink, double, and borne in great waves.

CLIMBING ROSES

Although many catalogs lump all climbing roses together, there are several types, each with its own cultural needs. Not true climbers, since they neither twine nor cling by holdfasts, they might be called scramblers. If not supported, the canes pile up until they manage to grow above the surrounding vegetation.

All need support, to which they must be tied, at least until they can crawl over a wall or pergola. Because of their need for winter protection in many areas, they are often planted against trellises hinged at the ground line so that the entire plant can be laid down for winter protection.

RAMBLER ROSES

Except for the so-called Baby Rambler (which belongs in the Polyantha class) these are cluster-flowered with small individual blooms, appearing in June or July on one-year old wood. Because they are quite susceptible to mildew and do not flower again after the early summer display, they are gradually losing favor but are still widely grown in some areas.

'DOROTHY PERKINS.' About the only variety in this class still found in commerce. Lovely in bloom, with its masses of clear pink flowers, it usually slumps into a yellowish-green mass of foliage, flecked with mildew, for the rest of the summer. One of the only climbers known by name to many gardeners. There are better ones.

Floribundas do well even for beginning rose-gardeners. Hardy and eager to grow, they produce many brilliant clusters of blooms.

Roses in miniature: The "tree" is rose-pink 'Midget', all of 12″ tall. The tiny bouquet is 'Twinkles', a bushy miniature with white blooms.

OTHER SMALL-FLOWERED CLIMBERS

Hard to find, but still in demand by sentimentalists, is 'Tausendschön.' Its rather shapeless blooms are borne in enormous sprays that vary from white through pale pink to pale buff. There are better climbers.

If they can be had, the 'Pemberton' climbers, which are really pillar roses growing from 7 and 10 feet in height, are excellent. They bloom off and on all summer and are fragrant. 'Clytemnestra' (soft salmon-orange), 'Penelope' (ice-cream pink), and 'Prosperity' (white, flushed pink) are desirable.

NOISETTE CLIMBERS

These are not for northern gardeners but are the pride of the South. 'Maréchal Niel' is perhaps the most beautiful climber in the world (unless that title belongs to 'Mermaid,' another southern exclusive). Great billows of fragrant double golden flowers, borne all summer long, smother the entire plant.

'Mme. Alfred Carrière' is also a Noisette, but survives as far north as New York City. Flowers are almost as wonderful as those of 'Maréchal Niel,' but pure white. Where hardy, this is *the* white climber.

LARGE-FLOWERED ONCE-BLOOMING HARDY CLIMBERS

These are of mixed ancestry, but all are large in size and usually flower only once a year.

'DOUBLOONS.' Although once-flowering, the blooming season is so long that it more than pays its way. Deep golden yellow, fragrant flowers.

'DR. VAN FLEET.' This delightful pale flesh-pink climber has been outdated by its everblooming sport, 'New Dawn.'

'MARY WALLACE.' This husky pink climber is still catalogued, but its season is too short to justify garden space today.

'MRS. ARTHUR CURTISS JAMES' (Golden Climber). Must be trained horizontally or it will not bloom for several years. Flowers are golden yellow, semi-double, and fragrant.

'PAUL'S SCARLET CLIMBER.' Of historic interest only it has been superseded by its everblooming sport, 'Blaze.'

'SILVER MOON.' This has been called a 'Yankee Mermaid.' Although not as fine a rose as that magnificent tender climber, it does give the same effect by moonlight. A rampant grower: allow it plenty of room. Slightly fragrant.

'THOR.' A husky grower that can cover a 30-foot stretch of fence with masses of double intensely fragrant, blood-red flowers in June and early July. This is an ideal rose where time does not permit much care; practically grows itself.

LARGE-FLOWERED REPEAT-BLOOMERS
(not including Climbing Hybrid Teas)

These large-flowering hardy climbers with their habit of blooming off and on during the summer and early fall have made most of the older once-flowering varieties obsolete.

'BLAZE.' Without question, the most popular climber in America today. Slightly fragrant, fire-engine red flowers borne in great masses on tall-growing climber in late June, with intermittent bloom throughout the summer and early fall, account for its popularity.

'BLOSSOMTIME.' Perhaps the only climber in this class that comes close to being everblooming. Flowers are of Hybrid Tea quality, very fragrant, and two-toned — salmon-pink with a light cerise reverse. Not very tall-growing, but lovely on a fence.

'DON JUAN.' Five-inch, fragrant, deep velvety red flowers on a healthy plant.

'DREAM GIRL.' An excellent repeat bloomer in coral, apricot, and salmon tones. Fragrant.

'DR. J. H. NICOLAS.' A slow starter but once it comes into bloom, it produces enormous deep rose-pink, fragrant flowers on long single stems. One of the best climbers for cutting.

'GOLDEN SHOWERS.' The first hardy repeat-bloomer among the large-flowered climbers. Beautiful long yellow buds make this an outstanding cut-flower variety. Not too rampant a grower. Fragrant.

'INSPIRATION.' Perhaps the best of the repeat-blooming pure pinks. Semi-double, very fragrant flowers that keep opening all summer and early fall.

'NEW DAWN.' A delicate shell-pink, fragrant climber. Strong grower. The everblooming version of 'Dr. Van Fleet.'

'TEMPTATION.' A changeable rose of interesting form. Colors range from medium pink to a bright carmine red. Flowers are fragrant. A tall grower.

'WHITE DAWN.' The pure white flowers are like gardenias. They are borne in great profusion. Not a rampant grower. It can be used as a groundcover.

MERMAID

This is a rose in a class by itself. It is a hybrid of *Rosa bracteata*, from which it inherits tremendous vigor, beautiful glossy dark green foliage and tenderness to cold. A single plant will cover a 30-foot stretch of fence. The creamy yellow flowers are enormous and are never absent from the plant during the growing season. Unfortunately, it is not reliably hardy north of the Ohio River and is often killed a bit south of that line.

CLIMBING HYBRID TEAS

Once considered exclusive to the Gulf Coast, California, and similar mild climates, Climbing Hybrid Teas are venturing farther and farther north each year. One magnificent specimen of Climbing 'Peace' has survived north of New York City for a decade.

However, they are a poor risk as outdoor plants north of the Alabama-Tennessee line. North of this area they are best handled in large tubs and moved to a sun-heated pit or bulb-storage cellar in winter.

No rose plant in the world is more striking than a well-grown Climbing Hybrid Tea in full bloom. It incorporates the beauty of the bush form but spreads that beauty over an area of many square feet at eye level and above, where it can really be seen. Since the varieties match those of the bush roses of the same name, no attempt is made to describe them here.

Those fortunate enough to live in regions of little or no frost can grow an even more exotic climber, the true Climbing Tea Rose, One of these, 'Gloire de Dijon,' is somewhat hardier and has survived in Philadelphia with protection. It is a strong, hardy climber which blooms constantly, producing its buff-pink, orange-shaded flowers in great masses. It is intensely fragrant.

BUSH AND SHRUB ROSES

These are roses for the man who has little time to spend dusting, spraying, and pruning. They thrive with minimum care.

Rosa alba. By many considered "the rose," having been grown for centuries. One of the roses used to produce attar of rose for the perfume trade. Grows 4 to 5 feet high; flowers usually double, white, 3 inches across and intensely fragrant.

Rosa centifolia (Cabbage Rose). Flowers usually pink, fragrant and 3 inches across. Four to 6 feet tall. Suckers freely. The old-fashioned Moss Rose is a variety.

Rosa damascena (Damask Rose). Another source of attar of rose. Intensely fragrant. Flowers pink or red. Bush 5 to 7 feet tall. An interesting variety is 'York and Lancaster,' symbol of the War of the Roses.

Rosa eglanteria. The Sweet Brier of English song and poetry. A bushy shrub 5 to 7 feet tall with foliage that is strongly aromatic in damp weather. Flowers not too conspicuous.

Rosa foetida (Austrian Brier). One of the few yellow roses. A vigorous shrub 7 to 10 feet tall with numerous spines. Flowers deep yellow with an unpleasant scent. 'Austrian Copper' has orange-scarlet flowers. 'Persian Yellow' is a double form.

Rosa gallica. The Provence or French Rose. Plant 3 to 4 feet tall. Suckers badly. Flowers a delightful pink.

Rosa hugonis. Widely planted, but subject to "oriental die-back," a disease which is disfiguring and makes this rose less desirable.

Rosa rugosa. Perhaps the toughest and easiest to grow of the shrub roses. Four to 8 feet tall, thorny. Makes a good barrier hedge. Flowers vary from white to deep red. Fruits of the rugosa rose have been waterborne along much of the New England coast and sprouted wherever they came ashore. From these volunteers, thickets an acre or more in extent have arisen and survive without care. At one time there were more than 30 rugosa varieties in American commerce, but many have been lost. Those that remain are all easy-care shrubs.

ROSES FOR HEDGES

The use of some strong-growing variety or species of rose for hedge purposes is a welcome change from the overplanted privet and barberry. The choice is wide. By proper selection of variety, hedges from 12 inches up to 8 feet can be grown anywhere. These can meet the old farmers' requirements of "pig tight, bull strong, and horse high."

Where cost is not a factor, the Grandifloras are an excellent choice. Not only do they produce a strong, vigorous hedge, but are superior in quality of bloom.

For a wicked barrier hedge which cannot be broken down and will be tight enough to turn cats and dogs, plant the climbing rose 'New Dawn' or 'Blaze' 12 inches apart. Allow the canes to grow upright to a height of 6 feet, then bend them to the ground and bury the tips. These will root, forming an impenetrable barrier against any form of life much larger than a mouse.

For low hedges, the Polyanthas are ideal. The Hybrid Teas are not too good for hedges because they need regular spraying and pruning. Hybrid Perpetuals that form tall bushes are better, but need to be set on 12-inch centers to make a hedge without gaps.

TREE ROSES

These are plants which have a stem of a species which makes strong upright growth on its own roots. When the stems reach a height of 4 or 5 feet, buds are inserted near the top. When these have "taken," the top is cut off and the buds form a new top.

Three different understocks are commonly used. For the North, strong rugosa stems of a special variety from Holland are used. Besides being hardier than other understocks, rugosa produces stems that are flexible enough to be bent over and covered for winter protection. Tree roses are particularly susceptible to winter injury because of their exposed position. Also a beetle is likely to girdle rugosa stems. This species suckers badly, so these must be watched for and removed before they weaken the budded plant.

For the South, a much better root and stem stock is IXL from California. It is killed by temperatures that drop lower than 5° above zero. For intermediate climates, such as Long Island and Washington, D.C., *Rosa multiflora*, trained to a single stem, can be used.

There is little use recommending varieties: tree roses are so scarce that the buyer must take what is available or go without. Victorian gardeners grew a form of tree rose that was sensationally beautiful — the Weeping Standard. These were produced by growing an unusually tall cane of *Rosa rugosa*, perhaps 7 to 8 feet high. Four buds from a climber (usually a Noisette) were inserted near the top of the cane. As soon as these had "taken," the rugosa top was cut away, leaving a head made up of long weeping canes. When these reached maturity and bloomed, the effect was that of a fountain of roses. Occasionally these Weeping Standards can be found listed in specialists' catalogs. They are well worth purchasing. A pair makes a spectacular gateway for a rose garden.

MINIATURE ROSES

Widely proclaimed as house plants, these really belong outdoors. They are hardier than Hybrid Teas and can be used for edgings or low plantings almost anywhere. Under conditions of severe exposure, their low stature makes winter protection easy.

For the miniature-minded gardener who wants to lay out a complete garden with these 6-inch specimens, miniature tree roses and climbers as well as bush forms are now available. Incidentally, the dwarf Alberta spruce, which can be had 5 to 6 inches tall in perfect conical form, with growth less than a quarter of an inch a year, is the perfect evergreen for landscaping these gardens.

11

House Plants: Winter Solace for Gardeners

House plants tide the devoted gardener over the long weeks that intervene between the first killing frost and the flowering of the winter aconites and snowdrops in the spring. The plants that we shelter indoors, originally wildlings, must now live under artificial conditions of light, heat, moisture, food, and air. If they are to thrive, these elements must be balanced carefully.

CONDITIONS REQUIRED BY HOUSE PLANTS

Light

Most often the limiting factor is light. Few rooms have enough daylight to balance the amount of heat to which house plants are subjected. But today, with the scientific control of light an established fact, there is promise, perhaps within the next decade, of complete success in bringing house plants into flower almost at will.

Meanwhile, except for those that do best in shade (principally kinds grown for their foliage), plants grown indoors over winter should be given the greatest possible amount of light. (African violets are an exception. See the special section on them later in this chapter.)

The exact light needs of most species have never been worked out scientifically. The data following come from various sources. Plants are amazingly accommodating in their ability to adjust to quite wide variations in light intensity. The limits given below are based on the plant's being grown at proper temperature and under good conditions of humidity and nutrition. When a plant is being grown at the lowest tolerable limit of light intensity, its food, temperature, and water should be reduced accordingly.

HIGH: Either in direct sunlight or bright, unshaded daylight.

Preference: 5,000 to 8,000 foot-candles for normal summer day. Best to supplement shorter winter day with electric light as described in Chapter 12.

Tolerance: 1,000 to 2,000 foot-candles for a 12-hour day.

MEDIUM: Lightly shaded environment. To test intensity, pass hand over plant. Shadow of hand should be clearly visible, but its outline slightly fuzzy.

Preference: 1,000 to 4,000 foot-candles for normal day.

Tolerance: 500 to 1,000 foot-candles for 12-hour day.

LOW: No direct sunlight. Shadow of hand passed over plants should be barely visible. It should be stressed that these plants do not necessarily *require* such low light intensities, but will *tolerate* them. All will do well at medium intensities.

HIGH	MEDIUM	LOW
Aloë variegata	*Aglaonema simplex*	*Aglaonema simplex*
Cissus quadrangularis	*Begonia rex-cultorum*	*Asplenium nidus*
Codiaeum variegatum	*Caladium bicolor*	*Ferns,* various kinds
Crassula arborescens	*Cissus antarctica*	*Ficus elastica decora*
Euphorbia, various species	*C. erosa*	*F. macrophylla*
Ficus exotica	*C. rhombifolia*	*F. pumila*
F. pandurata	*Dieffenbachia,* various species	*Hedera helix*
Gynura aurantiaca	*Dracaena,* various species	
Hedera helix	*Ficus,* various species	
Hoya carnosa	*Hedera helix*	
Kalanchoë blossfeldiana	*Ligularia kaempferi*	
Pelargonium hortorum	*Pandanus veitchi*	
Rhoeo discolor	*Peperomia,* various species	
Sansevieria, various species	*Philodendron,* various species	
Schefflera, various species	*Rhoeo discolor*	
	Schefflera, various species	
	Scindapsus aureus	
	Syngonium, various species	

Chapter 12 on growing plants under artificial lights will provide further guidance on the needs of plants under indoor conditions.

Temperature

House plants must usually live in temperatures suited to people. Most of them would be better off at 58° to 65°. This is true even of species that flourish outside when temperatures range toward 75° or more. The difference is due to the reduced light intensity in houses.

Actually, when at their lowest level of growth, say from mid-November to mid-January, many plants will tolerate readings of about 42° for fairly long periods. Tropical species are, of course, an exception to these low readings. To prevent their damage, a radiant-type electric heater attached to a thermostat will provide heat if temperatures drop suddenly.

Whenever possible, a separate plant room, such as a sun porch, should be provided where temperatures can be kept much lower than required for human comfort. When the room is being used, the heat can be raised temporarily. Plants can stand a brief spell at higher readings without harm.

Humidity

During winter, the air in most houses, even with humidification, seldom goes above 30 per cent relative humidity. Twenty per cent is common. This means that air around house plants is actually drier than that over the Sahara Desert where humidity readings are about 35 per cent. Think of how this might affect a plant which came originally from a tropical rain forest, or a maritime climate where the average humidity may be 80 to 90 per cent.

This is one of the reasons why heat-tolerant succulents and cacti, with their thick, specialized epidermis to protect them against water loss, do so well as house plants — even though they may get less light than they prefer.

Various devices have been used to increase humidity around house plants. Most central air-heating systems have humidifiers, but these do not raise the readings high enough to do much good. Individual units which can be placed near the plants are better, but expensive.

One of the simplest ways to add moisture to air is to pack ground sphagnum moss or peatmoss around the base of the plant and keep this slightly moist at all times. While fine for a plant or two, the effect is limited. A better method is to fill a flat pan (about 3 inches deep) to within an inch of the top with clean pebbles. If this is placed over a radiator and water is added, an amazing amount of moisture will go into the air. Insulation, such as two sheets of cement-asbestos board, will be needed between the pan and radiator if plants are to stand on the pebbles. Even then, probably only tropical species will thrive.

Similar pans can be placed on window sills, with water just covering the pebbles. Pots set on the pebbles will be to some extent self-watering.

Watering

Provision of water is related to humidity control. For instance, plants will do better if, once a week or so they are set in the bathtub and sprayed with a fine spray to wash the foliage. Since plants can absorb water through their leaves, these must be kept clean. In many instances, proper watering determines whether or not a plant will thrive or fail. It is hard to say whether more plants are killed by drowning or by desiccation. Some enthusiasts water heavily every day, saturating the soil so that all air is driven out. Others may allow plants to go for days or weeks without watering.

For the inexperienced, there are moisture meters that can be stuck into the soil to indicate whether it is dry, moist, or saturated. However, most house-plant growers prefer to feel the soil and judge that way. Except for succulents, soil should be kept constantly moist but never wet. Succulent plants, including cacti, should be watered well, then allowed to dry out before being watered again.

With most types of plant-growing containers, soil should be no higher than about ¾ inch below the rim. To determine the amount of water needed, fill this space and leave the pot alone until the water is absorbed. Then knock out the plant, and note how far down the moisture has penetrated. This will be a guide for future watering: enough water should be applied to moisten all the soil in the pot without leaving any excess. This depth will vary somewhat. During bright sunny weather, even in winter, pots lose moisture more rapidly than when skies are overcast. There will be a variation, too, between summer and winter. When the heat is on, the dry air takes out more water.

It may seem fussy to advise chemical analysis of water used on house plants, but even when dissolved chemicals are present in only a few parts per million, they can accumulate at a relatively rapid rate. Some water softeners also have a damaging effect. However, those that work on the ion-exchange principle (the kind sold for softening water for use in steam-electric irons) improve the water for plants. When only a few plants are grown, these may be convenient. Otherwise, it will pay to save rain water if ground water or municipal supplies are high in mineral content. Waters with a high mineral analysis are particularly bad when porous clay pots are used. They soak through the pot, evaporate, and leave salts behind. Glazed pots are then more practical because they take less water and do not allow salts to accumulate.

Air

Fresh air is quite as important to plants as to people. It should circulate freely in the room, without cold drafts striking the foliage. When a window must be opened in a small plant room, a thin sheet of polyethylene plastic on a frame that fits the window frame exactly will allow air to filter through so gently that the room will be freshened without the temperature dropping abruptly. Even so, opened windows may have to be dispensed with in zero weather.

The cooking and heating facilities of a house can often affect plants adversely.

Manufactured gas that leaks is particularly bad for plants and can quickly kill them. Natural gas, while nothing to fool with, does not affect them as much. To check whether your heating plant, gas stove, or hot water heater is leaking, grow a few tomato seedlings in the room. If any gas is leaking, they will quickly drop their leaves.

THE CULTURE OF HOUSE PLANTS

Soil

Even commercial growers have difficulty in getting good soil for house plants. For a large number of plants, it will pay to build your own supply. An ideal base material is the trimmings from lawn edging piled up and composted. Or use good sifted compost, adding a pound of good mixed complete fertilizer to every bushel of soil. If these materials are not available, prepare the following mixture: One bushel of good garden loam, half a bushel of leafmold or peatmoss, and one and a half pounds of a good mixed fertilizer.

If the soil seems heavy and water does not run through freely, add a peck or so of vermiculite or sand. Otherwise, buy one of the packaged mixes, which are available in bags of several sizes, also in wholesale lots. It will serve you well, though at somewhat greater expense than home-mixed soil.

Fertilizers

Most house plants need feeding only three or four times a year. The recommendations on commercial packages are often much in excess of what is needed, largely because tests using them were run in greenhouses, under very strong light. With moderate light, heavy feeding will cause trouble. Try at half the rates recommended. If growth seems long and weak, reduce the temperature and increase the light instead of adding more fertilizer. Because of the small amounts needed, the cost of fertilizers is relatively unimportant. Liquid plant foods are popular and convenient to use.

House plants can be used efficiently in an infinite number of ways — in cozy nooks or on spacious terraces, in period rooms or simply as colorful decorative features in a sunny expanse of window.

Potting

When a plant from the garden is to be potted and brought indoors, dig it with as much soil clinging to the roots as possible. Select a pot that will take this ball of soil. Fill in around the roots with the potting soil already recommended; water well and set in a light (but shaded) spot until the plant recovers from transplanting.

Repotting about every second year is sufficient for most house plants, but they should be examined yearly. To do this, hold the stem between two fingers, invert the pot, and tap lightly with the rim against a table or bench. The entire ball of earth with its root mass will come out of the pot. If the outside of this ball is only spotted with white roots, just beginning to mat, the plant can probably go another six months without repotting. But if the entire surface is a thick mass of white hair roots, the time for repotting has come. Wash off as much of the old soil as possible and repot one size larger: that is, from a 4-inch pot to a 5-inch, or from a 5-inch to a 6-inch.

Summer Care

Many house plants could not survive without a rest outdoors in summer. Released from artificial conditions, they build up vigor and prepare for another spell of adversity.

An ideal summer haven is under a tree that has deep roots and thin foliage. An oak or honey locust is excellent. The pots can be plunged into the soil or sit in a frame about as deep as the largest pot is tall. (Four boards nailed together will serve.) If pots are to be plunged, it pays to dig out to a depth of several inches and lay down a bed of well-washed steam cinders, gravel, or vermiculite.

Set shade-loving plants on the north side of the tree. Plunge the pots into soil up to their rims. If a frame is used, fill the space around the pots with soil, peatmoss, a mixture of sand and peatmoss, or with vermiculite.

Usually, the plants will need regular watering unless the summer is rainy. Plants in pots dry out more than those in the border. Keep them sprayed for insect control. Ever so often, give each pot a twist to keep the plant from rooting through the drainage hole into the soil. When night temperatures threaten to drop below 50°, bring the plants back into the house.

STARTING NEW HOUSE PLANTS

Midsummer is the time to consider next year's house plants. Make new cuttings of geraniums, impatiens, heliotrope, and other tender garden specimens. About mid-August sow seeds of 'Heavenly Blue' morning-glory in 4-inch pots for vines that will often bloom all winter indoors.

Spring-Flowering Bulbs as House Plants

About the easiest of all plants for the beginner are the so-called Dutch bulbs — tulips, hyacinths, narcissus, and crocus. In these, the bulb contains the flower bud, laid down the spring before, ready to bloom when given the proper conditions. By proper selection of species and varieties, a succession of bloom can be enjoyed from Christmas until the earliest tulips flower out of doors.

When buying bulbs for forcing, a good rule is to buy the largest available size. So few bulbs are needed that cost is not usually a factor.

Pots for Bulbs

The best container for bulbs to be forced is an old-fashioned red clay pot of the type known as a bulb pan. This is quite low and usually rimless in the smaller sizes. Put a crock or piece of broken pot over the hole, and about an inch of soil, and the pan is ready for planting. Since the bulbs are considered expendable, they need little or no room for root growth and can be planted practically touching. While some growers leave the tips of the bulbs exposed, it is better practice to cover them with about half an inch of soil.

Potted bulbs may be kept out of doors to root and brought into a 60° temperature on the dates indicated on the list. A coldframe is ideal, but an orange crate or similar wooden box can be used. Set the pots in the box on a thin bed of peat or sand, then fill the box to the top with the same material. As freezing weather approaches, throw straw or other protection around the box. When forcing time comes, the pots are brought inside. If a succession of flowering bulbs is wanted in the house, several boxes (or groups of pots) may be used, each for a separate forcing date.

Some bulbs can be forced earlier than others. The list below shows the earliest dates on which various tulips, narcissus, and hyacinths are best brought into a 50° temperature for forcing into bloom. It is assumed that bulbs have been planted as soon as available in fall and held under cool conditions.

SINGLE EARLY TULIPS

'Brilliant Star'	Dec. 10	'Olympiade'	Jan. 25
'Couleur Cardinal'	Jan. 15	'Prince of Austria'	Jan. 5
'General de Wet'	Jan. 5	'Sunburst'	Jan. 28
'Ibis'	Jan. 1	'White Hawk'	Jan. 1

'Paperwhites' are the easiest of all bulbs to grow indoors. Just plant them in pebbles (no soil), add water up to bases of bulbs, and set in cool, light window. The bulbs will bloom in about 6 weeks.

Hyacinths can be forced for early blooms. Set bulbs singly in 4" pots. Water well, then slip pot into plastic bag, leaving 6" of empty bag at top for shoot to grow. Set in cool, dark basement and keep soil moist. Remove bag and bring into warmth and light when stalk is about 6" high.

Tulips by the pot: In autumn, put 4 or 5 large bulbs in pot 8" wide. Add soil to cover bulb tips. Press soil down well and water. Cover with upturned empty pots and bury in outdoor soil frame until mid-January. When shoots are 3" to 4" high, bring into cool, dim room until buds grow well above leaves.

DOUBLE EARLY TULIPS

'Electra'	Jan. 15	'Peach Blossom'	Jan. 15
'Mr. van der Hoef'	Jan. 15	'Snowball'	Jan. 15
'Orange Nassau'	Jan. 15		

TRIUMPHS

'Alberio'	Jan. 10	'Elmus'	Jan. 15
'Crater'	Jan. 15	'Korneforus'	Jan. 15
'Elizabeth Evers'	Jan. 20	'Telescopium'	Feb. 1

DARWINS

'All Bright'	Jan. 15	'Princess Elizabeth'	Jan. 25
'Bartigon'	Jan. 15	'Prunus'	Jan. 15
'Campfire'	Jan. 15	'Red Pitt'	Jan. 5
'Cordell Hull'	Jan. 15	'Rose Copland'	Dec. 25
'Niphetos'	Jan. 15	'William Copland'	Dec. 25
'Philip Snowden'	Jan. 15	'William Pitt'	Jan. 5
'Pride of Zwanenburg'	Jan. 15		

COTTAGE TULIPS

'Albino'	Jan. 15	'Golden Harvest'	Jan. 10
'Carrara'	Jan. 15	'Mothers Day'	Jan. 25

NARCISSUS

'Carlton'	Jan. 10	'Laurens Koster'	Jan. 15
'Golden Harvest'	Jan. 1	'Rembrandt'	Jan. 10
'Imperator'	Feb. 15	'Scarlet Elegance'	Jan. 15
'King Alfred'	Jan. 15		

HYACINTHS

'Lady Derby'	Jan. 10	'Bismarck'	Jan. 5
'La Victoire'	Jan. 5	'Grand Maître'	Jan. 15
'Marconi'	Jan. 25	'King of Blues'	Jan. 25
'Pink Pearl'	Jan. 5	'Myosotis'	Jan. 10
'Queen of Pinks'	Jan. 25	'L'Innocence'	Jan. 10

Where controlled temperatures are available, the bulbs can be planted as soon as received, held at 48° in a dark cellar until the shoots are 2 to 3 inches above the pot rim, then brought into a 60° temperature and light. If this culture is followed, they are usually ready for forcing about one month ahead of the above schedule. Hyacinths, too, can be speeded up by being held at 50° and then brought in when the shoots are 4 inches above the pot.

There are two exceptions to the rule that a cool rooting period is necessary; these are the Triumph tulip varieties 'Nivea' and 'Ulmus.' If kept in a temperature of 48° for three weeks, then brought into a 60° light room, they will flower without further treatment.

SPECIAL HYACINTHS

Formerly, French Roman hyacinths were sold in quantity for early forcing, but they produced loose, weak spikes. Their place has been taken by varieties which have undergone a secret process in Holland whereby the bulbs are treated under controlled temperatures to speed up flowering. If these are planted as soon as received and kept at a temperature below 50° until December 1, they can be flowered very early. The variety 'Gertrude,' a clear pink, will usually flower for Christmas, other varieties soon after New Year's day.

MINOR BULBS

Some of the most delightful of all flowering plants are small bulbs such as *Muscari armeniacum, Iris reticulata*, and Dutch crocus. These can be planted, several to a 5-inch bulb pan, and stored outside to root along with the tulips. The only difference in handling is that they should be kept much cooler, preferably not over 45 to 48°. *Iris reticulata* is particularly desirable because of its rich violet fragrance.

OTHER BULBOUS HOUSE PLANTS

A number of other "bulbous" plants (most of which grow from tuberous roots) are well suited to indoor culture, though not to forcing. These include achimenes, amaryllis, tuberous begonias, fancy-leaved caladiums, calla lily, and gloxinia. For details, see the Plant Encyclopedia and Chapter 4.

CACTI AND OTHER SUCCULENTS

Of more than 2,000 species of cacti only a few of the readily available kinds are listed here. Because of its special uses and culture, the Christmas cactus is described later in this chapter. Most cacti require an alkaline soil, gritty, and well drained. To supply the lime, a little pounded plaster, ground limestone, or crushed eggshells can be added to a mixture of one part loam, three parts sand, and one part humus. Water cacti only enough to keep the stems from shriveling, at least in winter when growth practically stands still. The water should run through the pot freely. Keep the plants in full sun unless signs of sun burning show as browning or yellowing of the side toward the sun.

SMALLER CACTI (TO 12 INCHES TALL)

Ariocarpus retusus (Seven Sisters or Chaute). Flat, 4 to 7 inches wide, pink flowers.

Astrophytum asterias (Sand-dollar). Flat, about 3 inches across, ribbed body, yellow flowers.

Astrophytum myriostigma (Bishop's Hood). Striking yellow flowers, plants 6 inches across but low.

Chamaecereus silvestri (Peanut Cactus). Stems look like clusters of peanuts, orange-scarlet flowers.

Coryphantha robustispina (Devil's Pincushion). Name suggests shape. 2 to 4 inches across.

Echinocereus, various species. Plants 6 to 8 inches tall with long flowers in pink, yellow, and purple.

Echinopsis eyriesi (Easter-lily Cactus). Small globular plant with large white flowers.

Espostoa lanata (Sheep-wool Cactus). Even small plants are woolly.

Gymnocalycium schickendantzi (Pink Chin Cactus). Four-inch plant with pink flowers 2 inches long.

Lophophora williamsi (Peyote). The sacred mushroom of South American religious rites. Not impressive, but interesting because of this association. Flattened plants 3 inches across.

Mammillaria species. Many of the most interesting house-happy cacti are in this group, including Bird's Nest, Powder Puff, Thimble, and Golden Stars. Catalogs of cactus specialists will list many delightful varieties. There are over 200 species.

Opuntia microdasys (Rabbit-ears). This is the one cactus in the opuntia group that is small enough for indoors.

LARGER CACTI

Many cactus plants are so large that a good-sized greenhouse is needed to grow them. However, a number can be grown in 5- to 6-inch pots though they will not flower unless allowed to grow to maturity, when most of them are too large for the house.

Aporocactus flagelliformis (Rat-tail Cactus). The long stems are more like sausages than rat tails, about half an inch in diameter, and hairy. Flowers bright red.

Cephalocereus senilis (Old Man Cactus). Hoary even in youth, this may be 25 to 30 feet tall at maturity. Slow growing, however.

Echinocactus grusoni (Golden Barrel Cactus). Interesting for its beautiful clear yellow spines and red-and-yellow flowers. ˈ

Hylocereus undatus (Night-blooming Cereus). Too gawky to justify growing unless to amaze friends on the rare occasions when it flowers indoors.

Opuntia elata (Orange Tuna Cactus). Its flat oval stems are what most people think of as typical of cacti.

Tephrocactus glomeratus (Paper Spine Opuntia). Like the above, with true cactus-form flattened stems.

SUCCULENTS OTHER THAN CACTI

These require about the same culture as the cacti, except that they will tolerate somewhat more moisture.

Agave (Century Plant). Avoid agaves as house plants. They are likely to outgrow the room.

Aloë variegata. One of the most commonly grown of all succulents: striking green-and-white variegated leaves.

Crassula argentea (Jade Plant). Thick, fat leaves and a plant that seems to tolerate any abuse make this the most popular of all succulents.

Echeveria, various species (Hen-and-chickens). Rosette-forming plants that produce small colonies around the mother plant. Many beautifully colored variations within this genus, some with interesting, metallic high lights.

Cheiridopsis candidissima (Cigarette Plant). Paired ash-colored leaves 4 inches long with 3-inch pedicels for pale flesh-colored flowers.

Faucaria tigrina (Tiger's Jaw). Spotted jaw-shaped 2-inch leaves with curved teeth; bright yellow flowers 1 inch across.

Gasteria acinacifolia (Ox-tongue Plant). Similar to *Aloë variegata*, but with tongue-shaped leaves 1 foot long.

Haworthia cymbiformis (Cushion Aloe). A "push-down" version of the aloe, but with transparent "windows" in the tips of the leaves.

Kalanchoë blossfeldiana (Fire Plant). Perhaps the most commonly available succulent, but not too interesting. The red of its flowers is one of the harshest colors in nature.

Lithops species (Stone Faces). Odd little plants, from 1 to 3 inches across, that look exactly like pebbles when not in flower. Grow half-buried in sand to reduce evaporation. Transparent windows in the leaves admit light to the inner leaf cells.

Pleiospilos bolusi (Living Rock). Like the preceding, but larger. This species is a dull rusty orange with bright yellow flowers.

Sedum species. These form colonies like echeverias, but have fat banana-shaped leaves.

Sempervivum species. These rosette-forming hardy plants can be carried in a coldframe until after New Year's Day, then brought into the house for unusual foliage color display.

Stapelia species (Carrion Flower). The flowers are malodorous, but appear in summer when the plants are outdoors. They are striking in color, mottled and barred in vivid contrasts. Star-shaped, they give this genus the alternate common name of starfish flower.

If the collection is accessible to children or careless adults, avoid the euphorbias. They have wicked thorns, and exude a poisonous sap which can cause a severe dermatitis. Two of the most commonly grown are crown-of-thorns (*E. splendens*) and Medusa's head (*E. caput-medusae*).

FOLIAGE PLANTS

Indoor foliage plants are now being specified in architect's plans for monumental public buildings as well as for large elaborate residences. As a result of this tremendous interest, new and unusual species are being introduced so frequently that most of the existing lists are obsolete. Where a few years ago we had two species of philodendron, today it is a poor list that does not catalog twenty. Old-time favorites such as the cast-iron plant (aspidistra) and corn plant (pandanus) are being revived because of their ability to tolerate abuse and to survive under relatively low light intensities.

The one weakness of foliage plants is a monotony of color, even when variegated species are used. The number with leaves of colors other than green, white, or cream is quite limited.

FOLIAGE PLANTS GENERALLY AVAILABLE

Aglaonema simplex,
    Chinese Evergreen
Asparagus plumosus,
    Fern Asparagus
A. sprengeri, Emerald Feather
Aspidistra elatior, Cast-iron Plant
Codiaeum variegatum, Croton
Dieffenbachia, various species,
    Dumb Cane

Dracaena, various species,
    Dragon Plant
Fatshedera lizei, Fatshedera
Fittonia verschaffelti, Fittonia
Gynura aurantiaca, Velvet Plant
Ligularia kaempferi, Leopard Plant
Ligustrum lucidum, Glossy Privet
Liriope muscari, Blue Lily-turf

Livistona chinensis,
    Fountain Palm
Maranta leuconeura,
    Brazilian Arrowroot
Nephthytis afzeli,
    African Arrowhead
Ophiopogon jaburan, Lily-turf
Pandanus veitchi, Corn Plant
Peperomia obtusifolia,
    Watermelon-begonia
Phoenix roebelini, Baby Palm

Pilea microphylla, Artillery Plant
Pittosporum tobira,
    Japanese Pittosporum
Rhektophyllum mirabile,
    Rhektophyllum
Rhoeo discolor, Oyster Plant
Schefflera actinophylla,
    Queensland Umbrella Tree
Tradescantia fluminensis,
    Wandering Jew

PLANTS THAT WILL FLOWER INDOORS

If the light requirements can be met, and if careful attention is given to temperature, moisture, and air, as well as to potting soil and fertilizer, as described at the opening of this chapter, a number of plants can be brought into bloom in the house. The basic directions for culture will serve for most of these. But two of the most popular ones — the Christmas cactus and the African violet — require somewhat special treatments. Detailed information for these is therefore being provided. It follows the list immediately below, which names some of the most satisfactory of flowering plants for indoor culture.

Abutilon hybridum,
    Flowering Maple
Anthurium scherzerianum,
    Flamingo Flower
Ardisia crispa, Coralberry
Astilbe hybrids, Astilbe
Begonia feasti, Beefsteak Begonia
B. heracleifolia, Star Begonia
B. metallica, Bronze-leaf Begonia
B. rex-cultorum, Rex Begonia
Beloperone guttata, Shrimp Plant
Billbergia nutans, Air Plant
Camellia japonica, Camellia
Campanula isophylla,
    Star of Bethlehem
Chrysanthemum hortorum,
    Greenhouse Chrysanthemum

Cyclamen persicum, Alpine Violet
Episcia coccinea, Flame Violet
Ervatamia coronaria,
    Fleur d'Amour
Fuchsia hybrida,
    Florist's Fuchsia
Gardenia veitchi,
    Greenhouse Gardenia
Heliotropium arborescens,
    Heliotrope
Impatiens holsti, Patience Plant
Ipomoea purpurea, Morning-glory
Lantana camara, Lantana
Neomarica gracilis, Apostle Plant
Pelargonium domesticum,
    Lady Washington Geranium
P. hortorum, Common Geranium

Vines make fascinating house plants. Passion flower, below, can be started from cuttings rooted in water in fall.

Exotic wax plant demands plenty of sun. It is best grown from nursery plants as cuttings may be slow to bloom.

Hibiscus plants grow fast and bloom profusely if given lots of water and sun.

Spathiphyllum blooms from spring to September. It likes humidity.

Primula malacoides, Fairy Primrose
P. obconica, Hairy Primrose
P. sinensis, Chinese Primrose

Rhododendron varieties, Azaleas
Rosa chinensis, Fairy Rose
Senecio cruentus, Florist's Cineraria

TRAILING VINES, CLIMBERS, AND HANGING BASKET PLANTS

Campanula isophylla,
    Star of Bethlehem
Ceropegia woodi, Hearts-on-strings
Cissus quadrangularis, Grape Ivy
Cyanotis somaliensis, Pussy-ears
Cymbalaria muralis, Kenilworth Ivy
Ficus pumila, Creeping Fig
Hedera helix, English Ivy
Hoya carnosa, Wax Plant
Ipomoea purpurea, Morning-glory
Lantana montevidensis,
    Trailing Lantana

Philodendron, various species,
    Philodendron
Quamoclit pennata, Cypress Vine
Saxifraga sarmentosa,
    Strawberry Geranium
Scindapsus aureus, Ivy Arum
Senecio mikanioides, German Ivy
Thunbergia alata,
    Black-eyed Susan Vine

HOUSE PLANTS FROM SEED

The following plants can be grown from seed in a sunny window, if humidity is maintained and some artificial light is provided during the winter:

Abutilon hybridum,
    Flowering Maple
Antirrhinum majus, Snapdragon
Asparagus plumosus,
    Fern Asparagus
A. sprengeri, Emerald Feather
Begonia rex-cultorum, Rex Begonia
B. semperflorens,
    Fibrous-rooted Begonia
B. tuberhybrida, Tuberous Begonia
Calceolaria crenatiflora, Slipperwort

Calendula officinalis, Pot Marigold
Cuphea 'Firefly,' Cigar Flower
Episcia coccinea, Flame Violet
Exacum affine, German Violet
Kalanchoë blossfeldiana, Fire Plant
Mimosa pudica, Sensitive Plant
Saintpaulia ionantha, African Violet
Sinningia speciosa, Gloxinia

The following species can be grown from seed if sown in midsummer, in pots. The plants become fairly mature outdoors, and can be brought into the house for flowering. Put them in a very cool window (not over 50°).

Browallia speciosa, Sapphire Flower	*Myosotis sylvatica*
Ipomoea purpurea,	Wood Forget-me-not
'Heavenly Blue' Morning-glory	*Petunia hybrida,* Petunia
Lobelia erinus, Edging Lobelia	*Tropaeolum majus,* Nasturtium

CULTURE OF CHRISTMAS CACTUS: ZYGOCACTUS TRUNCATUS

One of the most popular of all house plants because of its blooming season is the Christmas cactus. Not the least of its attractions is the extreme longevity of some specimens. Plants half a century old are not uncommon. However, the culture of this cactus does offer several problems which cannot be worked out exactly, partly because of the difficulty of accurately identifying any one plant. At least half a dozen similar species are involved. To complicate matters further, specimen plants are frequently grafted onto stems of opuntia or pereskia to raise the lax, flopping branches above the pot rim.

As a result of this confusion, some supposed Christmas cactus plants may start blooming at Thanksgiving, others wait until Easter. The following directions for culture are not guaranteed to overcome these problems, but should produce flowers close to Christmas day if the specimen is a true *Zygocactus truncatus.*

The potting soil used should be the same as for other cacti. Water should not be allowed to stand on the surface but should run through freely.

However, unlike other cacti, the Christmas cactus likes plenty of water when in active growth. The soil should never dry out, yet never be wet. In the summer, pots should be plunged outdoors in light, filtered shade, such as is found under a honey locust. The soil should be kept moist. If no such spot can be found, full sun is better than heavier shade.

Use a light dose of liquid house-plant fertilizer every three weeks during the summer. In fall, the plants need a spell of cool weather, above 42° but below 68°, to trigger the production of flower buds. This is a critical point in their growth. Yet since this is a tender plant, do not risk exposing it to frost. Bring it indoors when night temperatures begin to drop below 42°.

At this point, Christmas cacti should be kept in a shady window until about mid-October, when they should go as close as possible to the glass in a sunny window. During this period, they should be watered only enough to keep the stems from shriveling. When flower buds begin to form, water the plants more frequently and feed every three weeks with liquid fertilizer until they bloom. If a plant dries out at any time during this period, the buds may drop off. Exposure to drafts may also cause bud drop.

Reduce watering and feeding after the plant has flowered until it shows signs of making vegetative growth; then water it freely until it is set outside for the summer.

SUCCESS WITH AFRICAN VIOLETS

The African violet, oddly enough, is not a violet at all. It belongs to the tropical genus saintpaulia in the gesneriad family. Its native home is in the rain forests of Africa, where it grows in pockets of woodsy soil in limestone cliffs. The air around it is so moist that it practically "drinks" through its leaves. Rotting plant material and limestone dust make up about all the soil found in the pockets where it grows. The decaying organic matter neutralizes the lime, so that the soil is slightly acid.

Light is screened through a canopy of leaves, but because of the location of these rain forests near the equator, does not vary much from twelve hours a day throughout the entire year. This gives a clue to proper culture.

Culture

SOILS. Few garden soils are naturally adapted to growing African violets, but they can be modified without too much trouble. (Many strange and wonderful mixtures are recommended, but these are unnecessarily complicated and expensive.) Start with a good garden loam, and add two parts of well-rotted organic matter — manure, leafmold, peatmoss, compost, or dust from an old stump. To this, add one part of either sand or vermiculite.

When mixed, this soil should allow water to run through freely, yet be so spongy that the mixture is quite moist. If your blend "balls" or sticks together, add more sand or vermiculite. The pH reading should be between 6.5 and 6.9.

FERTILIZERS. African violets need very little plant food. One research worker kept a plant alive for an entire year in a sterile solution without adding a single nutrient. Although it deteriorated slightly, it revived immediately when given a very light dose of complete plant food. Most directions prescribe two to ten times as much fertilizer as is needed. A light feeding once a month with a liquid fertilizer solution should give the plants everything they need for normal growth.

LIGHT REQUIREMENTS. An African violet plant needs 12 hours of daylight to flower. That light should be strong enough to read fine print easily. Direct sunshine, however, should be avoided. In an east window, a single glass curtain should be hung between the plants and the window when the sun is bright. Two such layers are needed in a west window in summer, three in a south window.

To measure light intensity, run your hand across the plant at high noon. If the shadow is so faint as to be barely discernible, light intensity is too low. If the shadow is fuzzy and indistinct, the intensity is about right. If the outline of your hand can be seen sharply, light intensity is too high.

HOW BIG A POT? Unlike many plants, which like to be root-bound before they will flower, African violets prefer a loose root run. That is, the walls of the pot should never be lined with fine white hair roots when the plant is inverted and removed from the container. At the same time, too large a pot wastes soil. A rule of thumb is to use a pot which measures half the spread of the leaves.

Clay pots are still considered best, although plastic containers are often used. The so-called azalea pot, which is lower than a standard type, is best, since African violets are not deep-rooting. A crock, a piece of broken pot, should cover the drainage hole. Over this, place a small handful of sphagnum moss or osmunda fiber. The old plant, knocked out of its pot, is then set on the sphagnum moss so that the old soil reaches to about half an inch from the rim, and soil is filled in around the roots. A light pressure with the thumb is about all the firming the soil needs.

A useful device to use when repotting large old plants is to cut a notch about 5 inches square out of one side of an 8-inch board. When slipped under the leaves, this will allow you to invert the entire plant in knocking it out of its old container. Because of the brittleness of African violet leaves, such a device is almost essential to doing this job without breaking off much of the foliage.

LEAFSTALK ROT. If a plant keeps losing its lower leaves, look to see if the leafstalks are touching the rim of the pot. Clay pots are porous and allow water to rise to the rim, where it evaporates. Since soil water carries soluble salts with it, these are left behind on the rim. As the leafstalk droops and touches the pot, the salts kill a few cells at this point, permitting rot to enter.

This trouble can be avoided by dipping the rims of the pots in paraffin before the African violets are planted. If already planted, insert a thin layer of aluminum foil or plastic film between the leaves and rims.

WATERING. Again going back to its native home for hints of its needs, think of the plant as living in a dripping tropical rain forest steaming with moisture. Most city apartments are too dry.

Where a special room is not available (many fans keep their best plants in the bathroom), provision for moistening the air should be made. The best device is a flat pan filled with pebbles placed over a warm radiator. The pan is kept filled with water up to the bottom of the pots. If the house is heated by steam, put a layer of cement-asbestos board between the pan and the radiator. If it is still too hot, raise the pan slightly with strips of wood.

Many plants like to dry out between waterings, but not African violets;

they do best when the soil is constantly moist but never wringing wet.

LEAF SPOT. Beginners with African violets are often shocked to see the leaves turn gray and die off. This is usually caused by watering the plant from above with cold or cool water. In tropical rain forests, the air moisture is warmer than the leaves. Watering with a spray from above to wash off the leaves is good practice, but the water should be just slightly warmer than room temperature. Syringing sometimes helps open double-flowered varieties that "ball" and refuse to open properly.

Much has been written about the necessity for washing off the leaves so they can "breathe." Actually, the transpiration pores are located on the underside, and washing is for its cosmetic effect alone.

TEMPERATURES. Growth at temperatures as low as 65° is slower but healthy. The plants can survive temporarily at as low as 42°, but are injured or killed at readings below this point. Readings of about 75° to 88° during the day should be maximum. In air-conditioned rooms, care should be taken that the plants are not in the direct blast from cooling ducts or fans.

At temperatures above 80°, particular care should be given to humidity to avoid dehydration. As temperatures rise, the capacity of the air to hold moisture is increased, and water may be pulled out of the plant unless humidity is provided. In greenhouses where humidity can be maintained at saturation, African violets have withstood 100° without injury.

Drafts are definitely bad for African violets. If a room must be aired, the slower the change is made, the better.

Propagation

African violets are easy to propagate from leaves, though this is a slower process than with some other plants. Select leaves that are mature, but not past their prime, and dark green in color. Old leaves (lighter in color) make poor propagating stock.

The leafstalk should be about 1½ inches long. This will allow the first cutting to grow from a leaf, after which the stem can be cut to ¾ inch and the rest of the leaf used to produce another plant. It will take about 12 weeks for a long cutting to root. If only a single plant is wanted, use a ¾-inch stem, and a new plant will be produced in about 8 weeks.

Make your cutting at night and allow it to lie on the table overnight. This dries off the cut end and helps prevent rotting. Then dip the cut end in a rooting hormone (sold in most seed stores and garden centers) and insert it in sand or vermiculite.

ROOTING MEDIUM. The most commonly used rooting medium today is vermiculite, which holds moisture better than sand. It should be moist but not wringing wet. Either pots or flats can be used. Sometimes a single

African violets from leaf cuttings: *Remove a middle leaf by pressing to side (1). Cut stem diagonally, leaving it about 1½" long (2). Insert in 2¼" pot of vermiculite (3). Stand pot in water until vermiculite is moist.*

Plantlets (4) should be ready for potting in 4 or 5 months. Separate them gently by hand (5). Discard any that are too small. Pot plants in 2¼" pots, using teaspoon as trowel (6). Do not *press soil mix firm.*

Enthusiast's reward: a window filled with African violets.

cutting is inserted in a 2½-inch pot filled with vermiculite and grown to repotting stage in this.

If sand is used, it is usually mixed 50-50 with peatmoss to help hold moisture.

Inverting a thin plastic bag over the pot or flat will reduce the need for watering; often no additional moisture will have to be added until the cuttings have rooted. As long as the inside of the plastic steams slightly, the moisture supply is adequate.

Diseases and Insect Pests

LEAF INJURY. Brownish tan or parchment-colored patches on the leaves, a scorched look or other leaf blemishes are usually due either to too much sun or to cold water applied to the leaves.

GAS INJURY. Natural gas causes little injury, but where manufactured gas is used, a leak will cause the plant to sag suddenly without apparent cause. Coal gas can be especially devastating. Watch out, too, for fumes from coal-burning grates or stoves.

NEMATODES. These cause considerable damage. Baking potting soil for an hour at 300° should kill them. Infected plants are best discarded.

MEALYBUGS. These white cottony insects work furtively under the foliage and are usually well-established by the time they are discovered. They look like misplaced bits of cotton. Underneath the "cotton" is a flat scale-like pest. If only a few of these are found, touch them with a bit of cotton wrapped on a toothpick and dipped in rubbing alcohol. Badly infested plants are hardly worth fussing with, unless they are particularly valuable. Three or four inspections should be made within a week to see that no new mealybugs have appeared.

MITES. Although mites are among the worst enemies of African violets, they are practically invisible (less than $\frac{1}{100}$th of an inch long). Suspect mites when leaves curl unnaturally, when young shoots are distorted or thickened, or when flowers are lopsided. Effective treatment involves such powerful poisons that they are not recommended for amateur use. Discarding affected plants is best practice. Immediate burning, where possible, will help to prevent spread of the infestation.

THRIPS. Tiny pests that feed by rasping, causing the plant to look burned. Lindane, malathion, or Diazinon will control them. Watch for a tiny lance-shaped insect about $\frac{1}{6}$ inch long, marked with a network of lines over head and body and with a lighter tail end. This is your enemy.

SANITATION FOR CONTROL. Always use new clean pots. Never introduce a new plant directly into your collection, but grow it in a separate room until you are sure it is healthy. Don't let decaying organic matter accumulate in humidifier trays or around pots. Propagate only from clean stock.

12

Gardening Under
Artificial Light

During the past two decades, the growing of plants wholly under artificial light has become an accepted part of gardening. While lights are sometimes used only on seedlings and cuttings, often the plants (notably African violets) spend their entire life cycle under lights.

The idea became practical just before World War II, when scientists at the U.S. Department of Agriculture began using fluorescent lights to grow seeds of quinine trees flown out of the Far East just ahead of the Japanese invasion. They found that if these were planted in sphagnum moss and the pots set under lights in a closed cabinet similar to a Wardian case, the seedlings could be grown to transplanting size without daylight.

There were problems, of course. Not the least of these was the exact spectrum or color range of light emitted by the fluorescent tubes. Various colors and combinations were tried. When plants were grown from seed, fairly good growth could be had with daylight-white tubes, but growth was shorter and healthier if light from incandescent bulbs was added. When cuttings were grown, they rooted faster if warm-white or soft-white tubes were used.

These differences were due to varying color needs of plants. Experimentation is still going on in an attempt to determine the ideal artificial light for plants at various stages of growth. Present recommendations for seedlings and plants on their own roots are to use daylight white to which a 25-watt incandescent bulb is added for each two 40-watt fluorescent tube. If the unit is to be used for rooting cuttings, regular warm-white tubes can be used without being supplemented.

African violets thrive in artificial light. These basement units are used for

If high-light intensities are wanted, tubes can be as close together as sockets permit, but should not be separated by more than 8 inches. Two 40-watt tubes 8 inches apart can cover an area 48 inches long and 16 inches wide.

One of the weaknesses of fluorescent light is that it does not project well. Plants must be kept quite close to the tube to receive much benefit. Fortunately, this is safe with fluorescents (*not* with incandescents) because of their low heat output. This can be reduced to a minimum by mounting the ballast on the outside of the growing unit.

DISTANCES BETWEEN TUBES AND PLANTS

The closer to the plants the fluorescent tubes can be brought, the greater the amount of light that will reach the plants. Many plants are tough enough not to be harmed when their leaves come in contact with the tubes. However, a separation of 3 to 4 inches is best — never more than 12 inches.

TEMPERATURES

For Growing

Even plants which normally grow at higher temperatures, such as African violets, do reasonably well at 68° when grown under artificial light in an enclosed case. Unless the unit stands in an unheated basement, heating devices are rarely needed. When an open layout with light tubes sus-

starting new plants and bringing exhibition specimens into full bloom.

pended over a table is used in a basement with an insulated boiler, electric cables in the soil controlled by a thermostat will probably be needed in winter.

For Seed Germination

Several factors other than actual thermometer readings must be considered when germinating seeds. (See Chapter 21.) Seeds that sprout at 68° present no problem; they can be sown *on top* of the vermiculite in flats or pots and kept in the fluorescent unit until ready for transplanting. The light given off by the fluorescent tubes, or by daylight-white plus incandescent, without natural daylight, will give short stocky growth.

More difficult to solve is the problem of species that require alternating temperatures. Perhaps no more uniform heat can be found outside a laboratory than that inside a fluorescent-lighted unit. The species that need alternating temperatures probably should be reserved for outdoor planting under conditions which will provide these readings naturally.

Plants that require lower temperatures either should be seeded outdoors early in spring, or grown in a fluorescent-lighted unit that is not enclosed, in a part of the basement where a temperature of about 55° occurs naturally. Those requiring a steady high heat can probably be given a warmer spot near a radiator where a fluorescent tube can be installed to provide light.

Once the seedlings have germinated, all will do well at 68° and can be put into the regular unit maintained at that temperature.

PLANTS TO GROW

African violets, gloxinias, and tuberous begonias are flowering plants that do well under artificial light and are a good choice for early efforts. Other species should be tried cautiously. Among plants often kept as reserves in the basement under lights, the following will tolerate fairly low light intensities.

Aglaonema modestum,
    Chinese Evergreen

Begonia rex-cultorum, Rex Begonia

Caladium bicolor,
    Fancy-leaved Caladium

Cissus antarctica, Kangaroo Vine

Dieffenbachia varieties,
    Dumb Cane

Dracaena varieties, Dragon Plant

Ficus varieties, Fig, Rubber Plant

Hedera helix, English Ivy

Pandanus varieties, Screw Pine

Philodendron varieties,
    Philodendron

Rhoeo discolor,
    Moses-in-the-bulrushes

(For even lower light intensties, try ferns, *Aglaonema modestum, Ficus elastica decora,* and *Ficus macrophylla.*)

DESIGN AND OPERATION OF UNITS

Although the construction of a unit (merely a closed box with tubes suspended in the top) is too simple to require elaborate plans, the wiring needs special mention. Electricity is extremely dangerous in the presence of moisture. Although condensation on the tubes is not a menace, always avoid touching the tube near the end. All extension cords used should be heavy. All connections should be covered so that water cannot splash on live contacts.

Drainage should be good, with a run-off provided for excess water. If the cabinet is high enough, shelves for germinating seeds that do not require light can be provided below the lighted space. As soon as germination has taken place, however, these plants must be moved into light at once.

If cost is not a factor, lights can be left on constantly. This will not affect the three flowering species recommended. However, if plants affected by short or long days are grown, a schedule must be worked out to fit their flowering habits or they may not bloom.

Where seedlings are being grown, a 16-hour day and an 8-hour night will give best results. This need not agree with the day outside. In areas where special rates are set up for heating water at night, the "day" can be fitted into the night schedule. However, the cost of operating a unit is not high.

13

Terrariums and Dish Gardens

Terrariums had their beginning early in the 19th century when Dr. N. B. Ward, an eminent London surgeon, invented a case for importing rare plants from distant countries.

A voyage of several months was not unusual then, and passing through several different climatic zones was rough on plants. Dr. Ward devised a case which was nearly airtight and created its own climate by conserving and condensing moisture given off by the plants inside. This became famous as the Wardian case.

The idea was adapted to their own use by others in England, Germany, and France. Our present-day terrarium, however, is as American as blueberry pie. It began when New England housewives found that partridgeberries (*Mitchella repens*) would live over winter in clear glass bowls with a bit of moss in place of soil. In the cool, moist air of stove-heated kitchens, "squaw bowls," as they were called, seldom needed the glass cover we use today. The moss would often contain bits of twinflower (*Linnaea borealis*), goldthread (*Coptis trifolia*), and flowering wintergreen (*Polygala paucifolia*), which would usually grow and thrive.

Terrarium gardens are planted today in almost any type of container that is made of reasonably clear glass, is big enough to hold suitable material, and can be closed with some sort of a lid. Even fruit jars, covered with plastic film, have been used.

The reason plants can survive for a long time in a closed case is that they give off moisture which condenses on the glass, falls back to the moss, and is picked up by the plant to continue the cycle. This makes a terrarium practically self-watering, able to go for weeks without added moisture. So long as condensation produces a light beading inside the bowl, watering is unnecessary.

Because of the close atmosphere inside a terrarium, precautions must be taken to avoid the growth of fungi. Wash the container with a strong chlorine solution two or three days before planting and let the chlorine evaporate before using it. Keep your hands washed with a detergent solution while you work. The soil medium you plan to use should be baked for an hour at 325° or steamed in a pressure cooker for at least 20 minutes.

For evergreens and northern plants, use half peatmoss or leafmold and half clean sand, with an ounce of powdered charcoal added to each pint of the medium. For lush-growing tropical plants use one part sand, one part peatmoss, shredded sphagnum moss, or leafmold, and three parts good mellow loam, not too high in clay.

As a base and for drainage under the soil, use a ¾-inch layer of pea gravel or torpedo sand. Over this place the sterilized medium. Set the plants in this and cover the surface with moss.

PLANTS FOR TERRARIUMS

MOSSES. No matter what is planted, a terrarium without moss seems incomplete. Gather it in the woods (you can rarely buy it) or use the dried kind sold by florists as sheet moss. When watered, it turns lettuce green. The color seems artificial when used with northern plants, but is just right for tropical material.

The term mosses is used rather loosely. Many plants which are not true mosses are collected for terrariums, including lichens, and liverworts. The club mosses (lycopodium and selaginella) — not true mosses — are also used. Even farther afield is a flowering plant *Helxine soleiroli*, sometimes called Irish moss, also baby's tears, mind-your-own-business, and fairy fern.

Whenever possible, collect your mosses in the wild and try to note whether they grow on granite rocks or in evergreen woods (indicating preference for acid soil), or on limestone rocks, in which case a little lime will be needed in the soil.

FERNS. Ferns are very much at home in terrariums, being shade-tolerant and usually moisture-loving. Again, choice is limited. About the only ferns offered in florists' shops, except for Boston fern, are the so-called table ferns — mixed species grown from spores of types that remain small for a

GARDEN IN A GLASS: *The ingredients include a large brandy glass with cover, moss or sphagnum moss, charcoal, rich topsoil, small stones, aquarium gravel, miniature fence, and tools. The plants are violets and Johnny-jump-ups. The results are pictured on a color page.*

Line one-quarter of glass with moss, green side out, or with damp sphagnum moss (left). Add soil and charcoal almost to edge of moss. Arrange stones and gravel for the "terrain" (center). Set plants in place with tongs; use a pencil to adjust final positions. Water lightly.

long time. They are practically never named. Most of them thrive in terrariums. The one exception is fern asparagus (*Asparagus plumosus*),
which is not a fern but a relative of table asparagus. Ask your florist to
eliminate it from a mixture of table ferns. Usually it rots quickly in a terrarium, but if it *does* survive, it becomes a rampant monster that chokes
out the other plants.

VINES. In small globes which barely have room for half a dozen partridge-berry plants, vines would be out of place, but in a large, rectangular terrarium they are lovely creeping up the glass. The creeping fig (*Ficus
pumila*) is a gem. If it is to thrive, it must not be overwatered. Beautiful
new close-jointed, small-leaved varieties of English ivy (*Hedera helix*)
are also suitable. The variegated green-and-white forms are particularly
lovely. Creeping snowberry (*Chiogenes hispidula*) is delightful sprawling
against the glass. It has an aromatic fragrance which can be enjoyed by
lifting the lid, and it has white berries that add a pleasant accent. Irish
moss (*Helxine solieroli*), already mentioned, is also vine-like.

FOLIAGE PLANTS. Except for the African violet (*Saintpaulia ionantha*)
and its near relatives, the episcias or flame violets, few plants can be expected to bloom under terrarium conditions. For color, small specimens
of dracaena can be used for about a year before they grow too large. Several species have brilliantly hued foliage.

Seedlings of evergreens are among some of the most useful foliage
plants for terrariums. In nature, they must survive for years on the damp
shaded forest floor before they can rise above the gloom; hence they are
fitted for life in a terrarium. Japanese yew (*Taxus cuspidata*) and hemlock (*Tsuga canadensis*) are the most shade-tolerant. If a rather poor soil
is used, they can be kept small for two or three years. Their attractive
foliage and ability to withstand regular shearing are added features.

Except for its avid roots, the arborvitae (*Thuja orientalis*) is desirable
and lovely with its soft green foliage. White- and blue-spruce seedlings do
beautifully if grown cool; they soon grow leggy in heat. Bar Harbor juniper is a splendid semi-prostrate species that grows slowly. Actually, practically any evergreen seedling will thrive if fairly deep soil, not too rich,
and quite sandy is used.

While partridge-berries seldom flower and set fruit in glass, new plants
with berries already formed can be added each fall. They will retain their
color all winter. The bunchberry (*Cornus canadensis*), although not long-
lasting, is beautiful too. Goldthread (*Coptis trifolia*) will sometimes
flower. Wintergreen (*Gaultheria procumbens*) is another berried plant
worth having.

Florists sell what are known as table palms — true palms that will remain small for a fairly long time. These are interesting and add a tropical
note to miniature landscapes. Smaller varieties of fibrous-rooted begonias
— sometimes called wax begonias — survive and often flower.

TERRARIUM CARE

One of the desirable features of gardens in glass is that they will survive for days, even weeks, without attention. When trouble does develop, as when mildew or decay invades a terrarium that has been growing for some time, it seldom pays to treat the problem in place. Remove everything, wash the container and lid with a chlorine solution and go over the plants carefully. Any that are rotting should be discarded. Others can be dusted with a slight puff of dusting sulfur, heeled in for an hour or two in damp moss to allow the sulfur fumes to dissipate, and then replanted.

DISH GARDENS

Bonsai, the dwarfed Japanese trees which have become a hobby for thousands of Americans, have brought a revival of the dish-garden fad of the mid-1930's. Although they usually feature one of the artificially dwarfed trees, practically any deciduous tree or woody shrub in seedling form can be used in combination with mosses, small plants, and even grasses to create an illusion of landscape.

CONTAINERS

Except when holding specimens of Bonsai that have strong vertical lines, the containers used are generally quite shallow, seldom more than 3 inches deep. The Japanese, who call these dish gardens Bonkei (pronounced bonn-kye) usually prefer hexagonal bowls made of a dull brown unglazed terra cotta. If glazed bowls are used, they should be in a low key to suggest earth. Long, oval, and rectangular bowls also are used. All have four or five holes for drainage.

Specialists do not secure rocks and other features to the container with cement, but this does save trouble if a sudden movement shifts the entire arrangement. If cement is used, it should be allowed to set completely. Then the container should be well washed to remove every trace. There is so little soil in these containers that the slightest amount of a foreign substance can cause harm.

DESIGNS

There are no set patterns; let your imagination run riot. Two things to avoid are overplanting and lack of attention to scale. If a rail fence is introduced into a landscape, for example, it should be the right size for the log cabin it is supposed to surround. No matter how appealing a human figure or animal may be, it should never be used if it is out of scale with the rest of the composition. The most difficult job of all is to work out perspective so that the horizon seems to be receding. Dozens of objects may have to be tried and shifted before the right combination is found.

SOIL

For most needled evergreens, use a soil that is a mixture of 2 parts sand, 2 parts sandy loam, and 1 part leafmold or peatmoss. For broad-leaved evergreens and deciduous plants, substitute a fairly good garden loam for the sandy loam. Too rich a soil will mean rapid growth and loss of the original proportions of the plants.

14

Greenhouses, Coldframes, and Hotbeds

While a discussion of cost may seem a dull approach to the quiet pleasure a greenhouse provides, misconceptions regarding expense are barriers that must be broken down before home-owners dare consider one. It is not true that home greenhouses cost fabulous sums. A perfectly satisfactory house — one that can produce thousands of plants and cuttings for the garden in a single year — can be erected for less than the cost of a good bicycle.

A current mail-order catalog lists clear vinyl plastic 4 mils thick (a mil is 1/1,000 of an inch), large enough in area to cover a house 6 by 10 feet, for less than $10. A simple wooden structure to support it should not cost more than $25. For the perfectionist who wants a glass-covered house, an even larger unit can be had for about $200.

These prices of course mean doing your own work, and do not include heat. Often no additional heat is needed if the greenhouse can be attached to a wall of the residence. If natural gas is available, several firms sell a satisfactory gas-heating unit for less than $30 that will heat a 10 by 10 house in zero weather. For a house used only in spring to produce bedding plants, small electric heating units are satisfactory. If a larger house is built later, these small heating units can be used as stand-by emergency equipment.

Unfortunately, the need to dispel the illusion of high cost obscures the principal reason for owning a greenhouse — the constant delight it provides. Until you have experienced the thrill of walking into your own glass or plastic house on a snowy winter day, you cannot realize the pleasure it represents. This is gardening at its best — comfortable, no stooping, and no weeds to fight.

It has been estimated that in Great Britain one gardener in 20 has a reasonable facsimile of a greenhouse; in the United States the figure is about one in 500! Yet our needs for a greenhouse far exceed theirs. Our more rigorous climate, the limited range of plant material we can buy from commercial growers, and the far higher prices we pay — all proclaim the need for this invaluable aid.

Perhaps the greatest satisfaction that comes from growing your own plants under glass is that it enables you to use them in masses. Instead of a dozen petunias purchased at a fancy price, you can have hundreds, all from a single packet of seed. Instead of being limited to the few colors and varieties offered by commercial growers, you can search the far corners of the world for seed of new and unusual varieties. A sample stock plant of some choice geranium or fuchsia can be multiplied by cuttings into a whole border of color at practically no cost.

DIFFERENT KINDS OF GREENHOUSES

The Plastic House

For every foot of conventional greenhouse being built by commercial growers today, probably 10 feet of plastic houses are going up. This does not mean that the plastic house is ten times as good, far from it, but it does indicate that hard-headed businessmen find a plastic structure perfectly adequate for growing plants. In spite of its drawbacks, it does a job at a price so low that the humblest gardener can own one.

What are the drawbacks? One is its temporary nature. Despite its frail appearance, a glass greenhouse is a strong structure. Houses as old as 70 years still stand, and they may have lost only an occasional pane of glass, whereas a single gale can tear off sheets of flexible plastic if it has been exposed to the weather just a few months too long. Never count on flexible plastic covering for more than one year's service.

Another drawback is that a plastic house is much tighter than one made of glass. As a result, excess moisture does not escape readily but condenses on the roof and drips down on the plants. Double glazing, with one plastic film inside and another outside solves the problem but is expensive.

The true role of the plastic greenhouse is to serve as an introduction to indoor gardening. The gardener can try out the idea, and if he enjoys the experience, he will want a more permanent structure. At the same time, many who erect plastic houses are so well satisfied that they continue using them. If they do their own work, they can replace the covering once a year (in fall) for about $10.

Prefabricated greenhouses like this one come complete, ready to be assembled, except for the foundations.

This roomy lean-to is 7′2″ by 18′10″. Prefab aluminum frame is weatherproof. Concrete block lower wall helps structure blend with house.

Rigid Plastic Houses

The ultimate covering for a greenhouse may be fiber glass, a corrugated sheet of glass fibers imbedded in a clear plastic. Hailstones do not damage this material, which can take all kinds of abuse. It is the one house that foils small boys who consider greenhouses perfect targets for stones or snowballs.

Another advantage is that the pitch of the roof is not important. With other coverings, an ideal angle must be worked out to capture maximum sunshine in winter — an angle that increases as we move north from the equator. With fiber glass, the individual fibers capture the sun's rays no matter what the angle and diffuse them through the interior. Light-meter readings taken in this type of house show nearly double the light of a glass house in early morning and late evening. This is not necessarily true at midday, except when the sun is quite low in the south during winter.

Fiber glass is perhaps the most expensive covering by the square foot, but because of its light weight, smaller framing members can be used, thus effecting savings in construction needs.

Glass Greenhouses

Nowadays prefabricated small houses are so low in cost that it hardly pays to attempt the do-it-yourself kind. Wide glass is the rule, which means more light on the benches. All sorts of labor-saving devices — automatic heating, watering, ventilating, and humidification can be had — at a price — to make the job of caring for a greenhouse less of a burden. Aluminum framing is ideal, and from some manufacturers, costs no more than wood. If a wood-framed house is built, by all means use bar caps of aluminum over the roof bars for practically permanent installation.

CONSTRUCTION MATERIALS AND EQUIPMENT

Wood for Greenhouse Members and Framing

The ideal wood for a greenhouse is old-fashioned heart cypress, a material that is extremely scarce today. Next best is clear redwood, a product that can be had but not cheaply. An added disadvantage (in the cheaper grades used for benches) is that it is soft and brittle. Nevertheless, redwood is perhaps the best buy in greenhouse lumber today.

If you are not certain that you will continue to operate a plastic house, and want to keep investment to a minimum, any reasonably strong, easy-to-work wood can be used. Such wood can be made almost as durable as heart cypress by treating it with copper naphthenate (sold under various trade names) mixed with fuel oil or kerosene and painted on. Pieces should be cut to final size before treating so that the ends (the most vulnerable part) can be soaked. Penta products (pentachlorophenol and its derivatives) also can be used, but should be allowed to dry for two to three weeks before plastic is applied. Never use creosote: even its fumes kill plants.

Foundations

A plastic house puts so little weight on its foundations that a simple post structure like a wooden fence will serve for closing in the lower part of the wall. A glass structure, however, must have solid footings that go below the frost line. Except that it is an ugly material, it is hard to beat concrete blocks for the wall itself.

Because a home greenhouse, particularly one covered with plastic, is a rather individual affair, there is no need to adhere strictly to standard dimensions, particularly as to the height of the lower wall. In most greenhouses, the outer edge of a bench rests on this wall. If you are tall, you need a higher bench, so make the wall high enough. There is nothing more annoying than trying to pot on a bench that is too high or too low.

Don't make the mistake of paving the entire greenhouse floor with cement. This will make the house so dry that humidity will be difficult to maintain. Cement walks are all right if you must have them, but clean gravel is better for humidity's sake.

Shape, Size, and Site

Few home properties offer much choice of site. An attached lean-to — the most common form of home greenhouse — practically always is built facing south or canted a trifle from that orientation.

Do not overlook the possibility of attaching a greenhouse to the side or the back of some structure other than the house. A tool shed or garage will serve. Against the drawback of not being able to walk from the house into your garden, is the advantage of keeping greenhouse mess off the living-room floor. Against the loss of an opportunity to use the house heating system is the advantage of being able to suit the heat to the needs of plants rather than people.

A distinct advantage of a detached location is that poisonous fumigants can be used without worrying about their getting into the house. If the size of the property will permit, the building of a separate head house has many advantages. It can provide space for a potting bench, for storing soil and pots, cabinets for sprays and dusts, and even add winter storage space for tender bulbs. Be sure to leave plenty of room for chairs. You'll be amazed how the boys in the neighborhood will drop in at night when they see your lights.

Soil

In commercial greenhouse operation soil is a serious problem. The home gardener, however, seldom loses his soil unless he gives a plant to a friend. He more than makes up this minor loss in the compost he produces. Usually he can borrow soil from the vegetable garden, use it for a season, and return it to the garden after a rest in the compost heap.

By the use of compost, purchased sand, a bag or two of vermiculite, plus peatmoss and leafmold, soil for a home greenhouse can be improvised easily. Any deficiency in natural richness can be supplied by fertilizer.

Summer Shading

In glass houses or those covered with clear polyvinyl, shading is essential. To cover glass, shading compounds that weather gradually and are easily removed in fall can be had from dealers in greenhouse supplies. Deluxe shading for orchids and other valuable plants is often provided by elaborate roll-up shading of slats.

Shading the plastic house is best done from the inside with saran netting hung under the rafters. War-surplus camouflage netting is also practical. It can be purchased cheaply, and a single net can be thrown over an entire small house without much trouble. Clip-on panels that fit against the underside of the rafters also can be used on small structures.

In the fiber-glass house, shade is no problem. In spite of the amount of light that the plastic admits, the rays are so diffused that no burning results.

Winter Lighting

Be sure to provide electric lights at intervals over the benches, because sooner or later you will want to try controlled lighting to advance or slow down flowering. Remember that humidity in a greenhouse is always high. All lights, therefore, should be in conduit and grounded. Wires without conduit are taboo. Use porcelain sockets throughout. Provide weatherproof outdoor convenience outlets in case you want to use an electric sprayer.

If the heating system is electrically controlled, consider buying a minimum temperature alarm that will warn you if the heat fails and temperature drops to a dangerous point. This should be operated by dry-cell batteries.

WHAT TO GROW

More often than not the problem is knowing what *not* to grow. For the man with a single-plant hobby, such as orchids or African violets, the decision is easy and management simple. With only one kind of plant to consider, he needs only one temperature range. Difficulty arises when plants of widely varying temperature requirements are wanted in a single house without divisions. In larger houses a partition can be installed, even if only of plastic, and an extra heating pipe can be added to the warm end. But this complicates matters where automatic ventilation is installed unless separate motors are used in each section. The best plan in the small house is to select a group of plants with similar heat demands. The extra heat needed for rooting cuttings and germinating seeds can be provided by an enclosed propagating case equipped with an electric hotbed cable.

Bulbs

Because of the limited room in most home greenhouses, bulbs are particularly useful. They do most of their growing in the dark and occupy bench space for only a few days before blooming. Part of this forcing period can even be spent under the benches in space which is otherwise chances of failure are much less than with other types of plants. Bulbs and foliage plants are the backbone of greenhouse planting; for their culture see Bulbs (Chapter 4) and House Plants (Chapter 11).

Bedding Plants for Outdoor Use

The raising of bedding plants is one of the real pleasures offered by a greenhouse. From a 50-cent packet of seed, you can produce enough petunias to fill a long border, or enough fibrous-rooted begonias to stage a dramatic show in some lightly shaded spot. Seeds that require high temperatures for germination (see Chapter 21), can be started in a closed propagating case. Once they have sprouted, they can be transferred to peat-fiber or bagasse pots and grown in the open house at a lower temperature. Timing of plantings is as follows:

JANUARY: Ageratum, *Asparagus sprengeri* and *A. plumosus* (for hanging baskets), fibrous-rooted begonias, annual carnations, annual chrysanthemums, coleus, Unwin dahlias, dusty miller (*Centaurea cineraria*), impatiens, lobelia, nierembergia, pansies, double and giant petunias, verbena, and *Vinca rosea*.

FEBRUARY: All of the January list can still be sown except fibrous-rooted begonias, annual chrysanthemums, lobelia, and *Vinca rosea*. Add *Salvia splendens* to the list.

MARCH: Sweet alyssum, antirrhinum (snapdragon), browallia, celosia, *Centaurea gymnocarpa* (a different dusty miller), Unwin dahlias, ipomoea ('Clark's Early Flowering' in pots), marigolds, nasturtiums (in pots), small-flowered petunias, *Salvia splendens, S. farinacea*, verbena, and zinnia.

FLOWERING POT PLANTS

Next to bulbs, flowering pot plants are best for greenhouses. They put on a brave show in the bench and can be moved into the house, where they are fully as effective as a bouquet of cut flowers that might have occupied ten times as much space. Some shrubs, grown as pot plants, can be forced into bloom, rested after flowering, and forced again the following year. In the list below, Sh indicates tolerance of shade.

Abutilon hybridum (Sh),
   Flowering Maple

Acacia, species (Sh), Mimosa

Ageratum houstonianum, Ageratum

Begonia, fibrous-rooted varieites,
   Wax Begonia

Begonia rex-cultorum, Rex Begonia

B. tuberhybrida, Tuberous Begonia

Bouvardia humboldti (Sh),
   Bouvardia

Browallia speciosa,
   Sapphire Flower

Calceolaria crenatiflora, Slipperwort

Camellia japonica, Camellia

Choisya ternata, Mexican Orange

Cyclamen indicum,
   Florist's Cyclamen

Cytisus canariensis (Sh),
   Florist's Genista

Daphne cneorum (Sh),
   Rose Daphne

Erica, various species (Sh), Heath

Euphorbia pulcherrima (Sh),
   Poinsettia

Hydrangea macrophylla (Sh),
   Florist's Hydrangea

Kalanchoë blossfeldiana, Fire Plant

Pelargonium hortorum,
   Florist's Geranium

Primula malacoides, Fairy Primrose

P. obconica, Hairy Primrose

P. sinensis, Chinese Primrose

Rhododendron indicum (Sh),
   Kurume and Indian Azaleas

Saintpaulia, African Violet

Schizanthus wisetonensis,
   Poor-man's Orchid

Senecio cruentus, Cineraria

Sinningia speciosa, Gloxinia

VEGETABLES IN THE GREENHOUSE

Most home greenhouses are too small for vegetables. Three forcing crops, however, are worth considering as interesting additions to the winter table. All are better when home-grown.

FORCED RHUBARB. Old clumps of rhubarb can be dug from the garden in late fall and placed in bushel baskets or other suitable containers. These should be stored against an outside wall, covered with leaves, and allowed to freeze. Placed under the greenhouse benches at intervals during the winter, they will grow up delicious pink stalks. If tar paper is used to keep light away from the plants, their color will be improved.

FORCED ASPARAGUS. The same technique will produce forced asparagus with a marvelous flavor — one of the great delicacies of the Victorian age, now almost forgotten.

FRENCH ENDIVE. As witloof chicory, this is imported from Belgium at a fancy price during the winter. Grow the roots in the summer vegetable garden. After a good freeze, dig them, being careful not to injure the crowns. Turn them upside down so that all the crowns are even. Cut the roots to a uniform 6-inch length and store them in a coldframe where temperatures are below 40° until wanted for forcing.

Use bottomless boxes about 14 inches deep for forcing, and place them under the greenhouse bench. Set the roots upright in the box, touching. Now fill in with a mixture of half peatmoss and half sand, and water to settle the mixture around the roots. Fill the box to within 2 inches of the top. The heads are ready for cutting when the leaves barely break the surface of the sand and peatmoss mixture. Do not let them grow beyond this length because the flavor is spoiled when they turn green. Cut the forced heads 1 inch above the crown and replant the roots for another crop.

THE SUN-HEATED PIT

Not all greenhouses are above ground. The sun-heated pit, perhaps the least expensive of greenhouses to build and operate, is a modification of the old sash houses used in the 19th century by commercial vegetable-growers. Such houses are no longer used because improved transportation brings in early spring vegetables from California and Texas.

A sun-heated pit may or may not be artificially heated. If it is, the apparatus is simple — an out-sized electric heater or a small coal stove in a corner, used only when bitter cold threatens to penetrate deep into the earth.

A pit is lighted only from the south. Since it is used exclusively during winter months when the sun is low in the southern sky, a north-facing sash would only waste heat. The room is an uneven span; that is, the north section slopes at a fairly gentle angle, while the south is nearly perpendicular. This is to trap every possible ray of sunshine. A modern improvement is to line the underside of the north roof with aluminum foil. More light is then reflected and less heat is lost during the night.

Although limited as a place to grow plants, a pit is more useful than one might imagine. A few camellia fanciers find that tubbed plants kept along the north wall of a pit can catch enough sun to grow better blooms than in a mixed house. By careful manipulation of a small electric heater, such cold-tolerant plants as calendulas and stocks can also be grown well. Forced hyacinths, tulips, and daffodils can be grown to perfection in a pit. In spring, seedlings of bedding plants can be started there too, and it is ideal for propagating cuttings in summer.

One drawback to a sun-heated pit (unless thermostatically controlled heat is added) is that the glass must be covered every night to conserve sun heat. The use of corrugated fiber glass partially does away with this in mild weather, but when the thermometer drops to zero, heavy padding is needed.

A means of ventilation is vital, because the temperature inside can build up rapidly on bright winter days. Hinging the glass with the opening at the bottom is the customary way of providing ventilation.

COLDFRAMES

By use of coldframes, hotbeds, cloches, and hotcaps, experienced gardeners protect early plants from cold and produce the first flowers and vegetables on schedule. There is no better place to root cuttings, multiply a valued bulb into dozens of bulbils, store vegetables for winter eating, and protect half-hardy perennials from winter-killing than a well-designed coldframe.

Essentially, a frame is a bottomless box with a glass top, either sunk into the earth slightly or with earth hilled around its sides. It slopes to the south to capture every stray ray of sunshine when sun is needed. (When dormant plants are stored in the frame, sun can do more damage than good.) The box can be made of wood, metal, brick, or concrete. Metal, unless insulated (which makes its cost high) loses heat too rapidly. Masonry construction is permanent but also costly. Most home garden frames are made out of 2-inch lumber. Because of the high cost of cypress, they are usually of a less durable wood, treated with copper naphthenate or pentachlorophenol. Custom has decreed that frames should be 6 feet wide from north to south, probably because the owner can then reach halfway across from either side.

Modern sashes for frames are glazed with a temporary covering of polyethylene or vinyl film, or covered with sheets of rigid fiber glass. Fiber glass is highly desirable because of the superior insulation it provides, and its better light-dispersing qualities. Frames with this type of glazing are less likely to heat up rapidly during bright weather early in spring. Their light weight makes them easy to handle, but unless they are fastened down, a light breeze will make them flutter, while a stiff wind could lift them and throw them for several yards. Always provide two lines of cord to secure them — one at the north end and one at the south end across the entire frame.

Winter management of a coldframe calls for slowly lowering the temperature inside, then keeping it at a steady reading until warmer weather returns in spring. Because sun striking through sash can raise temperatures to above freezing, a covering of some kind is needed during the winter. The newest material is glass wool bonded to waterproof plastic sheeting. This is lightweight, yet a superb insulator. The traditional covering is straw matting, but this gets wet and is nasty to handle. Discarded quilts and rugs make excellent hotbed mats but should be kept dry with an additional layer of plastic film. Do not use tar paper. Its dark color absorbs heat and makes trouble during sunny weather.

Ventilation of coldframes (and hotbeds) is important. During sunny weather when the thermometer is in the 20's and 30's, some air must be admitted. A brick or block of wood under the sash will provide this. Put the brick or block under the northern, or high, side so the hot air will rise and pass out of the frame.

For summer use, provide shades made of laths spaced one lath's width apart. Or use burlap or cheesecloth (two to three thicknesses of the latter). These shades should be supported about 2 feet over the bed to allow breezes to blow through while screening out the sun. A shaded frame is an ideal place to root cuttings, grow pansies and English daisies, and to produce bulbils from lily scales.

HOTBEDS

A hotbed is simply a coldframe with heat added. Fresh horse manure was formerly the source of heat. Today, unless a hotbed is warmed by pipes from a central heating system, it is probably heated by a thermostatically controlled electric cable. The cable is laid under the soil and protected by hardware cloth.

Another method is to heat the hotbed with electric lights suspended above the plants. Two 60-watt bulbs will heat a space 3 by 6 feet. The light supplements the weaker daylight of early spring and produces stronger, sturdier plants than can be grown in a cable-heated hotbed.

CLOCHES AND HOTCAPS

The cloche came to England from France but was never widely adopted by American gardeners. One reason is that our spring sunshine is much brighter than that in England, so that temperatures under these small glass hats rise too high for safety.

A modification of the cloche is, however, being used. Lengths of wire about 3 feet long are formed into a half circle and thrust into the ground at intervals along the row of plants to be protected and covered with a length of polyethylene film (not over 2 mils thick) to form a tunnel. Earth thrown over the edges of the plastic keeps it in place.

There is some movement of air through 2-mil polyethylene film so that generated heat moves out rapidly. The film is also somewhat milky, which cuts down heat absorption. Ends of the row can be left open in fine weather and closed if cold night temperatures are threatened.

Hotcaps are waxed-paper plant protectors for individual hills. They are used like cloches, but the amount of air they contain is less than can be trapped under a continuous cloche of polyethylene film.

15

Hobby Flowers: Chrysanthemums, Geraniums, Gladiolus, Peonies

CHRYSANTHEMUMS FOR AUTUMN COLOR

If you want your garden as colorful in October as it was in May or in mid-summer, plant chrysanthemums. These spectacular beauties, whose history can be traced back to the Orient for 2,500 years, come in more shapes and sizes than any other flowers you can grow outdoors. From clusters of thimble-size blooms to the gigantic "football" types, from daisy-like flowers to feathery spiders, from dwarfs that stand a little over a foot high to giants taller than yourself — you can make your choice or you can try them all. And in color you can have anything except blue, from brilliant yellows and reds to white, pink and soft muted shades of bronze, purple and gold. With flowering dates considered when selecting varieties, it is possible to brighten the garden from September until the first severe frost comes.

PLANTING CHRYSANTHEMUMS

The best time to plant chrysanthemums is from the middle of May to the middle of June. Their basic requirements are about the same as those of most popular flowers. They need a sunny location, fairly rich, well-drained soil, routine feeding and watering, and occasional spraying or dusting. They need no special care beyond that which is required by most other garden favorites. A bonus feature is that you can dig up chrysanthemums at any time — even when in flower — and transplant them to a spot where you want instant, dramatic effect.

Like most perennials, chrysanthemums make their best show when massed in groups of three or more plants of the same variety. You can plant them in straight or curved formal beds, in irregular drifts, or simply as color accents in three-plant clumps. Their colors can be grouped to produce either bold contrasts or subtle blends.

The shorter kinds should be planted 12 to 15 inches apart, the taller ones 18 to 24 inches apart if grown as bushes or 12 to 15 inches apart if grown for large blooms on a few stems.

Before planting, spread fertilizer fairly generously on the soil and then turn it to a depth of about 6 inches. One-half to 1 pound of standard complete plant food per 100 square feet is a satisfactory rate. Set the plants no deeper than they grew in the nursery and water them thoroughly after planting.

Chrysanthemums grow and flower best if fed lightly every two or three weeks from about two weeks after planting until the buds begin to show color. Use about one-half or one-third as much plant food as when you prepared the soil, and follow each feeding with a good watering.

Since they are shallow-rooted plants, chrysanthemums need regular watering during dry spells — about as frequently as you water your lawn. Don't keep the soil saturated, but never let it become really dry.

Like roses, chrysanthemums should be given a preventive spraying or dusting at least every two weeks. Use an all-purpose combination insecticide-fungicide and continue from the time you plant them until the flowers begin to open.

PINCHING FOR BUSHINESS

The popular Pompons, Decoratives, and other cluster-flowered bush types should be pinched to make them produce compact, well-shaped plants. This means pinching off ½ to 1 inch of the stem tip just above a leaf.

If a single-stem plant is set out about May 15, the tip is pinched off around June 1. The plant then makes several branches. Around July 1 the tip of each branch is pinched off and new branches then develop on each of the original branches. Thus you get a bushy, well-branched plant.

PRODUCING LARGE BLOOMS ON SINGLE STEMS

The big Incurve ("football"), Spider, and other large-blooming chrysanthemums, however, are not grown as bush-type plants. They are limited to one, two, or three stems, and one large flower is produced on each stem, the buds of the others being removed. The fewer the stems, the larger the blooms.

A plant of this type, set out in May will probably start to branch naturally sometime in June. Keep the two or three strongest branch shoots and pinch out all the rest. From then on, pinch out any side branches or tip branches as soon as they start to grow, thus restricting the plant to its two or three main stems. Stake the stems with 4- to 5-foot canes as soon as they need support. When buds begin to form, carefully pinch out the side buds of each cluster, leaving only the large center bud on each stem.

With experience, you will learn that you can control bloom quality, plant height, and flowering time to a considerable extent by systematic pinching and disbudding. Also, since flowering time is governed by day length (they are short-day flowers), you can advance their flowering by use of black shade cloth or delay it by the use of lights.

COLD-WEATHER PROCEDURE

Chrysanthemum flowers can stand moderate frosts, but if your area normally gets severe frosts before mid-October you'd better stick to September-flowering varieties. If you'd like to grow some of the choicer, later-blooming varieties, however, you can do so by protecting them at night with plastic film or light cloth. Drive a few tall stakes into the ground around the plantings and drape the material over them in the evening when a sharp frost is predicted. Make sure that the plants are covered all the way to the ground. Remove the material in the morning.

NEW PLANTS EVERY SPRING

Although chrysanthemums are perennials, it is best to start with new plants each year. Either make cuttings from old plants in the spring or buy rooted cuttings from commercial specialists. You can also make new plants by pulling the old ones apart into single-stem divisions in the spring. To protect the old plants from winter injury, cut them to the ground after they have frozen in late fall and cover them with a good layer of hay, straw, or evergreen branches.

TYPES OF FLOWERS

The chrysanthemum flower-head is made up of many small flowers or florets of two kinds. The ray florets, which look like petals, are incomplete, sterile flowers, bearing only stamens. The disk florets, which make up the center or disk of the flower-head, are complete, fertile, seed-producing flowers.

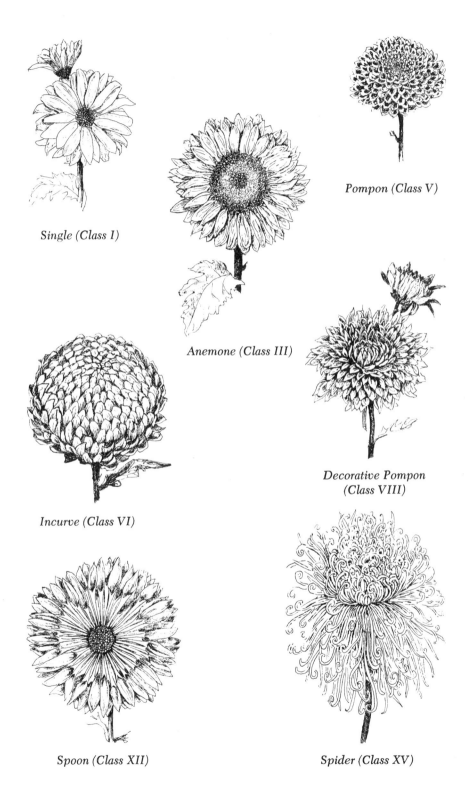

Single (Class I)

Anemone (Class III)

Pompon (Class V)

Incurve (Class VI)

*Decorative Pompon
(Class VIII)*

Spoon (Class XII)

Spider (Class XV)

The National Chrysanthemum Society recognizes 15 classes, based on the type of bloom. Choice varieties in the most popular of these classes are given below, with notes on color, height, and average blooming date. The other classes are: Semidouble, II; Irregular Anemone, IV; Irregular Incurve, VII; Decorative Reflex, IX; Regular Reflex, X; Irregular Reflex, XI; Quill, XIII; Thread, XIV.

CHOICE CHRYSANTHEMUM VARIETIES

SINGLE (CLASS I)

Ray florets in 1 to 5 rows. Disk more or less flat, disk florets short. Grown as bush-type plant.

'Ginny Lee,' white, 48 inches, Oct. 20
'Happiness,' yellow, 42 inches, Oct. 22
'Daphne,' pink, 36 inches, Oct. 20
'Buckskin,' bronze, 42 inches, Oct. 25
'Fred Stone,' red, 36 inches, Oct. 15
'Daisymum,' white, 24 inches, Sept. 25
'Gold Daisy,' yellow, 20 inches, Sept. 22

ANEMONE (CLASS III)

Ray florets broad, in 1 to 5 rows. Disk florets longer than in singles, forming prominent, rounded disk. Grown as bushy-type or 1- to 3-stem plant.

'Powder Puff,' yellow, 48 inches, Oct. 30
'Ethel Anderson,' bronze, 48 inches, Nov. 1
'Sincerity,' white, 52 inches, Oct. 25
'Yellow Sincerity,' 52 inches, Oct. 25

POMPON (CLASS V)

Ray florets broad, short, incurved, forming globular bloom. Disk florets concealed. Grown as bush-type plant.

'Irene,' white, 30 inches, Oct. 15
'Bright Forecast,' yellow, 30 inches, Oct. 15
'Masquerade,' pink, 36 inches, Oct. 25
'Red Doty,' 40 inches, Oct. 25
'Rosita,' pink, 20 inches, Sept. 15
'Chiquita,' yellow, 20 inches, Sept. 20
'Bronze Doty,' 40 inches, Oct. 25

INCURVE (CLASS VI)

Ray florets broad, long, incurved, forming large globular bloom. Disk florets concealed. Grown as 1- to 3-stem plant.

'Silver Sheen,' white, 60 inches, Oct. 20
'Mrs. H. E. Kidder,' yellow, 60 inches, Oct. 20
'Major Edward Bowes,' purple, 60 inches, Oct. 15
'Detroit News,' bronze, 60 inches, Oct. 20
'Mrs. David Roy,' red, 60 inches, Nov. 10
'Golden Age,' yellow, 36 inches, Sept. 25

DECORATIVE POMPON (CLASS VIII)

Ray florets short to medium length, reflexed, producing less rounded, more irregular bloom than Class V Pompon. Disk florets concealed. Grown as bush-type plant. Most of the popular garden chrysanthemums are in this class.

'Ostosa,' white, 24 inches, Oct. 10
'Charles Nye,' yellow, 40 inches, Oct. 5
'Elizabeth Hood,' pink, 36 inches, Oct. 15
'Carnival,' bronze, 36 inches, Oct. 15
'Jetfire,' red, 42 inches, Oct. 30
'Chippewa,' purple, 24 inches, Sept. 20
'Tanager,' red, 30 inches, Oct. 1
'Canary,' yellow, 30 inches, Oct. 1
'Eugene A. Wander,' yellow, 22 inches, Sept. 20
'Lee Powell,' yellow, 36 inches, Sept. 25

SPOON (CLASS XII)

Ray florets tubular, opening at ends to form spoon-like tips. Disk small. Grown as bush-type plant.

'Chester Newell,' white, 42 inches, Oct. 20
'Kimie,' yellow, 48 inches, Oct. 20
'Remember Me,' fawn, 48 inches, Oct. 20
'Yellow Spoon,' 48 inches, Oct. 10

SPIDER (CLASS XV)

Ray florets tubular, long, tips coiled or hooked. Disk small or concealed. Grown as 1- to 3-stem plant.

'Swan Ballet,' white, 60 inches, Nov. 1
'Luyona,' yellow, 72 inches, Oct. 25

'Emerald Isle,' green-white, 60 inches, Nov. 1
'Sunnyslope Glory,' pink, 72 inches, Oct. 25
'Waikiki,' bronze, 72 inches, Nov. 1
'Bunbu,' purple, 72 inches, Oct. 25

GERANIUMS FOR EXOTIC EFFECTS

Geraniums can keep a garden gay with luxuriant foliage and colorful bloom from spring to autumn frost. And so varied are these plants in appearance, texture, habit, and fragrance that no two beds or effects need be the same.

Before discussing where to plant geraniums and how to care for them, let us first clear up the bothersome matter of names. Use of the word geranium for any member of the geranium family — botanically the *Geraniaceae* — is sanctioned by long usage. This family includes several genera, two of which are of particular interest to gardeners. One of these is the genus geranium, comprising some 40 annual and perennial species found in various parts of the world, and called collectively "cranesbill" because of their long-beaked seed pods; a number of them are good subjects for wild gardens. The other is the genus pelargonium, which includes a score or more of South African perennials sometimes called "storksbill." Some of these (or forms descended from them) are the widely grown "geraniums" of florists and gardeners discussed here. They fall into several classes or types such as the Fish, or Bedding geraniums (*Pelargonium hortorum*); the Show, Fancy, or Lady Washington, which are varieties and hybrids of *P. domesticum*, and forms with popular names descriptive of their leaf shapes, habits, fragrance, and so forth, such as maple-, oak-, ivy-, grape-leaf, apple, and nutmeg. Although perennial in their mild native habitat, they are not hardy and can be used in northern gardens only as annuals or pot plants. In warm regions, they can remain in the ground the year around to become tall, sometimes almost woody, permanent features of the home landscape. Versatile and adaptable, they produce plants useful not only in window boxes and hanging baskets, but also as unusual covers for banks and rough ground, and in massed beds and borders.

CULTURE

Geraniums require only ordinary conditions and a minimum of care. Indeed, a geranium is one of the easiest of plants to grow. Do not pamper it or fuss over it, and it will give you abundant bloom. In average-good soil, you do not need to fertilize it, nor should you water it too much because actually it is a plant of semi-arid regions. However, if you want to confound your friends and have them ask, "Is *that* really a geranium?" a simple way to grow magnificent specimens is to feed them according to the "little and often" system. The first week, water them with a soluble plant food such as Grow-Chem; about two weeks later, use a slower-acting fertilizer such as Milorganite; still later, change to a quick worker like Vigoro. It seems better to vary the type of plant food rather than keep to the same one; the plants may get some nutrient from one kind that is lacking in others. As to watering, soak the soil thoroughly when you do it, but let it dry out completely between waterings.

OVERWINTER STORAGE

Although not winter hardy, geraniums *can* be carried over from one year to the next. Just before the first frost, dig them up, leaving a ball of earth around the roots; set them close together in an old apple box or similar container; fill in around them with sand, and put the box in a cool, well-ventilated basement or room that gets plenty of daylight. Examine it occasionally and if the sand gets really dry, moisten it slightly. Another storage method consists of digging the plants and hanging them upside down in a cellar, frost-free garage, or any cool place that is not too dry.

MAKING CUTTINGS

The propagation of geraniums by means of cuttings is an intriguing and productive activity. By following a few simple rules you can soon increase your supply of plants. Cuttings can be made at almost any time of year. If you want vigorous young plants in April for setting outdoors, make your cuttings about the end of October when you are storing your plants for the winter. The stock or parent plant which supplies the cuttings should be healthy, with stocky, short-jointed, non-flowering shoots. Cuttings should be from 2 to 4 inches long. When you have chosen the proper plant and shoots, cut straight across each shoot with a sharp knife, directly below a joint. Leave some leaves at the top but trim off the lower ones. Wrap the cuttings in newspaper and store them in a cool, well-ventilated place for about a week, or until a callus forms over the cut end. (This will help reduce losses from a disease called black leg.)

If you are making a lot of cuttings, plant them after they have callused in a seed flat filled to within a half-inch of the top with clean No. 2 sand, well soaked and firmed with a brick. Make holes about 2 inches apart with a pencil or skewer, insert the cuttings so that the lower two nodes are covered, and pack the sand firmly around them. Keep the flat moderately damp in a room of about 60° temperature. If it can be given mild heat from below (as by being placed on a radiator), rooting will be hastened but watering must be done oftener. If you want just a few choice plants, you can root the cuttings in sand in a large clay flowerpot or "bulb pan." Close the drainage hole of a 2-inch pot with a cork or wooden plug, place it in the center of the large pot, and insert the cuttings in the sand around it. Keep the little pot full of water and the cuttings will be assured ample moisture.

EFFECTS WITH GERANIUMS

There is almost no end to the stunning effects that can be created with geraniums, so indulge your imagination and experiment with different colors, heights, and foliage; plant geraniums in beds, pots, planters, or window boxes, singly or massed, and be sure to include some of the trailing ivy types for hanging baskets.

GLADIOLUS, A BARGAIN IN BEAUTY

The gladiolus has been called "everybody's orchid" because it is literally a beautiful bargain — a queenly flower which is easily grown by amateurs and costs little. It gives regal beauty to the garden — and what is more striking than an armful of freshly cut spikes taken indoors to create handsome line and color effects? In addition, gladiolus plants reproduce freely. While they are blooming, the bulbs are multiplying underground. (Technically, they are *corms* and the tinier ones are *cormels*, but as most catalogs call them bulbs and bulblets we shall follow common usage.)

A beginner can start with a neighbor's surplus bulbs, but it is better to buy some from a reputable seedsman or gladiolus specialist; the neighbor's variety may have deteriorated or be infested with the plant's one serious insect pest, thrips. Also, dealers offer an up-to-date choice of new varieties as well as the time-tried ever-popular older ones like 'Supreme', 'Lady Jane', and the famous 'Picardy.' You might start by buying nine pedigreed bulbs, three each of your favorite colors, for less than the price of a dozen cut gladiolus from the florist. Instead of losing them in a few days, you will cut your own flowers season after season while your stock of bulbs doubles or even trebles each year. In three years the original nine can build up a stock of about 240 fine bulbs, without making use of the bulblets.

The "upkeep" in time and labor is also small, because the gladiolus is not fussy. All kinds need sun, but in any ordinary climate and fertile soil grow as easily as onions. If you want them just for cutting, grow them in the vegetable garden.

BUYING THE BULBS

Choosing a type of gladiolus is mainly a matter of selecting for length of flower spike; the number of blooming florets it will carry (12 to 24);

and for the size, shape, and color of the florets. The bulbs can be ordered whenever the new catalogs arrive. However, purchase should not be delayed beyond April because planting begins as soon as the frosts have gone. Setting out some bulbs every ten days will give a succession of blooms until autumn frosts come; or you can choose varieties whose flowering seasons vary but overlap, to provide continuous flowering.

Many catalogs list days from planting to blooming for the varieties offered. Others use symbols: VE for very early (under 65 days); E for early (65-75); EM for early midseason (75-85); M for midseason (85-95); LM for late midseason (95-100), and L for late (over 100). In general, count on large bulbs normally giving blooms in from 80 to 90 days. It is a good idea to study the catalogs of two or more dealers; and it is educational as well as pleasant to visit a gladiolus farm at flowering time.

Do not worry unduly about types — such as Formal, Informal, Exhibition, Commercial. The gladiolus has long suffered from confused terminology and such distinctions are for the commercial grower and the specialists. Aside from color, the important factor is size — which ranges from massive giants down to "baby glads" which can be either hooded (Primulinus type), or open-faced true miniatures of the big fellows. While some argue that giant glads are better suited for the banquet hall or funeral parlor than for the average home, a large spike is imposing anywhere, and at flower shows it is usually the good big one that wins over the good small one.

A good catalog, besides indicating the size and color of florets, usually describes also any conspicuous marking, notes whether the floret is ruffled or hooded, gives the length of the spike, and tells how many buds can be expected to open at any one time.

The size of the gladiolus bulb you buy depends upon your purse and your patience. The larger ones cost more, usually bloom a little earlier and give more buds to the spike; they are recommended for the deep south. But Mediums and Smalls are popular and satisfactory. While blooming, they will be growing large bulbs for the next year. Retail catalogs usually simplify matters by offering Large, Medium, and Small bulbs; but of some varieties they may also offer, at about a tenth of the cost of large bulbs, economy bulblets from which a stock of flowering-size bulbs can be built up in a few years.

PLANTING AND CULTURE

As soon as the soil is warm in the spring, start setting out the bulbs, 3 to 5 inches deep (larger bulbs can go as deep as 8 inches for extra stalk support), spaced 3 to 6 inches apart in rows 2 feet apart or, if desired, in clumps among lower-growing flowers in beds or borders, working fertilizer into the bottom of the trench before placing the bulbs. There-after, the important thing is to keep out weeds, either by cultivating or by mulching — that is, covering the soil between shoots with old hay, straw, leaves, or peatmoss.

After a bulb is planted, it first sends up its sword-like leaf shoots which give the plant its name — gladiolus, from a Latin word meaning "little sword." Keep the plants moist (but not soaked) until the seventh leaf unfolds (indicating that the flower spikes will soon appear). During dry weather, supply water, especially when the spikes are forming, but after the flowers open, beware of overhead sprinkling which may spot the petals. And to insure good bulb growth for the following year, cut spikes carefully so as to leave 3 or 4 bottom leaves to make food for the under-ground parts. You should also pick off seed pods as soon as they form — unless, of course, you want to try raising some plants from seed.

Throughout the growing season, from the time the plants are 6 inches tall, spray them with a DDT solution (following the manufacturer's directions on the package), or use a 5 per cent DDT dust, every ten days or so to control the thrips, a tiny insect that feeds on and between the buds, rasping the tissues and seriously injuring the plants.

BULB STORAGE

At the season's end, when the stalks are yellow or have been killed by frost, dig the clumps, cut off the tops, and let the bulbs dry in the sun for a day. The original bulb will be found to have shriveled into a dry "mummy," but above and around it will have developed one or two prime-size bulbs, one or two smaller ones, and a whole lot of bulblets, pea-size or smaller — new planting stock During the next few weeks, break the clumps apart and discard the mummies and any bulblets you do not want. Do not bother to peel the larger bulbs, but do destroy any thrips they may carry. To do this, put the bulbs in a paper bag, throw in a handful of 5 per cent DDT dust, tie the bag shut, and shake it enough to dis-tribute the dust. The bulbs may then be stored right in the bags — one for each variety — or packed in paper or peatmoss in shallow cartons. Place these in a frost-free temperature (40°-45° is ideal) and in an ordinarily humid atmosphere, neither damp nor excessively dry. A shelf in the aver-age basement (not near the furnace) or in a warmed garage is ideal.

PEONIES ARE LOVELY

Peonies are among the easiest to grow of all perennials — if you live where winters are cold. In spite of the delicacy of their fragrant blos-soms, they are hardy, durable, and so long-lived that they will probably outlast you. However, they are not for the deep south or other warm-winter areas; they need an annual period of freezing weather in order to thrive and bloom.

The plant is attractive from early spring, when its reddish shoots appear, until it dies down in a blaze of autumn glory. Winter protection is never necessary, though beneficial in northern sections. Its blooming period is about two months. There are hundreds of varieties to choose from, ranging in color from purest white to the deepest of maroon reds. We are talking here, of course, about herbaceous peonies and primarily the common varieties of the species *Paeonia albiflora,* also called lactiflora, sinensis, and chinensis. The woody-stemmed "tree peonies," though related, belong to other species. Some of the new hybrids vary from 6 inches to 60 inches in height and bloom two or three weeks earlier than the others. Their flowers are from 2 to 12 inches across in a wide color range that includes yellow, lilacs, scarlets, greens, cherries, purples, and some that are almost black.

Peony flowers are of five distinct types. *Singles* have five or more true petals arranged around a circle of stamens, which in turn surround the carpels of future seed pods. *Japanese-type* blooms have five or more true petals around a center of more or less transformed stamens, called "staminodes." The *Anemone* type closely resembles the Japanese, except that the stamens have been transformed into small, narrow, petal-like "petalodes." The carpels are normal in both these types, which are often grouped together in catalogs. *Semidoubles* have several rows of petals and many stamens which may be intermingled with, or in rows among, the petals, or grouped in a central tuft. The carpels may be normal or more or less transformed into petals. *Doubles* have all their stamens, and often the carpels, transformed into petals, though occasionally true or abortive stamens may be found hidden among the petals; thus there are many subforms within the double type. Peony blossoms are long-lasting, lend themselves to many kinds of arrangements, and are unsurpassed for exhibition; but some fine show varieties have weak stems and need support in the garden. Peonies make handsome specimen plants and also do well in borders.

PLANTING PEONIES

Autumn is the best time of year to plant peonies, September in northernmost states, October in the midsection of the country, and November or December in mild climates. The site selected should be sunny. Peonies love sunshine and should have it for about half of each day — the more sun, the more bloom. Keep them away from big shrubs and trees whose roots would deprive them of food and moisture. Peonies are not fussy about soil, but cannot tolerate soggy ground. And place the plants where they can remain permanently for they dislike being dug up and moved.

It sets them back. The season following transplanting is a period of adjustment; newly set plants seldom bloom the following summer. After they become established, however, they grow larger each year, and produce more and more blooms.

Planting is a simple matter, but there are some things that you should know. First of all, the plant you purchase (unless it is a potted one in full growth) will be dormant and a very peculiar-looking affair. It will consist of a cluster of bare woody roots with a few buds (next year's shoots) at the top. Probably the roots will have been shortened by pruning. Dig a hole much wider and deeper than the size of these abbreviated roots. It should measure at least 1½ feet each way. If more than one peony is to be set, allow 3 feet spacing between the plants. Work some complete fertilizer into the bottom of the hole, where it will not come into direct contact with the roots. (Follow the manufacturer's directions as to the amount.)

When placing the plant in the hole, the important thing to watch is the depth of the buds below ground level. If they are too deep, the plant may fail to bloom. The best depth in the North is 2 inches, in central sections of the country it is 1½ inches, and in the South just below ground level. Allow for the fact that the plants will probably sink a little deeper as the soil in the hole gradually settles. Firm the earth carefully around the roots, then sprinkle it generously with water. In a severely cold climate the plant should be mounded with soil during the first winter. The mound should be removed in the spring.

Dividing and transplanting of old clumps is best done in the autumn, but can also be done in the early spring. One method is to dig the entire clump, wash the earth away so that the root structure can be seen, and cut the tangle into divisions carrying two or more buds apiece. Another technique involves removing a start from an old plant without disturbing the main clump. To do this, cut down through the plant with a spade, prying and digging out the wanted piece.

Once they are planted, peonies require little or no care. They are grateful for an annual early-spring feeding of any balanced plant food, and appreciate water during droughts, but they can survive a lot of neglect. When you pick flowers, try not to take more foliage than necessary. And never cut the plants to the ground before autumn. Leaves produce food of the plant's future growth, and removing them has a weakening effect. Do not let seed pods develop, because ripening them takes strength from the plant. The thing to do is to cut off each flower head when it begins to wither. Cut back to the top large leaf on the stem.

Peonies are remarkably free of diseases and pests. Ants crawling over the buds cause no direct damage, but may spread disease. They can be controlled by dusting the ground around the plant with chlordane. If stems or buds turn black and moldy, the plant probably has botrytis blight. This disease usually develops during damp weather, and among crowded plants where air circulation is poor. As a preventive measure, cut the plants to the ground each fall and burn the tops. Each spring, spray the emerging young shoots with captan, zineb, ferbam, or maneb (1½ tablespoons per gallon, plus a detergent) and continue spraying at 10-day intervals.

The reward for this very simple care is a mass of perfumed blossoms in the summer and ever increasing bloom as the seasons roll by.

RECOMMENDED PEONY VARIETIES

WHITE	RED	PINK

Early

WHITE	RED	PINK
'Christine' (J)	'Big Ben' (D)	'Dainty' (S)
'Festiva Maxima' (D)	'Gopher Beauty' (S)	'Kagawa' (J)
'Minnie Shaylor' (Semi-D)	'Mrs. Wilder Bancroft' (J)	'Mrs. Franklin D. Roosevelt' (D)
'Mme. de Verneville' (D)	*Officinalis Rubro-plena* (D)	*Officinalis Rosea-plena* (D)
Officinalis Alba-plena (D)	'Richard Carvel' (D)	'Therese' (D)
'Pico' (S)	'The Mighty Mo' (D)	

Midseason

WHITE	RED	PINK
'Isani-Gidui' (J)	'Imperial Red' (S)	'Gay Paree' (J)
'Kelway's Glorious' (D)	'Felix Crousse' (D)	'La Perle' (D)
'Krinkled White' (S)	'Mikado' (J)	'Mons. Jules Elie' (D)
'May Morn' (D)	'Kansas' (D)	Sarah Bernhardt' (D)
'Mother's Day' (D)	'Ruth Clay' (D)	'Sea Shell' (S)
'Sister Margaret' (D)	'Shawnee Chief' (D)	'Walter Faxon' (D)

Late

WHITE	RED	PINK
'Henry Sass' (D)	'Highlight' (D)	'Hansina Brand' (D)
'La Lorraine' (D)	'Karl Rosenfield' (D)	'Martha Bulloch' (D)
'Mary E. Nicholls' (D)	'Kickapoo' (S)	'Minuet' (D)
'Roberta' (J)	'Nippon Beauty' (J)	'Mischief' (S)
'Solange' (D)	'Phillippe Rivoire' (D)	'Mrs. Livingston Farrand' (D)
'Watchman' (S)	'Tempest' (D)	'Nippon Gold' (J)

D-Double   S-Single   J-Japanese

16

A Folio of
Conversation Gardens

THE CITY GARDEN

By city garden we mean here the small, intimate gardens close to the center of a great city where many handicaps must be overcome. The plants suffer from pent-up air trapped between brick walls and fences; from heat accumulated in brick and stone, and from the heavy shade cast by solid buildings. Or exactly the opposite may be true of a penthouse high above the streets where glaring sunlight, high winds, and lack of shelter make plant growth precarious.

Space is almost always a factor. Few city lots have room enough to permit elaborate landscaping. In one way, smallness is an advantage, because in most such gardens every ounce of stone, soil, plant material, and other essentials must be wheeled in by hand.

Of all the handicaps to the city garden, soot accumulation is perhaps the worst. Any plant selected must be able to tolerate it. Equally important, it must have smooth leaves which can be washed to remove grime.

Despite all these handicaps, some of the country's most delightful gardens grow close to the centers of our great cities. The Sutton Place area in New York, Old Town in Chicago, and the tiny patches behind old Beacon Hill houses in Boston are examples. Each carefully tended plot tells of a person who loved gardens enough to triumph over city conditions.

The Landscape Design

Most city gardens must be designed very simply — without elaborate focal points. Opportunities for framing distant views are practically non-existent except on a penthouse terrace. The area facing the street is usually so tiny that little or nothing can be done with it; 95 per cent of these gardens are in backyards.

A small-sized lot allows little room for hedges; tall fences or walls often are specified for the city garden, but these are a barrier against the free movement of air. The new perforated ceramic tiles, which form a pattern when laid, are better. They provide for a grill-like structure which permits air to circulate, but obstructs direct sight lines. If wooden fences are used, they should be made with staggered boards, so that air can move through them.

Privacy is, of course, even more difficult to achieve. Few city gardens are far enough from some tall building to be hidden from tenants on the upper floors. Sometimes a pergola can be built and vines trained across it to break up such sight lines.

Landscape Features

Because of the need for dramatic accents in a design of limited scope, the city garden particularly needs such objects as small pools, wall fountains, small pergolas, interesting statuary, or unusual plant material. The sound of running water is especially pleasant on a hot city night and should be provided whenever possible.

If masonry walls are used, vines can be trained against them in an interesting pattern, as is done so effectively in California. Roses on trellises, particularly the new climbers that flower off and on all summer, are highly attractive.

Gravel walks are particularly appropriate for such small gardens. They can be wet down so that they give off a cooling vapor. They allow water to move down into the soil instead of trapping it like concrete or asphalt. And they can be sprayed with modern weed-killers to keep them weed-free. If the right gravel is selected, such a walk can be highly decorative. Here we can learn much from the Japanese, whose use of white-and-gray washed pebbles reaches the status of a fine art. Granite chips also are highly decorative and can be had in unusual colors.

Space for outdoor living can be provided by paving an area with flagstone, slate, or brick. On such a terrace, the planter boxes and pots described at the end of this chapter are appropriate. To hide such utilities as garbage cans, plant a couple of good, solid evergreens such as Japanese yews.

Tucked inside its vine-covered fence, this city garden has a lawn, a terrace, a path, trees, a raised planter, and privacy without crowding.

PLANTS FOR CITY GARDENS

Plants selected for city gardens must be species that can survive in rather dry soils, and thrive in spite of heavy shade and smoke pollution. Evergreens will endure only if washed regularly to remove accumulated soot. If the soot clings, use a light solution of a dishwashing detergent. Spray it on, allow it to remain a minute, then hose it off.

DECIDUOUS TREES

Ailanthus altissima, Tree of Heaven
Aesculus hippocastanum,
 Horse Chestnut
Aralia spinosa, Devil's Walking-stick
Carpinus betulus,
 European Hornbeam
Cornus florida,
 Flowering Dogwood
C. mas, Cornelian Cherry
Elaeagnus angustifolia,
 Russian Olive
Fraxinus americana, White Ash
Ginkgo biloba, Maidenhair Tree

Liriodendron tulipifera, Tulip Tree
Magnolia soulangeana,
 Saucer Magnolia
M. stellata, Star Magnolia
Platanus acerifolia, London Plane
Quercus coccinea, Scarlet Oak
Q. palustris, Pin Oak
Salix babylonica, Weeping Willow
Sophora japonica,
 Chinese Scholar Tree
Tilia cordata, Little-leaf Linden
T. vulgaris, European Linden

EVERGREENS

Picea pungens, Colorado Spruce

Pinus mugo mughus, Mugho Pine

P. sylvestris, Scotch Pine

Taxus cuspidata, Japanese Yew

SHRUBS

Acanthopanax sieboldianus,
    Five-leaved Aralia

Amorpha fruticosa, Bastard Indigo

Aronia arbutifolia,
    Red Chokeberry

Benzoin aestivale, Spicebush

Berberis thunbergi,
    Japanese Barberry

Caragana arborescens,
    Siberian Pea Tree

Chaenomeles lagenaria,
    Japanese Flowering Quince

Cornus alba sibirica,
    Coral Dogwood

Deutzia scabra, Rough Deutzia

Forsythia, various species,
    Golden Bells

Hamamelis virginiana,
    Autumn Witch Hazel

Hibiscus syriacus, Rose of Sharon

Ligustrum amurense,
    Amur River Privet

Mahonia aquifolium,
    Oregon Holly-grape

Pyracantha coccinea, Firethorn

Rhamnus frangula,
    Alder Buckthorn

Rhus canadensis, Aromatic Sumac

R. copallina, Shining Sumac

Ribes alpinum, Alpine Currant

Sorbaria sorbifolia, False Spirea

Syringa, various species, Lilacs

VINES

The value of vines can best be appreciated after seeing some multistory brick apartment building turned into a soft mass of green by a few plants of Boston ivy, or the dense overlapping leaves of Dutchman's pipe forming a curtain which the eye cannot penetrate over a pergola. Because they are practically two-dimensional, vines can be grown on walls as backgrounds where no room exists for a regular shrub border.

Actinidia polygama, Silver Vine

Aristolochia durior,
    Dutchman's Pipe

Campsis radicans, Trumpet Vine

Celastrus scandens, Bittersweet

Lonicera japonica halliana,
    Hall's Japanese Honeysuckle

Parthenocissus quinquefolia,
    Virginia Creeper

P. tricuspidata, Boston Ivy

Polygonum auberti,
    Silver Lace Vine

GROUNDCOVERS

Groundcovers must often substitute for lawns in city gardens because of the difficulty of maintaining turf in dense shade. Even where some sun reaches the area, groundcovers should be considered because of the labor they save. Small plots of turf are a nuisance to trim and are usually subject to disease because of poor air circulation. The following are good city substitutes for lawns.

Aegopodium podagraria, Goutweed
Ajuga reptans, Carpet Bugle
Cotoneaster horizontalis,
   Rose Rockspray
Euonymus radicans, Wintercreeper

Hedera helix baltica, Baltic Ivy
Pachysandra terminalis,
   Japanese Spurge
Phlox subulata, Creeping Phlox
Vinca minor, Periwinkle

ANNUALS

Few annuals tolerate both shade and smoke. The following will do well with about five hours of direct sunshine a day. Of these, impatiens, lobelia, nicotiana, torenia, and *Vinca rosea* will survive in light filtered shade such as that found under an oak or an ash.

Ageratum	Larkspur	Salvia
Celosia	Lobelia	Snapdragon
Cleome	Marigold	Sweet Alyssum
Coleus	Nicotiana	Torenia
Coreopsis	Petunia	Verbena
Dianthus	*Phlox drummondi*	*Vinca rosea*
Four-o'clock	Portulaca	Zinnia
Impatiens		

PERENNIALS

Because of the short blooming season of most perennials, it is best to use only those which have attractive foliage when not in flower. This means planting them in rather large masses, since small groups of plants with mixed foliage do not give a calm, peaceful effect. Use at least six plants of a single species in a clump. With the small size of city gardens as a limitation, perennials may not be worth planting. To be considered are:

Ajuga reptans, Carpet Bugle

Aquilegia canadensis,
    American Columbine

Astilbe, various species, Spireas

Bergenia cordifolia,
    Siberian Saxifrage

Ceratostigma plumbaginoides,
    Plumbago

Convallaria majalis,
    Lily-of-the-valley

Dianthus barbatus, Sweet William

Digitalis purpurea, Foxglove

Hemerocallis, various species,
    Daylilies

Heuchera sanguinea, Coral Bells

Hosta, various species,
    Plantain Lilies

Phlox divaricata,
    Wild Sweet William

Bedding Plants

Plants in pots and tubs will need constant attention unless grown in self-watering pots. The dry, hot air of a closed-in garden takes moisture from the soil much faster than air in an open space. If the terrace receives a few hours of sunshine, geraniums in large tubs can be quite dramatic. Fuchsias are effective in shady spots, particularly if grown in tree form. Fancy-leaved caladiums and tuberous begonias are lovely, but die quickly in bad smoke areas.

Disease Control

Red-spider mites thrive in the close, dry air found in city gardens. They can be kept down by hitting the underside of foliage with a stream of water almost daily. Otherwise, standard miticides should be used regularly. Aphids are a nuisance too, but are readily controlled by regular spraying.

Penthouse Gardens

Plants on a rooftop can be exciting, but to handle them properly requires more information than can be given in a few paragraphs. Some very serious problems can be created by carelessly built boxes filled with soil. This is a job for a professional landscape architect who either knows his building engineering or consults with a regular architect. He will have to go into such details as roof drains (soil can play havoc with traps), allowable floor loads (soil is heavy), and internal transportation. A cubic yard of soil on top of a skyscraper can cost as much as a modern refrigerator!

Seaside landscape: *Raised planter holds imported topsoil for annuals and greenery. Concrete ring allows an extra depth of soil for tough little tree. Goundcover below is of pebbled concrete slabs and tanbark.*

THE SEASIDE GARDEN

Seashores and sand dunes are difficult to landscape, but with patience plants can be made to grow. Select plants that are resistant to salt spray and dry air — the protective mechanism is the same for both — and establish them in imported garden soil.

The initial problem is to hold food and moisture in the soil long enough to get the plants started. Once they are growing, their roots will go down deep enough to enable them to survive. One way to get an important tree or shrub started is to knock the bottom out of a barrel, sink the barrel to its rim in sand, and plant the tree in it, using rich garden soil. During the first two years, keep it well watered.

Soil itself is a problem on sand. Any fertilizer, humus, soil, or other material applied to sand works down until it disappears, often in a matter of a few days. The best treatment, if the cost is not prohibitive, is to have the area bulldozed out to a depth of 24 inches and the sand piled to one side. A layer of plastic or roofing paper is then laid over and covered with organic matter such as salt hay, straw, peatmoss, fish scrap, garbage, or compost. Sprinkle this layer (up to a foot deep) with a good mixed fertilizer, and replace the sand. If black soil or muck is available, it can be mixed with the sand. The layer of plastic or paper delays the loss of soil-building materials long enough for cultivated plants to form fibrous roots to hold the mass together and begin the formation of a true soil. By the time it disintegrates it is no longer needed.

HARDY SEASIDE PLANTS

TREES

Abies homolepis, Nikko Fir
A. veitchi,
    Japanese Purple-cone Fir
Acer pseudo-platanus,
    Sycamore Maple
Albizzia julibrissin rosea, Silk Tree
Caragana arborescens,
    Siberian Pea Tree
Elaeagnus angustifolia,
    Russian Olive
Fagus sylvatica, European Beech
Gleditsia triacanthos, Honey Locust

Juniperus virginiana keteleeri,
    Bottle-green Juniper
Maclura pomifera, Osage Orange
Nyssa sylvatica, Sour Gum
Picea glauca, White Spruce
Pinus mugo, Swiss Mountain Pine
P. nigra, Austrian Pine
P. nigra calabrica, Corsican Pine
P. sylvestris, Scotch Pine
P. thunbergi, Japanese Black Pine
Platanus acerifolia, London Plane
Populus alba, White Poplar

SHRUBS

Amelanchier canadensis, Shadblow
Arctostaphylos uva-ursi, Bearberry
Aronia arbutifolia, Red Chokeberry
Baccharis halimifolia,
    Groundsel Bush
Buddleia davidi, Butterfly Bush
Calluna vulgaris, Scotch Heather
Caryopteris incana, Blue Spirea
Clethra alnifolia, Sweet Pepperbush
Cornus amomum, Silky Cornel
C. baileyi, Red Dogwood
Cotoneaster divaricata,
    Spreading Rockspray
C. horizontalis, Rose Rockspray
Cytisus praecox, Warminster Broom
C. scoparius, Scotch Broom
Euonymus alatus,
    Winged Burning-bush
Gaylussacia baccata,
    High-bush Huckleberry
G. dumosa, Gopherberry

Hippophaë rhamnoides,
    Sea Buckthorn
Hydrangea macrophylla,
    House Hydrangea
H. petiolaris, Climbing Hydrangea
Hypericum calycinum,
    Aaron's Beard
Ilex glabra, Inkberry
I. opaca, American Holly
I. verticillata, Winterberry
Juniperus horizontalis,
    Creeping Juniper
J. sabina, Savin Juniper
Leiophyllum buxifolium,
    Sand Myrtle
Ligustrum amurense,
    Amur River Privet
L. vulgare, Common Privet
Myrica cerifera, Wax Myrtle
M. gale, Sweet Gale
M. pensylvanica, Bayberry

Prunus maritima, Beach Plum

Rosa blanda, Beach Rose

R. hugonis, Father Hugo's Rose

R. nitida, Shiny Rose

R. rugosa, Rugosa Rose

Sambucus canadensis,
     American Elderberry

Tamarix odessana, Caspian Saltbush

T. pentandra, Amur Saltbush

Taxus cuspidata, Japanese Yew

Vaccinium corymbosum,
     High-bush Blueberry

V. macrocarpon, Cranberry

V. vitis-idaea, Cowberry

Viburnum dentatum, Arrow-wood

ANNUALS

If shelter is provided and the soil is built up behind it, almost any annual suitable to the climate can be grown. The following list contains only those that are highly drought resistant and have some tolerance for salt.

Abronia umbellata, Sand Verbena

Ageratum houstonianum, Ageratum

Alyssum maritimum, Sweet Alyssum

Mesembryanthemum crystallinum,
     Ice Plant

Petunia hybrida, Petunia

Phlox drummondi, Annual Phlox

Portulaca grandiflora, Moss Rose

PERENNIALS

See remarks under annuals.

Aletris farinosa, Colic Root

Artemisia canadensis,
     Sea Wormwood

A. stelleriana, Old Woman

Asclepias tuberosa, Butterfly Weed

Baptisia australis,
     Blue False Lupine

Campanula rotundifolia,
     Bluebells of Scotland

Chrysopsis falcata, Golden Aster

Coreopsis grandiflora, Coreopsis

C. maritima, Sea Dahlia

Echinops ritro, Globe Thistle

Empetrum nigrum, Crowberry

Euphorbia corollata,
     Flowering Spurge

Gaillardia aristata, Blanket Flower

Glaucium flavum, Sea Poppy

Hemerocallis, various species,
     Daylily

Hibiscus palustris, Sea Mallow

Lantana camara, Yellow Sage

Lathyrus maritimus, Beach Pea

Limonium sinuatum, Sea Pink

Oenothera biennis,
     Evening Primrose

O. missouriensis, Missouri Primrose

Opuntia compressa, Prickly Pear

Silene maritima, Sea Campion

Solidago sempervirens,
     Beach Goldenrod

Thermopsis caroliniana,
  Aaron's Rod
Thymus serpyllum,
  Mother-of-thyme

T. vulgaris, Garden Thyme
Yucca filamentosa, Adam's Needle

GRASSES

Most of the grasses that will survive on beach sand are not sold commercially but must be collected locally and transplanted. If any domestic grass will succeed, it is a tall fescue. Both 'Alta' and 'Kentucky 31' fescues will send their roots down 3 feet for water. For lawns, seed at a heavy rate — 10 pounds to 1,000 square feet.

WARM-CLIMATE SEASIDE PLANTS

TREES

Acacia verticillata, Star Wattle
Araucaria araucana, Monkey Puzzle
A. bidwilli, Bunya Bunya
A. cunninghami, Moreton Bay Pine
A. excelsa, Norfolk Island Pine
Eriobotrya japonica, Loquat
Ficus retusa,
  Malayan Rubber Tree
Lagunaria patersoni,
  Australian Tulip Tree
Leptospermum laevigatum,
  Australian Tea Tree

L. pubescens, Silky Tea Tree
L. scoparium, Tea Tree
Libocedrus decurrens,
  Incense Cedar
Ligustrum ovalifolium,
  California Privet
Melaleuca armillaris, Bottlebrush
Metrosideros tomentosa, Iron Tree
Olea europaea, Olive
Prunus lyoni, Evergreen Cherry
Sabal palmetto, Palmetto

SHRUBS

Carissa grandiflora, Natal Plum
Cistus, various species, Rock-roses
Coccolobis uvifera, Sea Grape
Coprosma baueri, Mirror Plant
Echium fastuosum,
  Shrubby Viper's Bugloss
Elaeagnus pungens, Silverleaf
Escallonia rosea,
  Peruvian Honeysuckle

Euonymus japonicus,
  Evergreen Burning-bush
Genista monosperma,
  African Broom
Hakea laurina, Sea Urchin
Juniperus conferta, Sand Juniper
Lavatera assurgentiflora,
  American Tree Mallow
Lonicera nitida, Box Honeysuckle

Myoporum laetum,
    Bastard Sandalwood
Nerium oleander, Oleander
Phlomis fruticosa, Jerusalem Sage
Pittosporum crassifolium, Karo

Rhus integrifolia, Sourberry
Ruscus aculeatus, Butcher's Broom
Severinia buxifolia, Spiny Box
Spartium junceum, Spanish Broom

VINES

Bougainvillea spectabilis,
    Bougainvillea
Lycium halimifolium,
    Matrimony Vine

Muehlenbeckia complexa,
    Wire Vine

PERENNIALS

Ceratostigma plumbaginoides,
    Plumbago
Lavandula spica, Lavender

Mesembryanthemum edule,
    Hottentot Fig
Phormium tenax, New Zealand Flax
Romneya coulteri, Matilija Poppy

THE WILDFLOWER GARDEN

Wildflower gardens are suitable only for uncultivated areas such as woodlands and fields, and the banks of streams. On large properties they are logical extensions of formal beds and borders. Since all flowers are wild in some part of the world, one need not be a purist in making selections. Choose plants that grow naturally in your region, and exotics that are informal in habit and seem to suit your garden.

One caution is in order: when introducing an exotic species, be careful not to include a plant so aggressive that it will crowd out less vigorous, more desirable native species. The Japanese honeysuckle along the eastern seaboard and the water hyacinth in Florida have become pests. On the other hand, this ability to smother all obstacles is occasionally an advantage. Gardeners who might shudder at the thought of introducing creeping Jenny (*Nepeta hederacea*), into a wild garden might well consider it as a plant for some shaded area where few other plants will grow. But be sure that its spread is limited by concrete drives and walks or other barriers. Fortunately, new herbicides now permit gardeners to use these aggressive plants without fear that they will get out of hand.

Natural Associations

Two factors should be considered in the selection of plants for wild gardens — ecology and climate. Ecology deals with associations. Some

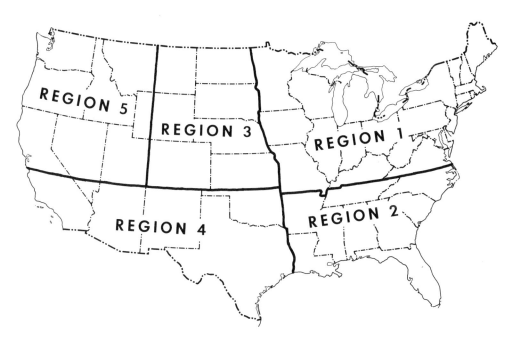

plants thrive in marshes and bogs, alpines live on rocks, while others do best in prairies and meadows. The limited number of desirable bog and marsh plants are mentioned in the description of water gardens. Alpines are treated under rock gardens. Woodland plants are those that belong on the forest floor. They are shade tolerant and usually must be able to survive with limited food and water supplies. As a rough guide to what plants may be grown in a given area, the country can be divided into roughly five regions (see map). In the following lists, if a plant is not marked with region numbers, it can be tried anywhere in the United States and Canada with the possible exception of Florida and the warmer parts of Texas and southern California.

Woodland Plants

The widest use of wildflowers is in planting the forest floor under trees. Except for parts of the Great Plains, about 90 per cent of all wild gardens are established artificially in such locations.

Unfortunately, many of our loveliest native woodland plants are difficult to transplant and must be seeded. They resent being moved unless grown in pots by specialists who understand their peculiar soil needs. It is almost impossible for amateurs to transplant them from the woods. If no dealer in trailing arbutus, Jack-in-the-pulpit, bloodroot, and gentian can be found, forget them and concentrate on easy plants like *Phlox divaricata*, English bluebells, wood asters, and Virginia bluebells.

PLANTS SUITABLE FOR WILD GARDENS

HERBACEOUS PLANTS

A few in the following list are woody or slightly woody plants, but they give the appearance of herbaceous plants and they blend well with them. For additional species, see the list of prairie wildflowers at the end of this chapter.

Actaea alba, White Baneberry

A. rubra, Red Baneberry

Amsonia tabernaemontana (2, 4), Blue Shadow

Anemone quinquefolia (1, 3, 5), Wood Anemone

Anemonella thalictroides (1, 5), Rue Anemone

Aquilegia canadensis, American Columbine

Aralia nudicaulis, Wild Sarsaparilla

Arisaema triphyllum, Jack-in-the-pulpit

Asarum canadense (1, 3, 5), Wild Ginger

Aster cordifolius, Blue Wood Aster

A. divaricatus, White Wood Aster

Astilbe species, False Spirea

Caltha palustris, Marsh Marigold

Camassia esculenta, Camass

Chimaphila maculata (1, 3, 5), Spotted Wintergreen

C. umbellata, Prince's Pine

Cimicifuga americana, Snakeroot

C. racemosa, Black Cohosh

Claytonia virginica, Spring Beauty

Collinsonia canadensis, Horse Balm

Cornus canadensis (1, 3, 5), Bunchberry

Corydalis sempervirens, Pale Corydalis

Dicentra cucullaria, Dutchman's Breeches

Dodecatheon meadia (1, 3, 5), Shooting Star

Epigaea repens (1, 5), Trailing Arbutus

Erythronium americanum (1, 3, 5) Trout Lily

Fragaria vesca, Wood Strawberry

Gentiana crinita (1, 5), Fringed Gentian

Hepatica americana (1, 3, 5), Hepatica

Impatiens biflora, Jewelweed

Iris cristata, Crested Iris

Lilium superbum, Turk's-cap Lily

Liparis liliifolia, Twayblade

Lobelia cardinalis, Cardinal Flower

L. siphilitica, Great Blue Lobelia

Lysimachia nummularia, Creeping Charlie

Maianthemum canadense,
    Canadian Mayflower

Mertensia virginica,
    Virginia Bluebell

Mimulus ringens,
    Allegheny Monkey Flower

Mitchella repens, (1, 3, 5),
    Partridge-berry

Mitella diphylla, Mitrewort

Muscari botryoides,
    Grape Hyacinth

Myosotis sylvatica,
    Wood Forget-me-not

Phlox divaricata,
    Wild Sweet William

Podophyllum peltatum, May Apple

Polemonium reptans, Bluebell

Polygala paucifolia, Gay Wings

Polygonatum biflorum,
    Solomon's Seal

Pyrola elliptica, Shinleaf

Sanguinaria canadensis, Bloodroot

Scilla nonscripta, English Bluebell

Smilacina racemosa,
    False Solomon's Seal

S. stellata, Starry Solomon's Seal

Staphylea trifolia,
    American Bladdernut

Streptopus roseus, Twisted Stalk

Thalictrum dioicum,
    Early Meadow Rue

Tiarella cordifolia, Foamflower

Trientalis borealis, Starflower

Trillium erectum, Wake-robin

T. grandiflorum, White Trillium

Uvularia grandiflora,
    Wood Daffodil

U. perfoliata, Mealy Bellwort

U. sessilifolia, Wild Oats

Veratrum viride, False Hellebore

Viola, various species, Violet

FERNS

Ferns are among the most valuable plants for woodland gardens. Their only drawback is their lack of color other than green, but this is more than offset by their period of delicate leafy growth. They are among the first plants to emerge in spring and some continue until after early frosts. A choice few are evergreen or nearly so (marked E below). Ferns are generally pest-free, and they demand little care. In the following list, those marked only for Region 1 will usually grow in moist areas along the coast in Regions 4 and 5, as well as in areas with damp soil along the southern Atlantic coast. They are not worth trying in dry sections of Regions 2, 3, 4, and 5.

Adiantum pedatum (1),
    American Maidenhair

Asplenium ruta-muraria (E) (1),
    Wall Rue

Athyrium filix-femina (1),
    Lady Fern

A. thelypteroides (1),
    Silvery Spleenwort

Botrychium dissectum (E) (1),
    Cutleaf Grape Fern

B. obliquum (1), Grape Fern

B. virginianum (1),
   Rattlesnake Fern
Cystopteris bulbifera (1),
   Bladder Fern
C. fragilis (1), Brittle Fern
Dennstaedtia punctilobula (1),
   Hay-scented Fern
Dryopteris species, Wood Ferns
Onoclea sensibilis (1),
   Sensitive Fern
Osmunda cinnamomea (1),
   Cinnamon Fern
O. claytoniana (1),
   Interrupted Fern

O. regalis, Royal Fern
Pellaea atropurpurea, Cliff Brake
Polypodium vulgare (E),
   Common Polypody
Polystichum acrostichoides (E),
   Christmas Fern
P. lonchitis (E),
   Mountain Holly Fern
P. munitum (E) (Moist woods 4, 5),
   Sword Fern
Pteretis nodulosa, Ostrich Fern
Pteridium aquilinum, Bracken
Woodwardia aerolata (Moist woods
   1, 4, 5), Chain Fern

PRAIRIE WILDFLOWERS

Open areas are usually suited to more sophisticated flowers, but many home-owners in semi-rural areas have open stretches where the cultivation of garden flowers would be too difficult and where naturalistic treatment solves a problem at less expense. Care must be taken to eliminate weeds (particularly quackgrass), which quickly kill out many beautiful species; otherwise little attention is needed. Just loosen the soil where seeds are to be planted or seedlings set out.

Achillea ageratum, Golden Yarrow
A. millefolium roseum, Rosy Milfoil
A. ptarmica, Sneezewort
Asclepias tuberosa, Butterfly Weed
A. verticillata, Whorled Milkweed
Aster ericoides, Heath Aster
A. novae-angliae,
   New England Aster
A. novi-belgi, New York Aster
Baptisia australis, False Indigo
B. tinctoria, Clover Broom
Delphinium ajacis, Rocket Larkspur
Echinacea angustifolia,
   Purple Daisy
E. purpurea, Hedgehog Coneflower
Helenium autumnale, Yellow Star

Helianthus annuus,
   Common Sunflower
H. tuberosus, Jerusalem Artichoke
Leonurus cardiaca, Lion's Tail
Liatris pycnostachya,
   Kansas Gayfeather
L. scariosa, Blazing Star
Linaria vulgaris, Butter-and-eggs
Linum lewisi, Prairie Flax
Lobelia siphilitica,
   Great Blue Lobelia
Lupinus perennis, Quaker Bonnets
L. subcarnosus, Texas Bluebonnet
Lychnis alba, Evening Campion
L. coronaria, Dusty Miller
L. flos-cuculi, Ragged Robin

Lysimachia vulgaris,
   Golden Loosestrife
Lythrum salicaria,
   Purple Loosestrife
Monarda citriodora, Lemon Mint
M. didyma, Beebalm
M. fistulosa, Wild Bergamot
Oenothera missouriensis,
   Missouri Primrose
O. speciosa, Showy Primrose
Penstemon, various species,
   Beardtongues
Phlox bifida, Sand Phlox
P. divaricata, Wild Sweet William
P. drummondi, Annual Phlox

P. maculata, Wild Sweet William
Rudbeckia fulgida,
   Orange Coneflower
R. hirta, Black-eyed Susan
Saponaria officinalis, Bouncing Bet
S. vaccaria, Cow Cockle
Silene armeria,
   Sweet-William Catchfly
Solidago, various species,
   Goldenrods
Thermopsis caroliniana, Aaron's Rod
Verbena bipinnatifida,
   Prairie Verbena
Yucca filamentosa, Adam's Needle

THE HERB GARDEN

Herbs are grown to add piquancy to cooking, for fragrance, and (in a rather limited way today) for medicinal use. They are seldom planted in masses, but as miniature gardens, easy to establish and to tend. A plot 6 feet square is all the space needed.

A special charm of the herb garden is its subtlety. Leaves of the plants are softly green or gray, the modest flowers generally are dressed in delicate lavenders and pinks, and the scents are elusive.

Culture

Herbs are essentially poor-land plants, developing their highest flavor and fragrance on less fertile soils baked by the sun. Adapted to survival in situations that few plants tolerate, they should be grown on sandy banks exposed to the full sun or on exhausted soils. They do not respond to heavy applications of fertilizer and, except for occasional weeding, need little care.

Practically all herbs crave full sunlight, yet seem to display their charms best when the area in which they grow is enclosed by walls, hedges, or heavy plantings. When exposed to winds, their delicate fragrance is often blown away.

Annual herbs are sown in early spring in the place where they are to grow. Few herbs transplant well. Perennials can be grown from seed sown early in spring, from divisions of older plants, or from cuttings. In the following list "A" means annual, "P" perennial.

CULINARY, MEDICINAL, AND FRAGRANT HERBS

ANGELICA (*Angelica archangelica*) P. Roots candied as confection, leaves boiled with fish, midrib of leaf blanched and eaten like celery, leaves and stems stewed with rhubarb. Several supposed medicinal virtues.

ANISE (*Pimpinella anisum*) A. Seeds used to flavor candies, bread, stews, soups, and wines. Bags filled with anise were used as a drag to train foxhounds.

BALM (*Melissa officinalis*) P. Leaves used to flavor egg dishes, tea, soups, stews, salads, and summer drinks. Add small amounts to tarragon vinegar. Some supposed medicinal virtues.

BASIL (*Ocimum basilicum*) A. Add to spaghetti sauce, steep in vinegar, use in tomato juice, stewed tomatoes, cream cheese, chopped meat. Flavor butter sauce for use with fish. (The newer 'Dark Opal,' a purple-leaved variety, has a flavor not liked by some: test it before using widely.)

BEE BALM (*Monarda didyma*) P. Dried and laid in linens like lavender, several industrial and medicinal uses. One of the few bright-flowered herbs.

BORAGE (*Borago officinalis*) A. Young leaves added to summer greens, steeped in hot water and iced as summer drink; adds a cucumber flavor to salads. Dried blue flowers add color to *pot pourri*.

BURNET (*Sanguisorba minor*) treat as A. Steep in vinegar, add leaves to salads, use in iced beverages. Several supposed medicinal uses.

CALENDULA (*Calendula officinalis*) A. Substitute for saffron; adds yellow color to soups and stews. Use in custards to give rich deep color.

CARAWAY (*Carum carvi*) A. Steep seeds in vinegar, mix with rye-bread dough; add to German-style potato salad and sauerkraut; use in apple pie, baked apples, spiced beets, goulash, cabbage and potato soups; coat the seeds with sugar as comfits. Several supposed medicinal values.

CHAMOMILE or camomile (*Matricaria chamomilla*) P. Used in tea, supposedly as medicine, but pleasant to many for itself.

CHERVIL (*Anthriscus cerefolium*) A. Adds a mild parsley-like flavor to egg dishes, salads, fish, melted butter for chicken, spinach soup. An essential ingredient in Béarnaise and Ravigote sauces.

CHICORY (*Cichorium intybus*) P. Roasted roots used with coffee or as substitute for it. Blanched leaves are the witloof or French endive of commerce.

CHIVES (*Allium schoenoprasum*) P. Hollow tubular leaves with a delicate onion flavor: use wherever onions may be used. Add to cream or cottage cheese, to butter sauce for new potatoes, to soups.

CORIANDER (*Coriandrum sativum*) A. Seeds and leaves have an unpleasant odor when fresh but become pleasantly aromatic when dry. Use crushed seeds in bread, cake, cookies; coat whole seeds with sugar as a confection. Try with various meats, cream cheese. Drop three seeds in demitasse of espresso coffee.

DILL (*Anethum graveolens*) A. Use entire seed-head in cucumber pickles; steep seeds in vinegar; add to fish, lamb stew, potato salad, tomato juice. Use chopped leaves in salads and in cream sauce for chicken.

FENNEL (*Foeniculum*, various kinds) A. Finocchio (Italian bulb celery) is one herb that does better in rich soils. Use bulb at base as salad or relish, or boil it as a green vegetable. Use chopped leaves in foods mentioned under coriander. Seeds of garden fennel are used to flavor fish sauce, cakes, spiced beets, cream cheese, and German sauerkraut.

GOOD KING HENRY (*Chenopodium bonus-henricus*) P. Use as a pot herb, like spinach.

HOREHOUND (*Marrubium vulgare*) P. Use dried stems and flowers as tea, or as infusion to flavor candy.

LAVENDER (*Lavandule spica*) P. True lavender has a much more pleasant odor than spike lavender. Use dried flowers for linen sachets.

LOVAGE (*Levisticum officinale*) P. Dried or fresh leaves substitute for celery leaves.

MARJORAM (*Origanum* species) treat as A. Use fresh or dried leaves in spaghetti sauce, with snap beans, roast lamb, egg dishes, salads. Steep leaves in vinegar.

MINT (*Mentha* species) P. Mint tea from leaves is refreshing. Steep leaves in vinegar for use with roast lamb.

NASTURTIUM (*Tropaeolum majus*) A. Green seeds add piquant flavor to salads. Leaves make good sandwiches.

PARSLEY (*Petroselinum crispum*) treat as A. Three different parsleys are grown: plain or Italian has the strongest flavor, curled is best for garnishing, Hamburg rooted is boiled as a vegetable. Uses too familiar to list, but try minced parsley in a cream soup.

ROSE GERANIUM (*Pelargonium graveolens*) tender P. Use dried leaves as you would lavender. Add green leaves to apple jelly.

ROSEMARY (*Rosmarinus officinalis*) P. Leaves flavor spaghetti sauce, other sauces, veal stew, soups, roast pork, fried potatoes. Many supposed medicinal uses.

SAGE (*Salvia officinalis*) P. Leaves in poultry stuffing, sage tea, sausage, with roast pork. Several supposed medicinal uses.

SAVORY (*Satureja hortensis* and S. *montana*) both A. and P. forms. Leaves in snap beans, salads, sausage, poultry stuffing, with roast pork or lamb.

TARRAGON (*Artemisia dracunculus*) P. Same uses as anise, but mainly used to flavor vinegar.

THYME (*Thymus vulgaris*) P. Add to practically any dish where other herbs have a place, but use lightly. Used also as a tea.

How to Dry Herbs

Drying herbs is an art. Moisture must be evaporated but, since some of the essential oils go off with the water, care must be taken not to overdry them. Leaves should barely reach the crumbling stage.

Drying in direct sun is not recommended: flavor and color are too rapidly lost. The best place for drying is an airy *dark* attic. If all light can be excluded, most herbs will retain their natural green color.

Do not tie too many stems in a single bunch — ten is maximum — and hang them from the ceiling, stem ends up. Watch carefully and take down as soon as leaves can be crumbled between the fingers.

Store in sealed containers to avoid loss of flavor. A drop or two of essential oil of the particular plant is added to most commercial herbs. This is not unethical: it merely restores an element which goes off too rapidly. Most druggists can supply essential oils of various herbs in small quantities.

THE ROCK GARDEN

If this delightful branch of horticulture had been called by the name the British now use — alpine gardening — we might have fewer of the rock puddings that are known as rock gardens. Early in the present century, rock gardening attracted many persons who thought that any pile of rocks would do and that all species less than 3 feet tall were "rock-garden plants" suitable for the center of the heap. Fortunately, the vogue collapsed.

A few knowledgeable enthusiasts, however, most of them members of the American Rock Garden Society, continued collecting and growing alpine plants in a more appropriate style. It is to them that we owe today's increasing interest in this charming art.

Certain parts of the United States offer opportunities for duplicating — at least in part — the mountainous conditions where these plants grow naturally. A home built on a rock ledge, or where some huge boulder thrusts its monolithic mass into the landscape, cries out for the use of rock-garden techniques. Because many species can work their roots into tiny crevices and find enough soil to survive, they can be used where other plants would soon die. There is a fitness about alpine plants in such a situation which makes anything else seem out of place.

Rock gardens do not belong on flat, level land. Those that are created artificially belong only in a public park or botanic garden, where an attempt is made to display many aspects of horticulture. Even then they should be well built and tucked away from other types of gardens that would mar their distinctive beauty. Never, never should a rock garden be placed where the works of man protrude obviously into the picture. It should suggest a wild garden, grown without help, to delight a chance wayfarer.

Mechanics

The first essential of a rock garden is drainage. This should not be a superficial provision decanting excess water: it should be what alpine enthusiasts call "sharp." That is, it should be capable of absorbing a heavy downpour while the rain is falling, not a few moments later. If the rocks themselves are porous, so much the better.

One way to insure the right kind of drainage is to lay out the run-off lines before construction begins, making certain that these have outlets. Over these, lay a foot-deep layer of steam cinders to cover the entire area of the garden.

Rocks

· Although care must be taken not to make rocks the most prominent element in the garden, their proper selection is extremely important. Whenever possible, use a native rock. By this is meant material from a surface rock structure; quarried blocks of limestone from below the surface would be completely out of place. A cut surface on stone is unthinkable: every exposed face should be weathered, show natural stratification, and look as if nature had placed it.

Round stones never look right in a rock garden. Tufa rock, while useful for its structure (it absorbs its own weight in water) is poor in color, lays badly, and looks unnatural. A relatively new pumice-like, lightweight rock from California has better color, is stratified, and absorbs even more water than tufa. While less desirable than a good native stone, its light weight is an advantage. Another virtue is that it can be carved easily with an ax or chisel yet is so abrasive that the edges do not last long. When a channel must be cut in a rock to conduct water, this material is ideal. Pools and drinking fountains carved in it look as if they had been formed naturally.

For lime-loving plants, limestone ledge rock is usually easy to find and lays beautifully. Granite for lime-haters is more difficult to manage: slate or shale is usually easier to handle.

Plants

Rock gardening is culture in miniature. We use a few well-chosen gems, placed with appreciation for their form and color as part of a composition. Because of the relatively small number of plants needed, growing from seed is usually unnecessary except for some rare species not otherwise available. Always get exact instructions for growing the species — or any special variety — from the dealer. Culture is often a highly involved process and no general directions will do.

Sun or Shade

Many feel that a shaded rock garden is an anomaly, forgetting the forest floor coverings of mountain woods and the lovely ferns clinging to the walls of ravines. Even in the Alps, above the timber line, many audacious alpine plants will be found clinging to crevices on northern slopes where the sun seldom shines.

At the same time, the ability to tolerate intense sunshine is a quality found in many alpine species. Few can stand the drip of moisture from trees, nor do they flourish where trees and shrubs block the free movement of air around them.

Soil

One mistake often made in constructing a rock garden is to assume that, because the amount of soil in small pockets is limited, it must be rich. Alpine plants set in rich soil either puff up and sprawl piggishly across the rocks, or sicken and die. Usually they die.

For true high alpines, a mixture of 4 parts of crushed granite or limestone chips (depending on which type of plant is being grown), 2 parts of torpedo sand (a size that will go through a ⅜-inch mesh), and 1 part leafmold is a good mixture. The stone should be small enough to go through ½-inch mesh, but less than 10 per cent of it should pass through ordinary fly screening. Such a mixture comes close to duplicating the mixture of stone and humus in which these alpine plants grow high in the mountains. It is not a true soil: the only plant food is that which seeps down from the disintegrating leaves of last year's growth, plus the nitrogen brought down in rain water — not a rich diet, but adequate.

The humus breaks down slowly — perhaps releasing 10 per cent of its contained nitrogen a year. If you are overly neat and remove dead leaves each fall, a small amount of leafmold should be worked into the mixture each spring.

For smaller plants, those from 2,500 to 4,000-foot elevations, a somewhat richer mixture is needed. This can be made up of 3 parts of a good garden loam that is not too high in clay, 2 parts of leafmold, and 2 parts of crushed limestone for lime-lovers. All the crushed limestone should pass through a ⅜-inch mesh and less than 10 per cent through ordinary screen wire. For acid-soil lovers, substitute crushed granite or slate for the limestone and use an acid peat (Swedish or German brand) for the leafmold. If domestic peats are used, test them to be sure they are positively acid. Incidentally, the small amount of acidity supplied by oak leafmold is not enough to worry about. It can even be used with lime-loving plants if the limestone ingredient is added.

Where plants are likely to become too rampant, they can be held in check by limiting the amount of soil allowed them and by controlling fertility. One reason for using humus as a source of nutrition is that it breaks down so slowly that plants are never pushed too hard by it.

Fortunately, because of the sharp drainage in a rock garden, the problem of acid soil becoming alkaline and vice versa is avoided. There is little washing from one pocket of soil to another. Also, because drainage is down, the danger of sublimation — solutions rising to the surface and evaporating, leaving lime — is practically nil. Thus it is possible to provide pockets of treated soil for each species, almost side by side.

Actually, most rock-garden plants will grow well at a pH of between 6.0 and 6.9. The lists below have been confined, as far as possible, to plants that present few problems.

A great deal of nonsense is written about the need of certain plants for alpine conditions. Stories about young lovers being killed in the Alps trying to find an edelweiss for their sweethearts are strictly for tourists. Edelweiss grows everywhere in limestone mountains, but not necessarily on the heights. It occurs in vast sheets in alpine meadows, and in eastern Siberia it is a roadside weed worse than our dandelions.

Water

Alpine plants live more on water than on nutrients. In true alpine country, moisture comes from below the plants as much as from above. Flowing down the mountain slopes under gravel, water keeps the roots of native plants constantly bathed in moisture, yet because of the porous character of the subsoil, air is never driven out. Many of the best rock gardens are built with a stream or trickle of water running through them; this keeps the drainage layer constantly moist.

Construction

Except for rather small rock gardens, those that can be fitted into natural ravines or glens, so much heavy earth and rock must be moved that construction becomes a professional job. The underlay of such a garden for drainage, for example, can involve the moving of several tons of earth. Unless tufa or pumice rock is used, stone is extremely heavy — 150 to 200 pounds to the cubic foot. This is a factor to take into consideration before deciding that you want a rock garden.

Placement of the rocks is not only a matter of artistic arrangement (a factor no book can hope to impart) but one of sound mechanical construction as well. Every stone has its natural bed — it has to *feel* right when laid on the soil. Move every piece, turning it over and around until it seems to settle naturally into position. If a stone doesn't nestle naturally into place, set it aside for use elsewhere and try another.

When laying rock against a slope, a basic rule is that the upper edge of the outer face must be higher than the comparable edge of the inner face. It must be so placed that when rain falls and strikes the upper surface, the water will be led back into the bank or wall. To help it get back into the soil, apply a thin layer of torpedo sand on the upper surface of each rock before the earth pocket is laid over it and the rock above put into place.

This provision may not be needed in areas such as Denver or in the mountains of California where rainfall is scant, yet will help absorb the brunt of sudden mountain storms when these occur. It is better to have to water more frequently and be able to absorb extra run-off than to lose an entire garden by washing.

Rock-Garden Walls

One place where a touch of formality can be tolerated is when alpine plants are set into crevices in a stone wall. This type of planting is an excellent solution for a tall retaining wall which might otherwise thrust a mass of unrelieved rock face into a pleasing landscape scheme. Such a wall must slope inward to catch rain on its face. Because of the weight pressing downward, such a wall must have a solid foundation, preferably cast concrete, as ugly as this is. However, the cement need go only to below frost level, since not all the weight will fall on the base. Part of the load will be taken by the earth fill behind the leaning wall. To make sure there will be no buckling, the fill back of it must be tamped solidly into place as the stone is laid.

The first layer of stone is best left unplanted. This layer should be placed on a bed of torpedo sand about 1 inch thick: much of the seepage from the slope back of the stone will drain out here. However, if the wall is more than 6 feet tall, better lay drainage tiles under the footing and away from the base. Stone is laid without mortar, but with layers of soil between each two courses. If the plants are available, they are best set in place and their roots covered as the wall goes up.

PLANTS FOR ROCK GARDENS

In the following list, shade-tolerant plants are marked s, acid-soil plants have an A, lime-lovers an L, and those for poor soil in scree are marked with a P.

PERENNIALS

Achillea ageratifolia, Aizoon   A. moschata (A), Musk Yarrow
A. clavennae (P), Silver Yarrow   A. tomentosa, Woolly Yarrow

Adonis amurensis,
   Amur Floss Flower
Aethionema coridifolium (L),
   Lebanon Stone Cress
A. grandiflorum (L),
   Persian Candytuft
Ajuga genevensis (s), Geneva Bugle
Alchemilla alpina,
   Alpine Lady's Mantle
Alyssum alpestre, Alpine Madwort
A. argenteum, Yellow Tuft
A. saxatile, Gold Dust
Androsace carnea (s),
   Pink Rock Jasmine
A. lanuginosa, Silver Rock Jasmine
A. sarmentosa (P),
   Himalayan Rock Jasmine
Anemone canadensis (s),
   Meadow Anemone
A. hupehensis (s),
   Dwarf Japanese Anemone
A. sylvestris (s),
   Snowdrop Anemone
Antennaria dioica rosea,
   Rosy Pussy-toes
Aquilegia alpina, Alpine Columbine
A. caerulea (s),
   Rocky Mountain Columbine
A. canadensis (SP),
   American Columbine
A. flabellata nana,
   Dwarf Fan Columbine
Arabis albida, Wall Rock Cress
A. alpina, Alpine Rock Cress
A. aubrietioides, Tufted Rock Cress
Arenaria balearica (s),
   Corsica Sandwort
A. grandiflora, Sandwort
A. montana, Alpine Sandwort

Armeria maritima, Common Thrift
Asperula odorata (s),
   Sweet Woodruff
Aster alpinus, Alpine Aster
Aubrieta deltoidea (L),
   Purple Rock Cress
Brunnera macrophylla,
   Siberian Forget-me-not
Campanula bellardi (P),
   Nodding Bellflower
C. carpatica (s),
   Carpathian Harebell
C. excisa (P), Alpine Bellflower
C. garganica, Italian Bellflower
C. portenschlagiana,
   Wall Bellflower
C. rotundifolia (s),
   Bluebells of Scotland
Cardamine pratensis (s),
   Bitter Cress
Ceratostigma plumbaginoides,
   Plumbago
Chimaphila maculata (s),
   Spotted Wintergreen
Corydalis lutea (s),
   Yellow Corydalis
Cymbalaria aequitriloba,
   Tiny Tim Ivy
C. muralis, Kenilworth Ivy
Dianthus alpinus (L), Alpine Pink
D. arenarius, Sand Pink
D. caesius (L), Cheddar Pink
D. deltoides (L), Maiden Pink
D. neglectus (A), Ice Pink
Dicentra canadensis (s),
   Squirrel Corn
D. cucullaria (s),
   Dutchman's Breeches
D. eximia (s),
   Plumy Bleeding-heart

A natural slope made an excellent setting for this well-developed rock garden. Southwestern climate allowed the use of many succulents.

Dodecatheon species (s), Shooting Stars

Douglasia vitaliana (p), Yellow Rock Jasmine

Draba aizoides (L), Whitlow Grass

D. olympica (L), Rock Beauty

Dryas octopetala, Wood Nymph

Epigaea repens (sa), Trailing Arbutus

Epilobium nummularifolium, Creeping Willow Herb

Epimedium species (s), Barrenworts

Erinus alpinus, Crevice Plant

Genista pilosa (a), Creeping Broom

G. sagittalis (a), Dwarf Broom

Gentiana acaulis (L), Slender Gentian

G. septemfida, Asian Gentian

G. sino-ornata, Chinese Gentian

Gypsophila repens (L), Creeping Baby's Breath

Helianthemum nummularium (LP), Rock Rose

Hepatica americana (L), Liverleaf

Houstonia caerulea (a), Bluets

Hypericum reptans, Creeping Goldflower

Iberis sempervirens, Evergreen Candytuft

Iris cristata (ps), Crested Iris

I. gracilipes (ps), Slender Iris

I. tectorum, Roof Iris

Leontopodium alpinum (L), Edelweiss

Linum alpinum, Alpine Flax

L. salsoloides, Eyed Flax

Lychnis alpina, Red Campion

Mentha requieni, Creeping Mint

Mitchella repens (A),
Partridge-berry

Mitella diphylla (s), Bishop's Cap

Myosotis scorpioides (s),
Perennial Forget-me-not

M. sylvatica (s),
Wood Forget-me-not

Nepeta mussini, Dwarf Catnip

Omphalodes verna (s), Navelwort

Papaver alpinum (L), Alpine Poppy

P. nudicaule (L), Iceland Poppy

Penstemon glaber,
Blue Beardtongue

P. heterophyllus,
Violet Beardtongue

Phlox adsurgens (PS),
Oregon Phlox

P. amoena, Sweet Phlox

P. divaricata (s),
Wild Sweet William

P. douglasi (P), Western Phlox

P. stolonifera (s), Running Phlox

P. subulata, Moss Pink

Phyteuma hemisphaericum (P),
Horned Rampion

P. scheuchzeri (P),
Italian Horned Rampion

Potentilla nepalensis,
Nepal Cinquefoil

P. tridentata (SP),
Wineleaf Cinquefoil

P. verna (P), Spring Cinquefoil

Primula auricula (SL), Auricula

P. bulleyana (s),
Chinese Mountain Primrose

P. denticulata (s), Indian Primrose

P. japonica (s), Japanese Primrose

Pulmonaria angustifolia,
Cowslip Lungwort

Pulsatilla vernalis (L),
Pasque Flower

Ramonda nathaliae, (SA),
Serbian Queen

R. pyrenaica (SA), Ramonda

Sanguinaria canadensis (s),
Bloodroot

Saponaria ocymoides, Soapwort

Saxifraga aizoides (PSL),
Arctic Rockfoil

S. apiculata (P), Hybrid Rockfoil

S. cochlearis (SL), Alpine Rockfoil

S. hosti, Silver Rockfoil

S. macnabiana, Spotted Rockfoil

S. moschata, Mossy Rockfoil

S. umbrosa (s), London Pride

Sedum acre, Golden Moss

S. album, White Stone Cress

S. dasyphyllum, Leafy Stone Cress

S. reflexum, Jenny Stonecrop

S. spurium, Running Rock Cress

Sempervivum arachnoideum,
Spiderweb Houseleek

S. soboliferum, Hen-and-chickens

Shortia galacifolia (A),
Oconee Bells

Silene acaulis (P), Moss Campion

S. alpestris, Alpine Catchfly

S. caroliniana (A), Wild Pink

S. schafta, Rose-tuft Catchfly

Thymus serpyllum,
Mother-of-thyme

Tunica saxifraga (P), Coatflower

Veronica gentianoides,
Gentian Speedwell

V. incana, Woolly Speedwell

V. pectinata, Comb Speedwell

SHRUBS IN THE ROCK GARDEN

Because shrubs are not found in the high Alps, a few purists decry the planting of shrubs in rock gardens. Others point to the shrubs and dwarfed trees growing below timber line in company with many of the plants recommended by specialists as alpine plants. Stiff, upright species have no place in the home rock garden. The following list recommends a few species that are not out of place in small gardens. Few of these have strong soil preferences; those that need an acid soil are marked A. Shade-tolerant species are marked s.

Andromeda glaucophylla (AS),
    Bog Rosemary

Buxus sempervirens suffruticosa,
    Dwarf Box

Cornus canadensis (AS),
    Bunchberry

Cotoneaster adpressa,
    Creeping Rockspray

C. dammeri,
    Trailing Rockspray

C horizontalis, Rose Rockspray

C. microphylla, Dainty Rockspray

Daphne cneorum (L),
    Rose Daphne

Erica carnea (A), Spring Heath

Euonymus radicans, Wintercreeper

Gaultheria procumbens,
    Wintergreen

Juniperus chinensis sargenti,
    Sargent Juniper

J. sabina, Savin Juniper

Kalmia angustifolia (AS), Lambkill

Leiophyllum buxifolium (AS),
    Sand Myrtle

L. lyoni (AS),
    Allegheny Sand Myrtle

Lonicera nitida, Box Honeysuckle

L. pileata, Privet Honeysuckle

Mahonia nervosa, Water Holly

M. repens, Creeping Barberry

Ononis fruticosa, Rest-harrow

Pachistima canbyi, Rat-stripper

Pinus mugo mughus, Mugho Pine

Potentilla fruticosa,
    Shrubby Cinquefoil

Rhododendron ferrugineum,
    Rusty Azalea

R. indicum, Indian Azalea

Rosa wichuraiana, Memorial Rose

Rosmarinus officinalis prostratus,
    Creeping Rosemary

Spiraea decumbens, Low Spirea

Taxus canadensis, Canadian Yew

T. cuspidata nana,
    Dwarf Japanese Yew

BULBS

Many bulbs are alpines. An example is the tulip, derived from species found originally at elevations 2,500 to 6,000 feet. Many of the tulip species do much better when planted under rock-garden conditions than when grown as border subjects. Some simply refuse to grow except under the sharp drainage and bright exposure of such situations.

Mums are at their best when planted for mass effect. In this planting, the two anemone-flowered varieties are "Medallion" and "Maiko"; the large-flowered pompons are "Pink Dream".

The artful use of flower beds and trees can provide an inviting front entrance despite a barren expanse of drive and parking area.

Waterlilies, waxen and fragrant, bring a cool, exotic beauty to garden pools.

African violets, America's favorite house plants: "Pink Fantasy" (top left), "Double Delight" (top center), "Geneva Beauty" (center left), "Pansy" (center), "Blue Sail" (bottom left), "Pink Cushion" (bottom center), and "Black Magic" (bottom right).

Allium karataviense, Rainbow Leek

A. moly, Lily Leek

Anemone blanda, Greek Anemone

Chionodoxa luciliae,
    Glory-of-the-snow

Colchicum autumnale,
    False Autumn Crocus

C. speciosum, Tall Autumn Crocus

Crocus biflorus, Scotch Crocus

C. speciosus, Lilac Autumn Crocus

C. susianus, Cloth-of-gold

C. zonatus, Eyed Autumn Crocus

Eranthus hyemalis, Winter Aconite

Erythronium americanum,
    Adder's Tongue

E. revolutum, Trout Lily

Fritillaria meleagris,
    Guinea-hen Flower

F. pudica, Golden Fritillary

Galanthus nivalis, Snowdrop

Leucojum vernum, Snowflake

Lilium cernuum, Lavender Lily

L. pomponium, Alpine Lily

L. pumilum, Coral Lily

Muscari botryoides,
    Grape Hyacinth

Narcissus bulbocodium,
    Hoop-petticoat Narcissus

N. cyclamineus,
    Portuguese Daffodil

N. jonquilla, True Jonquil

N. triandrus, Angel's Tears

Scilla nonscripta,
    English Bluebell

S. sibirica, Siberian Squill

Sternbergia lutea, Autumn Daffodil

Tulipa acuminata, Turkish Tulip

T. clusiana, Candystick Tulip

T. dasystemon, Dwarf Turkish Tulip

T. kaufmanniana, Waterlily Tulip

T. linifolia, Slender Tulip

T. patens, Persian Tulip

THE WATER GARDEN

Pond or pool, rill or stream, water almost inevitably becomes the focal point in any landscape scheme. It therefore behooves the gardener to consider the placement of aquatic features most carefully.

In the formal garden, the location is seldom a problem. No landscape detail is easier sited than a reflecting pool or fountain. Almost of necessity, it ends up as the focal center of the design as a dramatic accent at the end of the major axis.

Informal design, however, is another matter. Dark waters under trees are impressively dramatic, but arranging such a situation requires great skill. In general the amateur gardener would be well advised to avoid this situation unless no other solution for placement is available.

You should be aware, too, that practically all water surfaces in informal gardens reflect the sky in some way. To avoid introducing disharmonious lines in the reflected image, you will have to place the pool so that buildings, fences and other structures do not create strong vertical or horizontal shadows that would mar the visual effects.

Streams look best if they seem to arise from some distant, out-of-sight source. Even if they actually originate in a water tap at the corner of the property, you should plant out or hide the source so that the eye is deceived into imagining miles of up-stream country.

Perhaps the most difficult water feature to design properly is a small cascade or water fall. The secret is the form of the rim over which it flows. If this is a straight line of masonry, no amount of camouflage can hide the fact that it is purely artificial. If you will study natural water falls, you will see that the most pleasing effects occur when the rim is undercut and has a jagged and irregular edge.

It is important to remember, too, that though many people find the sound of running water soothing, others are disturbed by it, particularly at night. What may be a gentle murmur at dusk can become an insistent roar at two in the morning. If you want to have the moving water without the sound, allow the water to flow over gently sloping surfaces to reach a lower level.

Flowing water, and aquatic plants, you should remember, do not go together. The moving water injures plants both by its mechanical action and by its cooling effect. If there is any flow at all, it should be no more than a mere trickle.

Construction

Pools of plastic or fiber glass are convenient and usually less expensive than those built with concrete. They are perfectly adequate for waterlilies unless you plan to leave hardy waterlilies in place during the winter. Most of them are too shallow to provide the 3-foot depth necessary for that kind of gardening. Nevertheless, this need not be a serious drawback to their use. The pool can be drained and filled with straw, leaves or other material to provide the necessary winter protection.

A 36-inch pool is usually considered best for successful waterlily culture. There are, however, miniature species available that will flower well in 6 inches of water. This allows the roots to be enclosed in a 12-inch-deep box with enough room for growth at the surface.

In this day of ready-mix concrete, pools constructed in place are much easier to build than they once were. The one precaution that you should bear in mind is that the entire structure should be poured in a single operation. When bottom and side walls are poured separately, cracks usually occur where the two planes meet.

Most pool failures are due to lack of adequate drainage under and around the walls and bottom. The usual specifications call for a 6-inch base of cinders or coarse gravel. But unless you also install drain tile to permit water to flow away from the area around the pool, the cinder base

The water garden is the focus of this handsome formal design which sets off the lily pool with a portable garden of calla lilies and daffodils.

merely acts as a sump into which surface waters flow. Always provide an outlet for the tile lower than the bottom of the pool.

Drainage for the water inside the pool should be provided at this time. The inconvenience of trying to siphon off its contents often results in leaving the job undone, with resultant damage to the walls. Walls that slope outward so that the surface is wider than the bottom are also desirable. They allow an ice mass to rise without exerting damaging pressure.

Reinforcing rods or mesh are essential because of the tremendous weight of water contained in even a modest pool. The mesh should be bent upward at the point where the bottom joins walls. If you merely tie the pieces together with wire, you are inviting trouble.

Because of the depth of water needed for waterlilies, bog plants cannot be grown on the bottom. Unhappily, the usual method of providing for these plants — protruding pockets set in the walls — quite often form weak spots in the pool. They also prevent rising of the ice mass. A better method is to grow these plants in wooden boxes set on loose concrete blocks so that they stand just below the surface of the water.

If you build a concrete pool, wet it down several times a day for a week after the forms have been removed. Then fill it with water. Allow this to stand for two weeks, drain and refill. After another two-week period, drain and refill the pool once more before planting. A freshly poured pool is so filled with alkaline chemicals that unless this washing procedure is followed, plants may be injured or killed.

HARDY WATERLILIES

Two types of waterlilies are available — hardy and tropical. All belong to the genus nymphaea. The former cannot withstand actual freezing at the root, but will survive in water at a depth of three feet or more. If the pool is not that deep, water should be drained off and the boxes containing the waterlilies sprayed with phaltan to reduce fungus contamination. They should then be covered with a 2-foot layer of straw, peatmoss, wood shavings, or similar protection.

Some water gardeners prefer to carry lilies over in a cool basement (the temperature must be above freezing but below 40°) where they can be wet down occasionally.

In the pool they are best planted in wooden boxes about 18 inches by 18 inches and at least 10 inches deep. Soil should be a rich compost, but it should be free of fresh organic matter. Cover the soil with a 1-inch layer of torpedo sand, particularly if there are fish in the pool.

Fish, by the way, are an important asset. They destroy mosquito larvae and help clean up bits of organic matter. It is also a wise precaution to include a few snails as scavengers.

Those accustomed to thinking of waterlilies only as the pure white, fragrant wildings that float on woodland pools will find the cultivated colored varieties exciting. These are mostly French in origin. They come in colors ranging from palest yellow through pink and bronze to deep maroon. All of them open in the morning and close at night.

Good pinks are 'Marliac Flesh,' 'Marliac Rose,' 'Lucida,' and 'Eugenia de Land.' Favorite reds are 'James Brydon,' 'Escarboucle,' 'Gloriosa,' and 'Attraction.'

TROPICAL WATERLILIES

The tropicals are larger and more spectacular than the hardies, but they must have warm water to do well. North of the Ohio River, they should not be planted in the open until June 1 or they may rot. Along the Canadian border, night temperatures are usually too cool for them to prosper. Unless a greenhouse with a night temperature of 70° or over is available, most amateurs should not attempt to carry them over. It is better to buy new plants each year. Because they demand warm, still water, they are not suitable for natural streams or spring-fed lakes.

To force bloom, tropical waterlilies should be fed with a good chemical garden fertilizer and grown in a rich composted soil. Boxes should be at least 3 feet by 3 feet and not less than 1 foot deep.

Both day-blooming and night-blooming species are available. Most spectacular among the day bloomers are the blues and purples. 'Mrs. Edward Whittaker' and 'Blue Beauty' are excellent. 'August Koch' and

'Frances Beardsly Griffith' (syn. 'Royal Purple') are beautiful lavender and violet shades. 'General Pershing,' 'Castaliflora,' and 'Peach Blow' are excellent pinks. 'Mrs. George H. Pring' is a sensational large white.

Among the night bloomers, 'Juno' and 'Missouri' are the best. Both are white — and white is certainly the best color if the flowers are to be seen by moonlight. 'Mrs. George Hitchcock' and 'Emily Grant Hutchins' are pinks light enough to show up against dark waters. 'Frank Trelease' and 'H. C. Haarstick' are good bright reds, but they are hardly visible at night unless they are illumined by floodlights.

BOG PLANTS

To soften the edges of natural ponds and to provide contrast in artificial pools, bog plants and free-floating aquatics are often used. The draining of wet areas for agricultural lands has reduced the availability of material for this purpose because most of the stock sold is gathered from the wild rather than grown for the purpose. This limits the water gardener to what he can find, usually cattails, pickerel weed, water poppy, and parrot's feather. Many other plants are available commercially, if you prefer to buy material rather than collect it yourself.

FRAGRANT PLANTS FOR THE GARDEN

It is said that in ancient Arabian gardens flowers were arranged to produce a symphony of fragrance. Delicate and elusive scents that might otherwise be unnoticed welcomed the visitor when he entered the garden and lured him to those that were progressively headier.

Without thinking, we lift a new flower and smell it critically. Whether or not its fragrance pleases us depends, not upon its character, but upon our personal response to it. The scents of flowers exert a powerful influence upon human emotions, inspiring feelings that range from delight to depression or revulsion. And the response varies with the individual. Not without reason did John Gerarde remark in his famous *Herball* that "Syringa be too sweet, troubling and molesting the head in a strange manner."

Many attempts have been made to classify flower odors but with little success. There are too many qualities to be considered and, in addition, several "top notes," as perfumers call them, which confuse even an expert.

One of the most difficult of all flowers to classify for scent is the rose. As many as 15 different rose odors have been identified in Hybrid Tea varieties alone. These have been described as just about everything from freshly brewed tea to burnt chocolate.

To say a plant is fragrant does not necessarily mean that it is sweetly scented, nor does it mean that the flowers alone are scented. In the lists that follow, many plants smell pungent, spicy, musky, bitter, or otherwise, and in some it is the leaves, roots, or seeds instead of (or in addition to) the flowers that give off the odors. Not every plant would be grown especially for its fragrance, but all give off some sort of pleasant scent, at least (with most) when flowering.

HARDY FRAGRANT PLANTS

Annuals, shrubs, trees, vines, bulbs and perennials grown in the North

Abronia umbellata, Sand Verbena

Achillea filipendulina,
    Fernleaf Yarrow

A. millefolium, Common Yarrow

Akebia quinata, Five-finger Akebia

Alyssum maritimum,
    Sweet Alyssum

Anthemis nobilis, Camomile

A. tinctoria kelwayi,
    Golden Camomile

Anthoxanthum odoratum,
    Sweet Vernal Grass

Anthyllis montana, Ladyfingers

Aquilegia chrysantha,
    Yellow Columbine

Arabis alpina, Alpine Rock Cress

Asperula odorata, Sweet Woodruff

Asphodeline lutea, Jacob's Rod

Benzoin aestivale, Spicebush

Borago officinalis, Borage

Boussingaultia baselloides,
    Madeira Vine

Buddleia davidi, Butterfly Bush

Calycanthus floridus,
    Carolina Allspice

Catalpa ovata, Japanese Catalpa

Centaurea imperialis, Sweet Sultan

Centranthus ruber, Red Valerian

Cephalanthus occidentalis,
    Buttonbush

Cheiranthus cheiri, Wallflower

Chionanthus virginicus, Fringe Tree

Chrysanthemum parthenium,
    Feverfew

Clematis, various species, Clematis

Clethra alnifolia, Sweet Pepperbush

Convallaria majalis,
    Lily-of-the-valley

Corylopsis paucifolia, Winter Hazel

Crataegus, various species,
    Hawthorn

Crocus species and varieties,
    Crocus

Daphne cneorum, Rose Daphne

D. mezereum, February Daphne

Deutzia scabra, Rough Deutzia

Dianthus, species and varieties,
    Pinks

Dictamnus albus, Gas Plant

Dioscorea batatas, Chinese Yam

Elaeagnus angustifolia,
    Russian Olive

E. multiflora, Gumi

Epigaea repens, Trailing Arbutus

Erysimum murale,
    Siberian Wallflower

Eucharis amazonica, Amazon Lily

Exacum affine, German Violet

Fraxinus ornus, Flowering Ash

Galtonia candicans,
    Summer Hyacinth

Geranium robertianum,
   Herb Robert
Gleditsia triacanthos,
   Honey Locust
Gordonia alatamaha, Franklin Tree
Hamamelis species, Witch Hazels
Heliotropium arborescens,
   Heliotrope
Hemerocallis species, Daylilies
Hosta plantaginea,
   Fragrant Plantain Lily
Hydrangea petiolaris,
   Climbing Hydrangea
Iberis amara, Annual Candytuft
I. umbellata, Globe Candytuft
Iris species, Iris
Itea virginica, Sweet Spire
Lathyrus odoratus, Sweet Pea
Lavandula spica, Lavender
Leucojum vernum,
   Spring Snowflake
Leucothoë catesbaei, Fetterbush
Lilium species, Lilies
Lonicera species, Honeysuckles
Lupinus mutabilis, Lupine
Lychnis alba, Evening Campion
Lycoris squamigera,
   Hardy Amaryllis
Magnolia species, Magnolias
Maianthemum canadense,
   Canadian Mayflower
Mathiola bicornis, Evening Stock
M. incana, Ten-week Stock
Melissa officinalis, Lemon Balm
Milla biflora, Mexican Star
Mirabilis jalapa, Four-o'clock
Monarda didyma, Oswego Tea
M. fistulosa, Wild Bergamot
Myrica caroliniensis, Bayberry

Narcissus jonquilla, True Jonquil
N. tazetta, Polyanthus Narcissus
Nicotiana affinis,
   Flowering Tobacco
Oenothera, species,
   Evening Primroses
Paeonia, varieties, Peonies
Papaver nudicaule, Iceland Poppy
Pelargonium, species and varieties,
   Geraniums
Periploca graeca, Grecian Silk Vine
Philadelphus coronarius,
   Mock Orange
Phlox, species and varieties, Phlox
Pieris floribunda, Andromeda
Polianthes tuberosa, Tuberose
Primula veris, True Primrose
P. vulgaris, English Primrose
Pterostyrax hispida, Epaulette Tree
Peuraria thunbergiana, Kudzu Vine
Pyrus, various species,
   Flowering Crabs
Reseda odorata, Mignonette
Rhododendron, species, Azaleas
Rhus aromatica, Fragrant Sumac
Ribes aureum, Flowering Currant
Rosa, species and varieties, Roses
Rosmarinus officinalis, Rosemary
Sambucus canadensis,
   American Elder
S. nigra, European Elder
Santolina chamaecyparissus,
   Lavender Cotton
Saponaria officinalis, Bouncing Bet
Scabiosa atropurpurea,
   Sweet Scabious
Scilla nonscripta,
   English Bluebell

Symplocos paniculata,
    Asiatic Sweetleaf
Syringa, various species, Lilacs
Thymus serpyllum,
    Mother-of-thyme
Tilia, various species, Lindens
Tropaeolum majus, Nasturtium
Tulipa, certain varieties, Tulips
Ulex europaeus, Furze
Valeriana officinalis,
    Garden Heliotrope
Viburnum burkwoodi,
    Burkwood Viburnum

V. carlesi, Mayflower Viburnum
V. odoratissimum,
    Sweet Viburnum
Viola, species and varieties,
    Violets, Pansies
Vitex agnus-castus, Chaste Tree
Vitis species, Grapes
Wisteria floribunda,
    Japanese Wisteria
W. sinensis, Chinese Wisteria

HALF-HARDY AND TENDER FRAGRANT PLANTS

Practically the entire list of northern plants can be grown in the South. In addition, a great many species that are more or less tender can be used, among them some of the world's most fragrant plants.

Acacia, various species, Mimosa
Alpinia speciosa, Shellflower
Amaryllis belladonna,
    Belladonna Lily ·
Azara microphylla,
    Chilean Wall Vine
Boronia elatior, Boronia
Cestrum, species, Jasmine
Choisya ternata, Mexican Orange
Clerodendron fragrans,
    Glory-bower
C. thomsonae, Bagflower
Datura arborea, Angel's Trumpet
Diosma ericoides,
    Breath-of-Heaven
Eriobotrya japonica, Loquat
Eurya ochnacea, Cleyera
Gardenia jasminoides, Cape Jasmine
Gelsemium sempervirens,
    Carolina Yellow Jessamine

Hoya carnosa, Wax Plant
Hymenocallis calathina,
    Peruvian Daffodil
Jasminum, species, Jasmines
Murraya exotica, Orange Jasmine
Nerium oleander, Oleander
Osmanthus fragrans, Tea Olive
Passiflora caerulea, Passion Vine
Phillyrea decora, Mock Privet
Piqueria trinervia, Stevia
Pittosporum, various species,
    Australian Laurel
Schizopetalon walkeri,
    Almond Flower
Spartium junceum, Spanish Broom
Thevetia nereifolia,
    Yellow Oleander

HERBS WITH AROMATIC FOLIAGE, SEEDS OR ROOTS

Many culinary and medicinal herbs have clean-smelling aromatic foliage which is not precisely fragrant but very pleasing to the senses. Of those not listed above, the following are worth growing for their odor alone:

Acorus calamus, Sweet Flag

Anethum graveolens, Dill

Angelica archangelica, Angelica

Artemisia, species, Wormwood

Buxus sempervirens, Boxwood

Carum carvi, Caraway

Chrysanthemum balsamita, Costmary

Citrus bergamia, Bergamot

Comptonia asplenifolia, Sweetfern

Coriandrum sativum, Coriander

Dennstaedtia punctilobula, Hay-scented Fern

Foeniculum vulgare, Fennel

Hyssopus officinalis, Hyssop

Laurus nobilis, Bay-leaf Tree

Levisticum officinale, Lovage

Lippia citriodora, Lemon Verbena

Mentha, various species, Mint

Myrrhis odorata, Sweet Cicely

Nepeta cataria, Catnip

Ocimum basilicum, Sweet Basil

Origanum vulgare, Pot Marjoram

Pimenta officinalis, Allspice

Pimpinella anisum, Anise

Ruta graveolens, Rue

Santolina chamaecyparissus, Lavender Cotton

Satureja hortensis, Summer Savory

Tanacetum vulgare, Tansy

Thymus vulgaris, Garden Thyme

Vetiveria zizanioides, Vetiver

GARDENS TO ATTRACT BIRDS

Birds are under such pressure today that if many kinds are to survive in our more populous regions, they must have the help of man. Area spraying for mosquito and Dutch elm disease control, suburban sprawl that has destroyed millions of acres of nesting sites, land taken over for toll roads, and the draining of wet lands are robbing many birds of food and shelter at an alarming rate.

If every suburban property were to provide a bird corner, the pressure on our bird population would be greatly relieved. The corner should be located as far as possible from the street, where spray crews usually operate. Fog spray drops rapidly after 150 feet, so that the back lot lines of most properties are safe havens.

Shrubs that attract birds are usually thought of in terms of food, but food is only one of five basic needs which must be met if you want birds in your garden. In addition to food, birds need shelter from weather (particularly in winter), nesting sites, protection from predators, and a source of water.

The importance of water is often overlooked but in a dry area it will lure birds away from food. For winter, provide an electrically heated poultry water fountain. Twenty-one different species were counted in a single day at a winter feeding station equipped with such a fountain.

Protection from predators is sometimes difficult to assure. Where cats have run wild, it may be necessary to capture them in box traps and turn them over to the proper authorities for disposal. Released at a distance, they will return to the same spot. Cats will usually refuse to enter a thicket planted with sharp-thorned roses such as *Rosa alba*, 'New Dawn' climber, or *Rosa multiflora*. The last named species makes ideal cover on wild land, where its fruits provide food for birds, thorns to bar predators, and dense growth for shelter.

The most difficult problem is to provide protection for ground-nesting species. If rough land is available, planting dewberries is an ideal solution. They will also nest under the branches of a rose hedge but are more exposed there.

In carefully maintained suburban and city areas, birds have a difficult time finding nesting material. If this can be provided, they will accept it gratefully. Be careful, however, that any threads or rags put out are old and fragile. Beware of tough fibers like nylon which can strangle a robin if it catches around the neck. A supply of mud, high in clay, will attract robins and other mud-using species.

A cat-proof fence will protect any area that can be set aside as a home bird sanctuary. Not every tight fence is cat-proof: cats can climb even link fabrics. An ordinary chicken-wire fence, about 6 feet tall, is excellent. Make it without a top rail, and string it between poles that wobble. A cat trying to climb such a fence is frightened off with the first movement of the wire. Ordinary snow fencing with picket tops also makes a good fence and is largely self-supporting.

Cats as well as squirrels can be kept from climbing trees if cones of smooth metal at least 12 inches wide are placed around the trunks at least 6 feet above the ground. However, any tree within 20 feet of another tree or a building can be reached by an active squirrel. Squirrels can be trapped and transported at least 2 miles away from their point of capture; they do not seem to have a homing sense.

One of the most important needs of birds in winter is shelter from biting winds and sleet. A group of several evergreens such as arborvitae, spruce, or red cedar, planted to form a solid mass, will often be alive with birds on stormy days and nights. However, when roosting, they are easy victims for cats. Circle the grove with a temporary fence of chicken wire or snow fencing when fall migration begins and leave it in place until after the birds return in spring. This will allow migrants to roost in safety. Or if the landscape scheme permits, leave the fence in place permanently and plant it with a thorny climbing rose.

TREES AND SHRUBS THAT ATTRACT BIRDS

The following list includes both plants that supply food and those that provide nesting sites. Some, like the Japanese barberry, do both. Its fruits are never eaten until tastier foods are gone, but after that the bushes are soon stripped in winter. Those providing both food and shelter are marked *.

Aronia arbutifolia, Red Chokeberry

A. melanocarpa, Black Chokeberry

Benzoin aestivale, Spicebush

*Berberis thunbergi**, Japanese Barberry

*Betula lenta**, Sweet Birch

*B. nigra**, River Birch

B. papyrifera, Canoe Birch

*Celtis occidentalis**, Hackberry

Cornus species*, Dogwoods

Crataegus species*, Hawthorns

Elaeagnus angustifolia, Russian Olive

Euonymus europaeus, Spindle Tree

Gaultheria procumbens, Wintergreen

Gaylussacia baccata, Huckleberry

Hypericum prolificum, Shrubby St. Johnswort

*Juniperus communis**, Common Juniper

*J. virginiana**, Red Cedar

Larix decidua, European Larch

L. laricina, American Larch

Ligustrum vulgare, European Privet

Lonicera species, Honeysuckles

Mitchella repens, Partridge-berry

Morus alba, White Mulberry

M. rubra, American Mulberry

Myrica caroliniensis, Bayberry

M. cerifera, Wax Myrtle

Nyssa sylvatica, Tupelo

Parthenocissus quinquefolia, Virginia Creeper

P. tricuspidata, Boston Ivy

*Picea glauca**, White Spruce

*P. pungens**, Blue Spruce

Pinus species*, Pines

Prunus species*, Cherries and Plums

Pyrus species*, Asiatic Crabapples

*Rhamnus cathartica**, Common Buckthorn

*R. frangula**, Glossy Buckthorn

Rhus glabra, Smooth Sumac

R. typhina, Staghorn Sumac

Rubus species*, Blackberries and Raspberries

Sambucus canadensis, American Elder

S. nigra, European Elder

S. racemosa, European Red Elder

Shepherdia argentea, Buffalo-berry

Sorbus americana, American Mountain Ash

S. aucuparia, European Mountain Ash

Symphoricarpos orbiculatus, Coralberry

*Tsuga canadensis**, Canadian Hemlock

*T. carolinieniana**, Carolina Hemlock

Vaccinium corymbosum, High-bush Blueberry

V. pensylvanicum,   *Viburnum,* various species,
    Low-bush Blueberry   Viburnum

HERBACEOUS PLANTS

The food plants of many sparrows, finches, cardinals, and other seed-eaters are plants we consider weeds. With plowed fields now running up to the fence line and roadsides sprayed for weed control, this source of food is being destroyed rapidly. Certain garden flowers can replace the weeds. Letting annuals go to seed toward autumn does the garden no harm and the birds a great deal of good. Particularly attractive are amaranthus, annual aster, centaurea, sunflower, poppy, and zinnia. Birds will eat the seeds of practically all plants of the composite family. Sparrows are fond of the seeds of Oswego tea *(Monarda didyma)*.

THE INSTANT GARDEN

We live in a hurried age. Instant coffee, TV dinners, push-button paints, and other time-saving devices are now routine.

Bedding Plants

For those who cannot wait, there are even instant gardens. So important have these become that millions of home-owners today never sow seeds, but rely instead on ready-made annuals in full bloom for immediate effect. This practice has been encouraged by a number of big greenhouse operators, many of whom turn out a million or more such plants every spring. Nor is this custom confined to spring. Each year sees the grower offering plants later and later in the summer, to satisfy the demands of tardy gardeners.

Although these plants naturally cost more than seeds (a single petunia plant in bloom sells for more than a packet of seed that should produce 100 plants), the small size of many modern gardens makes the idea of instant glamour feasible. In a matter of minutes, for the price of a couple of seats for a good play, a home-owner can set out a border of 50 petunias in full bloom and edge them with as many blue ageratums. If he prefers, his local garden center or greenhouse can supply him with dozens of other annuals, from alyssum to zinnia.

What is more, he (or, more often, she) can select the exact colors wanted, instead of depending on catalog descriptions and illustrations that often fail to show the delicate shadings that are so important.

On the debit side, while annuals in full bloom are often beautiful when purchased, they may not remain so. In order to produce plants that will flower quickly in small flats or pots, breeders often have to sacrifice long period of bloom, compactness, and other desirable qualities. Quick-flowering may also mean quick dying. However, it is usually safe to select hybrid varieties, particularly of petunias. They flower earlier but usually keep flowering longer.

Other Plants

Not all instant glamour is confined to bedding plants. Nowadays, the sale of shrubs and even trees in five-gallon cans is a well-established practice. Although such nursery stock is usually fairly small, it is in active growth and, when sold, will give a quicker effect than dormant stock that must be cut back when planted and given time to grow new roots.

Whole hedges can be planted with such stock, if the pocketbook can take the blow. Planting is simple; garden centers selling such stock usually have special shears to cut away the can for instant planting.

Potted roses, in either old-fashioned clay pots or the larger tar-paper pots are available almost everywhere. Because of the smaller size of the clay pot, these are not too good a buy much after May 15; the growing root needs more room. The larger tar-paper pots, from 9 to 10 inches across, can usually be planted well into July. They are usually sold with flower buds already on them.

Later in the season — in fact, right into October — chrysanthemums can be set out in bud or in full bloom. The move does them no harm. An accent of bright color, a group of filler plants to replace spent annuals or bulbs, or an entire chrysanthemum border can be planted in this manner.

In a relatively short time, several summer-flowering bulbs can bring dramatic bloom into the garden. Ismene, the Peruvian daffodil *(Hymenocallis calathina)* will bloom in a few weeks if planted up to late July. The bulbs must be set deeply. The clusters of lavender-rose, amaryllis-like flowers of *Lycoris squamigera* will appear late in the summer, instead of July, if they are planted in midsummer. Both of these bulbs do best in rich soil.

The main problem is to find bulbs, corms, tubers, and potted plants of kinds that are normally offered for sale at a different season. If they can be located, fall-flowering crocus and the similar sternbergia, with bright yellow flowers, will bloom if planted as late as August. Corms of colchicum cannot be restrained from autumn flowering whether or not they are set in the ground. Their foliage appears in spring.

Lily bulbs that have been kept in cold storage sometimes bloom in September from a July planting. Tuberous begonias that are well established in pots are one of the most satisfactory of plants to transfer to the garden when in bloom. Foliage of elephant's ear *(Colocasia antiquorum)*, which grows rapidly when the large tubers are planted, can provide abundant green for the background of an "instant" garden.

Balled and Burlapped Stock

The development of container-planted stock has made us overlook the older balled and burlapped stock, which is often a better buy. Evergreens, deciduous shrubs, and large trees have been handled in this way for generations. A mature lilac, for example, can be purchased in full bloom. If grown from bare-root stock, it would require several years to attain blooming size. The spectacular saucer magnolia, *(Magnolia soulangeana)* is always sold in this way. It opens its huge pink and white flowers a day or two after planting.

Quick Lawns

Instant lawns can be achieved by laying sod. Often this costs little more than remaking a poorly handled seeded lawn. Sodding fell into disrepute early in the century because too often the turf used had been stripped from old pastures. Poorly cut, full of weeds, and weakened by years of hay cutting, it was seldom satisfactory.

Today's sod nurseries, using selected seed, and practicing complete weed control, produce accurately cut sod that can be laid without a sign of joints. However, the selection of a reliable firm to lay the sod is highly important. All too many landscapers try to buy sod at the lowest possible price and are likely to supply a product that is contaminated with *Poa annua*, knotweed, and other hard-to-control weeds. Insist upon seeing a lawn that was laid by the contractor you are considering, and be sure the lawn was laid at least a year before. Then talk to the owner and see how well satisfied he is with it.

The one thing to avoid when in a hurry is sowing a temporary lawn. This is always a waste of time and a source of dissatisfaction. About the only grass that will produce a reasonably good-looking lawn in a hurry is common or perennial rye grass, a fast-growing, dark green clump grass, which looks good for about two months and then goes to pieces. About August 1, just when it is at its best from spring seeding, it will have to be plowed under and all the trouble of establishing a new lawn must be experienced a second time. If you plan to seed your lawn, see Chapter 9 for directions.

Temporary Hedges

Where the expense of canned stock is too great, temporary hedges can be grown in a few weeks by using certain annuals. These are not usually available from florists as flowering plants, but must be seeded in place. The most vigorous of these, and the one that makes the most perfect screen is the castor bean, *Ricinus communis*. Unfortunately, it produces

PORTABLE GARDENS: *Planter-bench blooms colorfully on a terrace. Bright potted geraniums accent the charm of a rustic entryyard.*

curiously mottled poisonous seeds which are highly attractive to children. Either avoid using these plants where there are small children, or cut off the curious flower spikes as soon as they appear.

Tithonia speciosa, the Mexican sunflower, is another excellent hedge plant, forming a thick screen about 5 feet tall. Its flowers are a brilliant chrome-orange.

Kochia childsi, the Mexican fire-bush, is excellent for lower-growing hedges. The ostrich-plume celosia, 'Pride of Castle Gold,' if planted thickly, also produces a barrier about 3 feet tall.

THE PORTABLE GARDEN

Although at first glance they may seem ultramodern, portable gardens are centuries old — so old that their origin cannot be traced. Ancient Persian and Chinese paintings show potted plants as a part of everyday life, and records of early Greek civilization tell us that pots of growing wheat were displayed in the spring to celebrate Persephone's return from Hades.

For years the people of Italy and Spain have grown both ornamentals and fruits in pots and tubs outdoors, bringing them inside during unfavorable weather. Many a tub of figs grown by Italian-Americans in New

York, New Jersey and elsewhere came directly from such parent stocks. Even when protection was not needed, these Europeans found that growing plants in this way enabled them to change the garden picture at will.

A portable garden has many practical uses. It enables a tenant or temporary resident to take his garden with him when he moves. It also allows the restless housewife who likes to shift the furniture about to rearrange her plants to enhance a new decorative scheme.

In the United States, Californians have developed the idea beyond anything thought of in the past. Instead of limiting themselves to pots and tubs, they use elaborate planters and boxes, sometimes several feet long, containing a variety of flowering material. With several such boxes, an entire landscape scheme can be developed.

A common location for such planters is on the edge of a driveway or walk, usually where there is too little room for a regular border in open soil. A bare wall or box-like garage can often be made attractive by a well-placed box or two. Sometimes, English ivy is planted in such a box, then trained up the wall as a more-or-less permanent feature, but one that can be removed and used elsewhere, if desired.

The use of wooden platforms, about 5 by 5 feet, is a further extension of this idea. These platforms, made of some durable wood, or wood treated with a preservative, can be used to form terraces of any shape desired. Six such platforms, for instance, would form a terrace 10 by 15 feet, large enough to hold a picnic table and several chairs. If surrounded by a quick-growing hedge (see Chapter 6), a pleasant outdoor living room can be created in a single season. The following year the same platforms can be arranged in a different pattern, or the area can be extended by additional units.

Herbs in pots lend themselves to this type of gardening. For larger accents, tubbed specimens of rosemary and sage are attractive. These are fairly woody and make sizable plants if allowed to grow. Smaller specimens can spend the winter in a sunny kitchen window where they will serve a dual purpose. Since most herb gardens are small, all the perennial plants from such a garden might be wintered on shelves in a picture window.

Portable garden material can also be rented for special occasions. To create a setting for a garden wedding, tubbed tree roses and tree geraniums might be rented from a grower and used to form aisles leading to an altar created of palms and other exotics.

Large pots containing specimen plants in a home greenhouse can be kept on a low, sturdy platform on wheels. When they are wanted for interior decoration, they are easily rolled into the living or dining room. Wheeling, in fact, whether by means of a platform, cart, wheelbarrow, or dolly, is the most practical way of moving the heavy containers of plants in a portable garden.

17

Plants for Acid Soil

There is a large number of flowering plants, most of them members of the heath family *(Ericaceae)*, which demand an acid soil in order to grow well. Among them are some of the handsomest woody plants used in landscaping: rhododendrons and azaleas, mountain laurel, heather, sorrel tree, blueberries, and others. Many of these are evergreen. An alkaline soil is poison to them; lime and nitrate of soda are likely to kill them. Equally damaging are the hot dry winds of the desert and the winter blasts of the northern plains.

The areas in which the coveted acid-soil plants can be grown are therefore somewhat limited. But if yours is a region of mild winters and moderate summers, with a light, acid soil and abundant atmospheric moisture, you are lucky — and probably already growing them. Along the Pacific Coast, north from San Francisco to British Columbia, you can grow the world's best broad-leaved evergreens. So, in such regions, consult local nurserymen as to available and suitable varieties and their care.

On the East Coast, the more favored climate is near the ocean — in protected spots on Cape Cod or Long Island, or in the Chesapeake Bay area, where new Oriental species and British hybrids are being tried. Certain of them appear promising and, used in hybridization and selection work, may eventually augment our list of hardy ones.

Going inland to places a bit less mild, more of the standard varieties and fewer of the novelties are advised. As one goes north and south, the lists dwindle, but there remains a respectable group of "ironclad" sorts for New England and a wealth of evergreen azaleas for the southeast. Going west, one might use many from the Middle-Atlantic list in West Virginia, Kentucky, and Tennessee and the mountains southward. But

273

westward from New England, into central New York and Ohio, and onward touching Michigan and the Great Plains area, only the hardiest forms are feasible. Places like Kansas and Texas are not favorable for the culture of rhododendrons and other acid-soil plants, yet a few kinds are being successfully grown in those two states by people interested enough to give them special care.

The rhododendrons listed in the table are standard sorts usually carried by nurserymen. Many of the rarer, newer sorts are not included because they are mostly unavailable and are often inadequately tested. Since the war, even old, standard varieties have been scarce. You may have to depend, to some degree, upon collected wild material. In deciduous azaleas, this is often very good indeed, but as seedlings and wild plants are quite variable, it will pay to visit a nursery at flowering time and pick out the ones you prefer. In buying collected material (both rhododendrons and azaleas), specify plants which have been cut back and grown on in a nursery for several seasons.

Those safe for New England are mainly older sorts; few modern hybrids are of the "ironclad" type. The Catawba hybrid list in the table is based upon years of trial at the Arnold Arboretum near Boston, and elsewhere. Few new kinds for this region have appeared since 1880, but most of them are still quite beautiful even though regarded as obsolete in England and elsewhere. Perhaps more possibilities exist for the cold Northeast among the deciduous azaleas than in any other class. When grown on their own roots (not grafted) and given adequate water in early summer, they will flourish and survive a surprising degree of winter cold. Unthriftiness in summer generally means injury or death during the subsequent winter, and grafted azaleas are subject to such troubles.

If you live where the water is "hard," don't use it for watering but depend on the rains and conserve the soil moisture by maintaining a year-round very heavy mulch. For best results, rhododendron soil should test pH 4.5 to 5.0 in the conventional chemical acidity rating, in which pH 7.0 is neutral.

In planting, you can make one big bed, or set the plants in separate holes, but in either case dig 14 to 18 inches deep, and break up the subsoil to insure drainage. When planting in separate holes, make them twice as broad as the root balls. In filling them, mix in at least 50 per cent peat or sawdust; in a lime soil, use almost pure peat — as is done in Rochester, N. Y., where many fine plants of the heath family are grown.

Place a 4- to 8-inch layer of peaty soil in the hole, set the plant at about the depth it grew before, fill in with the peaty mixture, and water thoroughly. A mulch tends to keep the soil cool and moist. Use oak leaves or pine needles if possible; sawdust and peat are good but should be covered with leaves so they will not get so dry that rain runs off instead of soaking in. Oak leaves are acid and remain so a long time; the thinner leaves of maple and elm disintegrate rapidly, becoming somewhat alkaline. Pile on the leaves in fall up to 8 inches deep and leave them there, adding a fresh layer every year. As they break down they furnish valuable nutrients; in fact, many growers say this is all the fertilizer the plants need. In any case, do not use ordinary fertilizers, but special kinds made for acid-loving plants. Ammonium sulfate and acid phosphate are suitable. Rotted manure should be used only if the soil is acid enough to stand the ammonia it contains. A successful formula is 1 part potassium nitrate to 2 parts acid phosphate (superphosphate) mixed and applied in early spring at the rate of half a pint (1 trowel-full) around each 3-foot plant.

Given the above initial care, broad-leaved evergreens, azaleas, and other acid-soil plants will require almost none thereafter. Never use a hoe around them, for their roots are shallow and fine. Sometimes they may need to be sprayed but when once they are established, this is not a serious problem. Except in the South, where azalea flower-spot is prevalent, neither insects nor disease give much trouble, and they are usually controlled by the use of ordinary insecticides and fungicides. The rhododendron lace bug, which is occasionally troublesome, calls for spraying with nicotine sulfate or a good rotenone-pyrethrum preparation.

RECOMMENDED RHODODENDRONS AND AZALEAS

Here are the regions used in the table:

A. New England, Central New York, Northern Pennsylvania, Ohio, westward (including Michigan) to Central States.

B. Middle Atlantic States (including Metropolitan New York, Philadelphia, Washington), Virginia, North Carolina, and westward including Kentucky, Tennessee, and the mountains southward; also mild coast areas — Cape Cod southward.

C. The Lower South — Charleston, S. C. to Florida and westward through Alabama to the Gulf of Mexico.

D. The West Coast, from San Francisco northward through Portland and Seattle to Vancouver and Victoria.

SPECIES, VARIETIES, AND HYBRIDS	REGIONS	CHARACTERISTICS AND NOTES
R. catawbiense, R. maximum, and forms such as atrosanguineum, album elegans, album grandiflorum, 'Charles Dickens,' 'Caractacus,' catawbiense album, everestianum, 'Lady Armstrong,' 'Mrs. Chas. Sargent,' purpureum grandiflorum, roseum elegans.	A B C	Color range from white through blush and pink to rose, crimson, and lilac. Besides those named, many hardy seedling and old-time named varieties are available.

SPECIES, VARIETIES, AND HYBRIDS	REGIONS	CHARACTERISTICS AND NOTES
Other Catawba hybrids, *R. ponticum,* the *R. fortunei* group and its hybrids, such as the 'Dexter' hybrids (some fragrant).	B C	Good in the New York City and Philadelphia areas; some may be hardy northward.
R. thomsoni, griffithianum, fortunei, auriculatum, and others. 'Britannia,' 'Earl of Athlone,' 'Purple Splendour,' 'Cynthia,' others. Loderi and loderi hybrids, especially loderi 'King George' and 'Venus.'	D	All grow well in Pacific Northwest. A few may prove hardy in Region B. For larger list for West Coast, consult regional nurserymen. Wide range of colors; many brilliant.
R. carolinianum, minus, smirnowi, catawbiense compactum. R. micranthum. Hybrids such as 'Boule de Neige,' 'Henrietta Sargent,' myrtifolium, wilsoni and others.	A B	Colors, white light pink, lilac. *R. micranthum* with tiny white flowers is not handsome in bloom; leaves small, evergreen. Growth habit of these hybrids tends to be compact.
'Cunningham's White'	B	An early-blooming white hybrid.
R. chapmani	C	A native of Florida, very much like *R. carolinianum.*
R. augustini ('Tower Court' form), *R. campylocarpum, cinnabarinum roylei, griersonianum, haematodes, neriifolium, wardi.* Hybrids including 'Azor,' 'Butterfly,' 'Fabia,' 'Lady Chamberlain,' 'May Day,' 'Romany Chai,' 'Temple Belle,' and many others.	D	These include a vast array of forms and many additional species. Colors range from almost blue to bright red and clear lemon-yellow. Some of the hybrids have intermediate shades, as salmon-rose. Some have peculiarly shaped flowers.
R. arborescens (white), *calendulaceum* (yellow, orange), *cumberlandense* (orange, scarlet), *nudiflorum* (light pink), *roseum* (rose), *viscosum* (white), *vaseyi* (pink), *R. japonicum* (salmon, yellow), *molle* (orange, yellow), *R. schlippenbachi* (light pink), *poukhanense* (li-	A B C D	Native American azaleas, hardy even in sub-zero climates. Height ranges from 3 to 12 feet or more. Flowers are under 2 inches in diameter, except in japonicum and molle which are usually more than 2 inches across. Kaempferi will not succeed where tempera-

SPECIES, VARIETIES, AND HYBRIDS	REGIONS	CHARACTERISTICS AND NOTES
lac), *kaempferi* (bright salmon-rose), *mucronulatum* (lilac-purple).		ture goes 15° below zero.
R. *luteum* (yellow), *occidentale* (white and yellow), *pentaphyllum* (bright magenta), *reticulatum* (white), 'Ghent' and mollis hybrids.	B C D	'Ghent' and mollis hybrids vary in hardiness. The true occidentale is not very hardy.
R. *austrinum* (yellow, orange), *canescens* (white, pink), *prunifolium* (red, orange, yellow), *serrulatum* (white), *speciosum* (red).	C	Native azaleas of the Lower South, generally unsatisfactory north. Much like the northern wild azaleas in character.
R. *occidentale* (white, with yellow blotch).	D	There are some excellent forms and hybrids of this species.
R. *poukhanense* (lilac), *kaempferi* (red).	A B C D	Semi-evergreen in the North; evergreen in the South.
R. *obtusum*, large Kurume azaleas (white, pink, lilac), *mucronatum* (white), *indicum* (red), *malvaticum*, 'Glenn Dale' and 'Gable' hybrids.	B C D	Some Kurume azaleas grow to 6 feet. Untested 'Glenn Dale' hybrids may prove hardier and better than Kurumes.
R. *phoeniceum* (magenta), *simsi* (red), *scabrum* (scarlet), Indian Hybrid Azaleas, macrantha hybrids, malvatica hybrids.	C	The large Indian azaleas and their allies, famous in the Lower South; not hardy in the North.
R. *atlanticum* (white, pink), *canadense* (lilac, lavender), *micranthum, racemosum;* R. *wilsoni* and *myrtifolium* (hybrids).	A B	R. *atlanticum* is a coastal species, 18 inches tall; the white form is best. R. *canadense* is the Rhodora. Both are deciduous.
Kurume and malvatica azaleas, 'Glenn Dale' hybrids in small forms.	B C	Several types of dwarf Japanese azaleas do well in the South.
R. *hippophaeoides* and possibly some other Oriental species.		

SPECIES, VARIETIES, AND HYBRIDS	REGIONS	CHARACTERISTICS AND NOTES
R. triflorum, ledoides, williams- ianum and others. 'Temple Belle,' 'Bow Bells,' 'Blue Tit' and other hybrids.	D	There are many dwarf ever- green rhododendrons from Asia in many colors from blue to red and yellow.

GROWING BROAD-LEAVED EVERGREENS UNDER ADVERSE CONDITIONS

Gardeners who wish to grow broad-leaved evergreens where acid soils do not exist face some serious but not insurmountable problems. The most important single phase of their culture is their need for a certain kind of fungus, called a mycorrhiza, on their roots. This specialized fungus serves these plants in place of their root hairs and is therefore essential in the uptake of nutrients. If the mycorrhizal fungus is destroyed, the plant dies.

Another important requirement of these plants is for an outside source of certain plant hormones. Species that grow in alkaline soils seem able to manufacture them in abundance. Acid-soil plants, however, draw these hormones, which are growth factors, largely from bacteria that die and release them as they decay. Bacteria, in turn, obtain them from organic matter. For this reason, the soil for acid-demanding plants should contain at least 25 per cent of well-decayed organic matter. Chemical fertilizers do not seem to meet the needs of ericaceous species except temporarily.

Most plants in this group are quite shallow-rooted and subject to injury from the sun if the roots are not protected. An organic mulch is therefore useful. It also protects the mycorrhizae from drying out and from being injured or killed by too much heat. In short, what is good for the mycorrhizae is good for the plant.

Unlike deciduous plants, the need of evergreens for moisture continues all winter long. Their broad foliage gives off water continually, even when the soil is frozen. With frozen soil, there is no upward movement of water to replace that lost by evaporation. Broad-leaved evergreens do roll their leaves in cold weather to cut water loss, but in dry climates this is not enough. The use of screens or burlap wrappings to cut down evaporation and give protection against the winter sun is vital. Where exposure is unusually severe, the best winter protection is afforded by setting a ring of chicken wire or fencing around the plant, and filling this with oak leaves, pine needles, excelsior, or some other dry, fluffy material.

Changing the Soil Reaction

One of the most difficult problems in alkaline-soil areas is that of permanently altering the pH of the soil. This can be done temporarily, but the "buffering" ability of soil is enormous, and usually there is a slow return to its original reaction. If the pH of the available water supply is high, for instance, indicating alkalinity, the application of peatmoss, dusting sulfur, or ammonium sulfate will work for only a few weeks.

In limestone areas, the upward movement of ground water during dry weather will bring up moisture that is highly alkaline. Earthworms living in alkaline soils below a treated bed can undo your best efforts to keep the soil acid, for as they crawl to the surface they coat their tunnels with lime mixed with slime. To avoid this difficulty, dig to a depth of 24 inches and lay down a mixture of coarse and fine steam cinders. Earthworms will not burrow through such a layer. The cinders will also break the upward movement of limed water.

An ideal soil for these plants consists of about 1 part well-decayed organic matter, 1 part sand, and 1 part garden loam, with pH adjusted by the use of sulfur or other amendments to about 4.5. Don't assume that oak leafmold and peatmoss are acid; some leached oak leafmold may be alkaline. Also, while most imported brands are acid, domestic peats may be alkaline.

As we go west of Ohio, summer weather tends to be drier and drier. Summer drought is the rule over most of the Middle West. It is during these dry periods that winter-killing really occurs. A dry atmosphere dessicates the bark so that it becomes a poor conductor of nutrients between the various parts of the plant. When this semi-starved plant goes into winter, water moves with such difficulty up the injured bark that when water is given off by the foliage, it cannot be replaced.

Protecting the plants during summer dry spells is the first step toward increasing winter hardiness. If any large number of plants is involved, it may even pay to install a mist system to keep the air around them at a constant humidity. For a plant or two, the hose (preferably with a fog-nozzle installed) should be used at least twice a day during hot dry weather. This is in addition to whatever watering will be needed to keep the soil constantly moist (never saturated).

Feeding in mid-August is important, too. At this time the plant has completed its terminal growth for the year and begins to expand in branch diameter. This means the plant is storing nutrients which will be needed next spring. This stored food acts as an anti-freeze and reduces winter damage.

Although the use of organic material such as cottonseed meal, well-decayed cow manure, and compost is recommended, this summer feeding will do more good if it consists of either ammonium nitrate or ammonium sulfate.

The list of really tough varieties of azaleas is short. It includes: *Rhododendron kaempferi*, *R. poukhanense* and *R. schlippenbachi*; the natives, *R. canadense*, *R. calendulaceum*, *R. arborescens*, *R. vaseyi* and *R. mucronulatum*; and selected varieties of the 'Beltsville' hybrids.

OTHER PLANTS TOLERANT OF ACID SOILS

The magnificent explosion of color that marks the flowering of rhododendrons and azaleas often blinds us to the fleeting nature of their display. When it is over, we become aware that other plants are needed to supplement them.

Not all plants in the following list are broad-leaved evergreens (E). Some are needle-leaved evergreens or conifers (C), others are true deciduous plants (D), and a number of them are herbaceous (H), but all are included because of their ability to survive at pH readings as low or lower than those tolerated by rhododendrons.

Abies species (C), Firs

Acer pensylvanicum (D),
   Striped Maple

Andromeda glaucophylla (E),
   Bog Rosemary

Arctostapylos uva-ursi (E),
   Bearberry

Arethusa bulbosa (H),
   Dragon's Mouth

Calluna vulgaris (E),
   Scotch Heather

Camellia japonica (E), Camellia

Ceanothus delilianus 'Gloire de
   Versailles' (D), Ceanothus

C. prostratus (E), Mahala Mat

C. thyrsiflorus (E),
   California Lilac

Chamaecyparis thyoides (C),
   Southern White Cedar

Chamaedaphne calyculata (E),
   Leatherleaf

Chionanthus retusus (D),
   Chinese Fringe Tree

C. virginicus (D), Fringe Tree

Clethra alnifolia (D),
   Sweet Pepperbush

Comptonia asplenifolia (D),
   Sweetfern

Convallaria majalis (H),
   Lily-of-the-valley

Cornus canadensis, Bunchberry

Corylopsis paucifolia (D),
   Winter Hazel

C. spicata (D),
   Giant Winter Hazel

Cyrilla racemiflora (D),
   Leatherwood

Cytisus species (D), Brooms

Dicentra eximia (H),
   Plumy Bleeding-heart

Diosma ericoides,
   Breath-of-heaven

Empetrum nigrum (E),
   Crowberry

Erica species (E), Heaths

Exochorda species (D),
   Pearlbushes

Fagus grandiflora (D),
   American Beech

Fothergilla gardeni (D),
   Dwarf Alder

F. major (D), Witch Alder

Galax aphylla (E), Beetle-weed

Gordonia alatamaha (D),
   Franklin Tree

Ilex species (ED), Hollies

Iris cristata (H), Crested Iris

Kalmia angustifolia (E),
   Sheep Laurel

K. latifolia (E), Mountain Laurel

K. polifolia (E), Swamp Laurel

Larix decidua (D),
European Larch

Ledum groenlandicum (E),
Labrador Tea

L. palustre (E), Wild Rosemary

Leiophyllum buxifolium (E),
Sand Myrtle

Leucothoë catesbaei (E),
Fetterbush

Liatris scariosa (H), Gayfeather

Magnolia virginiana (D),
Sweet Bay

Menziesia pilosa (D),
Minnie Bush

Mitchella repens (E),
Partridge-berry

Monarda fistulosa (H),
Wild Bergamot

Myrica caroliniensis (D), Bayberry

M. gale (D), Sweet Gale

Osmanthus americanus (E),
Devilwood

O. aquifolium (E), Tea Olive

Oxydendrum arboreum (D),
Sourwood

Pernettya mucronata (E),
Prickly Heath

Pieris floribunda (E), Andromeda

P. japonica (E),
Japanese Andromeda

Quercus borealis (D), Red Oak

Skimmia japonica (E), Skimmia

Sorbus americana (D),
American Mountain Ash

Styrax japonica (D), Snowbell

Ulex europaeus (D), Furze

Vaccinium corymbosum (D),
High-bush Blueberry

V. macrocarpon (E), Cranberry

V. pensylvanicum (D),
Low-bush Blueberry

Vitex agnus-castus (D),
Chaste Tree

Zenobia pulverulenta (E), Zenobia

18

Vegetables for Flavor

You can enjoy gourmet vegetables only if you grow your own. Picked at the peak of flavor a few moments before they are to be cooked or made into a salad, they have a perfection which only those who have eaten such ambrosia can appreciate. Even if the home gardener mistakenly plants commercial varieties bred for shipping qualities rather than for taste, the difference will still be great. If he selects varieties used by gourmet gardeners and known to be superior, he can elevate dining to a fine art.

Do not be deterred from enjoying this experience by comments that home-grown vegetables cost more than those you buy. Any well-planned vegetable garden should return at least five dollars for every dollar spent on it. This alone would justify its existence, without the added boon of delectable produce.

GOURMET VEGETABLES FOR THE AMATEUR

Not all gourmet varieties can be found easily because seed dealers usually follow the course of least resistance, offering the same commercial types to home gardeners and commercial growers. These less desirable seeds will produce better vegetables than you can buy, but to enjoy the ultimate in quality, try to located the special strains listed below. Some are old varieties, still treasured because nothing better has been discovered. Typical is 'Blue Coco' bean, which has been listed for over 100 years by a French seed house, yet has never been equalled in flavor.

ASPARAGUS. Rust found in America prevents the growing of the finer French varieties. 'Paradise,' relatively new, grows quickly and has high flavor.

BEANS, GREEN BUSH. Those who have eaten the broad-podded Italian cut beans and loved them for their superb quality will enjoy 'Streamliner,' a similar bean. However, it must be used young as it may get stringy. It should always be planted as a first crop, even in late seasons, because it is resistant to rotting in cold soil. For a round-pod bean of high flavor plant 'Contender.'

BEANS, WAX. Old-time, high-flavored flat-podded wax beans seem to have disappeared from the market.

BEANS, POLE. Many experts consider 'Blue Coco' the finest. Pods are vivid purple but turn clear green when cooked. 'Kentucky Wonder' is a bean either loved or hated by gourmets. It is meaty, sometimes stringy, but has a strong "beany" flavor.

BEANS, BUSH LIMA. Breeders have spoiled lima beans more than any other vegetable trying to combine the small size of the "baby" lima with the flavor of the large-seeded type. Perhaps the best-flavored of modern lima beans is 'Fordhook 242,' with large seeds.

BROCCOLI. 'De Cicco,' a very early maturing broccoli, is best for early use, but for fall, the giant heads of 'Waltham' are better.

BRUSSELS SPROUTS. A new variety, 'Jade Cross,' has top flavor and does well almost everywhere. 'Catskill' is excellent if you can't find 'Jade Cross.' Always let Brussels sprouts be touched by frost before using to develop the flavor.

BEETS. Best-flavored beets in the world are the long English type, with roots like those of a carrot, but blood-red in color. 'Winter Keeper' and 'Long Season' are best, but late. Sow a short row of 'Ruby Queen' for early use.

CANTELOUPE. The old-time 'Emerald Gem' can occasionally be found and has the best flavor of all. 'Hearts of Gold' is a top-quality modern sort. 'Honey Dew,' while difficult to grow, has the green-flesh flavor of 'Emerald Gem.'

CARROTS. Because coreless types contain less fiber, they have better flavor. 'Touchon' and 'Sweetheart' are two good coreless varieties. 'Nantes Half Long' is wonderful too.

CAULIFLOWER. Most modern varieties are grown for whiteness, not flavor. Try 'Purple Head' — purple when picked, a pale greenish white when cooked.

CELERIAC. A truly gourmet vegetable, often overcooked. Large 'Smooth Prague' has the true old-time German celery-root flavor.

CELERY. Unfortunately, the European pink and red varieties do not do well in America. Next best is the white Pascal type. Sow 'Summer Pascal' for an early crop, 'Winter Pascal' for storage. 'Golden Self Bunching' is good, but the older 'Emperor' and 'Fordhook' have better flavor.

CHINESE CABBAGE. Perhaps the most underrated vegetable in the catalog. It makes a marvelous winter salad and stores well. Very tasty cooked as a green vegetable, too. Old-time varieties ('Wong Bok' or 'Pao Ting') cannot be planted before July 1 without running to seed. 'Nagoa Hybrid,' a new variety from Japan, can, however, be seeded in spring and will head up.

CORN. Although a glutton for space, it is perhaps the vegetable in which differences between commercial stuff and home grown are greatest. 'Aunt Mary's' probably combines more of the qualities wanted in a sweet corn than any other. Where Stewart's wilt is present and a hybrid variety must be used, 'Golden Cross Bantam' is about as good as any.

CUCUMBER. Try to find a source of seed for 'English Frame' cucumbers and grow them on your compost pile or in shallow depressions with 6 inches of well-rotted manure just under the surface. Otherwise, try 'Mandarin.'

EGGPLANT. 'Black Beauty,' an old-time variety, is still as good as any.

ENDIVE. Best flavored of all is 'Broad-leaved Escarole' ('Batavian White' or 'Florida Deep Heart'). Plant it after July 15 or it will turn bitter in summer heat. 'Rose Ribbed,' a cut-leaf variety, will head up and be sweet even in July heat.

LETTUCE. Shun the California crisp-head varieties. 'Matchless' (also called 'Deer Tongue') is a 'Butterhead' type of high flavor, which is very tender. It is fully as good as 'Bibb' or 'Limestone' but, unlike the latter, can be grown even in summer heat. For growing in coldframes for winter use, 'Bibb' is a shade better. 'Cos' or 'Romaine' is much overrated.

NEW ZEALAND SPINACH. For warmer sections where true spinach will not do well, a mixture of half New Zealand spinach (a different plant altogether) and half 'Fordhook' Swiss chard will be better than any other greens you can grow. The "flat sour" of New Zealand spinach (objectionable to many) is neutralized by the chard, while the earthy flavor of the latter is suppressed when cooked in this combination.

ONION. The world's best-flavored onion is 'Italian Red Bottle' or 'Red Tripoli,' but it can be grown only as a winter crop in California. 'Sweet Spanish' type (now available in hybrids) is best for home use and will grow in the North. However, it does not keep well: for winter use, grow 'Ebenezer.'

PARSLEY. For a true parsley flavor, grow 'Italian' or 'Plain.' For garnishing but with less flavor, grow 'Triple XXX Curled' or 'Champion Moss Curled.' For use in soups, to give a subtle parsley flavor, use 'Hamburg Rooted.'

PARSNIPS. 'Hollow Crown,' 'Long Smooth,' and 'All America' are excellent varieties.

PEAS. Except in favored spots where nights are cool (northern Wisconsin, New England, Pacific Northwest) about the only pea that will produce well is 'Wando,' which has better flavor than any peas you can buy. 'Little Marvel' is slightly better, but less heat resistant. For real pea country, plant 'World's Record,' 'Improved Gradus,' or 'Laxton's Progress.' For a gourmet's treat, grow 'Dwarf Grey Sugar' and cook pods and all.

PEPPERS. 'California Wonder' and 'Early California Wonder' are both excellent. For slicing as a relish, use 'Sweet Banana.' In northern sections with cool nights, 'Wisconsin Lakes' will mature.

PUMPKIN. Grow 'Butternut' squash instead: it makes better pies than pumpkin.

RADISHES. 'Burpee White,' a round early, is the ultimate in flavor. 'Giant Butter' is perhaps the finest round red. For hot-weather use, grow 'White Strassburg.'

RHUBARB. While used as a fruit, rhubarb is usually grown with vegetables. Here is one case where modern varieties are best: any of the newer all-red rhubarbs is superb.

RUTABAGA. 'Laurentian' is most generally satisfactory.

SPINACH. A poor crop except where peas will grow. 'Bloomsdale Long Standing' is best flavored and grows well.

SQUASH. If judged by the flavorless objects sold in commerce, no one would ever plant summer squash. But when you try 'Caserta' for the first time, you will experience a real treat, a completely different vegetable. For winter use, 'Butternut' (resistant to borer attack) is the one to grow. It has the highest quality.

TURNIPS. 'Just Right F-1' hybrid has better flavor than old-time varieties, plus tender foliage for those who like cooked turnip greens.

TOMATO. Good modern disease-resistant varieties include 'Wiltmaster,' 'Manalucie,' and 'Garden State.' For northern areas, try 'Firesteel' (somewhat acid). Two really choice old-time varieties are 'Giant Tree' (which can be grown as a "climbing" tomato) and 'Henderson's Richmeat.' Although Peter Henderson went out of business, others handle this variety.

PLANNING THE VEGETABLE GARDEN

Some crops occupy so much space that they are not worth growing in home gardens — potatoes, for example. At the same time, there is no way to enjoy one of the best of all gourmet dishes — marble-sized new potatoes boiled in their jackets and served with melted butter and parsley — unless you grow your own. Plant a short row for this purpose, but unless space is unlimited, don't grow potatoes for winter storage.

Sweet corn is a glutton for space too, but to be gourmet fare, corn must be home grown. If space is limited, sigh and mark it off the list. Garden peas, perhaps the most delicate of all vegetables, demand more in space than they are worth. However, 'Wando' can often be grown for fall use (it tolerates heat well) by planting it after some spring crop has been gathered.

Always work vegetable garden soil full time. As soon as one crop is gathered, seed another to take its place. Grow quick-maturing crops like radishes and lettuce between rows of tomatoes and other slow-maturing vegetables.

When it is too late to grow even vegetables, seed the vacant rows to rye for a cover crop ('Rosen' is a good variety of winter rye).

Layout and Soil

A great to-do is often made about the need for changing the locations of each crop from year to year to prevent disease. This idea has little value: the short distances that separate rows in a home garden offer no isolation. With adequate fertilizer use, there is no need to worry about soil exhaustion. Even the poorest soil will produce good vegetables if it is workable and if 30 to 40 pounds of a good mixed fertilizer, such as a 10-6-4 are applied to every 1,000 square feet before digging.

If your soil is stiff, heavy clay, better pass up such crops as carrots, parsnips, and long radishes. In their efforts to corkscrew into the soil, they will develop hard, woody fiber and be practically worthless. Do, however, plan to add compost and other organic matter to lighten the clay for root crops in future years.

Although winter rye is recommended as a cover crop to blot up any un-used fertility in soil after the growing season, don't sow this where the earliest vegetables are to grow. It makes such rank growth that when plowed under in spring, it rots too late to allow sowing of early crops.

To Lime or Not to Lime?

Most vegetables do best if the soil is just slightly acid. If a pH kit is used, the reading should be between 6.0 and 6.9. If below 6.0, lime should be added, but don't overdo it. Ground limestone is better than hydrated lime. For an explanation of pH, see Chapter 1.

Digging or Tilling

For those able to do the job, digging a garden by hand is a pleasant task. English garden enthusiasts even go to the trouble of double-digging — removing the surface soil, working up the subsoil, and replacing the topsoil. It isn't worth it. Most vegetables don't send roots that deep.

If physical labor is at a premium, a mechanical tiller should be used. Its one weakness is that if used at the same depth each time the garden is tilled, it will form a hard, pounded layer at the bottom of the tilled soil. In some cases true hardpan will form. To avoid this, change the depth of tilling each time.

Preparing to Plant

Allow the soil to settle for three or four days if possible before laying out the rows. Rows are best if they run north and south so that each crop gets its full share of sunshine. Don't try to run rows without a guide. Use a chalk line tied to stakes at the end of the row. A convenient trick is to mark a hoe or rake handle with brass tacks or escutcheon nails at intervals of 12, 18, 24, and 36 inches. This can then be used to measure the space between rows. Reserve one end of the garden plot for permanent crops such as asparagus and rhubarb.

Since planting directions accompany all seed and nursery orders, no attempt is made here to recommend spacing and culture. However, for what it is worth: despite the rigid rules these directions give for spacing plants, do not worry if you make a mistake and plant them too close together or too far apart. All plants are amazingly adaptable and will survive and produce in spite of minor errors.

A good man to consult if you want help in a hurry is your county farm adviser or county agent, whose office is usually in the courthouse at your county seat. He can help with insect and disease problems, but do not take his recommendations of varieties too seriously. He will be inclined to favor commercial types and not the less reliable home-garden varieties with high flavor.

19

Fertilizers for Cultivated Plants

The growth of plants is influenced by four elements — heat, light, food, and water. Of these, the gardener can usually do little about light and heat, but food and water are largely subject to his control.

Science is now in agreement that at least 15 elements are essential to the growth of green plants: carbon, hydrogen, oxygen, phosphorus, potassium, nitrogen, sulfur, calcium, iron, magnesium, boron, zinc, manganese, copper, and molybdenum.

We do little to control carbon in the open garden: plants take their supply from the carbon dioxide in air. It is perhaps the most important single element, for nearly half the weight of many plants is carbon. Water taken up by the roots is the source of the plant's needs in hydrogen and oxygen. The surplus oxygen is liberated as a gas. All the other chemical elements listed here are used in such small quantities that they are called minor or trace elements in plant nutrition.

DIFFERENCES BETWEEN PLANTS AND ANIMALS

There are fundamental differences as well as similarities between the feeding of garden plants and the nutrition of animals. They are alike in that every living thing — whether a human being, a giant sequoia, a fungus, or a mouse — must have some source of energy foods, sugars or starches that are "burned" by living cells as fuel in the process of living.

They differ in that green plants are able to manufacture their own energy foods out of simple carbon dioxide, water, and minerals from the soil, while animals must depend for energy upon the starches manufactured in plants.

Animals, including man, have organs capable of ingesting elaborate organic substances, whether of animal or vegetable origin, and by digestion, reducing these into simple compounds which can circulate through the body and be used. Plants, on the other hand, have no digestive apparatus. They are unable to break down elaborate foods and use them directly. What this means is that all complex organic fertilizers applied for use by green plants must be broken down into simple chemicals, almost in elemental form, before they can be of use. This is done by the micro-organisms of the soil — fungi, bacteria, and similar microscopic living things which are able to digest organic matter. In this process they use some of the energy contained in organic matter and built its nitrogen, phosphorus, potash, and other food elements into their own cells. When these micro-organisms die (and their life cycles are usually quite short) these elements, less a certain loss inevitable in the long chain of organism to organism, become available to plants.

ORGANIC FERTILIZERS

Here we have an explanation of the advantages and disadvantages of natural manures and other organic fertilizers. Obviously, these materials cannot begin feeding plants the moment they are applied. Various chains of bacteria are needed to complete their breakdown into the simpler forms required by plants.

Soil organisms are not always predictable in their working. They are fussy about pH, about aeration, and about their own food supply. At temperatures below 60°, most of them stop moving and feeding. Because their activity is low at this stage, they live longer, retaining the foods they have absorbed instead of releasing them for use by green plants. This is useful in fall, when unused fertilizer elements in the soil are taken up by bacteria and fungi which then proceed to go dormant until warm weather returns. They serve as a blotter, absorbing plant foods and conserving them for use in the spring.

The slowness with which organic fertilizers are released depends upon how they are bound up in the basic material. Dried blood is perhaps the most valuable single fertilizer in the world, since it contains every element needed by plants that is largely available as soon as water can dissolve it. Unfortunately, it commands such a high price for the manufacture of plastics and adhesives that little is now available for fertilizer use. At the opposite pole is humus, also a highly valuable organic source of nitrogen. Here, nitrogen is so tightly bound that at normal pH readings, it will be released at a rate of between 1 and 2 per cent a *year*. This means that it will remain as a source of fertility for half a century or more. The long "pay-out" of humus means little to the gardener raising a crop of lettuce, but when planting a lawn or a tree, whose roots may not be accessible again in his lifetime, it is the only material that can be used for "permanent" feeding.

Whatever organic matter is available for fertilizer use should be reserved for planting trees and shrubs and making lawns. Only if it can be spared from these more important purposes, should it be applied in the vegetable garden or perennial border. All garden soils should contain some organic matter, however, because of its beneficial effect on soil organisms (see Chapter 1).

Although the use of organic matter is highly recommended in the initial preparation of soils for turf, the old-time practice of applying an organic fertilizer to the lawn in late fall has little to recommend it. For one thing, it does not break down and do much feeding in the cool soils of fall. For another, it feeds certain fungi which are active at low temperatures and cause the various diseases lumped under the name snow mold. This does not mean an outright condemnation of such fertilizers if they have been used without causing difficulty in the past (as in warmer sections of the Southwest) but if snow mold attacks year after year, avoid all forms of organic fertilizer.

Delayed nitrogen burn is a puzzling condition which often occurs on lawn grasses (and can occur on other plants) caused by improper use of organic fertilizers, usually sewerage sludge. Because no immediate effect is observed after applying sludge to turf in early spring, amateurs often figure they have not applied enough and put on another dose. This does nothing at the time, but if weather conditions change suddenly and temperatures soar into the 90's, soil bacterial action may be so rapid that far more nitrogen is released than either the grass plants can absorb or the soil particles can buffer.

The result is nitrogen burn, exactly like that caused by application of too much chemical nitrogen, but seldom associated with the fertilizer used because the cause and effect are so widely separated.

CHEMICAL FERTILIZERS

The difference between chemical and organic fertilizers is largely one of complexity of the organics and the simplicity of the chemical types.

In general, we consider a fertilizer "chemical" if it is made of salts or similar materials in simple form which are either immediately available to plants or require only a slight change to make them so, sulfate of ammonia, for example. Acid-soil plants such as blueberries and rhododendrons can use ammonia, but for most alkaline-soil plants this must be converted by soil bacteria to nitrites and then to nitrates. Although tremendous differences are claimed by organic gardeners who favor "natural" fertilizers, these must all be broken down finally into the same ammonia-nitrite-nitrate products, which are released in a much shorter time by "chemical," or commercial, fertilizers.

Herein lies the advantage of the chemical fertilizers. They are available to plants almost as soon as applied, and they produce rapid response in growth. It is not unusual to apply a chemical fertilizer to a lawn and see the grass turn a darker green in two or three days. But immediate results mean rapid use of the material. The salts used for fertilizer are instantly soluble and move rapidly down the drainage system if not absorbed by the soil particles or taken up by micro-organisms. Almost all chemical plant foods must be applied at short intervals where maximum growth is wanted.

Because they do not depend upon soil bacteria to make them available, these fertilizers can be absorbed by plants in early spring. This makes them useful on lawns when grass is making rapid growth long before the soil warms up, and in late fall after it has cooled. Practically all market vegetable crops are fed chemically because growth can be kept at maximum by regular feeding.

The one valid criticism of chemical plant food is that of "burning" plants. If applied at rates higher than recommended (often very easy to do when overlapping with a fertilizer spreader), or if they are applied dry and not watered enough to dissolve all of the salts, most chemical fertilizers will draw moisture from plant tissues. Since a salt in complete solution cannot take up any more water, the obvious answer is either to water in the material as soon as applied, or to apply it dissolved in water. The advantages of liquid fertilizers have brought on a rash of claims for them which are not substantiated by results. They merely increase costs to extravagant figures for the amount of actual plant foods they contain. While convenient for use on house plants, they are certainly illogical for use on lawns and gardens.

High-analysis dry chemicals are available, to be mixed with water for application through a hose. These are often more economical than conventional garden fertilizers. Since they are pure plant food, with no added fillers or carriers, shipping costs per unit of fertilizer are lowered, thus in turn reducing their cost to the user.

LIGHTWEIGHT LAWN FERTILIZERS

As a convenience to women gardeners who cannot easily handle 50-pound bags, and also because of high shipping costs, lightweight lawn fertilizers have been developed. Practically all of these analyze about 20 per cent nitrogen, 10 per cent phosphorus, and 5 per cent potash, and are sold in bags weighing between 20 and 22 pounds. The application rate calls for one bag to 5,000 square feet. This, however, means applying only 8/10 of a pound of nitrogen to 1,000 square feet. The minimum feeding rate for bluegrasses is 4 pounds per 1,000. This would mean 5 applications during the growing season at the rate recommended.

Southern warm-season grasses, with their vigorous growth and high nitrogen demand, probably should be fed at double the 4-pound rate, which would mean either 8 applications a year, or applying the light-weight fertilizer at double strength, with some risk of burning.

UREAFORM NITROGEN

In an attempt to solve the problem of applying large amounts of nitrogen at one time, yet feeding plants over a long growing season, several methods of slowing down nitrogen release have been developed. The only one in regular commercial use at present is application of a new type of chemical called ureaform. It is a soft plastic made by reacting urea and formaldehyde. This plastic breaks down slowly and releases the nitrogen it contains at about the rate grass can absorb it. The breakdown is partly effected by soil chemicals and moisture, but is largely by bacterial action. As a result, ureaform fertilizer alone is slow to act in spring and does not release in late fall. However, it does do an outstanding job of feeding during warm weather.

Ureaforms, of course, supply only nitrogen and are not complete turf fertilizers. They are at their best as ingredients in mixed fertilizers, but if the plant is to benefit properly from their long-feeding advantages, at least 50 per cent of the mixture should be ureaform. Some quickly available type of nitrogen should be used for early feeding before soils warm up. One such mixed fertilizer uses four different sources of nitrogen other than the ureaform ingredient to give full-season feeding.

Straight ureaform is particularly valuable when used in planting nursery stock. The critical period for newly planted trees and shrubs is usually the first year of growth: if they are well fed then, they usually are able to survive and thrive whatever conditions occur later. Many nurserymen add a mixture of half sewerage sludge and half ureaform nitrogen to the soil in covering roots of newly planted stock.

FOLIAR FEEDING

Completely soluble plant foods are often applied in solution to the leaves of plants. These are absorbed and are almost instantly available to the plant. This is one reason why many liquid fertilizers have earned such a reputation for stimulating growth. However, costly liquids are not necessary: most dry fertilizers, if they are completely soluble, can be used in this way in liquid form.

One drawback to this method of feeding is that the effect is very brief. Indeed, it is over almost as soon as it has begun because only a limited amount of plant food can be applied to a leaf. For this reason, foliar feeding is mainly a device for quick stimulation. Unless you are willing to water almost daily, it cannot be relied upon for season-long feeding. As a supplement to regular soil fertilization, however, it has its place.

FERTILIZER FORMULAS

In order to use fertilizers properly, you must be able to calculate how much of each element a given product actually contains. Since nitrogen is the most costly ingredient and the element most often in short supply, the usual practice is to figure the quantity of this element and take the others for granted.

A great deal of fuss is made about ratios. Actually, almost the only time that ratio is really important is when low-phosphorus lawn fertilizers are essential to the proper functioning of pre-emergence crabgrass controls containing calcium arsenate. In practically no place where fertilizers are used is there such a thing as a perfect-ratio general fertilizer. This may sound like heresy to rose enthusiasts, who have been known to spend an entire evening session of a rose club arguing whether formula A was better than formula B, or vice versa. It is, nevertheless, a fact.

True, a fertilizer to fit exactly the needs of a specialty crop such as roses could be devised for a given soil under given cultural methods, but about the only advantage it would have would be to save a miniscule amount of one or more nutrient elements. The cost of working out the perfect fertilizer would probably be ten times that of the elements wasted.

Much of the pother about analysis arises from the fact that farmers, when planting a field of 50 to 100 acres to a single crop, find this factor important. By omitting a certain element, or including it only in exactly the right amount, a saving of several hundred dollars may be possible. However, when you are dealing in units of 1,000 square feet or less, running a soil analysis to see if a 5 per cent potash fertilizer is adequate, or whether 10 per cent is needed, would cost far more than the extra food element.

Still, it is worth remembering that fertilizers *can* be overused. Most experienced gardeners have seen lawns burned with too much nitrogen. But bear in mind that the damage would have been done whether the lawn fertilizer had 12 per cent phosphorus instead of 5, or 8 per cent potash instead of 4. It is the excess that is harmful, not the analysis.

What many people fail to understand is that plant roots are selective. So long as enough of each element is available to meet normal needs, and provided any excess can be buffered or absorbed in the soil, plants will thrive. The important thing is always to have enough, but never too much.

Since nitrogen is the most costly element, let us see how to figure it. The formula on the bag usually includes only three elements — nitrogen, phosphorus, and potash. These are the elements which all states insist must appear on the bag, stated in the formula. It is noted as a figure such as 10-10-10, or 4-12-4. The first stands for nitrogen, the second for phosphorus, and the third for potash. The figures given are percentages. In order to reduce them to pounds, consider them as one-hundredths, represented as decimals. That is, if we are dealing with a 10-8-6, we multiply the weight of the bag (say 50 pounds) by .10 to give us nitrogen, a total of 5 pounds; by .08 to give us phosphorus, a total of 4 pounds; and by .06 to give us potash, a total of 3 pounds.

Although you should consider what form of fertilizer is best for a particular purpose (chemical, organic, ureaform, mixed ureaform), in general you can assume that a pound of nitrogen in one form does the same work as a pound of nitrogen in another. Dividing the cost of the fertilizer by the number of pounds of nitrogen it contains is a simple way of figuring out whether you are getting your money's worth.

For example, a 50-pound bag of sewerage sludge at $4 looks like a tremendous bargain compared to a 25-pound bag of ureaform at $8. But when the sludge turns out to cost $1.33 a pound for nitrogen and the ureaform only 64 cents, it becomes obvious that the reverse is true.

USING FERTILIZERS

Although fertilizer bags always give specific directions for applying the products they contain, the instructions generally are of little use except as a rough guide to safe limits. Usually they err on the side of conservatism in order to avoid complaints of plant injury caused by overuse. In most instances the amounts indicated in the directions can be doubled with safety.

In the case of lawn fertilizers, overstating coverage is a survival of the day when one pound of actual nitrogen was considered a good application for 1,000 square feet of turf for an entire growing season. Today the consensus is that from four to eight times that amount is advisable where maximum luxury growth is wanted.

In general, heavy clay soils and those high in organic matter can safely absorb and store anywhere from two to ten times the rates recommended on bags. Poor, thin soils — the ones which need fertilizers most — unfortunately cannot be fed as heavily with safety to plants. Because they need more nutrient elements, and because they lose these faster than heavier soils, such soils must be fed oftener and in lighter doses — usually at the recommended rates.

Since most soils need and benefit from the elements in organic material, and since such material improves conditions for the vital micro-organisms, at least one fertilizer application during the year should be an organic material such as sludge, well-rotted compost, or animal manure. If these are not readily available, substitute peatmoss to which a chemical fertilizer has been added. Because the nutrient elements in such fertilizers are released only in warm soils, application during the summer months is best.

Since no two soils react in exactly the same way, every garden-owner must carefully observe how his land responds to various types of added plant foods. The one important thing to remember is that if a fertilizer is complete — if it contains all the minor or trace elements as well as the "Big Three" of nitrogen, phosphorus, and potash — plants will take what they need so long as the supply is adequate. If the pH reading of the soil (see Chapter 1) is kept between 6.0 and 6.9, all these elements should stay in available form.

(The special conditions surrounding the nutrition of acid-soil plants is covered in Chapter 17.)

20

Modern Weed Control

Modern weed control by means of chemicals has revolutionized many phases of agricultural and horticulture in less than two decades. However, chemicals were used long before that time. Iron sulfate mixed in a concoction called lawn sand was beloved of old-time English gardeners and did a fair job of controlling dandelions and plantains (with some incidental damage to fine turf grasses). Sodium chlorate, a highly flammable chemical, was used (often with explosive results) as a non-selective control in fields and driveways. Sodium arsenite, an intensely poisonous material that makes weed-control experts shudder when they see it in the hands of amateurs, has been used for the same purpose for more than 75 years.

All of these, however, lack the qualities of modern weed-control chemicals — selective action which provides killing power for a specific weed, a high degree of safety for the user, and ease of application. Take the case of the dandelion. Up to 1944, this was the No. 1 lawn pest. Today, the use of 2,4-D has reduced it to the status of a minor nuisance.

SOME CHEMICALS USED TODAY

HORMONE WEED-KILLERS. Both 2,4-D and 2,4,5-TP (Silvex) were originally called hormone weed-killers. They might more accurately be called absorption weed-killers, since they work after being absorbed through the leaves and roots of plants. By moving through the plant's vascular system they disrupt its normal functioning.

Even more important from the standpoint of the lawn-owner is that in certain formulations they work only against broad-leaved weeds. By stimulating abnormal growth of dormant root buds that exist in the cambium layers of broad-leaved weeds (but not in grasses), they cause a choking off of the normal movement of food and moisture between tops and roots. The plant then starves to death.

For the control of most broad-leaved weeds and narrow-leaved weeds such as clover or chickweed, a mixture of 2,4-D and 2,4,5-TP is used. This is relatively safe for the amateur if he reads and follows exactly the directions on the package, and also measures accurately the areas to be sprayed. Granular formulations of 2,4-D and 2,4,5-TP give good results and are a sensible choice for small areas.

Certain really tough weeds like creeping Jenny refuse to die when sprayed with this mixture. The leaves can be knocked off time after time but they still come back. Here, straight 2,4,5-TP (Silvex) can be used, but *not* if the lawn contains bentgrasses; it is toxic to that group. For bentgrass safety replace Silvex with MCPP.

AMINOTRIAZOLE. Although the excitement stirred up several years ago about cranberries and cancer has frightened many people away from this chemical, aminotriazole is safer than common table salt. It is one of the most valuable of all weed-killers in dealing with persistent, hard-to-kill, deep-rooted weeds. Its action on poison ivy, for example, is dramatic.

Aminotriazole works by destroying the plant's ability to make chlorophyll. On some plants, grass in particular, its effect is temporary. Because chlorophyll production is interrupted, the blades turn white but slowly return to a normal green. If the plant is a species where chlorophyll suppression is complete, as it is in poison ivy, the plant never recovers.

DALAPON. We have long needed a chemical that will kill only grasses. The discovery of dalapon gave us that product. At recommended rates, it will kill only grasses, leaving broad-leaved plants untouched. For example, the non-grass lawn plant dichondra, used widely in California, can now be freed of grasses by the use of dalapon.

Another use is on groundcovers, which formerly had to be dug up when quackgrass invaded them. After the soil had been supposedly cleared of quackgrass by mechanical means, the groundcover was then replanted. All too often, the owner discovered that almost invisible grass tips, broken off during the digging, were still alive to bring the infestation back in full force. With dalapon, quackgrass can be removed from such groundcovers as English ivy, prostrate junipers, pachysandra, *Euonymus radicans,* and others.

ENDOTHOL. One of the highly specialized problems in weed control is that of destroying *Veronica filiformis,* a mat-forming speedwell scarcely two inches tall. In some parts of the country this is regarded as a valuable groundcover, producing great sheets of sky-blue flowers even in quite dense shade. In others it is considered a noxious weed. In Ithaca, New York, where it was introduced by a professor at Cornell, it is called the "profesosr's weed," sometimes preceded by uncomplimentary adjectives. In Cleveland, Ohio, it became such a pest that several cemeteries used non-selective herbicides to kill all vegetation in an effort to control it.

However, the chemical Endothal has been found to control it selectively in turf. Endothal is highly toxic to *Veronica filiformis* and to other veronicas as well.

Knotweed, a wiry-stemmed, ground-hugging plant that is sometimes called "farmer's lawn," had resisted all attempts to control it chemically. Some golf-course superintendents consider it a worse pest than crabgrass. But a new material called Dicamba (Banvel D) now gives practically 100 per cent control of this pest. It controls mature knotweed without injury to lawn grasses.

CHEMICALS AND METHODS FOR CRABGRASS CONTROL

Pre-Emergence Treatment

Crabgrass is perhaps the most irritating, because it is almost diabolic in its special adaptation to survival in a mown lawn. Its life cycle practically complements that of common Kentucky bluegrass. It makes its best growth when drought, summer dormancy, and turf diseases have thinned out the permanent grasses. Its prodigious seeding habit, and the longevity of the seed even when buried, further increase its ability to compete. Although we have had post-emergence controls for this pest for years, they have been only moderately successful.

CALCIUM ARSENATE. It was not until the discovery of the effect of calcium arsenate on newly sprouting crabgrass seed that we had a chemical capable of controlling it. Lead arsenate had been used for about 30 years by golf-course specialists as a pre-emergence control, but had definite limitations — high cost, slow action when applied late in spring, considerable danger to the user (poisonous white arsenic dust floated in the air when it was applied), and often an adverse effect on grass vigor.

Dr. William Daniel of Purdue University found that a special grade of 85 per cent calcium arsenate would kill up to 100 per cent of sprouting crabgrass seeds. In order to work, the chemical had to be on the soil in time to "fix" on the upper inch. This meant that it should be applied before apple and flowering crab blossoms were fully open, or when the saucer magnolia opened its flowers.

The action of calcium arsenate (also lead arsenate) is highly interesting and illustrates how selective controls can be found for various weeds by a study of their internal workings. Seeds of crabgrass contain no reserves of phosphorus, while those of permanent grasses are well supplied. If no high-phosphorus fertilizers have been applied for two or three months before the application of calcium arsenate, sprouting crabgrass seeds will take up arsenic instead of phosphorus. (The two chemicals are enough alike to fool the seeds.) Seedlings of perennial grasses are able to thrust their roots through the treated layer before they run out of phosphorus, and are not affected.

Although calcium arsenate is perhaps the most widely used of pre-emergence crabgrass controls, it has definite limitations which should be kept in mind. It has been more successful in the Middle West than in the East, because of differences in soil pH. On eastern lawns which have been regularly limed it has been fully satisfactory, but on acid soils it has either failed to control or has caused some leaf injury. In the Middle West it has not affected the germination of permanent grasses, but in the Philadelphia-Washington area, it has injured them for two to three weeks after application. For this reason, in acid-soil regions a delay of three weeks in reseeding is recommended.

The second limitation is that it must not be applied at the same time as fertilizer. Severe burning may result if the two are applied together. However, a major advantage of calcium arsenate is that it has a long residual period, remaining active against crabgrass for as long as three years. It can therefore be applied in fall to take effect next year, and fertilizer can be safely laid down in spring. The product used should be low in phosphorus, such as a 20-5-5 or a 25-5-5. When applied in fall, calcium arsenate also kills common chickweed (but not mouse-ear chickweed), and gives fairly good control of *Poa annua*. It also controls white grubs, Japanese beetle larvae, and other injurious soil insects. When applied in spring or summer, calcium arsenate must be in place at least a week before crabgrass seedlings sprout.

In view of the serious limitations of this chemical and with newer pre-emergence materials now available, calcium arsenate is no longer recommended.

DACTHAL. This material is highly effective as a crabgrass killer, with up to 100 per cent control at turf Experiment Stations all over the United States. It is not as sensitive to soil pH as calcium arsenate and should be given preference in eastern states on lawns which are definitely acid in reaction and which have not been limed for two or three years. It does have an effect on seeds of permanent grasses; these should not be sown on Dacthal-treated soil for at least four weeks after treatment.

Since this means a delay in seeding past the best time for germination in spring, seeding should perhaps be delayed until August 15, unless you are willing to water three times a day to sprout seeds of permanent grasses and enable the seedlings to become established.

While Dacthal gives full-season control, it is definitely a one-year material. Dacthal can be applied at the same time as fertilizer without interaction. Dacthal is safe on Kentucky Bluegrass but sometimes injures fescues and bentgrasses.

SIDURON (Tupersan). This new crabgrass control material is probably the biggest and most recent breakthrough in the lawn industry. According to Du Pont, manufacturers of Siduron, the chemical sets up a blockade in the soil which attacks the root system of crabgrass but does not harm roots of desirable lawn grasses. Crabgrass roots are unable to penetrate the chemical barrier. One of its most unique characteristics is that one can apply Siduron at the time most grasses are seeded, particularly the cool season grasses which include bluegrass, tall fescue and red fescue. The exceptions in seeding time application are with carpet grass, centipede grass or common Bermuda grass. It may not be used when Bermuda grass is sprig-planted, however it does not affect sprigged Meyer Zoysia. Siduron can be used to control crabgrass after it has germinated to the one or two leaf stage.

ZYTRON. Where nimble-Will (*Muhlenbergia diffusa*) is also present, Zytron is a logical choice. Nimble-Will, which looks like a dull gray-green bentgrass, is today considered a worse pest than crabgrass in Ohio, Kentucky, and areas along the Ohio and Missouri rivers. Two applications of Zytron ten days apart should practically eliminate it. For crabgrass itself, Zytron has also been one of the most consistent performers of all in state university tests, practically always giving 100 per cent control. It can be applied even after crabgrass seed has begun to sprout, but is not effective if the seedlings have started to root.

Its one defect is its strong residual effect on seeds of permanent grasses and its tendency to injure these same desirable grasses. At recommended rates it will inhibit seed germination of permanent grasses for six to eight weeks following application. This means delaying all reseeding until fall. On overlaps and turns, turf injury may be serious if too much is applied. This material is *not* for the slapdash operator.

TRIFLURALIN. One of the newer chemicals, with some excellent reports from a number of stations, is Trifluralin. It is sold both with and without fertilizer added. Under rather unusual weather conditions, the material with fertilizer added has caused some severe turf injury in the hands of home-owners, but such effects did not show up in state university tests. Possibly failure to follow directions exactly was responsible.

Post-Emergence Treatment

Once crabgrass seed has sprouted, pre-emergence controls (with the possible exception of Trifluralin or Siduron) are of little value, and post-emergence chemicals must be used. While these will kill the plants that are already in the turf, more plants will appear as wave after wave of crabgrass seed germinates. If you insist upon a lawn in which no crabgrass plants are visible, five to eight sprayings may be necessary — a costly process.

DSMA, AMA. Of all the chemicals introduced during the past two decades for the control of young and mature plants of crabgrass, disodium mono-methyl arsonate (Sodar, DSMA) has proved the most effective. It is not without some danger to bluegrass turf if used carelessly, but when properly applied, it will kill crabgrass without injury to the desirable grasses and it acts quickly: if it has taken effect, the crabgrass will be curling the next day. It has practically no residual effect; grass seed can be sown the following day.

Even more powerful, but with somewhat greater chance of injury to the lawn, are the so-called AMA compounds (mixtures of octyl ammonium methyl arsonate and dodecyl ammonium methyl arsonate).

Both DSMA and AMA may seriously injure bentgrasses and fine-leaved fescues. Where these grasses are in a lawn and considered valuable, test these chemicals on an inconspicuous corner before applying them to the area.

GRASSY WEEDS IN LAWNS

Grass species other than crabgrass often disfigure lawns. Because of their resemblance in physical make-up to the desirable grasses, control of them presents some tricky problems.

Tall Fescues and Perennial Rye

Sometimes weedy grasses are inadvertently seeded by the owner. Even perennial rye grass, often included in cheap mixtures as a "nurse grass," can be a problem if it survives the first winter. When mature, it is tall and coarse and forms ugly clumps in an otherwise fine turf. Perhaps the worst grassy weed is tall fescue, particularly the variety 'Kentucky 31.' During the past ten years, this has been added to cheap seed mixtures in an effort to delude purchasers into believing they are getting Kentucky bluegrass, a much more desirable species.

Tall fescues, seeded at a heavy rate, are useful for permanent lawns when traffic is a problem. As seeded in cheap mixtures, a plant develops in nearly every square foot of lawn, where it produces a coarse, rough clump. Because of the widespread use of tall fescues, seeds are now blowing into lawns where they were not sown. Unfortunately, any chemical that will destroy perennial rye grass or tall fescues, will also kill the better grasses.

If the clumps are few and scattered, cutting them close enough to injure the crown will soon kill them. If an entire lawn is infested, some means of slicing through the crown is needed. Several makes of lawn renovators are available for such an operation (among them the Henderson Contour and the Verti-Kut). They can often be rented. Their blades revolve on a central axle like the knives of a hammer mill, and they will slice through clumps of meadow fescue, tall fescue, and other grasses of this type. They will also tear out great wads of dead and living bluegrasses, fine-leaved fescues and bents, but this action is actually beneficial and the turf soon heals.

Bentgrasses

Before World War II, mixtures of bluegrasses and bents were sold as "deluxe" or "estate" mixtures and were ranked as the quality lawns of the day. Since then, bent has come to be considered a weed. This is particularly true when it is mixed with 'Merion' Kentucky bluegrass. Because of the former widespread use of bents, these grasses are firmly established in lawns all over the United States. A single "string," released when a lawn is mowed, can blow into a turf of other grasses, take root and form patches of light green against the emerald of 'Merion.'

We have needed a good killer for bentgrass which would not injure bluegrasses. Although that need has not yet been fully met, 2,4,5-TP (Silvex) — not to be confused with 2,4,5-T — can be used for this purpose. Two or even three applications may be needed. A complete kill may take 6 weeks. This means that 18 weeks (practically an entire summer) may be needed, during which time brown patches of dying bent will be present. However, there is a bonus, because 2,4,5-TP also kills most broad-leaved weeds, including clover and both forms of chickweed.

Poa Annua

This was once sold at a high price as "the grass you don't have to mow." It grows about two inches tall, sets seed, and does not grow any taller. In early spring, when it is at its best, it has a beautiful clear emerald green color and, in solid stands, looks like perfect turf.

It is still widely used in the South for winter golf greens because it remains in active growth during cold weather. It is a winter annual, germinating in late October and growing whenever air temperatures go above 32° for even a few hours. By spring, the plant is mature and in June it sets seed. Because of its vivid green color, inexperienced lawnowners often gather the seed and sow it, hoping to spread it over an entire lawn. But the seed lies dormant until the following fall.

Unfortunately, Poa annua is so susceptible to several turf diseases that it seldom survives after the first of July. It dies suddenly, leaving large dead areas where it stood. It is a weed and should be eradicated.

Materials such as Dacthal and Betasan have shown some promise in controlling this weed. However, these materials must be used in the early to late August — to prevent germination of annual bluegrass seed — for three successive years.

Foxtail and Barnyard Grass

These tall coarse annual grasses can be controlled by the methods described for tall fescues. They are also susceptible to DSMA or AMA and often disappear after these are applied for crabgrass control.

POISON IVY

The most ubiquitous poisonous plant in the United States is the native poison ivy (*Rhus toxicodendron*), the familiar three-leaved vine or shrub that causes a severe rash when touched. Leaves, branches, roots — all parts of the plant are poisonous at any time of year. Most toxic of all is the smoke which comes when uprooted vines are burned. It grows in every state, and across southern Canada, surviving in dry, rocky areas as well as in rich, moist woodlands.

It varies in growth habit from place to place. In the Northeast it grows as a climbing or clambering vine; on the West Coast it is a shrubby, thick-leaved plant (the so-called poison oak), and there are additional variations elsewhere. The forms belong to the same species, and the regional forms can only be considered sub-species.

The leaves vary greatly in size and shape from region to region and even from plant to plant, some being smooth and sharply pointed at the tip, others being as wavy-margined as an oak leaf (hence "poison oak" as one of the names). All, however, have two traits in common — a longer stalk on the middle leaflet and a varnished appearance to the leaf surface. (Japanese lacquer comes from a close relative growing in Japan. Many persons have learned the poisonous quality of this substance through the use of lacquered mah-jongg sets.)

An American relative with equally irritating qualities is poison sumac (*Rhus vernix*), a small tree which fortunately confines itself to wet places. It is distinguished from the harmless shrubby sumacs by its pendent clusters of waxy gray berries instead of the erect spikes of fuzzy hard red fruits of the innocuous kinds.

All of the poisonous species of rhus contain the same irritant, urushiol, which is a non-volatile oily resin. The theory that sensitive individuals are poisoned by breezes that blow over poison ivy is a myth. The chances are, when they are unaware of contact with the plant itself, that irritation has come from a dog or other pet that has touched the foliage or from wearing clothes that have been exposed to it on some previous occasion. Even the dead branches are dangerous.

Poison ivy and poison sumac are readily killed by aminotriazole, which has certain selective properties so that it can be sprayed on some trees without injury. However, directions should be followed exactly. It can also be killed by Silvex. This chemical, however, is toxic to trees. If the bark under a poison ivy vine is wetted in spraying, injury to the tree may result. Ammonium sulfamate (sold as Ammate) is also effective against poison ivy.

NON-SELECTIVE WEED-CONTROL CHEMICALS

Around every home there are areas where you want to kill out all vegetation, such as along fences, on driveways and walks, and along the edges of lawns. In the past, sodium arsenite, a highly toxic chemical, was widely used, but with an unhappy record of accidental poisoning. Sodium chlorate, an explosively flammable chemical, was another.

Today, several products are available which will kill all vegetation for various periods of time. A simple mixture of 2,4-D, 2,4,5-TP, and dalapon gives excellent control for about six weeks.

This residual period, however, is not long enough to keep drives, walks, and other areas clean all season long. For one- to two-year control on railroad rights of way in areas around industrial plants and similar places, a number of long-lasting substituted-urea compounds are available.

An excellent product, for amateur use, which will give a full season's control if applied when weeds are small, or will control with two sprayings if they are mature, is based on a mixture of certain esters of dalapon and Silvex. It is no more toxic than common table salt. Because it does not spread sideways, it can be used to edge lawns by directing a fine narrow spray along the line to be killed out.

METHODS OF APPLICATION

Sprays

Originally all weed controls were used as sprays, and liquids are still the most effective and the most economical controls for weeds. When cost is a factor, or tough weeds a problem, spraying should always be considered because of its more certain action.

Nevertheless, spraying does have its disadvantages. The most serious of these is drift. Inexperienced users often pump hand-sprayers to a high pressure to avoid pumping too often. If a nozzle with a fine opening is used with a tank-sprayer pumped up to 40 pounds or more, a fine mist will be produced which, instead of falling on the lawn, will drift hundreds of feet, even if a breeze can barely be detected. Even after traveling a considerable distance, this mist can seriously injure tomatoes, roses, and other plants. Drift can be avoided by using lower pressures and a nozzle opening that produces a coarse drop. This coarse drop will hit the leaf and if the spray material is properly compounded, will "break" immediately and spread.

This does not eliminate another hazard of certain weed-killers, particularly 2,4-D and 2,4,5-TP. Both are volatile to some degree. Even the so-called low-volatile esters will pass into a vapor if applied when air temperatures are above 90° on a bright sunny day. Under these conditions, plant leaves may reach a temperature of over 100°, high enough to volatilize even low-volatile esters. At the same time, most weed-killers work poorly if air temperatures are below 70°. The best results can be had by spraying when air temperatures are between 75° and 80° on a day with a light cloud overcast.

Although most ester-type weed-killers penetrate the leaf within 20 minutes of contact, the safest course is to respray if rain falls within eight hours after application.

Dry Application

Because of the hazards of drift and volatility, the use of materials that can be applied dry has become popular. These are also easier to use, and convenience is often more important than cost. They are applied with an ordinary fertilizer spreader. While spreading in this way allows you to judge coverage better, there is always a tendency to overlap. With many weed-killers this can have serious results.

Another problem is that spreaders (particularly rented ones) are often out of adjustment and should be checked for accuracy before they are used to apply either weed-killers or fertilizers. Most application rates are given for 1,000 square feet. Cover a stretch of garage floor with paper for a distance of 10 feet. Fill the spreader, adjust it to the recommended opening, and roll it across the paper. The amount spread over the 10-foot stretch can then be weighed.

If the spreader is 24 inches wide, 20 square feet will have been covered. Since this is one-fiftieth of 1,000 square feet, multiplying the amount spread by 50 will give the coverage. If half a pound was deposited, this would mean 25 pounds to 1,000 square feet.

Dry materials must be applied when the grass is wet with dew, so that the weed-killer will cling to the leaves of weeds.

Fertilizer — Weed-Killer Combinations

These are obviously mismatched materials. We know that injury to grass by fertilizer is at its worst when the fertilizer particles adhere to grass blades. However, if the weed-killer particles do *not* adhere, they do not kill.

Equally important, the season for killing weeds seldom coincides with that for fertilizing. Such combinations sound like bargains (lawn food and weed-killer for the price of one) but they are not based on good lawn practice.

MECHANICAL CONTROL OF WEEDS

The use of chemicals cannot eliminate entirely the need for hand or tool weeding. In the perennial border a weed-killer would be as deadly to desirable plants as it would be to the weeds. Here hand weeding is a necessity. However, once the weeds have been pulled, they can be prevented from coming back by applying a granular material of Dacthal or Trifluralin, or by spraying with sesone, a chemical that inhibits growth of seedling weeds, but has no effect on mature plants.

In the vegetable garden, the hoe, wheel hoe, and five-pronged weeder are still the best controls. Not too well known, but a wonderful labor-saver is the English scuffle hoe. This is a flat blade set at right angles to the handle. *Pushed* against weeds, it cuts them off at the surface with practically no effort. The operator walks backwards as he weeds, and thus never steps on his work.

The value of mulches in weed control cannot be overestimated. The new black plastic sheet material, in which holes are cut for the plants, is the latest development in this field. If care is taken to see that plants under plastic mulch get enough water, it is almost an ideal material for mulching.

21

Plant Propagation: Foundation of Gardening

Propagation in the world's first gardens was from seed, and the object was the production of food. Primitive man would not have found it too difficult to associate seed, seedling, and mature plant as logical steps in bringing wild plants under his domination. He could observe this succession in nature. Propagation of garden plants today similarly follows procedures by which plants in the wild perpetuate themselves.

A seed contains in miniature the finished plant of the next generation, requiring only certain amounts of heat and moisture (and in some instances, light) to begin its cycle. Botanically, a seed is a fertilized ovule produced by a flowering plant. It is obviously a device to enable that plant to perpetuate its kind. Some plants, those we call annuals, could not survive if the yearly chain of plant to seed to plant were broken. Others, called perennials because they live for more than one year, are able to survive even though all of their seeds are destroyed. This is because they contain self-perpetuating tissues that enable them to live through periods of dormancy or adversity created by frost, drought, or other growing hazards.

Many of the tissues of such perennials, including roots, stems, and leaves, when removed from the plant and inserted in a suitable growing medium, are capable of generating roots and assuming an independent existence. The parts removed for propagation purposes are called cuttings, and the method is known as "cuttage," in contrast to "seedage." All propagation is to a considerable degree a variation of these two processes; even the more complex methods known as budding, grafting, inarching, and layering are merely different ways to make a new plant grow independently of its parent.

SEED GERMINATION: AN INTRICATE PROCESS

Home gardeners seldom fail with vegetable seeds, if they remember not to plant beans too early and otherwise recognize the differences between hardy and tender crops. Through centuries of selection, the hard-to-grow species have disappeared. Man cannot depend for his vital food supply on any but reliable vegetable crops.

The same cannot be said of flower seeds, since these have always been selected on the basis of beauty, rather than on utility and reliability. Flower seeds have been brought to American gardens from the far corners of the world and represent climates as varied as valleys in the high Himalayas and semi-deserts in South Africa.

Growing Flowers from Seed

Easy-to-grow annuals such as marigolds, zinnias, and phlox dominate the garden of the beginner, but as he gains experience he tries increasingly difficult species and runs into trouble in germinating their seeds. His failures are usually due to his ignorance of certain basic requirements.

MOISTURE — A LIMITING FACTOR. Seed will not begin to grow until it has imbibed moisture. This means something more than merely soaking up enough water, which all seeds will do (far too readily if exposed to high humidity). When a seed has absorbed water, not only are the starchy parts of the seed moist, but water has penetrated the oily embryo and created conditions favorable to germination. A few kinds of seed, if they dry out after they have taken up enough water to begin germination, start up again when moisture is supplied. Most bluegrass seed is of this type. With a majority of seeds, however, once the process of germination has begun, it cannot be temporarily halted, and the seed will die if deprived of water.

This is the greatest single source of complaint concerning seeds that fail to germinate. The seed is blamed when, actually, failure to maintain constant moisture has been responsible. More than a mere occasional wetting is called for; the soil must be kept *constantly* moist so that water can move from soil particles to the seed. If the soil dries out before the root hairs have emerged, the process may be reversed. Moisture will be drawn from the seed, thereby killing it. A dry spell of as little as half an hour can destroy the embryo. Unfortunately, seeds also need oxygen for germination. If the soil is kept too wet, the embryo may be suffocated for lack of air. For this reason, a seed-starting medium must be one which can blot up a great deal of water without becoming waterlogged.

MEANS OF SURVIVAL. Mechanisms of checks and balances inside the seed permit it to survive some adverse conditions. They may be a season of cold weather — during which the seed must remain dormant — lack of sunshine, or prolonged drought. A dozen or more combinations of heat, moisture, dormancy, season, and soil conditions may be involved.

TEMPERATURE REQUIREMENTS. The pansy is an excellent example of a seed with special requirements. If grown in a steady 70° temperature, it may germinate poorly or not at all, depending upon the age of the seed. It does better if temperatures go as high as 85° during the day, but drop to 70° at night. If, however, temperatures fluctuate between 90° days and 50° nights, viable seed sprouts strongly. This is apparently a mechanism which permits seed to ripen in late fall, drop to the soil after frost kills the foliage, and germinate in spring when warm sunshine heats the soil during the day, only to have it cool off at night.

Delphinium seed, too, often causes trouble. Sown in spring after the soil has warmed up, it seldom germinates. The same is true of its relative, the annual larkspur. Specialists who sow this seed in the greenhouse in winter have learned that they must hold temperatures between 50° and 55° for good germination.

Certain other seeds are still immature when they drop from the plant or are harvested. The embryo will not develop unless exposed to temperatures above freezing but below 42°. Many shrub seeds require this type of after-ripening.

ALTERNATING DORMANCY. The problem of a condition known as alternating dormancy is difficult to solve. This involves a rhythm within the seed which allows it to sprout soon after harvest, but not a few weeks later. If, however, the seed is not disturbed, it will sprout when a mechanism inside the seed again returns it to germinating condition. There are records of primrose seed which did not sprout until three years after sowing.

HARD SEED COATS. Some flowers, such as sweet pea and clover, have hard-coated seeds. In nature, these may lie dormant for years before the seed coat softens enough to permit germination. There are authentic records of seeds of the lotus (nelumbo) germinating 200 years after they were buried, but only after the hard seed coat was broken artificially. Such seeds do not germinate until fungi or bacteria have partially digested the seed coat, allowing moisture to enter.

LIGHT VERSUS DARKNESS. The role of light in seed germination is fascinating. Some seeds will not sprout if they are in darkness. Freshly harvested bluegrass seed, if raked in too deeply, will not sprout until washed out of the soil and exposed to light. To complicate the problem further, bluegrass seed also contains a natural inhibitor, ferulic acid, which also prevents the seed from sprouting even though all other conditions are favorable. The acid must be washed out, either by soaking, by natural rainfall, or by sprinkling, before the seed can begin growth.

COOLING TREATMENT. Many gardeners complain that they were sold old seed that failed to grow. This is practically never true when the seed comes from a reliable firm. Actually, the reverse may be true: it may be too fresh. Seeds of many annuals are not ready for germination when freshly harvested. Before they will grow, they must be cooled to 42° or below, then raised to about 68°. If, however, this same seed is stored over winter — even if not cooled — germination is much better. When specialists raise a crop in South America in order to gain a year in increasing some valuable new variety, it is often necessary to store the seed at cool temperatures before packeting it for sale. Some seeds that display this peculiarity are snapdragon, candytuft, carnation, dianthus, larkspur, lupine, *Phlox drummondi* (perennial phlox requires even longer chilling), stock, and sweet peas.

If you save your own seeds of these, be sure to give them cold treatment before sowing. The easiest way to do this is to mix the seed with damp sand and peat and hold it in the refresher pan of a refrigerator for three weeks before sowing.

BEST TEMPERATURES FOR ANNUAL FLOWER SEEDS

SPECIES	TEMP.	DAYS TO GERMINATION	REMARKS
Abutilon	68	8 to 25	
Ageratum	68-86	6 to 10	
Alyssum	68	6 to 15	Pre-chill fresh seed
Amaranthus	68-86	6 to 10	
Anchusa	68-86	9 to 24	
Antirrhinum	54	12 to 25	Pre-chill fresh seed
Aster (annual)	68-86	6 to 12	Try fresh seed at straight 86
Balsam, Bush	68	10 to 21	
Bells of Ireland	68-86	12 to 25	
Begonia	68	16 to 30	Seed needs light
Browallia	68	10 to 28	
Cardinal Climber	68-86	6 to 20	
Calendula	68-86	6 to 16	Likes cooler conditions when growing
Candytuft	68	6 to 14	Fresh seed needs either light or pre-chilling
Carnation	68	6 to 10	Pre-chill fresh seed
Celosia	68-86	6 to 14	Try 68 steady if no results

SPECIES	TEMP.	DAYS TO GERMINATION	REMARKS
Centaurea	68	6 to 15	Try 68-86 if no results
Chrysanthemum (annual)	68	6 to 15	Considerable seed in every sample without embryos
Cineraria	68	10 to 15	
Clarkia	54-91	5 to 12	Some stocks need light
Cleome lutea	54	15 to 35	
Cleome pungens	54-91	8 to 28	Fresh seed needs pre-chilling
Cobaea	68	10 to 20	Seed must be planted edge-wise
Convolvulus (see Ipomoea)	68-86	6 to 15	
Cosmos bipinnatus	68-86	6 to 15	
Cosmos sulphureus	86	6 to 15	
Cuphea	68-86	9 to 16	
Cynoglossum	68	7 to 25	
Dahlia	68-86	9 to 16	
Dianthus	68	6 to 16	
Didiscus	68	5 to 12	
Globe Amaranth	68-86	6 to 12	Lower temperature slower but stronger
Godetia	68	6 to 16	Pre-chill new seed
Gypsophila	68	8 to 24	
Heliotrope	68-86	14 to 20	
Hunnemannia	86	9 to 21	
Impatiens	68	5 to 20	
Ipomoea	68-86	6 to 15	'Heavenly Blue' may need warmer temperature
Kochia	68-86	5 to 8	
Larkspur	54	12 to 30	
Lobelia	68-86	7 to 20	
Marvel of Peru	68-86	6 to 12	
Marigold	68-86	7 to 15	
Nemophila	54	6 to 14	
Nierembergia	68-86	7 to 22	
Nasturtium	68	12 to 20	Fresh seed hard to germinate
Nicotiana	68-86	7 to 20	
Pansy	54-91	9 to 25	

SPECIES	TEMP.	DAYS TO GERMINATION	REMARKS
Petunia	68	5 to 14	
Perilla	68	7 to 22	
Phacelia	54	7 to 20	
Phlox drummondi	68	7 to 18	
Portulaca	68-86	4 to 14	
Pyrethrum	68-86	7 to 12	
Ricinus	68-86	8 to 22	Try steady 86 if no results
Salpiglossis	68-86	6 to 16	
Salvia	68-86	6 to 16	Try steady 86 if no results
Scabiosa	68-86	6 to 18	Try steady 86 if no results
Schizanthus	54	9 to 22	
Statice	68	7 to 22	Considerable non-viable seed in every sample
Stock	54-91	6 to 15	Needs light to germinate
Sweet Peas	68	7 to 12	Slower, stronger germination at 54
Torenia	68-86	6 to 16	
Verbena	68-86	7 to 22	Damps off easily; seed must be treated
Vinca rosea	68	8 to 22	
Viola	54-91	9 to 22	Some varieties must have light
Zinnia	68-86	5 to 12	

BEST TEMPERATURES FOR PERENNIAL FLOWER SEEDS

SPECIES	TEMP.	DAYS TO GERMINATION	REMARKS
Achillea	54-91	6 to 16	Needs light for germination
Adonis	54	10 to 60	
Alyssum saxatile	68	6 to 12	If no results try 68-86
Anchusa	68-86	8 to 28	
Anemone	68	Up to 80	Erratic germination
Anthemis	68	6 to 16	
Aquilegia	68-86	7 to 50	Hard seed is slow
Armeria	68	9 to 30	
Asclepias	68-86	7 to 22	Fresh seed may need chilling
Asparagus	68-86	10 to 40	
Asperula	54	12 to 22	
Aster alpinus	68	8 to15	Some chaffy seeds

SPECIES	TEMP.	DAYS TO GERMINATION	REMARKS
Bellis	68	5 to 14	
Briza	68-86	9 to 35	Needs light to germinate
Centranthus	54-91	6 to 16	Needs light to germinate
Cerastium	68	7 to 22	
Chrysanthemum	68	7 to 22	
Coreopsis	68	7 to 20	
Delphinium	54	10 to 30	
Dianthus	68	5 to 12	
Digitalis	68-86	6 to 15	
Doronicum	68	6 to 18	Some chaffy seed
Echinops	68-86	9 to 30	
Gaillardia	68	7 to 22	
Gentiana	68	10 to 30	Freeze first to 20 above, keep for 10 days, raise to 30, hold for a day and bring up to 68
Gerbera	68	9 to 16	
Geum	68-86	10 to 30	
Gloxinia	68	12 to 30	Needs light to germinate
Gypsophila	68	8 to 16	
Helianthus	68-86	5 to 16	
Heuchera	68-86	Up to 50	Must use seed treatment
Hollyhock	68	6 to 16	
Kniphofia	68-86	12 to 30	
Lathyrus latifolius	68	9 to 35	
Lavandula	54-91	12 to 50	
Lavatera	68	6 to 17	
Liatris	68-86	9 to 28	
Linum	54	12 to 35	
Lunaria	68	9 to 21	
Lupinus	68	6 to 20	
Lychnis	68	6 to 20	
Malcomia	68	5 to 16	
Malva	68	7 to 25	
Matricaria	68-86	6 to 16	
Myosotis	68	7 to 23	
Nepeta	68	9 to 35	

SPECIES	TEMP.	DAYS TO GERMINATION	REMARKS
Papaver	54	9 to 21	
Penstemon	68-86	7 to 20	
Phlox (perennial)	—	—	Needs freezing over winter
Primula	68	Up to 3 yrs.	Don't disturb old seed beds
Primula obconica	54-91	9 to 30	Needs light
Pyrethrum	68-86	8 to 20	Some seeds without embryo
Ranunculus	68	9 to 30	Some seeds without embryo
Rudbeckia	68-86	6 to 16	
Salvia	68-86	6 to 21	
Senecio	68	6 to 16	
Silene	68	6 to 20	
Statice	68	7 to 22	Some seed without embryo
Thalictrum	68	9 to 30	Some hard seed may take longer
Thyme	54-91	9 to 22	Must have light
Valeriana	54-91	8 to 20	Must have light
Viola	54-91	8 to 22	Some species must have light

In most cases, these are not fixed, arbitrary temperatures: they can often be varied 10° either way and some germination will occur. However, the closer readings can be held to these figures, the better the germination should be.

Vegetable Seed Germination

Although the same processes are involved in the germination of vegetable and flower seeds, far less difficulty is experienced with vegetables. Except for certain warmer sections of the country such as Florida, the Gulf Coast, and southern California, where certain cool-weather crops may be difficult to germinate in summer, practically all crops start growth readily if we pay attention to the differing demands of warm- and cool-weather species.

Even among these, there is considerable latitude. For example, the snap bean 'Streamliner' can be planted in quite cool soil without rotting and, unless it sprouts just before the last killing frost occurs, will make a crop.

Cool-season vegetables which can be planted as soon as the soil can be worked in spring are: asparagus, broad 'Windsor' beans, broccoli, Brussels sprouts, cabbage, carrot, cauliflower, Swiss chard, garden cress, kale, kohlrabi, leek, lettuce, onion, parsley, parsnip, smooth peas, pumpkin, radish, salsify, spinach, squash, and turnip. Tomatoes and New Zealand spinach can be seeded with these, though considered warm-season crops. Squash and pumpkin are similar, but somewhat hardier.

Warm-season crops should not be planted outdoors until apple blossoms, lilacs, and the earliest peonies are in bloom. These include snap beans, pole beans, lima beans, soy beans, sweet corn, cucumber, muskmelon, watermelon, and okra.

Long-season crops normally started indoors and set out as plants include eggplant, pepper, and tomato, although tomatoes are often direct-seeded with cool-season crops.

Vegetables involving special culture are: Chinese cabbage (do not seed until July 1), celery, and celeriac. All of these tend to shoot to seed if planted too early. If early celery is wanted, start it indoors at temperatures above 60°.

NEW PLANTS FROM CUTTINGS

The art of growing new plants from cuttings probably began with the willow, which produces new roots readily if a few inches of mature wood come in contact with damp soil. Primitive man might have observed this process and tested it with other species.

Initiation of roots from portions of aboveground parts has always seemed a mystery, yet is quite simple physiologically. Within the bark of most woody plants and under the epidermis of most herbs lie root primordia — bud-like structures that will spring into activity upon steady contact with moisture. Anyone who has grown English ivy on a stone wall or has seen *Ajuga reptans* crawling over a cement sidewalk has observed this process: even *without* contact with soil, the root initials begin to grow.

In theory, all plants which have a definite cambium layer — the dicots, as opposed to the monocots (grasses, orchids, lilies, and their relatives) — can be propagated by cuttings, but some are very difficult to increase by this method. Gardeners will do well to experiment with plants that they want to increase rapidly. For example, suckers on tomatoes root readily. Because young, vigorous-growing plants resist late blight better than older plants already in fruit, these suckers are worth rooting in early August and setting out to produce a fall crop after the main crop is all but dead.

Even annuals, such as marigolds and morning-glories, can be rooted for winter flowering indoors. Formerly, double petunias were carried over as stock plants and cuttings rooted each spring for the new crop. Because of the development of all-double varieties from seed, this is no longer necessary, but the owner of a small greenhouse will find it worthwhile to save particularly fine specimens for use as stock plants for producing cuttings.

Many tender perennials are propagated as bedding plants from cuttings.

A good example is lemon verbena. The seed is so poor that one plant from a hundred seeds is a common experience. As a result, practically all lemon-verbena plants have come from cuttings.

Propagation from cuttings has one important advantage over seedage: the plants produced are (except for rare sports) actually an extension of the original specimen, identical in genetic make-up, or inheritance.

When grown from seed, on the other hand, subtle variations creep in with each passage of the germ plasm from generation to generation. Two parents are involved and contribute equally to the seed so that differences are bound to materialize.

Softwood Cuttings

When a plant part is severed and rooted separately, three types of cuttings are involved. The first is the softwood cutting, a new section from a stem where lignification (wood formation) has not taken place. Common examples are cuttings of geraniums and fuchsias, made from growth forced on stock plants in early spring by feeding and watering and applying additional warmth to stimulate "breaks" or new shoots. When these shoots have formed several leaves, they are cut from the parent plant and inserted in a rooting medium.

The cut-off shoot of a geranium will serve to illustrate what happens inside a cutting. Old plants are lifted in late fall before freezing weather begins and kept as close to dormant as is possible with this flower. Only enough water is given to keep the plant tissues plump. Temperatures between 45° and 50° are best because growth is practically at a standstill. No fertilizer should be given at this time. Light is naturally low because of the reduced intensity of winter sunshine.

About mid-February, the old plant is stirred into life by increasing heat, light, and water. As soon as it begins to show signs of breaking into new growth, fertilizer is applied. In two or three weeks, strong new shoots are produced which form true softwood cuttings. When these have four or five new leaves, they are cut off from the main plant, leaving a bud or two at the base for the formation of more shoots.

Tradition holds that the cut should be made at a node — the spot where the leafstalk emerges, but this destroys the bud at that point and wastes material. Softwood cuttings will root at the lower end, whether cut at a node or not. The cut is usually made on a slant because this exposes more of the cambium for rooting.

After removal from the plant, cuttings are inserted or "planted" in a material that is light, airy, and quick-draining, yet able to retain moisture. They can be placed quite close together, even touching, as there is little leaf action at this stage.

NEW PLANTS FROM CUTTINGS: *Mature Geranium (1) yielded several good shoots. Cuttings, 2" to 4" long, were trimmed of all but top leaves, dipped in rooting hormone powder, and planted in imported peatmoss. Some "slips," like Impatiens (2), will produce strong roots in water.*

ROOTING MATERIALS. Sand is the traditional rooting medium but it drains so rapidly that cuttings must be watered two or three times a day to keep them from drying out. In modern practice, sand has been replaced by several other materials, or is mixed with an equal volume of imported peatmoss to improve its water-holding capacity. Imported peatmoss is used because it is definitely acid in reaction, and roots form more rapidly in an acid medium. Also, it is less likely than domestic peats to be contaminated with weed seeds and other foreign matter. Clean domestic peats are available, but should be checked for pH (they should be below 5.0 at least), and for contamination before using. Whichever you use, wet it thoroughly before mixing it with sand.

Sometimes vermiculite, an expanded mica product, is used with sand. Vermiculite can also be used alone but, because of its tremendous capacity for holding water, it can become saturated and slippery to handle. Saturation can be prevented by making the bottom of the propagating bench of screen wire, which allows free water to escape. Handled in this way, vermiculite is about the perfect rooting medium, requiring water only two or three times during the rooting period. When used in a closed propagating case, it may need watering only once — when the cuttings are inserted.

Perlite, a similar material but white in color, is used in the same way. It is alkaline in reaction, but does not contain enough free chemicals to make much difference. It does, however, produce better cuttings if watered once with an ammonium sulfate solution before inserting the cuttings.

Peatmoss is often used alone, particularly for rooting acid-loving plants, but has no real advantage over a sand-peat mixture and has some disadvantages. For this type of material, it is important to check both the sand and peat for pH, because some sands are alkaline.

PROPAGATING CASE. A closed case for the rooting medium, to prevent rapid evaporation, makes it possible to root cuttings with much less attention than is needed in an open flat. This is particularly useful when rooting both conifers and broad-leaved evergreens, both of which are slow and delicate to handle. The covering can be of glass, clear plastic, or fiber glass. Outdoors, a coldframe will serve in summer, but must be shaded to prevent heat building up under the glass. Where only one or two cuttings are to be made, Grandmother's trick of inverting a fruit jar over a rose "slip" can be used to advantage. But don't set it in a sunny window!

Cuttings root faster if their medium is slightly warmer than the air above. An electric hotbed cable under the sand (controlled by a thermostat) is a handy device for supplying this "bottom heat," as it is called.

HORMONE DIPS. Hormone — a powder into which the lower end of the stem is dipped — will give the cutting an extra supply of certain growth-stimulating chemicals which occur naturally in plants. Such a hormone will assure quicker, more complete rooting on easy-to-root species and may even result in formation of roots on species which cannot otherwise be propagated by cuttings. Most seed houses and garden centers can supply these hormones in ready-to-use powder form. A special technique is used by geranium specialists when applying rooting hormones. Dipped when the cutting is newly made, the wet end picks up too much of the material and often rots. To avoid this hazard, they make cuttings in the evening and allow them to lie all night on the open bench. By morning, the lower end is quite dry and can be dipped into the hormone powder and stuck in the usual way.

Plants to Propagate

While the following list is not complete, it will suggest the wide range of plants that can be increased from softwood cuttings. These are, it will be noted, mostly herbaceous plants.

Abutilon	Forsythia	Petunia
Alternanthera	Fuchsia	Rochea
Arabis	Helianthemum	Salvia
Aubrieta	Heliotrope	Scabiosa
Boronia	Hibiscus	Sedum
Cactus	Hypericum	Sophora
Calceolaria	Kerria	Tagetes (marigold)
Chrysanthemum	Lantana	Tecoma
Coleus	Leptospermum	Verbena
Cytisus	Linum	Veronica
Dahlia	Mesembryanthemum	Viburnum
Dianthus	Pelagonium	Viola
Erica	(geranium)	Vinca
Felicia	Penstemon	Zinnia

Half-hard or Hardened Greenwood Cuttings

While many woody plants can be propagated from softwood cuttings, hardened greenwood cuttings will make more rapid growth. These half-hard cuttings are made from shoots of the current year's growth, after this has begun to firm up, but before it is really woody. The way to check the condition is to bend over a shoot. If it crushes rather than snaps, it is probably too green. It should snap clean and not bend. If it bends over and hangs together, it is probably too old.

Roses are particularly easy to propagate by half-hard cuttings. A shoot that has just bloomed is usually in peak condition for rooting. The old flower is cut off and a cutting made with four or five good leaves on it. Use of a rooting hormone is recommended because roses sometimes root poorly.

All half-hard cuttings must be rooted in shade; they stand sunlight poorly. As soon as roots have formed, however, they should be potted up individually (the new bagasse fiber pots are ideal because of their excellent drainage) and grown on until well established.

Genera which do well from half-hard cuttings include the following:

Abelia	Euonymus	Myrtus
Azalea	Forsythia	Nerium
Boronia	Grevillea	Pelargonium
Bougainvillea	Hibiscus	Pernettia
Buxus	Hedera	Rosa
Camellia	Hoya	Solandra
Cassia	Hydrangea	Solanum
Cistus	Ilex	Spiraea
Clerondendron	Ipomoea	Stephanotis
Cytisus	Jacaranda	Syringa
Daphne	Jasminum	Tibouchina
Deutzia	Lavandula	Trachelospermum
Diervilla	Lavatera	Vinca
Escallonia	Leonotis	
Eugenia	Mahonia	

Hardwood Cuttings

Most hardy woody plants are best propagated from hardwood cuttings — sections of mature stems that have been defoliated by frost. Advantage is taken of the fact that woody plants store food for next year's growth which can be used to help produce roots. However, the plant must be tricked into moving this food to the rooting end. To do this, change the polarity of the twig by putting the end that was closest to the ground when on the plant uppermost in storage.

Twigs of the last season's growth are used, cut into lengths of 6 to 10 inches. If material is scarce, tamarix, maple, willow, and olive cuttings can also be made from two-year-old wood, but younger growth is better.

In warmer climates, such as found in California and on the Gulf Coast, storing to produce a callus is not necessary and may even be harmful. Here, the cutting is made from mid-November until late February and inserted into the rooting medium immediately after the lower end has been treated with a hormone for woody plants such as Rootone #10. (This is stronger than any hormone used on softwood cuttings.)

In cooler climates, the cuttings are tied in bundles (with all the lower ends headed in one direction) and the entire bundle is buried in damp sand, sand and peat, or even sawdust. Temperature around the bundle should be below 40° and may even drop to freezing.

In spring, just before woody plants leaf out, dig up the bundles and open them. Because of reversing the twigs, the lower end (which has been uppermost) will probably show heavy callusing — a fleshy white curd on the cambium. When planted callused end down in a light, rich soil in the open, such a cutting will usually form a mass of roots.

Evergreen Cuttings

Without a greenhouse or heated frame, evergreen cuttings are difficult to root. Those of conifers need to be taken in late fall — October or November — after a spell of light frosts or even light freezes. When possible, they are taken with a "heel," a sliver of the old branch attached to the base of the one-year-old wood from which the cuttings are made.

Before inserting in sand, strip the end of the cutting that will be buried in the rooting medium, and dip it in a hormone powder used for woody plants.

Spruces and hemlocks are often difficult to root because they exude a resinous gum so fast that rooting hormones are pushed off before they can go to work. To check this, dip the lower end of the cutting in hot water (between 130° and 150°; use a thermometer). Withdraw it quickly and treat it with a hormone powder.

Broad-leaved evergreens are even more difficult than conifers. While hormone powders help, they have not completely simplified propagation. Timing is very important. Cuttings should be taken as soon as branches have stopped making terminal growth and are beginning to swell in diameter. This is usually from the middle to the last of August. They can then be handled the same as softwood cuttings, but placed farther apart in the propagating case and kept severely away from sunshine.

Root Cuttings

Many woody plants produce what are called adventitious buds on their roots. These are bud beginnings which, if the plant is separated from its roots, will develop and produce new shoots. This habit can be quite annoying. If roots of a cherry tree, for example, come close to the surface under a lawn and are injured, adventitious shoots will spring up everywhere.

Most fruit trees will produce such shoots, but since the root is usually an understock and not a desirable variety, root cuttings are seldom used. At the same time, a home-owner who wants a crabapple hedge, might want to dig up an old specimen and, by cutting the roots into pieces 3 to 4 inches long and planting these along the hedge line, develop a hedge at practically no cost.

Bramble fruits (raspberries, blackberries, and dewberries) are easy to increase by root cuttings. Other plants easy to propagate in this manner are bouvardia, trumpet creeper, most citrus fruits, Oriental poppies, plumbago, lilacs (if on own roots) and persimmon.

In cooler climates root cuttings are usually made in fall, stored like hardwood cuttings, and planted out in spring. In the South, if bottom heat in a hotbed is used during winter months, a good-sized plant will be produced in a year.

From Scales

A special class of propagation is that of breaking up a mature lily bulb into separate scales, each of which will produce a small bulb or bulblet at the base if properly handled. Most healthy big bulbs can have a few scales removed from the outside without hurting the bloom.

The best time to do the scaling is probably soon after the plants have flowered. The bigger the scale, the more numerous will be the bulblets it will produce. These form best at quite high temperatures — between 90° and 100°. If any number of scales are to be grown, the construction of a "sweat box" is recommended. This is a closed propagating frame equipped with an electric hotbed cable. It should contain a mixture half sand and half peat, or of sand and vermiculite.

Since scales develop best when they are exposed to air, they should be laid on the surface of the rooting medium rather than buried in it. This is true whether they are handled in a sweat box, coldframe, or in the open garden. To prevent them from drying out, cover them with a half-inch layer of sphagnum moss. Since the scales do not need light to produce bulblets, the operation can take place in a dark warm cellar.

Scales tend to rot during propagation; to prevent this, treat with Arasan, Spergon, or Fermate. Dusting the scales with a hormone powder increases the percentage of "takes." Arasan is compatible with this material. At no time should scales be allowed to dry out. Keep them well watered, but not soaked.

If the scaling operation is carried on indoors, the scales can be kept growing if greenhouse space is available; or they can be stored at below 40° if it is not. In spring, plant them out in the garden at a depth of 2 inches. After the summer growth has been killed by frost the following fall, add 2 inches more of soil. Usually, a bulb produced from scales is big enough to set in permanent position the following spring.

Stem Cutting of Lilies

Lilium regale, L. umbellatum and several others can be propagated by pulling out the old stem as soon as it is through flowering and laying it in a shallow trench. Covered with a light sandy soil, the old stem will usually produce a bulbil at each axil.

LAYERING FORSYTHIA: *Tip of branch is bent down, buried in soil, and secured. Rootlets form, like those marked by arrow (2). New plant which grows from tip is fed by pipeline stem to parent (3).*

LAYERING AND AIR LAYERING

These are methods of making cuttings and rooting them while they are still attached to the parent plant. In regular layering, a branch is bent to the ground and its tip pinned down with a loop of wire or held by a clod of soil. In a few weeks (on most shrubs) the buried tip develops new roots and can be severed from the parent plant to be moved elsewhere. In a sense, strawberries are produced by layering; the runners produced by old plants are usually self-rooting, but are easier to handle if one of the bagasse fiber pots is filled with a light rich soil and plunged into the ground under a likely runner. When well-rooted, the new plant can be moved.

Air layering is an ancient art practiced by the Chinese for centuries. Today, it is commonly used to reduce the height of rubber plants that have stretched too high. A cut is made through the bark and slightly into the wood with an upward stroke of the knife. A toothpick is inserted to hold open the cut and the slit is dusted with a hormone powder. The Chinese did *not* have hormones but they did soak the moss used in the operation with urine, which contains a natural hormone.

A wad of sphagnum moss is then tied around the cut area and kept damp until roots form. The traditional method of protecting this from too-rapid drying-out was to split a flower pot and tie the halves around the moss. Plastic films are a better material, however. The film is wrapped over the moss and tied at both ends. Select a kind that is thin (not over two mils) so that air can move through it freely. Usually, the moss does not need to be wetted again until roots have formed.

When roots are seen filling the moss, the stem is cut off just below the air-layering section and potted as a new plant. The stub will then develop new side branches and leaves.

The same method can be used to root branches of trees. Although flowering crabs and magnolias may take as long as a year to develop a good root ball, they can often be propagated by this method. Apples, also cherries, pears, and plums will root better from air layering if a strip of bark is bleached out before the moss ball is applied. A strip of clean white writing paper about 1½ inches wide is wrapped around the stem and held in place with black plastic electrical tape. The tape should not touch the bark, but should cover as much of the paper as possible. After about 6 weeks, the paper can be removed and the bark will be found to have turned quite pale in color. When a moss ball is placed over this etiolated area, roots will form much more readily than on unbleached bark.

GRAFTING AND BUDDING

Grafting is the art of uniting a top or scion of one kind on a root or understock of another. Budding is a variation of grafting where the top that is used starts as a dormant bud. Inarching is a combination of layering and grafting, where both plants remain on their own roots until the union has been completed.

Budding

To see a professional rose budder at work, you would think this was one of the easiest of all propagating operations. Carrying a bud stick, he makes a T with two simple slits in the bark of a rose understock plant, deftly chips off a single leaf and its attached dormant bud from his bud

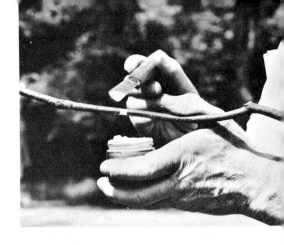

AIR LAYERING: *The materials necessary for practicing this ancient method of starting new trees include sphagnum moss, a sharp knife, rooting hormone, plastic film, and ties. First, make a cut through the bark or remove a small ring of it. Dust with hormone powder.*

Surround cut with moss which has been soaked and squeezed nearly dry.

Around the moss, wrap a piece of thin plastic film (not over 2 mils).

Bind plastic tightly at both ends with tape or stout plant ties.

When roots permeate sphagnum, cut branch free. Plant unwrapped root ball.

stick and slips the base of this leaf into the slits he has just made. A twist of a rubber tie, and the job is done.

As simple as it seems in the hands of an expert, budding is a highly delicate operation which must be timed closely. It must be done when cells in the cambium layer are actively dividing (but usually when the bud is dormant in the case of roses), so that it will not make growth that year. In the North, this usually means July. Fruit trees are often budded in May and June in the South; in this case the bud does grow the first year but produces a salable tree a year sooner than those budded later in the North.

When the understock is in right condition for budding, the bark will peel back easily, exposing the cambium or growth layer, when the T cut is made. The bud cut from the stick of budwood should have little or no wood attached; if a bit of wood is picked up accidentally in cutting, expert budders are able to peel it out. This means that the inserted bud has its cambium on the *bottom*, which is in full contact with the green cambium of the understock.

Bud sticks are cut from a desired variety, using new wood of the current season's growth. Usually, the tip buds and those near the base are discarded, since those from the middle of the branch are more likely to catch. Buds are always inserted on the north side of the understock, to keep them at least partially shaded.

Raffia is the traditional wrapping material but in commercial use is practically obsolete. Budding strips of rubber are now used; they lose their tension gradually and do not have to be cut away after the bud has "taken." However, for small operations when only a few buds are inserted, raffia can still be used, but should be cut away as soon as it is apparent that the bud is firmly anchored. If the bud shrivels and turns brown, make a cut on the opposite side of the stem, insert a new bud and tie.

The following spring, inserted buds will begin growing. As soon as they have produced strong shoots, cut off the top of the understock above the bud union. From then on, the top growth of the plant should all originate from this bud or the wood above it.

A great many variations on the simple T cut have been worked out, but these are not for the amateur.

Grafting

A grafted plant consists of two parts — the stock or rootstock and the scion or piece of stem, inserted in such a way that the cambium layers of both members are in direct contact. Under favorable growing conditions, stock and scion unite to form a unique plant — one which has characteristics not possible to find in either alone.

Occasionally, three parts are used — a rootstock, an intermediate stem, and the scion. This is often a means of propagating apples on rootstocks which are well suited for a particular situation but which do not form strong grafts with certain varieties. By inserting a third variety between stock and scion, one which is compatible with both, grafts can be made successfully.

There are a number of reasons for grafting. Perhaps the most important is to propagate fruits which do not come true from seed and which root with such difficulty from cuttings that commercial propagation is unprofitable by that method. All commercial varieties of apples must either be budded or grafted.

The propagation of specially colored foliage variations or unusually fine flowering specimens of certain ornamental trees and shrubs can only be done by grafting. Another use for grafting is to form living braces for trees that have narrow crotches likely to split unless braced. If rabbits or mice girdle the trunks of valuable trees during snowy months, these can sometimes be saved by prompt bridge grafting to carry food and water across the denuded area.

In some instances, grafting changes the characteristic flavor of fruits, not always for the better. In other instances, improvement may be marked.

The choice between budding and regular grafting is one of personal preference. Usually, budding is a little easier for the tyro; lining up different cambiums in a graft is not a simple matter.

Perhaps the only grafting operation that will be used to any extent by the amateur is the cleft graft, a method by which an apple tree of a poor variety can be changed to one which bears desirable fruit of one or more varieties. This is sometimes called top-grafting. In this operation, the old branches are cut to stubs and split with a special tool. Scions of the desired varieties are inserted in the splits. For making an occasional cleft graft, the special tool is not necessary; a stout chisel sharpened to a keen edge will do. After the graft has been made, it must be covered with grafting wax to keep it from drying out while the scion and stock are knitting. Grafting wax is usually available at seed stores or from mail-order houses.

DIVISION AND SEPARATION

Perhaps the simplest of all propagating operations is the division of old specimens into smaller plants. This is a continuing operation in the perennial garden. Except for a few species that resent being disturbed, such as peonies and the gas plant (*Dictamnus albus*), most perennials must be dug up, divided, and reset at fairly short intervals. Hardy chrysanthemums, in fact, should be lifted each spring, separated into single stem divisions and reset. If this is not done, the old clumps deteriorate. Hardy phlox clumps also do better if reset every two years. This also prevents the intrusion of volunteer seedlings that may sound off-color notes if allowed to grow uncontrolled.

Even peonies need lifting and dividing if they are not doing well. They are often planted too deep and fail to bloom as a result. In this case, dig the clump in early September, divide the fleshy root into sections (each with 3 to 5 pink buds). Reset the pieces with the uppermost bud about 1 inch below the surface of the soil.

Except in warmer parts of the country, the newer 'Pacific' hybrid delphiniums hardly justify dividing old clumps. They are not reliable perennials and are better replaced yearly with younger plants from seed. However, the older English varieties, as well as various species, can be taken up in early fall, split into sections of single stems and replanted. There must be a good cluster of eyes or buds at the base of each section.

Dahlia clumps should not be replanted as dug, but after winter storage in a cool place should be divided into single tubers, each of which must have a piece of the original stem and a live bud or eye attached. To simplify division, place the clumps on damp sand or peat in a warm light spot for a week or so to start the eyes in active growth.

Shrubs that form many stems can often be split into smaller specimens by inserting a spade into the center of the clump and driving it down through the roots. If, however, new young stock from cuttings can be used instead of such divisions, it will usually be found more satisfactory.

22

Pruning: Discipline for Plants

Opinions on the value and necessity for pruning differ widely. There are many who believe this operation is essential to shrub and tree survival. Impelled by this belief, they whack away without purpose and without understanding, just to prune.

Others argue: "Trees in the forest are never pruned, yet they survive." Of the two schools, the second is the more sensible, yet there is a middle ground in which knowing gardeners can exercise their judgment to give more pleasing form or greater usefulness to woody plants, rather than letting them grow according to their natural habit. For example, seedlings of beech or Chinese elm, whose heredity has destined them as tall forest trees, may serve our purposes better if planted so closely they can never reach that maturity and if clipped closely to form a hedge.

REASONS FOR PRUNING

Elimination of Dead Wood

Pruning serves many purposes, among them the removal of weak and dead wood, balancing of root and top growth, training of a hedge, improvement of form for flowering or fruiting or other decorative features, stimulation of flowering and fruiting, removal of competition among trees and shrubs in a landscape planting, creation of interesting patterns, and pleaching and plashing.

WHERE AND HOW TO MAKE PRUNING CUTS: *Make cut at slight angle, about ¼"
above bud (1, left). Do not make cut below bud (1, right, top) or stub will die
back, as shown in (2). Do not cut at too sharp angle (1, right, bottom) or it will
fail to heal properly (3).*

*Smooth side-of-stem cuts (4, left), trimmed with knife if necessary, will heal
well (5). Ragged cut (4, right) will not heal and may start decay. To head back
a plant and encourage bushiness, prune to just above branch (6, left, top); but
to eliminate low branches and encourage a high crown, remove branch flush
with stem (6, left, bottom). Do not prune branch between buds (6, right, top),
or prune stem or trunk between branches (6, right, bottom).*

Never before has removal of weak and dead wood been so important (particularly on elms) as it is today. Sanitation — the removal of every scrap of weak or dead wood that might harbor bark beetles — is as vital to Dutch elm disease control as is spraying with chemicals to kill these beetles. A combination of spraying and sanitation has held tree losses in many badly infested areas to as low as 1 per cent a year.

Dead wood itself is a symptom of decline rather than of disease. Dying of branches can usually be traced to one of the following causes:

Unfavorable soil nutrient conditions
Compaction of soil above roots
Unfavorable weather conditions
Falling water table or inadequate rainfall
Rising water table or excessive rainfall
Insect or disease attacks
Excessive crown density (shading out)
Inadequate crown density (sunscald)
Sooty or fume-laden air
Mechanical injury to trunk or limbs
Senility

Obviously, merely removing dead wood cannot correct the conditions responsible. If a change of drainage has lowered the water table, some means of supplying more moisture must be devised. Sometimes the remedy is impossible, as when polluted air is responsible. Some good can be done by removing the dead wood and washing off foliage, but more often a sensitive species must be replaced by one more resistant.

Removal of dead wood is particularly important with street trees because of the possible hazards from falling limbs. It also improves the health and appearance of the trees.

Senility can sometimes be delayed by proper reduction of the amount of top that an aging root system is called on to support. This should be considered in the case of older elm plantings. What is not appreciated is that elms are normally lowland trees, which may send out roots to cover an acre or more. When their roots are penned between a sidewalk and a curb, with all surface moisture drained away before it can penetrate, is it any wonder that elms reach senility before their time?

Transplanting Procedure

Pruning to balance root and top growth is equally important when trees are transplanted. Present practice, however, calls for removing much less wood than formerly, because of latex sprays now used to prevent water loss. The more top that is removed, the longer a tree or shrub will need to produce enough foliage to resume growth. Such practices as wrapping the trunk, hilling up lower branches with earth and shading with burlap are useful in allowing more wood to be retained.

Hedge Discipline

Pruning forced trees and shrubs can be to conform to a pattern or purpose we have in mind. Shearing, pruning, pleaching, or cutting back to form a hedge is perhaps the best example of this. Such shearing can be strictly formal, with plants used almost as plastic material to be molded into a desired form. This type of pruning becomes more common as architects learn to echo structural forms with trained plants.

Hedge training can also be informal, with just enough pruning to keep plants from growing out of hand but allowing them to retain something of their natural habit. This style is suited to many home gardens, where more formal hedges would look inappropriate and would call for too much time and effort. However, many severely modern houses demand closely disciplined plants trained in formal patterns.

For Finer Decorative Effects

Such discipline is not confined to hedges. Shrubs that are grown for their flowers or ornamental fruits, young growth or bark, can generally show off their features to better advantage if they are skillfully pruned. It is important to understand the growth habit in order to know when to prune for decorative effects.

Early Spring Bloomers

Some shrubs and trees, of which forsythia is an excellent example, flower so early in spring that it is obvious they bloom only on old wood, on which the buds were set the summer before. Removing of wood in late summer, fall, or early spring, therefore, means no blossoms. These plants should be pruned only after flowers have faded. The list of shrubs to be treated thus is quite long. Typical examples are amelanchier, caragana, chaenomeles, choisya, corylopsis, enkianthus, escallonia, exochorda, forsythia, philadelphus, physocarpus, ribes, shepherdia, *Spiraea vanhouttei*, syringa (lilac), and weigela.

Late Spring and Summer Bloomers

Some shrubs flower on new wood of the current season's growth. These can be pruned in late fall, if this is convenient, or during winter months, or very early in spring before growth begins. Typical species include shrub althea, buddleia, caryopteris, elsholtzia, hydrangea, and vitex.

Lilacs: Flower buds are fat, round-ish ones at tips (1). Slender tip buds (2) produce new growth and leaves. Prune stems with growth buds, not those with flower buds. Remove flowers when faded, but do not touch new shoots below flowers (3), for they will bear next year's blooms.

Forsythias bloom on second-year growths (1, right). First-year growth (1, left) produces only leaves. Prune after flowering, removing growths that have bloomed (2) and leaving unflowered first-year stems. Maintain natural form (3) by pruning a few of oldest stems close to ground each year.

Berried Shrubs

Whether these flower in early spring or on new wood does not change the fact that they are grown largely for their display of berries. They are best pruned only enough to keep them shapely, doing whatever pruning is necessary the moment the berries fall or are eaten by birds. Berberis, *Cornus mas*, cotoneaster, pyracantha, and symphoricarpos are examples. If these are allowed to go too long without some occasional trimming, severe cutting-back may be needed to bring them back into shape, which will mean a loss of bloom and fruit for at least one year.

Pruning Lilacs

The peculiar flowering habits of the lilac require special mention. If long branches are removed when cutting flowers, that section of the shrub may not flower again for three years. A year is required to form the twig on which the flowers will be produced, another year to lay down the two flowering buds just under the bud from which the flower cluster appears, and a year to bring this into bloom.

When cutting off faded lilac flowers, be careful not to remove the two fat buds on either side of the point at which the flower stem arises. These are next year's flower buds.

Broad-leaved Evergreens

As a rule, the less these are pruned, the better. Any cutting should be limited to removing long, "pushy" branches that are trying to outgrow the rest of the plant. Old flower heads should be removed as soon as they fade on rhododendrons and azaleas, but berried plants such as hollies and pyracantha must be left untouched if fruits are wanted.

Shrubs with Colored Bark

A number of shrubs are grown largely for their brightly colored bark, which is most brilliant on new shoots. When used in this way, they should be cut back to the ground early in spring to force young growth. Plants so treated include the shrubby dogwood, *Cornus alba*, *C. sibirica*, *C. stolonifera*, and *C. stolonifera flaviramea*, also *Kerria japonica*.

To Stimulate Flowering and Fruiting

On certain plants, flowers and fruits can be induced by pruning. For example, rambler roses bloom only on wood of the previous year's growth. If old shoots are left, they will not flower again until the dormant buds on

Yews are the easiest of all evergreens to prune. New growth starts at base of any leaf, and even old, bare trunks will send out new shoots if cut back. To shape and restrict growth, cut back branches as shown above.

Junipers often need yearly pruning to prevent ungainly growth. Young growth (left) has innumerable growth buds and can be pruned anywhere. Old growth (right) can only be cut back to side branch, not to old, branchless wood.

them have made short, stubby twigs. Even though flowers will come on these, they will be inferior to those on strong one-year-old wood. For this reason, the old wood is cut away immediately after flowering. New shoots will form from their stubs, and in another year these will give good bloom. The removal of leading shoots on apples and pears about the time of the June drop is another example of pruning for flowers and fruits.

Pruning for a View

We prune trees and shrubs in a landscape scheme to open up vistas and to prevent them from destroying the original pattern. This type of pruning is most often done in winter, with the foliage off deciduous trees, since the skeletal formation of the plant being treated is then visible. Evergreens, however, must be pruned as described above.

When cutting away branches to open up a vista, always cut to a bud that will send the new growth at an angle that will not block the view later. Buds can actually be "aimed" by noticing the way their tips are pointed: they will almost always continue in a straight line from the tip.

Letting in Air and Light

A similar purpose is served when plants are pruned to permit free air circulation or the entry of sunlight into areas being shaded by over-rampant growth. When there is competition among trees and shrubs in a landscape planting, ample food and moisture as well as air and light must be provided for all. Not all species grow at the same rate. When several are brought together in a single planting, competition is bound to arise. Pruning helps the entire planting by holding back the more aggressive members and giving the others a chance.

Plant Sculpture

Pruning to form interesting patterns and silhouettes is a tremendous subject. It embraces the highly specialized work of forming topiary specimens, espalier shrubs and trees against walls, and the trimming out of existing specimens to produce interesting shadows or patterns against backgrounds of structures, sky, or plant growth. The gardener becomes a sculptor, creating new forms with his plants.

Pleaching and Plashing

The pleached allée — a method of training where rows of trees are permitted to grow together to form a solid wall of green, is perhaps the most sophisticated form of pruning. It calls for a precision and care even greater than that needed to form topiary specimens, since the least variation from the selected line will produce an adverse effect. It calls for so much work that professional help is almost essential to its maintenance.

A simpler form of interwoven hedge is that used by French and British countrymen to form plashed hedges. In plashing, plants with tough wood, such as the hawthorn or holly, are planted side by side. Branches which grow at an angle from the main axis of the hedge are cut partially through near their bases and bent back so they can be woven into the main body. The result is a hedge so tough it can resist almost any impact, as American tank operators discovered when they tried to crash through plashed barriers on the sides of French roads during World War II.

Plashed barriers would be ideal crash absorbers on highways if it were not for the tremendous amount of handwork necessary for their original training. Once trained, the only pruning needed would be occasional removal of stray twigs that grow out of the main body of the hedge.

SOME RULES FOR PRUNING

The following standards set up for National Park Service contracts covering tree pruning are worth considering as a guide:

1. All final cuts shall be made flush with the remaining limb or trunk.

2. All cuts shall be painted with a suitable wound dressing.

3. Final cuts on limbs too large to hold with the hand shall be preceded by preliminary cuts from one to two feet beyond the final cut. Such preliminary cuts shall include an undercut to prevent stripping of the bark.

4. Dead wood, unhealed old stubs, and minor interfering branches should be removed routinely from every tree as work progresses. However, removal of live limbs, large interfering branches and suckers should be directed by a trained and experienced tree-worker or foreman only after a careful survey of the job.

5. Cutting back, shaping, or dehorning are usually done to accomplish a special purpose. These practices require knowledge and skill and should be done only on specific instruction and under careful supervision.

6. After the safety rope is crotched, men must stay in the safety saddle or bowline with the taut-line hitch kept tied until they are again on the ground. Even when working on a ladder, a safety line must be used.

7. Pole pruners, pole saws, or hand saws which are hung in a tree temporarily must be placed in a safe position. Make sure that the branch over which a pruner hook is placed will safely hold the load. Never place pruners on a wire.

8. A cut or badly worn rope must never be used as a safety rope.

9. Every rope must be inspected as it is uncoiled.

10. Look below and give plenty of warning before dropping a limb.

11. All limbs which might do damage if dropped free must be supported by ropes.

These rules are not mentioned because it is assumed many homeowners will be likely to put them into effect; instead, they are given because they emphasize one fact: tree pruning is a specialized job and not for the inexperienced amateur. Anyone who has occasion to trim or prune a mature shade tree once every four or five years has no business on the end of a sling or safety rope 40 or 50 feet in the air. This is one place where professional help is needed and is worth what it costs.

If in doubt where to get good help, ask the city forester or city manager of a good-sized town or city near you. They usually have firms of professionals they employ, who are usually far better than you will turn up by consulting an unrated listing somewhere.

23

The Garden Doctor

In some publications on gardening, more space is given to disease and insect control than to plants and cultural practices. As a result, many new gardeners feel that more peril than pleasure lies before them. Sensational books and cultists' magazines add to their confusion. No wonder the poor beginner falters.

It is true that tens of thousands of insects attack the plants we grow for food and ornament; still, our plants manage to survive. And if we use lethal dusts or sprays to control a particularly obnoxious pest, we go on living too.

Some gardeners never spray or dust, yet seem to enjoy the fruits of their gardens year after year without any particular trouble. By selecting species and varieties not subject to attack, it is possible to garden for years with no pests more serious than a few aphids in spring, or an errant caterpillar.

This is more true today than it was a decade or two ago. Spraying for mosquito control in areas of heavy population also kills a fairly wide range of insects that attack cultivated plants. Many gardeners can now grow broccoli, cabbage, and other members of the cabbage family without spraying or dusting because chemicals that control the mosquitoes also kill the fat green larvae of the cabbage butterfly. These do not, however, touch aphids, which some growers consider worse pests than worms.

Trouble-free Species

By eliminating plants which are subject to attack by certain pests, the need for controls is considerably reduced. For example, the common nasturtium is almost impossible to grow without attracting thousands of black aphids. The English broad 'Windsor' bean and the high-bush cranberry are similar magnets for these pests. Unless you are willing to spray for aphids, you had best avoid growing these plants. If, after you have planted a species you thought was pest-free, trouble develops year after year, common sense would dictate that it be dug out and replaced with something less sensitive.

Planting trouble-free species and relying only on area-spraying for mosquitoes does not provide complete immunity from insects. The presence of aphids may be noted by a syrupy drip on cars parked beneath aphid-infested trees. This honeydew, which is given off by aphids, will attract thousands of ants. It also serves as a propagating medium for a sooty mold.

If Dutch elm disease is present in your community, you will have to decide whether to spray to control the elm bark beetle that carries it, or face the almost certain prospect of losing your elms. You will be told that spraying will drive away or kill all birds. If your community has suffered from the population explosion which has taken over all vacant property and has cleaned out every thicket and copse where birds once nested, and if you do have area-spraying for mosquito control, the question has already been settled; the birds will already have gone. Communities which do a thorough job of spraying all accessible trees have managed to hold elm losses as low as 1 to 2 per cent; but *your* elms may not be in such a locality.

Obviously, the no-spraying type of program is not for the individual who wants everything perfect. Nibbled leaves and traces of disease will be present at all times, but usually not obtrusively so.

Middle-ground Control

A second type of program, the one practiced by most gardeners, calls for reasonably good sanitation, such as burning diseased and insect-infected plants in fall, and spraying only when a sensitive crop such as roses is grown in quantity.

There are variations of this program. Most gardeners recognize that diseases such as tulip fire and botrytis blight of peonies cannot be eradicated once the organisms have entered the plant. Therefore they will apply such preventive methods as spraying the ground with phaltan as peony shoots break through the soil and tulip leaves begin to unfold. It is important that gardeners who follow such a program understand that plant diseases *cannot be cured;* they can only be *prevented.*

Certainly, clean apples cannot be produced in the northeastern quarter of the United States without a regular program of spraying for codling moth and apple maggot — the pests responsible for wormy apples. Apple scab also requires preventive treatment.

The Show Garden

Perfectionists can achieve complete control of all pests only by regular preventive spraying. So many wide-range insecticides and fungicides are available today that good general-purpose sprays can be mixed, if care is taken to use compatible chemicals. With these, a single product is able to kill or otherwise control a great many different insects. The term "broad-spectrum" is also applied to such chemicals.

For regular control, such products are quite valuable. Their use often prevents some insect from building up to a point where the harm it does is obvious. Unfortunately, pesticides do not control all insects and diseases to the same degree. The fungicide phaltan, which has about the broadest spectrum of any commonly available material, works against such widely different fungus troubles as powdery mildew, rose blackspot, rust, and botrytis. However, if mildew alone invades an area, phaltan is not the perfect material for control. Here, a specialized chemical, such as Karathane or Actidione, will work better, even though it may not touch other common diseases.

WHEN TROUBLE STRIKES THE GARDEN

With 640,000 different insect species in the world and 35,000 to 40,000 of them a threat to plants in the United States, and with new pests likely to appear at any time, the task of presenting a comprehensive chart of identification and controls is obviously beyond the scope of any one book. Since first-class entomologists and plant pathologists are not found in every corner hardware store, many a gardener is left in a quandary. Trying to find a suitable insecticide for a strange insect, he discovers that most retail outlets can give him little or no help. Manufacturers' charts offer some assistance, but cannot illustrate all the pests. The State Agricultural Extension Service, or the County Agent should be able to offer help, but if devastation seems imminent, the best weapon against the newcomer is a mixture of two or three broad-spectrum materials — a shotgun prescription, but one likely to fit most plant pests. In using them, be sure to *read and heed each label.*

What to Look for on the Label

The weakest link in pest control is failure to read the label. Even professional men such as lawyers and doctors, accustomed to reading every word in documents pertaining to their own fields, have been known to skip carelessly through printed directions for garden sprays and come up with the wrong answer.

The first step is to read the analysis — the list of ingredients required by law. This is put on the label for your protection. It lists both active and inactive ingredients and gives the percentage of each. You can be sure of general control of insect pests if it contains two or three of the following chemicals: Diazinon, malathion, methoxychlor, Sevin and chlordane. These are usually safe on ornamentals.

When food crops are to be sprayed, use only chemicals that state clearly that they are for use on vegetables. Here, the question of safety to life and health requires the use of such chemicals as rotenone, cubé, and pyrethrum. In certain stages of growth (which will be specifically listed on the label), methoxychlor, Sevin and malathion will be included.

Among broad-spectrum fungicides, phaltan, captan, ferbam, maneb, zineb and sulfur are perhaps most widely used. Again, reading the label will give some clue to their possible effectiveness.

Watch particularly for limitations mentioned on the label. For example, sulfur should not be used at temperatures of 80° or over or foliage may be burned. If a vegetable spray label warns against spraying within 10 days of harvest, the statement is there for your protection. *Heed the warning!*

Turf fungicides are a field in themselves. Here the problem is one of controlling both leaf diseases and those that invade the soil and attack roots and rhizomes. Some broad-spectrum fungicides for turf that have proved effective are Dyrene, Kromad (Formula Z), Daconil and Tersan 1991 (Benomyl).

Seeking Expert Help

When these prescriptions fail to control a pest, accurate diagnosis of the disease is important. Golf-club members can do no better than consult the superintendent in charge of the greens for practical advice about turf diseases. Local farm advisers or county agents, employed by local, state, and federal agencies to help farmers, are always willing to look at samples brought to them. Most of them are trained entomologists and plant pathologists, but only those in counties adjacent to big cities will have much knowledge of turf.

If these sources fail and the problem is serious, samples can be sent to your State Agricultural Experiment Station. Remember that, in mailing samples, it is against the law to send live noxious insects through the mails. Put a little rubbing alcohol in a vial, insert the insect, and seal the stopper with tape. Wrap the vial with enough paper to absorb any alcohol that leaks.

In their anxiety to have plant-material samples arrive in good condition, amateurs often wrap them in aluminum foil. This does not work. Usually the plant arrives half-rotted. A couple of layers of paper toweling are much more effective.

When writing about a problem, do not make the entomologist or plant pathologist do all the guessing. It is hard enough to make identifications on the spot: the bug or branch he receives is only part of the story. Describe how and where the pest or disease attacks plants, when it appeared, and what plants it affects, and give any other pertinent facts you can supply.

COMMON INSECT PESTS

Ants are perhaps the most numerous in kind and quantity of all land-life populations. There are 8,000 species. Except for the big black carpenter ant, which eats holes in trees, houses, coldframes, and other wooden structure, the only species which do much damage are those that carry aphids ("plant lice") from place to place. The aphids are milked like cows for the sweet syrup they exude. Ants put aphids out to "pasture" and pamper them by moving them from one plant to another. Fortunately, either chlordane or heptachlor sprinkled around areas where ants are active quickly eradicates them.

The common name of "plant lice" identifies aphids. They are soft-bodied sucking insects, usually pear-shaped, so small that when seen in masses on the end of a branch they look like mildew. In color they may be gray, green, black, bright red, or whitish. Some are waxy or powdery.

When they are stroked by ants to induce them to give off honeydew, some of this sticky substance falls onto the supporting plant. Here it acts as a growth medium for a sooty fungus, usually found on shaded tree branches where the honeydew has dripped, but sometimes on plants beneath. Aphids also carry virus diseases. Because they hatch early in spring and are instantly active, they can do considerable damage before their natural enemies appear. Predators which control them include the lacewing fly larvae (called "aphid lions"), ichneumon wasps, ladybugs, the insidious plant bugs and others. If any of these helpful predators are seen feeding on aphids when you are about to spray, move them to an unsprayed plant before you start.

Most pesticide mixtures control aphids, but old-fashioned nicotine sulfate or rotenone will do as good a job and leave no residue harmful to the predators that keep them under control.

BAGWORMS. Tough bags one to two inches long, covered with bits of leaves from the infested tree, each hold a single female larva. Pick them off, preferably in winter and burn them. If young caterpillars are already crawling, Sevin, malathion or Diazinon will kill them.

BEETLES. Some of our worst garden enemies are mature beetles, but they may do their damage as borers, weevils, or curculios. Among the worst offenders in the garden are the smaller European elmbark beetle which carries Dutch elm disease, Mexican bean beetle, Colorado potato bug, Japanese beetle, Asiatic beetle, squash and diabrotica beetle.

It will pay to use a culture of milky spore disease, which is particularly effective on Japanese beetle grubs, and also infects about 35 other species. It is slow acting, but eventually effective. When a lawn is treated according to common practice, three years will be required before a grub-free turf can be expected. Zytrone will give one year control of grubs.

Beetles are easily killed with direct sprays of Sevin. For European elm bark beetle use Methoxychlor in March or April.

SPRUCE BUDWORM. A highly destructive pest, the spruce budworm has caused tens of millions of dollars damage to ornamental and forest trees. The dark reddish brown, yellow-striped caterpillars feed on the young tips of trees. Spray with Sevin or Methoxychlor when the caterpillars first appear in late July.

CHINCH BUG. This small bug with a black oval body and white wings with black markings gives off a foul odor when crushed. In Florida it is said to cause damage to lawns equal to the value of many of the state's leading agricultural and horticultural crops. An economic insect of great importance. The best chemical for control is Diazinon or Aspon.

CANKER WORMS. These are the "inchworms" that measured us for new clothes when we were children. There are spring and fall canker worms, both kinds feeding on tree leaves. They can be controlled by banding trees; first with a layer of cotton batting, then a strip of tar paper, with a sticky band of "tree tanglefoot" smeared around it.

CATERPILLARS. The larvae of moths or butterflies, called caterpillars, feed on a wide range of plants. The ones most commonly troublesome in gardens are the woolly-bear and tomato hornworm, also the iris borer and corn borer.

All seem to be quite sensitive to Sevin or Methoxychlor and can be killed when sprayed with these insecticides. For iris borer use Cygon when iris leaves are 2-3 inches tall and again when leaves reach 8-10 inches. Use care in handling these pests; many have poisonous hairs that can irritate the skin.

CICADAS. Except for the dramatic feeding of the 17-year locust, cicadas do little harm and are kept in check by a parasitic wasp, the digger wasp or cicada killer. For the control of the 17-year locust spray with Sevin.

CRICKETS. The common field cricket of the East is omnivorous and feeds widely. Use either a poison bran bait, or buy a commercial preparation. The Mormon cricket, a pest of the western plains, cannot fly; it can be killed with a dust of calcium arsenate. Soft dingy gray or gray-green caterpillars (there are other colors) that, overnight, cut off plants at the ground line are cutworms. Some hibernate in holes in lawns hidden under grass blades. Flooding will bring them to the surface. Use poison bran baits around vegetable plants and other crops on which they feed. Diazinon works well on lawns when flooded into the soil.

GRASSHOPPERS. Seldom present in epidemic numbers except around open fields and meadows. Chlordane will knock out serious invasions.

LEAFHOPPERS. Like aphids that hop; they are closely related. They feed by sucking, injecting certain toxins as they eat. They fly ahead of you as you walk through infested areas. Affected plants have a burnt look. On food plants, control them with rotenone (not easy — they fly away before you can hit them). If the crop is not to be harvested for at least two weeks, use Diazinon. This is the best control on ornamentals. Malathion also works well.

MEALYBUGS. These are scaleless "scale" insects, with soft bodies on which the conventional scale is replaced by soft woolly hairs or fibers. Like aphids, they give off a honeydew which lures ants and encourages sooty mold. They also harbor organisms of plant diseases that are carried to healthy plants by ants in the honeydew.

On house plants, touching the mass of cottony fibers with a swab of cotton dipped in alcohol is a safe, simple remedy. Outdoors, spraying with an oil emulsion such as Volck is perhaps the best remedy. Malathion, Diazinon or Cygon are effective when the crawlers or young hatch. If a spreader-sticker is added to these chemicals, they will also kill adult mealybugs.

MIDGES. Perhaps the only one of major importance in gardens is the rose midge, which mummifies the young growing tips. Watch for a reddish or brownish fly about 1/16 inch long or smaller that lays tiny yellow eggs on flower buds or young leaves. These hatch into small white maggots. A general-purpose spray used regularly will keep them under control.

MITES (red spiders). Technically, these are neither insects nor spiders, but they are bothersome pests. Suspect mites if leaves on deciduous plants or needles on evergreens begin to turn a yellowish green (usually after a warm dry spell). Shake the foliage over clean white paper: if tiny moving specks appear, barely visible to the naked eye, they are mites. Where only mites are involved, specific miticides, such as Tedion, Genite, Chloro-benzilate, or Kelthane, should be used. If the weather is cool (below 80° for at least eight hours after dusting or spraying), wettable sulfur either

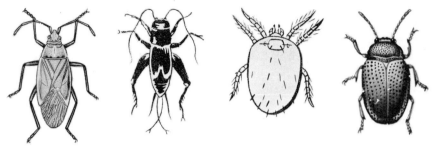

Boxelder Bug, Cricket, Chigger, Flea Beetle

SOME COMMON PESTS

There are hundreds of thousands of insect species — and scores of thousands of them exist in North America.

In the past their damage was largely controlled by the balance of nature — each had its enemies and predators, each fed upon lesser creatures. But in building cities and suburbs and turnpikes, in draining swamps and eliminating disease bearers and crop destroyers, man has altered the delicate balance.

Today we have learned to be selective in our attempt to control insect pests. Rachel Carson's Silent Spring *has made the public well aware of the potential dangers of poisonous residues and their possible effects on nature's pattern. Increasingly scientists are searching for biological methods to replace chemical controls. In some instances they have achieved re-*

Japanese Beetle, Lace Bug, Lygus Bug, Rose Chafer

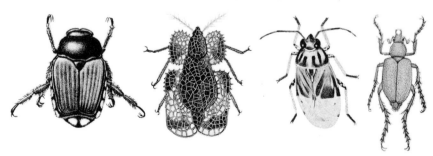

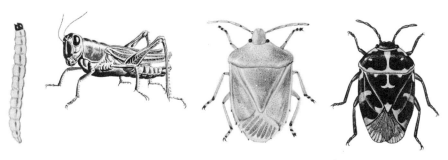

Flea Beetle Larva, Grasshopper, Green Stink Bug, Harlequin Bug

markable success. Over much of the eastern seaboard, for example, the "milky disease," spread by a parasitic wasp imported from Korea, has reduced the Japanese beetle from a menace to a nuisance. The control of the destructive screwfly — by the sterilization of the males — is an equally spectacular story.

Biological controls, when possible, are generally preferable. But they are not always feasible. Chemical methods are often necessary, and when properly administered, they are both effective and safe. Today they are essential in many agricultural operations. To teach people to use them carefully and wisely is the pressing problem.

On these pages are pictures of some of the most common garden pests. They may (or may not) be a problem in your locality. Learn to recognize them. Learn to combat them selectively. And remember: — Don't kill every bug you see. Many of them are your friends.

Sod Webworm, Sod Webworm Moth, Tick

as a dust or spray is cheaper and just as effective as newer chemicals, but may burn foliage at higher temperatures. Directing a strong stream of water regularly onto all parts of evergreens is an effective way to keep down these pests.

MOTHS. The codling moth of apples, perhaps the worst pest in this group as far as the gardener is concerned, is controlled by chemicals applied on a definite schedule. Write your State Experiment Station for a copy of their recommendations.

The gypsy moth in New England and parts of New York State is the subject of special bulletins by both the U.S.D.A. and state stations. These should be in the hands of all gardeners in gypsy-moth territory.

PSILLIDS ("hopping plant lice"). They resemble aphids but have longer legs. The two most common species are the boxwood and laurel psyllids. Spraying with malathion or Diazinon as new growth begins, and repeating this three weeks later, usually cleans them out.

SAWFLIES. The European pine sawfly is a major pest on pines, denuding young growth of needles. The larvae are beautifully camouflaged to look like pine needles. Before new growth starts, watch for a slight curling and yellowing of old needles, on which the larvae feed until young shoots appear. Spray with Methoxychlor, Sevin or Meta Systox R in the spring, and repeat a month later.

The red-headed pine sawfly is similar but has two broods. Spray for the first brood toward the end of June and repeat August 1. The red head differentiates it from the European species. Sides are spotted black.

SCALES. These are among the most persistent and difficult of all insects to control. Only females remain to feed on plants. You can generally identify scales by the presence of bits of hard matter on the stems of plants; they are juicy when squeezed. Some shell-less scales are soft, however. Usual control in cooler regions is to use an oil spray when the plants are dormant. In warmer sections, a white summer oil emulsion such as Volck must be used. Ask your State Agricultural Experiment Station to identify specimens and advise you of the hatching date in your area. When young crawlers are hatching, spray with malathion or Diazinon. Some species have several generations a year.

SLUGS AND SNAILS. Best control for these pests is a bait containing metaldehyde and a poison. Metaldehyde will lure them for a distance of several feet. Sanitation is important in slug and snail control. Clean up all decaying wood and trash, remove fallen leaves promptly, do not leave flat stones or bits of wood under which they can hide at night. If slugs keep attacking certain plants, surround the plants with a ring of hydrated lime; this serves as a barrier.

THRIPS. These curious insects are largely fitted for rasping — scraping away the skin on leaves, flowers, and stems and drinking the sap that exudes. As a result of this type of feeding, infested plants take on a peculiar burned appearance which to the expert at once indicates the presence of thrips. Malathion, Diazinon or dimethoate (Cygon) must be applied every week or so to offset an attack.

PLANT DISEASES

Diseases are much more difficult to diagnose than insect damage because, if visible at all, the causal organisms are often impossible to see with the naked eye. Moreover, other types of injury — frost damage, wind burn, sunscald, and deficiency diseases either mask those caused by bacteria, fungi, or viruses, or resemble them. Disease control is a complex phase of plant care.

The remedy for diseases caused by mechanical injury or chemicals is obvious. Eliminate the cause of trouble. But it is important to understand that, once a plant has been invaded by a virus, fungus, or bacterium, external application of a spray or dust will do nothing to cure plant parts already infected. All spraying or dusting in this field is preventive; its purpose is to protect new growth from infection and to destroy the organism responsible before it can infect other plants.

Virus diseases are particularly difficult to understand because they often occur in plants without visible symptoms. They may exist in one species or variety without harm, yet be capable of causing severe injury to others. Virus diseases are often suppressed by cold and stimulated by heat, so that a plant which seems perfectly healthy when set out in early spring may suddenly show severe mottling or other virus symptoms when warmer weather arrives.

Physiological Troubles

Faulty environment, which is usually easy to correct, will often give the effect of disease in a plant. Wilting, for instance, while it may be caused by disease, may also indicate a lack of water.

Injury may result from either too high or too low a temperature. Blossoms on tomato plants may drop off if air temperatures at night go below 50°. They also tend to shuck off when night readings are 80° or 90°.

Excess soluble salts in soil can also cause disease-like symptoms. Some minor elements are particularly ambivalent. For example, many plants need boron in amounts as low as two or three parts per million; if this element is present in concentrations of ten parts per million or higher, severe injury may occur.

Lack of air in the soil, particularly when caused by soil compaction, can make plants look diseased. Loosening of the soil is the obvious remedy.

Since light is all-important to plant growth, shade can cause physiological diseases and at the same time prevent sunshine from destroying certain light-sensitive fungi. By delaying maturity in the fall, shade can also make plants more susceptible to frost damage.

Injury by fumes and gas is often puzzling and has been known to occur as long as a year and a half after exposure. A leaking gas main under frozen soil may allow trapped gas to travel 100 feet or more and injure or kill vegetation which seems far removed from the source of injury.

A blacktop driveway may also produce harmful fumes, as well as heat, which will kill sensitive plants several feet from the paved area.

Smoke injury, formerly prevalent only in cities, is now accompanying the spread of industrial operations and becoming serious in the suburbs. The effect of smog on plants in California is well known.

Injury caused by misuse of chemical weed-killers can be serious and mystifying (Chapter 20). One such spray applied to a pond is known to have entered an underground watercourse and killed trees a mile or more away. Control of water weeds is better left to commercial applicators who are familiar with the hazards involved and who carry insurance against damage. If insecticides or fungicides have been improperly used, the injury usually follows the application so closely that it is easy to diagnose.

BLACKSPOT. Perhaps the classic disease for the home gardener is blackspot on roses. The name is so descriptive that it needs no elaboration. Spores falling on a leaf will germinate if kept moist continuously for six to eight hours. During prolonged rainy periods, however, they are usually washed off mechanically before they can sprout.

Dew condensing on leaves at night makes infection inevitable unless the leaf is coated with a residual fungicide. Spraying at intervals of five to seven days with an effective chemical such as Actidione or phaltan is standard practice with most amateurs who live in blackspot country, however, a new fungicide called Benomyl (Benlate) has been very effective in controlling blackspot as well as powdery mildew. Applications are effective for 2-3 weeks.

Usually, because blackspot is active only in warm weather, it becomes less infectious in fall, but conditions at that time are favorable to the development of powdery mildew, so protective coatings of a fungicide are still needed. Since both phaltan and Actidione (and many other fungicides) are also effective against powdery mildews, the same regular spray program is usually continued until the leaves fall. Where rose rust is also a problem, these same two fungicides are effective. Where blackspot is almost unknown, as in the San Francisco area, but mildew is a constant problem, a specific control such as Karathane is preferred.

RUST INFECTIONS. Rust shows up as rusty-red patches or irregular areas on green leaves. One of the most devastating economic diseases in the world is wheat rust, whose cost to agriculture runs in the millions. A disease which often causes double trouble for the gardener is apple rust, which not only attacks flowering crabs, apples, pears, quinces, and many other members of the rose family, but also red cedar (*Juniperus virginiana*) in the East and the incense cedar (*Libocedrus decurrens*) in the West. There are several sub-races of this disease.

Spores falling on cedars in fall produce brown galls; the so-called cedar apples. Small at first, these may swell to the size of a golf ball by spring. During a wet spell they soften, turn bright orange and become covered with long fingers, or telia. By a peculiar series of events, too long to describe, spores float to apple leaves where they germinate and produce rusty-red patches — typical apple rust. The rust patches in turn produce spores to start the cycle over again.

Planting flowering crabs and red cedars close to each other means asking for trouble. If only one or two cedars grow in the vicinity, cutting off the cedar apples will break the chain of infection. Asiatic flowering crabs are practically resistant and should be given preference over native kinds whenever possible.

Blister rust of five-leaved pines is a similar alternate-host disease; both pines and gooseberries (or currants) must grow in the same neighborhood to enable it to survive. In states where the white pine is an important timber tree, planting gooseberries or currants is prohibited by law.

Rust diseases most commonly occurring in gardens include snapdragon rust (use rust-resistant varieties), chrysanthemum rust, hollyhock rust, rose rust and the apple rust already mentioned.

MILDEW INFECTIONS. Mildews are readily recognized by the whitish or grayish film they lay on foliage. Perhaps the commonest form is powdery mildew on lilac leaves in late fall. This does not seem to be firmly attached and in early stages can often be washed off with a hose. It occurs on lilacs so late in fall that it does no harm and is usually left untreated. It does, however, destroy the foliage and flowers of many fall-blooming annuals such as zinnias.

The powdery mildews are readily controlled with a spray of wettable sulfur, but this should not be used if temperatures above 80° are expected within 24 hours after application. Chemicals such as phaltan, Benomyl (Benlate), Actidione and Karathane are used where plant injury must be kept to a minimum.

Downy mildews, sometimes called white rust, do not seem to invade foliage as quickly as powdery mildews do, but are much more harmful when they finally do break through the leaf epidermis. The mycelium, or root-like structure, once it is inside the leaf, deeply penetrates the spaces between plant calls. Downy mildews are felted rather than dusty and are not readily washed off even in early stages of infection.

Late blight of potatoes and tomatoes are typical downy mildew infections, causing weakening and premature death of the plants and stopping production long before frost. Many newer fungicides, particularly zineb and ziram, can be used as preventive sprays. Directly seeded tomato plants usually are more resistant and do not deteriorate as rapidly as transplants. Cucumbers, lima beans, most members of the cabbage family, and spinach are also subject to downy mildews.

WILT DISEASE. About the only important wilt disease in home gardens is aster wilt. It is best controlled by growing wilt-resistant varieties.

DISEASES OF TURF

Only within the past two decades have turf diseases been widely recognized as threats to quality turf. Common Kentucky bluegrass, for example, was believed to "go dormant" in summer and the condition was taken as a matter of course. Since World War II, "dormancy" has been recognized as the result of leaf-spot diseases, largely caused by Helminthosporium fungi. An interesting experiment is to gather a handful of so-called "dormant" turf of common Kentucky bluegrass and see how many small patches of yellow, with a darker center, can be seen on the blades. The same organisms also attack most of the named varieties which improve on some quality of the common type. Some are slightly resistant. 'Delta,' 'A20,' 'Fylking,' 'Pennstar,' 'Park,' 'Windsor,' 'Newport,' 'Arboretum' and 'C-1' are all infested to some extent under favorable conditions. 'Merion' is the most resistant, but is somewhat affected by other fungi — Pythium and Curvularia, Fusarium roseum and stripped smut. This produces a condition known as "fading out" which under midwest conditions has been best controlled by a mixture of Actidione and thiram. In the East, a Dyrene mixture has been used effectively in one state.

Snow mold is a puzzling disease to many. Patches of dead grass, pinkish gray, whitish, ecru, or some other color, depending upon the organism responsible, show up when the snow melts. Around these dead patches the live green grass stands out in strong contrast.

These are caused by several peculiar fungi that grow only at temperatures between 23° and 42°, particularly active if covered with snow or if there is a thick thatch or duff of dead matter on the surface. Spraying with a suitable turf fungicide (Dyrene, Cadminate and others) just before the soil freezes in the winter is recommended. Repeat the spraying in spring when the snow disappears if the infestation has been serious in previous years.

Sanitation is important. Mow the grass as long as it keeps growing and remove all clippings. Avoid organic fertilizers. Use a lawn renovator to remove thatch or duff. If hedges or fences cut off free air circulation, removing these will often stop snow mold.

Nothing else in the garden can match the springtime beauty of flowering trees. The waxy blooms of magnolias (top left) are graceful. Crabapples (bottom left) have the added charm of fragrance. And, for something exquisitely delicate, there are the flowering cherries (right).

Hyacinths mean fragrance as well as color. Here a drift of light lavender "Sapphire" is tucked into a hard-to-mow spot beside a tree.

Ivy-edged beds of iris and daffodils, and pink geraniums in pots keep the accent on flowers in this well-planned outdoor living area.

A garden in a glass brings spring into the house long before it happens outside. For ingredients and instructions, see Chapter 13.

Rust on 'Merion' bluegrass is a problem in some years, but does not develop if proper care is taken. Mow the lawn every week (it develops on new growth), feed the turf at least 4 pounds of actual nitrogen per year, and keep the grass short — not over 1¼ inches. Overwatering produces soft, tender growth that is readily attacked by rust. All bluegrasses are infected by this disease, but, because they are in less active growth than 'Merion' in summer, usually escape a serious and conspicuous attack. Actidione seems to be a specific for control, but the cultural remedies are more effective.

Two new diseases have recently given Merion a hard time. Fusarium Blight usually occurs after 2 or 3 days of 85-90 degree temperature. The disease has a very characteristic pattern development. Affected grass first shows a yellowing in areas that are either circular, crescent-shaped or streaked. In addition, centers of green grass, apparently healthy plants, occur in circles of dead grass and have taken the name "Frog eye." This disease has been found in New York, New Jersey, Pennsylvania, Ohio, Michigan and Maryland. Apply Tersan 1991 (Benomyl) in two applications 14 days apart, one in early June and one in late June.

In the second new disease — striped smut — long yellow-green streaks develop on the leaves. As the disease progresses these streaks become gray in color. In the final stages the leaf splits exposing black spore masses of the fungus, leaf blades then turn brown, wither and die. Apply Tersan 1991 (Benomyl) once in the fall.

Romantic stories about the origins of fairy ring in lawns say they are caused by the devil churning his butter on the lawn, by fairies dancing in the moonlight, or by witches weaving spells. Actually they are visible evidence that the mycelium, or root-like structure, of some mushroom is growing on buried organic matter. As it grows, it digests nutrients in the wood, using some of them for further growth, but releasing others to the grass growing above. The grass in the outer ring is at first a darker green because of this extra food, but dies for lack of food and water when the supply fails. As the mycelium spreads outward, the dark green ring spreads with it, leaving a weakened turf inside the ring.

Puncturing the ring with holes made with a special tube and pouring a solution of phaltan or wettable sulfur, into the holes will often kill the mycelium. To make the tool, cut a 36-in-wide length of electric conduit and sharpen the lower end so it will cut a core of earth. Drive this to a depth of about 10 inches (you can feel the cutting edge hit the felted mycelium) and withdraw it. A length of ½-inch dowel is useful in pushing out the core of earth removed. Fill the holes with vermiculite to allow air to reach the area under the mycelium.

Another way to control fairy ring is to use a root-irrigator of the type used for watering trees. If it has a chamber for applying insecticides, use a fungicide cartridge or mixture. Drive the tube to a depth of about 10 inches and turn on the water until the area inside the ring is soft and puffy.

Most of the other vague, hard-to-define diseases of turf are best controlled by the regular application of a broad-spectrum turf fungicide such as Kromad, Dyrene, Diconil, Fore, Tersan 1991.

Virus Diseases

Aster yellow is the virus disease most often encountered by the home gardener. It is carried by leafhoppers, and if these can be kept away, healthy asters can be grown. The plant may turn yellow, but, if infested late in growth, only the blossoms may be hit. These turn an ivory yellow, usually on one side, and fail to develop properly. Infected plants should be destroyed. Spraying at one-week intervals to control the leafhoppers usually protects the rest.

ANIMAL PESTS

RABBITS are the most common animal pests. The best control is a 1-inch wire mesh fence, at least 2 feet higher than any expected snowfall, entirely around the area to be protected. A female cat is another excellent control measure; she will find the young in their nests and drive away the adults. Commercial repellents are available for spraying on woody plants for winter protection.

MOLES are readily controlled in lawns by treating the soil with calcium arsenate (which will also serve as a pre-emergence control of crabgrass, if that is a problem), or with a soil-insect control such as dieldrin, chlordane, or heptachlor. These chemicals kill the insect food of moles. No mole will continue to push its nose through hundreds of feet of soil if it finds nothing there to eat.

SQUIRRELS can be effectively controlled only by shooting or trapping them.

WOODCHUCKS must be attacked in their burrows. Cyanogas, used according to manufacturers' directions, or a pint of carbon disulfide poured down the hole and sealed in will usually do the trick. Just be sure the woodchuck is inside. The same treatment works for chipmunks.

MICE can be controlled with commercial poison baits, but dusting the area where they walk with dieldrin will usually eliminate them. They lick their paws and are killed.

Pesticide recommendations change from year to year and from state to state. Some states have a pesticide regulator program which prohibits persons from buying certain pesticides. Check with your land grant college or the Coop Extension Agent (County Agent) for latest pesticide information.

24

Garden Equipment
and Construction

A garden is held in place, protected, divided up, and framed by structures — fences and retaining walls, steps, paths, and terraces. Beautifully groomed flower beds and smooth lawns are products of well-used rakes and hoes and mowers. The handsome show depends on backstage efforts, on structures and equipment that are seldom the center of attraction, sometimes hidden, but always essential to the beauty, health, and safety of the things that are meant to be noticed.

It doesn't pay to skimp backstage. The collapse of a two-foot brick planter wall probably won't injure anyone. But it can mean the loss of your favorite flowering plants. Terraces that develop cracks or turn into muddy lakes whenever it rains bring endless headaches. Inefficient, make-do tools end in trouble where it hurts the most — in the muscles of your back. But with care and little, if any, extra expense, you can run the backstage of your garden the right way.

GARDENING EQUIPMENT

Whether your garden is large or small, you will need the proper tools to care for it properly. Not very many, and not necessarily expensive — but the right ones. The investment you make for this equipment will be tailored to fit your needs and your purse. If you shop around, you *can* find a special tool for nearly every imaginable gardening job. Naturally, you won't indulge yourself in a clutter of gadgets and equipment, but if you do have special needs, you will do well to browse through the catalogs and visit suppliers until you find the tools that best fit your requirements. But if you are a back-yard gardener like most of us, you will probably find that a set of *good, basic* tools is all you'll want or need.

But be sure that they are well-made tools, not the tinny sort. The investment in quality pays off in healthier plants and less work. A shovel with a sharp slicing edge and a handle the correct length for your height is worth its weight in liniment.

At the head of your list of basic tools go a *shovel* and a *spade*. A *shovel*, with its spoon-like blade set at an angle with the handle which allows you to scoop without stooping, is for moving loose, soft earth. Get a lightweight one, and don't use it for prying up boulders. There are other tools for that. The short ones with D-shaped handles *look* handy, but remember that you have to crouch when you use them. With a long-handled shovel, you can often work standing up. As for that tailor-made handle length: hold the shovel so that its blade lies flat along the ground; if you can grasp the end of the handle with little or no bending, that is the shovel and handle length for you.

A *spade* is not for shoveling. It is for spading — that is, for slicing into soft or hard-packed earth and turning it or lifting it up. The blade and handle form almost a straight line, so you can push down with your foot, hands, and shoulders. And for spading work, the short D-shaped handle is an advantage (unless you are very tall and the handle is very short). The steel of the blade should be hard enough to hold its slicing edge and the handle stout enough to take the strain when you yank at it to loosen up a clump of old roots. A spade has to take a lot of strain, so you will do well to avoid the dime-store spades that are likely to bend or crumple when the going gets rough. A rectangular *garden spade* will do good general duty around your lot. A *nurseryman's* or *drain spade*, which has a narrower, longer blade of heavy-gauge steel and a rounded cutting edge, may be a better buy, however. It won't lift up as much dirt, but it cuts more easily, and its slightly curved shape is useful for transplanting.

The old-fashioned *hoe* is now manufactured in several new back-saving shapes. It will do all of the jobs it used to do — and many more. Start with a plain *hoe*. Later on, if you want and need them, you can buy the special-duty models. A *soil-knife* or *v-cultivating hoe*, for instance, has a small, wedge-shaped blade and gooseneck shank which add up to efficiency and accuracy — you can slice a single shoot of grass or clover with it. The *beet-hoe* has corners where the ordinary hoe has curves; its blade is a bit heavier, and its three cutting edges make it the ideal tool for cultivating and weeding. For getting at the weeds that lurk under shrubs, a *scuffle-hoe* is the best answer. You set the V-shaped blade flat on the ground (the

Where you build, what you build, and what you build around it should (and does) reflect the kind of person you are.

handle angle allows you to do this without stooping), then "scuffle" it back and forth. The sharp edges, front and back, do the rest.

A *metal rake* is a must. Two are better: one of regular width and a narrow one for raking between close rows of plants.

Wooden rakes are for gathering up leaves and grass clippings, but most gardeners prefer *flexible metal* or *bamboo rakes* for this job because they are so much easier to use. Remember that they are designed to be used like brooms: sweep, don't pull.

Among your basic hand tools you should have a *trowel*, a *hand fork*, and a claw-like *cultivator*. A metal *dibble*, which pokes holes for seeds and seedlings, is handy, too. But, if you are not fussy about equipment, you can make your own by sharpening a six-inch length of broomstick.

If you add to these a pair of sturdy pruning shears, some sharpened stakes of various lengths, a good supply of plant ties, and a foot-square plank securely fastened to an upright handle (for tamping and smoothing plots of earth), you have a set of tools equal to almost any garden task.

If, however, you garden seriously, you will find much use for a *spading fork*, a tough earth-loosener with its four pronged "blade" angled like a spade not a pitchfork, and a *spading shovel*, which has the shape and long handle of a shovel plus the sharpness and straight-line thrust of a spade. Later on you can reward yourself with a long-handled *"speedy cultivator"* to keep the flower beds in shape, and a *weed spud*, a double-pointed metal scoop also on a long handle, which goes after surface-rooted weeds such as dock and plantain.

Lawns, of course, require some special equipment: edgers, spreaders, for reseeding and fertilizing, and mowers. The old man-powered mowers are rapidly giving way to power machines, which come in dozens of styles and sizes — so many and so rapidly changing that no garden guide could list and describe them adequately. Don't over-buy. Don't be unduly impressed by soft seats and brilliant colors. Make a sensible estimate of the job to be done and then go to a reliable dealer who will help you to select the correct machine for your needs. (A little shopping around is a good idea, too. No supplier has everything.) When you get the machine home, read the instruction book *all* the way through, so that you know how to operate the device most easily and effectively. Then put the book in a place where you can find it when you want to disassemble the machine for repairs or cleaning.

Cleaning is perhaps the most neglected of garden jobs. Everybody knows that a clean, bright tool works better and lasts longer than a dirty one. Yet few of us care for garden equipment properly. You will do well to make it a rainy-day routine to clean and refurbish your tools. A rub-down with an oily cloth and then a dry one is usually all that is required to keep them in decent shape. Used crank-case oil is good for this job, though it should be strained through a cloth to remove some of the carbon.

A small box of sand with a little of the oil in it is the best possible place to keep your hand tools. Hoes and weeders and other edged tools, of course, must also be sharpened occasionally.

Wood turns up in the garden in many guises — as frames for hotbeds and cold frames, as edging, pergolas, garden seats, and fences. It is a convenient, easy-to-use, low-cost material.

For best results, only the more durable species and grades should be used. If, for reasons of economy, less durable kinds are used, they should be treated with preservatives. You should be aware, however, that after the cost of treatment is added to the price of inexpensive lumber, you may find little or no savings, and that using a better grade would actually have been a better buy.

For example, garden grade redwood, perhaps the most durable wood generally available today, costs only 35 to 50 per cent more than species that will last less than half as long in contact with earth. To treat the less desirable wood so that it will approximate redwood in durability will usually cost you as much as you have saved — and your time and work besides.

This is not intended to be a 100 per cent endorsement of redwood, without qualification. It does have its defects. Unless you personally select the pieces you need out of a pile in the lumber yard, you are likely to wind up with a number of lengths that are soft, brittle and brashy, and not suitable for garden use. If you can, go down to the stacks and pick your own stock, choosing boards and dimension lumber that feel hard and heavy. Such redwood will last many years longer than inferior grades.

Another fault of redwood is that ordinary nails driven into it are eaten away by the acid it contains. Use only galvanized iron, brass, or aluminum fastenings.

Oak is another wood that is hard on unprotected iron under moist conditions. It is, however, an excellent wood except for its tendency to warp if not saturated with oil. It makes excellent garden furniture and equipment if it has been soaked in tung oil for several days, then dried before cutting.

Cedar can be similarly treated with oil, but soak it *after* treatment with a wood preservative such as zinc naphthenate. Western edge grain fir and old white pine are also excellent woods. The stiles of old white pine doors are marvelous for this purpose.

Plywood

Marine grade plywood, the kind used for boats, is the only grade of plywood that can stand up to the weather. It is not cheap, and unless the

Fences are for protection and privacy; they enclose beauty and exclude what is extraneous. Modern or traditional, they can be built to be both useful and beautiful.

unique qualities of plywood are needed — thin sections of unusual strength, for example — ordinary lumber is usually more economical to use. But plywood *is* easy to use, reliable (if properly chosen), and for many jobs a time-saving bargain.

Chemicals For Wood Preservatives

By far the most useful chemical for the treatment of wood that is to be in contact with plants is copper naphthenate, a copper "soap" that soaks into the pores and becomes an insoluble preservative. About 90 per cent of the copper naphthenate used in the United States is sold under the trade name Cuprinol. However, there is a second form of Cuprinol, a zinc compound, which you may sometimes prefer to use.

Copper naphthenate does have one disadvantage: it bleeds through practically any paint (even the new water-solubilized outdoor latex products) and produces green stains. Where a greenish color is not objectionable, you can use this preservative freely, because it is by far the longest lasting wood preservative that can be applied at home. Or you can avoid discoloration by using copper naphthenate only on the parts of wooden structures that are to be in contact with soil. Other parts can be treated with the other form of Cuprinol, *zinc* naphthenate. This preservative is clear in color and does not stain paint. Unhappily, it is not quite as durable.

Copper and zinc naphthenate are not available in all supply stores, but they are for sale in many large hardware stores and lumber yards. The copper form can usually be bought through dealers in greenhouse supplies.

Several variations of pentachlorophenol, called penta compounds in the trade, are more widely available through lumber yards. These are also good wood preservatives and, if allowed to dry very thoroughly before they come in contact with living plants, are excellent for garden use.

One preservative you should avoid at all costs is creosote. For at least two years after treatment, creosoted wood can injure or kill plant life. In fact, except for its disagreeable odor, it would make a good weed-killer for unplanted areas.

Garden Furniture of Wood

Garden tables, benches, and lounge chairs can be purchased about as cheaply as they can be made. Commercially produced redwood and western fir furniture, everywhere available, is well designed and ready to use. So, unless you especially enjoy working with wood, it does not pay to make your own picnic tables, benches, and similar equipment. If you do decide to build your own garden furniture, you should first read a reliable guide on the subject. Whatever you make should be designed with the weather in mind. Slats of seats, for example, should run from front to back rather than crosswise, so water will not pocket. The legs should be designed so that edge grain rather than end grain is in contact with the soil or with terrace paving. It is pleasant to design your own outdoor furniture, but for good results it requires more specialized knowledge than most household carpenters have.

Fences

Fences are ordinarily homemade, though ready-cut designs in sections are sold by many lumber yards. The design depends on the style of your house and garden, the purpose of the fence (for privacy, background, shade, and the like) and your budget.

Wood rots, and even well painted fences begin to sag eventually. One simple way to prolong their appearance — and one that is sadly neglected — is to treat the danger spots occasionally with a good wood preservative. Keep a can of copper or zinc naphthenate handy and from time to time brush a little on places where two pieces of wood come in contact. This little resting-time care will yield years of dividends.

Needless to say, all post ends buried in soil or imbedded in concrete should stand in a copper naphthenate solution overnight before being planted. To neglect this simple treatment is to invite early sorrow.

One final word: make the gates wide — wide enough to drive a wheelbarrow or small tractor through without barking your knuckles. And some place, if you can, install a removable section that will admit something as large as a truck. You'll be grateful — years later perhaps.

OUTDOOR LIVING AREAS

In western parlance, almost any outdoor area used as living space is a patio, whether it is attached to a residence or not. Call it what you will, it seems to have become an American institution, a useful (sometimes), pleasant part of the new wide-windowed houses that try to make the outdoors and indoors one. Too often, however, the well-intended patio turns out to be more headache than pleasure — too small to be useful, but just big enough to ruin the looks of the garden; a bare, awkward slab unconnected with the landscaping and plants that struggle to give the rest of the yard some beauty and grace. At its worst, the patio can become a back-yard obstacle course of cracked concrete or jumbled bricks.

Architects tell you that the patio must be a part of the whole design of your garden. That is good in theory, but not always easy to accomplish since you may be dealing with a stretch of rigid, unnatural material. Using an irregular shape, instead of a rectangle, will often help solve the problem. So will occasional unpaved areas, spaces within the terrace which you can fill with flowers or shrubs. Plants in pots and tubs will bring the garden to the patio. If they are reasonably portable, you can rotate them with plants from other parts of the yard so that the best blooms are always where they can do the most good.

From the practical standpoint, the patio, if it is to be useful, must be near an entrance to the house, preferably the one which provides the shortest route to the kitchen. It may be out in the open, partially sheltered from direct sun by lattice work or even completely roofed. No one formula is "best," for each location is a special complex of weather, wind, sea, and rain. In areas where mosquitoes and summer showers are both unknown, the only problem is shelter from the sun when the outdoor living space is to be used during the day. In other areas, chilly winds at night may call for baffles and barriers.

The elaborate outdoor fireplaces and barbecues constructed mainly as sales features in some new houses are often used once or twice and then abandoned because a pitiless afternoon sun or a plague of insect pests make outdoor dining unpleasant. In almost any part of the United States east of the Mississippi River, a barbecue *porch*, enclosed by screen wire and with a right roof overhead is a sensible investment. It will make outdoor entertaining truly enjoyable — rain or shine, bugs or no bugs.

If the roof is constructed of corrugated panels of fiber glass (a rigid plastic), the feeling of being out-of-doors is not lost. If you want maximum light, translucent white panels are the answer. If you feel that on bright days these would be too glaring, try colored panels. Yellow gives a lovely sunlit effect, even in cloudy weather. Soft pink shades give an artificial glow, but definitely improve the appearance of everyone underneath. Green is ice cool — but it plays havoc with skin color! Test the effect of different colors by holding a sheet of the plastic between you and the sun.

PATIO MATERIALS AND CONCRETE PAVING

Outdoor living areas can be paved with concrete or other flat-level materials. Usually, however, a home-owner wants beauty as well as utility. He looks for a surface texture that complements the building materials of the house, the fences and walls and other garden structures. Brick, quarry tile, slate, and bluestone are all popular. And all of them can be laid on a sand over crushed stone or some other bed which provides adequate drainage. This is a job you can do for yourself, if you're strong, actively interested, and not averse to toting bricks and stone.

You should be warned, however, that in the long run (especially if a large area is to be covered), stone and brick terraces are usually more weatherproof and enjoyable when laid with mortar joints. This is not a job for most gardeners. It is best left to the professionals. More expensive to begin with, perhaps, but in the long run more economical and pleasurable.

Concrete is, of course, a superior, long-lasting material. It *can* be used in ways which are attractive, but seldom in great slabs and expanses. Irregular shapes are a help. So are planters. But if you do use concrete, it must be in well-designed areas. The concrete must be well made and well laid — which means that it is likely to be expensive.

For areas where frost is a problem, a new type of mix called air-entrained concrete is best. It is made by forcing millions of microscopic bubbles into the mix. These tiny expansion joints act as reinforcement against frost action. It can be had in ready-mix form.

A home-owner should think twice before tackling the job of laying concrete over a large area. Not only is considerable strength called for, but it takes more skill than most people have to level a 9- or 10-foot width of terrace in the time concrete remains workable. Even when ready-mix concrete can be obtained, few amateurs are able to distribute the standard 2-yard load before it begins to set up. All in all, paving any sizable area in concrete is not a project to be taken lightly.

You can solve some of the problems of handling concrete by dividing the terrace area into a series of rectangles divided by a framework of wood. Use only redwood, cedar, or cypress, the so-called toxic softwoods. If you elect to mix your own concrete, you can prepare a batch that will fill only two or three rectangles, and thus give yourself the time you need to do a proper job of leveling and smoothing. Even if you have a load of ready-mix delivered, you start, at least, with the concrete distributed among the rectangles instead of in an uncooperative lump that has to be distributed quickly before it turns into a rock. Drainage will be less of a problem, too. Give each rectangle a slight hump at its center and rainwater will drain off along the framework.

Those who feel able to cope with jobs big enough to make a load of ready-mix practical, should be warned to make adequate preparations for the arrival of the truck. First, think of how the delivery is to be made. A ready-mix delivery truck is as big as a small garage — difficult, if not impossible, to squeeze into narrow driveways. It's high, too — and that means that it may not be able to get in under the electric or telephone wires that you have never noticed up there. The spout from that truck can usually reach no more than 8 or 10 feet. When this massive thing arrives, you will have no time to make last-minute preparations. The concrete will come pouring out, and you had better have the foundation stone in place, packed firm and wet down before you hear the roar of the motor. Forms should be in place, tools ready, and an emergency box on hand to hold whatever excess won't go into the forms. Since you don't dare order exactly the amount needed, it's a good idea to have some secondary project set up so that you can use any excess.

Estimate the job carefully. The following recommendations including a

Terraces and walks offer infinite possibilities for variation in material, shape, design, and texture. Here are four that express something of the infinite variety of outdoor living.

slight surplus to allow for waste. For a 5-inch layer (about the thinnest practical for a home driveway) divide the area by 60. This will give the amount of concrete needed in yards of mix. Thus a driveway that measures 600 square feet will require 10 yards of mix. Place your order well in advance of the delivery day. Check at least a day in advance to be sure that delivery will be on time.

Do not forget expansion joints, one at least every 8 feet.

Place and finish as quickly as possible; working cement past its setting time is fatal to good work.

Cure properly. Keep the surface wet down for at least a week. Cover it with burlap or damp sand. By building a 1-inch deep rim on all sides, you can keep the surface under water. This is called pounding, and is by far the best way to cure concrete. Or cover it with plastic or building paper after soaking it well.

DRIVEWAYS

If driveways could be eliminated, homes would be cooler, fit into their surroundings more naturally, and extra space would be available for gardening. Unfortunately, passageway must be provided for the ubiquitous automobile. Not only must we provide service areas for the family car (or cars), but space for off-street parking by guests.

On a wide lot, a Y turn to allow a turn without backing out on a busy street is a great convenience, but admittedly it is wasteful of space. Sometimes such turns are used for off-street parking, but their value is questionable, particularly if the family car must be driven out when others are in the driveway behind it. More usable is a turnaround, but to be practical, a turn for modern cars should be at least 40 feet wide, which isn't feasible unless the lot is at least 80 feet wide. For a full-sized turning court at the garage, an area of at least 45 by 45 feet is needed. Compact cars take less space, of course, but even the most devoted small-car fancier has friends with larger ideas and larger cars.

We are talking about a large area of hard surface, and when you think of it in relation to heat absorption or reflection, the modern automobile seems something less than a blessing. Such an area paved with concrete, and on the sunny side of a house, can easily reflect enough heat to raise the living room temperature several degrees. With blacktop, the amount of heat *reflection* is reduced, but heat *absorption* is increased; on a very hot day the asphalt becomes something of a "radiator," adding its warmth to the area around and above it.

There is no pat answer to this problem. Cars are here to stay, and so are parking areas. The best you can do, probably, is to plant tall trees to shade completely these heat-generating areas. They will add beauty — and deliver several degrees of comfort.

Driveway Drainage

The most common defect in homemade paving projects is poor drainage. Plan for it properly before it is too late. A watertight covering over the soil concentrates rain and melting snow into a stream that flows down whatever grade exists. This is often a problem with terraces; with driveways it can be much more troublesome. A common complaint is that water drains all the way from the street down into the garage, where it freezes in winter. The only solution to that is to divert the water, and if city or village ordinances prohibit running storm drains into city sewers, a dry well is the best answer.

Materials For Driveway Paving

ASPHALT: This material acquired a bad reputation from early products that were soft and sticky in hot weather. Today, properly formulated asphalt is as rigid and durable as concrete and usually costs much less to lay. Defects do appear in time, but they are usually rather easy to repair.

On firm soil, a layer of crushed stone, washed gravel, or clean washed steam cinders is all that is needed as a base for blacktop. (But you should treat the soil underneath with a long-lasting, non-selective weed killer.) This layer should be at least 3 inches deep. It should be rolled with a roller weighing at least 350 pounds. For normal driveway use at least 2 inches of topping should be applied. In California and Florida, where frost action does not have to be considered, a 1-inch layer is feasible; a 2-inch layer is better.

Do-it-yourself paving with asphalt is possible. The basic materials are cheap; most of blacktopping cost is labor. However, this means using cold-mix products which are less durable than hot-mixed, professionally applied material. The latter produces a paving in which stone or gravel forms the aggregate, with hot asphalt substituting for Portland cement in conventional concrete.

Sometimes the material used for hot application by commercial pavers is sold for home use, but the results are usually unsatisfactory. Heavy rolling and tamping are necessary to solidify the material properly, and since few home-owners have the necessary equipment for the job, the drives often remain soft for weeks after they have been laid down.

EMULSION-BONDED SAND SURFACE: The cheapest and quickest drive to lay is one in which clean gravel, steam cinders, or crushed stone are coated with a quick-setting water emulsified asphalt (quite a bit thinner than that used as a cold-mix). After the surface has been coated, sand is swept over it to take up excess asphalt and to help fill the voids. The stone at the surface should be between ½ and ¾ inch in diameter.

A crude type of concrete, practical for even the unskilled amateur, is called soil-cement. Not all soils can be used. Heavy clay or a soil high in organic matter will not work. Ordinary loam or sandy loams, however, will serve well. A layer of soil about 6 inches deep is mixed with cement and then allowed to set. The work must be done in dry weather to avoid premature setting of the cement before it has been mixed with the soil.

GARDEN WALKS

Whatever the architect may think, the gardener almost always decides that the less obtrusive the walks are, the better. Brick, bluestone, and slate, as attractive as they are in texture and color, are to him artificial notes which contribute little to his plants. For him paving is a nuisance to be tolerated rather than emphasized. He may make an exception of a walk in a formal garden, yet even there he would rather see it subordinated to the plants. Wherever possible, he is happy to replace walks and drives with grass.

A fundamental principle of garden design is that a path must seem to go somewhere. Even when it is introduced only to create a landscape effect and has no actual destination, it should disappear behind some object such as a building or a shrub. A path that looks purposeless is merely a distraction.

Except in formal designs, or where heavy traffic demands sturdy construction some loose, soft, and inconspicuous material is usually preferable. A gravel or tanbark path is generally better than one of brick or cut stone. Where a more durable material is needed, blacktop is a good compromise; its color tends to fade into the background.

Whatever kind of surfacing material is used, a path must have a firm foundation and adequate drainage. A layer of at least 3 inches of clean steam cinders, gravel, or crushed stone will provide both. If you can use this base layer as a path for a month or so, you will have a better finished path. After that, tamp it thoroughly and fill any hollows that develop before you pave it. If you plan to use slate, brick, or bluestone laid with mortar joints, the drainage layer should be at least 6 inches thick.

The use of one of the substituted area weed-killers or some other nonselective chemical on the soil before laying down gravel, cinders, or stone is always good practice. Weeds have been known to grow right through blacktop.

STEPS

Changes in levels are always a problem. If the land falls off too sharply to make a gentle workable slope, your only alternative is to build some kind of step. Perhaps the best way to describe the ideal garden steps is to say that they should be designed so that you can walk down them in the dark without fear of tripping and falling. This means that the ratio of the rider to the tread must be right, the surface smooth, and the run generally straight ahead. Curved stairs, beautiful as they may be in a Colonial hallway, are a menace outdoors.

Ideally, the risers should be regular — usually not lower than 6 inches or higher than 9. The treads should be at least 10 inches wide, though on a long slope they can be much wider. The important thing is that they be at *regular* intervals — not arranged as booby traps for the unwary.

Like masonry walls, steps should have a deep foundation. If they are of masonry, they should be laid with sound mortar joints. It is possible, and often desirable, however, to make steps of materials which blend more pleasantly with the growing parts of the garden — steps of railroad ties and soil fill, and the like. For details of their construction, see illustrations.

STEPPING STONES

Stepping stones are attractive in the garden, but they are perhaps better in theory than in practice. Keeping grass weeded and well mowed between them is a Herculean task — labor which might well be used more profitably in caring for attractive plants. Where stepping stones *are* called for by a landscape design (they are, for example, a basic in Japanese gardens), the use of a non-selective weed-killer around each flagstone will reduce the amount of care needed. Fortunately, Japanese design calls for bare earth around stepping stones.

MASONRY WALLS

However they are used, as decorative features or to achieve a change of level, masonry walls must be solidly built. Much more than foundation walls, they are exposed to frost action and weathering. Joints should be "shoved" — a term used by masons to indicate that the individual brick or stone unit is laid on a full bed of mortar and then shoved into place to squeeze out all voids in the mortar. Such joints are slow and expensive to make, but they are more durable — and that they must be if the wall is to stand firm in the garden. Foundations for walls of any height must extend below the frost line. Over most of the northern half of the country, this means at least 36 inches below the soil surface.

By and large, any sizable wall laid up in mortar is a job for a mason. But there is at least one exception. More and more home-owners, especially those who like to do their own garden construction, are finding out about concrete masonry blocks. These king-sized "bricks" are made of Portland cement and coarse aggregates. The weight, texture, and porosity of the blocks depend on the aggregate: sand, crushed rock, and gravel make heavyweight units; pumice, expanded shale, or cinders produce light ones. The lightweight blocks are easier to work with and tough enough for

SLOPE-HOLDING FACT SHEET

There are several ways of holding sloping land to prevent erosion and of terracing it to provide a series of level areas. The simplest and most popular is by means of retaining walls made of stone, concrete, or blocks. A wall not over 4' high is usually easy to build and presents no problems to the average do-it-yourselfer. If it has to be much higher than that, or if the site conditions are unusually difficult, you'd do well to get some advice from an engineer, landscape architect or builder before tackling it. The principles of building retaining walls are illustrated below. Other methods of holding slopes are on the next page.

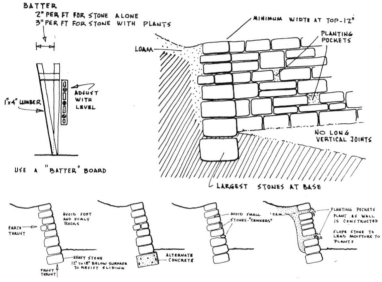

STONE WALLS WITHOUT MORTAR

Dry-stone walls are constructed by fitting rocks together in mosaic fashion, with weight and friction holding them together. Each stone should rest on parts of two others below, so no long vertical joints are formed and the weight is well distributed. Largest stones should be in lower courses. Flattest ones should be saved for top course which should be as level as possible. A solid bedding is essential. Dry walls up to 3 or 4 feet high should have a base of large stones or concrete slab below ground. This is not for frost action, but to resist sliding. The walls should slant backward to provide strong resistance against pressure from the earth being retained. A batter (slant) of 2 to 3 inches horizontally to each vertical foot is usually recommended.

WALLS OF SOLID CONCRETE

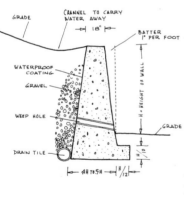

Drawings and Information: Thomas A. Barton

Concrete retaining walls are of two types: gravity (which depends on its own weight and shape to resist pressure) and reinforced (which utilizes strength gained with metal reinforcing). Both must be designed to avoid overturning, sliding forward, or failure at any point in height. Planning for drainage is vital since a solid wall acts as a dam to underground moisture. A layer of loose porous material behind the wall, with a line of tile at its base to carry away water that filters down, will reduce sub-surface pressure. "Weep holes" also help. They are tiles or pipe, sloped through the lower part of the wall at 6 to 10 foot intervals. Some batter is desirable. In cold climates, slant the back side too, so any frost-action pressure will be deflected upward.

USING CONCRETE BLOCK

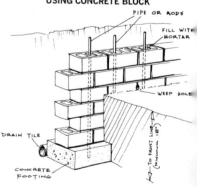

Concrete or cinder-block walls often need additional strength to withstand earth pressures. This can be attained by inserting pipes or rods through the block openings and filling these spaces with mortar. A coating of water-proof material such as tar on the back of wall will help prevent water seeping through the joints.

Slopes exceeding 30 degrees are liable to erosion and often difficult to make attractive even with hardy groundcovers. Here, in diagram form, are some prac-

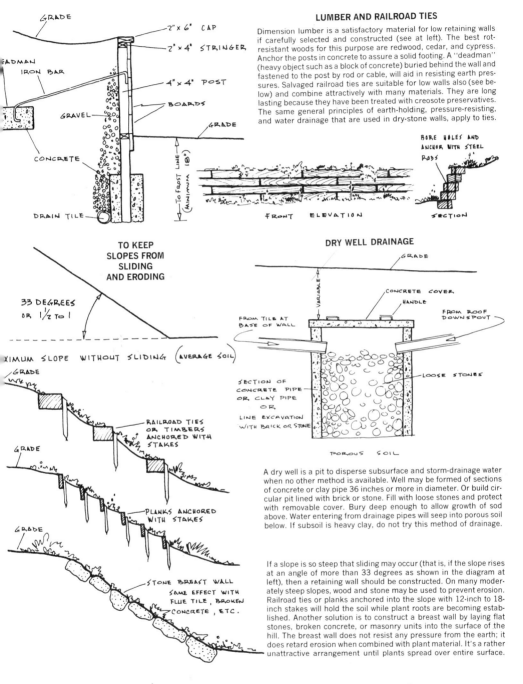

GRADE
2" x 6" CAP
2" x 4" STRINGER
4" x 4" POST
BOARDS
GRADE
DEADMAN
IRON BAR
GRAVEL
CONCRETE
TO FROST LINE (MINIMUM 18")
DRAIN TILE

LUMBER AND RAILROAD TIES

Dimension lumber is a satisfactory material for low retaining walls if carefully selected and constructed (see at left). The best rot-resistant woods for this purpose are redwood, cedar, and cypress. Anchor the posts in concrete to assure a solid footing. A "deadman" (heavy object such as a block of concrete) buried behind the wall and fastened to the post by rod or cable, will aid in resisting earth pressures. Salvaged railroad ties are suitable for low walls also (see below) and combine attractively with many materials. They are long lasting because they have been treated with creosote preservatives. The same general principles of earth-holding, pressure-resisting, and water drainage that are used in dry-stone walls, apply to ties.

BORE HOLES AND ANCHOR WITH STEEL RODS

FRONT   ELEVATION   SECTION

TO KEEP SLOPES FROM SLIDING AND ERODING

33 DEGREES OR ½ TO 1

MAXIMUM SLOPE WITHOUT SLIDING (AVERAGE SOIL)

GRADE
RAILROAD TIES OR TIMBERS ANCHORED WITH STAKES

GRADE
PLANKS ANCHORED WITH STAKES

GRADE
STONE BREAST WALL
SAME EFFECT WITH FLUE TILE, BROKEN CONCRETE, ETC.

DRY WELL DRAINAGE

GRADE
VARIABLE
CONCRETE COVER
HANDLE
FROM ROOF DOWNSPOUT
FROM TILE AT BASE OF WALL
LOOSE STONES
SECTION OF CONCRETE PIPE OR CLAY PIPE OR LINE EXCAVATION WITH BRICK OR STONE
POROUS SOIL

A dry well is a pit to disperse subsurface and storm-drainage water when no other method is available. Well may be formed of sections of concrete or clay pipe 36 inches or more in diameter. Or build circular pit lined with brick or stone. Fill with loose stones and protect with removable cover. Bury deep enough to allow growth of sod above. Water entering from drainage pipes will seep into porous soil below. If subsoil is heavy clay, do not try this method of drainage.

If a slope is so steep that sliding may occur (that is, if the slope rises at an angle of more than 33 degrees as shown in the diagram at left), then a retaining wall should be constructed. On many moderately steep slopes, wood and stone may be used to prevent erosion. Railroad ties or planks anchored into the slope with 12-inch to 18-inch stakes will hold the soil while plant roots are becoming established. Another solution is to construct a breast wall by laying flat stones, broken concrete, or masonry units into the surface of the hill. The breast wall does not resist any pressure from the earth; it does retard erosion when combined with plant material. It's a rather unattractive arrangement until plants spread over entire surface.

tical ways of building serviceable retaining walls that do not exceed 4 feet in height and other suggestions to keep slopes from sliding.

most garden jobs. However, they are difficult to find in some regions (the blocks usually are made locally, since their weight makes them expensive to transport, and the aggregates used are generally the ones available nearby). Shop around several lumberyard and masonry supply dealers before you make your selection and place an order.

As a rule, cinder blocks should be avoided. Often they contain bits of iron which will produce rust stains which disfigure the landscape.

Though concrete blocks don't lend themselves to delicate or subtle effects, in open, lattice-work designs they can look surprisingly light. They do handle with relative ease, come in a wide variety of patterns which allow for many solid or open designs, and, once you have learned how to set them, they go up in a comparative hurry. For some suggested designs and the method for building with blocks, see illustrations.

Even with blocks, masonry laid in mortar is fairly costly — and to skimp on the work is foolish economy. For this reason many people prefer dry walls — those laid up without mortar with stones set so that frost will not dislodge them. To reduce frost action, the stones should rest on a well-drained foundation. A trench filled with broken bits and pieces of stones is the usual base. However, if the trench happens to run across the natural line of drainage, it may fill with water, freeze, and cause more damage than it prevents. So, if you do build over a trench, make sure that it has an outlet to a lower spot so that any water it intercepts will drain away. If it holds any amount of water, your hard work will be destroyed at the first freeze.

If they are to serve as a retaining wall, stones should be set so that they slope backward toward the bank. Not only will this "batter," or angle, make the wall more secure; it will also drain the surface water back into the bank and make it easier for you to use the wall for planting as a rock garden.

Plant Encyclopedia

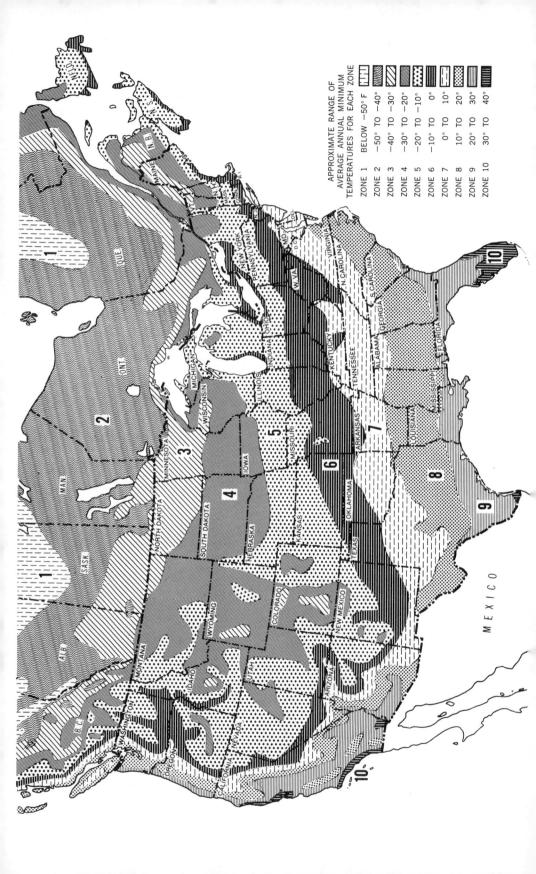

APPROXIMATE RANGE OF
AVERAGE ANNUAL MINIMUM
TEMPERATURES FOR EACH ZONE

ZONE 1   BELOW −50° F
ZONE 2   −50° TO −40°
ZONE 3   −40° TO −30°
ZONE 4   −30° TO −20°
ZONE 5   −20° TO −10°
ZONE 6   −10° TO   0°
ZONE 7   0° TO 10°
ZONE 8   10° TO 20°
ZONE 9   20° TO 30°
ZONE 10   30° TO 40°

PLANT ENCYCLOPEDIA

Here is a list of some 2,000 ornamental plants that are mentioned in this book. They represent a selection from among ten times that number that are available for the widely varied climatic zones of the United States and Canada. Where special requirements need to be met, cultural notes are provided. Uses are suggested and a brief description is given of each.

The first name given is the botanical name — generally the one by which the plant can be located in a catalog. Where the name preferred by botanists differs greatly, this is added in parentheses. Next come the common name or names believed to be in most frequent use.

For woody plants and a few herbaceous ones you will find the zone range (e.g., Zones 5-8) in which they can be grown. In some cases the zone numbers are lettered 'a' and 'b'. The 'a' refers to the colder parts of each zone (more northerly, higher, distant from water, etc.); 'b' to the warmer parts (more southerly, lower, closer to water, etc.). You can easily decide whether you are located in the colder or warmer part of your zone.

No list of hardiness ratings can be completely accurate. Most are based on empirical information, and it is well known that within a very short distance — sometimes no more than a city block — a matter of altitude, air drainage, or other situation may create a micro-climate, too small to map, that will kill a plant supposedly hardy in that zone. A plant's tolerance of drought, need for high humidity, or resistance to prolonged cold or excessively warm spells will affect its apparent hardiness. In California, for instance, more northerly perennials may not tolerate the steady heat of lower altitudes, but may thrive in the same zone at a higher elevation. In the North, a lack of snow cover or continued cold without relief will often kill otherwise hardy plants.

Hardiness figures should not deter gardeners from the pleasures of experimenting, particularly on a large property where there are plenty of other trees or shrubs to fill the space if one of marginal hardiness succumbs. The results, while often disappointing, can sometimes be highly rewarding. On a small property, however, where the loss of a single woody plant can be a tragedy, it is wiser to acquire only the kinds that are known to be both sturdy and hardy in the immediate area.

ABELIA. *A. grandiflora.* Glossy Abelia. z 6b-10a. Half-hardy shrub to 5 ft., flowering from July to frost. Honey-suckle-like flowers ¾ in. long, white, flushed pink. Does best in well-drained soil with considerable organic matter. Full sun. Sometimes forced for winter bloom.

ABIES. Fir. Among our best ever-greens for ornamental planting. Prefer acid soils, well-drained but moist.

A. balsamea. Balsam Fir. z 2-7. America's favorite Christmas tree, but difficult to transplant and use orna-mentally. To 70 ft. Interesting 2½-in. violet-purple cones.

A. cilicica. Cilician Fir. z 4-8. Soft green foliage; bark ash-gray. To 90 ft. One of the few firs good in warmer climates.

A. concolor. Colorado Fir. White Fir. z 3-8. One of the most widely planted of all firs in the U.S. Some-what smoke-tolerant in cities. Too often, its ultimate height of 125 ft. is overlooked, and it becomes an over-grown, out-of-place specimen. Needles are bluish. Many varieties are available.

A. homolepis. Nikko Fir. z 4-7. Rich green color and symmetrical growth make this a valuable landscape sub-ject. To 75 ft.

A. lasiocarpa. Rocky Mountain, Ari-zona, or Cork Fir. z 5-7. The fir known as *A. arizonica* is probably only a vari-ety of this species. Of little value ex-cept in clear sunny country; in the East it deteriorates rapidly. Valuable for a region where few other ever-greens thrive. To 90 ft. Interesting purple cones.

A. nordmanniana. Nordmann Fir. z 4-7. Popular and widely planted. To 90 ft.

A. veitchi. Japanese Purple-cone Fir. z 4-6. Of the easiest culture but re-sents lime in any form. Fast-growing and a good landscape subject. To 70 ft.

ABRONIA. *A. umbellata.* Sand Ver-bena, Wild Lantana. Fragrant rose-pink flowers in showy heads that re-semble those of the verbena. Vine-like habit, rooting at the joints. Excellent hanging-basket plants. Start seeds early and treat as an annual. In mild climates sow seed in fall, after removing husks. Often slow to germinate.

ABRUS. *A. precatorius.* Rosary Pea, Wild Licorice. z 9-10. Grown for the bright red seeds with striking black eye, used for beads and rosaries. They are poisonous, however, and should not be chewed. A vine to 10 ft. Needs support. Red to purple flowers, rarely white.

ABUTILON. *A. hybridum.* Flowering Maple. z 9-10. Herb or shrub. Seeds in commerce are usually a mixture of several species and interspecific hybrids. Leaves like those of a maple. Bell-shaped white, rose, orange, or yellow flowers, 1-3½ in. across, veined or striped with red. Can be grown from seeds or cuttings. Used as house plants and for bedding out. Perennial.

ACACIA. Mimosa, Wattle. z 9-10. Evergreen flowering shrubs. Small, puffy, bell-shaped flowers, usually yellow, in clusters. Most are richly fragrant. All are confined to warmer parts of California and Florida.

A. baileyana. Cootamundra Wattle, Winter Acacia. Showy shrub or small tree with striking blue-green compound foliage. To 25 ft.

A. decurrens. Silver, Green, or Purple Wattle. Several forms, all trees nearly 50 ft. high at maturity. Golden yellow flowers in racemes. Very striking, deep green foliage. To 50 ft.

A. longifolia. Sydney or Golden Wattle. Shrub or small tree with unusually long leaves. Finger-like clusters of soft lemon-yellow flowers. To 20 ft.

A. verticillata. Star Wattle, Star Acacia. Finger-like clusters of flowers form the "stars" that give this plant its common name. Interesting small tree or tall shrub. To 15 ft.

ACANTHOPANAX. *A. sieboldianus.*

Five-leaved Aralia. z 5-8. Rather stiff stems make this shrub awkward in appearance, but it is widely used because of its resistance to city smoke. To 9 ft. Greenish white flowers. *A. s. variegatus* is a variety with white-edged leaves.

ACANTHUS. *A. mollis.* Bear's Breech. z 6-10. The leaf form of classic Greek architecture. Perennial to 2 ft., with leaves to 2 ft. long, prickly on the edges. Rose, lilac, or whitish flowers in 1½-ft. spikes. July-Aug.

ACER. Maple. Among the best trees for autumn color. Prefer light soils but thrive elsewhere if soil is not waterlogged. Difficult to grow grass under most species because of the dense shade. They form girdling roots readily; examine soil at the base of trunk regularly and remove these roots if they form. Deciduous.

A. campestre. Hedge Maple. z 3-7. Round-headed tree, 50 ft. or more at maturity but can be kept lower by pruning. Excellent fall color. If allowed to fruit freely, does not live long.

A. circinatum. Vine Maple. z 5-7. Small, round-headed tree to 40 ft. Like *A. campestre,* but does better in uplands. Will tolerate lowland conditions. Beautiful fall color.

A. ginnala. Amur Maple. z 3-6. Shrub or tree to 20 ft. One of the better small trees. Excellent fall color.

A. japonicum. Full-moon Maple. z 7-9. To 15 ft. Not to be confused with *A. palmatum,* the true Japanese maple. A smaller plant. The variety *A. j. filicifolium* is beautifully cut; *A. j. aureum* is yellow-leaved until midsummer. All turn rich red in autumn.

A. macrophyllum. Oregon Maple. z 7-9. From Vancouver to southern California, this is one of the best street and shade trees. To 100 ft. Deep green, leathery foliage to 1 ft. across, turning yellow or orange in the fall. Fragrant flowers in drooping racemes.

A. negundo. Box-elder. z 2-8. A messy tree to 70 ft., harboring a disagreeable striped beetle that invades houses. Only virtue is that it will grow anywhere, even on the Great Plains.

A. palmatum. Japanese Maple. z 6-9. This small, highly ornamental species is one of the finest of all tall shrubs or small trees; to 20 ft. Many different leaf shapes and colors; outstanding fall color. Numerous horticultural varieties.

A. pensylvanicum. Striped Maple, Moosewood. z 2-4. Conspicuous green bark, striped white, striking in winter. To 35 ft. Grows only in cool regions.

A. platanoides. Norway Maple. z 4-8. A dense-foliaged tree, widely planted for street use but casts such dense shade that grass cannot grow under it. To 100 ft. Many interesting forms such as globe-headed, pyramidal, and purple- or maroon-leaved. Dull yellow in autumn.

A. pseudo-platanus. Sycamore Maple. z 5-8a. Somewhat less compact than the preceding. To 100 ft. at maturity.

A. rubrum. Red or Swamp Maple. z 3-9. A well-grown specimen becomes a torch of red-and-gold fire in autumn. To 120 ft. A desirable street and landscape tree.

A. saccharinum. Silver Maple. z 4b-9. The leaves have a striking silvery reverse. To 120 ft. Cut-leaf form is popular, but wood too brittle for a street or shade tree.

A. saccharum. Sugar Maple. z 4-8. An excellent street tree. To 120 ft. Outstanding fall color.

A. spicatum. Mountain Maple. z 3-5. Really a tall shrub, to 20 ft. Brilliant fall color.

A. tataricum. Siberian Maple. z 4-6.

Tree or shrub to 20 ft. Another valuable small tree for modern houses. Bright yellow in autumn.

ACHILLEA. Yarrow. Hardy perennials. *A ageratifolia.* Aizoon. z 3-9a. A desirable rock-garden plant, 6-8 in. tall, with tufted silver foliage, white flowers. Summer.

A. ageratum. Golden or Sweet Yarrow. z 4-9a. Dome-shaped heads of small clustered yellow flowers on stems that grow 12-24 in. high. July-Aug.

A. argentea. See *A. clavennae.*

A. clavennae. Silver Yarrow. z 4-9a. Prostrate rock plant to 1 ft., with grayish foliage, deeply cut leaves. White flowers June-July.

A. filipendulina. Fernleaf Yarrow, Golden Yarrow. z 3-9a. Showy clusters of yellow flowers on 3-ft. stems. Considered a weed, but a desirable garden species where it fits in. The flowers can be dried for winter bouquets. Aromatic foliage, sometimes dried as an herb. The variety *A. f. roseum* is widely grown for its rose-red flowers on 18-in. stems. Summer.

A. millefolium. Milfoil, Common Yarrow. z 3-9a. Normally white-flowered, but rose-colored and pink forms are available. Although weedy, it is a satisfactory perennial. Aromatic foliage. Stems to 18 in. July.

A. moschata. Musk Yarrow. z 3-9a. A low-growing, tufted, rock-garden plant to 6 in. White flowers in spring.

A. ptarmica. Sneezewort, Milfoil. z 4-9a. The type has loose, wide flower heads but is seldom grown. Best known for several double-flowered varieties such as 'Boule de Neige' and 'The Pearl,' with dense heads of white flowers and aromatic foliage. Flowers most of the summer. To 24 in.

A. tomentosa. Woolly Yarrow. z 3-9a. Largely grown in rock gardens, but a good edging plant. To 12 in. Prefers sandy soil. Yellow flowers June-Sept.

ACHIMENES. A tender, rhizomatous plant. See Bulbs (Chapter 4).

ACIDANTHERA. *A. bicolor*. Summer-flowering cormous plant. See Bulbs (Chapter 4).

ACONITUM. Monkshood, Wolfbane. z 3-8. Herbaceous perennials with hooded flowers in shades of white, blue, or yellow on long spikes. Flowers late summer to early autumn. Fleshy, poisonous roots. Do not plant where children or animals can get at them. Rich soil with a pH of 5 to 6 and partial shade.

A. fischeri. A badly mixed species with many different plants sold under this name. Should have brilliant blue flowers Sept.-Oct. To 6 ft. White varieties are available. Best to check in bloom before planting in permanent location.

A. lycoctonum. Yellow Monkshood, Yellow Wolfbane. Color varies; creamy-yellow varieties are weak in color and should be avoided. Stems 4-6 ft.

A. napellus. Common Monkshood, Aconite. Blue flowers on 4-ft. spikes. White and pale blue varieties available. Very poisonous.

ACORUS. *A. calamus*. Sweet Flag. z 3-9. Marsh-loving plant of the arum family, with iris-like leaves, yellow-striped in one variety. For the bog garden.

ACTAEA. Baneberry. *A. alba*. White Baneberry, White Cohosh. z 3-7. Showy perennial with terminal clusters of white flowers in spring; to 18 in. Poisonous white berries with conspicuous black eye. Rich woodsy soil, but does not like acidity. Rock and wild gardens; borders.

A. rubra. Red Baneberry. z 3-7.

Like above, but with poisonous red berries.

A. spicata. Herb Christopher, Black Baneberry. Similar to preceding but with purplish black berries.

ACTINIDIA. *A. arguta*. Bower Arguta, Tara Vine. z 4-8. A dense-foliaged tall woody vine with spotted white flowers ¾ in. across. Yellowish edible fruit.

A. polygama. Silver Vine. z 4-8. Not to be confused with silver lace vine. Variegated foliage gives it this common name. Like preceding, but fruit is bitter.

ADENOPHORA. *A. communis*. See *A. lilifolia*.

A. lamarcki. Mountain Gland Bellflower. z 5-8. Flowers similar to a campanula on 20-in. stems. A rare blue rock species from Transylvania. Propagate all adenophoras by seeds or cuttings in spring. Use care with roots.

A. lilifolia. Ladybell, Gland Bellflower. z 5-8. Fragrant, pale blue bell-shaped flowers 1¼ in. long in pyramidal panicles. To 3 ft. Perennial blooming in summer.

ADIANTUM. *A. pedatum*. American Maidenhair Fern. z 4-8. One of America's best-loved ferns. Prefers lightly shaded woodsy soil. Finely divided leaves to 1½ ft. Black stems.

ADLUMIA. *A. fungosa*. Allegheny Vine, Mountain Fumitory, Mountain Fringe. z 5-9. A biennial but self-seeds freely. Daintily cut leaves much like those of bleeding-heart. White or purplish flowers, ½ in. long in panicles. Summer. Prefers shady, slightly acid woodsy soil.

ADONIS. *A. amurensis*. Amur Floss Flower. z 5-8. Perennial. Golden yellow flowers in May, 2 in. across, sometimes double. To 18 in. Needs a rich, loamy soil.

A. annua. Pheasant Eye, Floss Flower. Annual from seed, to 18 in. Bright red cupped flowers ¾ in. across with darker center. June-July.

A. vernalis. Spring Ox-eye, Spring Adonis. z 5-8. Perennial to 10 in. Yellow flowers to 3 in. across in May. Useful rock-garden plant. Also white and double-flowered varieties.

AEGOPODIUM. *A. podagraria.* Bishop's Weed, Goutweed, z 4-8. A rampant perennial weed, but invaluable as a groundcover for problem places where few other plants will grow. Commonest form is *A. p. variegatum,* with white-and-green leaves. To 8 in. Mowing occasionally will keep it neat. Can be killed with Silvex (2,4,5-TP) if it gets out of hand.

AESCULUS. Horse Chestnut, Buckeye. Desirable deciduous shade trees for the open lawn, but most kinds not suited to streets because of the messy fruits.

A. carnea. Red Horse Chestnut. z 4-8. A hybrid between *A. hippocastanum* and *A. pavia* with 8-in. panicles of pale pink to rosy-red flowers in May. To 40 ft.

A. glabra. Ohio Buckeye. z 4-8. Its fruits are a folklore remedy for rheumatism if carried in the pocket. To 30 ft. Greenish yellow flowers in 6-in. panicles are less conspicuous than those of the true horse chestnut.

A. hippocastanum. Horse Chestnut. z 3b-10. A majestic tree, to 100 ft., covered in May or June with 8-in. spikes of hyacinth-like white flowers. The variety *A. h. baumanni* has double flowers and does not produce the objectionable fruits of the single form. The famous street tree of Paris.

A. parviflora. Bottlebrush Buckeye. z 5-6. A shrub, coarse and somewhat weedy, to 12 ft. White spiky flowers Aug.-Sept. Desirable in the wild garden.

A. pavia. Red Buckeye. z 5-6. Small tree or tall shrub to 20 ft. with bright red flowers.

AETHIONEMA. *A. coridifolium.* Lebanon Stone Cress. z 5-8. Perennial 4-10 in. tall, bushy with blue-gray leaves and clusters of pinkish to lilac-pink flowers in May or June. Desirable rock-garden plant; prefers alkaline soils. 'Warley Rose' is a variety superior in color.

A. grandiflorum. Persian Stone Cress, Persian Candytuft. z 5-8. Perennial to 14 in. Like above except for size.

AGAPANTHUS. *A. africanus* (*A. umbellatus*). Blue Lily-of-the-Nile, African Lily. z 9-10. See Bulbs (Chapter 4).

AGAVE. A large genus (over 300 species). z 9-10. Succulent and semi-desert plants. About the only species widely grown is *A. americana,* the century plant or American aloe (it is not an aloe). Trunkless leaves 5 ft. long. Flower stalk produced only after 15-20 years. Used as tub plant in the North. Many other species deserve attention from some specialist for use in southwestern gardens. Propagated by seeds and suckers.

AGERATUM. *A. houstonianum.* Garden Ageratum, Floss Flower. z 8-10. Grown as an annual in North but is a tender perennial. Propagated by seeds and cuttings. Slow from seed. Feathery balls of tiny blue flowers in abundance make this a popular edging plant. 'Fairy Pink' is really a dull pinkish blue. White varieties are dull. Up to 14 in.

AGLAONEMA. *A. modestum* (*A. simplex*). Chinese Evergreen, Chinese

Water Plant. A soft-stemmed tender perennial to 3 ft., grown as a foliage house plant. Old plants often flower.

AILANTHUS. *A. altissima.* Tree of Heaven, Stink Tree. z 5-9. Widely publicized as a rare and valuable shade tree but actually an arboreal weed. Will grow practically anywhere in any soil, its one virtue. Soft, punky wood. Compound leaves like those of a walnut. To 60 ft. or more. Odor of male flowers is obnoxious. Can become a pest as it sprouts from every root injury and seeds profusely. Deciduous.

AJUGA. *A. genevensis.* Geneva Bugle. z 5-9. Differs from the following in its taller flower spikes to 14 in. and the fact that it does not form runners.

A. reptans. Carpet Bugle. z 5-9. Whether this is a valuable groundcover or a pestiferous weed depends upon one's needs. Will quickly cover ground in almost full shade. Aggressive creeping perennial to 1 ft. Attractive spoon-shaped leaves and whorls of blue-violet flowers in spring. White- and pink-flowered forms are available. Varieties with unusually colored foliage are in commerce.

AKEBIA. *A. quinata.* Five-finger Vine. z 5-9. A desirable woody vine for shady places. Five-parted leaves and inconspicuous but fragrant purplish flowers in spring. Berries, seldom produced in the North, are edible. Night-flowering. Propagated by seeds, cuttings, root divisions. Requires sun and good drainage.

ALBIZZIA. *A. julibrissin.* Silk Tree, Pink Mimosa. z 7-10a. Plumy pink flowers like those of true mimosa on a deciduous tree not usually more than 30 ft. tall. Subject to the mimosa webworm, limiting its usefulness where this pest occurs. The variety *A. j. rosea* is handsomer and hardier.

A. lebbek. Woman's-tongue Tree, Lebbek Tree, Siris Tree, East Indian Walnut. z 10. Interesting greenish yellow flowers in axillary heads on a deciduous tree to 50 ft. Pods to 1 ft.

ALCHEMILLA. *A. alpina.* Alpine Lady's Mantle. z 4-9. A mat-forming perennial to 8 in. with silver foliage. Flowers, not conspicuous, in July.

A. vulgaris. Lady's Mantle. Like above, but with 15-in. spikes of greenish yellow flowers in July.

ALETRIS. *A. farinosa.* Star Grass, Colic Root. z 5-8. An acid-soil plant to 3 ft. that tolerates seaside conditions but only if soil is acid (pH 5.0). Grass-like foliage, tubular white flowers in slender spikes in July.

ALLIUM. Ornamental Onions. Relatives of the leek, onion, and garlic, with interesting flowers in ball-shaped heads. All of the following produce bulbs. Some are used in rock gardens. Most species are hardy North.

A. giganteum. Giant Garlic. z 5-9. Or farther north with protection. A spectacular ball of blue, 4 in. across or larger on stem to 4 ft. in midsummer. A real conversation piece.

A. karataviense. Rainbow Leek. z 5-8. Grown largely for its broad leaves like those of a tulip, blue-green veined with lilac-blue. Dull white flowers on 10-in. stems in globose umbels to 3 in. across.

A. moly. Lily Leek. z 5-9. Bright yellow ball-like umbel of flowers 3 in. across on 14-in. stems in July. The moly of classical fame.

A. schoenoprasum. Chives. z 4-9. An herb usually sown from seed but also propagated by dividing the clump. Grown in sunny windows for kitchen use. Its small globes of lilac flowers in July make it an interesting edging plant.

ALNUS. Alder. *A. vulgaris.* Black Alder. z 4-8. Although a tree to 80 ft. in the wild, usually grown as a clump at much lower height. A valuable landscape specimen, particularly in spring, with delicate, yet vivid green foliage. Grows well in moist places. Deciduous.

ALOE. *A. succotrina.* Perennial to 4 ft. Thick, succulent leaves with white margins; 1¼ in. long, red flowers.

A. variegata. See House Plants (Chapter 11).

ALONSOA. *A. acutifolia.* Maskflower. z 10. A bushy perennial to 3 ft., propagated by stock plants carried over in a greenhouse. Reddish-lipped flowers (there is a white) with mask-like markings. Pot plant, grown as annual in gardens.

ALPINIA. *A. speciosa.* Shellflower. z 8-10. To 12 ft. Leaves 2 ft. long. A member of the ginger family with showy, fragrant, orchid-like flowers, white tinged purple, with yellow lip variegated brown and red. An interesting greenhouse perennial.

ALSTROEMERIA. *A. aurantiaca.* Peruvian Lily. z 7-10 (farther North with protection). See Bulbs (Chapter 4).

ALTHAEA. *A. rosea.* Hollyhock. z 4-8. Tall (to 9 ft.). See Biennials (Chapter 2).

ALYSSUM. *A. alpestre.* Alpine Madwort. z 4-9a. Grayish mound, not over 4 in., with racemes of bright yellow flowers in late June or July. Perennial herb or subshrub for rock gardens and borders, in sun.

A. argenteum. Yellow Tuft. z 4-9a. To 15 in. Woolly, silvery leaves and deep yellow flowers, off and on all summer. Perennial.

A. maritimum (actually *Lobularia maritima,* but seldom so catalogued).

Sweet Alyssum. An annual to 1 ft. in the North; may survive winter south of z 9. White, pink, and lavender varieties. Perhaps the most widely used edging plant.

A. saxatile. Basket-of-gold, Gold Dust, Golden Tuft. z 4-9a. Popular perennial alyssum. Grayish leaves in dense mats bearing golden or citron-yellow flowers. April-May.

AMARANTHUS. *A. caudatus.* Love-lies-bleeding, Tassel Flower. Deep pinkish red "rat-tail" flowers on 3-ft. stems. A popular old-fashioned annual. Grows anywhere, but flowers are bigger in rich soil.

A. tricolor. Fountain Plant, Joseph's Coat. Bright-foliaged annual, 12-30 in. Grown mostly for foliage of green, yellow, and red. Several varieties available.

AMARYLLIS. *A. advena.* Oxblood Lily. See Bulbs (Chapter 4).

A. belladonna. Belladonna Lily. z 8-9. See Bulbs (Chapter 4).

Amaryllis hybrids. Sold as dormant bulbs in early winter, these bulbous plants produce huge saucer-shaped flowers on a tall, stout scape, in white, red, rose, and striped white-and-red. Flowering is erratic, except in specially prepared bulbs from Holland which flower for Christmas. Leaves may appear before, during, or after flowering on different varieties. Potted bulbs can be carried over summer outdoors and brought in for flowering again.

AMELANCHIER. *A. canadensis.* Shadblow. z 5-8. Its clouds of white flowers in April make this a favorite shrub or tree in northeastern U. S. To 40 ft., deciduous. Reddish purple edible but tasteless berries in July.

A. stolonifera. Dwarf Juneberry. z 3-6. A sprawling shrub to 4 ft. Forms large colonies by underground stems. Sweet berries used in jellies and jams.

Was an important food for American Indians. Prefers moist soil.

AMMOBIUM. *A. alatum.* Winged Everlasting. Bushy annual to 36 in. Conspicuous wings or flanges on stems. Silvery white composite flowers to 2 in. across. Can be dried for winter bouquets.

AMORPHA. *A. canescens.* Leadplant. z 3-5. One of the few summer-flowering shrubs with blue flowers. Hoary gray foliage, 6-in. flower spikes. To 3 ft. Prefers cool situation. Blooms July-Aug.

    A. fruticosa. Bastard Indigo. z 4-8. Shrub to 15 ft. Green foliage, dull bluish or purplish flowers in 6-in. clusters in June.

    A. nana. Dwarf Leadplant. z 2-6. A miniature version of *A. canescens.* To 1 ft.

AMPELOPSIS. *A. brevipedunculata.* Porcelain Creeper. z 5-8. Woody vine to 30 ft. Grown largely for exquisitely colored berries, lilac turning to porcelain blue in fall. Arbors, walls.

    A. japonica. Porcelain Creeper. z 6-9. Fruit similar to above, but plant tuberous-rooted.

AMSONIA. *A. tabernaemontana.* Blue Shadow. z 5-8. A stout perennial to 24 in. Blue funnel-shaped flowers ¾ in. long, few, in terminal clusters, May-June. Likes a cool, moist location.

AMYGDALUS. *A. communis.* Flowering Almond. z 6b-8. Tree to 25 ft. The nut-producing variety has several ornamental forms with pink or white flowers, 1½ in. across, some double. The name flowering almond is also applied to *Prunus glandulosa* and *P. triloba.*

    A. nana (Prunus nana). Dwarf Russian Almond. z 3-6. A shrub not over 4 ft. Snowy white or pink double flowers in spring.

ANAGALLIS. *A. arvensis.* Pimpernel, Poor-man's Weatherglass. Weedy, sprawling annual with white or red ¼-in. flowers that close in bad weather. May become a pest.

ANCHUSA. *A. azurea.* Alkanet, Bugloss. z 4-8. Sturdy perennial to 3 ft. or more. Brilliant blue flowers ¾ in. across, summer and autumn. Several cultivated varieties usually listed as *A. italica.*

    A. capensis. Cape Forget-me-not, Cape Alkanet. z 8-10. Biennial to 18 in. Blue flowers ¼ in. across, sometimes marked with red or white. Blooms in summer or fall. Pot plant.

ANDROMEDA. *A. glaucophylla.* Bog Rosemary, Gray Andromeda. z 1-4. Creeping broad-leaved evergreen shrub not over 12 in. Must have very acid soil. Small urn-shaped pinkish flowers May-June. Good bog plant. May be listed as *A. polifolia.*

ANDROSACE. *A. carnea.* Rock Jasmine. z 5-8. Rock-hugging perennial not over 3 in. White or rosy-pink flowers in tiny umbels in spring.

    A. lanuginosa. Silver Rock Jasmine. Like above, but with silver hairs. Pink flowers.

    A. sarmentosa. Himalayan Rock Jasmine. Like above, but 5 in. tall, spreading by runners. Woolly foliage. Rose-colored flowers, ¼ in. across. Clustered rock gardens, low borders.

ANEMONE. Windflower. z 3-8 except *A. japonica,* z 5-9. The name windflower is a misnomer; they do best in sheltered locations. Hardy perennials with white, rose, red, purplish flowers, 1-3 in. across, some fibrous-rooted, some tuberous. Like rich sandy loam. Wild borders, colonizing.

    A. alpina. Pasque Flower, Mountain Windflower. Roots tuberous, transplants poorly. To 8 in. Reddish purple or violet cup-shaped flowers, cream inside, to 3 in. across, in late May. Best raised from seed. A yellow form is rare.

A. *blanda*. Blue Windflower, Greek Anemone. Azure blue flowers on 6-in. stems. Tuberous rooted (tubers sold with other spring-flowering bulbs in fall). White and pink varieties are available.

A. *canadensis*. Meadow Anemone. Perennial to 2 ft. with 2-in. white flowers May-Aug. Not too showy but a good wildflower. Its creeping rootstocks may be a nuisance in the perennial border.

A. *coronaria*. Poppy Anemone, 'St. Brigid's' Anemone, 'De Caen' Anemone. See Bulbs (Chapter 4).

A. *hupehensis*. Dwarf Japanese Anemone. A lovely fall-flowering fibrous-rooted perennial with clusters of nodding pink or mauve flowers on 12- to 15-in. stems. Otherwise identical with A. *japonica*.

A. *japonica*. One of the finest fall-flowering perennials, from Sept. to frost on 2-ft. stems. Purple, red, rose, white flowers, to 3 in. across. Semi-double varieties last longer in flower.

A. *nemorosa*. European Wood Anemone. To 8 in. Cupped purple, white, or reddish violet solitary flowers 1 in. across, April-May.

A. *pulsatilla*. Pasque Flower. Blue, purple, or lilac upright bell-shaped flowers to 2½ in. across on 10-in. stems; silky-hairy leaves. April-blooming gem for the rock garden.

A. *quinquefolia*. American Wood Anemone, Windflower. White flowers, smaller than A. *nemorosa*, nodding like the bulbous snowdrop in May. A double form is in commerce.

A. *sylvestris*. Snowdrop Anemone. One or two fragrant white flowers 2 in. across in spring on a stem 8-18 in.

tall, the leaves three-parted. Rock garden.

A. *virginiana*. Tall Anemone. White or greenish flowers to 2½ in. across on 2-ft. stems. June-Aug. A wildflower.

ANEMONELLA. A. *thalictroides*. Rue Anemone. z 4-7. Perennial with white or pink flowers to 1 in. across in 8 in. terminal umbels. March-June. Delicately cut foliage. To 9 in. Needs woodsy soil in light shade.

ANETHUM. A. *graveolens*. Dill. An ancient Asiatic and Mediterranean herb, 2-3 ft., with finely cut leaves useful in salads. Clusters of small yellow flowers which yield the dill seeds of commerce. Grown as an annual.

ANGELICA. A. *archangelica*. Angelica. Stout biennial or perennial to 6 ft. Inconspicuous white or greenish flowers in terminal umbels. Quite fragrant. Stems used as base for making angelica candy.

ANTENNARIA. A. *dioica*. Pussy-toes. Furry Everlasting. Woolly foliage, ¼ - in. heads with white or rose bracts suggesting its common name. To 1 ft. Forms mats and may become a pest. Prefers open dry places and sandy soil. Perennial. A. *d. rosea* is a rose-colored variety.

ANTHEMIS. A. *nobilis*. Camomile. z 3-8. A somewhat weedy perennial to 1 ft., with aromatic foliage, sometimes used for tea. Finely cut leaves. Can be used as grass substitute for lawns. White ray flowers, 5 in. across on 12- in. stems. Double white and yellow forms available.

A. *tinctoria*. Golden Marguerite, Ox-eye Camomile, Yellow Camomile. z 5-8. Useful perennial with finely-cut fragrant foliage and 2-ft. stems of bright yellow flowers. The variety A. *t. kelwayi* has richer color and darker foliage July-Aug.

ANTHOXANTHUM. *A. odoratum.* Sweet Vernal Grass. Zone 5-8. Sweet smelling. To 2 ft.

ANTHRISCUS. *A. cerefolium.* Chervil, Salad Chervil. Annual herb, to 2 ft. combining flavors of parsley and celery. Deeply cut foliage. Widely used in French cookery.

ANTHURIUM. *A. scherzerianum.* Flamingo Flower. Tailflower. Greenhouse or house plant with striking leaf-like spathes, 3 in. long, red or rose. A tail-like spike drops from center of the spathe. Must have 60° or over at night to flower. Keep roots covered with soil, as they tend to work to surface of pot.

ANTHYLLIS. *A. montana.* Ladyfingers. z 4-7. Clover-like fragrant flowers in showy spikes, purple or pink, to 12 in., on plants with striking white-silky foliage. June. Perennial.

ANTIGONON. *A. leptopus.* Coral Vine, Confederate Vine, Mountain Rose. z 9-10. Climbs to 40 ft. in the South. Of easiest culture even in poor soils. Pink or white flowers in long drooping clusters.

ANTIRRHINUM. *A. majus.* Snapdragon. One of the most popular annuals. Dwarf types to 8 in., intermediate to 20 in., and tall to 36 in. (taller when grown as greenhouse cut flowers). Often a reliable perennial south of Ohio River if given light protection. In the North, fall sowing outdoors gives earlier bloom. Flowers rose, red, purple, yellow, and white; sac-shaped, 2-lipped, 1½ in. long in racemes.

APIOS. *A. tuberosa.* Ground Nut, Wild Bean, Potato Bean. z 5-8. Odd, pea-like brownish flowers in clusters in midsummer, with fragrance of violets. Vine to 8 ft. Tuberous roots were a favorite Indian food. Prefers sunny, sandy soil. Wild garden.

APOROCACTUS. *A. flagelliformis.* See House Plants (Chapter 11).

AQUILEGIA. Columbine. z 3-9a. A valuable group of fibrous-rooted perennials, the low-growing forms suitable for rock gardens. Petals and sepals generally of contrasting colors: white, blue, lavender, yellow, red. Most species have long spurs. Prefer light soils and an open situation. Resent too much water in summer after flowering. Propagated by division in spring.

A. alpina. Alpine Columbine. Long-spurred blue flowers, 2 in. wide on 10-in. stems. July-Aug. Rock gardens.

A. caerulea. Rocky Mountain Columbine, Long-spurred Columbine. Parent of most of the modern hybrids. To 3 ft. Originally bluish purple flowers to 2 in. across with long spurs in May-June. Hybrids of many colors: McKana hybrids are particularly fine.

A. canadensis. American Columbine. Clear yellow flowers with red spurs. Blooms in May on 12-18-in. stems. Does well in partial shade on woodsy soil. For garden.

A. chrysantha. Yellow Columbine. Showy, fragrant, all-yellow flowers on 2-ft. stems. Blooms May-Aug.

A. flabellata. Dwarf Fan Columbine. Lilac flowers on 15-in. stems, July-Aug. The variety *A. f. nana* is much shorter, with white flowers.

A. vulgaris. Common Columbine. With *A. caerulea*, parent of most garden hybrids. Original type blue, purple, or white on 2-ft. stems, June-July.

ARABIS. *A. albida.* Wall Rock Cress. z 5-8. A rock-garden perennial not over 1 ft. tall with downy whitish foliage. Fragrant white flowers to ½ in. long in loose racemes. April. Several garden varieties.

A. alpina. Alpine Rock Cress. Less downy and more slender than above. This and previous species confused and mixed in commerce.

A. aubretioides. z 5-8. A tufted, compact rock-garden plant with small felted white leaves and pink or purple flowers in May. Must have sharp drainage and sandy soil. A true alpine.

A. rosea (*A. muralis*). Rosy Rock Cress. z 5-8. Biennial to 10 in. Tufted hairy foliage and white or rosy flowers in spring.

ARALIA. *A. chinensis* (*A. elata*). Angelica Tree. z 6-10. Handsome thorny tree, to 25 ft. with long compound leaves. Large hairy white flower clusters in summer, glossy black fruit. There are varieties with white or golden variegated foliage.

A. nudicaulis. Wild Sarsaparilla. z 4-6. Perennial herb to 1 ft., surviving in almost pure sand and valuable for that reason. Inconspicuous ball-like clusters of greenish yellow flowers in summer.

A. spinosa. Devil's Walking-stick, Hercules Club. z 5-8. Like *A. chinensis* but with heavier thorns. Planted closely, forms impenetrable barrier hedge. Whitish flowers in panicles to 4 ft. long.

ARAUCARIA. Tender evergreens related to the pines. Tall trees in Florida and California. Often grown as pot plants in north. Large woody cones, scale-like, overlapping leaves.

A. araucana. Monkey Puzzle. z 7b-10. The hardiest species. Interesting stout spiny leaves and odd twisting growth. Resistant to salt spray. To 100 ft.

A. bidwilli. Bunya Bunya. z 9-10. Similar to above but less hardy. To 150 ft.

A. cunninghami. Moreton Bay Pine, Hoop Pine. Somewhat less stiff than two preceding species. To 150 ft. Resistant to salt spray.

A. excelsa. Norfolk Island Pine. z 10. Perhaps the araucaria most commonly grown as a pot plant. Use only erect tips for cuttings or resultant plants will not grow straight. To 200 ft. in frost-free areas. Also a valuable timber tree. Resistant to salt spray.

ARBUTUS. *A. menziesi.* Madrona, Oregon Laurel. z 8-10. Striking tree to 100 ft. Grows only on West Coast from British Columbia to California. Handsome white flowers in erect 6-in. clusters in May, followed by bright orange fruits.

A. unedo. Strawberry Tree. z 8-10. Similar to preceding, but not over 30 ft. Difficult in dry sections: does not like humidity. Flowers white or pinkish, 1/3 in. long, in 2-in. clusters in fall. Insipid, but edible, strawberry-like fruits.

ARCTOSTAPHYLOS. *A. uva-ursi.* Bearberry, Kinnikinnick. z 3-5. Evergreen shrub. Running stems often 6 ft. long, rooting at joints. Small pinkish or white wing-shaped flowers in terminal clusters. Evergreen foliage turns bronze in fall. Must have acid soil, sandy and well drained. Difficult to transplant. Groundcover. Ornamental.

ARCTOTIS. *A. grandis* (*A. stoechadifolia*). African Daisy. Woolly-leaved annual to 2 ft. with white or pale blue ray flowers in heads to 3 in. across. Hybrids with wider color range, including red and yellow, are available.

ARDISIA. *A. crispa.* Coralberry, Coral Ardisia. z 8b-10a. Subtropical shrub, also grown as greenhouse plant for Christmas. Bright 1/4-in. coral-red berries lasting longer than those of holly. To 1 ft.

ARENARIA. *A. balearica.* Corsican Sandwort. z 5-8. Thick, glossy green, oval but tiny leaves on a creeper only 3 in. tall make this an outstanding rock-garden plant. Small white flowers are unimportant. Needs moisture during summer months.

A. *grandiflora.* European Sandwort. z 5-8. Somewhat more upright than preceding (to 10 in.) with longer, silvery leaves. Flowers larger. Otherwise identical.

A. *montana.* Alpine Sandwort. z 4-8. Like a narrow-leaved A. *balearica,* to 4 in., otherwise similar.

ARETHUSA. A. *bulbosa.* Dragon's Mouth, Wild Pink. z 3-5. Interesting bulbous-rooted bog orchid with solitary leaf and solitary 2-in. flower, rose-purple with fringed yellow lip, hooded. To 10 in. Soil pH 4.5 to 5.0.

ARGEMONE. A. *mexicana.* Mexican Poppy. Large orange or yellow flowers like Oriental poppies, 2 in. across, on 3-ft. stems. Seeds narcotic and purgative, especially when smoked with tobacco. Sale prohibited in some states, but a beautiful garden flower. Grown as an annual of easiest culture. Plants need room; space 2 ft. apart.

A. *platyceras.* Crested Poppy, Prickly Poppy. Leaves and stems prickly, bluish gray. Flowers on 3-ft stems, usually white, sometimes purple, to 2 in. across.

ARIOCARPUS. A. *retusus.* See House Plants (Chapter 11).

ARISAEMA. A. *triphyllum.* Jack-in-the-pulpit, Indian Turnip. z 4-8. The familiar arum of rich, moist woods with pulpit-like spathe. Perennial to 3 ft. Roots, when heated to drive off astringent taste, were eaten by American Indians, but are too acrid for present-day taste. For wild gardens.

ARISTOLOCHIA. A. *durior.* Dutchman's Pipe, Pipe Vine. z 4b-9. Sometimes catalogued as A. *sipho.* Vigorous, woody, hardy vine to 30 ft., with large heart-shaped leaves that cast complete shade. If used on wooden structures, should be cut to the ground every fourth year to permit examination of wood's condition, as rot often develops under this vine. Interesting curved yellowish green flowers, to 3 in. long, the "pipes" of its name.

A. *elegans.* Calico Flower. Popular greenhouse vine related to above but tender. Flowers more conspicuous, spotted purple and brown.

ARMERIA. Thrift. Sea Pink. Often listed in catalogs as statice. A. *maritima.* Common Thrift. z 4-8. Perennial to 1 ft. Narrow leaves in a tufted rosette. White or rose-purple flowers in globular heads 1 in. across. May-June.

ARONIA. A. *arbutifolia.* Red Chokeberry. z 4-9a. A clean-foliaged shrub of wide usefulness. To 8 ft. Grows on practically any soil. Showy white flowers in terminal clusters in early spring, red berries in fall. The variety A. a. *brilliantissima* is in commerce.

A. *melanocarpa.* Black Chokeberry. z 4-8. Lower-growing than above (to 4 ft.), with black fruits.

ARTEMISIA. A. *abrotanum.* Southernwood. Divided greenish gray aromatic foliage. Perennial to 4 ft. Flowers yellowish white, not conspicuous.

A. *absinthium.* Wormwood, Absinthe Plant. z 4-9. Silky white leaves, yellowish flowers. To 3 ft. The herb used to flavor the liquor absinthe. Perennial.

A. *albula.* Silver King Artemisia. z 4-9. Perhaps the most widely planted of this genus. Perennial to 3 ft., striking silvery foliage, good for drying.

A. *canadensis.* Wild Wormwood, Sea Wormwood. z 4-9. Perennial to 2 ft. Largely grown in seaside and wild gardens.

A. dracunculus. Tarragon, Estragon. z 5-9. The flavoring plant from which tarragon vinegar is made. Ornamental qualities unimportant. Perennial.

A. stelleriana. Beach Wormwood, Dusty Miller. Old Woman. z 4-8. Interesting white woolly foliage. To 2 ft. Grows well in sand and near the sea. Good tall groundcover. Yellow flowers in summer.

ARUNCUS. *A. sylvester* (*A. dioicus*). Goatsbeard. z 4-8. Produces spire-like white flowers in clusters on stems to 7 ft. tall. Perennial. Partially shaded moist soil. June-July.

ASARUM. *A. canadense.* Wild Ginger. z 2-4. Low spreading perennial with kidney-shaped leaves, to 8 in. Needs light shade and soil that is constantly moist (but never waterlogged) and high in humus. An ideal groundcover in moist woods. Flowers purple-brown, hidden close to ground. April-May.

A. caudatum. z 7-9. A western species hardy only in moist coastal areas of northwest Pacific.

ASCLEPIAS. *A. tuberosa.* Butterfly Weed, Orange Milkweed, Pleurisy Root. z 3-8. Brilliant orange flowers in clusters in Aug.-Sept. Rough hairy foliage. Perennial, to 3 ft.

A. verticillata. Whorled Milkweed, Horsetail Milkweed. z 4-8. To 2 ft. Greenish white flowers. Perennial. Useful in wild garden, largely for ornamental seed pods in fall.

ASPARAGUS. *A. plumosus.* Fern Asparagus. Not a fern, but delicate fernlike foliage with leaves reduced to scales, used by florists as filler. A dainty house plant, tall and climbing. Used as a groundcover in the South. Propagation a specialist's job; buy started plants.

A. sprengeri. Emerald Feather. A 6-ft. climber, similar to above but with wider leaflets. Best as a hanging-basket vine or for porch boxes.

ASPERULA. *A. odorata.* Sweet Woodruff. z 5-8. A low-growing, fragrant perennial (to 8 in.) much used as a groundcover. Dried leaves added to May wine. Prefers shade and moist soil. Flowers white.

A. orientalis (*A. azurea setosa*). Blue Woodruff. Low-growing, spreading annual (to 1 ft.), easily grown from seed. An ideal temporary groundcover. Tolerates shade but does not bloom there. Flowers blue in forked clusters.

ASPHODELINE. *A. lutea.* Jacob's Rod, Asphodel. z 5-9. The classic asphodel of the Greeks. Perennial with fleshy roots and flower stems. To 30 in. Fragrant yellow flowers 1 in. long, in finger-shaped clusters. June.

ASPHODELUS. *A. albus.* Asphodel. z 5-8. Similar to above, but with white flowers. June.

ASPIDISTRA. *A. elatior.* Cast-iron Plant. A house plant so tough "only a florist can kill it." In z 8-10 sometimes used as a foliage plant for edging. Stiff, wide, lance-shaped dark green leaves. To 2½ ft.

ASPLENIUM. *A. nidus.* Bird's-nest Fern. Its undivided fronds curl to form the typical bird's nest. Bright green foliage. House plant; hardy out-of-doors in z 10.

A. ruta-muraria. Wall Rue, Wall Spleenwort. z 5-8. A native fern for planting in crevices of rock walls; otherwise of little ornamental value. To 6 in.

ASTER. Annual asters belong under callistephus, which see. True asters are mostly perennial. As garden subjects, appreciated in England long before they were in America, their native home. Some outstanding low fall-flowering varieties were bred in England. All are plants of the open border, thriving in good garden soil. Division every other year is advised to keep clumps from deteriorating.

A. *alpinus.* Alpine Aster, Rock Aster. z 4-9a. Less than 10 in. tall, with blue, rose, white, or violet flowers in May. Needs good drainage.

A. *amellus.* Italian Starwort. z 5-9. One of the few good asters of European origin. To 18 in. Rough leaves. Purple to deep purple flowers in Aug.

A. *cordifolius.* Blue Wood Aster. z 3-6. One aster that thrives in partial shade. To 4 ft. Much branched. Violet or blue flowers. Late summer.

A. *divaricatus.* White Wood Aster. z 3-6. Possibly only a variety of the above.

A. *ericoides.* Heath Aster. z 4-8. Tiny white ray flowers in clusters, that, in masses, resemble white heather. To 3 ft. Good wild-garden subject.

A. *laevis.* Smooth Aster. z 3-9. Blue or violet flowers 1 in. across in large heads on 4-ft. stems. Many garden varieties available. One of the few asters thriving in the South.

A. *novae-angliae.* New England Aster, Michaelmas Daisy. z 3b-8. A favorite perennial in England where many fine named varieties originated. White, pink, red, purple, blue, and lavender flowers. Wide range in height — 8-60 in. — depending on variety. Aug.-Sept.

A. *novi-belgi.* New York Aster. z 3b-8. Bluish violet flowers 1 in. across on 2-ft. stems in Aug.-Sept. A number of named varieties.

A. *sericeus.* Silvery Aster. z 3-9b. Much-branched, with interesting silvery foliage. Violet-blue flowers 1½ in. across on 2-ft. stems. Late-summer flowering.

ASTILBE. False Spirea. (Spirea is a common name applied to a confused group of plants, some belonging to aruncus or spiraea; note spelling difference between botanical and common names.) Useful because they thrive under difficult conditions including shade and city smoke. Perennials, with tough woody stems.

A. *chinensis.* Chinese False Goatsbeard. z 5-8. Flowers in slender panicles, white, tinged rose. July-Aug. Useful for naturalizing. To 2 ft.

A. *davidi.* Florists Spirea. z 6-9. Showy panicles of rose flowers on stems 12-20 in. tall in summer (or forced for spring bloom). Many named varieties in commerce with white, cerise-red, or purplish flowers.

A. *japonica,* Japanese False Goatsbeard. z 5-8. Much like A. *chinensis,* but with denser flower panicles. To 3 ft.

ASTROPHYTUM. See House Plants (Chapter 11).

ASYSTASIA. A. *coromandeliana.* Coromandel. z 9-10. A creeping groundcover for warmer parts of Florida and California. White or purple tubular flowers, 1 in. or more long in 6-in. racemes. Can be made to climb to 4 ft.

ATHYRIUM. A. *filix-femina.* Lady Fern, Female Fern. z 5-7. Bright green leaves, 3 ft. long. An easy-to-grow fern for shady places. Several horticultural forms.

A. *thelypteroides.* Silvery Spleenwort. z 5-7. Sometimes catalogued as A. *acrostichoides.* To 30 in. tall. Useful in shady woods.

AUBRIETA. A. *deltoidea.* Purple Rock Cress, Rock Mustard. z 5-8b. Mat-forming perennial 3-6 in. Purple, violet or pink flowers in June. Thrives in border or rock garden.

AUCUBA. A. *japonica.* Gold-dust

Tree, Japanese Laurel. z 7b-10a. Evergreen shrub grown for its attractive glossy foliage and scarlet berries (produced only on female plants). The gold-dust tree is a form with spotted yellow leaves. To 10 ft., but often grown as pot plant. Prefers half-shade and moist soil.

AZALEA. Although botanists classify azaleas as rhododendrons, in horticulture they are usually separated. Azaleas have thinner leaves, sometimes deciduous, sometimes evergreen, with thinner-petaled flowers than rhododendrons. Covered in detail in Chapter 17.

AZARA. *A. microphylla.* Chilean Wall Vine. z 8-10. Actually a sprawling shrub rather than a vine, clambering over walls. To 12 ft. Clusters of small, inconspicuous but fragrant greenish yellow flowers in late winter. Orange berries.

BABIANA. *B. stricta.* Baboon Flower, z 9-10. See Bulbs (Chapter 4).

BACCHARIS. *B. halimifolia.* Groundsel Bush. z 5-8. Shrub growing largely in brackish marshes; useful near the sea. Will grow in open sun in ordinary soil. Six to 10 ft. tall. Small fuzzy white flowers in clusters. Fruits white.

BAPTISIA. *B. australis.* Blue False Lupine, False Indigo, Wild Indigo. z 5-8. Perennial. Lupine-like flowers in June, indigo-blue. Full sun on rather poor light soil. To 6 ft.

B. tinctoria. Clover Broom. Yellow False Lupine, Yellow False Indigo. z 5-8. Similar to above. Yellow flowers. To 3 ft.

BEGONIA. Except for *Begonia evansiana* (hardy to z 7), these are tender plants either grown as house plants or, in summer, as bedding plants. Some have fibrous roots, others tuberous. All have soft, succulent stems and can-not tolerate dry conditions. A moist, loamy soil in partial shade is best for all grown outdoors. Fibrous-rooted bedding types are often grown from cuttings, but are easy from seed.

B. coccinea. Angel-wing Begonia. A large plant with long wing-like leaves and coral-red flowers.

B. evansiana. Hardy Begonia. z 7. Flower stems to 18 in., large single pink flowers. Has survived zero weather in southern Ohio and in Washington, D.C. Tuberous.

B. feasti. Beefsteak Begonia. A thick hairy-edged leaf on a plant often seen in barber shops and old-fashioned kitchens. Flowers light pink, but not important. So easy to propagate, few florists stock it. Rhizomatous.

B. heracleifolia. Star Begonia. Hairy creeping stems with coarse leaves on long stalks. Leaves roughly star-shaped. White or rose flowers to 1 in. across. Reliable house plant, 2-4 ft. Rhizomatous.

B. metallica. Bronze-leaf Begonia. Leaves with interesting metallic sheen, rich green with pale reverse. Leaf stems quite hairy. Flower stems 2 ft. with clusters of profuse pink flowers.

B. rex. Rex Begonia, King Begonia, Beefsteak Begonia. The plants in commerce are not the true species, but a mixture which Bailey classifies as *B. rex-cultorum.* A bewildering group with many varieties, some of considerable beauty with green, purple, gray, blue, or bronze foliage.

B. semperflorens. Fibrous-rooted Begonia, Wax Begonia, Ever-flowering Begonia. The florist's bedding begonia, grown in vast numbers for reliable bedding in shade. Many hybrids, ranging from 6 in. to 2 ft. Waxy, glossy leaves of bright green, bronze, or red. White, pink, and carmine flowers. Certain winter-flowering types grown only in the greenhouse, such as 'Chatelaine,' 'Cincinnati,' and 'Gloire de Lorraine.' These are specialists' plants, not for the amateur.

B. tuberhybrida. Tuberous Begonia. See Bulbs. (Chapter 4).

BELLIS. *B. perennis.* English Daisy, Bachelor Button (in England). See Biennials (Chapter 2).

BELOPERONE. *B. guttata.* Shrimp Plant. Interesting long fingers of dull orange with overlapping scales like a shrimp's shell make up the flowers. Tender. Good house plant. To 1½ ft.

BENZOIN. *B. aestivale.* Spicebush, Benjamin Bush, Spicewood. z 4-8. Botanists class this as *Lindera benzoin,* but present name is preferred in commerce. Aromatic deciduous shrub to 12 ft. (usually lower) with small yellow flowers before leaves. Fruit scarlet. Lovely yellow fall color. Tolerates partial shade and city conditions.

BERBERIS. Barberry. An interesting group of shrubs, usually spiny and used as barrier plants. Some cannot be sold because they are alternate hosts of wheat rust. Only those which can be legally sold are listed here. Berries not palatable, but eaten by birds in winter when other fruits are gone.

B. aggregata. Salmon Barberry. z 6-10. Densely branched shrub, deciduous, to 8 ft. Salmon-colored berries in fall. Horticultural varieties available. Excellent hedge plant.

B. buxifolia. Magellan Barberry. z 7-9. To 8 ft., the variety *B. b. nana* to 4 ft., variety *B. b. pigmaea* to 3 ft. Evergreen shrub with orange-yellow flowers and purple berries, mostly grown along the Pacific coast.

B. darwini. Darwin's Barberry. z 8-9a. Striking evergreen to 6 ft. Golden yellow flowers in long clusters, unusual for a barberry. Fruits dark purple.

B. julianae. Wintergreen Barberry. z 5b-10a. The hardiest evergreen barberry; survives but foliage may burn as far north as z 5. Dark glossy leaves, dark bluish berries with conspicuous bloom. To 6 ft.

B. koreana. Korean Barberry. z 6-9. Distinct from, but no better than, *Berberis thunbergi.* Somewhat coarser plant and less hardy. Deciduous.

B. mentorensis. Mentor Barberry. z 4b-9. A hybrid between *B. julianae* and *B. thunbergi.* In z 4-6 it is deciduous, farther south it is evergreen. Forms a stiff, impenetrable hedge 3-5 ft. tall. Tolerates drought.

B. thunbergi. Japanese Barberry. z 3-10a. Next to privet, the most commonly planted deciduous hedge. Tolerates city conditions. Arching branches to 6 ft. Tolerates shearing. Brilliant autumn color. Variety *B. t. erecta* (true-hedge barberry) is stiffly upright. Variety *B. t. minor* (box barberry) is an excellent low-growing substitute for boxwood.

B. vernae. Coral Barberry. z 6-10. Dense, compact deciduous shrub to 6 ft. Coral-colored fruit.

B. wilsonae. 'Tom Thumb' Barberry. z 7-9. Evergreen, sprawling, sometimes partially erect shrub. May scramble to 6 ft. Not fully rust-resistant, but sometimes planted.

BERGENIA. *B. cordifolia.* Siberian Saxifrage. z 5-9. Its thick, fleshy, tropical-looking leaves belie its Siberian name. Clusters of large bright pink flowers partially hidden by the leaves. A coarse but interesting perennial, to 20 in., which usually draws attention. May.

BETULA. Birch. *B. lenta.* Sweet Birch, Black Birch, Cherry Birch. z 4-6. Aromatic bark used as wintergreen flavoring. Symmetrical tree to 75 ft. Deciduous.

B. maximowicziana. Monarch Birch. z 6-7. A striking tree to 100 ft. with flaking bark. Deciduous.

B. nigra. River Birch, Red Birch. In spite of its botanical name, it is seldom called black birch, a name applied to two other species. Grows 60-80 ft. Needs a moist soil. Except for its value as a bird tree, of little interest.

B. papyrifera. Canoe Birch, Paper Birch, White Birch. z 2-6. This is the most popular of all birches, usually planted in clumps of three to five stems. Difficult to keep alive south of z 4 because it is attacked by bronze birch-bark borers. Best on soil continuously damp; lowering of water table causes this tree to "stag head" or die off at the top. To 100 ft.

B. pendula. European White Birch. z 3-8. Similar to the above and equally touchy. The weeping form is lovely where it survives. To 60 ft.

B. populifolia. Gray Birch. z 4b-7a. Often substituted for *B. papyrifera,* but a poorer tree. Bark beautiful when young but matures quickly to a dull gray. It is useful for rough stony land where little else grows, and as bird cover. To 30 ft.

BIGNONIA. *B. capreolata.* Cross Vine, Trumpet Flower. z 7-10a. Vigorous summer-flowering vine with beautiful coral-orange, trumpet-shaped flowers 2 in. long in heavy clusters. Sometimes kills back on new growth in North. Sometimes grown north of z 7, where it is root-hardy, but bloom is too sparse on new wood to do it justice. Evergreen in South.

B. venusta. Flame Vine, Roof-on-fire. z 9-10. Botanically, *Pyrostegia ignea,* but listed under present name in most catalogs. Next to bougainvillea, the most striking of all tropical vines. Like the preceding, but larger flowers of more brilliant color. Flowers off and on during the year.

BILLBERGIA. *B. nutans.* Air Plant. Leaves 1½ ft. long, ½ in. wide. An interesting house plant with drooping green flowers edged blue, with scarlet bracts. If grown indoors the year round, needs extra moisture in summer but can tolerate ordinary houseplant culture in winter.

BOCCONIA. *B. cordata.* Plume Poppy, Tree Celandine. z 5-8. Another victim of botanical juggling, now *Macleaya cordata,* but never so catalogued. A striking perennial to 6 ft. Long, foamy, plumy white flowers. Valuable as background in perennial borders. July-Aug.

BOLTONIA. *B. asteroides.* Giant Aster, False Camomile, Thousand-flowered Aster, False Starwort. z 4-8. Bold perennial 4-8 ft. tall with large heads of white starry flowers, sometimes tinged lilac or purple, late summer to early fall. May become weedy if it self-seeds. Rear-of-the-border species.

BORAGO. *B. officinalis.* Borage. Hairy-leaved hardy annual with fragrant, vivid blue flowers (some white or purple) late summer to early fall. To 2 ft. Excellent bee plant. Used as pot herb for cucumber-like flavor.

BORONIA. *B. elatior.* Boronia. z 10. Evergreen shrub to 4 ft. with intensely fragrant or aromatic flowers ½ in. long which vary on the same plant from white, through purple to rose, red, and blue. A greenhouse plant in the North.

BOTRYCHIUM. *B. dissectum.* Cutleaf Grape Fern, Moonwort, z 3-7. Fern to 18 in. tall in open woods, but not where soil is strongly acid. Spores borne in clusters like grapes. The variety *B. d. obliquum* has broader leaf segments.

B. virginianum. Rattlesnake Fern. z 3-8. Like above but more variable in height, to 2½ ft. Useful as ground-cover in shady woods.

BOUGAINVILLEA. *B. spectabilis.* z 10. The most glorious of all vines for warmer sections with great billows of brilliant, papery bracts in orange, cerise, crimson, mauve, and purple surrounding the inconspicuous flowers in late winter and spring. Sometimes almost too vivid. Tall growing; often covers trees and low buildings. The species *B. glabra* flowers most of the year, but the flowers are less interesting.

BOUSSINGAULTIA. *B. baselloides.* Madeira Vine, Mignonette Vine. z 9-10. Tall-growing creeper with fleshy tubers. North of z 7 grown as tender vine; tubers stored for the winter. Flowers have the odor of mignonette, white in drooping clusters sometimes 1 ft. long. They fade to sooty gray as they age. Tiny bulb-like tubercles that form in the leaf axils will produce new plants if rooted in damp sand.

BOUVARDIA. *B. humboldti.* Bouvardia. Shrub grown in greenhouses (a favorite wedding flower), and sometimes as a house plant. Intensely fragrant white tubular flowers 2½ in. long and half as wide. Grows 2-4 ft.

BRACHYCHITON. *B. acerifolium.* Flame Tree, Bottle Tree. z 9-10. Brilliant scarlet flowers make this one of the most striking trees in Florida and southern California. To 60 ft. Flowers in midsummer, then drops all its leaves. Shining black fruits to 4 in. across.

B. populneum. Kurrajong, Bottle Tree. Similar to above but with yellowish white flowers stained red within, smaller fruit. To 60 ft.

BRACHYCOME. *B. iberidifolia.* Swan River Daisy. Tender annual to 18 in. Slender plants with daisy-like flowers 1 in. across in blue, sometimes white or pink.

BRIZA. *B. maxima.* Quaking Grass. Ornamental annual grass to 2 ft. with pendulous bronze spikelets in late summer.

BRODIAEA. *B. uniflora.* Triplet Lily, Spring Starflower. z 8-10. See Bulbs (Chapter 4).

BROUSSONETIA. *B. papyrifera.* Paper Mulberry. z 6-9. A tree to 50 ft. but usually lower. Some fascinating gnarled old specimens in colonial Williamsburg. Widely used because of its ability to stand salt air and poor soil. Can be a nuisance if it suckers.

BROWALLIA. *B. speciosa.* Sapphire Flower. A much-neglected annual with vivid sapphire-blue petunia-like flowers 2 in. across; a better flower than the blue petunias now in commerce. Tolerates partial shade. Makes an excellent house plant. Can be propagated from cuttings.

BRUNNERA. *B. macrophylla.* Siberian Forget-me-not. z 4-8. Sometimes listed as *Anchusa myosotidiflora.* Short-lived perennial with blue flowers like forget-me-nots, ¼ in. across in showy clusters on 18-in. stems. May.

BUDDLEIA. *B. davidi.* Butterfly Bush, Summer Lilac. z 5-9. Shrub (but tops usually winter-kill to the ground north of z 6). Fragrant flowers appear on new wood in lilac-like spikes to 10 in. in shades of purple, cerise, white, and pink. To 10 ft. where wood is perennial; new wood grows to 5 ft. in North.

BUPHTHALMUM. Ox-eye. Weedy daisy-like plants usually collected from the wild. Useful in the wild garden for their yellow flowers with brown eyes, borne late in summer.

BUXUS. Box. *B. japonica koreana.* Korean Box. z 5-8. Usually catalogued as shown, but more accurately called *Buxus microphylla koreana.* To 2 ft. Hardier than *B. sempervirens,* but less attractive in color in winter and spring. Leaves winter-burn.

B. sempervirens. Common Box. z 6-10a. Perhaps the choicest of all evergreen shrubs with glossy dark green aromatic foliage. Some describe the odor as cat-like. Mature specimens may reach 25 ft., but only after a century or more. Colonial Williamsburg boasts a collection of many horticultural forms.

B. sempervirens suffruticosa. Dwarf Boxwood. z 6-10a. Although a variety of the preceding, it is so distinct in its extremely compact form as to deserve special mention. Outstanding as formal edging. Excellent house plant if a moist atmosphere can be maintained. Useful in terrariums.

CALADIUM. *C. bicolor.* Fancy-leaved Caladium. Tuberous foliage plants. See Bulbs (Chapter 4).

C. candidum. See Bulbs (Chapter 4).

CALCEOLARIA. *C. crenatiflora.* Slipperwort, Pocketbook Flower. Greenhouse or house plants grown for their unusual bag-like flowers. These are yellow, orange, or dull red, spotted brown or purple. Because of special culture required, plants are usually purchased. Tender perennial to 2½ ft.

CALENDULA. *C. officinalis.* Calendula, Pot Marigold. A pot herb as well as a desirable bedding annual, to 2 ft. Flowers used for yellow color and flavor in soups. Daisy-like flowers 2 in. across, white, yellow and orange. Subject to the same virus disease — yellows — as annual asters.

CALLICARPA. *C. americana.* Beautyberry, French Mulberry. z 6-9a. Bluish flowers, May-July. Lovely violet-blue berry-like fruits in clusters on a 4-6 ft. shrub. A white-fruited form also available.

C. dichotoma. Hardy Beautyberry. z 5b-9a. Like above but lower. May tolerate a few more degrees of cold, yet not much more resistant. To 4 ft.

C. giraldiana. Large-fruited Beautyberry. z 6-9a. Taller than either of the above, to 8 ft. Pink flowers, July-Sept. Striking violet-purple fruit.

C. japonica. Japanese Beautyberry. z 7-9a. The most profuse-fruiting species but less hardy. To 5 ft. Flowers pink or whitish, in Aug. Fruit violet or white.

CALLIRHOE. *C. involucrata.* Purple Poppy Mallow. z 6-8. Deep-rooted perennial, with sprawling stems to 12 in. Mauve purple flowers, June-Aug. Prefers fairly dry soils.

CALLISTEMON. *C. lanceolatus.* Bottlebrush. z 8b-10. A shrub or small tree to 20 ft. Brush-like loose spikes of yellow flowers with bright red stamens. Grows in sandy soils; tolerates salt air.

C. rigidis. Stiff Bottlebrush. z 8b-10. Similar to above but flowers more compact and stiff. Shrub 6-10 ft.

C. speciosus. Tree Bottlebrush. z 8b-10. Flowers like *C. rigidis,* but a medium-sized tree to 40 ft.

CALLISTEPHUS. *C. chinensis.* Annual Aster, China Aster. A favorite old-time annual that is losing ground because it is hit by both aster yellows and aster wilt. Yellows can be partially controlled by spraying with DDT to kill leafhoppers that carry the virus. Wilt-resistant varieties are available, but do not always resist wilt found in Middle West. To 2½ ft.

Violet, purple, blue, rose, or white flowers 5 in. across. Condensed and dwarf forms also.

CALLUNA. *C. vulgaris.* Scotch Heather, Ling. z 5-8. Spikes of densely packed tiny florets in 10-in. racemes, lilac-purple in the type, but in cultivated varieties from white to deep red. Flowers July-Oct. on coastal islands of New England, where it has become naturalized. Winter-flowering in California. A perennial worth trying where light acid, sandy soils and cool moist air in winter are common. To 3 ft.

CALOCHORTUS. *C. venustus.* Mariposa Lily, White Mariposa. z 5-10. See Bulbs (Chapter 4).

CALONYCTION. *C. aculeatum.* Moonflower, Bona Nox. (May be listed with ipomaea in catalogs.) Perennial south but grown as annual climber in the northern U.S. Seed germination may be speeded up by notching. Fragrant tubular white flowers, often banded with green, to 6 in. across, opening only at night.

CALTHA. *C. palustris.* Marsh Marigold, Cowslip. z 4-8. Most commonly grown form is *C. palustris flore-pleno*, with double yellow buttercup-like flowers 2 in. across — April-June. Though a marsh plant, will grow to 2 ft. in border in rich damp soil.

CALYCANTHUS. *C. floridus.* Sweet Shrub, Strawberry Shrub, Carolina Allspice. z 5b-10a. Shrub to 8 ft. with odd, reddish chocolate, fragrant flowers to 2 in. across in summer. Prefers moist rich soil, tolerates light shade. Called simply "shrub" in some parts of the South.

CAMASSIA. *C. esculenta.* Wild Hyacinth, Camass, Missouri Hyacinth. z 4-9a. See Bulbs (Chapter 4).

CAMELLIA. *C. japonica.* Camellia, Japonica. z 7-10a. Popular evergreen ornamental shrubs for mild climates and for greenhouse culture in North. Experimentally, their culture is being pushed as far north as Norfolk and Long Island, but they are not reliably hardy there. Prefer acid soil. Winter-flowering. Their wax-like flowers vary from red to rose and white, are often double and 5 in. across. About 25 ft. high.

CAMPANULA. Bellflower. All kinds are hardy to z 5. Bellflowers usually are blue-flowered, are among our most useful perennials, ranging in height from the near prostrate bluebells of Scotland to towering chimney bellflowers with 6-ft. spikes. With 300 species in cultivation, the choice is bewildering, but the following are good and are generally available.

C. bellardi. Nodding Bellflower. Useful in rock gardens; 4-6 in. high, with solitary nodding blue flowers ½ in. long. Probably *C. pulsatilla* and this species are mixed in the trade; differences too slight to be important to the gardener. Also called *C. caespitosa.*

C. calycanthema. Canterbury Bells. Probably only a variety of *C. medium;* see Biennials (Chapter 2).

C. carpatica. Carpathian Harebell. White, sky blue, and deeper blue, solitary, nodding flowers to 2 in. across on 10-in. stems in early summer and from time to time thereafter. One of the best perennials for a blue edging.

C. excisa. Alpine Bellflower. A species for the rock garden, about 5 in. tall, with pale blue, nodding, solitary flowers to ½ in. long.

C. garganica. Italian Harebell. Like *C. carpatica,* with more conspicuous and more numerous flowers of somewhat deeper blue. A really desirable perennial. Branches trailing; to 10 in.

C. isophylla. Star of Bethlehem, Ligurian Bellflower. Not reliably hardy north of z 7, but widely grown as a hanging-basket plant indoors; lovely when covered with showers of white or pale blue saucer-shaped flowers, 1 in. across.

C. latifolia. Great Bellflower. Large purplish blue bells on 4-ft. stems. The variety *C. l. macrantha* has flowers 2¼ in. wide. A white is also available.

C. medium. Canterbury Bells, Cup-and-saucer Flower, Hose-in-hose. Biennial to 4 ft. See Biennials (Chapter 2).

C. persicifolia. Peach Bells. White or blue nodding flowers to 1½ in. long on 3-ft. stems. Many interesting July-flowering varieties, including doubles.

C. portenschlagiana. Wall Bellflower. Its clumsy specific name has probably held back this truly handsome perennial (formerly called *C. muralis*). Rich blue-purple nodding flowers to 1 in. long (1 to 3 together) on 6-in. stems. Rock garden.

C. pyramidalis. Chimney Bellflower. To 5 ft. Strong spikes of pale blue flowers about 1 in. long in July. Not hardy north of z 6 without winter protection. Often grown as a pot plant. Difficult from seed.

C. rotundifolia. Bluebells of Scotland. Nodding clear lavender-blue flowers to 1 in. on 10-in. stems off and on all summer. Easily naturalized. Tolerant of seaside conditions. Good rock-garden plant. Hardy to z 4.

CAMPSIS. *C. radicans.* Trumpet Vine, Trumpet Creeper. z 4b-9. Tall woody climber seldom flowering until 5 years old. Orange-scarlet trumpet-shaped flowers to 2 in. across in striking clusters. 'Mme. Galen' is a hybrid between this and a more tender species, but just as hardy, with larger, more vivid flowers.

CANNA. Showy summer-flowering tuberous plant. See Bulbs (Chapter 4).

CARAGANA. *C. arborescens.* Siberian Pea Tree. z 2b-9a. One of the hardiest of all small trees or tall shrubs. Finely divided leaves, showy yellow flowers in clusters in June followed by pea-like pods. Prefers exposed position, full sun, dry soil. To 20 ft. but dwarf forms are available for hedging. Deciduous.

C. maximowicziana. Russian Peashrub. z 2b-9a. To 6 ft. with bronze-yellow flowers in June. Not too attractive but one of few shrubs hardy on Great Plains. Deciduous.

CARDAMINE. *C. pratensis.* Cuckoo Flower, Lady's Smock. z 4-8. Perennial to 18 in. with white or rose-colored flowers. Double varieties available. In warmer sections must have light shade and moist soil. In z 4-5 will tolerate full sun if moist. Rock and bog gardens. June.

CARDIOCRINUM. *C. giganteum.* Giant Lily. See *Lilium giganteum.*

CARDIOSPERMUM. *C. halicacabum.* Balloon Vine, Heart Seed. Usually grown as an annual vine, but may live over in warmer sections. To 10 ft. Clusters of small white flowers in summer, 3-angled, balloon-shaped pods about 1 in. diameter. Naturalized in many parts of U.S.

CARISSA. *C. grandiflora.* Natal Plum, Amatungula. z 9-10. Tropical evergreen shrub with fragrant white or pink flowers to 2 in. across. Fruit an edible berry 1-2 in. long, scarlet when ripe. Makes dense hedges to 12 ft. Good seaside plant.

CARPENTERIA. *C. californica.* California Mock Orange. z 8-10. Evergreen shrub to 10 ft., similar to the mock orange of the East. White fragrant flowers 2-3 in. across in June-July, single or a few in a cluster.

CARPINUS. *C. betulus.* European Hornbeam. z 3-9. Tree to 75 ft. but lower as grown here. Makes a dense, tight hedge. Does not transplant well; move with balled roots, or plant as seedlings. Birch-like foliage, catkins to 5 in. The variety *C. b. fastigiata* has more upright growth.

C. caroliniana. American Hornbeam, Blue Beech, Ironwood, Water Beech. Lower growing than preceding and tends to form multiple trunks. Somewhat easier to transplant. To 30 ft.

CARUM. *C. carvi.* Caraway. A culinary annual or biennial herb to 2 ft. tall, worth growing for fragrant foliage alone.

CARYA. All hardy z 4-8 except pecan. Useful deciduous nut-bearing ornamental and crop nut-bearing trees that transplant poorly; best started from nuts. Stratify seed over winter and sow in spring. Those with edible nuts bear more freely on rich soils, but on poor soils produce better-flavored nuts.

C. alba. Mockernut. Of little value as food; nuts hard to crack and yield is small. Large and ornamental. To 90 ft. Winter buds.

C. glabra. Pignut. Smooth-barked tree to 100 ft. Nuts astringent.

C. laciniosa. Shellback Hickory, Big Shagbark. Interesting tree with peeling, shredded bark, to 120 ft. Nuts hard to shell, but edible.

C. ovata. Shagbark or Shellbark Hickory. Bark shaggier than preceding. About as tall, but nuts easier to crack. The only hickory with good fall color (yellow).

C. pecan. Pecan. z 6-9. At maturity to 150 ft., one of the tallest eastern

trees. The familiar pecan of commerce and a good landscape subject.

CARYOPTERIS. *C. incana.* Blue Spirea, Bluebeard. z 6-9. Hoary-leaved shrub to 4 ft. Bluish purple or blue flowers ¼ in. long in verbena-like heads in Sept. Good for seaside and sandy soil.

CASSIA. *C. marilandica.* American or Wild Senna. z 6-9. Perennial to 4 ft. Racemes of pea-like yellow flowers in July-Aug.

CASTANEA. Chestnut. Since the virtual elimination of the American chestnut by blight, Chinese chestnuts have been planted, but cannot replace either American or Spanish chestnuts in flavor. Resistant hybrids of native chestnut are being distributed by Connecticut nurseries. European trees, formerly depended on for nuts, now rapidly succumbing to blight.

C. crenata. Japanese Chestnut. z 5-8. To 30 ft. More useful in breeding new varieties than as an ornamental or nut tree.

C. dentata. American Chestnut. Virtually extinct, except in hybrids.

C. mollissima. Chinese Chestnut. z 5-8. An awkward tree, overrated as an ornamental. To 50 ft. Largely useful for breeding.

C. sativa. Spanish Chestnut. z 8-9. Susceptible to chestnut blight, but survives as isolated specimen. A noble tree to 90 ft., round-headed when mature. Nuts twice the size of American chestnuts.

CASUARINA. *C. cunninghamiana.* Australian Beefwood, She-oak, Australian Pine. z 9b-10. An odd tree with jointed branches and scale-like leaves. Desirable street tree, 40-60 ft. tall. Salt-tolerant.

C. equisetifolia. Horsetail Tree, Beefwood, She-oak. Like preceding but taller, to 70 ft. and less compact. May sucker.

C. stricta. Coast Beefwood. z 9b-10. Leaves like other casuarinas but growth shrub-like with drooping branches. Usually under 30 ft.

CATALPA. Attractive deciduous trees, mostly native species, surviving under adverse conditions from Maine to the Great Plains of Nebraska and Arizona. All produce attractive large trusses of white flowers with curiously spotted throats (June-July) that resemble those of horse chestnuts. Large heart-shaped leaves provide substantial shade. Long thin pods are formed in late summer, popular with children as "Indian cigars." Valuable for their rapid growth and profuse bloom.

C. bignonioides. Indian Bean, Common Catalpa, Cigar Tree. z 5-9. To 60 ft. Leaves ill-smelling if bruised. A grafted globe-headed form is the umbrella catalpa, sold as *C. bungei.*

C. ovata. Japanese Catalpa. z 5-9. Sometimes sold as *C. kaempferi.* Fragrant, cream-colored flowers with a distinct purple spot. About 30 ft high.

C. speciosa. Western Catalpa, White Mahogany, Catawba, Hardy Catalpa. z 5-9. Except that leaves are not ill-smelling, much like *C. bignonioides.* to 60 ft.

CATANACHE. *C. caerulea.* Cupid's Dart, Blue Succory. Hardy perennial to 2 ft. similar in appearance to cornflower, with blue ray flowers to 2 in. in midsummer. Dried flowers used as everlastings.

CEANOTHUS. *C. americanus.* New Jersey Tea, Red Root, Indian Tea. z 4-9. Eastern member of a striking group of shrubs called "California lilacs," but less conspicuous than its western relatives. To 3 ft. White flowers in flat clusters in summer.

C. delilianus. 'Gloire de Versailles,' 'Gloire de Plantières.' z 7-9. Beautiful hybrids with profuse lilac-like flowers July-Aug. Often grown as espaliers on walls. From 3 to 12 ft.

C. prostratus. Mahala Mat. z 8-10. A striking prostrate shrub with blue flowers in summer.

C. thyrsiflorus. Blue Blossom, California Lilac. z 7-10. Shrub to 20 ft., flowering in great billows of blue on California hillsides. Evergreen foliage. White-flowered varieties known.

CEDRELA. *C. sinensis.* Toona. z 9-10. Deciduous tree to 50 ft., shedding leaves late. Cedar-like wood. Honey-scented white flowers in long hanging panicles.

CEDRUS. Cedar. *C. atlantica.* Atlas Cedar. z 7-9. True evergreen cedar to 50 ft. Striking blue-green foliage; forms with variegated foliage known, also weeping forms.

C. deodara. Deodar Cedar. z 7. Like preceding but foliage less stiff. To 100 ft.

C. libani. Cedar of Lebanon. z 6-9. Like above, but foliage rich dark green. Tends to form multiple trunks; trim to one stem if so wanted. To 50 ft.

CELASTRUS. *C. scandens.* Waxworks, Bittersweet, False Bittersweet. z 4-8. A vigorous woody vine with scrambling stems. Yellow fruit splits to show bright scarlet berry.

CELOSIA. *C. cristata.* Cockscomb. Annual to 3 ft. The old-fashioned cockscomb of grandmother's day has been bred to many lovely pastel shades. The new 'Gilbert' varieties are particularly outstanding. New brighter reds also known. Flat velvety flower heads, often dried as everlastings.

C. plumosa. Cockscomb. Annual. Instead of plushy flowers of preceding, this species produces long feathery spikes of brilliant yellow, orange, or red. Both tall and compact types known.

CELTIS. Hackberry. Trees with elm-like foliage, often suggested as replacement for American elm, but a fungus, called witches' broom, produces knotty, compact growth, invisible when tree is in leaf. This does no harm, however, and produces a denser tree.

C. australis. California Hackberry. z 6-9. To 80 ft. Purplish green fruit, edible but insipid. Grows to 70 ft.

C. laevigata. Sugarberry, Mississippi Hackberry. z 6-9. Up to 90 ft.

C. occidentalis. Common Hackberry, Nettletree. z 4b-9a. Except for its more rounded, compact form, difficult to distinguish from American elm. Insipid but edible blackish fruits. To 120 ft.

CENTAUREA. *C. candidissima.* Dusty Miller. So catalogued, but correctly is *C. cineraria.* Another dusty miller is *Senecio cineraria.* These are much confused in commerce; when the form you want is secured, propagate from cuttings. Perennial to 1 ft. or more, grown for its finely cut gray foliage.

C. cyanus. Bachelor Button, Cornflower, Bluebonnet. Among the most popular of annuals, with ragged blue flowers all summer. White, red, and pink varieties are known. 'Blue Boy' is a particularly desirable variety. To 2 ft.

C. gymnocarpa. Dusty Miller. A perennial to 2 ft., grown from seed as an annual for its white felted leaves. Can also be propagated from cuttings. See *C. candidissima.*

C. imperialis. Giant Imperial. Stately annual, possibly only a variety of *C. moschata.* To 3 ft. with thistle-like flowers in white, cream, lilac, purple, or pink. Sweetly fragrant.

C. macrocephala. Showy Knapweed. z 5-8. Hardy perennial. Yellow thistle-like heads 4 in. across, on 3-ft. stems.

C. montana. Mountain Bachelor Button, Mountain Bluet. z 5-8. Perennial to 2 ft. Silvery leaves and blue flower heads to 3 in. across. The variety *C. m. citrina* has lemon-yellow flowers. White and rose-colored forms are also known.

C. moschata. Sweet sultan. Like *C. imperialis,* but somewhat shorter. Same color range; fragrant flowers.

CENTRANTHUS. *C. ruber.* Red Valerian, Jupiter's Beard, Scarlet Lightning. z 6-8. Perennial. Crimson or soft red spurred flowers in heads on 30-in. stems. Fragrant. June-July.

CENTROSEMA. *C. virginianum.* Butterfly Pea, Conchita. Annual twining vine with pea-like purple or white flowers and 5-in. pods.

CEPHALANTHUS. *C. occidentalis.* Buttonbush, Button Willow. z 5-9. Woody shrub to 20 ft. White ball-like heads of flowers to 1 in. across, July-Sept. Tolerates wet soil but survives in shrub border.

CEPHALOCEREUS. *C. senilis.* See House Plants (Chapter 11).

CEPHALOTAXUS. *C. drupacea.* Green Plum-yew. z 6-8. Similar to yew (taxus), but with broader needle-like leaves, green fruit. Shrub-like in cultivation, to 30 ft. in the wild. Prefers a damp seaside location. Evergreen.

C. fortunei. Purple Plum-yew. z 7-9a. Like preceding, but plant is broader at maturity. Purple fruits.

CERASTIUM. *C. tomentosum.* Snow-in-summer. z 4b-10a. Woolly-leaved perennial for gray effects. White star-like flowers. To 6 in. A relative of mouse-ear chickweed and as likely to become weedy. Survives in almost pure sand, one reason it remains in commerce. White flowers in early summer.

CERATONIA. *C. siliqua.* St. John's Bread, Carob, Wild Locust. z 9-10. Evergreen tree to 50 ft. Red flowers; leathery, fleshy, edible pods 12 in. long. These are the "wild locusts" on which John the Baptist presumably fed. Trees of one sex only; plant both male and female if pods are wanted.

CERATOSTIGMA. *C. plumbaginoides.* Plumbago, Leadwort. z 6-10. Sprawling 1-ft. perennial, sometimes woody, bearing flat clusters of clear sky-blue flowers resembling those of woods phlox, Aug.-Sept. Useful groundcover and rock-garden plant.

CERCIDIPHYLLUM. *C. japonicum.* Katsura Tree. z 4b-9a. A neglected tree, often multiple-trunked, to 40 ft. Heart-shaped leaves, brilliant fall color. Rich moist soil.

CERCIS. *C. canadensis.* Redbud, Judas Tree. z 5b-9. Irregularly shaped tree to 40 ft. with blackish bark and intense purple-pink pea-like flowers ½ in. long in April. Pure white and double pink forms are known.

C. chinensis. Chinese Redbud. z 6b-10a. Larger, more striking flowers than preceding, to ¾ in. More of a shrub than a tree. Less hardy. To 50 ft.

C. siliquastrum. Judas Tree. z 7-10a. Much like *C. canadensis,* but larger flowers (¾ in.), both white and purple-pink. To 40 ft.

CEREUS. Retained as a name here because the plant known as night-blooming cereus is usually so catalogued. A much confused group of plants. Species in three genera are sold as night-blooming cereus — *Selenicereus pteranthus, Nyctocereus serpentinus,* and *Hylocereus undatus.* All open fragrant white many-petaled flowers at night on climbing cactuslike plants.

CEROPEGIA. *C. woodi.* Hearts-on-strings, Rosary Vine. An interesting greenhouse vine with curious heart-shaped leaves that seem suspended on green strings. Best grown as a hanging-basket specimen to show off this habit. Purplish pink flowers, usually in pairs, ¾ in. long.

CESTRUM. *C. diurnum.* Day Jasmine. z 9-10. Woody shrub to 15 ft. with fragrant white flowers opening during the day. Jan.-April.

C. nocturnum. Queen-of-the-night, Night Jasmine. z 9-10. Like preceding but night flowering. Intensely fragrant.

C. parqui. Willow-leaved Jasmine. Except for its leaves, much like preceding, but shorter. Also night-flowering. Greenish white flowers 1 in. long, fragrant.

C. purpureum. Coral Jasmine, Purple Cestrum. Flowers like other forms but purple or rose. A sprawling shrub or vine to 10 ft.

CHAENOMELES. *C. japonica.* Dwarf Japanese Quince, Dwarf Flowering Quince, Japonica. z 5-9a. Still listed in some catalogs under cydonia. Shrub to 3 ft. Does well in city locations. Brick-red flowers to 1½ in. long, in clusters, resembling single roses. Tart greenish yellow fruits used for jelly. The variety *C. j. alpina* is more or less prostrate. March-April.

C. lagenaria. Japonica, Japanese Flowering Quince. Like above, but to 6 ft. Makes a good hedge if a horizontal wire is woven through branches to hold them together. March-April.

CHAMAECEREUS. *C. silvestri.* See House Plants (Chapter 11).

CHAMAECYPARIS. *C. lawsoniana.*
Port Orford Cedar, White Cedar,
Oregon Cedar, False Cypress. z 6b-
9a. Excellent evergreen for moist locations near the sea on acid soils; dies
out in regions with less than 40 in.
rainfall. Blue-green or green foliage,
usually drooping branches. Golden
and variegated forms known. To 150
ft.

    C. nootkatensis. Alaska Cedar, Sitka
Cedar, Nootka Cedar, Yellow Cypress.
z 5b-9a. Like preceding, but taller at
maturity. Not a commonly used ornamental, but desirable. To 175 ft. Give
wind protection North in winter.

    C. obtusa. Hinoki Cypress. z 5-8.
This is the retinospora or temple cedar
of Japan. To 120 ft. in Japan, but usually much less here. Like the above in
moisture and soil preferences. Many
horticultural forms, some of which
mature at a height of 8 ft. or less.
C. o. compacta and *C. o. filicoides* are
two of these.

    C. pisifera. Sawara Cypress. z 5-9.
Much like *C. obtusa*, though taller at
maturity.

    C. thyoides. Southern White Cedar,
False Cypress. z 6-10. Native of Gulf
Coast. Less attractive than above spe-
cies, but will tolerate drier conditions,
though it grows in bogs and swamps.
Very acid soil. To 75 ft.

CHAMAEDAPHNE. *C. calyculata.*
Leatherleaf. Evergreen bog shrub with
urn-shaped white flowers ¼ in. long
in 4-5 in. racemes, April-June. To 5
ft. *C. c. nana*, to 1 ft., will grow in
damp, peaty pockets in rock gardens,
where it is a desirable plant.

CHAMAEROPS. *C. humilis.* Low Fan
Palm. z 9-10. A fan palm with a
short stubby trunk 3-5 ft., but sometimes to 20 ft. Easy to grow.

CHEIRANTHUS. *C. allioni.* See *Erysimum asperum.*

C. cheiri. English Wallflower. Perennial to 2½ ft. See Biennials (Chapter 2).

CHEIRIDOPSIS. *C. candidissima.*
See House Plants (Chapter 11).

CHELIDONIUM. *C. majus.* Celandine Poppy. z 4b-8. Weedy biennial
or perennial 1-2 ft. tall. Blue-green
leaves, yellow poppy-like flowers to
⅔ in. across. Supposedly blooms when
swallows return north in spring.

CHELONE. *C. glabra.* White Turtle-
head, Shellflower. z 3-8. Perennial,
often found in swamps, but does well
in normal soil. Two to 3 ft. tall with
white snapdragon-like flowers to 1 in.
across. July-Aug.

    C. lyoni. Purple Turtlehead. z 4-8.
Like preceding but has reddish purple
flowers.

CHENOPODIUM. *C. bonus-henricus.*
Good King Henry, Mercury. z 5-8.
Weedy perennial to 2½ ft., often
grown as spinach substitute.

CHILOPSIS. *C. linearis.* Desert Willow, Mexican Catalpa, Flowering Willow. z 8-10. Desert species found near
streams and springs. Small shrub or
tree to 20 ft. Willow-like leaves;
trumpet-shaped, 2-in. flowers, lavender, veined yellow within, in terminal
racemes. Spring, summer. Deciduous.

CHIMAPHILA. *C. maculata.* Spotted
Wintergreen, Pipsissewa. z 3-5. Woods
plant for acid soil. Difficult to transplant. Must have native mycorrhiza
on roots; dig with soil in which they
grow. Evergreen prostrate perennial
with leathery leaves, veined white.
White nodding flowers in umbels during summer. To 10 in. Wild garden.

    C. umbellata. Wintergreen, Prince's
Pine, Pipsissewa. z 3-5. Like above
but somewhat taller.

CHIOGONES. *C. hispidula.* Creeping Snowberry. z 3-5. Evergreen creeper similar to preceding but less difficult to transplant. Tiny white flowers May-June and white berries borne above mat of small leaves.

CHIONANTHUS. *C. retusus.* Chinese Fringe Tree. z 6-10. Less showy than the following and less hardy. Panicles of white bloom in June-July. To 20 ft.

C. virginicus. Fringe Tree. z 5-10. Tree to 30 ft. Panicles of white flowers in showy sprays. May-June. Needs acid soil to survive.

CHIONODOXA. *C. luciliae.* Glory-of-the-snow. See Bulbs (Chapter 4).

CHOISYA. *C. ternata.* Mexican Orange. z 9-10. A shrub to 10 ft. with fine evergreen foliage and intensely fragrant 1-in. white flowers in early spring. Sometimes a greenhouse plant.

CHRYSANTHEMUM. See also Chapter 15. *C. balsamita.* Costmary, Mint Geranium, Lavender Geranium. z 5-8. Not a mint, geranium, or lavender, but suggests these in its fragrance. Hardy perennial to 30 in. Inconspicuous white flowers.

C. carinatum (*C. coronarium*). Annual Chrysanthemum. A half-hardy annual, valuable for its daisy-like flowers with heavy petals, marked with contrasting rings. Colors mostly tints of yellow, cream, and white with maroon or black rings at base. To 3 ft.

C. coccineum. Pyrethrum, Painted Daisy. z 5-8. Large, showy, daisy-like flowers in red, pink, lavender-pink, and white, sometimes double. Popular summer-flowering perennial, 1-2 ft. Plants are short-lived; divide every other year or grow new from seed.

C. hortorum. Greenhouse Chrysanthemums, Hardy Garden Chrysanthemums. z 5-8. This is an artificial name invented to cover hybrids of *C. morifolium.* Perhaps the most widely

grown cut flower today. Grown by the acre under shade in Florida for cut flowers. Bewildering range of sizes, forms, and colors from tiny buttons to large "football" chrysanthemums. So-called hardy chrysanthemums are shallow-rooted and so are not reliably hardy in the open where much thawing and freezing occurs.

C. maximum. Shasta Daisy. z 4-9. Striking large white daisy-like flowers to 6 in. across on 2-ft. stems. Short-lived perennial, often grown as a biennial to insure better bloom. Plants tend to heave in winter; a mulch is useful. Hardiness depends upon their not heaving; if this can be prevented, they can survive freezing.

C. parthenium. Feverfew. z 4-8. May be catalogued as matricaria or pyrethrum. Aromatic flowers and foliage. An old-fashioned herb. Stems to 30 in. Creamy or yellowish fluffy flower heads, ¾ in. or less across.

C. tchihatchewi. Turfing Daisy. z 5-9. (Also listed as matricaria.) Small-flowered, low-growing perennial with finely cut foliage, grown in Europe (and sometimes in U.S.) as a lawn substitute. Tolerates mowing without injury.

CHRYSOPSIS. *C. falcata.* Golden Aster. z 4-6. A wildflower useful in sand and at the seashore. Perennial to 1 ft. Aster-like flowers ⅓ in. across in long stiff heads. July-Aug.

CICHORIUM. *C. intybus.* Chicory, Succory. Perennial to 6 ft. with thick roots used as a substitute for coffee. Tops forced for salads. Vivid blue ray flowers 1½ in. across. Sometimes grown as ornamental. Summer.

CIMICIFUGA. *C. americana.* Bugbane. z 6-8. A native woodland plant to 6 ft. Clustered spikes of small white flowers bloom in early fall. Moist, shady situations.

C. racemosa. Black Snakeroot, Black Cohosh. z 3-7. Bold perennial 5-8 ft. Rich woods or in shady borders. Flowers small and white in loose clusters, July-Aug.

C. simplex. Lower than *C. racemosa,* 3 to 5 ft. high, with tiny white flowers in graceful, arching racemes, in autumn.

CINNAMOMUM. *C. camphora.* Camphor Tree. z 8b-10. A clean, shapely specimen used as a street tree South. To 50 ft. Commercial source of camphor. Flowers yellow in panicles.

C. cassia. Cassia-bark Tree. z 8b-10. Bark and dried buds used as adulterant for commercial cinnamon. Not much planted, but seen occasionally in southern California. To 40 ft.

CISSUS. *C. antarctica.* Kangaroo Vine. z 10. Sometimes grown outdoors in z 10, but more commonly a house plant with clean shiny 4-in. toothed leaves.

C. erosa. z 10. Similar to, but less common than, *C. quadrangularis.*

C. quadrangularis. Grape Ivy. z 10. Leaves like a grapevine. A favorite house plant; thrives under abuse.

C. rhombifolia. Much like preceding, but less commonly seen.

CISTUS. Rock-rose. z 7-9. Low shrubs 2-6 ft., with wide-open purple, mauve, or white flowers to 2½ in., thriving in full sun in light, well-drained, limestone soil. Transplants poorly and best grown from seed, in position. Separate species seldom available in commerce; mixtures may contain unusual types. Rock garden.

CITRUS. *C. bergamia.* True Bergamot. z 10. Small spiny evergreen tree to 18 ft. Inedible fruits produce a fragrant oil much used in perfume. Rarely grown (as a curiosity) in Florida or California.

Several species of citrus (which includes oranges, lemons, and their relatives) will flower indoors.

CLADRASTIS. *C. lutea.* Yellow-wood, Gopher-wood, Kentucky Yellow-wood. z 5b-8. Deciduous tree, 30-50 ft., valued for showy drooping clusters of white 1-in. fragrant flowers in a ring. June.

CLARKIA. *C. elegans.* Showy annual with ragged flowers on stems to 3 ft. White, rose, purple, and pink flowers during summer, but tending to burn out in hot climates. Good greenhouse plant. Tolerates light shade.

CLAYTONIA. *C. virginica.* Spring Beauty, Mayflower, Grass Flower. Perennial with narrow lance-shaped leaves, white ¾-in. flowers tinged pink, in May. Wild garden or shaded woods. Dies out in dry soil. Plants go dormant soon after flowering and are best moved then. Be sure to mark when in bloom so they can be located.

CLEMATIS. Virgin's Bower. Although usually thought of as vines, some members of this genus are true herbaceous perennials. All prefer rich, yet light, well-drained soil. Vine forms are particularly useful for covering fences, unsightly buildings, and dead trees.

C. fremonti. Prairie Bell. z 4-9. Perennial to 15 in. with nodding, bell-shaped purple solitary flowers about 1 in. long during spring and summer. Stands considerable drought. Useful border plant.

C. heracleaefolia. Dwarf Chinese Clematis. z 4-9. A perennial, but stems woody in late summer. Light blue to deep blue 1-in. tubular flowers on 30-in. stems, resembling a loose hyacinth stalk. Fragrant.

C. integrifolia. Dwarf Virgin's Bower. z 3b-8. A subshrub to 3 ft. Violet-blue or white flowers, urn-shaped, to 1½ in. long, June-July. Interesting plumy fruits.

C. jackmani. Jackman's Clematis. z 5-8. Perhaps the most widely grown showy hardy vine, with many garden varieties. Original species has vivid purple star-shaped flowers to 2½ in. in profusion on 10-ft. vine, July-Sept. White, red, lavender, and cream-colored varieties are known.

C. montana. Mountain Clematis. z 6b-10a. Woody vine to 20 ft. White fragrant star-shaped flowers to 2 in. across in clusters. May. Plumy fruits. A lovely pink-flowered variety is known.

C. recta. Dwarf Virgin's Bower. z 4-9. Valuable hardy perennial to 3 ft. with fragrant white flowers to 1 in. across in large clusters. June-Aug.

C. texensis. Scarlet Clematis. z 4b-10. Vivid scarlet urn-shaped flowers to 1 in. long, solitary and nodding on vine 5-6 ft. Also pinkish varieties. July-Sept.

C. virginiana. Woodbine, Old-man's Beard, Love Vine. z 4-8. Vine to 20 ft. found all over eastern U.S. Male and female flowers on separate vines. White flowers to 1 in.; female flowers bear feathery fruits. Blooms Aug.-Sept.

C. vitalba. Traveler's Joy, Withywood, Old-man's Beard. z 5-9. Much like preceding, but taller.

CLEOME. *C. lutea.* Yellow Spider Flower. A Western native annual, with clear yellow spider-like flowers. To 3 ft. Sometimes available from dealers in wildflower seeds. Tolerates dry soil.

C. pungens. (Often so listed, but actually *C. spinosa.*)

C. spinosa. Spider Flower. Annual to 5 ft. Interesting spider-like flowers in white, mauve, and pink. Self-sows, but colors do not come true. Pungent foliage.

CLERODENDRON. *C. fragrans.* Glory-bower. z 9b-10. Shrub to 8 ft. Pale pink or white fragrant flowers 1 in. across, clustered like hydrangea. The double form is usually sold.

C. thomsonae. Bagflower, Bleeding-heart Vine. z 9b-10. Woody vine much grown on Gulf Coast and in California for showy crimson flowers with large white calyx, borne in branching recemes. May kill back in cold winters but it flowers on new wood and will recover.

C. trichotomum. Harlequin Glory-bower. z 8-10. Shrub or dwarf tree to 15 ft. Fragrant flowers Aug.-Sept. Similar to *C. fragrans* but flowers white with reddish brown calyx in panicles. Conspicuous blue fruits set inside the reddish clayx cling until November.

CLETHRA. *C. acuminata.* White Alder. z 7-9. Small tree or shrub to 18 ft. Flowers in nodding clusters, white, not fragrant. Aug.-Sept. Must have acid soil.

C. alnifolia. Sweet Pepperbush, Spiked Alder. z 3b-9. Shrub to 10 ft. with white or pink, strongly fragrant flowers in erect racemes, 5 in. long. Aug.-Sept. Acid soil.

CLIANTHUS. *C. dampieri.* Glory-pea. z 9b-10. Scrambling woody plant to 4 ft. Pea-like flowers, vivid scarlet, with black blotch at base, to 3 in. long.

CLINTONIA. *C. pulchella.* An incorrect name for *Downingia pulchella,* which see. (The true clintonias are small, northern woodland plants of the lily family.)

COBAEA. *C. scandens.* Cup-and-saucer Vine, Cathedral Bells, Mexican Ivy. Quick-growing annual vine to 25 ft. if started early indoors. Bell-like flowers, 2 in. long and 1½ in. wide, greenish violet or violet, sometimes white. One of the best annual vines for covering unsightly objects quickly.

COCCOLOBIS. *C. uvifera.* Sea Grape, Sea Plum, Beach Plum. z 10. Small Florida tree or large shrub with fruit resembling bunches of grapes, sometimes used for jam or jelly. Leathery foliage resists salt spray.

COCOS. *C. australis.* Coco Palm, Pindo Palm. z 9-10. Now more accurately *Butia capitata.* Trunk to 18 in. diameter and 15 ft. long; tree to 25 ft. Egg-shaped yellowish or reddish fruit.

C. plumosa. Queen Palm, Plume Coconut. Still catalogued under this name but now *Arecastrum romanzoffianum.* Smooth-trunked palm to 30 ft. The palm most commonly grown as a house plant.

CODIAEUM. *C. variegatum.* Croton. z 9b-10. Bright-colored tropical foliage plant, shrub, or small tree to 10 ft. Foliage is poisonous and should not be accessible to children. Leaves strikingly mottled in green, yellow, brown, maroon, or bronze. Useful as bedding plant South, house plant North.

COLCHICUM. *C. autumnale.* Autumn Crocus. See Bulbs (Chapter 4).

COLEUS. *C. blumei.* Foliage Plant, Oriental Rug Plant, Coleus. Tender perennial with bright-colored foliage, often grown from seed as an annual, but also grown from cuttings. So widely used it is often known only as "foliage plant." To 3 ft. Trailing forms are known. House plant and also for bedding in shade.

COLLINSIA. *C. bicolor.* Chinese Houses. Spikes of interesting blue-and-white 1-in. flowers in pagoda form. To 2 ft. Grown as an annual. Tolerates shade.

C. canadensis. Horse Balm, Richweed, Citronella. z 3-8. Coarse, minty perennial to 4 ft. Flowers ½ in. long,

in panicles to 1 ft. Not the source of citronella oil. Woody soil in shade. Good for waste places.

COLLOMIA. *C. biflora.* Chilean Plume. Annual, to 2 ft., similar to gilia. Red, white, or yellow flowers in heads surrounded by leafy bracts, in summer.

COLOCASIA. *C. antiquorum.* Elephant Ear. A decorative large-leaved tropical herb, with leafstalks rising directly from an underground tuber. In some varieties, leaves have purplish markings.

COLUTEA. *C. arborescens.* Bladder Senna. z 5-9. Hardy shrub to 15 ft. with pea-like yellow flowers in branched clusters. May-July.

COMPTONIA. *C. asplenifolia.* Sweetshrub, Sweetfern. z 3-8. Not a fern but a richly aromatic shrub with fern-like leaves. Usually not over 3 ft. tall. Used to cover dry sandy banks or waste places. Of little garden value otherwise.

CONVALLARIA. *C. majalis.* Lily-of-the-valley. z 4-8. A perennial with underground creeping rootstocks. These produce "pips" often sold for winter forcing (they bloom in three weeks). Outdoors, a useful groundcover, with long lance-shaped leaves and racemes of nodding, strongly fragrant, bell-shaped white flowers (rarely pink). Pips and fruits are poisonous; keep away from children. An invaluable plant for city use, thriving where few others live. A good shade plant. If it becomes a nuisance, it can be killed with Silvex (2,4,5-TP).

CONVOLVULUS. Both beautiful vines and vicious weeds fall in this genus. Bindweed, deep-rooted and all but impossible to kill, is one of the latter. Most of the desirable varieties classed as ipomaea (morning-glory), which see.

C. japonicus. California Rose, Japanese Rose. Introduced as an ornamental but a noxious weed. Often sold at flower shows as a "sensational new flower" but should never be introduced into the garden. Sometimes used to bind banks, but once established cannot be eradicated. Perennial, twining stem to 20 ft. Pink flowers, solitary, to 2 in. across.

C. sepium. Rutland Beauty. Like the preceding, often sold for garden use, but another vicious weed difficult to eradicate.

C. tricolor. Dwarf Morning-glory. As delightful as its relatives are vile. A much-neglected low edging plant. In the variety 'Royal Ensign,' this was the favorite annual of the late Mrs. Francis King, who gave away hundreds of seed packets. Morning-glory flowers, on a 5- to 9-in. plant, are 1½ in. across, and a vivid royal blue, perhaps the most intense blue in garden flowers.

COOPERIA. *C. pedunculata.* Fairy Lily, Rain Lily, Prairie Lily. z 9-10. See Bulbs (Chapter 4).

COPROSMA. *C. baueri.* Mirror Plant. Despite the unpleasant odor of its leaves, a good hedge plant. To 20 ft. Tolerates shearing. Semi-evergreen foliage. Sweet white or greenish flowers; oval orange-yellow fruits ⅓ in. long. Tolerates seaside conditions.

COPTIS. *C. trifolia.* Goldthread. z 3-6. Tiny plant with creeping rootstocks, occasionally grown in rock gardens; prefers peaty, slightly acid soil, in damp shade. Under a mulch, the leaves are evergreen. A good terrarium plant.

CORDYLINE. *C. australis.* Australian Dragon Tree, Ti Tree. z 9-10. The plants sold as dracaena by florists belong here as does the Ti plant, widely used by flower arrangers. Foliage plants of palm-like appearance, often with variegated leaves. To 40 ft.

COREMA. *C. conradi.* Rough-leaf, Broom Crowberry. z 3-7. A low, bushy shrub related to the crowberry, not over 18 in. Thrives on acid soil of pH 4.5 to 5.0. Tolerates sandy soil. Useful groundcover.

COREOPSIS. *C. drummondi.* Golden Wave. A fine annual, 1 to 2 ft. high. Bright yellow to orange flowers.

C. grandiflora. Perennial Tickseed. z 4-9a. A useful perennial to 2 ft. with bright yellow daisy-like flowers in heads to 2½ in. across. Double varieties available. Summer blooming.

C. maritima. Sea Dahlia. z 5-9. Perennial to 30 in. with hollow leafy stems, yellow flowers in heads to 2½ in. across, solitary on 12-in. stems. Survives only in dry climates and prefers sandy soil at seashore.

C. tinctoria. Calliopsis. Easily grown annual to 2½ ft. Yellow flowers marked with reddish brown. Many varieties, some dwarf. In bloom all summer.

CORIANDRUM. *C. sativum.* Coriander. Annual culinary herb to 3 ft. Mentioned in the Bible and still grown for flavoring. Leaves strong-smelling; seeds used.

CORNUS. Dogwood. Valuable genus of trees and shrubs, most of which bear fruits attractive to birds. All thrive in most good garden soils.

C. alba. Coral Dogwood, Tartarian Dogwood. z 3-8. Shrub to 10 ft. with bright red branches; colorful in winter. Flat white umbels of flowers to 2 in. across, followed by white fruits with a bluish cast. Several garden varieties.

C. alternifolia. Pagoda Dogwood,

Pigeonberry, Blue Dogwood. z 2-9. Shrub or small tree to 15 ft. White clusters of flowers to 2½ in. across in May-June followed by blue fruit with distinct bloom. To grow as a tree, trim to single stem.

C. amomum. Silky Cornel, Silky Dogwood. z 2-9. Shrub to 10 ft., gray-purple stems. White flowers to 2½ in. across in June, followed by pale blue fruits. Tolerates sand.

C. baileyi. Red Dogwood. z 3-8. Shrub to 10 ft., usually growing on lake shores or in sandy wastes. Reddish bark, but not the bright red of *C. alba.* White flowers to 2½ in. across, May-June. Blue-white fruits.

C. canadensis. Bunchberry, Ground Cornel, Crackerberry. z 1-4. Woody perennial to 9 in. Bright red fruits against rosettes of leaves barely 4 in. tall make this interesting. Groundcover in light shade. Prefers rotting acid moss as a growing medium.

C. controversa. Giant Dogwood. z 5-8. Tree to 60 ft. in its native Japan, but none this size known in U.S. Much like *C. alternifolia* in fruit, leaf, and flower.

C. florida. Flowering Dogwood, Spindlewood. z 5-9. One of America's favorite small flowering trees. Shining white four-petaled bracts are followed by showy scarlet fruits. Prefers light filtered shade on somewhat acid soil. Pink, red, and double-flowered white forms are available. Also weeping and variegated-leaf forms. Autumn color a rich glowing red. To 40 ft.

C. kousa. Kousa Dogwood. z 5b-9a. Somewhat smaller than preceding but with more pointed, later flowers. Fruits are pink, in clusters.

C. mas. Cornelian Cherry. z 5-8. Tall shrub or small tree to 15 ft. Tiny yellow clusters of flowers in Feb. during mild winters, March-April otherwise. Much neglected winter-flower-ing species. Fruits scarlet, cherry-like, and edible but quite tart. Does well under city conditions.

C. nuttalli. Pacific Dogwood z 7-9a. Western counterpart of *C. florida* but a taller tree. Flowers have six bracts instead of four; white, occasionally pink. Fruits orange or red. To 75 ft.

C. racemosa. Gray Dogwood. z 3-8. Shrub to 10 ft. with smooth gray bark and clusters of white flowers in June. White fruit.

C. sanguinea. Bloodtwig Dogwood. z 3-8. Except that this species bears black fruit and is more tolerant of smoke conditions, much like *C. alba.* To 12 ft.

C. stolonifera. Red-osier Dogwood. z 3-8. Shrub to 10 ft. Much like *C. alba,* except that it suckers. Also a yellow-twigged variety.

CORONILLA. *C. emerus.* Scorpion Senna. z 6-9. Shrub to 9 ft. with pea-like yellow flowers in crown-shaped umbels. May-Sept.

C. varia. Crown Vetch. z 5-8. Sprawling perennial, vine-like, to 2 ft. Useful for holding banks or as border plant. Pinkish flowers ½ in. long in dense crown-like clusters. June-Oct.

CORYDALIS. *C. bulbosa.* Fumewort. z 5-8. Annual to 6 in. Flowers similar to bleeding-heart, purplish or rose. Likes shade.

C. lutea. Yellow Corydalis. Annual similar to preceding but with ½-in. pale yellow flowers. To 8 in. May be perennial south of z 7. May-Aug.

C. nobilis. Spotted Fumewort, Noble Fumewort. z 4-8. Perennial 6-9 in. White 1-in. flowers, tipped yellow, purple spot. May-June.

C. sempervirens. Pink Fumitory, Pale Corydalis. Annual. Pale pink flowers to ¾ in. long, tipped yellow. To 2 ft.

CORYLOPSIS. *C. pauciflora.* Winter

Hazel. z 6-9. Shrub to 6 ft. Fragrant yellow flowers to ¾ in. in Feb.-March. Valuable for winter bloom where hardy.

C. spicata. Giant Winter Hazel. z 6-9. Like preceding, but flowers twice as large.

CORYLUS. *C. avellana.* European Hazel, Purple Hazel. z 4-9. Shrub or small tree to 15 ft. Fruit is filbert of commerce. The variety *C. a. fusco-rubra* has purple foliage; unusual ornamental.

CORYPHANTHA. *C. robustispina.* See House Plants (Chapter 11).

COSMOS. *C. bipinnatus.* Garden Cosmos. Annual 4-6 ft. Daisy-like flowers, white, pink, or red, with yellow centers, to 3 in. across. Does best in lighter soils. July to frost.

C. sulphureus. Golden Cosmos. Like above, but lower-growing with orange-yellow flowers.

COTINUS. *C. americanus.* See *Rhus cotinoides.*

C. coggygria. See *Rhus cotinus.*

COTONEASTER. The rocksprays are reliable shrubs with clean small-leaved foliage, not used as much as their quality warrants. Berry-like red fruits (except *C. lucida*, which is black) eaten by birds. Some are evergreen.

C. acuminata. Hairy Rockspray. z 4-9. Deciduous, to 12 ft. Pink flowers in June. Bright red fruit.

C. adpressa. Creeping Rockspray. z 5b-9. Excellent groundcover, prostrate, deciduous. Flowers pinkish; fruit red. Good rock-garden plant.

C. dammeri. Trailing Rockspray. z 6-9. Like above, but evergreen and roots along stem.

C. dielsiana. Diels Rockspray. z 6-9. Height 3-6 ft. Unusually showy bright red fruit.

C. divaricata. Spreading Rockspray.

z 5b-9. Height 3-7 ft. One of the best in this genus. Good seaside plant. Bright red fruit.

C. francheti. Franchet's Rockspray. Height 4-10 ft. Semi-evergreen. Orange-red fruit.

C. frigida. Himalayan Rockspray. z 8. Height 7-20 ft. Sometimes tree-like (can be trained to a single stalk for this use). To 25 ft. Dense clusters of white flowers, May-June. Persistent fruit.

C. horizontalis. Rose Rockspray. z 6-10a. Low, almost trailing shrub to 3 ft. Evergreen in South but deciduous north of z 5. One of the best.

C. hupehensis. Chinese Rockspray. z 6-10a. Height 4-6 ft. Graceful arching branches. White flowers in clusters in May.

C. lucida. Hedge Rockspray. z 4-8. Height 4-10 ft. Glossy leaves. Pink flowers in May; black fruit. Best species for hedges. Deciduous.

C. microphylla. Dainty Rockspray. z 7-10a. To 3 ft. Good rock-garden plant. Dense, spreading, evergreen branches.

C. multiflora. Redberry Rockspray. z 6-10. To 10 ft. White flowers. Conspicuous bright red fruit ⅜ in. in diameter.

C. pannosa. Silverleaf Rockspray. z 7b-10a. Evergreen in California. To 10 ft. Underside of leaf woolly-white.

C. racemiflora soongorica. Glory Rockspray. z 4b-9. Normally 3-6 ft., but there are 12-ft. specimens at Morton Arboretum. Foliage whitish beneath. White flowers.

CRASSULA. *C. arborescens.* See House Plants (Chapter 11).

C. argentea. Japanese Rubber Plant, Japanese Laurel, Jade Plant. z 9-10. Neither a rubber plant nor a laurel. In California a shrub to 10 ft. See also House Plants.

CRATAEGUS. Hawthorns, Thorn-apples, Haw. All hardy z 5-9a. The genus crataegus is a source of irritation to botanists because it refuses to divide into neat species, but cross-pollinates and produces intermediate types at will. The following are fairly well fixed, but even so, may vary from nursery to nursery. Best selected as specimens in bloom. All have white or creamy flowers in corymbs except 'Paul's Scarlet' hawthorn. May-June. Deciduous.

C. cordata. Washington Thorn. Sometimes catalogued as C. phaeno-pyrum. Boldly upright, round-topped tree, 20-30 ft.

C. crus-galli. Cockspur Thorn. Long, wicked spines make this one of the best barrier hedges. Height 15-25 ft.

C. lavallei. Lavalle Hawthorn. A hybrid to 15-20 ft. Stout thorns. Fruit hangs on until March. Valuable bird-food tree.

C. mollis. Downy Hawthorn, Red Haw. 18-25 ft. Stiff thorns. Fruit 1 in. in diameter; used for jellies.

C. monogyna. English Hawthorn (name also applies to C. oxyacantha; see below). To 30 ft. Double flowers; some pink or red forms are known.

C. oxyacantha. English Hawthorn (but see preceding). Height 15-30 ft. Many cultivated varieties, including the striking double-flowered red, 'Paul's Scarlet' hawthorn.

CRINODENDRON. C. dependens. White Lily Tree, Lantern Tree. z 9-10. To 30 ft. White flowers, ¾ in. long, urn-shaped, in spring.

C. patagua. Red Lily Tree. z 9-10. Like above but with urn-shaped crimson flowers, 1-1¼ in. long.

CRINUM. z 7-10. See Bulbs (Chapter 4).

CROCUS. z 4-9. Sold as bulbs (ac-tually corms) in fall. Both spring-flowering and fall-flowering types are available. Most species have a delicate fragrance. Spring-flowering types can be forced indoors. See House Plants (Chapter 11) and Bulbs (Chapter 4). All under 8 in. in height.

C. aureus. Dutch Crocus. The familiar yellow spring species.

C. biflorus. Scotch Crocus. Mostly purple, striped or splashed white with yellow throat. Spring flowering.

C. sativus. Saffron Crocus, Saffron. See Bulbs (Chapter 4).

C. speciosus. See Bulbs (Chapter 4).

C. susianus. Cloth-of-gold. Interesting orange-yellow flowers with brownish centers in spring. Good rock-garden plant.

C. zonatus. Eyed Autumn Crocus. See Bulbs (Chapter 4).

CRYPTOMERIA. C. japonica. Japanese Temple Cedar, Sugi, Japanese Cedar. z 6b-9a. Stately pyramidal tree 75 to 125 ft. Planted around temples in Japan. Must have high humidity and damp soil. Evergreen C. j. lobbi is a more compact form.

CUCURBITA. Gourds, Pumpkins, and Squashes (various species and many varieties). Species include C. maxima (autumn, winter, and 'Hubbard' squashes), C. moschata (crookneck squash and 'Cushaw' pumpkin — possibly butternut squash belongs here), and C. pepo (field pumpkin and vegetable marrow). Because of the ease with which many of these intercross, botanical identification is not too accurate; selection by variety is advised.

CUMINUM. C. cyminum. Cumin. Cultivated as a culinary herb. To 6 in. Small white or rose flowers in umbels.

CUNNINGHAMIA. C. lanceolata. Chinese Fir. z 8-9. (Sometimes survives to Washington, D.C.) A striking evergreen much like cryptomeria. In England, the redwoods are placed in this genus. Evergreen tree to 80 ft.

CUPHEA. *C. hyssopifolia.* A small shrub with tubular white and violet flowers. Sometimes used as a ground-cover in California and Florida.

C. ignea (*C. platycentra*). Cigarette Plant, Cigar Flower. A small shrub that flowers the first year from seed, therefore grown as an annual. Tubular flowers, red with ashy-white ends. Cuphea 'Firefly' has open red flowers. Both are useful as house plants.

CUPRESSUS. *C. arizonica.* Arizona Cypress. z 6b-9. Evergreen, 30-40 ft. Blue-green needles. One of the few evergreens tolerating exposed situations in dry soil.

C. sempervirens. Italian Cypress. z 7b-9. Evergreen, to 75 ft., the cypress of history. Also grown as a shrub; globe forms are known.

CYANOTIS. *C. somaliensis.* Pussy-ears. House plant. Blue or purple flowers in clusters on 9-in. stems. Perennial.

CYCLAMEN. *C. indicum.* Florist's Cyclamen, Alpine Violet. House plant. Nodding flowers — white, lilac, rose or carmine; odorless. Culture is a specialist's job; purchase plants.

C. coum (z 7b-9), *C. europaeum* (z 6-9), and *C. neapolitanum* (z 7b-9) are small-flowered species 4-5 in. high. Rock garden.

CYDONIA. Japanese Quince. See CHAENOMELES.

CYMBALARIA. *C. aequitriloba.* Tiny-Tim Ivy. z 6-9. A miniature version of *C. muralis;* useful groundcover in rock gardens.

C. muralis. Kenilworth Ivy, Aaron's Beard. A popular house plant, vine-like to 3 ft. Kidney-shaped leaves. Flowers inconspicuous, lilac, pink, or white. Often used in hanging baskets.

Sometimes escapes and self-seeds outdoors.

CYNOGLOSSUM. *C. amabile.* Hound's Tongue, Chinese Forget-me-not. z 4-8. Biennial to 2 ft.; blooms the first year. Grown as an annual. Forget-me-not type of blue flowers. June-Oct. Tolerates light shade.

CYPERUS. *C. papyrus.* Bulrushes, Papyrus. z 9-10. The plant in which Moses was hidden. Tender aquatic for lily ponds and greenhouse pools. Stems to 8 ft. Leaves reduced to sheaths. The paper plant of the Egyptians.

CYRILLA. *C. racemiflora.* Leatherwood. z 6-9. Semi-evergreen tree to 30 ft. Small white flowers in racemes, June-July. Acid soil. Sometimes a shrub.

CYSTOPTERIS. *C. bulbifera.* Bladder Fern, Bulblet Fern. Berry Fern. z 4-7. Fronds 18-24 in., deep green. Bulb-like bodies under leaf can be used to propagate new plants. Shade, limestone soil.

C. fragilis. Bottle Fern, Brittle Fern. z 3-6. Like *C. bulbifera* but shorter; leaves quite brittle.

CYTISUS. Broom. Its common name is also applied to other species. Shrubs with scaly leaves and pea-like flowers in clusters. Those listed are hardy to z 6 in sheltered places, except *C. canariensis,* which is grown mainly in greenhouses. Prefer poorer soils, which may be mildly acid.

C. albus. Dwarf White Broom. (Also listed as *C. leucanthus.*) Shrub, 18-24 in., yellowish white flowers in June.

C. canariensis. Genista. Called genista by florists, but not a true genista. Evergreen shrub to 6 ft., forced for its fragrant bright yellow flowers in winter. Grown outdoors in California.

C. nigricans. Spike Broom. Shrub to 3 ft. Bright yellow flowers. June-July. May flower again in fall.

C. praecox. Warminster Broom. Shrub 8-10 ft. Profuse light yellow flowers in May.

C. purgans. Provence Broom. Shrub 30-36 in. Fragrant yellow flowers. May-June.

C. purpureus. Purple Broom. Sprawling shrub to 24 in. Scattered flowers along branches, white, purple or pink. A weeping form grafted on tall stems is an interesting plant.

C. scoparius. Scotch Broom. Shrub 4-9 ft. The hardiest form. Bright yellow flowers. May-June. Many color variations.

DAHLIA. Tender late-summer-flowering plants grown from tubers. See Bulbs (Chapter 4).

DAPHNE. *D. cneorum.* Rose Daphne, Garland Flower. z 5b-8a. Evergreen shrub to 1 ft. Fragrant pink flowers in terminal clusters. April-May.

D. genkwa. Lilac Garland Flower. z 5-9a. Deciduous shrub to 3 ft. with clusters of pale lilac, fragrant flowers on naked branches in April.

D. mezereum. February Daphne, Mezereon. z 5-8. Like *D. genkwa;* intensely fragrant flowers, orchid-purple, in March-April. Fruits poisonous. Partial shade and pH of 6.5 to 7.5.

D. 'Somerset.' z 5-9. Plant sold under this name is the same as *D. burkwoodi,* 2-4 ft., evergreen. White flowers turning pale pink, April.

DATURA. *D. arborea.* Angel's Trumpet. z 9-10. Tree to 12 ft. Long trumpet-shaped white flowers with green stripe. Musk-like odor. Black poisonous seeds attractive to children. Sometimes carried over winter in root cellars in the North.

D. metel. Dopeweed. Annual 4-6 ft.

Tubular white, yellow, or violet flowers to 7 in. long. Juice narcotic.

D. stramonium. Jimson Weed, Jamestown Weed, Thorn-apple. Annual weed, to 5 ft., tropical, but naturalized over most of U.S. White or violet flowers 4 in. long. Spiny fruits with shiny black, very poisonous seeds that are tempting to children. A dangerous plant; three seeds have been known to cause death.

D. suaveolens. Angel's Trumpet, Floripondio. z 9-10. Much like *D. arborea* but with longer white flowers.

DAVIDIA. *D. involucrata.* Dove Tree. z 6b-9a. Deciduous tree 50-60 ft. with showy, white, dove-like flowers, May-June.

DELONIX. *D. regia.* Royal Poinciana, Flame-of-the-forest, Flamboyant, Peacock Flower. z 9-10. To 40 ft. Considered by many the world's most spectacular tree. Brilliant scarlet claw-like flowers with a yellow stripe, 3-4 in. across, mostly in summer. Pods 2 ft. long, about 2 in. wide.

DELPHINIUM. Larkspur, Rocket. The hybrid delphinium is perhaps the most striking of all blue perennials. Pacific Hybrid strains, to 7 ft., are particularly outstanding but are best grown as biennials in colder climates. While all species have poisonous juice (sometimes used as a folk remedy for lice) they seldom cause poisoning. Annual species can be fall-sown in warmer climates; they do not do well in heat.

D. ajacis. Annual Larkspur. Height, 18-48 in. Long spikes of white, blue, lavender, pink, or purple flowers, June-Aug. Seeds may be poisonous.

D. chinensis. Siberian, Chinese, or Bouquet Larkspur. z 4-8. Dwarf biennial or perennial, 12-20 in. See Biennials (Chapter 2).

D. elatum. Candle Larkspur, Bee

Larkspur. z 4-8. Parent of most of the tall perennial delphiniums in commerce. Perhaps all varieties listed as D. *hybrida* belong here. To 6 ft., with spikes of blue flowers.

D. *nudicaule*. Red or Scarlet Larkspur. z 7-9. A most disappointing species. Hard to grow and has been a failure as a parent of red hybrids. Height 12-24 in.

DENNSTAEDTIA. D. *punctilobula*. Hay-scented Fern, Boulder Fern, Cup Fern. z 3-4. Fronds 3 ft. long. Prefers moist, shady soil covering rocks. Leaves have a hay fragrance. Good wildflower plant.

DENTARIA. D. *diphylla*. Twinleaf. Toothwort, Pepper Root. z 4-8. Perennial 8-12 in. Pinkish flowers with white centers. May. Shady woods.

DESMODIUM. D. *canadense*. Beggar's Lice. Tick Trefoil. Tick Clover. z 9-10. Perennial wildflower with clover-like flower. To 5 ft.

DEUTZIA. D. *gracilis*. Slender Deutzia. z 5-10. Shrub to 6 ft. Arching branches, white flowers.

D. *lemoinei*. Lemoine's Deutzia. z 4b-8. Shrub to 7 ft. Like D. *gracilis* but sturdier. The variety D. *l. compacta* to 4 ft. White flowers ¾ in., in large corymbs or panicles.

D. *scabra*. Rough Deutzia. z 5-10. 'Pride of Rochester,' a double form, is popular. White flowers, to ¾ in. long, June-July. Tolerates smoke. Shrub to 7 ft.

DIANTHUS. Low-growing perennial and annual plants with gray-green foliage and usually fragrant flowers. Do not tolerate heat well. The gillyflowers of Shakespeare. Carnations and Sweet Williams belong here. Most are hardy z 5-9, but plants are short-lived.

D. *alpinus*. Alpine Pink. Low-growing rock-garden perennial, 3-4 in.

Rose-colored or crimson flowers, 1½ in. across, with darker eye, solitary.

D. *arenarius*. Sand Pink. Perennial 6-15 in. Fragrant white flowers.

D. *barbatus*. Sweet William. Perennial to 2 ft., usually grown as biennial. See Biennials (Chapter 2).

D. *caesius*. Cheddar Pink. Mat-forming perennial, 3-10 in. Fragrant rose-colored flowers, solitary or a few on a stem.

D. *caryophyllus*. Carnation, Clove Pink. So widely grown in greenhouses that its value as a border flower is often overlooked. Annual border carnations are true perennials; best plants can be saved and propagated by cuttings. Intensely fragrant flowers make this a favorite wherever clove pinks or true carnations are grown.

D. *chinensis*. China or India Pink. Biennial or perennial, 12-18 in., grown as annual. Slightly fragrant flowers to 1 in. across in lilac, pink, white, and red. July.

D. *cruentus*. Blood Pink. Perennial to 1 ft. with tufted grayish foliage. Blood-red flowers in July.

D. *deltoides*. Maiden or Meadow Pink. Prefers rock gardens but grows in the open border. Six-in. stems, mat-forming; crimson-eyed pink, white, or red flowers in June.

D. *neglectus*. Ice Pink, Glacier Pink. Dwarf tufted plants, ¾ in. Reddish purple flowers, not fragrant.

D. *plumarius*. Scotch Pink, Cyclops, Grass Pink. Many garden forms, some with fringed or double flowers, rose to purple, and fragrant. Plants 8-12 in. tall with matted blue-gray foliage. Sometimes flowers all summer.

DICENTRA. D. *canadensis*. Squirrel Corn, Turkey Corn. z 3-8. Perennial plant to 1 ft., with feathery foliage. White flowers tipped purple, nodding, in racemes. Rich, shaded woods. Wild-flower. April.

D. cucullaria. Dutchman's Breeches, White Eardrops. z 3-8. Like *D. canadensis* but with white flowers tipped yellow. Both die down after flowering in April. Perennial.

D. eximia. Plumy Bleeding-heart. z 3-8. To 24 in. Racemes of rose-pink flowers in summer.

D. spectabilis. Bleeding-heart. z 3-8. An old garden favorite with pink heart-shaped flowers in drooping racemes. A white-flowered form is known. To 24 in. Perennial.

DICHONDRA. *D. repens.* Dichondra. z 5-9. A creeping subtropical vine used as a grass substitute. On the Gulf Coast it is considered a noxious weed. *D. carolinensis* is similar, but less hardy. Latter used in Florida as a groundcover.

DICTAMNUS. *D. albus.* Gas Plant, Burning-bush, Fraxinella, Dittany. z 4-8. Stout-stemmed perennial to 4 ft. White, rose, or purple flowers, 1 in. long, in racemes, emit vapor that will ignite on a still night. Pungent, somewhat disagreeable odor. Seeds sown in fall sprout in spring.

DIDISCUS. See TRACHYMENE.

DIEFFENBACHIA. Dumb Cane. A number of interesting tropical foliage plants. If chewed, leaves numb the tongue and throat. Grown only as a house plant in U.S.

DIERVILLA. *D. lonicera.* Gravel-weed, Bush Honeysuckle. z 3-7. Shrub to 3 ft. Small yellowish flowers in June.

D. rivularis. River Bush Honeysuckle. z 4-8. Shrub to 6 ft. Yellowish brown flowers in terminal clusters. June. Damp soil. Suckers.

D. sessilifolia. Wood Honeysuckle. Shrub to 5 ft. In shady woods. Similar to *D. rivularis.*

DIGITALIS. *D. purpurea.* Foxglove, Devil's Fingers, Finger Flower. Perennial to 4 ft., but usually grown as a biennial. See Biennials (Chapter 2).

DIMORPHOTHECA. *D. hybrida.* Cape Marigold. Those in commerce have been so interbred that botanical relationships are mixed. Grown as annuals to 18 in. White, red, yellow or orange daisy-like flowers all summer long.

DIOSCOREA. *D. batatas.* Chinese Yam, Cinnamon Vine. z 4-10. Tropical vine, but tubers (to 3 ft. long, deep in earth) often survive in the North, though top kills to the ground. Clusters of cinnamon-scented flowers in leaf axils in summer. Small axillary tubers.

DIOSMA. *D. ericoides.* Breath-of-heaven, Buchu. z 10. Heath-like shrub to 2 ft. Fragrant white flowers borne in profusion. Aromatic foliage. Grown in greenhouses North.

DIOSPYROS. *D. kaki.* Japanese Persimmon, Kaki. z 6-9. To 40 ft. Edible golden fruits to 3 in. across, puckery when not fully ripe. Glossy foliage, yellowish flowers ½ in. long in spring. Deciduous.

D. virginiana. American Persimmon. z 5-9. Like *D. kaki* but 1½-in. fruits much more astringent until after frost. Deciduous. To 50 ft. or more.

DODECATHEON. Shooting Star, American Cowslip. Small perennials usually in rich woodland soils in shade. Not too amenable to cultivation. Interesting flowers like small cyclamen blooms in pale lavender, pink, and white. Selection of species in American commerce is limited.

DOLICHOS. *D. hosei.* Sarawak Bean. z 9-10. Twining tender perennial forming mats of vines with pea-like flowers. Florida groundcover.

D. lablab. Hyacinth Bean, Lablab. Annual vine (perennial in tropics) to 25 ft. Flowers in dense clusters like a hyacinth spike. White or purple.

DOMBEYA. *D. wallichi.* Pink Ball. z 9-10. Tropical tree to 30 ft. Leaves very woolly underneath. Dense hanging heads of pink or red flowers.

DORONICUM. Leopardbane. z 4-6. Several species, all much alike and all short-lived unless divided every other year. To 24 in. tall, yellow daisy-like flowers in spring. Perennial.

DOUGLASIA. *D. vitaliana.* Yellow Rock Jasmine. z 5-7. Prostrate, tufted, hairy perennial with tubular yellow flowers, solitary or paired.

DOWNINGIA. *D. pulchella.* A western annual, 3-6 in. tall, with showy deep blue flowers with lower lip splotched white, yellow, and purple. Often incorrectly listed as *Clintonia pulchella.*

DOXANTHA. *D. unguis-cati.* Glory Flower. Cat's-claw Vine. z 8-10. Tropical evergreen vine. Yellow trumpet-shaped flowers with orange streaks to 3 in. long and 4 in. across. Grown in greenhouses North.

DRABA. *D. aizoides.* Whitlow Grass. z 5-8. Tufted hairy perennial, sulfuryellow flowers in spring. Interesting rock-garden plant. To 4 in.

D. olympica. Rock Beauty. z 5-7. Even smaller than *D. aizoides.* Orange flowers.

DRACAENA. Dragon Plant. Botanically, most dracaenas in commerce are cordyline. Interesting tropical foliage plants with woody stems and long spade-shaped leaves, often mottled or veined with contrasting colors. Popular house plants.

DRYAS. *D. octopetala.* Wood Nymph, Mountain Avens. Entire plant including flower stems less than 2 in. tall. Woolly leaves, upright white flowers, 1-1½ in. across.

DRYOPTERIS. Wood Fern. *D. bootti.* Boott's Wood Fern. z 3-8. Leaves to 2½ ft. Will tolerate shade in fairly dry spots.

D. cristata. Crested Wood Fern. z 3-8. Striking, feathery fronds to 30 in. long.

D. filix-mas. Male Fern. z 5-9. Nearly evergreen fronds to 4 ft. long, 1 ft. wide. One of the most widely used ferns for shady places.

D. hexagonoptera. Winged Wood Fern, Broad Beech Fern. Triangular fronds 15 in. long, 12 in. wide at base.

D. intermedia. Toothed Wood Fern, Fancy Fern. z 4-9. Fronds, to 18 in., nearly evergreen.

D. linnaeana. Oak Fern. z 4-9. Triangular fronds 11 in. long, 11 in. wide at base.

D. marginalis. Marginal Shield or Wood Fern. z 2-7. Handsome nearly evergreen fern with large fronds, broad at the base, growing in rosette fashion. Ideal in rocky open woods.

D. noveboracensis. New York Fern. z 4-9. Pale green fronds to 24 in. long.

D. phegopteris. Narrow Beech Fern, Long Fern. z 3-6. Triangular fronds 9 in. long, 8 in. wide at base.

DUCHESNEA. *D. indica.* Mock Strawberry, Barren Strawberry. z 5-8. Resemble strawberries in fruit and leaf, but fruit inedible. Trailing perennial useful as groundcover, but may become weedy. Yellow solitary flowers.

DURANTA. *D. repens.* Skyflower, Florida Lilac, Golden Dewdrop. z 9-10. Shrub or small tree, 10-20 ft. Spiny drooping or trailing branches bear ½-in. lilac flowers in summer. Will survive in z 8 but is killed to ground, flowering on new wood the following summer.

ECBALLIUM. *E. elaterium.* Squirting Cucumber. z 5-9. Herbaceous vine. Odd fruits that squirt seeds if pulled from the vine. Both male and female plants needed if fruits are to form. More curious than beautiful.

ECCREMOCARPUS. *E. scaber.* Glory Flower. z 8-10. Woody vine, 12 ft. in the South. Sometimes grown as an annual in the North. Showy orange-red tubular flowers 1 in. long in terminal racemes.

ECHEVERIA. See House Plants (Chapter 11).

ECHINACEA. *E. angustifolia.* Purple Daisy, Pale Coneflower, Hedgehog Coneflower. z 3-8. Weedy, coarse perennial, 18-24 in., with distinctive high-centered, rose-purple, daisy-like flower.

E. purpurea. Purple Coneflower. z 3-8. Somewhat darker flowers than *E. angustifolia* and taller, to 4 ft.

ECHINOCACTUS. *E. grusoni.* See House Plants (Chapter 11).

ECHINOCEREUS. Clump Cactus. Although grown as house plants these are not long-lived under such conditions and should be renewed frequently from specialists (mostly in California). See House Plants (Chapter 11).

ECHINOCYSTIS. *E. lobata.* Wild Balsam Apple, Mock Cucumber. Annual vine with puffy, papery, weak-spined fruits. Carries the virus of cucumber mosaic and has been dropped by most seed dealers for this reason.

ECHINOPS. *E. ritro.* Globe Thistle. z 4-8. Height 18-24 in. Perennial. Round, blue, thistle-like flowers. Survives on seashore. Give plants at least 12 in. in row; they need room.

ECHINOPSIS. *E. eyriesi.* See House Plants (Chapter 11).

ECHIUM. *E. fastuosum.* Shrubby Viper's Bugloss. z 9-10. Shrub 4-6 ft. Gray, hairy-leaved. Dark purple or blue flowers with red stamens, in cylindrical spikes.

ELAEAGNUS. *E. angustifolia.* Russian Olive, Oleaster. z 3-9. Deciduous shrub or small tree, 10-20 ft. Silvery leaves. Inconspicuous, green, fragrant flowers. Egg-shaped mealy fruits, sweet and edible. Tolerates seaside sand. Good wild-bird food.

E. argentea. Silverberry, Wolfberry. z 3-9. Shrub to 10 ft. with silvery leaves; deciduous. Fragrant flowers May-June.

E. multiflora. Gumi. z 5-9a. Shrub 6 ft. Silvery foliage; deciduous. Scarlet edible fruit. Resistant to city smoke. Good wild-bird food.

E. pungens. Thorny Silverleaf. z 7-10a. Spiny shrub, 10-15 ft. Evergreen leaves, silvery beneath. Seaside plant. Flowers silvery white, in axillary clusters in fall, very fragrant.

ELSHOLTZIA. *E. stauntoni.* Mint Shrub. z 5-8. Shrub 2-4 ft. Valuable for spikes of lavender flowers (about 8 in. long) in Sept.-Oct.

EMILIA. *E. flammea* (*E. sagittata*). Tassel Flower, Devil's Paintbrush, Flora's Paintbrush. Annual, often weedy. Tufted orange or scarlet flowers on 18-in. stems. Sometimes catalogued as cacalia.

EMPETRUM. *E. nigrum.* Crowberry. z 1-4. Evergreen prostrate shrub to 10 in. Flowers tiny, fruit a black berry. Acid soil groundcover. Tolerates seaside conditions and thrives on gravelly soil. In far north, occasionally found on limestone rocks.

ENKIANTHUS. *E. campanulatus.* Bellflower Tree. z 5-8. Shrub or small tree 15-25 ft. Small bell-shaped yellow-orange flowers veined red in May. Acid soil. Difficult to transplant.

EPIGAEA. *E. repens.* Trailing Arbutus, Mayflower, Ground Laurel. z 1-5. Prostrate evergreen shrub. The most fragrant North American flower. White or pinkish ½-in. flowers in clusters, April-May. Difficult to grow — needs mycorrhiza. See Chapter 17. Transplant only with ball of earth. Grows only as a wildflower in fairly dry woods.

EPILOBIUM. *E. angustifolium.* Fireweed, Giant Willow Herb. z 1-5. Perennial to 8 ft. Willow-like leaves. Reddish purple flowers (sometimes white) 1¼ in. across, in loose racemes. Damp soil. Wildflower and bee plant. Usually appears after forest fires in the North.

E. nummularifolium. Creeping Willow Herb. z 4-8. Rock-garden perennial, 8 in. Pink or white flowers ¼ in. across, neat, bronzy, round leaves. Excellent groundcover over bulbs.

EPIMEDIUM. *E. alpinum.* Common Barrenwort. z 4-8. Rock-garden and groundcover perennial, to 10 in. The only variety in commerce is *E. a. rubrum,* with red-margined leaves and bright red spurred flowers in May-June.

E. macranthum (*E. grandiflorum*). Longspur Barrenwort. z 4-8. Like *E. alpinum* but with flowers pure white, violet, and red. Longer spurs.

E. pinnatum. Persian Barrenwort. z 4-8. Similar to *E. alpinum* but with creeping rootstocks and brilliant yellow, red-spurred flowers.

EPISCIA. *E. coccinea.* Flame Violet. An African-violet relative, grown as a house plant to supply clear red colors lacking in saintpaulia. Culture identical (see African violet section in Chapter 11). Many other interesting species in commerce, but not widely distributed.

ERANTHIS. *E. hyemalis.* Winter Aconite. See Bulbs (Chapter 4).

ERICA. Heath. Shrubs, sometimes tree-like, of the open moors and heaths of Europe. All require acid soil. A mycorrhizal relationship probably exists for all. Cannot tolerate winter winds or dryness at the root. Small white, rose, or yellow flowers in loose clusters, urn- or bell-shaped; sometimes fragrant.

E. arborea. Tree Heath. z 7-9. To 20 ft. Fragrant white flowers winter or early spring.

E. carnea. Winter Heath. z 6-8. To 12 in. with sprawling branches. Bright red flowers March-May (earlier in warm regions). White and rose varieties known. Good rock-garden plant.

E. mediterranea. Darnley Heath. z 7b-9a. To 10 ft. Deep red or white flowers April-May.

E. scoparia. Besom Heath. z 6-9. Eight to 10 ft. Greenish white flowers, May-June.

E. stricta. Corsican Heath. z 7-9. To 8 ft. Rose-purple flowers in July.

ERIGERON. *E. aurantiacus.* Orange Fleabane, Orange Daisy. z 4-8. Perennial to 10 in. Daisy-like double orange flowers in summer.

E. coulteri. Mountain Daisy. z 6-9. Perennial, 12-20 in. White or lilac flowers 1½ in. across in summer.

E. speciosus. Showy Fleabane. z 4-9. Perennial, 15-30 in. Rose or purple flowers like those of fall asters. Best of the fleabanes. Blooms in summer.

ERINUS. *E. alpinus.* Crevice Plant. z 4-8. Perennial, 3-4 in., tufted, bearing white, purple, or rose flowers ½ in. across in spring. Must have sharp drainage and partial shade.

ERIOBOTRYA. *E. japonica.* Loquat, Japanese or Chinese Plum. z 8-10. Evergreen tree to 20 ft. Grown mostly for its edible, slightly acid, plum-shaped fruits. White fragrant flowers ½ in. across in conspicuous hairy clusters in spring. Tolerates seaside conditions.

ERVATAMIA. *E. coronaria.* Fleur d'-Amour, Adam's Apple, Crape Jasmine. z 9-10. Sometimes sold as *Tabernaemontana coronaria.* Evergreen shrub 5-8 ft. Intensely fragrant white flowers to 2 in. across, resembling gardenias in double form. Also grown as a house or greenhouse plant in the North.

ERYNGIUM. *E. amethystinum.* Eryngo, Blue Sea Holly. z 5-8. Perennial to 24 in. Holly-like leaves and tiny blue flowers in dense ½-in. heads. July-Aug.

E. maritimum. Sea Holly. Like *E. amethystinum* but smaller, to 1 ft. Mentioned by Shakespeare.

ERYSIMUM. *E. asperum.* Siberian Wallflower. z 3-7. Perennial to 30 in. Common name is confusing; actually from North America. Short-lived and often grown as a biennial. Clusters of brilliant yellow or orange four-petaled flowers in early summer. See Biennials (Chapter 2).

E. murale. Wallflower. Biennial but usually grown as an annual. To 20 in. Similar to *E. asperum.*

ERYTHRONIUM. *E. americanum.* Yellow Adder's Tongue, Trout Lily, Dogtooth Violet. z 4-8. Perennial, 4-6 in. Yellow nodding flowers to 2 in. long. Rock-garden plant. A favorite of children for generations. Prefers rich, moist woods.

E. revolutum. Western Trout Lily. z 6-9. Perennial bulb, to 12 in. White, nodding flowers turn purple with age. Rock garden.

ESCALLONIA. *E. montevidensis.* Peruvian Honeysuckle. z 7-9. Shrub or small tree 10-20 ft. New growth somewhat sticky. Fragrant white flowers in clusters.

E. rosea. Rose Peruvian Honeysuckle. z 8-10. Evergreen shrub to 15 ft. Rose-colored fragrant flowers in loose clusters in summer. *E. rubra* similar with red flowers.

ESCHSCHOLTZIA. *E. californica.* California Poppy. Annual to 24 in. Brilliant yellow or orange poppy-like flowers to 3 in. across in summer.

ESPOSTOA. *E. lanata.* See House Plants (Chapter 11).

EUCALYPTUS. Australian Gum Tree. Tall evergreen subtropical trees (sometimes shrubs) mostly with aromatic foliage. Not hardy north of z 9. Tolerate dry conditions. Wood often brittle (though some species are valuable timber trees), and falling twigs are messy. However their quick growth and interesting forms and foliage make them popular in California as ornamentals. Small white, yellow, or reddish flowers in umbels, or heads, have odd little caps.

E. amygdalina. Peppermint Gum. To 300 ft. Foliage has peppermint fragrance.

E. botryoides. Bastard Mahogany, Bangaley. To 150 ft. Interesting furrowed bark.

E. globulus. Blue Gum. To 300 ft. The most widely planted Australian gum. Bluish foliage. Smooth bark.

E. maculata. Lemon Gum, Spotted Gum. To 125 ft. Only the variety *E. m. citriodora* is widely planted; it has lemon-scented foliage.

E. polyanthemos. Australian Beech. To 150 ft. Beech-like foliage.

E. robusta. Mahogany Gum, Swamp Mahogany. To 100 ft. with shaggy bark.

E. rostrata. Red Gum. To 150 ft. Next to blue gum, the most popular species.

E. rudis. Desert Gum. To 100 ft. Rough, persistent bark.

E. sideroxylon. Red Ironbark, Silver Ironbark. To 100 ft. Shaggy red or black bark. Silver Ironbark has silvery foliage.

E. tereticornis. Slate Gum, Gray Gum. To 150 ft. Smooth gray bark that peels off yearly.

E. viminalis. Manna Gum. To 300 ft. Pendulous branches.

EUCHARIS. *E. amazonica* (*E. grandiflora*). Amazon Lily. z 9b-10. Greenhouse bulb in the North, outdoors in the South. Pure white, fragrant, showy, lily-like flowers to 3 in. across on 2-ft. stems.

EUCOMMIA. *E. ulmoides.* Hardy Rubber Tree. z 5-8. Tree to 50 ft. Elm-like with latex-containing sap of no commercial value. Inconspicuous flowers in April before leaves appear.

EUGENIA. *E. paniculata* (*E. myrtifolia*). z 8-10. Evergreen tree or shrub, 10-20 ft. Grown largely for rose-purple fruits ¾ in. in diameter used for jelly. White ½-in. flowers intermittently throughout the year. Shrub forms often used for topiary work.

EUONYMUS. Spindle Tree, Burning-bush. A diverse group of plants including creepers, shrubs, and trees, some evergreen, others deciduous. They thrive in a wide range of soils. Many have vivid autumn colors. Many consider *Euonymus alatus*, with cerise-pink leaves, the most beautiful of all autumn-colored shrubs.

E. alatus. Winged Burning-bush. z 3b-10. Curious corky winged twigs. Purple fruits. The variety *E. a. compactus* seldom exceeds 5 ft. Slow-growing. Glorious rose-red autumn color. Deciduous.

E. americanus. American Burning-bush, Skewerwood. z 4-8. To 8 ft. More open than *E. alatus*, without winged branches. Fruits pink with scarlet capsules when open. Deciduous.

E. atropurpureus. Wahoo, Burning-bush. z 4-8. Shrub or small tree, 8-20 ft. Scarlet capsules open to crimson centers. Deciduous.

E. bungeanus. Winterberry. z 3-8. Shrub or small tree to 16 ft. Showy orange fruits. Deciduous.

E. europaeus. Spindle Tree. z 4-9. Tree or shrub, 8-20 ft. Red or pink fruits. Tolerates seaside conditions. Deciduous.

E. japonicus. Japanese Burning-bush. z 7b-10a. Shrub to 15 ft. Interesting pinkish fruit. Evergreen.

E. japonicus microphyllus. To z 6. Somewhat hardier than the parent species. To 4 ft. Good substitute for boxwood. Evergreen.

E. latifolius. Bleeding-heart Tree. z 6-9. Shrub or tree, 9-20 ft. Bright red fruits. Deciduous.

E. obovatus. Running Bittersweet, Running Strawberry-bush. z 4-8. Procumbent shrub, 12 in. Good groundcover. Deciduous.

E. patens (*E. kiautschovicus*). Shrub, 4-8 ft. Lower branches tend to sprawl. Source from which stock is purchased is important; strains supplied by eastern nurseries hardy only to z 7, but stock from Nebraska has survived in z 4. A valuable hedge species. Semi-evergreen.

E. radicans carrierei. Shrubby Wintercreeper. z 5-10. To 3 ft. Shrub with light green, thick leaves. An excellent low edging shrub. However, some strains can be trained to climb. Confused with the variety *E. r. vegetus*. Newer botanical classification is *E. fortunei carrierei*, but seldom so listed. Evergreen or semi-evergreen.

E. radicans coloratus (*E. fortunei*). Bronze-leaf Wintercreeper. z 5-10. Creeper or climbing vine. Dark green leaves develop maroon-colored reverse in winter. One of the best ground-covers for shade, rooting as it runs and forming dense mats. Foliage persistent through winter, sometimes dropping in spring.

EUPATORIUM. *E. ageratoides.* White Snakeroot, Richweed. z 5-8. Perennial, to 30 in. White flowers similar to ageratum in summer. Should not be planted near areas where cattle graze; causes milk sickness.

E. coelestinum. Hardy Ageratum, Blue Boneset, Mistflower. z 4-9. Like *E. ageratoides* but flowers are blue and plant is not poisonous. Aug.-Sept.

EUPHORBIA. All euphorbias contain a milky juice that may cause severe blistering if it touches the skin.

E. corollata. Flowering Spurge, Milk Purslane. z 3-8. Perennial to 30 in. Grown largely for the white petal-like appendages on the top of the stalks, in summer.

E. marginata. Snow-on-the-mountain. Annual to 2 ft. Upper leaves conspicuously variegated green and white. Sap is poisonous. A popular old-fashioned plant.

E. pulcherrima. Poinsettia. Shrub to 10 ft. The popular Christmas plant in the North with brilliant scarlet leafy bracts (white and pink varieties also known). A weedy shrub in California.

EUPTELEA. *E. polyandra.* Autumn Flame Tree. z 5-9. Shrub or tree to 35 ft. Grown mainly for bright young foliage, reddish at first, changing to green. Brilliant gold and red fall color.

EURYA. *E. ochnacea.* Cleyera. z 6-9. Small shrub grown chiefly for its camellia-like foliage. Small creamy-white fragrant flowers like those of camellia.

EXACUM. *E. affine.* German Violet, Arabian Violet, Arabian Gentian. Biennial to 24 in. Grown as a tender annual for summer flowering in shade, or as a summer pot plant. Fragrant lavender-blue ½-in. flowers.

EXOCHORDA. *E. giraldi.* Pearlbush. z 5-9. Shrub to 10 ft. White, red-tinged flowers in spring in spikes like spires. Acid soil.

E. racemosa. Pearlbush. z 5-9. Shrub like *E. giraldi* but with pure white flowers.

FAGUS. Beech. *F. grandifolia.* American Beech, Red Beech, White Beech. z 4b-8. Tree to 90 ft. Sometimes used for hedges but difficult to transplant. Tolerates, but does not prefer, acid soil. Fall foliage yellow. Somewhat less refined than *F. sylvatica..*

F. sylvatica. European Beech. z 5-8. To 100 ft. One of the noblest of all shade trees with clean gray bark and graceful drooping branches, often spreading 100 ft. across. Many beautiful horticultural forms — weeping, purple-leaved, cut-leaved, etc. Red fall foliage. Deciduous.

FATSHEDERA. *F. lizei.* z 8-10. A botanical curiosity — a true bigeneric hybrid between *Hedera helix* and *Fatsia japonica.* Leaves like English ivy but much larger and thicker. Evergreen shrub not over 6 ft.; used as a vine in California.

FATSIA. *F. japonica.* Japanese Aralia. z 8-10. Evergreen shrub or small tree 10-20 ft. Large palmate leaves. Much planted for tropical effects.

FAUCARIA. *F. tigrina.* See House Plants (Chapter 11).

FELICIA. *F. bergeriana.* Kingfisher Daisy, Blue Daisy, Blue Marguerite. Annual 5-8 in. Not large, but its clear blue flowers are lovely.

FICUS. Fig. *F. carica.* Common Fig. z 8-10. Shrub or tree to 25 ft. Although grown for its edible fruits, the plant is ornamental, with large leaves, hairy below. The varieties that bear on new wood often fruit even when cut down by frost in colder climates, and roots survive if protected, even to New Jersey. Whether this is the fig mentioned in the Bible is not clear.

F. elastica. Rubber Plant, Rubber Tree. z 9b-10. Evergreen shrub or tree to 60 ft. in its tropical home. Its familiar long oval leaves, glossy green with red-tinted reverse, make this a favorite house plant. Of late, many improved varieties for house-plant use have been introduced.

F. exotica. z 9b-10. A house-plant name of uncertain standing; probably only a variety of *F. elastica*. Grown outdoors in California.

F. lyrata. Fiddleleaf Fig. Much like *F. elastica*, but the leaves have a restricted area in blade, suggesting the shape of a violin.

F. macrophylla. Moreton Bay Fig, Bigleaf Fig. z 9b-10. Evergreen tree to 60 ft. in nature. White fruit spotted purplish. House plant. Popular outdoors in California.

F. pandurata. Probably only a synonym of *F. lyrata*.

F. pumila. Creeping Fig. z 9-10. An old-time favorite vine for covering brick walls in conservatories. Mat of heart-shaped leaves. Groundcover. Desirable terrarium plant.

F. radicans. Not as vigorous as *F. pumila;* a variegated variety is known. Trailing.

F. retusa. Malayan Rubber Tree, Shady Fig. Evergreen tree to 30 ft. Useful shade tree in southern Florida. Tolerates salt spray.

F. sycamorus. Sycamore. z 8-9. Deciduous tree to 60 ft.

FIRMIANA. *F. simplex.* Chinese Parasol Tree, Phoenix Tree. z 8-10. Deciduous tree to 60 ft. resembling the plane tree. Tolerates shade. Hand-

some green bark. Greenish fruits to 5 in. long separate into leaf-like bodies bearing seeds.

FITTONIA. *F. verschaffelti.* Handsome house plant with 4-in. oval leaves, red veined.

FOENICULUM. *F. vulgare.* Fennel. Pot herb, perennial, but grown as annual. To 5 ft. Interesting as an ornamental because of fragrance and also because of its mention by Shakespeare.

FONTANESIA. *F. phillyreoides.* Syrian Privet. z 7-9. Foliage similar to that of common privet. To 10 ft.

FORSYTHIA. Golden Bells. z 5-8. Several very early-flowering fragrant shrubs with profuse yellow bloom before the leaves appear. Most have long arching branches. Root readily when ends touch soil and tend to form colonies unless grubbed out periodically. The species *F. ovata* is the hardiest, with amber-yellow blossoms. Flower buds often winter-kill but plants are hardy. Height 5-10 ft.

FOTHERGILLA. *F. gardeni.* Dwarf Alder. z 6-8. Dwarf shrub to 3 ft. Foliage with silvery reverse. White flowers before leaves appear, in spikes. Acid soil.

F. major. Witch Alder. z 6-10. Shrub 7-10 ft. Similar to *F. gardeni.* Scarlet or orange autumn color.

FRAGARIA. *F. vesca.* Wood Strawberry. z 6-8. Useful groundcover in shady woods. True strawberry foliage. White flowers to ½ in. Fruit sometimes white. To 1 ft.

FRANKLINIA. See GORDONIA.

FRAXINUS. Ash. *F. americana.* White Ash. z 5-8. Shade tree to 120 ft. Leafs out late and loses foliage early; desirable where spring and fall sunshine are welcome indoors. Shallow-rooted; hard to grow plants under this tree.

F. caroliniana. Water Ash. z 7-9. To 50 ft. Grows only in swampy soils: useful for wet places, otherwise unimportant.

F. excelsior. European Ash. z 4-9. To 140 ft. The tree mentioned by Shakespeare.

F. 'Moraine.' Moraine Ash. z 6-9. A small round-headed tree to 30 ft. Sometimes attacked by borers.

F. ornus. Flowering Ash, Manna Ash. z 6-9. To 40 ft. Whitish flowers, quite fragrant. Probably the parent of *F. 'Moraine.'* The gum that exudes from injured bark is edible.

F. pennsylvanica. River Ash, Red Ash. z 3-9a. Like *F. americana* but hardier. Survives on the Great Plains. To 60 ft.

F. quadrangulata. Blue Ash. z 4-9a. Tree to 60 ft. or more.

FREESIA. Greenhouse bulb. See Bulbs (Chapter 4), also House Plants (Chapter 11).

FREMONTIA. *F. californica.* Flannel Bush, Leatherwood. z 8b-10. Shrub 6-10 ft. Lobed leaves with flannel-like reverse. Showy yellow flowers 2 in. wide.

FRITILLARIA. *F. imperialis.* Crown Imperial. z 4-10. A stiffly erect bulbous plant about 3 ft. tall, bearing a crown of leaves at the summit directly above a circle of pendulous, orange-red, lily-like flowers. Spring.

F. meleagris. Guinea-hen Flower, Checkered Lily, Snake's-head, Toad Lily. z 4-10a. See Bulbs (Chapter 4).

F. pudica. Golden Fritillary, Yellow Fritillary. z 7-9. Bulb. Plant to 9 in. with nodding yellow or orange bell-shaped flowers tinged purple. Flowers ¾ in. long in clusters of 1-3.

FUCHSIA. *F. hybrida.* Florist's Fuchsia. z 9-10. Though grown outdoors in frostless areas, they do not like hot, dry air. Greenhouse plants in the North, sometimes used for bedding. Striking bell-shaped flowers to 3 in. long in contrasting colors — pink-white, purple-rose, etc. Will grow to 5 ft., usually lower as used. Hanging-basket types are known.

F. magellanica. Hardy Fuchsia. z 8-10. Shrub to 20 ft. if not cut down by frost. The variety *F. m. riccartoni* will survive in z 6b.

GAILLARDIA. *G. aristata.* Blanket Flower. z 5-8. Summer-flowering perennial to 3 ft. with golden daisy-like flowers to 4 in. across. Tolerates dry soils and seaside conditions.

G. pulchella. Indian Blanket, Annual Blanket Flower. Annual to 20 in. Yellow ray flowers to 2 in. with central halo of rose-purple at base of petals. 'Burgundy' is a solid brick red in color.

GALANTHUS. *G. elwesi.* Giant Snowdrop. z 5-9. See Bulbs (Chapter 4).

G. nivalis. Snowdrop. See Bulbs (Chapter 4).

GALAX. *G. aphylla.* Galax, Beetleweed. z 5-9. Stemless perennial evergreen with nearly rounded leaves, used by florists for wreaths, in corsages, etc. Must have damp, rich, acid woodsy soil. Wild-garden subject. White foamy flowers on spikes in summer. To 2½ ft.

GALEGA. *G. officinalis.* Goatsrue. z 5-8. Perennial to 3 ft. with distinct feathery foliage and purple-blue pea-like flowers in terminal clusters. Summer-flowering. White and pink forms are known.

G. orientalis. Caucasian Goatsrue. z 5-8a. Like *G. officinalis,* except to 4 ft.

GALIUM. *G. verum.* Yellow Bedstraw, Our Lady's Bedstraw. z 5-8. Traditionally, the straw on which the

Christ Child lay. Weedy perennial to 36 in. with bristly leaves. Tiny yellow flowers make good bouquet fillers.

GALTONIA. *G. candicans.* Summer Hyacinth. z 7-10. See Bulbs (Chapter 4).

GARDENIA. *G. jasminoides.* Cape Jasmine. z 8-10. Greenhouse shrub in the North, grown for its intensely fragrant, waxy-white flowers 3 in. across, like wide-open white roses. Flowers often double. In the South, an evergreen shrub to 6 ft.

G. veitchi. A variety of *G. jasminoides* with larger, extremely double, flowers.

GASTERIA. *G. acinacifolia.* See House Plants (Chapter 11).

GAULTHERIA. *G. procumbens.* Wintergreen, Checkerberry, Ground Holly, Spiceberry, Teaberry. z 1-5. Prostrate creeping plant with oval leaves, bristly at edges. Source of an extract formerly used for flavoring gums and dentifrices (now produced synthetically). Inconspicuous white flowers. Scarlet fruit a source of bird food. Acid soil.

GAYLUSSACIA. *G. baccata.* Black Huckleberry, High-bush Huckleberry. z 3-8. Shrub to 3 ft. Berries similar to, but less tasty than, true blueberries. Flowers in May, fruit in early July. Good bird-food and seaside subject.

G. dumosa. Gopherberry, Bush Huckleberry. z 4-8. Like *G. baccata* except 18 in. tall.

GELSEMIUM. *G. sempervirens.* Carolina Yellow Jessamine. z 8-10. Woody evergreen vine with intensely fragrant yellow flowers to 1½ in. long in dense clusters. Long blooming. Not a true jasmine. Juice is dangerously poisonous. Can be used as a groundcover.

GENISTA. *G. monosperma.* African Broom. z 8-10. Nearly leafless shrub with green-barked stems (they serve as leaves). Pea-like white fragrant flowers in racemes. March-April. To 10 ft. Tolerates seaside conditions.

G. pilosa. Creeping Broom. z 6-9. Prostrate nearly leafless green stems, warty. Yellow pea-like flowers in clusters. May-June. Good rock-garden plant.

G. sagittalis. Dwarf Broom. z 6-9. Similar to *G. pilosa* but branches not warty. To 1 ft. June-flowering. Rock garden.

G. tinctoria. Dyer's Greenweed. z 5-8. Upright shrub 2-3 ft. Profuse yellow flowers, June-Aug. Several horticultural forms. Yields dye materials.

GENTIANA. *G. acaulis.* Stemless Gentian. z 4-8. Perennial to 4 in. The common blue gentian of English rock gardens. Flowers dark blue, spotted inside, 2 in. long. *G. alba* is a white form of this.

G. crinita. Fringed Gentian. z 4-8. Wildflower that cannot be transplanted. Biennial to 3 ft. Start only from seed. Showy blue-fringed flowers to 2 in. in Sept.-Oct.

G. lutea. Bitterwort, Yellow Gentian. z 5-8. Source of gentian-root extract used medicinally. Perennial to 3 ft. Pale yellow 1-in. flowers in dense cymes, July-Aug. Coarse foliage, but a good border plant.

G. septemfida. Asian Gentian. z 5-8. Perennial to 18 in. Dark blue flowers 2 in. long in clusters, Aug.-Sept. Rock garden.

G. sino-ornata. Chinese Gentian. z 5-8. Perennial to 6 in. Striking pale yellow flowers dotted purple, Aug.-Sept. Spreads by stolons; may become weedy.

GERANIUM. *G. maculatum.* Wild Geranium. z 5-8. Perennial to 2 ft.

Purple or rose-purple flowers, April-May. Wildflower plant.

G. pratense. Meadow Cranesbill. z 5-8. True geraniums such as this differ from the florist's geranium, pelargonium. Perennial 18-30 in. Round leaves, purple or white flowers ½ in. across in summer.

G. robertianum. Herb Robert, Redshanks, Fox Geranium. z 5-8. Sprawling biennial with 18-in. stems. Red-purple flowers ¼ in. long in summer. Fragrant. A subject for woods or thicket.

G. sanguineum. Blood Geranium. z 5-8. The most satisfactory geranium for the open border. Perennial to 15 in. White, pink, pale purple, or rose-purple flowers in early summer.

G. wallichianum. Late Cranesbill. z 5-8. Prostrate rock-garden perennial to 6 in. Flowers purple to 2 in. across in summer.

GERBERA. *G. jamesoni.* Transvaal or Barberton Daisy. z 8-10a. Slender perennial to 1½ ft. with narrow-rayed daisy-like flowers to 4 in. across in white and tones of salmon, pink, and violet.

GEUM. *G. chiloense.* Common Avens. z 5-8. Bright scarlet cup-shaped flowers 1½ in. across (double forms resemble tiny roses) make this a popular garden perennial. Yellow, scarlet, and orange varieties are available. To 20 in., summer-flowering.

G. montanum. Mountain Avens. z 5-8. Like *G. chiloense* but only 12 in. high, with golden flowers in summer.

G. triflorum (*G. ciliatum*). Apache Plume. z 4-8. Quite different from *G. chiloense* and *G. montanum.* Purple flowers on 18-in. stems, not too conspicuous; grown for the striking airy seed heads that form later.

GILIA. *G. capitata.* Thimble Flower.

Annual to 24 in. Thimble-like blue flowers in stalked clusters.

GINKGO. *G. biloba.* Maidenhair Tree. z 5-9. Picturesque, wide-spreading tree to 60 ft. (sometimes taller). One of the best street or park trees, but only male trees should be planted. The fruits of female trees have an obnoxious odor. There is a columnar variety better for home landscapes than the type. Deciduous. Clear yellow foliage in fall.

GLADIOLUS. See Chapter 15.

GLAUCIUM. *G. flavum.* Horned Poppy, Sea Poppy. z 5-8. Orange-yellow poppy-like flowers on branching stems of this biennial make it a useful plant for seaside locations. To 30 in. tall. The variety *G. f. tricolor* has parti-colored flowers.

GLEDITSIA. Honey Locust. z 5-9. Tall deciduous trees, usually thorny. Not particular about soil, honey locusts make excellent shade trees. Tolerant of city conditions.

G. triacanthos. Common Honey Locust. Handsome trees to 120 ft. (usually less in cultivation). Gives pleasant, light shade. Fine-textured leaves. Inconspicuous flowers. There is a thornless variety.

GLOBULARIA. *G. vulgaris.* Globe Daisy. z 6-8. Perennial to 12 in., blue (sometimes white) globe-shaped flowers in May. Needs partial shade; rock-garden plant.

GLORIOSA. *G. rothschildiana.* Glory Lily, Climbing Lily. z 9b-10. Weak, climbing vine to 6 ft. Flowers to 3 in. long like *Lilium superbum,* but crimson with yellowish base to petals. Blooms in spring in Florida and California, in summer when grown as tender bulb North. Handle like gladiolus.

G. superba. Similar to *G. rothschildiana,* but to 12 ft. Flowers later.

GLOXINIA. Listed here under this name, though now classed as sinningia. Greenhouse tuberous-rooted plant with hairy leaves readily injured by careless watering. Striking trumpet-shaped flowers to 3 in. or more long in early summer. Violet, red, white, or spotted blooms. Need shaded glass in greenhouse. Start up tubers in Feb.-March in a mixture of sand and peat at 75°; when well rooted, pot up and grow to blooming. After flowering, store pots without removing earth until ready to start up again at gladiolus temperatures.

GODETIA. *G. amoena.* Farewell-to-spring, Satin Flower. Annual to 2 ft. Striking 2-in. flowers in pink, blue, lilac, or white. Does not do well in summer heat; start early in peat-fiber or bagasse pots and set out before sun becomes too strong in spring. Tolerates light shade.

GOMPHRENA. *G. globosa.* Globe Amaranth. Slender branching annual 1-3 ft. tall with clover-like heads of flowers used as everlastings, in white, yellow, violet, or red.

GORDONIA. *G. alatamaha* (*Franklinia alatamaha*). Franklin Tree. z 6-9. Half-evergreen tree to 20 ft. Fragrant cup-shaped white flowers to 3 in. across in late autumn. A choice species.

G. lasianthus. Loblolly Bay, Bastard Magnolia. z 8-10. Nearly evergreen tree to 60 ft. Fragrant white cup-shaped flowers to 2½ in. in July-Aug.

GREVILLEA. *G. robusta.* Silk Oak. z 9-10. In California a street or landscape tree to 125 ft., but wood is brittle and messy. Bright orange flowers in 4-in. racemes appear on bare branches in spring. Grown as a pot plant North, to 3 ft. Readily raised from seed.

G. thelemanniana. Jewel-flower

Shrub. z 8-10. Shrub to 5 ft., with pinkish flowers tipped green in long racemes. Drought-tolerant.

GYMNOCALYCIUM. *G. schickendantzi.* See House Plants (Chapter 11).

GYMNOCLADUS. *G. dioica.* Kentucky Coffee Tree. z 5-8. Feathery foliage on a tree to 100 ft. Greenish white flowers in clusters in spring, followed by thick red-brown pods to 10 in., used in colonial days as a coffee substitute.

GYNURA. *G. aurantiaca.* Velvet Plant, Violet-leaf. Tender house plant with succulent leaves covered with violet-purple hairs. Often used for bedding. Needs sun to develop color.

GYPSOPHILA. *G. cerastioides.* Baby's Breath. z 5-8. Creeping downy-leaved perennial. Flowers to ⅔ in. across, white with pink veins, in early summer.

G. elegans. Annual Baby's Breath. Annual to 15 in. with soft loose panicles of white flowers ¼ in. across, widely used as fillers in cut-flower arrangements. June to frost. Also pink, rose, and carmine forms.

G. paniculata. Baby's Breath. A popular and easily grown perennial to 3 ft. A profusion of airy white flowers in branched clusters bloom most of the summer. Excellent for bouquets, as well as in the border. Many varieties, some with double flowers.

G. repens. Gypsum Pink, Mistflower, Creeping Baby's Breath. z 5-8. Perennial to 6 in. Prostrate or trailing. Small white or rose-colored flowers.

HAKEA. *H. laurina.* Pincushion Flower, Sea Urchin. z 9-10. Tall shrub or small tree to 25 ft. Globular clusters of crimson flowers followed by egg-shaped fruits. Evergreen.

H. pugioniformis. Dagger-leaf,

Needle Shrub. z 9-10. Shrub to 8 ft. Needle-like leaves, stiff and tipped with spines. White flowers in dense clusters. Evergreen.

HALESIA. *H. carolina.* Carolina Silverbell, Snowdrop Tree. z 5-8b. Deciduous tree to 30 ft. Interesting, white, bell-shaped flowers to ¾ in. long in loose clusters. May. Prefers a sheltered location in woods.

H. diptera. Silverbell Tree, Snowdrop Tree. z 6b-9. Deciduous tree to 30 ft. Flowers larger than *H. carolina.* May.

H. monticola. Tisswood, Mountain Silverbell. z 6-8. Tree to 45 ft. in cultivation, taller in the wild. Flowers similar to *H. diptera.* May. Pink-flowered specimens are rare.

HALIMODENDRON. *H. halodendron.* Salt Tree. z 6-8. Despite its name, a shrub to 5 ft. Pea-like pale purple flowers in racemes. May-June. Salt and alkaline tolerant.

HAMAMELIS. *H. japonica.* Wintergold, Japanese Witch Hazel. z 5-8. Shrub or small tree to 25 ft. Bright yellow flowers ¾ in. long appear during January or February thaws. In cold winters, may flower as late as March.

H. mollis. Chinese Witch Hazel, Winter Hazel. z 6-8. Like *H. japonica* except flowers are reddish at base.

H. vernalis. Spring Witch Hazel, Spring-gold. z 6-8. Shrub to 6 ft. flowering Jan.-March. Yellow with orange base. Branches force readily after midwinter.

H. virginiana. Common Witch Hazel, Autumn Hazel. z 4-8. Shrub to 15 ft. Blooms Sept.-Nov. Bright yellow flowers to ¾ in. long.

HAWORTHIA. *H. cymbiformis.* See House Plants (Chapter 11).

HEDERA. Ivy. Evergreen vines. *H.*

canariensis. Algerian Ivy. z 9-10. May be only a form of *H. helix.*

H. helix. English Ivy. z 6-9. Perhaps the best-loved vine in the world. Useful as a groundcover, for masking bare walls and covering dead trees. Also valuable as a house plant. Leaves are poisonous; cattle should not be allowed to graze on them. Many forms. Until ready to flower, has more or less cut leaves; mature leaves are simple, heart-shaped. The variety *H. h. baltica* (Baltic ivy) is hardy to z 5 but only in winter shade.

HEDYSARUM. *H. coronarium.* French Honeysuckle, Sulla Clover. z 6-9. Shrub-like perennial to 4 ft. Pea-like red flowers, sweetly fragrant in summer. A white-flowered form is available.

HELENIUM. *H. autumnale.* Sneezeweed, False Sunflower, Yellow Star. z 5-8. Coarse branching perennial to 6 ft. Lemon-yellow daisy-like flowers to 2 in. with darker disk. Autumn-flowering. Several improved varieties available.

HELIANTHEMUM. *H. nummularium.* Sun Rose, Rock Rose. z 5-8. The species sometimes listed as *H. mutabile* and *H. vulgare* belong here. Perennial to 12 in. with 1-in.-wide yellow flowers in summer. Desirable rock-garden plant, particularly in improved varieties.

HELIANTHUS. *H. annuus.* Annual Sunflower. Annual to 12 ft. with orange-yellow blooms. The familiar giant disk-flowered plant with head 12 in. or more across. Seeds make excellent bird feed.

H. tuberosus. Jerusalem Artichoke, Girasole, Canadian Potato. z 3-8. Stout perennial to 10 ft. Grown for its edible potato-like tubers. Particularly used by diabetics, since the starch it contains does not affect them adversely. A plant widely eaten by American Indians. Flowers to 3½ in. across, 2-3 on stalk.

HELIOPSIS. *H. laevis* (*H. helianthoides*). False Sunflower, Ox-eye, Orange Sunflower. z 4-8. Perennial to 5 ft. Yellow, gold, or pale orange flowers in loose heads. Summer.

HELIOTROPIUM. *H. arborescens.* Heliotrope, Cherry Pie. Tropical perennial, grown as an annual bedding plant, to 48 in. Intensely fragrant flat heads of purple or lilac flowers ½ in. long make this a favorite. Fragrance varies. When grown from seed, select best specimens for propagating by cuttings.

HELLEBORUS. *H. niger.* Christmas Rose, Black Hellebore, Winter Rose. z 5-8. Perennial to 12 in. Grown for its white to pale purple buttercup-like flowers to 2½ in. across. These may open in late fall if freezing weather is favorable, at Christmas under snow, or in late spring. Protecting plants with a glass-covered frame usually insures Christmas bloom. Poisonous.

H. orientalis. Lenten Rose. Similar to *H. niger*, but flowers are greenish and bloom in spring.

HELXINE. *H. soleiroli.* Irish Moss, Baby's Tears, Fairy Fern. z 9-10. Moss-like plant used as a groundcover in warm regions, but must be kept moist at all times. A favorite delicate foliage plant for house use, particularly in terrariums.

HEMEROCALLIS. Daylily. See Chapter 3.

HEPATICA. *H. americana.* Liverleaf, Mayflower. z 4-8. Perennial to 6 in. Lavender, pink, or white flowers to 1 in. across in early spring. Light shade in woodsy soil, not too acid.

HESPERIS. *H. matronalis.* Dame's Violet, Sweet Rocket, Dame's Rocket. z 5-8. Old-fashioned perennial or biennial, self-sowing freely. To 30 in. tall with lilac-purple or rose-pink flowers to ½ in., which emit fragrance at night. Spring and summer.

HEUCHERA. *H. sanguinea.* Coral Bells, Alumroot. z 4-8. Perennial with rounded or lobed leaves and 20-in. stems topped with tiny coral-colored bells. Blooms for several weeks in summer. Prefers light shade. Smoke resistant. Good groundcover. White forms are available.

HIBISCUS. *H. moscheutos.* Swamp Rose Mallow, Marsh Mallow, Sea Hollyhock. z 5-8. Perennial 3-7 ft. Wide bell-like flowers to 8 in. across in Aug.-Sept. Rose and white forms. The variety called *H. palustris* is merely a narrow-leaved variety of this.

H. rosa-sinensis. Rose of China, Shoeblack Plant, Chinese Hibiscus. z 9-10. Shrub to 10 ft. with huge spider-like flowers to 6 in. across in red, pink, coral, buff, orange, yellow, and near-white. Often grown in greenhouses in the North.

H. syriacus. Shrub Althea, Rose of Sharon. z 5b-8. Shrub to 12 ft. valued for its late summer bloom, in Aug.-Sept. Typical hibiscus flowers to 3 in. across in pure white, eyed-white, rose, clear blue, and crimson.

HIERACIUM. *H. aurantiacum.* Orange Hawkweed, Devil's Paintbrush. z 4-8. Whether this belongs in the perennial border or is a weed depends upon the individual. It can be pesty and invasive. Brilliant tufted orange flowers. To 20 in.

H. umbellatum. Narrow-leaved Hawkweed. z 5-8. Not quite as weedy as *H. aurantiacum*, but similar. To 3 ft., with golden yellow flowers.

HIPPEASTRUM. See AMARYLLIS.

HIPPOPHAE. *H. rhamnoides.* Sea Buckthorn. z 4-8. Spiny shrub or small tree to 20 ft. or more. Silvery foliage, inconspicuous flowers followed by egg-shaped orange-yellow fruits. Male and female trees are needed if fruit is wanted. Valuable seashore plant.

HOLODISCUS. *H. discolor.* Rock Spirea, Creambush. z 6-8. Wide shrub to 12 ft. with white felted leaves. Showy white flowers in long clusters. July. Tolerant of sandy soils.

HOSTA. *H. caerulea.* Blue Plantain Lily. z 5-8. Large spade-like leaves resembling a giant plantain leaf. Flower stem to 30 in. with clusters of pale or deep blue lily-like flowers in summer. Tolerates light shade.

H. japonica (*H. lancifolia*). Japanese Plantain Lily. z 5-8. Similar to *H. caerulea* except flowers are more lavender in color.

H. plantaginea (*H. subcordata*). Fragrant Plantain Lily. z 5-8. Deeply ribbed leaves. Flower stalk to 30 in., bearing fragrant white flowers in August.

HOUSTONIA. *H. caerulea.* Bluets, Quaker Ladies, Innocence. z 5-8. Perennial to 6 in. Pale blue, violet, or white four-petaled flowers ½ in. across with yellow eye. Grows only in moist meadow soils.

HOVENIA. *H. dulcis.* Japanese Raisin Tree. z 5-8. Deciduous tree to 25 ft. Striking broad-oval leaves on long stalks. Raisin-like fruit is edible but not too tasty. Sandy loam soil.

HOYA. *H. carnosa.* Wax Plant, Wax Rose. z 9-10. Vine to 8 ft. or more with wheel-shaped flowers, pinkish white, pink center, ½ in. across, in summer. Marked fragrance. Delightful house plant.

HUMULUS. *H. japonicus.* Hop Vine. Fast-growing annual vine. Not too attractive but useful as quick cover for ugly objects. The tendrils may cause a severe rash.

HUNNEMANNIA. *H. fumariaefolia.* Golden-cup, Mexican Tulip Poppy. Grown North as tender annual. Showy yellow 3-in. poppy-like flowers with orange stamens, July-Sept. To 2 ft.

HYACINTHUS. For culture see Chapter 4. *H. orientalis.* Dutch Hyacinth. z 5-8. Popular spring-flowering hardy bulb. Dense spikes of intensely fragrant 1-in. flowers in white, pink, carmine, lavender, and purple. Valuable for forcing. See House Plants (Chapter 11). Dutch-Roman and French-Roman hyacinths produce smaller, but earlier, flowers. To 1½ ft.

HYDRANGEA. *H. arborescens grandiflora.* Snow-hill Hydrangea, Wild Hydrangea, Seven Bark. z 5-8. Ball-like clusters of white flowers on deciduous shrubs to 5 ft. An old favorite "snowball."

H. macrophylla. House Hydrangea, Hortensia, Florist's Hydrangea. z 6-8. Shrub to 12 ft. The familiar Mother's Day plant with white, pink, or blue ball-like heads of flowers. It is wood-hardy in z 5, but flower buds kill in most winters. To produce blue flowers, soil must be treated with alum. In alkaline soil, same varieties are pink.

H. paniculata grandiflora. Pee-gee Hydrangea. z 4-8. The most satisfactory hardy hydrangea with huge balls of whitish flowers in summer, turning pink with age. Although this may grow to 20 ft., it is best cut back severely each spring and allowed to flower on new wood.

H. petiolaris. Climbing Hydrangea. z 5-8. Why this magnificent vine is not growing against every wall where it survives is a mystery to all horticulturists. A marvelous plant with true hydrangea flowers in summer. Self-adhering, climbing by rootlets. Tolerates seaside conditions. To 25 ft. Flowers in circular clusters.

H. quercifolia. Oakleaf Hydrangea. z 7-9. Shrub to 6 ft. with lobed leaves like those of an oak. White flowers in June, later turning dull purplish pink, in panicles to 12 in.

HYLOCEREUS. *H. undatus.* Night-blooming Cereus. Suitable for indoor culture where there is ample space for its high-climbing stems.

HYMENOCALLIS. *H. calathina.* Basket Flower, Peruvian Daffodil, Spider Lily. z 7-10. Tender bulb. See Bulbs (Chapter 4).

HYPERICUM. *H. aureum.* St. Johnswort. z 6-9. Shrub to 3 ft., with blue-green foliage; flowers to 2 in., like single golden roses with protruding stamens.

H. bucklei. Carolina St. Johnswort. z 6-9. Subshrub to 10 in., used mainly as an undercover or groundcover. Scattered 2-in. golden flowers.

H. calycinum. Aaron's Beard, Rose of Sharon. z 6-9. Evergreen subshrub to 12 in. Clustered yellow flowers to 2 in., July-Sept. Grows on sandy soils and in shade.

H. coris. Corsican St. Johnswort. z 7-9. Like *H. calycinum* but with narrower leaves and flowers to ¾ in., in July-Aug.

H. densiflorum. Bush St. Johnswort. z 6-9. Evergreen shrub to 6 ft. Golden yellow flowers about ½ in. across in dense clusters.

H. moserianum. Goldflower. z 8. Shrub to 2 ft. Garden hybrid, one of the best cultivated hypericums. Flowers to 2½ in. long, solitary or clustered. Midsummer flowering.

H. olympicum. Green St. Johnswort. z 8-10. Subshrub to 12 in, with 2½-in.-wide flowers in clusters in summer.

H. patulum. Japanese St. Johnswort.

z 7-9. Evergreen shrub to 30 in. Solitary golden flowers 2 in. wide, July-Sept. The variety *H. p. henryi* is hardy to z 5b, with larger flowers.

H. prolificum. Bush Broom. z 4-8. Evergreen shrub (deciduous North) to 5 ft. Yellow flowers ¾ in. across in terminal clusters, July-Sept.

H. reptans. Creeping Goldflower. z 7-9. Prostrate shrub: stems root as they run. Yellow flowers to 1¾ in. wide, solitary. Good rock-garden plant.

HYSSOPUS. *H. officinalis.* Hyssop. z 6-8. A flavoring herb to 18 in. but not positively identified as the true hyssop of the Bible. White or blue flowers to ½ in. long in 5-in. spikes.

IBERIS. Candytuft. *I. amara* (*I. coronaria*). Rocket Candytuft. Hardy annual. White fragrant flowers in hyacinth-like spikes. To 12 in. A favorite for cutting.

I. saxatilis. Rock Candytuft. z 7-9. Shrubby perennial, evergreen foliage, 6 in. tall. White flowers in corymbs in early summer.

I. sempervirens. Perennial Candytuft. z 4-8. Evergreen perennial in mild climates, dying down elsewhere. White flowers in long finger-shaped clusters. Best of the perennial candytufts. To 1 ft. May.

I. umbellata. Globe Candytuft. Annual to 16 in. Similar to *I. amara* but not fragrant. Pink, red, violet, or purple flowers.

ILEX. Holly. *I. aquifolium.* English Holly. z 7-9. Evergreen tree to 35 ft. The traditional Christmas Holly with spiny leaves and bright red berries. Requires a soil of pH 4.5 to 5.0. Both male and female plants; be sure both sexes are planted if berries are wanted.

I. cassine. Dahoon, Yaupon. z 8-10. Evergreen shrub or tree to 20 ft. Oblong leaves, often without spines. Fruit yellow or red.

I. crenata convexa. Boxwood Holly, Japanese Holly. z 5b-9. Handsome evergreen shrub to 8 ft. with small round leaves like boxwood. Tolerates shearing. Does not require as acid a soil as other hollies. The variety *I. c. microphylla* has smaller leaves (½ in. long or less) and tolerates more cold than the type.

I. glabra. Inkberry, Bearbush, Winterberry. z 5-8. Evergreen shrub to 6-8 ft. South. Deciduous or semi-evergreen north of z 8. Tolerates seaside conditions and damp soil. Grow with a mulch rather than cultivate; roots resent disturbing. Black berries.

I. opaca. American Holly, White Holly. z 6-9. Similar to, but not as desirable as, English Holly, though it is hardier. To 50 ft.

I. verticillata. Winterberry, Black Alder, Dogberry. z 4-9. Deciduous shrub to 10 ft. with bright red berries in fall, much cut for florist decorations and being exterminated by this use.

I. vomitoria. Yaupon, Cassena. z 8-10. Evergreen tree to 20 ft. with bright red berries. Leaves used to make a strongly purgative tea used by American Indians in ceremonies.

IMPATIENS. *I. balsamina.* Garden Balsam. Tender annual to 24 in. Brilliantly colored flowers like old-fashioned roses in orange, rose, white, purple, and coral. Sow in open in May. Needs rich garden soil, constantly moist for best results.

I. holsti. With *I. sultani*, comprises the group of plants known as patience plants, touch-me-not, snapweed. Tender perennial grown as an annual. Used as pot plant indoors or as a bedding plant for shade. To 24 in. Shiny lance-shaped leaves and spurred flowers to 1¾ in. in scarlet, pink, white, rose, etc. New dwarf plants are particularly valuable for bedding in shade.

INDIGOFERA. *I. decora.* Chinese Indigo. z 6-10. Originally a source of the dye indigo, but now an ornamental plant in greenhouses in the North. A shrub to 2 ft. in the South. Pea-like pink or white flowers about ¾ in. long in racemes.

I. gerardiana. Indian Indigo. z 6-10. Shrub 6-10 ft., rose-red pea-like flowers in racemes.

IONOPSIDIUM. *I. acaule.* Diamond Flower. Annual to 4 in. with tiny violet or white flowers at the end of thread-like stalks. Sometimes grown as a pot plant North in greenhouses. Tolerates damp ground.

IPOMOEA. *I. leari.* Morning-glory, Dawnflower. z 8-10. Tropical vine with showy tubular flowers often 5 in. across, blue with white throat, turning pink as they fade. Perennial.

I. pandurata. Perennial Moonflower, Scammony, Wild Sweet Potato. z 6-10. Native vine with swollen root sometimes weighing as much as 100 lbs. White tubular flowers with purple throat to 4 in. across.

I. purpurea. Common Morning-glory, 'Heavenly Blue' Morning-glory. Annual vine to 20 ft. Tubular blue, white, purple, or pink flowers about 3 in. across. One of the most satisfactory of all annual vines. Excellent house plant if started early outdoors in pots.

IRIS. *I. cristata.* Crested Iris. z 5-9. Native wildflower, perennial to 6 in. Flowers blue to white, crest yellow, light fragrance. June.

I. dichotoma. Vesper Iris. z 5-8. Perennial to 2 ft. Greenish white flowers splashed lavender in August. Often flowers so freely the plant dies, but seeds quickly.

I. germanica. Common Iris, German Iris. z 4-8. This genus is a mixture of several species including *I. florentina*, the orrisroot iris. Hardiness varies with the species in the particular variety. Flower stems to 4 ft. in June. Brilliant shades of blue-white and bluish pink.

I. gracilipes. Slender Iris, Crested Japanese Iris. z 5-9. Rock-garden perennial to 12 in. Slender leaves, flowers pale lavender, veined white, with yellow "target" at center. June-flowering.

I. kaempferi. Japanese Iris. z 5-9. Perennial to 30 in. Perhaps the most striking of all iris. Huge saucer-like flowers to 6 in. across in blue, white, rose, and ivory, curiously veined and mottled. Flowers early in July. Needs moist soil until flowering period is over.

I. orientalis. Yellow Iris. z 4-8. A doubtful name. Probably the species known as *I. ochroleuca.* Perennial to 4 ft. Pale yellow to rich yellow flowers in June. Moist soil. Another species called *I. orientalis* is a perennial to 24 in., with rich blue-purple flowers, but this is rare in commerce. Probably only a variety of *I. sibirica.*

I. pseudacorus. Water Iris, Yellow Flag. z 4-8. Bright yellow flowers. Naturalized in parts of eastern United States. To 3 ft. June-flowering. Flowers sometimes veined purple.

I. pumila. Dwarf Iris. z 4-8. Perennial to 6 in. Many varieties with delightful small flowers in blues, whites, and yellows. Good for rock garden. April-flowering.

I. reticulata. Netted Iris. z 7-9. A bulbous plant scarcely 5 in. tall. Bright purple flowers with yellow throat. Intense violet fragrance. Feb.-March. A greenhouse plant North.

I. sibirica. Siberian Iris. z 4-8. Perennial with narrow grass-like leaves and white, blue, lilac, or purple flowers in late June. Tolerates moist soil.

I. tectorum. Roof Iris. z 7-9. Evergreen perennial to 10 in. Lavender or blue-purple flowers in April. Grown on reed-thatched roofs in Japan. *I. t. album* has white flowers on shorter stems.

I. xiphioides. English Iris. z 8-9. So like *I. xiphium* that they can be treated together.

I. xiphium. Spanish Iris, Bulbous Iris. z 8-9. Reliably hardy only in z 8-9, but if planted late, so that the plants do not make top growth in fall, it can be grown for one season in z 5-7. Stems to 18 in. with purple, yellow, blue, and white typical iris flowers.

ITEA. *I. virginica.* Virginia Willow, Sweet Spire. z 5-8. Deciduous shrub to 6 ft. Willow-like foliage, showy 6-in. racemes of fragrant yellow flowers, June-July. Good red color in fall.

IXIA. African Iris. z 7-9. See Bulbs (Chapter 4).

JACARANDA. *J. acutifolia.* Jacaranda. z 9-10. Plants offered under this name in commerce are probably *J. mimosifolia.* Tree to 50 ft. (often grown as a tall shrub). Fern-like hairy leaves. Showy purple-blue flowers, funnel-shaped, to 2 in. long, in April-June. Although deciduous, it holds its leaves until March in Florida.

J. cuspidifolia. Violet Tree. z 9-10. Like *J. acutifolia* but lower (to 30 ft.) with smaller flowers. Less spectacular.

JAMESIA. *J. americana.* Shagbark Shrub. z 6-10. Deciduous shrub to 4 ft. Fragrant white or pink flowers to ½ in. in dense clusters or cymes, May-June. Showy orange-red autumn foliage.

JASIONE. *J. perennis.* Sheep Scabious, Sheep's Bit. z 6-9. Perennial to 12 in. Blue flowers in 2-in. globular heads in summer.

JASMINUM. *J. floridum.* Golden Jasmine. z 7-10. Semi-evergreen shrub to 3 ft. Golden yellow fragrant flowers ½ in. across in clusters. July.

J. grandiflorum. Catalonian or Spanish Jasmine. z 8-10. A shrub or scrambling vine to 4 ft. Fragrant white flowers to 1½ in. across in clusters during summer. Grown as a pot plant North. Source of jasmine perfume.

J. humile. Italian Jasmine. z 7-10. Shrub to 20 ft. Like *J. grandiflorum* but with clusters of bright golden yellow 1-in. fragrant flowers in summer and fall.

J. nudiflorum. Winter Jasmine. z 6-9. Shrub to 15 ft. Fragrant yellow flowers 1 in. across and solitary in early spring. May be nipped by frost north of z 8.

J. officinale. Common White Jasmine. z 7-9. Vine to 30 ft. Clusters of intensely fragrant white flowers to ¾ in. across in summer.

J. sambac. Zambac, Tea Jasmine, Arabian Jasmine. z 10. Sprawling shrub or vine to 6 ft. Clusters of white flowers 1 in. across turning purple with age. Intensely fragrant.

JUGLANS. Walnut. *J. californica.* California Walnut. z 8-10. Tree to 60 ft. Of little horticultural interest but sometimes used in landscaping.

J. cinerea. Butternut, White Walnut. z 4-8. Tree to 100 ft. Typical walnut foliage. Nuts are oily and rich.

J. nigra. Black Walnut. z 4-8. Tree to 125 ft. Weedy growth and not too satisfactory as a shade tree. Difficult to grow grass or other plants under it because of toxic effect of fallen leaves. Rich, oily nuts.

J. regia. Persian or English Walnut. z 6-9. Tree to 100 ft. with silvery bark. The wood of this tree is the Circassian walnut of commerce, particularly if strongly figured.

J. rupestris. Texas Walnut. z 8-10.

Tree to 30 ft. Not too important in horticulture.

JUNIPERUS. *J. barbadensis.* Bermuda Juniper. z 9-10. Typical evergreen of the Caribbean. Tree to 70 ft., usually wider than tall at maturity. Peeling bark. Needles with silvery reverse.

J. chinensis. Chinese Juniper. z 3-9. A variable species; some almost prostrate and shrub-like, others trees to 50 ft. Clean green evergreen foliage and hardiness make this a favorite evergreen. *J. c. sargenti* is a low, creeping shrub. An excellent groundcover.

J. chinensis pfitzeriana. Pfitzer Juniper. z 4-8. One of the forms of *J. chinensis*, but so widely used as to merit separate mention. Perhaps the most commonly used spreading evergreen, to 10 ft. tall and as wide, gray-green foliage; pyramidal.

J. communis. Common Juniper. z 2-6. Tree or shrub to 20 ft. The blue-black fruit is the source of the flavoring ingredient in gin.

J. conferta. Sand Juniper. z 7-9. A prostrate evergreen suited to sandy soils and seaside.

J. excelsa. Greek Juniper. z 7-9. Pyramidal evergreen to 50 ft. with blue-green needles. The variety *J. e. stricta,* sold in the U.S., is not of this species, according to the Arnold Arboretum.

J. horizontalis. Creeping Juniper, Savin. z 2-7. One of the many creeping or prostrate forms of juniper. Thrives in sandy soils and at seaside. Several horticultural varieties. The Waukegan juniper (*J. h. douglasi*) is distinct because of the rich purple color of its needles in winter.

J. mexicana. Ozark White Cedar. z 7-10. Evergreen tree to 30 ft. Useful as it is the one juniper that thrives in hot climates.

J. sabina. Savin Juniper. z 4-8.

Spreading evergreen to 10 ft. sometimes 12 ft. across. Tolerates city conditions and limey soil. Some object to a "cat-like" odor of foliage.

J. scopulorum. Colorado or Western Red Cedar. Like *J. virginiana,* but tolerates dry hot conditions of the Great Plains. Many forms and varieties. See *J. virginiana.*

J. squamata meyeri. Meyer Juniper. z 4-8. Shrub to 6 ft. Branches stiffly upright. Needles strongly lined with white, glaucous.

J. virginiana. Red Cedar. z 2-8. Slender upright evergreen to 40 ft. Fine-needled, many horticultural forms. Favorite bird food of the cedar waxwing. Not desirable near apples, hawthorns, and crabs; it is an alternate host of apple rust. *J. v. keteleeri,* the bottle-green juniper, resists salt spray.

KALANCHOE. *K. blossfeldiana.* See House Plants (Chapter 11).

KALMIA. *K. angustifolia.* Sheep Laurel, Dwarf Laurel, Lambkill. z 2-8. Evergreen shrub to 3 ft. Lavender-pink flowers to ½ in. across in corymbs or terminal clusters June-July. Needs moist acid soil and partial shade. Foliage poisonous to grazing animals.

K. latifolia. Mountain Laurel, Calico Bush. z 5-8. Shrub or small tree, 5-10 ft. Evergreen. Rose-colored flowers to 1 in. across in terminal corymbs or clusters in May-June. Moist acid soil and partial shade. Like *K. angustifolia,* poisonous to livestock.

K. polifolia. Swamp Laurel. z 4-8. Low shrub to 2 ft., a bog-garden species; of little importance otherwise.

KERRIA. *K. japonica.* Japanese Rose, Globe Flower. z 5-8. Shrub to 8 ft. Flowers like yellow roses, single or double, to 2 in. across, in early summer. Tolerates partial shade.

KNIPHOFIA. Red-hot Poker, Torch Lily. z 8-10. See Bulbs (Chapter 4).

KOCHIA. *K. childsi.* Burning-bush, Belvedere, Mexican Fire-bush, Summer Cypress. Annual to 3 ft. Grown principally for its bright-colored foliage, mingled green and rose-red. Makes excellent temporary hedges. The specific name is artificial; it is a variety of *K. scoparia.*

KOELREUTERIA. *K. paniculata.* Golden-rain Tree, Varnish Tree. z 5-9. Deciduous tree to 30 ft. One of the few yellow-flowered hardy trees. Flower panicles to 1½ ft. Bright papery pods in long clusters in midsummer.

KOLKWITZIA. *K. amabilis.* Beauty-bush. z 5-8. Shrub to 10 ft. Showy honeysuckle-like flowers in June, pale pink with yellow throat. Deciduous.

LABURNUM. *L. alpinum.* Scotch Laburnum. z 6-8. Shrub or small tree to 30 ft. Golden yellow flowers in pendulous clusters. June. All parts of tree are poisonous if eaten.

L. anagyroides. Golden-chain Tree. Bean Tree. Shrub to 30 ft. Like *L. alpinum* except flower clusters are shorter and it blooms two weeks earlier. Pods or beans are poisonous and a potential danger to children.

LAGERSTROEMIA. *L. indica.* Crape Myrtle. z 7-10. Deciduous shrub or tree to 20 ft. Striking white, purple, or carmine flowers in trusses resembling lilacs in effect. Fills a nostalgic place in Florida for northerners pining for lilacs. Good autumn color.

LAGUNARIA. *L. patersoni.* Tulip Tree. (Do not confuse with *Liriodendron tulipifera.*) z 9-10. Evergreen tree to 50 ft. A Pacific Island species, it tolerates seaside conditions. Flower, 2½ in. across, resembles a pink hibiscus more than a tulip.

LAMIUM. *L. maculatum.* Spotted Dead Nettle. z 4-8. Straggly perennial to 1½ ft. of easiest culture. White splash on leaf is quite conspicuous; red-purple flowers like those of mint, not too striking. Chewing leaf may temporarily paralyze the tongue.

LANTANA. *L. camara.* Red Sage, Yellow Sage. z 9-10. A shrub to 4 ft. in the South; a bedding plant in the North. Common name is confusing; it resembles a verbena more than a salvia (true sage). Red, yellow, and orange flowers in flat heads to 2 in. on the same plant.

L. montevidensis. Trailing Lantana. z 9-10. Similar to *L. camara*, but a trailing vine-like shrub with lavender or lilac flowers. *L. sellowiana* is a synonym for this species.

LAPAGERIA. *L. rosea* (see also nolana). Chilean Bellflower. z 9-10. Striking woody vine, tall-growing. Leathery foliage and rose-pink bell-shaped flowers 4 in. long, solitary, or few together. Sometimes forced in the North.

LARIX. *L. decidua.* European Larch. z 4-8. Deciduous tree to 100 ft. A conifer, but sheds its needles in winter. Delicate foliage makes this a popular tree. Prefers rich moist soil.

L. laricina. American Larch, Hackmatack, Tamarack. z 2-6. Tree to 60 ft. Similar to *L. decidua* but narrower in growth. Must have boggy, acid soil.

L. leptolepis. Japanese Larch. z 5-8. Handsome tree with bluish green needles, to 80 ft. Otherwise Like *L. decidua* and *L. laricina*. Less susceptible to canker than other species.

LATHYRUS. *L. latifolius.* Perennial Sweet Pea, Everlasting Pea. z 5-8. Lacking the odor of the annual sweet pea and likely to become weedy, this plant is of limited value. White or pale pink to magenta-pink flowers.

L. maritimus. Beach Pea, Salt Pea. z 2-5. Native along the North Atlantic coast, this semi-vining perennial is a useful dune or seaside plant elsewhere. Violet-magenta flowers. May-June.

L. odoratus. Sweet Pea. Annual vine to 6 ft. An old-fashioned favorite returning to popularity with introduction of new heat-resistant varieties. Inoculation of seed with legume culture recommended. Large flowers of many colors, fragrant, 1-4 on a stem.

LAUROCERASUS. *L. caroliniana.* Carolina Cherry Laurel, Laurel Cherry. z 7-9. Evergreen tree to 35 ft. Glossy rich green foliage makes this a favorite shrub or tree. Excellent for hedges; tolerates shearing. Small cream-colored flowers in racemes.

L. officinalis. Cherry Laurel, English Laurel. z 7-9. Evergreen tree or shrub to 20 ft. Many horticultural forms. Used like *L. caroliniana*. Properly, *Prunus laurocerasus*.

LAURUS. *L. nobilis.* Laurel. Bay-leaf Tree, Sweet Bay. z 8-10. Probably the true laurel of classic literature. A tree, but grown as an evergreen tub plant in various sheared forms. In the North, must be carried over winter in frost-free storage.

LAVANDULA. *L. spica.* True Lavender, French or Spike Lavender. z 6-9. Sometimes listed as *L. vera* or *L. officinalis*. Woody perennial to 3 ft. Grown for its sharply fragrant lavender-colored flowers ½ in. across, dried for sachets. July-Aug.

LAVATERA. *L. assurgentiflora.* American Tree Mallow. z 9-10. Woody perennial to 10 ft. Showy pinkish purple flowers 2¼ in. across, 1-4 in axils. Makes an excellent quick hedge, reaching full height in a single season from seed.

L. trimestris. Annual Tree Mallow. Annual to 3 ft. White or rose-red 4-in. flowers in summer of typical mallow form.

LAYIA. *L. elegans.* Tidy Tips. Hardy annual to 20 in. Daisy-like yellow flowers to 2 in. with neat white tips.

LEDUM. *L. groenlandicum.* Labrador Tea. z 1-5. Evergreen shrub to 3 ft. A bog-loving species demanding acid soil. Cannot tolerate high summer heat.

L. palustre. Bog Rosemary, Crystal Tea, Wild Rosemary. z 1-5. Except for smaller foliage, much like *L. groenlandicum.*

LEIOPHYLLUM. *L. buxifolium.* Box Sand Myrtle, Sleek-leaf. z 5-8. Evergreen shrub to 18 in. Glossy green foliage, terminal clusters of small white flowers May-June. Bog conditions in acid soil needed despite reference to sand in common name.

L. lyoni. Allegheny Sand Myrtle. z 5-8. Lower and more spreading than *L. buxifolium,* but probably only a variety.

LEONTOPODIUM. *L. alpinum.* Edelweiss. z 4-7. Woolly perennial 6-12 in. with white woolly flowers. Romantic tales about this growing only in high Alps and gathered at risk of life and limb are pure fiction; it thrives under ordinary rock-garden culture.

LEONURUS. *L. cardiaca.* Motherwort, Lion's Tail. z 4-8. Weedy mint-like perennial, rather coarse. To 4 ft. Pink-spotted white flowers to ⅓ in. in woolly spikes give this its common name. For wildflower gardens only.

LEPACHYS. *L. pinnata.* Coneflower. z 4-8. Coarse perennial to 5 ft. Showy yellow flowers about 3 in. across with high brown central cone. Summer.

LEPTOSPERMUM. *L. laevigatum.* Australian Tea Tree. z 8-10. An evergreen shrub or tree to 30 ft. Has no connection with tea plant of commerce. Will grow on sand and hold it from blowing. White flowers to ¾ in. in early summer.

L. pubescens. Like *L. laevigatum* but more shrub-like as usually grown.

L. scoparium. Flea Myrtle, Tea Tree. Evergreen shrub or tree to 20 ft. Dense foliage and white ½-in. flowers. Dwarf species with silky foliage is known.

LEPTOSYNE. *L. stillmani.* Golden Wave. Tender annual to 18 in. Catalogued under this name, but botanists insist it is a coreopsis. Flowers like others in this genus, but stems are fleshy or succulent. Bright yellow heads of daisy-like flowers.

LESPEDEZA. *L. japonica.* Similar to the more frequently seen *L. thunbergi* but with white flowers.

L. thunbergi. Bush Clover, Dusty Clover. z 5-8. Shrub to 6 ft., usually kills to ground in winter but flowers on new wood. Valuable for drooping clusters of rose-purple flowers in Sept.-Oct.

LEUCADENDRON. *L. argenteum.* Silver Tree. z 8-10. Tree to 30 ft. Striking silky silver leaves.

LEUCOJUM. *L. vernum.* Spring Snowflake. See Bulbs (Chapter 4).

LEUCOTHOE. *L. catesbaei.* Fetterbush. z 5-8. Evergreen shrub to 6 ft. Drooping clusters of white flowers in April-May on arching branches. Acid soil in light shade.

L. racemosa. Pepperbush, White Osier, Sweetbells. z 5-8. A deciduous shrub, unlike others in this genus. Upright growth to 10 ft. Terminal clusters of white fragrant flowers to ⅓ in. long in May-June.

LEVISTICUM. *L. officinale.* Lovage. z 4-8. A celery-like perennial herb, 3-6 ft., useful in flavoring soups and salads.

LEYCESTERIA. *L. formosa.* Himalayan Honeysuckle. z 8-10. Deciduous shrub to 6 ft. Striking spikes of drooping, purplish, funnel-shaped flowers to ¾ in. with reddish bracts. May-Sept.

LIATRIS. *L. pycnostachya.* Kansas Gayfeather, Prairie Pine, Prairie Snakeroot. z 4-8. Perennial to 4 ft. Dense wand-like spikes of rose-purple flowers in summer or early fall. Often gathered from the wild for florist use.

L. scariosa. Blue Blazing Star. Gayfeather, Button Snakeroot. z 5-8. Like *L. pycnostachya*, except flowers less dense and somewhat interrupted on stalk.

LIBOCEDRUS. *L. decurrens.* Incense Cedar, White Cedar, California Arborvitae. z 6-10. Handsome evergreen resembling the eastern arborvitae. Columnar or pyramidal to 90 ft. Thrives on the Pacific Coast; little grown in the East.

LIGULARIA. *L. kaempferi.* Leopard Plant. z 8-10. Half-hardy perennial with kidney-shaped leaves, to 2 ft. Light yellow flower heads to 2 in. across. The spotted form is a popular house and window-box plant in the North.

LIGUSTRUM. Privet. *L. amurense.* Amur River Privet. z 4-9. Woody shrub to 12 ft. Sold as a substitute for California privet, which it resembles. Does not do too well as a hedge plant; tends to get leggy and die out. *L. vulgare* is more satisfactory where California privet is not hardy.

L. japonicum. Japanese Privet, Wax Privet. z 7-10. Evergreen shrub to 10 ft. Useful evergreen hedge plant where hardy.

L. lucidum. Glossy Privet. z 7-10. Evergreen shrub or tree to 30 ft.

Smooth, glossy leaves, white flowers in 10-in. clusters in Aug.-Sept. Used in tree form as street tree in Florida.

L. nepalense (*L. indicum*). Nepal Privet. z 9-10. Evergreen shrub or small tree, useful for hedges in California.

L. obtusifolium. Ibota Privet. z 5-8. A better shrub for hedges than *L. amurense*, otherwise similar. The variety Regel's privet is widely planted for its graceful arching branches; grow as a specimen rather than in hedges. Grows 6-10 ft. high.

L. ovalifolium. California Privet. z 6-10. Despite its name, California has much better species for hedges than this. Its wide use in z 5, where it kills to the ground, has given this a bad name, but farther south, where it is semi-evergreen, it is a useful hedge. To 15 ft.

L. vulgare. Common Privet, Prim. z 5-9. Deciduous shrub in the North, semi-evergreen in the South, to 12 ft. Perhaps the most satisfactory privet for hedges where true evergreen types are not hardy. Variegated forms are known. The shrub called 'Golden Vicary' belongs here, as does 'Lodense' privet, which can be kept low.

LILIUM. See also Chapter 3. *L. auratum.* Goldband Lily. z 5-8. Hardy bulb to 6 ft. One of the most striking of all lily species with broad ivory petals conspicuously marked with gold and crimson. To 12 in. across. Fragrant. Blooms in July. It is difficult to grow; some of its new hybrids are much more satisfactory.

L. candidum. Madonna Lily, Annunciation Lily. z 5-8. Hardy bulb to 4 ft. Waxy white flowers to 3 in. long. Another difficult lily; one of the few tolerating alkaline soil. Must be planted in July to early September when bulbs are dormant.

L. cernuum. Lavender Lily. z 6-8. Were it not for its unusual color, would probably not be grown; not too spectacular. Flowers to 1½ in., lavender, spotted purple. Fragrant. To 2 ft.

L. chalcedonicum. Scarlet Turk's-cap Lily. z 5-8. Hardy bulb to 4 ft. Vermilion-scarlet flowers, sometimes spotted darker. July. Smell is objectionable to many.

L. giganteum. Giant Lily. z 6-9. Growing this lily is considered the ultimate test of a gardener's skill. Enormous stems to 12 ft., drooping white flowers stained purple in throat to 6 in. long and fragrant. Requires light shade and rich woodland soil. Main bulb dies after flowering, leaving offsets. Botanists classify under cardiocrinum.

L. hansoni. Hanson's Lily. z 5-8. To 4 ft. Tall spikes of fragrant golden flowers, purple-spotted, 1½ in. long and fragrant. June-July.

L. longiflorum. Easter Lily, White Trumpet Lily, Bermuda Lily, Florist's Lily. z 7-10. To 4 ft. The well-known Easter lily with flowers 7 in. long and fragrant. Grown in gardens South. The variety *L. l. giganteum* is often confused with the true *L. giganteum.* *L. harrisi* is a variety.

L. martagon. Turk's-cap Lily, Martagon Lily. z 5-8. To 5 ft. Nodding turban-shaped rose or dark purple flowers spotted purple-black, to 2 in. long, make this a favorite. The white form is particularly fine. June.

L. monadelphum. Caucasian Lily. z 5-8. To 6 ft. Four- to 5-in. nodding bell-shaped flowers, deep yellow, wine red at the base, with tiny black dots. Somewhat lime-tolerant. June.

L. pomponium. Alpine Lily. z 5-8. A Martagon or Turk's-cap-type lily with sealing-wax red flowers 2 in. across on 2½-ft. stems. Odor not pleasant. June-July.

L. pumilum. Coral Lily. z 5-8. Long known as *L. tenuifolium.* To 2 ft. Nodding brilliant bright scarlet flowers, turban-shaped. May. The variety 'Golden Gleam' is larger with golden flowers.

L. regale. Regal Lily. z 5-8. The most widely planted of all lilies. To 4 ft. Trumpet-shaped flowers, white within, stained red or purplish outside, golden throat, to 6 in. long. Intense fragrance. Many hybrids and horticultural varieties are better than the original. June-July.

L. speciosum. Japanese Lily, Queen Lily, Orchid Lily. z 5-8. Because it flowers late, it is seldom seen at its best outdoors. Lovely white flowers to 4 in. long, variously spotted and stained crimson to rose, on 4-ft. stems. Fragrant. Hybrids between this and *L. auratum* are among the finest of all garden flowers.

L. superbum. American Turk's-cap Lily, Wild Tiger Lily, Eastern Turk's-cap Lily, Swamp Lily. z 4-8. To 8 ft. with as many as 35 flowers. Typical Turk's-cap flowers, orange-red, spotted brown with distinct green star in center. Tolerates boggy conditions, yet grows in garden soils.

L. testaceum. Nankeen Lily. To 7 ft. Nodding fragrant flowers pale peach or ivory-rose in color to 3 in. across. Supposedly a hybrid between *L. candidum* and *L. chalcedonicum.* One of the choicest of all lilies. June-July.

L. tigrinum. Tiger Lily. An old-fashioned favorite, with numerous, dark-spotted, orange-colored flowers at the summit of a tall, leafy stem. Petals, to 4 in. long, are curved completely backward. Stamens and stigma are purple. Can be propagated from the small bulbils that form in the leaf axils.

LIMONIUM. *L. sinuatum.* Sea Lavender, Statice, Sea Pink. z 5-8. Perennial 1-2 ft. Grown for its panicles of blue flowers, usually dried for winter arrangements. Tolerates sand and seashore conditions.

L. suworowi. Annual Statice. Annual similar to *L. sinuatum*, to 18 in. Can be planted successively for continuous bloom in summer. Useful for winter bouquets, when dried.

LINARIA. *L. dalmatica.* Toadflax. z 5-8. Perennial 2-4 ft. Yellow flowers like delicate snapdragons in summer.

L. vulgaris. Butter-and-eggs, Common Toadflax. z 5-8. Weedy perennial similar to *L. dalmatica*, but with orange beard.

LINDERA. *L. benzoin.* See *Benzoin aestivale.*

LINNAEA. *L. borealis.* Twinflower. z 1-3. Creeping perennial, evergreen leaves, fragrant rose-pink flowers bell-shaped and in pairs, to ⅓ in. long and fragrant. June-Aug.

LINUM. *L. alpinum.* Alpine Flax. z 5-8. Perennial dwarf flax to 6 in. Bright blue fleeting flowers in spring.

L. flavum. Yellow Perennial Flax, Golden Flax. z 5-8. Perennial 1-2 ft. Golden yellow flowers, ¾ in. across in July.

L. grandiflorum rubrum. Flowering Flax. Hardy annual 1-2 ft. Bright red flowers to 1½ in. in July.

L. lewisi. Prairie Flax. Perennial 2-3 ft. Bright blue flowers 1½ in across in summer. Wildflower.

L. perenne. Blue Perennial Flax. z 5-8. Perennial 18-24 in. Bright sky-blue flowers to 1 in. in June. A white form is known.

L. salsoloides. Eyed Flax. z 6-8. Semi-evergreen perennial to 8 in. White flowers with purple eye. Rock-garden plant.

LIPARIS. *L. liliifolia.* Twayblade. z 5-8. Perennial orchid to 10 in. Not too conspicuous. Yellow flowers, veined red, clustered on 6-in. stem. May-July. Wildflower for light shade in rich soil.

LIPPIA. *L. canescens.* Carpet Grass. z 9-10. Creeping spreading plant grown as a groundcover in Florida.

L. citriodora. Lemon Verbena. z 9-10. Tropical shrub to 8 ft. South, with verbena-like flowers and strong lemon odor when leaves are crushed. Spikes of white flowers. Greenhouse plant North.

LIQUIDAMBAR. *L. formosana.* Formosa Sweet Gum. z 8-10. Majestic tree to 120 ft. Foliage similar to *L. styraciflua.*

L. styraciflua. Sweet Gum, Autumn Flame Tree. z 5-8. Tree to 140 ft., with star-shaped leaves. The sweet gum has probably the most magnificent autumn color of all trees. Needs moist, rich soil.

LIRIODENDRON. *L. tulipifera.* Tulip Tree. White Poplar, Whitewood. z 5-8. Deciduous tree to 150 ft. Bell-shaped, green flowers, marked with yellow, resembling tulips. One of the best landscape trees but needs rich, moist soil.

LIRIOPE. *L. muscari.* Blue Lily-turf. z 6-9. Hardy perennial to 18 in. Evergreen grass-like leaves. Blue flowers in terminal clusters or racemes. Groundcover for shady places in the South. Sometimes a house plant in the North. For the lily-turf exploited as a "lawn grass" see OPHIOPOGON.

L. spicata. Creeping Lily-turf. z 5-10. Evergreen grass-like foliage to 8 in.; pale pink flowers in August. Excellent groundcover for shade, creeping by underground runners.

LITHOPS. See House Plants (Chapter 11).

LITHOSPERMUM. *L. canescens.*

Hairy Puccoon, Gromwell. z 5-8. Hairy perennial to 18 in. Orange flowers in terminal clusters.

L. *prostratum* (*Lithodora diffusa*). Gentian Gromwell. z 7-9. Prostrate evergreen subshrub to 12 in. Deep blue flowers with violet-colored veins. Rock-garden plant.

LIVISTONA. *L. chinensis.* Fountain Palm, Chinese Fan Palm. z 9-10. As grown in tubs, a palm with distinct fan-like leaves. In the South, a tree to 30 ft., leaves sometimes 6 ft. wide.

LOBELIA. *L. cardinalis.* Cardinal Flower, Scarlet Lobelia. z 4-8. Wand-like perennial to 4 ft. with vivid scarlet ½-in. flowers in July-Sept. A semi-bog plant, surviving in the border only if kept constantly moist.

L. *erinus.* Edging Lobelia. Tender annual to 8 in. and perhaps the most striking blue-flowered edging plant available. Clouds of sky-blue or cobalt flowers to ¾ in. across all summer long, some with white eye. Trailing forms available. Tolerates light shade.

L. *siphilitica.* Great Blue Lobelia. z 5-8. Similar to *L. cardinalis,* but flowers a deep bluish purple and it prefers drier soil. To 3 ft. Aug.-Sept. White forms available.

LOBULARIA. *L. maritima.* See *Alyssum maritimum.*

LONICERA. Honeysuckle. *L. claveyi.* Clavey Dwarf Honeysuckle. z 4-8. A hybrid shrub not more than 4 ft. Foliage lettuce green, flowers unimportant. Excellent low hedge plant.

L. *dioica.* Small Honeysuckle, Small Woodbine. z 4-8. A scrambling, lax shrub. Flowers to ½ in. in terminal clusters, yellow, tinged purple, May-June. Deciduous.

L. *fragrantissima.* Winter Honeysuckle, Wintersweet. z 5b-8. Deciduous shrub to 9 ft. White, very fragrant flowers during winter thaws Jan.-March. A choice plant.

L. *heckrotti.* Hybrid Honeysuckle. z 5-8. Spreading deciduous shrub to 3 ft. Purple flowers, yellow within, in terminal clusters borne over a long period in summer.

L. *japonica.* Japanese Honeysuckle. z 4b-8. Semi-evergreen vine to 30 ft. Fragrant white flowers tinged purple and yellow in June. Escaped all over the East where it is now a rampant weed, smothering everything it grows on. The variety *L. j. halliana,* Hall's honeysuckle, is not quite as rampant, yet must be used with care.

L. *ledebouri.* California Honeysuckle. z 9-10. Deciduous shrub to 9 ft. Orange flowers tinged scarlet, June-July.

L. *maacki.* Manchurian Honeysuckle. z 5-8. Deciduous shrub to 15 ft. Large white fragrant flowers fading to ivory, May-June. Bright red fruit in fall.

L. *morrowi.* Morrow Honeysuckle. z 4-8. Deciduous shrub to 8 ft. White flowers, fading to yellow, May-June. Good bird-food plant.

L. *nitida.* Box Honeysuckle. z 6b-9. Semi-evergreen shrub to 5 ft. Fragrant white flowers Sept.-Oct. Purple fruit. Its glossy leaves are outstanding. Tolerates seaside conditions.

L. *periclymenum.* Woodbine. z 5-8. Woody climber to 20 ft. Fragrant white flowers tinged red in terminal clusters. June-Aug. Red fruit Aug.-Sept.

L. *pileata.* Privet Honeysuckle. z 7-9. Spreading semi-evergreen shrub to 1 ft. Fragrant white flowers April-May. Good rock-garden plant.

L. *sempervirens.* Coral Honeysuckle, Trumpet Honeysuckle. z 5-8. Woody climber, evergreen in the South, deciduous in the North. Small flowers in terminal clusters, bright apricot or red outside, yellow inside. April-May. Purple fruit. May-Aug.

L. standishi. Late Winter Honeysuckle. z 5-8. Semi-evergreen shrub in the South, deciduous in the North. Ivory-white fragrant flowers to 2½ in. March-April. Extends season of *L. fragrantissima*, though not as desirable a plant. To 8 ft.

L. syringantha. Lilac Honeysuckle. z 5b-8. Semi-evergreen shrub in the South, deciduous in the North. Fragrant pinkish flowers, to ½ in., May-June. Red fruit.

L. tatarica. Tatarian Honeysuckle, Bush Honeysuckle. z 4-8. Deciduous shrub to 10 ft. Almost too easy to grow; practically the first plant recommended when a tall, quick-growing screen is wanted. White or pink paired flowers to 1 in., May-June; conspicuous red fruit, July-Aug. Excellent summer bird-food plant.

L. thibetica. Tibetan Honeysuckle. z 5-8. Spreading deciduous shrub to 5 ft. Fragrant rose-purple ½-in. flowers, May-June; red fruit, Aug.-Sept.

LOPHOPHORA. *L. williamsi.* Peyote, Mescal Buttons. See House Plants (Chapter 11).

LUNARIA. *L. biennis.* Peter's Pence, Honesty, Moonwort, Satin Flower. Annual or biennial. See Biennials (Chapter 2).

LUPINUS. *L. hartwegi.* Annual Lupine. Annual to 3 ft. (actually a perennial, but flowers readily the first year). Tall spikes of pea-like flowers, bicolored rose and blue, July-Sept.

L. luteus. Golden Lupine. Annual to 2 ft. Fragrant yellow flowers. June-July.

L. mutabilis. Annual to 3 ft., similar to *L. luteus.* Fragrant white flowers with violet or yellow markings on upper petals. June-July.

L. perennis. Quaker Bonnets, Wild Lupine. z 4b-9. Perennial 1-2 ft. Grows best on sandy soils; difficult to collect from the wild. Collect seed and sow where it is to grow. Wildflower. White to blue flowers. June-July.

L. polyphyllus. Perennial Lupine. z 5-8. Perennial to 5 ft. Purple, white, or yellow flowers. June-Sept.

L. subcarnosus. Texas Bluebonnet. Annual to 12 in. Blue flowers with white or yellow patch. May.

LYCHNIS. *L. alba.* Evening Campion. z 4-8. Biennial or perennial plant to 2 ft. Sticky, hairy foliage, fragrant white flowers to 1 in. across at night in summer in few-flowered clusters. An escape and weedy in the East. Double form is finest.

L. alpina. Red Campion, Arctic Campion. z 1-5. Perennial to 9 in. pink flowers, ½ in., in dense terminal heads. April. White and red forms also available.

L. chalcedonica. Maltese Cross, Jerusalem Cross, Scarlet Lightning. z 4-8. Hairy perennial to 30 in. Eye-dazzling scarlet flowers, about 1 in. across, in dense terminal heads. June-July. Other color forms and doubles are available.

L. coeli-rosa. Rose of Heaven. Garden annual 12-15 in. Rose-pink solitary flowers during the summer. Red or purple forms also available.

L. coronaria. Mullein Pink, Dusty Miller, Rose Campion. z 5-8. Perennial to 30 in., grown mostly for its white woolly foliage. Terminal flowers, 1 in. or more across, solitary, bright crimson, white, or pink.

L. flos-cuculi. Ragged Robin, Cuckoo Flower. z 5-8. Weedy perennial to 20 in., stem under flowers sticky. Red or white flowers to 1 in. across in loose clusters. Sometimes double. May-June.

L. haageana. Shaggy Campion. z 5-8. Hybrid perennial to 12 in. with orange-red or scarlet flowers to 2 in. across. May-June.

L. viscaria. German Catchfly. z 5-8. Perennial to 15 in. Sticky stem below flower. Red-purple flowers, ½ in. across in clusters. May-June.

LYCIUM. *L. halimifolium.* Matrimony Vine, Boxthorn. z 5-8. A rank, weedy, woody vine of little beauty, but useful for covering unsightly objects. Scarlet-orange, poisonous fruits.

LYCOPODIUM. Club Moss. Several species of trailing evergreens with small needle- or scale-like leaves; variously known as ground pine, ground cedar, running pine. Useful in terrariums. Gathering in large quantities for Christmas greens (as is done commercially) threatens destruction of the species.

LYCORIS. *L. radiata.* Guernsey Lily. z 8-10. Half-hardy bulb. See Bulbs (Chapter 4).

L. squamigera. Hardy Amaryllis. z 5-8. See Bulbs (Chapter 4).

LYSIMACHIA. *L. nummularia.* Moneywort. Creeping Charley, Creeping Jenny (but see *Nepeta hederacea*). z 5-8. Prostrate perennial with stems rooting at joints, yellow solitary flowers in summer. A good groundcover. If it gets weedy, may be controlled with 2, 4-D.

L. vulgaris. Golden Loosestrife, Willow-wort. z 5-8. Stout erect perennial to 4 ft. Willow-like leaves, panicles of yellow flowers in summer.

LYTHRUM. *L. salicaria.* Willow-herb, Purple Loosestrife. Woody perennial with upright stalks of tiny bright purple-red flowers. To 3 ft. July-Aug. 'Morden's Pink' is a superior variety.

MAACKIA. *M. amurensis.* Amur Yellow-wood, Manchurian Butterfly Tree. z 5-8. Deciduous tree to 40 ft. Erect clusters of white pea-like flowers to ⅓ in. July-Aug. A much-neglected tree.

MACLURA. *M. pomifera.* Osage Orange, Prairie Orange. z 5-8. Shrub or small tree to 50 ft. Tough, spiny wood made this first choice for farm hedgerows in pioneer days, producing barriers "horse-high, bull-strong, and pigtight." Gnarly, round fruits 4-5 in. across like warty green oranges are favorites with flower arrangers. Deciduous.

MAGNOLIA. *M. acuminata.* Cucumber Tree, Yellow Magnolia. z 5b-9. Deciduous tree to 100 ft. Greenish yellow flowers, to 3 in., less conspicuous than other magnolias. Red fruit to 4 in. Foliage turns clear yellow in fall.

M. denudata. Yulan Magnolia. z 5-8. Deciduous tree to 40 ft. Striking hairy buds open to large, white, fragrant, cup-shaped blooms to 6 in. April-May.

M. fraseri. Fraser Magnolia. z 5-8. Deciduous tree to 45 ft. Huge creamy-white, fragrant, typical magnolia blossoms in June, sometimes 11 in. across. Should be planted where the bull bay is not hardy.

M. grandiflora. Bull Bay, Bigleaf Magnolia, Evergreen Magnolia. z 7-9. Evergreen tree to 100 ft. Large, cup-shaped, fragrant white flowers to 8 in. in July-Sept. and huge oval glossy green leaves, rusty-woolly on reverse. The favorite southern tree.

M. salicifolia. Anise Magnolia. z 5b-8. Deciduous tree to 30 ft. More graceful and airy than other magnolias. Fragrant white flowers with purple base, 4 in. across, opening before the leaves. April-May.

M. sieboldi. Oyama Magnolia, Korean Magnolia. z 6-9. Deciduous shrub or tree to 15 ft. Cup-shaped fragrant white flowers 4 in. across. June-July.

M. soulangeana. Saucer Magnolia. z 4-9. Deciduous shrub or small tree to 30 ft. Perhaps the most widely planted species; fragrant flowers to 6 in. across, nearly white inside, purplish pink outside, depending on the variety. Flowers open before leaves appear. May.

M. stellata. Star Magnolia. z 5-8a. Deciduous spreading shrub or small tree to 12 ft. Many-petaled white fragrant flowers 3 in. across before leaves appear. April-May. *M. s. rosea* has pink flowers.

M. tripetala. Umbrella Tree. z 5-8a. Wide-spreading deciduous tree to 40 ft. Typical umbrella shape. White cup-shaped flowers 10 in. across (but with unpleasant odor) appear with the leaves. April-May.

M. virginiana. Sweet Bay, Swamp Laurel, White Bay, Swamp Bay. z 5b-8. Semi-evergreen tree to 60 ft. in the South, but a deciduous shrub in the North. Intensely fragrant white flowers 3 in. across appear with the leaves. May-June. Prefers bog conditions with acid soils.

M. watsoni. Watson Magnolia. z 7-9. Deciduous tree to 25 ft. Creamy-white fragrant flowers with pink sepals, to 6 in. across, in June.

MAHOBERBERIS. *M. neuberti.* Bastard Holly-grape. z 6-8. A botanical oddity, an intergeneric hybrid between mahonia and berberis. Evergreen or semi-evergreen shrub to 6 ft. Some leaves resemble those of barberry, others mahonia. Not known to flower.

MAHONIA. *M. aquifolium.* Oregon Holly-grape. z 5-9. Evergreen or semi-evergreen shrub to 6 ft. with leaves closely resembling those of English holly. Fragrant yellow flowers in racemes. April-May.

M. bealei. Leatherleaf Holly-grape. z 6a-9. Evergreen shrub to 10 ft. Tough glossy compound leaves (each leaflet like a holly leaf). Conspicuous racemes of fragrant lemon-yellow flowers. March-April. Suggests a tropical plant in appearance.

M. nervosa. Water Holly, Oregon Grape. A lower *M. aquifolium,* but with more conspicuous flowers. To 2 ft. Black-blue fruits are edible.

M. repens. Creeping Barberry. z 5-8. Evergreen shrub to 10 in. with underground creeping stems. Excellent groundcover with typical mahonia foliage.

MAIANTHEMUM. *M. canadense.* Canadian Mayflower, Wild Lily-of-the-valley. z 4-7. Creeping perennial with sparse foliage and short stalks of small white bells in racemes. Wildflower or groundcover.

MAJORANA. *M. hortensis.* Sweet Marjoram. Perennial culinary herb, grown as an annual in cool climates, the most fragrant of the various kinds of marjoram. A small bushy plant with white flowers, raised from seeds or cuttings.

MALCOMIA. *M. maritima.* Virginia Stock. Annual to 12 in. with pink, white, red, or purple flowers about ½ in. long. Make successive sowings as blooms last only a short time. A favorite in Victorian gardens.

MALOPE. *M. trifida.* Mallow-wort. Annual mallow to 3 ft. Rose or purple mallow-like flowers on tall stalks all summer.

MALUS. The Apples. Though botanists now place apples into the genus malus separate from pyrus, the malus species have been retained here in pyrus, which see.

MALVA. *M. moschata.* Musk Mallow, Musk Rose. Perennial to 2 ft. Pink or white mallow flowers to 2 in. across in summer. Will grow in garden soils, but tolerates moist soil as well.

MAMMILLARIA. See House Plants (Chapter 11).

MARANTA, *M. leuconeura.* False Arrowroot, Brazilian Arrowroot. Tropical foliage plant to 12 in. Bluish green foliage with white bands along the veins. White flowers, striped purple.

MARRUBIUM. *M. vulgare.* Horehound, Hoarhound. z 5-8. Perennial herb with aromatic white woolly foliage. Whitish flowers in summer. Escaped over most of eastern U.S.

MATHIOLA. *M. bicornis.* Evening Stock. Annual to 15 in. Small scattered purple flowers about ¾ in., strongly fragrant at night. Sometimes lives over as a biennial. Tolerates light shade.

M. incana. Ten-week Stock, Gilly-flower, Brompton Stock. Biennial or perennial plant 1-2 ft. More often grown as a half-hardy annual. Strongly fragrant, pink, white, blush, chamois, or violet flowers about 1 in. long.

MATRICARIA. *M. chamomilla.* German Camomile, Chamomile. Annual to 2 ft., strong-scented foliage used for teas and medicinally. Flower heads 1 in. across, with white rays.

M. inodora. Scentless Camomile, Corn Mayweed. Annual to 2 ft., grown for the flat heads of white flowers, 1½ in. across.

M. tchihatchewi. Turfing Daisy. z 5-8. Low-growing perennial sold as a lawn substitute. To 10 in., but can be kept mown to lawn height: doesn't flower when so grown.

MELALEUCA. *M. armillaris.* Bottlebrush, Tea Tree. z 9-10. Shrub or tree to 20 ft. White flowers in 2-in. spikes resembling a bottlebrush. Tolerates seaside conditions, even muddy or swampy tidal areas.

M. decussata. Lilac Bottlebrush, Tea Tree. z 9-10. Similar to *M. armillaris* but with lilac-colored flowers.

M. hypericifolia. Hillock Tree, Red Bottlebrush, Dotted Bottlebrush. z 9-10. Similar to two preceding species but with red flowers.

MELIA. *M. azedarach.* Bead Tree, Chinaberry, China Tree, Texas Umbrella Tree. z 7-10. Deciduous or semi-evergreen tree to 45 ft. Purplish fragrant flowers. Small yellow fruits. Luxurious tropical-appearing compound leaves make it a favorite.

MELILOTUS. *M. alba.* White Sweet Clover, Bokhara Clover. z 4-9. Biennial to 10 ft. More of a forage plant than a garden subject, but sometimes grown for its sweet-scented flowers.

MELISSA. *M. officinalis.* Lemon Balm, Bee Balm. z 5-8. Mint-like perennial with lemon-scented foliage, grown as a flavoring; sometimes used medicinally.

MENISPERMUM. *M. canadense.* Moonseed, Yellow Perilla. z 5-9. Woody vine to 12 ft. Inconspicuous flowers. Grape-like fruit.

MENTHA. Mint. z 5-8. The mints are an important group of hardy perennial garden plants, used in many ways. All have strongly aromatic foliage, square stems, opposite leaves, and small, lipped, white, pink, or purplish flowers in clusters, heads, or spikes.

M. arvensis. Corn Mint, Field Mint, Wild Pennyroyal. z 4-8. Perennial to 2 ft.

M. piperita. Peppermint, Brandy Mint. z 4-8. The mint grown for essential oil of peppermint. Tends to become weedy, spreading by underground stems. Perennial to 3 ft.

M. requieni. Creeping Mint, Corsican Mint. z 7-9. Creeping herb with tiny round leaves and mauve flowers, interesting rock-garden subject.

MENZIESIA. *M. pilosa.* Minnie Bush. z 5-8. Deciduous shrub to 6 ft. Small bell-shaped white or pink drooping flowers. May-June. Not too ornamental, but will tolerate very acid soil.

MERATIA. *M. praecox.* Winterscent, Wintersweet. z 7-10. (Often listed as *Chimonanthus praecox.*) Deciduous shrub to 10 ft. Yellowish fragrant flowers about 1 in. wide bloom practically all winter.

MERTENSIA. *M. virginica.* Virginia Bluebell, Virginia Cowslip. z 5-8. Perennial to 3 ft. with nodding blue 1-in. flowers in early spring, turning pink with age. Plant dies down soon after flowering and can be moved only then. Does best in rich moist woodlands.

MESEMBRYANTHEMUM. *M. crystallinum.* Ice Plant, Sea Fig, Sea Marigold. z 9-10. Prostrate perennial with glistening white branches and leaves, small white or cerise daisy-like flowers, sometimes so profuse as to cover rocks with sheets of vivid color. Leaves sometimes eaten like spinach. Tolerates seaside conditions well.

M. edule. Hottentot Fig. z 9-10. Prostrate perennial with woody crown. Showy yellow daisy-like flowers to 3 in. across, followed by large edible fleshy fruits. Excellent groundcover. Tolerates seaside conditions.

METASEQUOIA. *M. glyptostroboides.* Dawn Redwood. z 5-8. Deciduous (but coniferous) tree to 150 ft. A recent discovery of a tree heretofore known only from fossils. Present specimens in U.S. too new to determine limits of hardiness, final height, etc. In China, a magnificent specimen to 150 ft. Foliage resembles that of hemlocks, but falls in winter. Perhaps the fastest-growing of all hardy trees, to 6 ft. in a single year.

METROSIDEROS. *M. tomentosa.* Iron Tree, Ironwood, Rata. z 9-10. Tree to 50 ft. Foliage white-felted underneath. Rich red flowers in dense terminal clusters. Wood perhaps the hardest of all trees. Tolerates seaside conditions.

MICHELIA. *M. fuscata.* Banana Shrub. z 9-10. Evergreen shrub to 15 ft. Young leaves coated with a brownish fuzz. Brownish yellow flowers edged with light scarlet to 1½ in. Their strong banana fragrance is offensive to some.

MILLA. *M. biflora.* Mexican Star, Prairie Star. z 9-10. Tender bulb. Starlike, white, fragrant flowers 2 in. across on 12-in. stems. In the North, handle like gladiolus.

MIMOSA. *M. pudica.* Sensitive Plant, Humble Plant. z 9-10. Perennial with finely divided mimosa foliage. When touched, leaves fold and collapse for several minutes. Lavender or rose-purple flowers in heads, seldom seen when this is grown as a house plant in the North. Naturalized in Florida as a roadside weed.

MIMULUS. *M. fremonti.* Monkey Flower. Annual to 8 in. Lipped crimson flowers 1 in. long bear a fancied resemblance to monkey faces. Tolerates light shade and damp ground.

M. luteus. Yellow Monkey Flower. z 3-9. Perennial to 3 ft. Deep yellow flowers with inner spots, in loose terminal clusters in summer.

M. moschatus. Musk Plant. z 6-9. Perennial, sprawling, to 1 ft. Pale yellow, brown-dotted flowers to ¾ in. have a musky odor.

M. ringens. Allegheny Monkey Flower. z 5-8. Branching perennial to

3 ft. Violet flowers to 1½ in., two-lipped. Wildflower subject.

MIRABILIS. *M. jalapa.* Marvel of Peru, Four-o'clock. Perennial grown as an annual. To 3 ft. Light-green, willow-shaped leaves. Fragrant tubular flowers with a flat corolla, white, yellow, pink, and carmine, sometimes splashed and striped, opening in the late afternoon. The fleshy roots sometimes live over if protected by heavy snow cover, or can be stored like dahlias.

MITCHELLA. *M. repens.* Partridge-berry. Creeping evergreen perennial for wild gardens in shade. Excellent in terrariums with its showy scarlet berries.

MITELLA. *M. diphylla.* Bishop's Cap, Mitrewort. z 2-8. Perennial to 18 in. White flowers in terminal racemes to 8 in., deeply cut resembling a mitre. April-May. Light shade in woods, shaded rock garden, or wild garden.

MOLUCELLA. *M. laevis.* Molucca Balm, Bells of Ireland, Shellflower. Grown as an annual for the 2-ft. spikes of nodding, fragrant green bells, used in floral arrangements. Can be dried for winter bouquets.

MOMORDICA. *M. balsamina.* Balsam Apple. Tropical vine, grown in the North as an annual for its curious warted fruits, orange, egg-shaped, to 3 in. long. Formerly used in folk medicine.

M. charantia. Balsam Pear. Taller growing than *M. balsamina.* Pear-shaped, orange-yellow fruits split open to show bright red seeds.

MONARDA. *M. citriodora.* Lemon Mint. Not a mint, but a lemon-scented annual to 1 ft. Flowers white or pink, shaggy.

M. didyma. Oswego Tea, Bee Balm.

z 4-8. Perennial to 3 ft. Bright scarlet shaggy 2-in. flowers in terminal clusters. Birds eat the seeds in fall and winter.

M. fistulosa. Wild Bergamot. z 5-8. Perennial to 30 in. Lavender or lilac-purple flowers, 1½ in., shaggy, with bergamot odor, but not the source of oil of bergamot. White varieties are known.

MORUS. *M. alba.* White Mulberry. z 2-8. Deciduous tree to 50 ft. Introduced originally as food for silkworms. Insipid fruits, but birds prefer them to cultivated fruits.

M. rubra. American Mulberry, Red Mulberry. z 4-8. Somewhat taller than *M. alba* with purplish red fruits, equally attractive to birds.

MUEHLENBECKIA. *M. complexa.* Wire Vine, Maidenhair Vine. z 9-10. Vine with tough, wiry stems. Not too important horticulturally, but if neglected survives without attention. Sometimes grown in hanging baskets.

MURRAYA. *M. exotica.* Orange Jasmine. z 9-10. Evergreen shrub to 10 ft. Very fragrant, white, bell-shaped flowers bloom intermittently throughout the year. Fragrance resembles that of orange blossoms.

MUSCARI. *M. armeniacum.* Grape Hyacinth. z 5-8. See Bulbs (Chapter 4).

M. botryoides. Bluebells, Starch Hyacinth, Grape Hyacinth. z 5-8. See Bulbs (Chapter 4).

MYOPORUM. *M. laetum.* Bastard Sandalwood. z 9-10. Evergreen shrub or tree to 15 ft. White, bell-shaped flowers ⅔ in. across spotted purple. Tolerates seaside conditions.

MYOSOTIS. *M. dissitiflora.* Early Forget-me-not. See Biennials (Chapter 2).

M. palustris. A form of *M. scorpioides.*

M. scorpioides. Perennial Forget-me-not. z 4-8. To 1½ ft. The common forget-me-not of gardens. Escaped and naturalized in the East. Pale blue flowers with yellow eye bloom off and on all summer. Also white and pink forms.

M. sylvatica. Wood Forget-me-not. Annual or biennial. See Biennials (Chapter 2).

MYRICA. *M. caroliniensis.* Bayberry. z 4-9a. Semi-evergreen shrub to 8 ft. Strongly aromatic foliage. Sometimes listed as *M. pensylvanica.* Grayish green berries gathered for wax to make bayberry candles.

M. cerifera. Wax Myrtle, Tallow Tree, Bayberry. z 6-9. Evergreen, or nearly so, shrub or tree to 30 ft. Aromatic gray-green berries. Prefers peaty soil.

M. gale. Sweet Gale. Bog Myrtle, Swamp Myrtle. z 1-5. The northern low form of *M. caroliniensis.* To 4 ft. tall. Prefers boggy acid soils.

M. pensylvanica. See *M. caroliniensis.*

MYRRHIS. *M. odorata.* Sweet Cicely. Perennial herb to 3 ft. Grown for its aromatic foliage.

MYRTUS. *M. communis.* Myrtle. z 9-10. Evergreen aromatic shrub to 10 ft. Grown principally for its foliage. A greenhouse plant in the North.

NANDINA. *N. domestica.* Sacred Bamboo, Heavenly Bamboo, Christmas Berry. z 7b-10. Evergreen shrub (not a bamboo) to 8 ft. Large panicles of tiny white flowers June-July, followed by bright red berries in fall.

NARCISSUS. Daffodil. Spring-flowering bulbs. See Bulbs (Chapter 4). For forcing types see House Plants (Chapter 11).

N. barri. Barr's Narcissus. z 5-8. Stems 12-15 in. A hybrid group, between *N. poeticus* and *N. incomparabilis.* The corona about half the trumpet length.

N. bulbocodium. Hoop-petticoat Narcissus. z 6-8. Stems 8-10 in. Bright yellow or citron-yellow oddly formed flowers, like a dancer's ballet skirt. A lovely small early narcissus.

N. cyclamineus. Portuguese Daffodil. z 5-8. Stems 10-15 in. Cyclamen-like flowers in lemon yellow.

N. incomparabilis. z 5-8. Stems 12-15 in. Yellow crown and segments, the former only half as long as the latter.

N. jonquilla. True Jonquil. z 5-8. To 18 in., yellow flowers in clusters of 2-6. The tube, 1-in. long, about one-half as long as the segments. Rush-like foliage.

N. leedsi. z 5-8. A hybrid group with solitary white flowers, yellow ruffled-edged crown nearly as long as the segments.

N. poetaz. Bunch-flowered Narcissus. z 6-8. Hybrid between *N. poeticus* and *N. tazetta* with pleasant fragrance. Bunch-flowered, much like *N. tazetta.*

N. poeticus. Poet's Narcissus. z 5-8. To 20 in. Popular because of its late flowering period, overlapping the tulips. Chalky-white segments, flat and wide-spread, cup much shorter than the segments, edged red or orange.

N. tazetta. Polyanthus Narcissus. z 7-9. To 24 in. The 'Paperwhite' and 'Chinese Sacred Lily' belong here. Bunch-flowered, the tube about 1 in. long, much shorter than the segments. Favorite varieties for forcing in pebbles and water.

N. triandrus. Angel's Tears. z 5-8. To 12 in. White flowers, cup half the length of the segments. A lovely plant for rock gardens.

NEMESIA. *N. strumosa.* Nemesia.

Tender annual to 2 ft. Dainty flowers in terminal clusters, yellow, brown, pink, white, blue, crimson, or buff, often combining two shades in a single flower. June-Sept. Must be started early as it dislikes heat.

NEMOPANTHUS. *N. mucronata.* Mountain Holly, Prick Timber. z 4-8. Deciduous shrub to 8 ft. Holly-like leaves turning yellow in fall. Fruit a dull-red berry. Needs a cool, woodsy soil.

NEMOPHILA. *N. insignis.* Baby-blue-eyes. Annual to 6 in. Clear blue bell-shaped flowers borne in profusion in summer. White forms are known. Tolerates shade and moisture.

NEOMARICA. *N. gracilis.* Twelve Apostles, Apostle Plant. z 9-10. Unusual flowers, iris-like, to 2 in. across, make this an interesting house plant. Formerly known as *Marica gracilis.*

NEPETA. *N. cataria.* Catnip, Catmint. z 5-8. An herb with a sharp aromatic fragrance, for some reason highly attractive to most cats (some will not touch it). Perennial to 3 ft. Straight stems with flowers like those of the mints.

N. hederacea. Creeping Jenny, Gill-over-the-ground. z 4-8. Creeping perennial with scalloped round leaves and small spikes of purple flowers like miniature snapdragons. Only two of its common names are given (it has over 30). Sometimes listed as *Glecoma hederacea* or *Nepeta glecoma.* Can be a persistent weed if allowed to invade gardens. Highly useful groundcover in shade otherwise.

N. macrantha. Giant-flowered Catnip. z 5-8. Perennial to 10 in. with typical mint-like flowers, some 2 in. long. Sometimes listed as *Dracocephalum grandiflorum.*

N. mussini. Dwarf Catnip. z 5-8.

Perennial to 2 ft. Like the taller form, much liked by cats, which may destroy a planting left unprotected. Excellent groundcover and does not become weedy as does *N. hederacea.* Excellent rock-garden plant. Small pale blue flowers in clusters, grayish foliage.

NEPHTHYTIS. *N. afzeli.* African Arrowhead. House plant resembling the Chinese evergreen (which is often sold as nephthytis by florists).

NERINE. *N. sarniensis.* Guernsey Lily. z 8-10. Semi-hardy bulb to 24 in. Crimson flowers 1½ in. long, often 10 to a cluster, in early spring. Plants die down after flowering and should be allowed to rest until Aug. if forced indoors.

NERIUM. *N. indicum.* Sweet Oleander. z 9-10. Evergreen shrub to 8 ft. Fragrant pink or white flowers, 2 in. across, in terminal clusters. All parts of the plants are dangerously poisonous, as is honey collected by bees from oleander blossoms.

N. oleander. Oleander. z 9-10. Evergreen shrub to 20 ft. Like *N. indicum* but taller. Equally poisonous.

NEVIUSIA. *N. alabamensis.* Snow Wreath. z 5b-8. Deciduous shrub to 6 ft. Produces great billows of 1-in. flowers, creamy white, in July.

NICOTIANA. *N. affinis.* Flowering Tobacco, Jasmine Tobacco. Annual to 20 in. with tubular, creamy white flowers opening towards evening. Heavy fragrance. A favorite old-time annual, but warn children against its toxic properties. Tolerates light shade.

N. hybrida. Largely, colored varieties, red, pink, and crimson, of *N. affinis.*

NIEREMBERGIA. *N. caerulea* (*N. hippomanica*). Cupflower. Although a perennial in the South, usually sown as an annual, though an occasional plant may live over. Bright violet-blue cup-shaped flowers on 9-in. stems practically smother the plant in summer.

NIGELLA. *N. damascena.* Love-in-a-mist, Devil-in-a-bush. Annual to 18 in. with white or light blue flowers 1½ in. across at the ends of branches, thread-like petals forming the "bush" of its common name.

NOLANA. *N. triplicifolia.* Chilean Bellflower. Perennial but grown as an annual. Spreading stems, purple spotted, to 1 ft. Bell-shaped flowers 2 in. across with violet-blue corolla and white and yellow throat.

NYMPHAEA. Waterlily. See Chapter 16.

NYSSA. *N. sylvatica.* Black Gum, Sour Gum. Tupelo. z 5-9. Deciduous tree to 75 ft. Its star-shaped leaves turn dull gold, orange, and rose-purple at first, then the most vivid scarlet of any forest tree; outstanding autumn color. Tolerates seaside conditions.

OCIMUM. *O. basilicum.* Sweet Basil. An annual herb to 3 ft. grown for its aromatic foliage; strong clove or bay-leaf flavor. White or purplish ½-in. flowers. The new 'Black Opal' variety does not have good flavor; useful only as an ornamental.

OENOTHERA. Evening Primrose. *O. acaulis.* Biennial Sundrop. z 4-8. Day-flowering prostrate plant, with white or pink cup-shaped flowers nearly 4 in. wide in early summer.

O. biennis. Biennial Evening Primrose. z 4-8. Night-flowering weedy biennial to 6 ft. Cup-shaped flowers 1-2 in. July-Aug. Interesting because of use to illustrate principles of genetics. *O. lamarckiana,* the supposed product of an early breeding experiment, is a variety. Tolerates seaside conditions.

O. drummondi. Texas Evening Primrose. Annual to 20 in. Flowers yellow or cream color, 3 in. across. Night-blooming. Fragrant.

O. lamarckiana. Dotted Evening Primrose. z 5-8. A supposed variety of *O. biennis,* but with much larger flowers. Stem dotted red. July-Aug.

O. missouriensis. Missouri Primrose, Missouri Sundrop. z 5-8. Day-blooming perennial to 1 ft. Showy yellow flowers to 4 in. July-Aug. Though it tolerates seaside conditions, it is at its best on the Great Plains, but needs some irrigation in dry weather.

O. speciosa. Showy Primrose, White Evening Primrose. z 4-8. A weedy, aggressive perennial to 4 ft. Flowers white, aging pink, 3 in. across, July-Aug.

OLEA. *O. europaea.* Olive. z 9-10. Evergreen tree to 25 ft. Silvery rough leaves, fragrant white flowers to 1½ in. followed by fruits green at first (at which stage they are pickled for green olives), black when fully ripe. An interesting ornamental with a long history extending back to Biblical times.

OMPHALODES. *O. verna.* Venus Navelwort, Creeping Forget-me-not. z 5-8. Perennial to 8 in., creeping but with erect flowering spear-like stalks. Flowers blue or white, ½ in., in spring. A good groundcover.

ONOCLEA. *O. sensibilis.* Sensitive Fern. z 3-8. Rather coarse fern 2-4 ft. tall, with fronds that curl slightly when picked. Useful in moist soil or wild gardens.

ONONIS. *O. fruticosa.* Rest-harrow. z 7-9. Deciduous shrub 2-3 ft. Clover-like leaflets. Pea-like white flowers, splashed with red or rose-pink in summer. Rock-garden plant.

ONOPORDUM. *O. acanthium.* Scotch Thistle, Robert Bruce, Cotton Thistle. z 5-8. Biennial thistle to 5 ft. with bristly white or silvery foliage and typical thistle heads 2 in. across in pale purple. Except for its symbolism in connection with the Scottish people and nation, it would probably be little planted. Can be weedy.

OPHIOPOGON. *O. jaburan.* Lily-turf, Jaburan. z 5-9. Botanists sometimes class this as *Mondo jaburan.* Long, grass-like leaves, white flowers in short terminal racemes. Promoted as a grass substitute, but dies out if moved. A favorite groundcover in the South.

O. japonicus. Dwarf Lily-turf. Cemetery Plant, Summer Grape Hyacinth, z 5-9. While this grass-like groundcover will survive to Boston, its winter color is poor and it looks drab in summer. In the South it is a favorite graveyard plant. To 12 in. Blue flowers on stems resemble those of grape hyacinth.

OPUNTIA. *O. compressa.* Prickly Pear, Barberry Fig, Barbary Fig. z 6-9. The only cactus really hardy in northeastern U.S. Typical flat oval joints with bright yellow flowers 2-3 in., in July. Tolerates seaside conditions.

O. elata. See House Plants (Chapter 11).

O. microdasys. See House Plants (Chapter 11).

ORCHIS. *O. maculata.* z 5-8. Native orchid up to 1½ ft. with small pink flowers. May-Aug. Rock or wildflower garden. Needs rich, moist woods soil and shade.

ORIGANUM. *O. vulgare.* Pot Marjoram, Wintersweet, Wild Marjoram, Oregano. z 5-8. Strong-flavored herb which imparts the typical flavor of many Italian dishes, such as pizza and spaghetti. True sweet marjoram (*Majorana hortensis*) is much milder in flavor.

ORNITHOGALUM. *O. arabicum.* Bird's Eye. z 6-9. Tender bulb. See Bulbs (Chapter 4).

O. thyrsoides. Darling Chinkerinchee. z 8-10. Tender bulb to 1½ ft. with large dense flower clusters. See Bulbs (Chapter 4).

O. umbellatum. Sleepy Dick, Star of Bethlehem, Summer Snowflake, z 5-8. See Bulbs (Chapter 4).

OSMANTHUS. *O. americanus.* Devilwood, Tea Olive. z 8-10. Evergreen tree to 35 ft. Fragrant greenish flowers in May. Needs acid soil.

O. aquifolium. See *O. ilicifolius.*

O. fragrans. Sweet Tea Olive. z 8-9. A favorite conservatory plant in the North, with white, intensely fragrant flowers. In the South, a tree to 25 ft., flowering in April.

O. ilicifolius. Holly Olive. z 7-9. Shrub to 20 ft. Many horticultural forms with purple, yellow, or variegated foliage. Fragrant white flowers. June-July.

OSMUNDA. *O. cinnamomea.* Cinnamon Fern. z 5-8. Tall, coarse fern to 5 ft. Young leaves covered with rusty hairs. Center leaves cinnamon-brown as spores ripen. Prefers low wet lands.

O. claytoniana. Interrupted Fern, Clayton's Fern. z 5-8. Tall, coarse fern to 4 ft., with breaks or interruptions in the fronds. A wet lowland plant.

O. regalis. Royal Fern, Flowering Fern. z 3-10. Huge, coarse fronds to 6 ft. make this the most tropical-appearing of all hardy ferns. It survives even under tropical conditions. One of our most striking wild plants.

OSTROWSKIA. *O. magnifica.* Giant Bellflower. z 7-9. Perennial to 5 ft.

Three to 5 flowers ¾ in. across, blue, in terminal clusters, bell-like.

OSTRYA. *O. virginiana.* Hop Hornbeam, Ironwood, Leverwood. z 4-8. Deciduous tree to 30 ft. Except for its extremely tough wood, it resembles the birch or hornbeam.

OXYDENDRUM. *O. arboreum.* Sourwood, Sorrel Tree. z 5-8. Deciduous tree to 40 ft. Fragrant white flowers, ⅓ in. across, in drooping 10-in. clusters. Midsummer. Foliage turns brilliant scarlet in fall. Hard to transplant; requires acid soil.

OXYPETALUM. *O. caeruleum.* Southern Star. The plant in commerce, grown as an annual, does not match the descriptions of various plants in this genus. An annual with intense sky-blue star-like flowers 1 in. across in clusters of 4-8.

PACHISTIMA. *P. canbyi.* Rat-stripper. z 5-8. A dwarf shrub to 10 in. with tiny holly-like leaves and inconspicuous flowers. Lack of an attractive common name has hurt this useful low-growing plant, used for groundcover, edging, facing shrub, and anywhere a dwarf-size plant is needed. Evergreen.

PACHYSANDRA. *P. procumbens.* Allegheny Spurge. z 6-8. To 1 ft. Evergreen perennial in the South, deciduous in the North. Procumbent with olive-green leaves. Spikes of white flowers, sometimes stained purple, are attractive. April-May. As a groundcover, not as good as *P. terminalis.*

P. terminalis. Japanese Spurge. z 4-8. Perennial to 1 ft., spreading by runners. Thick, glossy olive-green foliage overlapping to form a complete groundcover. Probably the most widely planted of all perennials for this purpose. Prefers acid soil, but grows on alkaline; part or full shade.

PAEONIA. Peony. Spectacular in the June garden, with their large upturned, cup-like blooms, peonies need to be supplemented with other species for continuous bloom. All have wide palmate leaves, borne on stems 18-36 in. tall. One species, the tree peony, is a woody shrub. Perennial. See also Chapter 15.

P. albiflora. Early White Peony. z 3-7. The parent of many garden varieties. To 3½ ft. White, pink, and red flowers, single in the species, double or semidouble in garden hybrids.

P. corallina. Probably the peony of Shakespeare. A European species to 3 ft. with rose-red flowers; does well in partial shade.

P. moutan. Tree Peony. z 5-8. So catalogued, but to botanists, *P. suffruticosa.* Woody shrub to 6 ft. Flowers white, yellow, pink, and red to 1 ft. across. Named varieties in commerce are so badly mixed that selection in bloom in the nursery is advised when possible.

P. officinalis. Common Peony. z 3-7. With *P. albiflora,* parent of most garden varieties. To 3 ft.

P. tenuifolia. Fern-leaved Peony. z 4-7. An old-fashioned garden favorite, with finely divided ferny foliage and brilliant rich scarlet or crimson flowers 3-4 in. across in early May. To 18 in.

PALIURUS. *P. spina-christi.* Jerusalem Thorn, Christ Thorn. z 7-9. Spiny shrub or tree to 18 ft., said to be the tree from which the crown of thorns for the Crucifixion was made. Small greenish yellow flowers in clusters. June-July.

PANDANUS. *P. veitchi.* Corn Plant, Screw Pine. House plant with leaves like those of field corn, variegated with white, 2-3 ft. long. So readily propagated from suckers that it is widely distributed.

PAPAVER. Poppy. *P. alpinum.* Alpine Poppy. z 5-8 Perennial to 4 in., producing 10-in. flower stalks with typical poppy flowers, yellow or white, fragrant. Rock-garden plant.

P. bracteatum. Blood Poppy. z 5-8. Perennial to 3 ft., hairy leaves. Blood-red flowers to 4 in. across. May-June.

P. nudicaule. Iceland Poppy. z 2-6. Perennial to 1 ft. May be grown as a biennial. Needs light soil and good drainage. Often self-sows. Fragrant flowers in shades of white, pink, red, yellow, and orange. May-June.

P. orientale. Oriental Poppy. Stout-stemmed perennial to 4 ft. Huge tissue-papery flowers in brilliant tones of red, scarlet, pink, and near orange, as well as white. Of easy culture, except that it can be moved only after the foliage dies down in July and before it grows again in early September.

P. rhoeas. Corn Poppy, Field Poppy. Annual. Some authorities say that the wild red form of this species was the "lily-of-the-field" to which Christ referred. To 3 ft., flowering in early summer. Flowers red, pink, or white. Shirley hybrids an improved form. The poppy that grew in Flanders Field. Can be seeded in late fall for early spring bloom.

P. somniferum. Opium Poppy. Tall annual (to 3 ft.) with white, pink, or red flowers, 3-4 in. across.

PARKINSONIA. *P. aculeata.* Ratama, Jerusalem Thorn, Palo Verde, Horse Bean. z 8-10. Shrub or tree to 30 ft. Spiny branches, compound leaves, and clusters of fragrant yellow flowers. Used as a hedge plant.

PARROTIA. *P. persica.* Iron Tree. z 5-8. Shrub or small tree to 15 ft. Foliage resembles that of witch hazel. Grown largely for its persistent, brightly colored autumn foliage.

PARTHENOCISSUS. *P. quinquefolia.* Virginia Creeper, American Ivy, Woodbine. z 4-8. Tall-growing vine with 5 leaflets, clinging to walls and trees by disk-tipped tendrils. Bright scarlet foliage in fall.

P. tricuspidata. Boston Ivy. z 5-8. Similar to preceding but a neater, more compact grower. Perhaps the best vine for covering brick houses in North.

PASSIFLORA. *P. caerulea.* Passion Vine. z 9-10. Woody tropical vine to 20 ft. The odd blue-purple, pink, and white flowers supposedly symbolize the Crucifixion. Grown as a house plant in the North.

PAULOWNIA. *P. tomentosa.* Empress Tree, Purple Catalpa. z 6-8. Deciduous tree to 50 ft. with bright violet clusters of fragrant, 2-in. flowers resembling those of the catalpa. May-June. A striking plant, but not long-lived.

PELARGONIUM. Geranium. In this group are the cultivated geraniums used for house, container, and bedding plants. (Wild geraniums belong to the genus geranium.) For culture and selection of pelargonium varieties, see Geraniums in Chapter 15.

P. domesticum. Lady Washington Geranium, Fancy Geranium, Show Geranium. House plant, quite similar in appearance to common geraniums, but of more difficult culture. Large pansy-like flowers with darker spots on white, pink, or red grounds. Of straggling habit unless regularly pinched. They are best grown for winter flowering under glass.

P. graveolens. Rose Geranium. House plant grown for its aromatic foliage, which is high in the essential oil, geraniol, the basis for many modern rose perfumes. A favorite "smelling herb" among Victorian ladies, who carried a leaf of it to church to sniff during long sermons. Rose or pink flowers in small umbels.

P. hortorum. Fish Geranium, Common Geranium. z 9-10. House plant in the North, garden plant (even in hedges) in the South. Some claim to detect a fish-like odor in the petals. Single or double flowers in long trusses, white, pink, red, or orange.

PELLAEA. *P. atropurpurea.* Cliff Brake. z 4-8. Fern to 1 ft. Tough and leathery. For wildflower or rocky cliff planting.

PENNISETUM. *P. ruppeli.* Fountain Grass. z 5-8. Feathery seed heads on 3-ft. stems over gracefully arching foliage. Perennial. *P. cupreum* is a variety with bright copper-colored seed heads.

PENSTEMON. *P. glaber.* Blue Beard-tongue. z 3-8. As a class, the penstemons are much-neglected perennials. True American natives, they are at home in our continental climate. Smooth-stemmed perennial to 2 ft. Flowers like large snapdragons (to 1¼ in.), blue or purple. In summer.

P. heterophyllus. Violet Beard-tongue. z 7-9. Smooth shrub to 5 ft. Purple flowers. Rock-garden plant for California.

P. rupicola. z 5-9. Hardy rock-garden species to 5 in. Crimson flowers.

PEPEROMIA. *P. crassifolia.* z 10. Thick-leaved perennial plant to 12 in. Used as a groundcover in Florida.

P. obtusifolia. Watermelon-begonia. Fleshy-leaved house plant; oblong leaves with reddish margins suggesting a cut watermelon.

PERESKIA. A group of leafy shrubs in the cactus family, one (*P. aculeata,* Barbados gooseberry) grown in tropical climates for its fruit. Also used as stock for grafting the Christmas cactus.

PERILLA. *P. frutescens crispa.* Beefsteak Plant. Annual to 2 ft. with pairs of intensely hued dark red leaves. Propagated by cuttings in the North; self-sows in warmer regions.

PERIPLOCA. *P. graeca.* Grecian Silk Vine. z 7-9. Woody vine to 40 ft. Greenish brown wheel-shaped fragrant flowers in summer. Silky fruits follow.

P. sepium. Chinese Silk Vine. Like *P. graeca* except that leaves are narrower and smaller.

PERNETTYA. *P. mucronata.* Prickly Heath. z 7-9. Evergreen shrub to 2 ft. Urn-shaped typical heath flowers, white or pinkish, but grown principally for the bright red or lilac-colored fruits (berries) that persist in winter. Needs moist, open, sunny, acid soil; seems to thrive best on the Pacific Coast, failing on the Gulf Coast.

PEROVSKIA. *P. atriplicifolia.* Silver Sage, Russian Sage. z 6-8. Shrubby deciduous plant with sage-like foliage, aromatic when crushed. Blue spike-like flowers in Sept. Will survive in z 5 but tops kill back; flowers on new wood. To 5 ft.

PETALOSTEMON. *P. purpureum.* Red Tassel Flower, Prairie Clover. z 5-8. A much-neglected handsome perennial to 3 ft., with flowers in dense spikes, the individual florets pea-like, purple or rose-violet. Good wildflower for the Great Plains.

PETROSELINUM. *P. crispum.* Parsley. The familiar garnish for dinner plates, a low herb with tightly crisped leaves of bright green, usually grown as an annual.

PETUNIA. Unquestionably America's most popular annual today; enough seed sold to produce one billion plants annually if well grown. Treated as annuals, though actually tender perennials. Selected types can be carried over as stock plants and propagated by cuttings. Most of present-day varieties are hybrids. Large-flowered and fringe types, as well as doubles, need an early start if flowers are wanted before mid-July. Small-flowered types do better if sown directly in the ground. Fragrant. Shade-tolerant.

PHACELIA. *P. campanularia.* California Bluebell. Annual to 8 in. Deep blue bell-shaped flowers marked with white. Tolerates semi-desert conditions and grows at seaside.

PHALARIS. *P. arundinacea picta.* Reed Canary Grass, Ribbon Grass. z 4-8. White-, green-, and yellow-striped leaves; an old-fashioned variegated plant still in favor. To 6 ft.

PHASEOLUS. *P. caracalla.* Corkscrew Vine, Snailflower. z 9-10. Perennial vine to 20 ft. Purple or yellow, pea-like, fragrant flowers but with a keel shaped like the shell of a snail.

P. coccineus. Scarlet Runner Bean. Annual vine to 12 ft. Showy crimson or rose-red flowers in summer followed by mottled red pods. The British eat the seeds, which they consider a delicacy, but this must be a cultivated taste since few Americans find them palatable. A white variety, Dutch case-knife bean, with white flowers and green pods, is perhaps the least edible of culinary varieties in existence.

PHELLODENDRON. *P. amurense.* Amur Cork Tree. z 4-8. Deciduous tree to 50 ft. A clean, quick-growing tree that should be planted more; makes a fine round-headed specimen with deeply fissured bark, aromatic leaves and flowers, and conspicuous black fruits in winter.

PHILADELPHUS. Syringa, Mock Orange. Although syringa is the botanic name of our lilacs, it is also a tradi-

tional common name for this group of desirable June-flowering shrubs, noted for their fragrant white flowers, in small clusters or racemes.

P. coronarius. Mock Orange. z 4-8. Deciduous shrub to 10 ft. White, intensely fragrant 1½-in. flowers with definite orange-blossom scent in June.

P. incanus. Woolly Mock Orange. z 4-8. Similar to *P. coronarius,* but foliage woolly beneath.

P. lemoinei. Hybrid Mock Orange. z 4-8. A race of choice shrubs developed by Lemoine, mostly June-flowering with fragrant white flowers, blooming intermittently later. Somewhat lower than *P. coronarius* and *P. incanus* as a class.

PHILLYREA. *P. decora.* Mock Privet. z 7-9. Evergreen shrub to 10 ft. resembling privet. Small fragrant white flowers in dense clusters in April-May, followed by black fruits.

PHILODENDRON. A large group of easy-to-grow house plants with heart-shaped glossy leaves on clambering vines. The new varieties introduced since World War II constitute a bewildering array of varying leaf forms. Valued as indoor foliage plants, as vigorous outdoor vines clinging to tree bark in warm climates.

PHLOMIS. *P. fruticosa.* Jerusalem Sage. z 5-8. Deciduous shrub to 4 ft. with white or ivory woolly foliage and whorls of sage-like yellow flowers in summer. Tolerates seaside conditions.

PHLOX. See also Chapter 3. *P. adsurgens.* Oregon Phlox. z 7-9. Prostrate evergreen perennial to 10 in. Pink or white flowers in loose clusters. Must have well-drained acid soil; best on West Coast, failing in the East.

P. amoena. Sweet Phlox. z 5-8. Spreading perennial to 10 in. Typical phlox flowers, purple, sometimes pink or white to ¾ in. across, in tight heads, early spring. A good rock-garden plant.

P. bifida. Sand Phlox. z 5-8. Low tufted hairy perennial to 6 in. Pale violet to violet flowers, with violet tube, appearing a week before *P. subulata.* Tolerates dune sand conditions.

P. divaricata. Blue Woods Phlox, Wild Sweet William. z 4-8. Perennial to 18 in., spreading by vigorous creeping stems, which root as they run. Sky-blue flowers to 1½ in. in May. Good groundcover and wildflower in open woods.

P. douglasi. Western Phlox. Tufted perennial to 10 in. across. Single flowers that are white, lavender, or purple, ½ in. across in spring.

P. drummondi. Annual Phlox. A hardy, colorful plant to 1½ ft., with flattish clusters of flowers in white, rose, purple, buff, and combinations, some fringed or star-shaped, on dwarf, medium, or giant-size plants.

P. maculata. Wild Sweet William. z 5-8. Perennial to 3 ft. with stems spotted purple. Purple-pink flowers. June-July. Wildflower.

P. ovata. Carolina Phlox. z 4-8. Perennial to 2 ft. Purple flowers 1 in. wide in loose clusters. May-June.

P. paniculata. Perennial Phlox, Garden Phlox. z 4-8. Stiffly upright perennial to 42 in. Wide range of color in garden varieties. July-Aug. Backbone of the late summer garden.

P. procumbens. Trailing Phlox. Probably no more than a variety of *P. amoena.*

P. stellaria. Star Phlox. Annual. A variety of *Phlox drummondi* with star-shaped flowers ¾ in. across, in a wide range of colors. To 12 in.

P. stolonifera. Creeping Phlox. z 4-8. Similar to *P. divaricata* in habit but lower-growing; violet or purple flowers to ¾ in. in June.

P. subulata. Ground Pink, Moss Pink, Flowering Moss, Creeping Phlox. z 4-8. Evergreen creeping perennial forming dense mats of foliage from which rise waves of brilliantly colored ¾-in. flowers in May. Commonly planted and available in a wide range of colors.

P. suffruticosa. Perennial Phlox, Garden Phlox. z 4-8. Like *P. paniculata,* but earlier flowering and lower in habit. Fragrant flowers.

PHOENIX. *P. canariensis.* Canary Island Palm. z 9-10. A handsome palm with leaves 15 to 20 ft. long; tree to 60 ft. at maturity. Widely planted as an avenue tree in California. One of the hardiest of palms; needs fertile soil.

P. dactylifera. Date Palm. z 10. Grown for its sweet fruit, the date of commerce. As an ornamental, less desirable than *P. canariensis.*

P. reclinata. Spiny Feather Palm. z 10. Tends to form multiple clumps, to 20 ft. tall. Similar to *P. canariensis* but not as hardy.

P. roebelini. Pygmy Palm, Baby Palm. z 9-10. Palm not over 6 ft. with graceful drooping leaves; the potted palm so fashionable for decoration in Victorian days.

PHOTINIA. *P. serrulata.* Christmas Berry. z 7-9. Evergreen shrub or tree to 30 ft., resembling a hawthorn. Shiny oblong leaves, reddish in young stage. Clusters of white flowers followed by bright red berries in fall and early winter.

P. villosa. Low Christmas Berry. z 5-8. Similar to *P. serrulata,* except deciduous, somewhat more hardy, and less tall (to 15 ft.).

PHYSALIS. *P. alkekengi.* Winter Cherry, Chinese Lantern, Strawberry Tomato. Perennial to 2 ft. with invasive creeping rootstocks that are difficult to eradicate. Grown for its red-orange, globular, hollow fruits 2 in. across, which are dried for winter arrangements.

PHYSOCARPUS. *P. monogynus.* Mountain Ninebark. z 5-8. Deciduous shrub to 3 ft. with multi-layer peeling bark. Flowers in white terminal clusters in early summer.

P. opulifolius. Ninebark. z 4-8. Similar to *P. monogynus* but about twice as tall.

PHYSOSTEGIA. *P. virginiana.* Obedient Flower, False Dragonhead. z 4-8. Perennial to 4 ft. with 1-in. flowers in spikes, like snapdragons, violet-pink or white, in summer. Wildflower.

PHYTEUMA. *P. hemisphaericum.* Horned Rampion, Stemless Bellflower. z 5-8. Low perennial, not over 6 in., with blue or white heads of flowers like a campanula, with long, curved, and horn-like buds. Blooms in early summer.

P. scheuchzeri. Italian Horned Rampion. z 6-8. Taller than *P. hemisphaericum,* to 1½ ft., but otherwise similar.

PICEA. Spruce. *P. abies.* Norway Spruce. z 2-7. Perhaps the most widely planted cultivated coniferous evergreen in the U.S. Stately pyramidal tree to 150 ft., but usually much lower in cultivation. Many horticultural varieties.

P. bicolor. Alcock Spruce. z 5-8. Pyramidal conifer to 75 ft. Needles marked with two white stripes.

P. engelmanni. Engelmann Spruce. z 2-6. A noble coniferous evergreen to 150 ft., lower in cultivation. Clean blue-green foliage.

P. glauca. White Spruce, Skunk Spruce. z 1-6. Coniferous evergreen to 100 ft. Graceful drooping branchlets, rich blue-green foliage. The Black Hills spruce is a variety. The variety

P. g. conica is the dwarf Alberta spruce which grows scarcely an inch a year.

P. omorika. Serbian Spruce. z 5-8. Coniferous evergreen to 100 ft. Ascending branches. Does better in the East and South than other spruces.

P. polita. Tigertail Spruce. z 5-7. Stiffly spreading coniferous evergreen to 100 ft. Foliage dark glossy green.

P. pungens. Colorado Spruce. z 1-6. The famous Koster's blue spruce and Colorado blue spruce belong here. While marvelous trees, they are perhaps more often misused than any other coniferous evergreen. Should be planted at a distance from a house where their blue color creates an illusion of great space. To 125 ft.

PIERIS. *P. floribunda.* Andromeda, Mountain Fetterbush, Lily-of-the-valley Shrub. z 5-9. Broad-leaved evergreen shrub to 3 ft. Nodding white fragrant flowers like lily-of-the-valley in 5-in. panicles in May. Must have acid soil.

P. japonica. Japanese Andromeda. z 6-9. Similar to *P. floribunda,* but taller and with more erect flower stalks. April-May.

PILEA. *P. microphylla.* Artillery Plant. Tropical annual, used in the South as a groundcover, but as a house plant in the North. Grown for its neat fern-like foliage. Flowers explode pollen.

P. nummulariaefolia. Creeping Charley. z 10. Florida groundcover similar to *P. microphylla* but lower.

PIMENTA. *P. officinalis.* Allspice, Pimento Bush (but not pimiento). z 10. Aromatic tree to 40 ft., grown for the commercial production of allspice. Fragrant foliage and white flowers.

PIMPINELLA. *P. anisum.* Anise. Annual to 2 ft., grown for its richly aromatic seeds used as a condiment.

PINUS. Pine. *P. banksiana.* Jack Pine, Scrub Pine, Gray Pine. z 4-6. An inferior coniferous evergreen but useful for rough plantings and poor soil. Will grow on sand dunes.

P. calabrica. Corsican Pine. z 6-9. Possibly a variety of *P. nigra.*

P. canariensis. Canary Island Pine. z 9-10. Coniferous evergreen to 100 ft., but seldom that tall in cultivation. Bluish green young growth.

P. caribaea. Cuban Pine, Slash Pine. z 9-10. Coniferous evergreen to 75 ft. One of the few good southern pines; tolerates seaside conditions.

P. cembra. Swiss Stone Pine. z 5-8. Grows very slowly to 60 ft.

P. cembroides. Piñon, Mexican Stone Pine. z 8-10. Coniferous evergreen to 20 ft. One form, *edulis,* has edible seeds, the popular pine or piñon nuts used as food.

P. coulteri. Big-cone Pine. z 6-9. Splendid coniferous evergreen to 75 ft. Huge cones, to 14 in. long, often sold for Christmas decoration.

P. densiflora. Japanese Red Pine. z 5-8. Coniferous evergreen to 90 ft. Also an umbrella-headed form known as the Japanese Umbrella Pine.

P. flexilis. Limber Pine, Western White Pine. z 6-8. To 70 ft. Today, the most important source of white pine lumber.

P. griffithi. Himalayan Pine. z 6-9. To 100 ft. Distinctive gray-green bark.

P. halepensis. Aleppo Pine. z 8-10. To 60 ft. The characteristic pine of Italy. Does well in the Southwest.

P. monticola. Western White Pine. z 6-9. Similar to *P. flexilis,* but with much larger cones, to 11 in.

P. mugo. Swiss Mountain Pine. z 4-8. A tree to 25 ft., but the species is seldom grown. Instead the dwarf form *P. m. mughus,* the mugho pine, is widely grown. It is prostrate or nearly so, to 4 ft. and much wider than tall. A popular evergreen for facing hedge or evergreen borders.

P. nigra. Austrian Pine. z 5-8. To 80 ft., usually lower. The one pine that will tolerate city conditions for any length of time. Unfortunately, badly subject to borer attack. *P. n. calabrica,* the Corsican pine, is a good tree for the seashore.

P. palustris. Longleaf Pine, Yellow Pine. z 8-10. Fast-growing pine for the southern states, to 100 ft. at maturity. Leaves to 18 in. long. Wood so hard it cannot be worked if allowed to age in the stack for more than a year.

P. parviflora. Japanese White Pine. z 5-8. A grafted tree as sold in commerce, with low picturesque form; final height depends on height of graft.

P. peuce. Macedonian Pine. z 4-8. Pyramidal pine to 50 ft. Slow-growing.

P. pinea. Italian Stone Pine. z 8-10. Pine to 60 ft. at maturity, but much less in cultivation. Stiff, bright green needles 6 in. long.

P. ponderosa. Bull Pine, Western Yellow Pine, Ponderosa Pine. z 5-8. Almost too big for an ornamental, growing rapidly and reaching 150 ft.

P. radiata. Monterey Pine. z 9-10. Highly picturesque tree with irregular wind-swept form to 30 ft. Grows only in a limited range along the California coast.

P. resinosa. Norway Pine, Red Pine. z 1-7. Quick-growing timber tree of limited horticultural use except in windbreaks and background plantings. To 100 ft.

P. strobus. White Pine, Weymouth Pine, Northern White Pine. z 3-7. A noble timber tree with fine, soft, bluish green needles. Its texture makes it useful in landscaping. To 100 ft. Several horticultural forms available.

P. sylvestris. Scotch Pine. z 3-7. Not a fir, as it is sometimes called. Irregular tree to 75 ft. at maturity. Susceptibility to borers limits its usefulness in landscaping. Tolerates seaside and city conditions.

P. taeda. Loblolly Pine. z 5-9. The characteristic tall, sparse pine of Tidewater Virginia near Williamsburg. Not too useful except for naturalistic planting.

P. thunbergi. Japanese Black Pine. z 5-7. Similar to P. nigra, but faster-growing. Tolerates seaside conditions.

PIQUERIA. P. trinervia. Stevia. z 10. Perennial to 3 ft. Largely forced in greenhouses in the North for its fragrant white flowers in winter. Too straggling and irregular to use outdoors in the South, though it survives.

PITTOSPORUM. P. crassifolium. Karo, Australian Laurel. z 9-10. Evergreen shrub or tree to 30 ft. Red or purple ½-in. flowers in clusters. Tolerates seaside conditions.

P. tobira. Japanese Pittosporum, Tobira. Shrub to 15 ft., evergreen. Greenish white, sweetly fragrant flowers ½ in. long in terminal clusters. Forced as a tub or pot specimen in greenhouses in the North.

PLATANUS. P. acerifolia. London Plane Tree. z 5-8. A hybrid between P. orientalis and P. occidentalis. Highly satisfactory street tree with picturesque tan bark that peels off in patches, revealing a white underbark. Tolerates seaside and city conditions. Perhaps the world's No. 1 street tree. Up to 100 ft.

P. occidentalis. Buttonwood, American Plane Tree, Sycamore. z 5-8. Larger than the London plane (in girth it is perhaps our largest shade tree) and to 150 ft. tall, but not as tolerant of adverse conditions. Too messy for street use.

P. orientalis. Oriental Plane Tree. z 8-10. Not known in American commerce, though one of the parents of the London plane (P. acerifolia), which is used in its stead.

PLATYCODON. P. grandiflorum. Balloon Flower, Japanese Bellflower. z 4-8. Perennial to 2½ ft. Deep blue, single flowers to 3 in. across. June-July. The dwarf ballon flower, P. mariesi, is only a variety of this. One of the few midsummer blues.

PLEIOSPILOS. P. bolusi. See House Plants (Chapter 11).

PODOCARPUS. P. elongatus. African Yellow-wood. z 8-10. Conifer to 70 ft. with flat needles like yew, but much wider and longer. Although a tree in nature, it is used almost entirely as a foliage plant in large pots or tubs.

P. macrophyllus maki. False Yew. z 8-10. Although the species is a tree to 70 ft., with foliage similar to that of P. elongatus, the variety maki is a tub or pot plant to 6 ft.

PODOPHYLLUM. P. peltatum. Mandrake, Mayflower, May Apple. z 4-8. Perennial with umbrella-like leaves to 18 in. tall, nearly that wide. White, strongly scented flowers 2 in. or more across are borne in the leaf axils in May. Yellow apple-shaped fruits in summer, edible. Woods soil in shade. Wildflower.

POLEMONIUM. P. caeruleum. Jacob's Ladder, Charity, Greek Valerian. z 4-8. Perennial to 3 ft. Striking blue flowers 1 in. across in clusters. A variety has white flowers.

P. reptans. Bluebell, American Abscess Root. z 4-8. Perennial to 1 ft. Light blue flowers to ¾ in. in loose drooping clusters.

POLIANTHES. P. tuberosa. Tuberose. Tender bulb. See Bulbs (Chapter 4).

POLYGALA. P. paucifolia. Flowering Wintergreen, Gaywings, Fringed Polygala. z 1-8. A perennial about 1 in.

high. Reddish purple flowers in small clusters. Must have acid soil; wild-flower. Also used in terrariums.

POLYGONATUM. *P. biflorum.* Solomon's Seal. z 4-8. Perennial to 3 ft. with broad lance-shaped leaves and greenish white flowers in drooping umbels.

POLYGONUM. *P. auberti.* Silver Lace Vine, Fleece Vine, Lace Vine. z 4-8. Tall-growing vine to 25 ft., twining. Produces long clusters of fragrant greenish white flowers towards the top of the plant in Aug. Quickly covers any support.

POLYPODIUM. *P. vulgare.* Common Polypody, Wall Fern. z 4-9. An easily grown fern to 2 ft. Thrives best in woodsy soil, at a pH of 4.5.

POLYSTICHUM. *P. acrostichoides.* Dagger Fern, Christmas Fern. z 4-8. Evergreen fern to 2 ft. Can be grown as a house plant.

P. lonchitis. Mountain Holly Fern. z 5-8. Similar to the Christmas fern except that leaflets are slightly wider.

P. munitum. Sword Fern, Giant Holly Fern. z 5-8. Evergreen fern with leaves to 3½ ft.

PONCIRUS. *P. trifoliata.* Hardy Orange. z 6-9. Deciduous shrub or tree to 20 ft. with fierce spines which make an impenetrable hedge. Fragrant white flowers to more than 2 in. long similar to orange blossoms. Orange-like acid fruit to 2 in.

POPULUS. Poplar. *P. acuminata.* Plains Cottonwood. z 1-6. Not worth mentioning as an ornamental except that it will survive on the Great Plains where little else will. Tree to 45 ft.

P. alba. Abele, Silver Poplar, White Poplar. z 4-8. Deciduous tree to 90 ft. Another tree for problem locations. Tolerates seaside conditions.

P. balsamifera. Cottonwood, Balsam Poplar, Tacamahac. z 1-8. Sturdy tree to 90 ft. Will grow anywhere. The firewood of the plains.

P. bolleana. A variety of *P. alba* with a sharply vertical columnar crown like the Lombardy poplar but a better tree.

P. candicans. Balm of Gilead, Balsam Poplar. z 4-8. Tree to 90 ft. with sticky buds.

P. deltoides. Carolina Poplar, Cottonwood. z 4-8. The true Carolina poplar is *P. canadensis,* a fairly good quick-growing tree. *P. deltoides* rots at the heart so quickly that it is worthless as a landscape species.

P. fremonti. California Cottonwood. z 8-10. Tree to 90 ft. tolerant of dry California regions along watercourses.

P. grandidentata. Bigtooth Aspen. z 3-8. Weedy tree to 60 ft. Quaking leaves.

P. laurifolia. Siberian Poplar. z 4-8. Tree to 45 ft. Little used for landscaping.

P. nigra italica. Lombardy Poplar. z 2-8. Tall, narrow, columnar tree to 80 ft. Perhaps the most widely planted screen tree, but inferior to both *P. bolleana* and *P. simoni* in fastigate form. Subject to disease.

P. simoni. Simon Poplar. z 3-8. Narrow-headed tree to 35 ft., the fastigate form most widely planted. There is also a weeping form, seldom seen.

P. tremula. Aspen, European Aspen. z 1-8. Round-headed tree to 80 ft. with quaking leaves. From Africa, yet hardy far north.

P. tremuloides. Quaking Aspen. z 1-8. Tree to 90 ft. Used largely for pulpwood, but its glorious golden autumn color commends it for special effects.

PORTULACA. *P. grandiflora.* Moss Rose, Portulaca, Sun Moss, Jewel

Plant. Prostrate annual with jewel-like flowers 1 in. across, resembling semi-double roses in white, yellow, pink, cerise, and purple. Tolerates hot, dry situations, including seashore. The variety 'Jewel' is double the size of others, in light purple-violet.

POTENTILLA. *P. fruticosa.* Shrubby Cinquefoil. z 5-8. Low deciduous shrub to 4 ft. Bright showy yellow or cream-colored flowers to 1¼ in. across in clusters. June. Prefers soil with pH of 7.0 or above, but will tolerate almost any situation.

P. nepalensis. Nepal Cinquefoil. z 5-8. Hairy perennial to 2 ft. Showy five-petaled flowers 1 in. across, red, in clusters. July-Aug. Rock-garden plant.

P. tridentata. Wineleaf Cinquefoil. Perennial to 1 ft. Turns red in fall. Flowers white, ¼ in., in clusters. July-Aug. Rock-garden plant.

P. verna. Spring Cinquefoil. z 5-8. Matted perennial to 6 in. Golden yellow flowers in clusters in spring. Rock garden.

PRIMULA. Primrose. *P. acaulis.* English Primrose. A variety of *P. vulgaris,* which see.

P. auricula. Eyed Primrose, Auricula. z 5-8. Perennial to 8 in. More difficult to grow than most hardy primroses. Eyed flowers in wide color range. April-May. Leaves usually downy or felted. Does best in the rock garden.

P. bulleyana. Chinese Mountain Primrose. z 5-8. Stout perennial to 30 in. Flowers to 1 in., deep yellow in candelabra form. June. Bog garden or moist situation in rock garden.

P. denticulata. Indian Primrose. z 5-8a. Perennial to 1 ft. Woolly or powdery foliage. Small flowers in dense clusters, lilac or purple, in May.

P. elatior. Oxlip. z 5-8. Perennial

to 8 in. Showy yellow flowers to 1 in. across, umbels. April-May. Good flower for naturalizing in light filtered shade.

P. japonica. Japanese Primrose. z 6-9a. Perennial to 2 ft. Glistening flowers, 1 in. or more across, on whorled stalks, white, pink, or violet. June-July. Rock garden.

P. malacoides. Fairy Primrose, Baby Primrose. Tender perennial to 1½ ft. grown as a greenhouse pot plant. Pale lilac or light pink flowers, Jan.-April (under glass) on whorled stalks.

P. obconica. Hairy Primrose. Tender perennial to 1 ft. Grown under glass, 1-in. flowers pink or lilac, Jan.-April. Hairs on leaves highly irritating to some; plants are barred by most hospitals.

P. officinalis. English Cowslip. See *P. veris.*

P. sinensis. Chinese Primrose. Tender perennial to 8 in., grown under glass, flowering Jan.-April. Flowers with striking darker eye, 1½ in. across, in umbels. Various colors. The variety *P. s. stellata,* the star primrose, is popular.

P. veris. Common Primrose, Cowslip. z 5-8. Sometimes listed as *P. officinalis.* Perennial to 8 in. Clear yellow flowers with orange eye, in May. Rock garden or naturalizing in woodlands.

P. vulgaris. English Primrose, Prim. z 5-8. Perennial to 6 in. Yellow flowers. April-May. Improved varieties include a clear blue, pink, and other colors. Also listed as *P. acaulis.*

PRINSEPIA. *P. uniflora.* Hedge Prinsepia. z 5b-8. Deciduous spiny shrub to 6 ft. Clusters of small creamy flowers in March-April, on arching branches. Black-purple fruit follows.

PROSOPIS. *P. juliflora.* Mesquite. z 9-10. Far from a beautiful tree or shrub, but survives in the desert where nothing else will grow. To 9 ft. Of some value as a honey plant.

PRUNUS. *P. americana.* American Wild Plum, Yellow Wild Plum. z 5-8. Small tree to 30 ft. White flowers in spring, yellow (sometimes red) small plums good for jams and jellies.

P. amygdalus. Almond. z 8-10. The almond of the Bible, seldom grown as an ornamental. While tree survives farther north than indicated, flower buds may be killed.

P. angustifolia. Chickasaw Plum. z 6-9. Tree to 12 ft. Very twiggy or spiny. White flowers about ½ in. in clusters in spring. Red or yellow fruit. The Sand Plum is the variety *P. a. watsoni.*

P. armeniaca. Apricot. z 7-9a. Tree to 20 ft., grown principally for its round orange fruit, but also for its ornamental flowers 1 in. across in early spring. However, these appear so early that they are usually killed except in California. Supposed to be the "apple" Eve gave to Adam.

P. besseyi. Sand Cherry, Hansen Bush Cherry. z 1-7. Semi-prostrate shrub to 4 ft. Black edible sweet fruits follow small white April flowers. Tolerates seaside conditions.

P. cerasifera pissardi. Pissardi Purple-leaf Plum. z 5-8. The original species is a small tree used as understock for commercial cherries. The purple-leaved variety is a shrub or small tree with purple leaves, large mauve flowers, and maroon fruits in fall.

P. glandulosa. Flowering Almond. z 5-8b. Not the true almond. Shrub to 5 ft., covered with pink flowers about ⅓ in. across before foliage appears. Many horticultural forms, some white, some double.

P. ilicifolia. Holly Plum, Islay, Ever-green Cherry. z 9-10. Evergreen shrub or small tree with holly-like leaves. White flowers ⅓ in., in racemes. April. Black or red small fruit, barely edible. Thrives only in California. Sometimes used for hedges.

P. laurocerasus. Cherry Laurel. See *Laurocerasus officinalis.*

P. lyoni. Evergreen Cherry. z 9-10. Evergreen tree to 25 ft. Possibly only a form of *P. ilicifolia* except that leaves are not bristly. Tolerates seaside conditions.

P. maritima. Beach Plum. z 4-8. Deciduous shrub to 6 ft. Grown for its round purple or black fruits with a delicate flavor; used for beach-plum jam, a Cape Cod specialty. Prefers sandy soil and sea air.

P. persica. Flowering Peach. z 5-8. Botanists prefer to call this *Amygdalus persica,* but it is usually listed as shown here. Lovely airy pink, white, or variegated flowers to 2 in. across in spring. Tree to 18 ft., short lived.

P. serotina. Black Cherry, Choke Cherry. z 2-8. Deciduous tree to 80 ft. Timber one of our best native woods, but trees tend to become arboreal weeds. Intensely fragrant white flowers in drooping clusters in May. Fruit sour, black, sometimes used for cherry liqueurs. If foliage wilts, it develops prussic acid and can kill livestock.

P. serrulata. Japanese Flowering Cherry. z 5-8. Tree of various sizes and growth habits with conspicuous flowers to 1½ in., white or pink, single or double, in April; not fragrant. While trees will survive in z 5, flower buds are often killed. In this aspect, flowering cherries are less satisfactory than the flowering crabs.

P. spinosa. Blackthorn, Sloe. z 4-8a. Thorny shrub or tree to 12 ft. Largely grown for its thorny branches, used for walking sticks in Ireland. Fruit used to flavor sloe gin.

P. subhirtella. Rosebud Cherry, Japanese Flowering Cherry. z 5-8a. Tree to 25 ft. The variety usually grown is *P. s. pendula,* with graceful fountain branches wreathed in soft pale pink flowers, to ¾ in. across, in May. An autumn-flowering variety (seldom matures flowers in z 5) is known.

P. tomentosa. Nanking or Manchu Cherry. z 2-8a. Shrub or tree to 10 ft. White flowers to ¾ in., May, followed by bright red edible fruits.

P. triloba. Flowering Almond, Flowering Plum. z 5-8. Not a true almond, although botanists class it as an amygdalus. Shrub to 10 ft. The variety *P. t. flore-plena* is generally grown; it has bright pink double flowers to 1½ in. that smother the entire plant in May.

PSEUDOLARIX. *P. amabilis* (*P. kaempferi*). Golden Larch. z 5-8. A deciduous coniferous tree to 100 ft. Light green needles turn golden yellow in fall. Prefers acid soils.

PSEUDOTSUGA. *P. taxifolia.* Douglas Fir. z 7-9 for the western form, z 4-8 for the Rocky Mountain form. Coniferous evergreen. In the Pacific Northwest may reach 300 ft. This form, however, is less hardy than that found in the Rockies, which matures at lower height. One of the finest of all evergreens for landscaping.

PTERETIS. *P. nodulosa* (*P. pensylvanica*). Ostrich Fern. A large coarse fern to 7 ft., suitable for background planting in a moist spot in the wild garden.

PTERIDIUM. *P. aquilinum.* Bracken. z 2-8. A wide-leafed fern, to 4 ft. tall and sometimes 3 ft. wide. Coarse and not too attractive, but useful for wild places and as bird cover.

PTEROSTYRAX. *P. hispida.* Epaul-ette Tree. z 5-9. Tree to 50 ft. Ten-in. panicles of white, flag-like fragrant bloom in June. A striking tree not enough planted.

PUERARIA. *P. hirsuta* (*P. thunbergiana*). Kudzu Vine. z 7-9. Woody rampant vine climbing to 50 ft. if given support. Kills to the ground north of z 7, but to z 5 the roots survive and will cover a 25-ft. trellis with new growth in a single year. Used for forage or groundcover in the South. Cultivation in California is forbidden by law.

PULMONARIA. *P. angustifolia.* Cowslip Lungwort. z 5-8. Perennial to 12 in. Mottled leaves, purplish or lilac flowers, on stalks that uncurl as flowers open. Rock garden.

PULSATILLA. *P. vernalis.* Pasque Flower. See *Anemone pulsatilla.*

PUNICA. *P. granatum.* Pomegranate. z 7-9a. Shrub or tree to 20 ft., somewhat spiny. Orange-red flowers, solitary or clusters, to 1½ in. Grown for its many-chambered brownish yellow or red fruits. Each chamber contains a slightly acid pulp that surrounds the seeds. Mentioned in the Bible. In its younger stage cultured as a pot plant.

PYRACANTHA. *P. coccinea.* Firethorn, Everlasting Thorn. z 5-9. Semievergreen shrub to 8 ft. Bright orange-red fruit conspicuous in fall. Flowers white, inconspicuous. The variety *P. c. lalandi* is the hardiest. Farther south, a yellow-fruited variety can be grown.

PYROLA. *P. elliptica.* Shinleaf, Lesser Wintergreen. z 1-6. Evergreen perennial to 10 in. Olive-green leaves. Fragrant, waxy, greenish white flowers in loose clusters, June-July. Wildflower.

PYRUS. The crabapples have been retained here rather than put into malus; a survey of American catalogs shows more so listed. However, botanically, they belong in malus. Pears, however, remain in the genus pyrus.

P. arnoldiana. A variety of *P. floribunda,* which see.

P. atrosanguinea. Carmine Crab. z 6-8a. A hybrid crab much like *P. floribunda,* but flowers a deeper rose color and not fading.

P. baccata. Siberian Crab. z 2-8. Tree to 40 ft. Small white flowers. April-May. Red or yellow fruit follows. A jelly crab.

P. calleryana. Chinese Sand Pear. z 4-8. Tree to 40 ft. Largely used as an understock for grafting. However, it deserves attention as a brilliantly colored tree in autumn on sandy, acid soils in the East.

P. coronaria. Garland Crab, Sweet Crab, American Crab. z 4-8. A common wildling east of the Mississippi. Tree to 18 ft. Rose-colored flowers to 1 in., changing to white, tart green fruits in fall. Subject to cedar apple rust.

P. floribunda. Showy Crab. z 4-8. Wide-spreading tree to 25 ft. Great billows of pink buds in spring open pale pink, to 1¼ in. across, and fade to white. Always admired. *P. arnoldiana* is similar, but with larger individual blooms, lighter in color.

P. halliana. Hall Crab. z 5-8. Tree to 18 ft. Flowers deep rose, to 1½ in., fruits purple. The variety *P. h. parkmani* has double flowers.

P. ioensis. Prairie Crab. z 3-8. Tree to 30 ft. The typical crab of the Midwest. Fragrant white or rose-tinted flowers, 1-2 in. across. Fruit is green and acid, but makes good jelly. The variety Bechtel's has double pink flowers like small roses. Subject to cedar apple rust.

P. sargenti. Sargent Crab. z 5-8. Shrub to 8 ft. Spiny, wide-branching.

One-in. white flowers. Desirable because of low habit in front of taller crabs.

P. spectabilis. Chinese Crab. z 5-8. Tree to 25 ft. with bright red buds, opening flesh pink and fading white to 2 in. One of the showiest crabs. Fruit not useful, but birds eat it.

P. theifera. Tea Crab. z 5-8. Tree to 20 ft., broader than tall. Fragrant white or pink flowers. Greenish fruit. The Chinese dry the young leaves for tea; they have a definite tea-like flavor.

QUAMOCLIT. *Q. coccinea.* Star-glory, Star Ipomoea. Annual vine to 10 ft. with heart-shaped leaves. Bright scarlet starred flowers to 1½ in. long with yellow throat. Often confused with *Q. pennata.*

Q. pennata. Cypress Vine. Similar to *Q. coccinea,* but with finely divided leaves and funnel-shaped scarlet flowers.

Q. sloteri. Cardinal Climber. A cross between *Q. pennata* and *Q. coccinea,* with abundant flowers and deeply lobed triangular leaves.

QUERCUS. Oak. *Q. agrifolia.* Coast Live Oak, California Live Oak, Encina. z 8-10. Evergreen tree to 100 ft.

Q. alba. White Oak. z 3-8. America's noblest tree if pasture-grown where it can develop its majestic rounded form. To 100 ft. Specimens 7 ft. in diameter are known.

Q. bicolor. Swamp White Oak. z 3-8. Similar to *Q. alba,* but only 70 ft. at maturity, often less.

Q. borealis. Northern Red Oak. z 4-8. A fine shade tree to 70 ft., fast growing. Leaves pale beneath, deep red in late fall. See also *Q. rubra.*

Q. coccinea. Scarlet Oak. z 3-8. Tree to 80 ft. Brilliant scarlet foliage in fall; best color of any oak.

Q. ile . Holm Oak, Holly Oak. z

8-10. Evergreen tree to 60 ft. with typical holly leaves.

Q. ilicifolia. Scrub Oak. z 1-7. Tree to 35 ft., useful largely for sandy soils and rough land; often picturesque but seldom ornamental.

Q. lobata. California White Oak, Valley Oak. z 8-10. Tree to 100 ft. Resembles eastern white oak.

Q. macrocarpa. Mossy-cup Oak, Burr Oak. z 3-8. Interesting largely for the fringed acorn caps. Tree to 100 ft.

Q. marilandica. Blackjack Oak. z 5-8. Tree to 50 ft., usually less. Of little importance horticulturally except on rough land.

Q. montana. See *Q. prinus.*

Q. nigra. Water Oak. z 6-10. Semi-evergreen tree to 80 ft. Often confused with the live oak, but a poorer, less durable, tree.

Q. palustris. Pin Oak. z 4-8. Tree to 80 ft. A noble tree, with regular conical form and dense branches, intense fall color. One of our most valuable oaks for landscape use.

Q. phellos. Willow Oak. z 6-9. Tree to 60 ft. Long, narrow leaves like a willow.

Q. prinus. Chestnut Oak. z 3-8. Tree to 100 ft. Leaves resembling those of chestnut. Sold in commerce as *Q. montana.*

Q. rubra. Red Oak. z 6-8. Fast-growing, wide-spreading tree to 75 ft. Foliage rich red in autumn. The name *Q. rubra* is also sometimes given to the northern red oak (*Q. borealis*).

Q. suber. Cork Oak. z 8-9. Tree to 60 ft. with spongy bark which produces the cork of commerce. Evergreen.

Q. velutina. Black Oak, Yellow Oak, Quercitron. z 5-9. Bold upright tree of rapid growth to 100 ft. or more. Lustrous green foliage, dull red in fall. Bark nearly black.

Q. virginiana. Live Oak. z 8-10. Evergreen tree to 60 ft. For many years, the basic timber used in American fighting ships. Practically always draped with Spanish moss when seen in Florida.

RAMONDA. *R. nathaliae.* Serbian Queen. z 6-9a. Delicate low perennial with hairy leaves. Lavender-blue flowers with yellow eye. Rock garden.

R. pyrenaica. Ramonda. z 6-9a. Similar to *R. nathaliae*, but only 3 in. tall. Purple flowers.

RANUNCULUS. *R. acris flore-pleno.* Butter Rose, Soldier's Buttons, Buttercup. z 4-8. Handsome bright yellow flowers like tight roses on 30-in. stems. Perennial. May-June.

R. repens. Creeping Buttercup, Creeping Crowfoot. z 4-8. Good groundcover, forming dense mats, but also a weedy invasive perennial. Can be controlled with 2,4,5-TP if it becomes undesirable. The double form is lovely when in flower; bright yellow, tight buttons 1 in. across.

RAPHIOLEPIS. *R. indica.* Indian Hawthorn. z 9-10. Evergreen shrub to 5 ft. Showy terminal panicles of pinkish white ½-in. flowers resembling hawthorn.

R. umbellata. Yeddo Hawthorn. z 9-10. Similar to *R. indica* but taller and with white flowers ¾ in. across, and fragrant.

RESEDA. *R. odorata.* Mignonette. Annual to 2 ft. Greenish and dull orange flowers of little beauty but grown for their intense fragrance. Sometimes a cut-flower crop in greenhouses.

RHAMNUS. *R. cathartica.* Common Buckthorn, Hart's Thorn, Rhineberry. z 1-8. Thorny deciduous shrub to 20 ft. Not too regular in habit but tolerates some shearing for hedges. Black fruits favored by birds. Old-time folk remedy.

R. frangula. Glossy Buckthorn, Alder Buckthorn. z 1-8. Smoother, more compact plant than *R. cathartica.* Good city shrub and bird food, to 12 ft. Red fruits, turning black.

R. purshiana. Cascara Sagrada, Bearberry, Shittimwood, Chittamwood, Cathartic Plant. z 7-9. Shrub or tree to 30 ft. The dried bark yields the cathartic drug of its common name.

RHEKTOPHYLLUM. *R. mirabile (Nephthytis picturata).* Arrowhead. Tropical climber used as a vining house plant when young. Long, arrow-shaped leaves variegated with pale green; wavy margins.

RHODODENDRON. Rhododendrons and Azaleas. Acid-soil plants of the heath family, containing some of the finest of ornamental shrubs for regions where the soil is or can be made suitable. See Chapter 17.

RHODOTYPOS. *R. tetrapetala.* Jetbead. z 5-8. Deciduous shrub to 6 ft. Solitary white flowers like single roses 2 in. across. May-June. Jet-black beadlike fruits follow.

RHOEO. *R. discolor.* Moses-in-the-bulrushes, Oyster Plant, Boat Lily. House plant. Common form has overlapping boat-shaped leaves. Small white flowers in dense umbels within two curious boat-shaped bracts.

RHUS. *R. canadensis.* Aromatic Sumac. z 3-8. Spreading shrub to 3 ft. with a resinous-aromatic odor. Birds eat the fruits. Interesting fall color. Sometimes listed as *R. aromatica.* Tolerates city smoke.

R. copallina. Dwarf or Shining Sumac. z 5-8a. Shrub or tree to 20 ft. Spiky clusters of greenish flowers, conspicuous red fruit. Tolerates sandy soils and city conditions.

R. cotinoides. American Smoke Tree. Chittamwood. z 5b-9. Large shrub or small tree to 20 ft. or more. Conspicuous airy flower spikes like puffs of smoke in July. Brilliant fall color. Does best in light soils. Often listed as *Cotinus americanus.*

R. cotinus. Smoke Tree. z 5b-8. Wide-spreading deciduous shrub 10 to 15 ft. Airy flower clusters, made up of purplish green hairs, resemble rising smoke at a distance. A striking specimen shrub on broad lawns. Often listed as *Cotinus coggygria.*

R. glabra. Smooth Sumac. z 3-8. Shrub or small tree to 20 ft. Spiky green flowers in dense terminal panicles. June-July. Conspicuous red fruiting spikes. Birds feed on them.

R. integrifolia. Sourberry. z 8-10. Evergreen shrub or tree to 20 ft. White or pinkish hairy flower spikes followed by rich red, hairy fruits.

R. laurina. Laurel Sumac. z 9-10. Evergreen shrub with smooth, entire (undivided) leaves. Dense panicles of small greenish white flowers, followed by white spiky fruits. To 15 ft.

R. ovata. Sugarberry, Sugarbush. z 8-10. Evergreen shrub to 10 ft. with smooth, entire leaves. Native to deserts of the Southwest, little grown elsewhere. Short dense spikes of yellow flowers; deep red, hairy fruits.

R. typhina. Staghorn Sumac. z 4-8a. Deciduous shrub or tree to 25 ft. Typical sumac flowers and fruits; best of the horticultural species. The variety *R. t. laciniata* has finely cut foliage. Glorious red autumn color. Valuable bird tree.

RIBES. Currant. *R. alpinum.* Mountain Currant, Alpine Currant. z 5-8a. Deciduous shrub to 8 ft., usually lower as grown. Flowers are unimportant: grown mostly as a low hedge plant.

Subject to a die-back disease in some areas.

R. aureum. Flowering Currant, Golden Currant. z 2-8a. Deciduous shrub to 6 ft. Drooping clusters of strongly fragrant yellow flowers in May. Purple-brown fruit.

R. grossularia. Gooseberry. z 2-7. Spiny shrub to 4 ft. Small fruit, but sometimes used ornamentally. Inconspicuous flowers. Green, yellow or purple-brown fruit.

R. odoratum. Golden Currant, Buffalo Currant. Deciduous shrub to 6 ft. Showy fragrant yellow flowers in drooping clusters. Difference between this species and *R. aureum* unimportant; both are mixed in commerce.

R. sanguineum. Flowering Currant, Winter Currant. z 2-9. Deciduous shrub to 9 ft. without thorns. Many-flowered clusters of showy red flowers. April-May. A desirable landscape plant.

R. sativum. Garden Currant. z 2-7. Deciduous shrub to 5 ft., thornless. Grown for its bright red (sometimes ivory) fruit used for currant jelly. Makes a good ornamental, but needs regular pruning.

RICINUS. *R. communis.* Castor Bean, Palma Christi, Castor-oil Plant. Annual to 15 ft. Quick-growing plant with huge palmate leaves, sometimes maroon or bright red in color. Fruits are spiny pods containing beautifully marked poisonous seeds. Should not be planted where children can reach them. Valuable for quick hedges or backgrounds around new homes.

ROBINIA. *R. hispida.* Rose Acacia, Pink Locust. z 5-8a. Deciduous shrub to 6 ft. Branches are brittle and snap off easily. Flowers in clusters, rose-purple or pink. May-June. Taller-growing forms are available.

R. pseudoacacia. Black Locust, False Acacia, Yellow Locust. z 4-8a. Tree to 80 ft. While the wood is very hard, it is not tough and snaps off easily. Promoted widely as a street tree, but hazards of breaking limbs in wind and sleet storms make this use inadvisable. Also badly susceptible to borer injury. Fragrant white flowers in long panicles in June. Conspicuous seed pods.

ROMNEYA. *R. coulteri.* Matilija Poppy, California Tree Poppy. z 6-10. Subshrub to 7 ft. Solitary flowers, like white poppies with paper-thin petals, fragrant, and 6 in. across. Tolerates seaside conditions.

ROSA. Rose. The genus which contains the true roses. For the culture and selection of garden varieties, see Chapter 10. (The word rose is also applied to many unrelated plants such as sun rose (*Helianthemum nummularium*) and Christmas rose (*Helleborus niger*).

ROSMARINUS. *R. officinalis.* Rosemary. z 7-9a. Evergreen shrub to 6 ft. in the South, lower in northern range. Long narrow leaves, strongly aromatic, gray-green, hairy. Light blue ½-in. flowers in short racemes. April-May. Used as a hedge plant in the South. A prostrate form, creeping rosemary, is used in rock gardens.

ROYSTONEA. *R. regia.* Royal Palm. z 10. Majestic palm to 70 ft. or more, with smooth gray trunk bulging near the middle. Grows only in Florida; does not succeed even in warmer parts of California.

RUBUS. Brambles, Blackberries, and Raspberries. Thorny shrubs, many with long arching branches that root at the tip. Most bear edible fruits. Few are ornamental and the majority are weedy.

R. odoratus. Flowering Raspberry.

z 3-8. Perennial to 6 ft. with bristly or hairy stems, but not thorny. A showy shrub with broad maple-like leaves and conspicuous rose-purple flowers 2 in. across. Worthless fruit.

RUDBECKIA. This genus of mostly bright yellow daisy-like flowers has been developed into plants with monstrous blooms in various patterns of deep red and yellow, called Gloriosa Daisies. Though perennial, they are generally grown as annuals.

R. bicolor. Black-eyed Susan, Thimble Flower. Annual to 2 ft. with hairy leaves. Yellow daisy-like flowers 2½ in. with purplish black stain at base, central disk black, ¾ in. high.

R. fulgida. Orange Coneflower. z 5-8. Perennial to 2 ft. Daisy-like flowers to 3 in. across, golden yellow with orange base, central disk purplish black.

R. hirta. Black-eyed Susan. Annual wildflower to 3 ft. Much like *R. bicolor* and *R. fulgida.*

R. laciniata hortensia. Golden Glow. z 5-8. A popular perennial of Victorian days; still used to a limited extent but weedy in appearance. To 12 ft. tall with large heads of ragged double yellow flowers to 4 in. across, the disk barely visible as greenish yellow central dots.

R. triloba. Brown-eyed Susan. z 6-9a. Biennial to 5 ft. Typical rudbeckia daisy-like flowers 2½ in. across, but central disk is dull brown.

RUSCUS. *R. aculeatus.* Jew's Myrtle, Butcher's Broom. z 9-10. In cooler sections known only as a red-dyed stiff plant, the flattened branches resembling leaves, used for Christmas decorations or stuck in cemetery wreaths. In California, grown as a leafless evergreen plant. To 3 ft. Red or yellow berries to ½ in.

RUTA. *R. graveolens.* Rue, Herb of Repentance, Herb of Grace. z 6-8.

Evergreen subshrub to 3 ft., grown for its bitter aromatic foliage. The leaves can be irritating to the skin in hot weather; handle carefully if perspiring.

SABAL. *S. palmetto.* Cabbage Palm, Palmetto. z 8b-10. Palm to 60 ft. with round palmate leaves, hardiest of our native palms. Thrives under seaside conditions.

SAGINA. *S. subulata.* Pearlwort. z 5-8. Moss-like evergreen perennial. Tiny white pearl-like flowers smother the plant. July-Sept.

SAINTPAULIA. *S. ionantha.* African Violet. See House Plants (Chapter 11).

SALIX. Willow. *S. alba.* White Willow. z 1-8. Deciduous tree to 75 ft. Undersides of leaves are gray and silky. The variety *S. a. vitellina*, golden willow or golden osier, has bright yellow twigs, conspicuous in winter.

S. babylonica. Weeping Willow. z 4-8. Deciduous tree to 40 ft. with long pendulous branches, fresh yellow-brown bark when young. Catkins before leaves.

S. blanda. Wisconsin Weeping Willow. z 5-8. Hybrid similar to *S. babylonica* but with bluish green leaves.

S. caprea. Goat Willow, Sallow. z 5-8. Deciduous tree to 25 ft., often shrub-like. Bright yellow catkins in early spring.

S. discolor. Pussy Willow. z 1-8. Shrub or small tree to 20 ft. Catkins, before leaves, are the familiar pussy willows.

S. elegantissima. Thurlow Weeping Willow. z 5-8. A Japanese tree to 35 ft. with unusually long drooping branches and leaves bluish green beneath.

S. lucida. Shining Willow. z 2-8. Shrub or tree to 18 ft. Catkins appear with the leaves. Foliage glossy on both sides.

S. *matsudana contorta.* Nanking Willow, Corkscrew Willow. z 5b-8a. Deciduous tree to 40 ft. with unusual spiraled branches, upright in growth. A striking subject if planted against the open sky.

S. *nigra.* Black Willow. z 3-8. Deciduous tree to 35 ft. Purple-black bark. Excellent background plant because of its dark color effect. Catkins with leaves.

S. *pentandra.* Laurel Willow, Bay Willow. z 3-8a. Deciduous tree to 60 ft. Showy yellow catkins in early spring. Shining foliage like that of the laurel.

S. *purpurea.* Purple Osier, Purple Willow. z 5-8. Twigs are purple when young. Only form in general commerce is S. *p. nana,* to 3 ft.

SALPIGLOSSIS. S. *sinuata.* Painted Tongue. Half-hardy annual to 3 ft. Large funnel-shaped flowers to 2½ in. long, with interesting venation, in shades of yellow, scarlet, and almost blue, mostly with yellow throats. Does well on light sandy loam soils.

SALVIA. S. *argentea.* Silver Clary. Sage. z 6-8. Half-hardy biennial to 4 ft. Downy-white foliage. Showy rose-white, purple-white, or yellowish flowers ¾ in. across in long panicles.

S. *bicolor.* Spanish Sage, Blue-and-white Sage. z 6-8. Biennial to 3 ft. Sticky, hairy leaves. Bright bluish violet and white flowers in racemes to 2 ft. long.

S. *farinacea.* Blue Sage, Mealycup Sage. z 8-10. Perennial to 3 ft., but grown as an annual in the North. Spikes of gray-blue flowers with white calyx. Sometimes forced under glass.

S. *officinalis.* Garden Sage. z 5-9a. Hardy subshrub to 2 ft. with gray-green aromatic foliage used for flavor-ing and medicinally. Planted close together and sheared, it makes an excellent hedge for herb gardens.

S. *pratensis.* Meadow Sage. z 5b-8. Perennial to 3 ft. Brilliant blue flowers sometimes stained blood-red, to 1 in. long, in racemes. White and red, or pure white varieties exist.

S. *splendens.* Scarlet Sage, Firecracker Plant. A tender shrub but grown entirely as a tender bedding plant. Can be started either from seed or cuttings. Dwarf varieties not over 10 in., taller sorts to 4 ft. Brilliant scarlet flowers, 1½ in. long, in upright racemes all summer from mid-July. Harsh in color but good for bold effects.

S. *sylvestris.* Wood Sage. z 5-8. Perennial to 3 ft. Purple-violet flowers in long racemes; leaves below flowers are colored also.

SAMBUCUS. S. *canadensis.* American Elder, Elderberry. z 3-8a. Deciduous shrub to 9 ft. with hollow stems that are brittle and snap easily. Fragrant, ivory-white flowers in flat umbels. June-July. Purplish black berries used for jellies and elderberry wine. Excellent bird food. Good seaside plant.

S. *nigra.* European Elder. z 5-8a. Deciduous shrub to 25 ft. Yellowish white flowers in flat umbels, intensely fragrant. July. Black fruits, used as described above. Birds eat the berries avidly.

S. *racemosa.* Red-berried Elder, European Red Elder. z 5-8a. Deciduous shrub to 12 ft. Like S. *nigra* but flowers earlier. April-May.

SANGUINARIA. S. *canadensis.* Bloodroot, Woods Poppy, Redroot, Tatterwort, Indian Plant. z 3-6. Perennial wildflower sending up a single leaf and a solitary white flower on an 8-in. stalk in April. Dies down completely after flowering. The double-flowered form is a good garden plant.

SANGUISORBA. *S. minor.* Salad Burnet, Toper's Plant. z 5-8. Perennial to 2 ft. Edible leaves, a supposed cure for hangovers. Juice supposedly a styptic. Used as a tall groundcover.

SANSEVIERIA. *S. trifasciata laurenti.* Bowstring Hemp, Mother-in-law's Tongue, Snake Plant, Leopard Lily. Tender perennial with stiff erect leaves about 2 ft. long. The present species typical of the many others used as ornamental house plants. Distinctly marked white-and-green or yellow-and-green foliage. It is said that only a florist can kill a sansevieria; it will stand more neglect than almost any other plant, but overwatering is harmful.

SANTOLINA. *S. chamaecyparissus.* Lavender Cotton. z 7-9 (to z 5 with winter mulch). Woody perennial to 2 ft. with evergreen silvery foliage. Yellow flowers in globular heads to ¾ in. across at ends of branches. Grown mostly for its fragrant silvery foliage.

SANVITALIA. *S. procumbens.* Golden Stars. Annual to 6 in. with yellow daisy-like flowers about 1¾ in. across. Good rock-garden annual.

SAPONARIA. *S. calabrica.* Soapwort. Annual with sticky, hairy stems and pale rose ½-in. flowers.

S. ocymoides. Creeping Soapwort. z 5-8a. Trailing perennial to 9 in. Bright pink flowers in loose clusters, calyx stained purple, May-June. Good rock-garden plant.

S. officinalis. Bouncing Bet, Common Soapwort. z 4-8a. Stiff perennial with light green foliage, to 2 ft. Pale pink or white fragrant flowers, 1 in. across, in dense clusters. May-Sept. The single form is weedy, but the double form is a handsome plant.

S. vaccaria. Cow Herb, Cow Cockle. Annual to 3 ft. Flowers ⅓ in. across are a rich pink in loose cymes. Often weedy.

SASSAFRAS. *S. albidum* (*S. variifolium*). Sassafras. z 4-8. Deciduous tree to 60 ft. Aromatic foliage, bark, and roots. Undivided, mitten-shaped or 3-lobed leaves. Richly fragrant yellow flowers in 2-in. racemes open before the leaves. Dark blue fruit on red stalks. Bark of the root used medicinally and for a beverage. Brilliant flame-red, purple, and gold foliage in fall.

SATUREJA. *S. hortensis.* Savory, Summer Savory. Annual herb to 18 in., grown for its aromatic leaves used in flavoring. Pink, purplish, or white flowers.

S. montana. Winter Savory. z 6-9. Low shrub to 15 in. Used like *S. hortensis.*

SAURURUS. *S. cernuus.* Lizard's Tail. z 5-9. Wetland perennial to 5 ft. with heart-shaped leaves. Fragrant white flowers in 6-in. dense spikes.

SAXIFRAGA. Rockfoil, Saxifrage. Perennials, usually low-growing, at home on rocks. All of the following are reasonably hardy except *S. sarmentosa.*

S. aizoides. Arctic Rockfoil. z 1-4. Mat-forming perennial to 7 in. Tiny orange-yellow flowers on branching stalks, solitary or several together. June-July. Cannot stand hot climates.

S. apiculata. Hybrid Rockfoil. z 5-8. To 3½ in., mat-forming. Loose clusters of small yellow flowers. June-July.

S. cochlearis. Alpine Rockfoil. z 5-8. To 9 in. in tufted clumps. Spoon-shaped leaves. Loose clusters of white flowers ¾ in. across in spring.

S. cordifolia. See *Bergenia cordifolia.*

S. crassifolia (*Bergenia crassifolia*). Rockfoil, Siberian Tea, Leathery Saxifrage. z 6-8. To 1½ ft. Lilac or rose-pink flowers.

S. hosti. Silver Rockfoil. z 5-8. Stout perennial to 2 ft. Rosettes of leaves encrusted as though whitewashed. White ½-in. flowers in panicles, sometimes dotted purple.

S. macnabiana. Spotted Rockfoil. z 5-8. To 18 in. Rosettes of encrusted leaves, white flowers, spotted purple, in summer. Hybrid.

S. moschata. Mossy Rockfoil. z 5-8. Tufted perennial to 5 in. Greenish yellow flowers, occasionally white or purple, in spring.

S. sarmentosa. Strawberry-geranium, Aaron's Beard, Beefsteak Saxifrage. z 8-10. House plant (ground-cover in warm climates) with runners like a strawberry, to 2 ft. Round scalloped leaves, reddish below, white-veined above. Often grown as a hanging-basket house plant. White flowers, to 1 in. across.

S. umbrosa. London Pride. z 5-8. Perennial to 1 ft. Rosettes of leaves, reddish beneath. White flowers to ⅓ in., spotted pink, in loose umbels.

SCABIOSA. *S. atropurpurea.* Sweet Scabious, Mourning Bride. Annual to 3 ft. Fragrant flowers, in wheel-like heads to 2 in. across, white, pink, red, purple.

S. caucasica. Blue Scabious. z 5-8. Perennial to 30 in. Wheel-like flowers, white, light blue, or deep lavender, bloom in summer.

SCHEFFLERA. *S. actinophylla.* Australian or Queensland Umbrella Tree. A tree in Australia, but here grown as a tall house plant. Bold shiny compound leaves and rugged constitution make it a good plant for this use.

SCHINUS. *S. molle.* California Pepper Tree, Mastic Tree, Peruvian Mas-

tic. z 9-10. Evergreen tree to 30 ft. with graceful drooping branches. Yellowish white flowers in branching terminal clusters in summer. Pendent clusters of small rose-red fruits persist through early winter.

SCHIZANTHUS. *S. wisetonensis.* Poor-man's Orchid, Fringe Flower, Butterfly Flower. Annual to 4 ft. White, pink, blue, to carmine-brown flowers. Upper lip suffused with yellow. Prefers cool conditions. Grown as a pot plant in greenhouses in the North in winter.

SCHIZOPETALON. *S. walkeri.* Almond Flower. Annual to 10 in. White fragrant flowers in terminal racemes. June to frost.

SCIADOPITYS. *S. verticillata.* Japanese Umbrella Pine. z 6-9. Slow-growing evergreen conifer, never reaching its ultimate height of 120 ft. here. Needles (actually flattened branchlets called cladophylls) in umbrella-like whorls. Needs moisture to do well.

SCILLA. *S. hispanica* (*Scilla campanulata*). Spanish Bluebell, Spanish Jacinth. z 5-8. See Bulbs (Chapter 4).

S. nonscripta (*Scilla nutans*). English Bluebell, English Blue Squill, Wood Hyacinth. z 5-8. See Bulbs (Chapter 4).

S. sibirica. Siberian Squill. z 5-8. See Bulbs (Chapter 4).

SCINDAPSUS. *S. aureus.* Pothos, Ivy Arum, Hunter's Robe, Devil's Ivy. Tender climbing plant with oval lance-shaped leaves, green splashed yellow. A popular house plant; several varieties.

SEDUM. *S. acre.* Wall Pepper, Mossy Stonecrop, Golden Moss. z 5-8a. Evergreen creeping perennial to 5 in. Forms mats of fleshy leaves. Terminal clusters of bright yellow flowers to ½ in. June. Valuable groundcover for dry places and rock gardens but often becomes weedy.

S. *album*. White Stonecrop, Worm Grass. z 5-9a. Similar to S. *acre*, but slightly taller and with white flowers in July.

S. *dasyphyllum*. Leafy Stonecrop. z 5-9a. Tufted evergreen perennial only 2 in. tall. Flesh-colored flowers ¼ in. across, yellow at base. June.

S. *reflexum*. Yellow Stonecrop, Jenny Stonecrop. z 5-8. Carpeting, creeping evergreen. Flowers on 1-ft. stalks in summer, golden yellow, ⅝ in. across.

S. *spurium*. Running Rock Cress. z 5-8. Weedy, red-stemmed evergreen perennial to 5 in. tall. Pale pink ½-in. flowers in summer.

SELAGINELLA. S. *kraussiana*. Club Moss. Creeping perennial forming a mossy mat, rooting at joints; flowerless. Often a volunteer under greenhouse benches; used to cover unsightly pots.

SEMPERVIVUM. S. *arachnoideum*. Cobweb Houseleek, Spiderweb Houseleek. z 7-9a. Succulent perennial with rosettes of leaves to 4 in. connected by cobwebby filaments. Grown for use in bedding, the bright red flowers seldom seen.

S. *soboliferum*. Hen-and-chickens. z 6-8a. To 9 in. Rosettes 1½ in. across, outer leaves tinged brown. Pale yellow flowers in 4-in. panicle. Offsets round and break away from parent plant to start new colonies.

S. *tectorum*. Roof Houseleek, Oldman-and-woman. z 5-8. To 12 in. Rosettes 3-4 in. across. Pink to red 1-in. flowers. The most commonly grown of all the houseleeks: has escaped in some parts of the U.S.

SENECIO. S. *cineraria*. Dusty Miller. One of several gray-leaved plants bearing this name. (See *Centaurea*

cineraria, C. *gymnocarpa*, *Artemisia stelleriana*, and *Lychnis coronaria*.) A hardy, bushy perennial to 2½ ft. with leaves cut into many narrow lobes. Flowers inconspicuous. Valuable as a blender among bright flowers.

S. *cruentus*. Florist's Cineraria. Tender greenhouse plant with many vivid daisy-like flowers in purple, cerise, blue, and lavender, all marked with white.

S. *mikanioides*. German Ivy, Parlor Ivy. House plant with ivy-like leaves (but not an ivy). Tender climbing perennial. Stems may be woody at base.

SEQUOIA. S. *gigantea*. Big Tree, Redwood. z 6-9b. The famous redwood of California. To 300 ft. or more. Hardier than supposed; it survives along the Ohio River. One planting near Geneva, N.Y., lived from 1870 to 1940. Foliage similar to that of the hemlock. However, metasequoia is more reliably hardy and should be given preference in colder areas.

S. *sempervirens*. Giant Redwood, Coast Redwood. z 7-9b. A less hardy tree than S. *gigantea*, but otherwise similar.

SEVERINIA. S. *buxifolia*. Spiny Box. z 9-10. Spiny evergreen shrub to 3 ft. Used largely for hedges; inconspicuous flowers. Tolerates seaside conditions.

SHEPHERDIA. S. *argentea*. Buffaloberry, Wild Oleaster. z 1-7. Deciduous shrub to 15 ft. Conspicuous silvery leaves, downy on both sides. Edible tart red fruit: good for jelly. Bird food.

SHORTIA. S. *galacifolia*. Oconee Bells. z 6-8. Shade-loving perennial with 8-in stems of nodding white bell-shaped flowers in spring or early summer. Rock garden.

SILENE. S. *acaulis*. Moss Campion, Moss Catchfly, Cushion Pink. z 5-8.

Tufted perennial to 2 in. Purple-red, solitary, ½-in. flowers. May-Aug.

S. alpestris. Alpine Catchfly. z 5-8. Creeping perennial to 6 in. tall, stems sticky. Glossy white ½-in. flowers in loose clusters in summer.

S. armeria. Sweet-William Catchfly, None-so-pretty. Annual to 2 ft. Pink flowers ⅔ in. across in compact cymes, in summer.

S. caroliana. Wild Pink. z 5-8a. Perennial to 10 in., upper part of stem sometimes sticky. Flowers white or pink, 1 in. across, in thin terminal clusters, in May.

S. maritima. Sea Campion. z 5-8a. Perennial to 1 ft. Glossy foliage, flowers white to ¾ in., 1-4 on stems, June. Tolerates seaside conditions.

S. schafta. Rose-tuft Catchfly, Moss Campion. z 5-8a. Spreading perennial to 6 in., leaves in a rosette. Purple or rose flowers, 1-2 on a stalk, in late summer or autumn.

S. virginica. Fire Pink, Indian Pink. z 5-8a. Showy perennial to 10 in. Bright crimson flowers, 1 in. or more across. June-Aug. Difficult of culture. Prefers sandy soil in light shade.

SILPHIUM. *S. laciniatum.* Pilotweed, Compass Plant, Rosinweed. z 4-9. Weedy perennial to 10 ft., with daisy-like yellow flowers in heads to 5 in. across. July-Sept. A coarse plant for wild gardens.

S. perfoliatum. Cup Plant, Indian Cup. Similar to *S. laciniatum* but less tall.

SILYBUM. *S. marianum.* Holy Thistle, Lady's Thistle, Milk Thistle. Annual to 4 ft. Glossy, silvery, spiny leaves that are edible. Flower heads to 2½ in., purple-red. Good for dried flowers for winter bouquets.

SINNINGIA. See GLOXINIA.

SKIMMIA. *S. japonica.* Skimmia. z

7b-10. Evergreen shrub to 4 ft. Grown for the bright red fruit clusters. Though small, its white flowers are intensely fragrant. April-May. Needs acid soil.

SMILACINA. *S. racemosa.* False Solomon's Seal, Wild Spikenard. z 4-8a. Perennial to 3 ft. Lance-shaped leaves on drooping stems, terminating in clusters of greenish white flowers. Needs open shade and rich woodsy soil.

S. stellata. Starry Solomon's Seal. z 2-5. Bears a small cluster of starry white flowers at the tip of a 2-ft. stalk in early summer. Will spread through open places in the wild garden.

SOLANUM. *S. dulcamara.* European Bittersweet, Blue Nightshade, Climbing Nightshade. z 5-8a. A poisonous weed, which should never be cultivated, but sometimes is by the inexperienced. Scrambling vine to 8 ft. in length. Flowers in loose clusters, violet with yellow-green spots. Fruit a showy red berry, poisonous, but carried by birds.

SOLIDAGO (various species). Goldenrod. The native American goldenrods are much more appreciated and used in England than in America. Since they are seldom offered in trade, plants for garden use must be collected from the wild. Species of plants that grow singly are much more desirable than those that colonize. Particularly recommended is *S. sempervirens,* the beach goldenrod. z 5-9. A large vigorous plant with a basal rosette of more or less evergreen leaves. It tolerates seaside conditions.

SOPHORA. *S. japonica.* Chinese Scholar Tree, Japanese Pagoda Tree. z 5-8. Deciduous tree to 50 ft. Round-headed spreading form with feathery compound leaves. Showy 12-15-in.

panicles of white pea-like flowers. July-Sept. A handsome tree too little planted.

S. *secundiflora*. Mescal Bean. z 9-10. Evergreen shrub or small tree to 30 ft. Fragrant violet-blue pea-like flowers 1 in. long in 4-in. terminal racemes. May survive in z 8b if planted against a south wall.

SORBARIA. S. *aitchisoni*. Kashmir False Spirea. z 6-9. Deciduous shrub to 10 ft. Spirea-like, white flowers in erect 10-in. panicles. July-Aug. Leaves like those of mountain ash.

S. *sorbifolia*. False Spirea. z 2-8a. Deciduous shrub to 6 ft. Similar to S. *aitchisoni*, but hardier and blooming earlier.

SORBUS. S. *americana*. American Mountain Ash, American Rowan Tree. z 3-7b. Deciduous tree to 30 ft. Smooth bark, compound leaves. White flowers in terminal clusters. May-June. Bright orange-red fruits, like miniature apples, avidly eaten by birds. Best on slightly acid soil.

S. *aucuparia*. European Mountain Ash, Rowan Tree, Service Tree. z 3-8a. Deciduous tree to 50 ft. Much like the American species, but larger, and with many interesting horticultural varieties, such as one used for preserves, one with pendulous branches, and one with golden fruit.

SPARAXIS. S. *grandiflora*. Wandflower, Harlequin Flower. z 9-10. See Bulbs (Chapter 4).

SPARTIUM. S. *junceum*. Spanish Broom. Weaver's Broom. z 7b-10. Deciduous shrub to 10 ft. Green rush-like stems and small, sparse, blue-green leaves. Fragrant pea-like yellow flowers in terminal racemes to 18 in. long. June-Sept. May flower year around in warm climates. Tolerates seaside conditions.

SPIRAEA. Spirea. Note difference in spelling of botanical name and common name. Deciduous shrubs with quantities of small white or pink flowers in compact or elongated clusters. Among our most valuable shrubs, but a few overplanted.

S. *bumalda*. 'Anthony Waterer.' z 5-8a. To 2 ft. White to deep pink flowers. June-July.

S. *decumbens*. Low Spirea. z 7-9a. Rock-garden plant, to 10 in., with white flowers. June.

S. *thunbergi*. Thunberg's Spirea. z 5-8a. To 5 ft., white flowers. April-May. Does not do well in highly alkaline soil.

SPIRONEMA. S. *fragrans*. Mexican Wandering Jew. z 10. Weak-stemmed perennial with waxy white fragrant flowers in clusters, used as a groundcover in Florida, as a hanging-basket plant in greenhouses in the North.

STACHYS. S. *officinalis* (S. *betonica*). Wood Betony, Horse Mint, Woundwort. z 5-8a. Perennial to 18 in. Coarse, bold plant with opposite leaves and lipped flowers of purple, white, or lilac in terminal spikes. June-July.

S. *olympica* (S. *lanata*). Woolly Woundwort, Lamb's Ears, Rabbit's Ears. z 5-8a. Perennial to 18 in., grown mainly for its soft, white downy foliage. Small, purple flowers.

STAPELIA. See House Plants (Chapter 11).

STAPHYLEA. S. *colchica*. Caucasian Bladdernut. z 5-8a. Deciduous shrub to 12 ft. of open habit with five-parted leaves. Fringed white flowers to ¾ in. across in erect or nodding clusters in May.

S. *trifolia*. American Bladdernut. z 3-7a. Shrub to 14 ft. Like S. *colchica*, but with three-parted leaves and flower clusters all nodding. May. Seed capsules of both inflated.

STATICE. See ARMERIA.

STELLARIA. *S. holostea.* Easter Bells, Greater Stitchwort. z 4-8a. Sprawling perennial to 20 in. Showy white flowers to ¾ in. across in loose clusters. May-June. Related to the weedy chickweed, and sometimes too rampant.

STEPHANOTIS. *S. floribunda.* Madagascar Jasmine. Waxflower, Queen's Crown. z 9-10. Tropical woody vine, 15 ft. or more. Heavy evergreen foliage, leathery. White flowers, 1-2 in. long, intensely fragrant, in clusters in leaf axils. A well-defined crown surrounds the opening of the corolla tube. Widely grown as a cut flower in the North; often used in wedding bouquets.

STERNBERGIA. *S. lutea.* Autumn Daffodil, Winter Daffodil. See Bulbs (Chapter 4).

STEWARTIA. *S. ovata.* z 6-9. Shrub to 15 ft. White flowers, 2½-3 in. across, bloom in summer. *S. o. grandiflora* is similar, but flowers have purple stamens.

S. pseudo-camellia. False Camellia. z 7-9. Deciduous shrub or tree to 50 ft. White 5-petaled flowers, cup-shaped, 3 in. across. July-Aug.

STOKESIA. *S. cyanea* (*S. laevis*). Stokes Aster. z 5-8a. Perennial to 18 in. with fluffy thistle-like flowers, the heads to 4 in. across, purplish blue. Aug. Needs a dry situation to survive winter.

STREPTOPUS. *S. roseus.* Twisted Stalk. z 5-8a. Perennial wildflower to 30 in. Flowers grow on short, twisted stems from the axils of the leaves. Nodding, bell-shaped, pink or white ½ in. long. For wild garden in damp shade, soil pH below 5.0.

STYRAX. *S. americana.* Snowbell, Storax. z 7-9. Tender deciduous shrub of wet places, with heavy bright green oval leaves and loose clusters of scented white flowers. To 9 ft.

S. japonica. Snowbell, Storax. z 5b-8a. Deciduous shrub or tree to 30 ft. Drooping clusters of fragrant, white, fringed flowers. June-July. Prefers acid soil, pH 5.5 to 6.0.

S. obassia. Snowbell, Storax. z 5b-8a. Deciduous shrub or tree to 30 ft. Resembles *S. japonica*, but flowers, while more profuse, are partly obscured by foliage.

SYMPHORICARPOS. *S. albus.* Waxberry, Snowberry. z 4-8a. Deciduous shrub to 4 ft. Small pink bell-shaped flowers. June-Aug. Grown largely for its conspicuous round white berries.

S. chenaulti. Spotted Indian Currant. z 5-8a. Deciduous shrub to 6 ft. Grown largely for its rose-red fruits, spotted white.

S. mollis. Creeping Snowberry. z 5-8a. Prostrate or sprawling shrub with round white fruits as on the upright form.

S. orbiculatus. Indian Currant, Coralberry. z 5-8a. Similar to *S. chenaulti* except that fruit is not spotted; it is red-purple. Birds love this species, although they seldom eat other snowberries.

SYMPLOCOS. *S. paniculata.* Asiatic Sweetleaf. z 5-8a. Deciduous shrub or tree to 30 ft. Fragrant white flowers in clusters 3 in. long; bright blue fruit in fall.

SYNGONIUM. *S. podophyllum albo-lineatum.* African Arrowhead. Tender house plant with deeply lobed leaves, marked with white. Vine, but often sold as "table plant" with two or three leaves developed.

SYRINGA. Lilac. As a botanical name,

this applies strictly to lilacs, but it is also used (though not botanically) as a common name for the plants we call mock oranges, which belong in the genus philadelphus.

S. *japonica* (S. *amurensis japonica*). Japanese Tree Lilac. z 4-8a. Deciduous shrub or small tree to 30 ft. Typical upright lilac-shaped clusters of flowers, white or ivory, but without fragrance.

S. *pekinensis*. Pekin Lilac. z 4-8. Deciduous shrub to 15 ft., otherwise similar to S. *japonica*.

S. *persica*. Persian Lilac. z 4b-10. Deciduous shrub to 6 ft. Flower clusters looser and less striking than in the common lilac, usually near-white to pale mauve in color. Considered the best species for hedges.

S. *vulgaris*. Common Lilac. z 4-7. The parent of the French hybrids and other desirable varieties in commerce. Deciduous shrub to 20 ft. Fragrant, white, blue, and violet flowers.

TAGETES. Marigold. *T. erecta*. African Marigold, Giant Marigold, Aztec Marigold. Annual to 4 ft. Yellow or orange flowers to 6 in. across, usually double.

T. patula. French Marigold, Dwarf Marigold. Branching annual generally less than 1 ft. tall. Flower heads about 1 in. across, yellow, orange, maroon, mixed. Double or single flowers. One of the best edging annuals. (The marigold of Shakespeare is a calendula.)

T. tenuifolia pumila (*T. signata*). Miniature Marigold. Annual to 10 in. Single marigold flowers, barely 1 in. across, yellow, orange, or yellow and maroon. Edging plant.

TAMARIX. *T. odessana*. Caspian Saltbush, Tamarisk. z 5a-8. Deciduous shrub to 6 ft. with slender upright branches. Pink, feathery panicles of bloom. July-Sept. Tolerates sand, al-

kaline soil, and seaside conditions.

T. parviflora. Saltbush, Tamarisk. z 6-8a. Deciduous shrub to 15 ft. with somewhat arching dark purple branches. Feathery plumes of purplish pink flowers April-May.

T. pentandra. Amur Saltbush. z 5-8a. Deciduous shrub to 15 ft., the arching branches purplish. Feathery panicles of pink or rose-pink flowers. Aug.-Sept.

TANACETUM. *T. vulgare*. Tansy. z 4-8a. Perennial to 3 ft. Finely cut fern-like leaves, highly aromatic. Tight heads of flowers in flat umbels, bright yellow, like clusters of brass buttons.

TAXODIUM. *T. distichum*. Bald Cypress, Swamp Cypress, Southern Cypress. z 5b-8, but very slow-growing north of z 7. Deciduous conifer to 150 ft. Grows in low land, on wet soil; seldom used horticulturally.

TAXUS. Yew. *T. baccata*. English Yew. z 5-7. Needle-leaved evergreen shrub or tree to 50 ft., available in many named horticultural forms. Lustrous dark green leaves. Bright red, berry-like fruit. Japanese yew has largely supplanted the taller form in commerce.

T. baccata repandens. Dwarf English Yew. z 6-8. Nearly prostrate evergreen, useful low-growing and hardier form of the taller English yew. Does poorly in dry areas.

T. canadensis. Canadian Yew, Ground Hemlock. z 3-7. Spreading semi-prostrate evergreen, useful as a groundcover in light shade. Cannot survive exposure to winter wind and sun. Good rock-garden plant. Grows to 3 ft.

T. cuspidata. Japanese Yew. z 4-8a. Evergreen shrub or tree to 40 ft. Similar to English yew in appearance, but more tolerant of dry air and other adverse conditions. Can be had in many forms, from low spreaders to pyramidal trees. Endures seaside conditions, survives city smoke, and does well as a small plant in a terrarium. *T. c. nana* is a dwarf form.

T. media. Hybrid Yew. z 5-8a. Cross between *T. baccata* and *T. cuspidata.* A number of fine horticultural forms such as *T. m. hicksi,* Hicks yew.

TECOMA. *T. stans (Stenolobium stans).* Yellow Elder. z 8-10. Deciduous or semi-evergreen shrub or tree to 20 ft. Showy yellow tubular flowers like those of the trumpet vine. One of the most useful subtropical shrubs.

TECOMARIA. *T. capensis.* Cape Honeysuckle. z 9-10. Evergreen sprawling shrub or vine (can be trained either way). Scarlet or orange-red flowers (yellow in one variety), 2 in. long.

TEPHROCACTUS. *T. glomeratus.* See House Plants (Chapter 11).

TETRAPANAX. *T. papyriferus.* Rice-paper Plant. z 8-10. A plant resembling both fatsia and aralia, and at one time or other classified in both genera. Shrub or small evergreen tree. Grown for its handsome large leaves, 1 ft. across and heart-shaped.

TEUCRIUM. *T. chamaedrys.* Germander, Wall Germander. z 5b-8a. Subshrub to 12 in. or more, with ½-in. leaves toothed around the edge. Used as an edging plant. Evergreen in the South but loses its foliage in the North. A substitute for boxwood in rose gardens. Red-purple or rose flowers, ¾ in., spotted red and white, on loose spikes. Aug.-Sept.

THALICTRUM. *T. aquilegifolium.* Meadow Rue, Feather Columbine. z 5-8a. Perennial to 3 ft., with foliage like that of columbine (aquilegia). Minute and feathery flowers in showy terminal clusters of white, dark purple, rose, or orange in different varieties.

T. dioicum. Early Meadow Rue, Silverweed. z 5-8a. Woodland wildflower to 2 ft. with minute inconspicuous flowers and columbine-like foliage. Needs low, moist soil.

T. flavum. False Rhubarb. z 5-9. Perennial to 4 ft. Yellowish flowers in a panicle resembling that of rhubarb.

THERMOPSIS. *T. caroliniana.* Yellow False Lupine. Aaron's Rod. z 5-8a. Perennial to 4 ft. Flowers resemble those of the lupine, but clear brassy yellow. Good wildflower. Endures seaside conditions.

THEVETIA. *T. nereifolia.* Yellow Oleander. z 9-10. Evergreen shrub or small tree to 25 ft. Foliage resembles that of the oleander. Flowers in a cyme, yellow, showy, fragrant, and 2-3 in. long.

THUJA. *T. occidentalis.* American Arborvitae, Northern White Cedar. z 3-7. Coniferous evergreen to 60 ft., with scale-like leaves closely pressed against fan-shaped branches. A valuable landscape species, with many horticultural forms, from low globes to pyramidal trees.

T. orientalis. Japanese Arborvitae, Chinese White Cedar. z 6-8. Lower and bushier than *T. occidentalis;* also includes many horticultural forms. Seedlings used in terrariums.

THUNBERGIA. *T. alata.* Black-eyed Susan Vine, Clock Vine. Perennial, but grown as an annual. Oval leaves on trailing stems. Flowers to 1½ in. long, buff, yellow, orange, or white, with vivid black-purple central spot. Outstanding as a hanging-basket plant.

T. grandiflora. Skyflower. z 8b-10. Woody evergreen vine. Bears brilliant blue (sometimes white) flowers to 3 in. across in drooping racemes. Aug.-Dec.

THYMUS. *T. serpyllum.* Carpeter, Creeping Thyme, Mother-of-thyme. Small creeping subshrub with tiny aromatic leaves and great sheets of reddish purple flowers in summer. The most popular of the low-growing thymes. Many horticultural varieties. Good low groundcover for sunny places.

T. vulgaris. Common Thyme, Garden Thyme. z 5-8a. Perennial to 8 in., hoary foliage, tiny purple flowers, in whorls. May-June. The culinary herb. Tolerates seaside conditions.

TIARELLA. *T. cordifolia.* Foamflower, False Mitrewort. z 5-8a. Perennial wildflower to 1 ft. with broadly heart-shaped basal leaves and foam-like clusters of small white flowers on an erect stalk. The variety *T. c. marmorata* has bronzy foliage that turns rich maroon in fall. One of our better wildflowers.

TIGRIDIA. *T. pavonia.* Shellflower, Tigerflower. Tender bulb. See Bulbs (Chapter 4).

TILIA. *T. americana.* American Linden, Lime, Basswood. z 5-8a. Deciduous tree to 120 ft. Heart-shaped leaves. Greenish white flowers, very fragrant, in long-stalked drooping clusters. June.

T. cordata. Little-leaf Linden, Small-leaved Linden, Lime Tree. z 5-8a. Deciduous tree to 90 ft. Yellowish white fragrant flowers. June-July. The lime tree of English literature.

T. euchlora. Crimean Linden. z 5-8a. Smaller (to 50 ft.), but similar to *T. cordata.* Tips of branches slightly pendulous.

T. heterophylla. Southern Linden. z 5-8. A southern counterpart of *T. americana,* to 60 ft.

T. petiolaris. Weeping White Linden. z 6-8. Identical with *T. tomentosa* except for pendulous branches.

T. platyphyllos. Big-leaf Linden. z 5-8a. Deciduous tree to 120 ft. Much larger leaves than on other lindens, flowers whiter, otherwise similar.

T. tomentosa. Silver Linden, White Linden. z 5-8. Deciduous tree to 100 ft. Downy white lower surface of leaves makes tree striking in a breeze.

T. vulgaris (T. europaea). European Linden, Lime Tree. z 5-8a. This tree is rarely seen in cultivation in America. *T. cordata* is usually supplied under the present name.

TITHONIA. *T. speciosa.* Mexican Sunflower, Goldflower of the Incas. In Mexico, a woody herb, but farther north, grown as an annual. Rough leaves resembling the sunflower on plants to 6 ft. with brilliant scarlet-orange flowers to 3 in. across, also similar to sunflower. Rapid grower; makes splendid annual hedge or screen.

TORENIA. *T. fournieri.* Wishbone Flower, Blue-wing Flower. Tropical perennial grown as an annual to 12 in. Lipped flowers violet, yellow, and blue, sometimes white, 1 in. across, somewhat resembling pansies. Useful as an annual in shade.

TORREYA. *T. californica.* California Nutmeg, California Yew. z 8-10. Needle-leaved evergreen tree to 70 ft., but may be deciduous in parts of z 8. Resembles true yews except for the egg-shaped, purple-stained green fruits.

T. nucifera. Japanese Cedar. z 5b-9a. Quite similar to *T. californica* but hardier.

T. taxifolia. Stinking Cedar. z 7b-9a. Needle-leaved evergreen tree to 40 ft. Purple fruit. Foliage has a fetid odor if crushed.

TRACHELOSPERMUM. *T. jasminoides.* Star Jasmine, Confederate Jasmine. z 8-10. Twining woody evergreen vine. White fragrant 1-in. flowers, star-like, in long-stalked cymes. A long-time favorite in the South. Sometimes used as a groundcover.

TRACHYCARPUS. *T. fortunei.* Hemp Palm, Windmill Palm. z 8b-10. Short-trunked palm, to 30 ft., much lower as grown in tubs. Fan-shaped leaves. The only rival of the palmetto for hardiness.

TRACHYMENE. *T. caerulea (Didiscus caeruleus).* Blue Laceflower. A pretty annual to 2 ft. Slender stems bear pale blue to lavender flowers, resembling those of Queen Anne's lace. Good pot plant. Blooms all summer.

TRADESCANTIA. *T. fluminensis.* Wandering Jew, Spiderwort. House plant with prostrate stems, oval leaves, green above, purple below in the most commonly grown form. A variegated form has watermelon striping. So readily propagated that florists seldom stock it.

T. virginiana. Spiderwort, Snake Grass. z 5-8a. Perennial to 3 ft. Broad grass-like leaves. Purple, blue, violet, red, or white 3-petaled flowers in leaf axils.

TRIBULUS. *T. cistoides.* Caltrops. A weedy perennial used as a groundcover in Florida; not in general commerce.

TRIENTALIS. *T. borealis.* Starflower. z 2-8a. Perennial wildflower not generally cultivated but good in moist shade. To 9 in. White star-shaped flowers above a whorl of pointed leaves. June.

TRILLIUM. *T. erectum.* Wake-robin, Birthroot, Purple Trillium. z 2-8a. Perennial wildflower to 15 in. with three broad leaves in a whorl at tip of stem. Three-petaled flowers, one to a plant, liver-colored (sometimes paler), with a disagreeable odor. April-May.

T. grandiflorum. Great White Trillium, Trinity Lily, White Wake-robin. Perennial wildflower to 18 in. Flowers to 3 in. across, waxy white fading to flesh color, in May. A double form is particularly handsome. One of our finest native plants.

TRITONIA. *T. crocata.* Flame-freesia, Blazing Star, Montbretia. Tender bulb. See Bulbs (Chapter 4).

TROLLIUS. *T. asiaticus.* Asiatic Globe Flower. z 4-8a. Stout perennial to 2 ft. Bronzy leaves. Ball-shaped bright orange flowers. May.

T. europaeus. Mountain Globe Flower, European Globe Flower. Perennial to 2 ft. Lemon-yellow flowers, globular, 1-2 in. across.

TROPAEOLUM. *T. majus.* Nasturtium, Indian Cress. Annual, either dwarf or climbing. Large five-petaled fragrant, scarlet-yellow flowers, irregularly cornucopia-shaped, with a spur. Round leaves, the stalk attached at the center, with a peppery flavor. Both buds and leaves are used as flavoring, the buds sometimes pickled like capers.

T. peregrinum. Canary-bird Flower. Tender annual vine to 8 ft. Pale yellow flowers 1 in. across with two large petals, three small ones, and a green spur. Five-lobed leaves. Good house plant.

TSUGA. *T. canadensis.* Canadian Hemlock, Hemlock Spruce. z 3-7. Evergreen conifer to 80 ft. Branches droop in older specimens. Perhaps the best of all evergreens for hedging; it tolerates hard shearing and will also grow in shade. Does not do well in Middle West: it needs moist air as found in seacoast states. A valuable bird tree, both for shelter and food.

T. caroliniana. Carolina Hemlock, Spruce Pine. z 5-8a. Somewhat lower than *T. canadensis* but otherwise similar, except that the needles do not grow in an even plane along the branchlets.

T. diversifolia. Japanese Hemlock. z 5-8a. Much like *T. canadensis;* to 80 ft.

T. sieboldi. Oriental Hemlock. z 6-8a. Much like *T. diversifolia,* except for horizontal branching.

TULIPA. Tulips. Spring-flowering bulbs. See Bulbs (Chapter 4). For forcing types, see House Plants (Chapter 11).

T. acuminata. Turkish Tulip. z 5-8a. To 15 in. Light yellow flowers, marked with red lines. Needs rock-garden conditions to survive.

T. clusiana. Candystick Tulip. z 5-8a. To 12 in. Small fragrant white flowers with purple base, striped red. Prefers rock-garden conditions.

T. dasystemon (*T. tarda*). Dwarf Turkish Tulip. z 5-7. To 5 in. tall, with several flowers from a bulb, yellow, edged white, greenish yellow reverse. Needs rock-garden conditions.

T. fosteriana. 5-7b. To 12 in. Enormous scarlet flowers, darker base. Parent of many brilliant new hybrids.

T. kaufmanniana. Waterlily Tulip. z 5-7. To 8 in. with broad leaves, very early flowers creamy white or light yellow, yellow centers and red markings. Best in the rock garden.

T. linifolia. Slender Tulip. z 5-7b. Narrow grass-like leaves. Crimson flowers with pointed petals, blue base. Rock-garden species. To 10 in.

T. patens. Persian Tulip. z 4-7b. To 9 in., fragrant yellow flowers, darker yellow base. Rock-garden species.

TUNICA. *T. saxifraga.* Coatflower, Saxifrage Pink, Tunic Flower. Tufted perennial to 10 in. spreading. Tiny lilac or pink flowers in terminal branching clusters, similar to those of dianthus.

TURRAEA. *T. obtusifolia.* Ribbon Flower. z 9-10. Tropical shrub to 3 ft. White flowers 1½ in. long with narrow ribbon-like petals at ends of branches.

ULEX. *U. europaeus.* Furze, Gorse, Whin. z 6-9. Leafless shrubs, thorny, to 4 ft. Pea-like, fragrant, bright yellow flowers, ¾ in. long, in spring in the North or the year around in frostless climates. Needs protection north of z 8. Moist acid soil.

ULMUS. Elm. *U. americanus.* American Elm. z 4-8. Noble deciduous tree to 120 ft. No longer recommended for general planting until a satisfactory control can be established for Dutch elm disease.

U. fulva. Slippery Elm. z 4-8a. Also subject to Dutch elm disease.

U. glabra. Scotch Elm. z 5-8a. Also subject to Dutch elm disease.

U. parvifolia. Chinese Elm. z 5-8. A handsomer tree than the Siberian elm, but less hardy. Also highly resistant to Dutch elm disease and a good windbreak tree. To 40 ft.

U. pumila. Siberian Elm. z 2-7. While this species is somewhat subject to Dutch elm disease, it is highly resistant. It is one of the most satisfactory of all trees for windbreak planting on the Great Plains, where it is not close to present centers of infection. To 60 ft.

UMBELLULARIA. *U. californica.* Balm of Heaven, Bay Tree, Spice Tree, California Laurel. z 8-10. Evergreen tree to 70 ft. Pleasantly aromatic foliage. Prefers moist soil.

UNGNADIA. *U. speciosa.* Mexican Buckeye, Texas Buckeye, Spanish Buckeye. z 9-10. Shrub or small tree to 30 ft. Glossy leaves, bright rose 1-in. flowers in clusters before the leaves. April-May.

URSINIA. *U. pulchra.* Orange African Daisy. Annual to 1½ ft., much-branched; orange daisy-like flowers with purple disk, 2 in. across.

UVULARIA. *U. grandiflora.* Bellwort, Merrybells, Strawflower, Wood Daffodil. z 3-8a. Perennial wildflower to 18 in. Stout forked stem with drooping yellow bell-shaped flowers 1½ in. long. April-May. For shade, preferably in peaty soil.

U. perfoliata. Mealy Bellwort, Mohawk Weed. z 3-9. Slender perennial wildflower to 18 in. Pale yellow bell-shaped drooping flowers to 1½ in. April-May. For shade, in peaty soil.

U. sessilifolia. Wild Oats. z 3-8a. Tubular greenish yellow flowers, 1¼ in. long, drooping in fancied resemblance to oats. April-May.

VACCINIUM. *V. corymbosum.* Highbush Blueberry, Whortleberry, Swamp Blueberry. z 4-8a. Deciduous shrub to 15 ft. Small white or pink urn-shaped flowers in clusters in May. Blue-black berries. Although usually grown for fruit, a highly ornamental shrub. Needs acid soil. Tolerates seaside conditions. Birds fight man for the fruit.

V. macrocarpon. Cranberry. z 3-6. Low plants grown for the commercial cranberry, but useful for low places near the sea (they will tolerate salt spray). Acid soil.

V. pensylvanicum (*V. angustifolium*). Low-bush Blueberry. z 1-5. Deciduous shrub to 2 ft. Usually grown only for its fruit, though the low plants are quite handsome, particularly when in fruit and again in autumn with crimson-colored leaves. Excellent bird food. Acid soil.

V. vitis-idaea. Cowberry, Lingonberry, Foxberry, Red Whortleberry. z 1-4. The lingonberry of Scandinavian countries. A smaller, sweeter version of the cranberry. Good groundcover in acid soil for the far North. Tolerates seaside conditions.

VALERIANA. *V. officinalis.* Garden Heliotrope, Valerian. z 5-8a. Perennial to 5 ft. Intensely fragrant lavender, pink or white flowers in compact rounded heads at the summit of the plant. Old folk remedy.

VENIDIUM. *V. fastuosum.* Jewel Daisy, African Daisy. Annual to 1½ ft. Leaves hoary when young, green when older. Bright orange daisy-like flowers with purplish black disk, to 4 in. across.

VERATRUM. *V. viride.* False Hellebore, White Hellebore, Green Hellebore, Indian-poke. A poisonous plant of wet places, sometimes used in the wild garden. Can be confused with *Gentiana lutea* (which is used medicinally) with fatal results. Stout perennial to 6 ft. with large bright green plated leaves. Greenish yellow flowers 1 in. across, in dense, tall panicles.

VERBASCUM. *V. longifolium.* Italian Mullein. z 6-9. Biennial to 4 ft. Lower leaves felted white or ivory. Stout stem with bright yellow flowers in terminal spikes.

V. olympicum. Greek Mullein. z 6-8. Biennial or perennial to 5 ft., felted leaves in a broad basal rosette. Yellow flowers in a terminal spike, 1 in. across, with prominent white stamens.

VERBENA. *V. erinoides* (*V. laciniata*). Tender perennial grown as annual to 12 in. Lilac-colored flowers on taller stems in clover-like heads. Tolerates dry soils.

V. hortensis. Common Verbena, Garden Verbena. Complex hybrids of tender perennials grown as annuals. To 10 in. Fragrant brilliant red, rose, purple, lilac, and blue flowers in flat clusters, appearing in late summer from seed, earlier if grown from cuttings. They usually survive early frosts and continue to flower with early chrysanthemums.

VERONICA. Shrubby species. These are now classed as hebe by botanists, but are still offered under the present name by nurserymen. Mostly woody evergreens hardy only in California. Because of limited distribution, no effort is made here to list species. They are, however, highly desirable and worth planting when available. Herbaceous species retain the name veronica.

V. chamaedrys. Angel Eyes, Germander, Speedwell. Perennial to 18 in. Racemes of small blue flowers 6 in. long. May-June.

V. filiformis. Professor's Weed. z 5-8a. Perennial to 2 in., but flowering first year from seed. Mat-forming, invasive; can become weedy. Forms bright sheets of pale blue flowers in light shade. May-Sept.

V. gentianoides. Gentian Speedwell. Perennial to 15 in. Flowers blue, veined darker, in long racemes. June. Rock-garden plant.

V. incana. Woolly Speedwell. z 5-8a. Silver-gray perennial to 2 ft. Six-in.-long racemes of clear blue flowers in July.

V. longifolia. Slender Speedwell. z 5-8a. Perennial to 2 ft. Dense terminal racemes of lilac-blue flowers. July-Sept.

V. pectinata. Comb Speedwell. z 6-8a. Prostrate hoary perennial, evergreen, forming thick mats of silvery foliage. Deep-blue flowers with white centers on 5-in. spikes. May-June.

V. spicata. Cat-tail Speedwell, Rat-tail Speedwell. z 5-8a. Perennial to 2½ ft. Flowers in dense terminal racemes, blue (occasionally rose) in summer. Tolerates sandy soil.

V. virginica. Culver's Root, Black-root. Now classed as *Veronicastrum virginicum.* Perennial wildflower to 1 ft. Leaves in whorls. Small white flowers in several terminal racemes. A folk remedy in Colonial days.

VETIVERIA. *V. zizanioides.* Vetiver, Khus-Khus. z 8-10. Perennial grass with stout rootstock; strongly aromatic and the base of many Oriental perfumes. Also used medicinally by the Arabs. Unimportant as an ornamental, but often grown for use as sachet, like lavender.

VIBURNUM. *V. burkwoodi.* Burkwood Viburnum. z 5b-8a. Hybrid shrub to 8 ft., most closely resembling its *Viburnum carlesi* parent. Semi-evergreen. White flowers, sometimes slightly pink, strongly fragrant, in clusters.

V. carlesi. Mayflower Viburnum. z 5-8a. Deciduous shrub to 5 ft. Clusters of fragrant flowers, individually resembling the Mayflower (*Epigaea repens*) in odor, color and form. April-May. Often grafted on *Viburnum lantana*, which may sucker and kill out tops.

V. dentatum. Arrow-wood. z 4-8a. Deciduous shrub to 12 ft. Straight, sparsely forked branches resembling arrow shafts. White flowers in long-stalked clusters to 3 in. across. May-June. Blue-black fruits, loved by birds. Foliage beautifully subtle in fall with soft rose tints predominating. Tolerates seaside conditions.

V. lantana. Wayfarer Tree. z 5-8a. Deciduous shrub to 12 ft. White flowers in flattish clusters to 4 in. across, May-June, followed by berries, green, turning red, then black, but soon consumed by birds.

V. odoratissimum. Sweet Viburnum. z 8-10. Striking evergreen shrub to 10 ft. Deep green foliage. Pale pink flowers in 3-in. cymes in summer. Sometimes raised in greenhouses in North.

V. tomentosum. Doublefile Viburnum. z 5-9. An excellent viburnum for specimen use or mass planting. Deciduous to 9 ft. with spreading, horizontal branching habit. Flat clusters of white flowers in May, followed by red berries, which turn blue-black in the fall. Soft red autumn foliage. Especially recommended among the fine varieties is *V. t. sterile* (Japanese snowball) with larger flowers than the type.

VINCA. *V. minor.* Common Periwinkle, Running Myrtle. z 4-7b. Prostrate evergreen creeper with glossy dark green leaves, rooting as it runs. Five-petaled flowers of clear lavender-blue. May-June. 'Bowles' variety flowers intermittently all summer. Excellent groundcover in shade. Tolerates city conditions.

V. rosea. Periwinkle, Madagascar Periwinkle. Tender perennial or subshrub grown as an annual, to 2 ft. Smooth glossy dark green foliage and neat habit make it a desirable annual hedge plant. White or pink flowers, to 1½ in. across, plain or with red eye. Everblooming. Must be seeded very early if summer bloom is wanted. Tolerates light shade.

VIOLA. *V. blanda.* Sweet Violet. z 2-8a. Small low-growing perennial wildflower with solitary fragrant white flowers in early spring.

V. canadensis. Canadian Violet. Yellow-eye Violet. z 1-5. To 1 ft. Fragrant white flowers with distinct yellow eye, stained purple outside. Early spring.

V. cornuta. Tufted Pansy, Horned Violet. z 5-8a. Perennial to 6 in. Many horticultural varieties ranging from white and yellow to purple. Violet-blue in species. Fragrant. Summer-flowering.

V. odorata. Florist's Violet. z 6-8a.

The intensely fragrant violet, either single or double, so popular in Victorian days. Deep violet, rarely rose and white. Garden varieties are available.

V. tricolor. Johnny-jump-up, Viola, Baby Pansy. Smaller than the garden pansy but a true perennial, self-seeding prolifically. Hardy, long-flowering, mostly in combined purple, white, blue, and pale yellow.

V. tricolor major (*V. tricolor hortensis*). Pansy, Heart's-ease. Short-lived perennial (but often living over). See Biennials (Chapter 2).

VITEX. *V. agnus-castus.* Chaste Tree, Hemp Tree, Monk's Pepper. z 7-10 (can be grown in z 5-6 if tops are allowed to winter-kill; it flowers on new wood). Shrub or small tree to 10 ft. Foliage hairy beneath, aromatic if crushed. Short dense terminal spike of pale blue or lilac flowers. July-Aug.

VITIS. *V. kaempferi* (*Vitis coignetiae*). Japanese Ornamental Grape. z 5-8a. Tall woody grapevine with leaves sometimes 1 ft. across, a brilliant crimson in fall. Blue-black, inedible fruit.

WATSONIA. *W. fulgens.* Bugle Lily. Tender bulb. See Bulbs (Chapter 4).

WEDELIA. *W. trilobata.* Wedelia. z 9-10. Creeping groundcover plant, rooting as it runs, yellow-rayed flowers. Grown in Florida.

WEIGELA. z 5-8a. Popular summer shrubs with clear red or pink flowers to 1½ in. in abundance. Among choice varieties are 'Cardinal Flower' and 'Eva Rathke.'

WISTERIA. *W. floribunda.* Japanese Wisteria. z 5-8a. Woody twining vine to 20 ft. or more. Pendulous clusters of pea-shaped flowers, 18-30 in. long, delicately fragrant, lavender, pink, white, or purple. May-June.

W. sinensis. Chinese Wisteria. Taller growing than *W. floribunda,* but with flower clusters about half the length.

WOODSIA. *W. glabella.* Woodsia. Small tufted fern about 6 in. tall, growing naturally in scanty humus or moss on shaded limestone rocks. Needs similar situation when cultivated in wild garden.

WOODWARDIA. *W. areolata.* Chain Fern. z 4-8. Native fern with triangular fronds to 15 in. Must have rich, moist soil.

XANTHOCERAS. *X. sorbifolia.* Chinese Flowering Chestnut, Yellowhorn. z 5-8a. Deciduous shrub to 15 ft. Leaves like mountain ash. Showy white flowers about 1 in. across with orange or red blotch, in 10-in. racemes in May.

XANTHORHIZA. *X. apiifolia* (*X. simplicissima*). Shrub Yellow-root, Yellow-root. z 5-8a. Deciduous shrub to 2 ft. Minute purple-brown flowers in 4-in. drooping racemes. April-May.

YUCCA. *Y. filamentosa.* Adam's Needle, Bear Grass. z 5b-10. Long-pointed bayonet-like leaves. Flower stalk to 10 ft., bearing globular white flowers 2 in. long in erect panicles in July. Tolerates seaside conditions.

ZANTEDESCHIA. Calla Lily. z 9-10. See Bulbs (Chapter 4).

ZANTHOXYLUM. *Z. americanum.* Toothache Tree, Angelica Tree, Prickly Ash. z 5-8a. Deciduous shrub or tree to 20 ft. Inconspicuous greenish white flowers. April-May.

ZEBRINA. *Z. pendula.* Wandering Jew. Tender house plant differing only technically from *Tradescantia fluminensis,* which see. Both species are used in Florida as groundcovers.

ZELKOVA. *Z. serrata.* False Elm. z 5-8a. Tree to 100 ft., much like the American elm, except for the latter's pendulous branches. Often planted as a substitute where Dutch elm disease has killed off elms. Deciduous.

ZENOBIA. *Z. pulverulenta.* Gray-lady Shrub. z 6-9. Semi-evergreen shrub to 6 ft. Grayish foliage. White bell-shaped flowers to ½ in. in terminal racemes. May-June. Acid soil.

ZEPHYRANTHES. *Z. atamasco.* Atamasco Lily, Zephyr Lily, Fairy Lily. z 6-9. See Bulbs (Chapter 4).

Z. candida. z 7-9. See Bulbs (Chapter 4).

Z. grandiflora. Common Zephyr Lily. z 7-9. See Bulbs (Chapter 4).

ZINNIA. *Z. elegans.* Zinnia, Youth-and-old-age. Annual to 3 ft. Because of its ease of culture, wide color range, and variation in height, the annual zinnia is among the three most popular flowers for summer bloom in America. Nearly every color except blue.

ZYGOCACTUS. *Z. truncatus.* See House Plants (Chapter 11).

INDEX

The bold face type indicates the major entry in any indexed subject. In plant listings in which several species are listed, the major entry for either the genus or the first of the species is bold-faced.

Cutworms, 345
Cyanogas, 354
Cyanotis somaliensis, 188, **412**
Cyclamen, **412**; *C. indicum*, 212, 412; *C. coum*, 412; *C. europaeum*, 412; *C. neapolitanum*, 412; *C. persicum*, 186
Cyclamens, florist's, 212, **412**
Cyclops, 414
Cydonia. see Chaenomeles
Cymbalaria aequitriloba, 253, **412**; *C. muralis*, 188, 253, 412
Cynoglossum, 311; *C. amabile*, 23, **412**
Cyperus gracilis, 146; *C. papyrus*, **412**
Cypress vine, 188, **463**
Cypresses, 88, **403**, 475. *See also Chamaecyparis* species.
  Cupressus species, 87, 111, **412**
  summer. *see* Mexican firebush
Cyrilla racemiflora, 280, **412**
Cystopteris bulbifera, 244, **412**; *C. fragilis*, 244, 412
Cytisus, 280, 319, 320, **412-13**; *C. albus* (*C. leucanthus*), 100, 412; *C. canariensis*, 103, 212, 412; *C. nigricans*, 100, 413; *C. praecox*, 237, 413; *C. purgans*, 100, 413; *C. purpureus*, 100, 413; *C. scoparius*, 99, 237, 413

DDD, 342
DDT, 342, 344, 345, 348, 349
DSMA, 301
Dacthal, 300
Daffodil garlic. *see* Lily leek
Daffodils, **58-59**, 60. *See also Narcissus* species.
  autumn, **62**, 257
  Peruvian, 53, **65**, 264, 269, 430
  wood. see *Uvularia grandiflora*
Dagger fern. *see* Christmas fern
Dagger-leaf, 103, **426-27**
Dahlia, **65**, 311, 319. *See also* Dahlias.
Dahlias, 53, **65**, 211, 311, 319, 328
  sea, 238, **408**
Dahoon, 89, **430**
Dainty rockspray, 256, **410**
Daisies. *see Chrysanthemum* species; *Echinacea* species; *Erigeron* species; *Rudbeckia* species; African daisies; English daisies; Globe daisies; etc.
Dalapon, **297**, 304
Damask rose, 168
Dame's rocket. *see* Dame's violet
Dame's violet, 32, **428**
Dandelions, 296
Daphne, 320, **413**; *D. burkwoodi*, 413; *D. cneorum*, 98, 212, 256, 262, 413; *D. genkwa*, 103, 413; *D. mezereum*, 100, 262, 413; *D. 'Somerset,'* 413
Daphnes. *see Daphne* species
Darling chinkerichee, **66**, 450
Darnley heath, 103, **418**
Darwin's barberry, 103, **393**
Date palm, 455
Datura, **413**; *D. arborea*, 264, 413; *D. metel*, 413; *D. stramonium*, 413; *D. suaveolens*, 413
Davidia involucrata, 86, **413**
Dawn redwood, 445
Dawnflower, 116, **431**
Day jasmine, 402
Daylilies, 32, **35-42**, 145, 235, 238
'De Caen' anemone, 63-64
Dead wood, pruning, 329-31

Delonix regia, 88, **413**
Delphinium (larkspur), 22, 28, 31, 234, 309, 310, 311, 313, 328, **413-14**; *D. ajacis* (annual larkspur), 23, 244, 309, 413; *D. chinensis*, 28, 413; *D. elatum*, 413-14; *D. nudicaule*, 414
'Delta' bluegrass, 131
Dennstaedtia punctilobula, 244, 265, **414**
Dentaria diphylla, 414
Deodar cedar, 400
Desert gum, 88, **419**
Desert plants, 75. *See also* Cacti.
Desert willow, 104, **403**
Design, landscape, **123**, 231
Desmodium canadense, 414
Deutzia, 320, **414**; *D. gracilis*, 101, 414; *D. lemoinei*, 101, 414; *D. lemoinei compacta*, 100, 414; *D. scabra*, 103, 233, 262, 414
Deutzias, 100, 101, 103, 233, 262, 320, **414**
Devil-in-a-bush. *see* Love-in-a-mist
Devil's fingers. *see* Foxglove
Devil's ivy. *see Scindapsus aureus*
Devil's paintbrush, 428. *See also* Tassel flower.
Devil's pincushion, 183
Devil's walking stick, 232, **388**
Devilwood, 281, **450**
Dewberries, 266, 321
Dexone, 342, 352, 353
Diabrotica beetle, 344
Diamond flower, 24, **431**
Dianthus (pinks), 31, 145, 146, 234, 262, 310, 311, 313, 319, **414**; *D. alpinus*, 253, 414; *D. arenarius*, 144, 253, 414; *D. barbatus*, 28, 235, 414; *D. caesius*, 253, 414; *D. caryophyllus. see* Carnations; *D. chinensis*, 23, 414; *D. cruentis*, 414; *D. deltoides*, 253, 414; *D. neglectus*, 253, 414; *D. plumarius*, 414
Diazinon, 342, 344, 345, 348
Dibbles, 358
Dicentra, **414-15**; *D. canadensis*, 253, 414-15; *D. cucullaria*, 242, 253, 415; *D. eximia*, 31, 253, 280, 415; *D. spectabilis*, 31, 415
Dichondra, 145, 146, 297, **415**
Dichondra carolinensis, 145, 146, **415**; *D. repens*, 415
Dictamnus albus, 32, 262, **415**
Didiscus, 311. *See also Trachymene.*
Dieffenbachia, 172, 185, 198, **415**
Dieldrin, 344, 345, 349, 354
Diels rockspray, 410
Diervilla, 320, **415**; *D. lonicera*, 100, 415; *D. rivularis*, 101, 415; *D. sessilifolia*, 101, 415
Digger wasps, 345
Digging in vegetable garden, 286
Digitalis (foxglove), 27-28, **28-29**, 313; *D. purpurea*, 29, 235, 415
Dill, 247, 265, **386**
Dimenthoate, 349
Dimite, 348
Dimorphotheca, 146; *D. hybrida*, 23, **415**
Dioscorea batatas, 115, 262, **415**
Diosma ericoides, 103, 111, 264, 280, **415**
Diospyros, **415**. *See also* Persimmons; *D. kaki*, 88, 415; *D. virginiana*, 82, 415
Diseases, 194, 235, 339-43, **349-54.**
  See also specific plants.

Dish gardens, 199, **203-4**
Disodium monomethyl arsonate, 301
Distictis, 146
Dittany. *see* Gas plant
Division and separation, 327-28
Dodecatheon, 254, **415**; *D. meadia*, 242
Dogberry. *see Ilex verticillata*
Dogwood violet. *see Erythronium americanum*
Dogwoods, 267, 334, **408-9**. *See also Cornus* species.
Dolichos hosei, 145, **415**; *D. lablab*, 115, 416
Dombeya wallichi, 416
Doors, plantings by, 123, **124-25**
Dopeweed, 413
Dormancy, **75-76**, 309
Doronicum, 32, 313, **416**
Dotted bottlebrush, 104, **444**
Dotted evening primrose, 449
Doublefile viburnum, 482
Douglas fir, 86, **462**
Douglasia vitaliana, 254, **416**
Dove tree, 86, **413**
Downingia pulchella (*Clintonia pulchella*), 24, **416**
Downy hawthorn, 83, **410**
Downy mildew, 351-52
Doxantha unguis-cati, 416
Draba aizoides, 254, **416**; *D. olympica*, 254, 416
Dracaena, 172, 185, 198, 202, 408, **416**
Dracocephalum grandiflora, 448
Dragon plant. *see Dracaena*
Dragon tree, Australian, 88, **408**
Dragonhead, false, 33, **456**
Dragon's mouth, 280, **389**
Drain spade, 356
Drainage, 139, 249, 258-59, 369, 370
Driveways, 121, 126-27, 128, 350, **368-70**
Drooping bottlebrush. *see Melaleuca armillaris*
Dry walls, 374
Dryas octopetala, 254, **416**
Drying of herbs, 248
Drying yards, 121
Dryopteris, 244, **416**; *D. bootti*, 416; *D. cristata*, 416; *D. filixmas*, 416; *D. hexagonoptera*, 416; *D. intermedia*, 416; *D. linnaeana*, 416; *D. marginalis*, 416; *D. noveboracensis*, 416; *D. phegopteris*, 416
Duchesnea indica, 144, **416**
Dumb cane. *see Dieffenbachia*
Duranta repens, 104, **416**
Dusty clover. *see* Bush clover
Dusty millers: *Artemisia stelleriana*, 145, 238, **390**
  Centaurea, 211, **401**
  Lychnis coronaria, 244, **441**
  Senecio cineraria, 471
Dutch crocus, **61**, 182, 411
Dutch elm disease, **91-94**, 331, 340, 344
Dutch hyacinth, 429
Dutch iris, 59
Dutchman's breeches, 242, 253, **415**
Dutch-Roman hyacinth, 429
Dwarf Alberta spruce, 109, 170, **456**
Dwarf alder, 102, 103, 280, **422**
Dwarf arborvitae, 100, 109
Dwarf boxwood, 103, 109, 111, 256, **396**
Dwarf broom, 254, **424**
Dwarf burning-bush. *see Euonymus alatus compactus*
Dwarf catnip, 145, 255, **448**
Dwarf Chinese clematis. *see*

493

497

505

BLACK AND WHITE PICTURE CREDITS
Harry H. Baskerville, Jr., p. 360 top; Thomas A. Barton, p. 372, 373; Ernest Braun, p. 92, 106; Clint Bryant, Armstrong Nurseries, p. 164 top; G. M. and H. V. Daetz, p. 323; George de Genaro, p. 113 top, 126 bottom, 177 bottom, 367 top; F. M. Demarest, p. 126 top, 177 bottom, 366 top; Gladys Diesing, p. 259; Jack Fields, p. 41; Hence Griffith, p. 176 top; Art Homes, p. 271 top; Jackson & Perkins, p. 164 bottom; Harold Johns, p. 74, 75; Wendell Kilmer, p. 325; Kranzten Studios, Inc., p. 107, 357 top; Lawrence Studio, p. 124 bottom; Lord and Burnham, p. 207; J. Horace McFarland Company, p. 53 center line, 154 top left, 164 center; Lew Merrim, p. 19, 21, 25, 140, 149, 193, 196, 197; Phil Palmer, p. 113 center, 257 bottom; Charles R. Pearson, p. 74; George E. Peterson, p. 366 top; Warren Reynolds, p. 75, 113 bottom, 176 bottom, 187 center left, center right, bottom, 232, 254, 271 bottom, 317 bottom, 360 bottom, 361 top, 367 bottom; John Robin, p. 361 bottom; John Robinson, p. 236, 378; Roche, p. 10, 49, 143, 180 top right, 317 top, 333 bottom right; Roger Sturtevant, p. 124 top; Nan Tucker, p. 180.

COLOR PICTURE CREDITS
Following page 32: Warren Reynolds; Gottscho-Schleisner. Following page 64: Jeannette Grossman; Gretchen Harshbarger. Following page 128: Lisanti; Robert McGinnis. Following page 160; Lisanti (2). Following page 224: George de Gennaso at Sunnyslope Gardens; Kranzten Studios. Following page 256: Maris/Ezra Stoller Associates; Harold Becker. Following page 320: Robert McGinnis, Guy Burgess, F. M. Demarest; Lisanti. Following page 352: Hahn-Millard; F. M. Demarest.